EDWARD
GIBBON

THE DECLINE AND
FALL OF THE
ROMAN EMPIRE
(VOLUMES 4, 5, & 6)

———————————————

In the last three volumes of his master-work, Edward Gibbon continues to display that lucidity and literary vigor, almost unmatched in historical writing, that is his hallmark. He tells the story of the Eastern Roman Empire at Byzantium from its inception to the rise of the Islamic civilization that would eventually supplant it, to its final dissolution in the fall of Constantinople in 1453. In chronicles that are continually propelled by Gibbon's sensitivity to the percussive beat of time and change, we can see the nature of his mind fully reveal itself in all its rationality, acerbic irony, and fatalistic wisdom.

EVERYMAN'S LIBRARY

EVERYMAN,
I WILL GO WITH THEE,
AND BE THY GUIDE,
IN THY MOST NEED
TO GO BY THY SIDE

EDWARD GIBBON

The Decline and Fall of the Roman Empire

with an Introduction by
Hugh Trevor-Roper

VOLUME 4
(Chapters XXXVII–XLVI)

EVERYMAN'S LIBRARY

Alfred A. Knopf New York Toronto

192

THIS IS A BORZOI BOOK

PUBLISHED BY ALFRED A. KNOPF, INC.

First included in Everyman's Library, 1910
Introduction Copyright © 1994 by Hugh Trevor-Roper
Typography by Peter B. Willberg

ISBN 0-679-43593-X
LC 93-1857

Library of Congress Cataloging-in-Publication Data
Gibbon, Edward, 1737–1794.
The decline and fall of the Roman Empire.
p.   cm.—(Everyman's library)
Includes bibliographical references.
1. Rome—History—Empire, 30 B.C.–476 A.D.
2. Byzantine Empire—History—To 527.
I. Title. II. Series.
ISBN 0-679-43593-X
DG311.G5   1993   93-1857
937'.09   CIP

Book Design by Barbara de Wilde and Carol Devine Carson

Printed and bound in Germany by
Mohndruck Graphische Betriebe GmbH, Gütersloh

THE DECLINE AND
FALL OF THE
ROMAN EMPIRE

———

CONTENTS OF
FOURTH VOLUME

———

CHAPTER XXXVII

Origin, Progress, and Effects of the Monastic Life – Conversion of the Barbarians to Christianity and Arianism – Prosecution of the Vandals in Africa – Extinction of Arianism among the Barbarians

CONTENTS

CHAPTER XXXVIII

*Reign and Conversion of Clovis – His Victories over the Alemanni,
Burgundians, and Visigoths – Establishment of the French Monarchy in
Gaul – Laws of the Barbarians – State of the Romans – The Visigoths of
Spain – Conquest of Britain by the Saxons*

CONTENTS

CHAPTER XXXIX

*Zeno and Anastasius, Emperors of the East – Birth, Education, and first
Exploits of Theodoric the Ostrogoth – His Invasion and Conquest of Italy –
The Gothic Kingdom of Italy – State of the West – Military and Civil
Government – The Senator Boethius – Last Acts and Death of Theodoric*

xi

CONTENTS

CHAPTER XL

*Elevation of Justin the Elder – Reign of Justinian – I. The Empress
Theodora – II. Factions of the Circus, and Sedition of Constantinople –
III. Trade and Manufacture of Silk – IV. Finances and Taxes –
V. Edifices of Justinian – Church of St. Sophia – Fortifications and
Frontiers of the Eastern Empire – VI. Abolition of the Schools of Athens,
and the Consulship of Rome*

CONTENTS

CONTENTS

CHAPTER XLI

Conquests of Justinian in the West – Character and the first Campaigns of Belisarus – He invades and subdues the Vandal Kingdom of Africa – His Triumph – The Gothic War – He recovers Sicily, Naples and Rome – Siege of Rome by the Goths – Their Retreat and Losses – Surrender of Ravenna – Glory of Belisarius – His Domestic Shame and Misfortunes

xiv

CONTENTS

CHAPTER XLII

State of the Barbaric World – Establishment of the Lombards on the Danube – Tribes and Inroads of the Sclavonians – Origin, Empire, and Embassies of the Turks – The Flight of the Avars – Chosroes I. or Nushirvan King of Persia – His prosperous Reign and Wars with the Romans – The Colchian or Lazic War – The Æthiopians

CONTENTS

CHAPTER XLIII

*Rebellions of Africa – Restoration of the Gothic Kingdom by Totila –
Loss and Recovery of Rome – Final Conquest of Italy by Narses –
Extinction of the Ostrogoths – Defeat of the Franks and Alemanni –
Last Victory, Disgrace, and Death of Belisarius – Death and Character
of Justinian – Comets, Earthquakes, and Plague*

CONTENTS

CHAPTER XLIV

Idea of the Roman Jurisprudence – The Laws of the Kings – The Twelve Tables of the Decemvirs – The Laws of the People – The Decrees of the Senate – The Edicts of the Magistrates and Emperors – Authority of the Civilians – Code, Pandects, Novels, and Institutes of Justinian: – I. Rights of Persons – II. Rights of Things – III. Private Injuries and Actions – IV. Crimes and Punishments

CONTENTS

CONTENTS

CHAPTER XLV

Reign of the younger Justin – Embassy of the Avars – Their Settlement on the Danube – Conquest of Italy by the Lombards – Adoption and Reign of Tiberius – Of Maurice – State of Italy under the Lombards and the Exarchs of Ravenna – Distress of Rome – Character and Pontificate of Gregory the First

CONTENTS

CHAPTER XLVI

Revolutions of Persia after the Death of Chosroes or Nushirvan – His Son Hormouz, a Tyrant, is deposed – Usurpation of Bahram – Flight and Restoration of Chosroes II. – His Gratitude to the Romans – The Chagan of the Avars – Revolt of the Army against Maurice – His Death – Tyranny of Phocas – Elevation of Heraclius – The Persian War – Chosroes subdues Syria, Egypt, and Asia Minor – Siege of Constantinople by the Persians and Avars – Persian Expeditions – Victories and Triumph of Heraclius

CONTENTS

CONTENTS OF FIFTH VOLUME

CHAPTER XLVII

Theological History of the Doctrine of the Incarnation – The Human and Divine Nature of Christ – Enmity of the Patriarchs of Alexandria and Constantinople – St. Cyril and Nestorius – Third General Council of Ephesus – Heresy of Eutyches – Fourth General Council of Chalcedon – Civil and Ecclesiastical Discord – Intolerance of Justinian – The Three Chapters – The Monothelite Controversy – State of the Oriental Sects – I. The Nestorians – II. The Jacobites – III. The Maronites – IV. The Armenians – V. The Copts – VI. The Abyssinians

CONTENTS

CHAPTER XLVIII

*Plan of the last two [quarto] Volumes – Succession and Characters of the
Greek Emperors of Constantinople, from the Time of Heraclius to the Latin
Conquest*

CONTENTS

CONTENTS

CHAPTER XLIX

Introduction, Worship, and Persecution of Images – Revolt of Italy and Rome – Temporal Dominion of the Popes – Conquest of Italy by the Franks – Establishment of Images – Character and Coronation of Charlemagne – Restoration and Decay of the Roman Empire in the West – Independence of Italy – Constitution of the Germanic Body

CONTENTS

CONTENTS

CHAPTER L

Description of Arabia and its Inhabitants – Birth, Character, and Doctrine
of Mohammed – He preaches at Mecca – Flies to Medina – Propagates his
Religion by the Sword – Voluntary or reluctant Submission of the Arabs –
His Death and Successors – The Claims and Fortunes of Ali and his
Descendants

CONTENTS

xxviii

CONTENTS

CHAPTER LI

The Conquest of Persia, Syria, Egypt, Africa, and Spain, by the Arabs or Saracens – Empire of the Caliphs, or Successors of Mohammed – State of the Christians, &c., under their Government

CONTENTS

CHAPTER LII

The Two Sieges of Constantinople by the Arabs – Their Invasion of France, and Defeat by Charles Martel – Civil War of the Ommiades and Abbassides – Learning of the Arabs – Luxury of the Caliphs – Naval Enterprises on Crete, Sicily, and Rome – Decay and Division of the Empire of the Caliphs – Defeats and Victories of the Greek Emperors

CONTENTS

CONTENTS

CHAPTER LIII

*State of the Eastern Empire in the Tenth Century – Extent and Division –
Wealth and Revenue – Palace of Constantinople – Titles and Offices – Pride
and Power of the Emperors – Tactics of the Greeks, Arabs, and Franks –
Loss of the Latin Tongue – Studies and Solitude of the Greeks*

CONTENTS

CHAPTER LIV

*Origin and Doctrine of the Paulicians – Their Persecution by the Greek
Emperors – Revolt in Armenia, &c. – Transplantation into Thrace –
Propagation in the West – The Seeds, Character and Consequences of the
Reformation*

CHAPTER LV

*The Bulgarians – Origin, Migrations, and Settlement of the Hungarians –
Their Inroads in the East and West – The Monarchy of Russia –
Geography and Trade – Wars of the Russians against the Greek Empire –
Conversion of the Barbarians*

CONTENTS

CHAPTER LVI

*The Saracens, Franks, and Greeks, in Italy – First Adventures and
Settlement of the Normans – Character and Conquest of Robert Guiscard,
Duke of Apulia – Deliverance of Sicily by his Brother Roger – Victories of
Robert over the Emperors of the East and West – Roger, King of Sicily,
Invades Africa and Greece – The Emperor Manuel Comnenus – Wars of the
Greeks and Normans – Extinction of the Normans*

CONTENTS

CONTENTS

CONTENTS OF
SIXTH VOLUME

CHAPTER LVII

The Turks of the House of Seljuk – Their Revolt against Mahmud, Conqueror of Hindostan – Togrul subdues Persia, and protects the Caliphs – Defeat and Captivity of the Emperor Romanus Diogenes by Alp Arslan – Power and Magnificence of Malek Shah – Conquest of Asia Minor and Syria – State and Oppression of Jerusalem – Pilgrimages to the Holy Sepulchre

CONTENTS

CHAPTER LVIII

Origin and Numbers of the First Crusade – Characters of the Latin Princes – Their March to Constantinople – Policy of the Greek Emperor Alexius – Conquest of Nice, Antioch, and Jerusalem, by the Franks – Deliverance of the Holy Sepulchre – Godfrey of Bouillon, First King of Jerusalem – Institutions of the French or Latin Kingdom

CONTENTS

CHAPTER LIX

Preservation of the Greek Empire – Numbers, Passage, and Event of the Second and Third Crusades – St. Bernard – Reign of Saladin in Egypt and Syria – His Conquest of Jerusalem – Naval Crusades – Richard the First of England – Pope Innocent the Third; and the Fourth and Fifth Crusades – The Emperor Frederic the Second – Louis the Ninth of France; and the two last Crusades – Expulsion of the Latins or Franks by the Mamalukes

CONTENTS

CHAPTER LX

Schism of the Greeks and Latins – State of Constantinople – Revolt of the Bulgarians – Isaac Angelus dethroned by his Brother Alexius – Origin of the Fourth Crusade – Alliance of the French and Venetians with the Son of Isaac – Their Naval Expedition to Constantinople – The Two Sieges and Final Conquest of the City by the Latins

CONTENTS

CHAPTER LXI

Partition of the Empire by the French and Venetians – Five Latin Emperors of the Houses of Flanders and Courtenay – Their Wars against the Bulgarians and Greeks – Weakness and Poverty of the Latin Empire – Recovery of Constantinople by the Greeks – General Consequences of the Crusades

CONTENTS

CHAPTER LXII

The Greek Emperors of Nice and Constantinople – Elevation and Reign of Michael Palæologus – His false Union with the Pope and the Latin Church – Hostile Designs of Charles of Anjou – Revolt of Sicily –War of the Catalans in Asia and Greece – Revolutions and present State of Athens

CONTENTS

CHAPTER LXIII

*Civil Wars, and Ruin of the Greek Empire – Reigns of Andronicus, the
Elder and Younger, and John Palæologus – Regency, Revolt, Reign, and
Abdication of John Cantacuzene – Establishment of a Genoese Colony at
Pera or Galata – Their Wars with the Empire and City of Constantinople*

CONTENTS

CHAPTER LXIV

Conquests of Zingis Khan and the Moguls from China to Poland – Escape of Constantinople and the Greeks – Origin of the Ottoman Turks in Bithynia –Reigns and Victories of Othman, Orchan, Amurath the First, and Bajazet the First – Foundation and Progress of the Turkish Monarchy in Asia and Europe – Danger of Constantinople and the Greek Empire

CONTENTS

CHAPTER LXV

*Elevation of Timour or Tamerlane to the Throne of Samarcand –
His Conquests in Persia, Georgia, Tartary, Russia, India, Syria, and
Anatolia – His Turkish War – Defeat and Captivity of Bajazet – Death of
Timour – Civil War of the Sons of Bajazet – Restoration of the Turkish
Monarchy by Mohammed the First – Siege of Constantinople by Amurath
the Second*

CONTENTS

CHAPTER LXVI

Applications of the Eastern Emperors to the Popes – Visits to the West of John the First, Manuel, and John the Second, Palæologus – Union of the Greek and Latin Churches promoted by the Council of Basil, and concluded at Ferrara and Florence – State of Literature at Constantinople – Its Revival in Italy by the Greek Fugitives – Curiosity and Emulation of the Latins

CONTENTS

xlvii

CONTENTS

CHAPTER LXVII

Schism of the Greeks and Latins – Reign and Character of Amurath the Second – Crusade of Ladislaus, King of Hungary – His Defeat and Death – John Huniades – Scanderbeg – Constantine Palæologus, last Emperor of the East

CHAPTER LXVIII

Reign and Character of Mohammed the Second – Siege, Assault and Final Conquest of Constantinople by the Turks – Death of Constantine Palæologus – Servitude of the Greeks – Extinction of the Roman Empire in the East – Consternation of Europe – Conquests and Death of Mohammed the Second

CONTENTS

CHAPTER LXIX

State of Rome from the Twelfth Century – Temporal Dominion of the Popes – Seditions of the City – Political Heresy of Arnold of Brescia – Restoration of the Republic – The Senators – Pride of the Romans – Their Wars – They are deprived of the Election and Presence of the Popes, who retire to Avignon – The Jubilee – Noble Families of Rome – Feud of the Colonna and Ursini

CONTENTS

1

CONTENTS

CHAPTER LXX

Character and Coronation of Petrarch – Restoration of the Freedom and
Government of Rome by the Tribune Rienzi – His Virtues and Vices, his
Expulsion and Death – Return of the Popes from Avignon – Great Schism of
the West – Reunion of the Latin Church – Last Struggles of Roman Liberty
– Statutes of Rome – Final Settlement of the Ecclesiastical State

CONTENTS

CHAPTER LXXI

Prospect of the Ruins of Rome in the Fifteenth Century – Four Causes of Decay and Destruction – Example of the Coliseum – Renovation of the City – Conclusion of the whole Work

CONTENTS

TEXTUAL NOTE

The History of the Decline and Fall of the Roman Empire was first published between 1776 and 1788 in six quarto volumes. A revised edition appeared during Gibbon's lifetime and he was working on a second revision at the time of his death. Several annotated editions appeared during the nineteenth century, culminating in the text presented here which is taken from the magisterial version in seven volumes edited by J. B. Bury between 1896 and 1900. Bury collated Gibbon's three versions to produce what has since been regarded as the definitive text.

Bury's edition was accompanied by a formidable battery of notes and appendices, mainly of interest only to the specialist and many of them now superseded by more recent scholarship. We have not reprinted these. Instead, the present text includes, besides Gibbon's own extensive notes (complete), the light annotation prepared by Oliphant Smeaton for the first Everyman edition in 1910 and revised in 1936 by Christopher Dawson, whose *The Making of Modern Europe* is still a highly regarded textbook. The notes, which are usually restricted to matters of fact, draw on the commentaries of previous editors, including Bury, Milman, Smith and Guizot; on the authorities consulted by Gibbon himself; on ancient texts discovered since Gibbon's time; and on the work of contemporary scholars. While archaeology and events have in some instances overtaken Smeaton, his commentary has withstood the test of time remarkably well. It is for the most part lucid, vigorous and concise.

Readers interested in Roman studies since Dawson's time are directed to the *Cambridge Ancient History* and the *Cambridge Medieval History* which contain detailed bibliographies.

[Footnotes printed in square brackets were written by Oliphant Smeaton for the 1910 edition.]

INTRODUCTION
TO VOLUMES 4 – 6:
THE EASTERN EMPIRE

———

Gibbon's *Decline and Fall of the Roman Empire* was planned by him, from the beginning, to be a continuous narrative from the high noon of the Empire under the 'Antonine' rulers in the second century down to the capture of Byzantium by the Ottoman Turks in 1453. At one time indeed he wavered, thinking that he might close his account with the extinction of the Empire in the West in 476 – i.e. at the end of the last chapter (chapter XXXVIII) in his third volume. His 'General Considerations' at the end of that chapter would then be an appropriate epilogue to the whole work. However, he took care to leave his options open and soon he returned to his original idea. After a year's vacation, he resumed his pen and moved on from Rome to Byzantium.

The first of his new volumes, Volume IV, was written mainly in London but finished, after his emigration and the interruption which it entailed, in Lausanne. In it he maintained the same steady pace as before, carrying the story through the sixth to the early seventh century. This was an important and well-documented period and for the facts Gibbon had two invaluable guides in the ultra-papist Counter-Reformation cardinal, Caesar Baronius, 'firm and hard as the rock of Peter', and the pedestrian but accurate Jansenist scholar Sebastian le Nain de Tillemont, 'the patient and sure-footed mule of the Alps' who 'may be trusted in the most slippery paths'. It was also a period in which, in spite of the Gothic conquest of Italy, some semblance of historical continuity and imperial unity was maintained. In Italy Theodoric the Ostrogoth, 'a Gothic king who might have deserved a statue among the best and bravest of the ancient Romans', continued Roman institutions and paid lip-service to the sovereignty of Constantinople; and after his death, that sovereignty was forcibly reasserted by the Emperor Justinian.

Imperial authority was then re-established, and secured by Roman fortresses, in Italy, North Africa and Spain; Roman law was formulated in the greatest of all its codifications and although the spoken language of Byzantium was Greek, Latin remained the language of government. Officially it was still the Roman Empire.

However, the successes of Justinian's long reign did not last. Though his laws and his buildings endured, his conquests did not. The Western Mediterranean had been reconquered only to be re-lost, and after the Emperor's death in 565 the Empire itself was threatened. The barbarian Lombards replaced the romanized Goths in Italy; the Avars, pouring into the Balkan provinces, 'alternately bathed their horses in the Euxine and the Adriatic'; and from Asia the revived Persian monarchy returned to the attack: its armies reached the Bosphorus and besieged Constantinople itself. The besiegers were finally driven off by the new Emperor Heraclius, but the whole structure of the Empire had been shaken by these attacks and it would never be the same. In retrospect the age of Justinian appears as the Indian summer of the historic Roman Empire, and modern historians see the reign of Heraclius (610–641) as the beginning of a new age of distinctive 'Byzantine' history.

This great disjuncture was not caused only by events within the Empire: it was emphasized and made permanent by a revolution further east. It was in the reign of Heraclius that Mohammed created a new power in Arabia and that his immediate successors began those lightning conquests which would destroy the age-old political balance of Rome and Persia. Within a few years Muslim armies would overthrow the Persian Empire, sever Syria, Egypt and the Maghreb permanently from Christendom, and conquer Visigothic Spain. From now on, both Rome and Byzantium changed their character. Rome became the spiritual capital of the Western barbarians, Byzantium the exposed outpost of Greek Christian civilization in the face of successive invaders from North and East.

Having reached this great turning-point, and observed the widening panorama before him, Gibbon conceived a new plan, which he would announce in the first chapter of his fifth volume (chapter XLVIII). With Byzantine history after Heraclius he had, he admitted, little sympathy, and he would have 'abandoned without regret the Greek slaves and their servile historians'. But, he reflected, 'the fate of the Byzantine monarchy is *passively* connected with the most splendid and important revolutions which have changed the state of the world'. He therefore decided, while keeping the history of the Byzantine Empire as the central thread of his work, to divert his main interest, or at least his sympathy, to its external relations: to the pressure upon it, and the interaction with it, of the more dynamic 'barbarian' societies around it: in the East, its successive Muslim assailants; in the West, the Catholic 'Franks' and their high-priests, the Popes of Rome who, from the eighth century onwards, would challenge the authority of Emperor and Church in Constantinople, recognize a new Roman Empire in the West – the Germanic Empire of Charlemagne – and seek to impose their own rigid doctrines on the more sophisticated and flexible Christians of the East.

Indeed, it is the long, tortuous and bitter dialogue between the two Churches, rather than the political 'decline' of Byzantium, which will form the unifying theme of Gibbon's last two volumes. In the six centuries after Heraclius 'sixty phantom kings' will 'have passed before our eyes and faintly dwell on our remembrance', but the contest with Rome, with its alternation of moods and intensity, will remain constant to the very end. His tale is thus a tale of two cities, and to them, after our excursions among the Arabs, the Bulgarians, the Magyars, the Russians, the Normans, the Mongols and the Turks, he will ultimately lead us back. Constantinople, in its final agony, will then make a positive, if still passive contribution to the most splendid and important of all revolutions, the rise of European civilization; and so we shall return 'from the captivity of the new to the ruin of ancient Rome, and the venerable name, the interesting theme, will shed a ray of glory on the conclusion of my labours'.

So ambitious a plan demanded a vast range of knowledge. It also required a quickening of pace. Gibbon's first four volumes had covered a little over four centuries. Now eight centuries had to be compressed into the two volumes which were all that he allowed himself for the completion of his work.

That work was punctually completed as planned: an extraordinary feat of erudition and virtuosity. The historical sources were now less accessible, the path less trodden. After the sixth century he had to 'take leave for ever' from Tillemont, 'that incomparable guide whose bigotry is overbalanced by the merits of erudition, diligence, veracity and scrupulous exactness', and to rely, for much of the time, on tendentious evidence and his own judgement. However, he mastered the evidence and his judgement was seldom at fault. Of course he made some errors, but they are remarkably few; his critical spirit was always alert; and his narrative is always vivid. Some of his most brilliant passages are to be found in these last two volumes: his accounts of Mohammed and the rise of Islam, of the iconoclastic movement in Byzantium, and of 'the long and disgraceful servitude' of the Papacy in the ninth and tenth centuries; his narratives of the Norman conquest of Sicily and of the Crusades; his excursions into the history of the Mongols and the Turks; and his concluding chapters on the dramatic siege and conquest of Constantinople and on the changing fortunes of the medieval city of Rome.

Throughout this history of the Dark and Middle Ages Gibbon continued to apply the new method of interpretation inspired by Montesquieu. Just as he had formerly used the Theodosian Code not as a mere compilation of laws but as a means of understanding the social structure of the Constantinian Empire, and thus appreciating the social revolution caused by the adoption of Christianity, so he now used the Code and the Pandects of Justinian and the 'Basilics' of the 'Macedonian' Emperors as a means of understanding sixth- and tenth-century Byzantium. He deduced the character of the Visigothic and Lombard societies from their laws, wrote to England to secure the Institutes of Timour (or Tamerlane), and plunged into 'the immense labyrinth of the *jus publicum* of Germany'. In studying barbarian societies he was not content with chronicles and narrations: he asked the questions which a modern social historian would ask: questions of diet, economy, family and social structure.

Perhaps the most striking example of this is his examination of the nomadic societies of the steppes whose movements caused such displacement of peoples: the Huns in the fourth and fifth and the Tartars or Mongols in the thirteenth century. Here he drew on a wide variety of sources – Greek and Roman writers from Herodotus onwards, the Franciscan friars who visited the courts of the great Mongol khans, the reports of the Jesuits in Peking whom he reproves for their 'blind admiration' of the Chinese Empire, and the French translations of Manchu and Chinese documents available in his time. These works he read critically, looking for evidence not only of political events but of social causation, and he often (as he once wrote in another context) 'deduced my own consequences, beyond the holy circle of the author'. The result is a very modern interpretation. Indeed, the greatest modern authority on the Mongols begins an essay on the social history of Mongol nomadism with a close examination of Gibbon's enquiry into the subject, explaining that 'Gibbon is worth quoting at this length, because he sets out so many of the facts, and raises so many of the questions, that must still be considered by the social historian who deals with such a people as the Mongols.'[1]

Gibbon's treatment of oriental history is indeed one of the most interesting aspects of his work. We know from his *Memoirs* that he had always been interested in it: that as a boy he had read all that he could find about 'the Arabs and the Persians, the Tartars and the Turks', and that at Oxford he had wished to learn Arabic. Dr Johnson's *boutade* that he had once been a Mohammedan may well be a recollection of that fact. He was also a friend of the greatest of English orientalists, Sir William Jones, who was a fellow-member of the Club in London and another declared disciple of Montesquieu. Gibbon showed both his knowledge and his sure judgement in oriental history when he insisted, against the prevailing view of the anti-clerical French *philosophes*, that the Nestorian inscription of Si-ngan Fu (or Sian) in China was genuine, and he was well

[1] Owen Lattimore, 'The Social History of Mongol Nomadism', in *Historians of China and Japan*, ed. W. G. Beasley and E. G. Pulley-blank, Oxford, 1961, pp. 328–331.

aware of the interrelation of Eastern and Western history. As a modern Chinese historian has written,[1] 'from the Pisgah height of his universal historical learning, Gibbon could clearly see how the East and West affect each other and co-relate in a causal way events apparently unrelated'.

The most dramatic direct collision of East and West in the Middle Ages was the Crusades. This was a subject which exercised all the 'philosophic historians' of the Enlightenment. In general, reacting against their theologically minded predecessors, they had seen the Crusades as wild enterprises, the expression of fanaticism, barbarism and delusion, but at the same time as economically advantageous to the West since they enriched the Italian cities by the commerce of the East. This had been the view of Voltaire, Robertson and Adam Smith. Gibbon however was more radical. To him the Crusades were almost entirely harmful. Even when viewed from a parochial Western position, they 'checked rather than forwarded the maturity of Europe'. The lives and labour which were buried in the East could have been 'more profitably employed in the improvement of their native country'; industry would then have 'overflowed in navigation and trade and the Latins would have been enriched and enlightened by a friendly correspondence with the climates of the East'.

Only in one accidental respect did Gibbon see the Crusades as beneficial, 'not so much in producing a benefit as in removing an evil': they undermined the 'Gothic edifice' of feudalism. Gibbon hated 'the oppressive system of feudalism' and his language about it is invariably strong. It was supported, he wrote, 'by the arts of the clergy and the swords of the barons' while 'the larger portion of the inhabitants of Europe was chained to the soil without freedom or property or knowledge'. He allowed that the authority of the clergy operated as 'a salutary antidote: they prevented the total extinction of letters, mitigated the fierceness of the times, sheltered the poor and the defenceless, and preserved or revived the peace and order of civil society'. But to the feudal

---

[1] C. S. Ch'ien, 'China in the English Literature of the 18th century', in *Historians of China and Japan*, p. 316.

lords he would allow no such extenuation. Their 'iron weight' oppressed the people and crushed 'every hope of industry and improvement'. However, the Crusades, if they achieved nothing else, at least indirectly weakened this 'martial aristocracy'. Impoverished by 'those costly and perilous expeditions', the feudal lords were obliged to grant 'charters of freedom which unlocked the fetters of the slave, secured the farm of the peasant and the shop of the artificer, and gradually restored a substance and a soul to the most numerous and useful part of the community'. Gibbon's chapter on the Crusades reveals his deeply felt hatred of foreign conquest and of social immobility. 'There is nothing perhaps more adverse to nature and reason,' he wrote, 'than to hold in obedience remote countries and foreign nations in opposition to their inclination and interest'; and it is in a tone almost of satisfaction that he records the ultimate failure of that whole imperialist adventure. After two centuries of heroism and barbarity the Muslims recovered control of Syria and Palestine, and 'a mournful and solitary silence prevailed along the coast which had so long resounded with the World's Debate'.

Whatever their effects on the Western countries which launched them, for Byzantium the Crusades were an unqualified disaster. The first of them had come in response to the appeal of the Emperor Alexius Comnenus in order to save the Holy Land from the infidel Seljuk Turks. The fourth, in 1204, never reached the Holy Land: the Crusaders stopped on their way and sacked Christian Constantinople. The richest city in Christendom, which had survived the attacks of Persians, Avars and Arabs, was wrecked and vandalized from within by new barbarians from the West. 'The martial aristocracy' of France then imposed its 'iron weight' on the peasantry of Greece, and the mercantile aristocracy of Venice took over its profitable harbours and islands. For sixty years Frankish usurpers ruled as Emperors of an impoverished Byzantium, now renamed New France; Catholic worship was forcibly imposed on the Greek Church; and the religious breach which had opened before the First Crusade was deepened and made permanent by the resentment of the conquered people. When Greek resistance finally evicted the Franks (though not the

Venetians), the restored Empire was a shadow of its former self. Under the last and longest of its dynasties, it survived only as a client-state of its more powerful neighbours, and only an accident – the distraction of the Turks by the meteoric career of Tamerlane – postponed its final capture. In the course of its prolonged agony three Emperors travelled personally to Italy to seek again the dangerous support of the West, which was offered only on an intolerable condition: the 'reunion' of the Churches by subjection to Rome. In their despair, the Byzantine rulers would have paid the price, but the people would not. They preferred (they said) the turban of the Turk to the tiara of the Pope; and that is what they got. In Gibbon's time they had it still.

In spite of these melancholy events, Gibbon contrived to end on a confident note. The desperate diplomacy of the last Greek Emperors brought them and their cultivated officers out of their complacent isolation and into Italy at a fortunate historic moment: the moment when the *élite* of Italy were turning from the scholastic orthodoxy of discredited Popes towards the classical past and seeking to recover not only (like Cola di Rienzo) the grandeur of imperial Rome but also (like Petrarch) the long lost intellectual and literary inheritance of Greece. Gibbon was never reluctant to touch lightly on discredited Popes: read his splendid accounts of John XII in chapter XLIX and of John XXIII in chapter LXX; but his serious concern now was with that wonderful conjuncture which saved the legacy of Antiquity. Not all of it indeed: much of it had already been lost – some of it perhaps in the sack of Constantinople in 1204 – but enough; and how narrowly even that had survived! Who could have guessed that Byzantium would last so long, a single and ultimately fragile link between ancient Hellenism and the modern world? In the end, that perhaps was its greatest achievement. 'We may tremble at the thought,' wrote Gibbon, 'that Greece might have been overwhelmed, with her schools and libraries, before Europe had emerged from the deluge of barbarism: that the seeds of science might have been scattered by the winds before the Italian soil was prepared for their cultivation.'

In his last chapter Gibbon remembered that day in October

1763 when he had seen the bare-footed friars singing vespers in the temple of Jupiter and had contemplated tracing the history not then of the Empire but of the City of Rome through this memorable transformation. Now he returned to that original idea. The imperial city had indeed been ruined in those centuries of 'barbarism and religion', but not, he insisted, by the barbarians. The Gothic invaders, 'so injuriously accused of the ruin of Antiquity', had neither the time nor the strength nor the will to destroy 'the solid piles of Antiquity'. 'From these innocent barbarians' the reproach may be transferred to '*those* barbarians who alone had time and inclination to execute such laborious destruction': to 'the Catholics of Rome' – and, not least, to the upstart Popes of the Renaissance who used the Coliseum as a quarry from which to build their ostentatious palaces. Afterwards, in his *Memoirs*, still remembering that day in 1763, Gibbon would describe the completion of his work with the words which are so familiar and yet so impossible not to quote:

I have presumed to mark the moment of conception; I shall now commemorate the hour of my final deliverance. It was on the day, or rather night, of the 27th of June [1787], between the hours of eleven and twelve, that I wrote the last lines of the last page, in a summer-house in my garden. After laying down my pen, I took several turns in a *berceau* or covered walk of acacias, which commands a prospect of the country, the lake and the mountains. The air was temperate, the sky was serene, the silver orb of the moon was reflected from the waters, and all Nature was silent. I will not dissemble the first emotions of joy on recovery of my freedom and, perhaps, the establishment of my fame. But my pride was soon humbled, and a sober melancholy was spread over my mind, by the idea that I had taken an everlasting leave of an old and agreeable companion, and that whatsoever might be the future date of my *History*, the life of the historian must be short and precarious.

Having completed his work, Gibbon took the three last volumes to England to be printed. He spent the autumn with Lord Sheffield at his country house, Sheffield Place, correcting the proofs. His preface was dated 1 May 1788, from Lord Sheffield's London house in Downing Street, and the volumes were published a week later. The publisher celebrated the event by a dinner at which a commendatory ode by Gibbon's friend, the poet William Hayley, was read.

Gibbon's fame was now well established. Only the clergy continued their attacks, and indeed extended them; for they now found a new front against which to direct them. This was what even Gibbon's defender, the Greek scholar Richard Porson, would describe as his 'rage for indecency': an indecency which was generally relegated to the footnotes and protected by 'the obscurity of a learned language'. The most notorious of such notes described the strip-tease act of the Empress Theodora, the wife of Justinian, in her unreformed days as a prostitute on the stage. Gibbon leaves the quotation in the original Greek of the Byzantine historian Procopius, from which I shall not presume to release it. The clergy were perhaps particularly irritated by his comment, 'I have heard that a learned prelate, now deceased, was fond of quoting this passage in conversation'. The prelate is said to have been William Warburton, Bishop of Gloucester, the swashbuckling literary tyrant whose pretensions to scholarship had once been punctured by Gibbon. The Bishop of Norwich was so shocked by this quotation that he went through the whole of Gibbon's work extracting the indecent passages in order to hold them up for execration; but he was forestalled by the edition of *The Gentleman's Magazine*, who published such a list, without comment, and was duly reproached by a correspondent for printing 'filthy extracts from a silly book'. I am told that Cecil Rhodes was so stimulated by this note that he hired a classical scholar to translate all Gibbon's Greek and Latin quotations, but was disappointed by the meagre result.

These attacks by 'the rigid censors of morals' surprised Gibbon. They had not been levelled at his earlier volumes, he noted, so why now? And had not Theodora's exploit been told in print by a clergyman, 'an instructor of youth' – indeed the headmaster of Winchester? But publicly he took no notice of these or of any other critics, and absolutely refused to be tempted or bullied into controversy. He left them all to be forgotten, as they soon were. 'It would be strange,' Macaulay would write in 1850, 'if, in so large a work as Gibbon's there were nothing open to just remark', but in fact 'how utterly all the attacks on his *History* are forgotten!' However, in more recent times, with the expansion of Byzantine studies, and the great increase in archaeological and iconographical evidence, more serious criticisms have been made, not so much of Gibbon's historical accuracy as of his general interpretation of Byzantine society and civilization. Even if they do not name him, modern byzantinists often, as they write, have him in their eye.

Apart from points of detail, they make two general charges against him. First, they challenge his whole concept of 'decline'. Gibbon, they say, like other writers of his time, subjected history to the distorting categories of 'progress' and 'decadence', 'progress' being progress towards their own form of society, 'decadence' the renunciation of it: an anachronistic and unhistorical criterion, rightly rejected by the more conservative German historians of the nineteenth century who insisted that every society, and every age, should be seen in its own context and judged by its own standards. That the Eastern Roman Empire, like the Western, declined in power and extent, and ultimately fell, is of course undeniable; but to extend the concept of decline from mere power to politics and morals is to pre-empt objective judgement. Byzantium under the 'Macedonian' and Comnenian dynasties was still a vigorous political system, the richest and most sophisticated society in Christendom; it converted and thereby civilized the Slavs and sent missionaries to the East; its social organization deserves to be studied independently of its politics; its art and architecture are admired today; and it was a bulwark, or at least a breakwater, against the successive tides of invasion from the East.

The second general charge is that Gibbon by his dismissive treatment of the Byzantine Empire, and the great reputation of his work, positively retarded Byzantine studies. These studies had begun in sixteenth-century Germany and had been powerfully forwarded in seventeenth-century France, especially by the Benedictines of St Maur and by the greatest of early byzantinists, Charles du Fresne du Cange. These scholars had edited and published the Byzantine chronicles and had made it possible to reconstruct the history of the Empire. But Gibbon, though he venerated these precursors and acknowledged his debt to them, effectively, by his negative attitude towards Byzantium, undermined their work and 'damped enthusiasm for Byzantine research for nearly a century'.[1]

There is substance in both these charges, but they are in themselves somewhat anachronistic since they presume the resources and the mentality of a later age. The disparagement of Byzantium was general among eighteenth-century 'philosophic' writers. Montesquieu declared that the history of the Byzantine Empire was only 'a tissue of revolts, seditions and treacheries'. Voltaire described its records as 'a worthless collection of speeches and miracles'. In England, Horace Walpole told Gibbon – before Gibbon had begun to write on it – that he was sorry that he 'should have pitched on so disgusting a subject as the Constantinopolitan history'. All these judgements were based, directly or indirectly, on the texts edited by the great antiquarian scholars of the previous century, and perhaps were legitimate deductions from them. Perhaps those texts, which Gibbon had read more closely and critically than anyone, had themselves 'damped enthusiasm' for the subject; for in the hundred years since their publication, no modern scholarly narrative of Byzantine history had been published. The point had been made by Montesquieu. What we need, he wrote, in a private memorandum, is 'a history of Byzantium, instead of all those folio volumes of detestable authors which we have'. I am afraid that those folios of detestable authors were the great Paris *Corpus* of Byzantine writers. Gibbon's work, itself inspired by Montesquieu, was, in effect, the answer to Montesquieu's prayer.

Gibbon was certainly unsympathetic to Byzantium. If we are to understand his lack of sympathy, it too must be seen in its context: the context not merely of eighteenth-century historiography but also of his personal philosophy, which transcends it. In my introduction to the first three volumes of this edition I summarized that philosophy and need not recapitulate it here. It was a philosophy of public spirit, civic

[1] George Ostrogorsky, *History of the Byzantine State*, translated by Joan Hussey, Oxford, 1956, p. 6.

virtue, Machiavelli's *virtù*. Such virtue, Gibbon believed, both required and itself generated political freedom and a plural, competitive society. Any society, even a barbarian society, can throw up great individuals and no society, however civilized, is immune from human accident or folly; but high civilization, characterized and authenticated by original thought and great literature, depends for its stability on pluralism and liberty. Judged by this criterion, Gibbon believed, Byzantium had failed. Its citizens spoke Greek and called themselves Roman, but they no longer respected the values of the Greek city-states or the Roman republic. In this it marked a further 'decline' from the Western Empire. The Western Empire may have been a political despotism, but the old republican 'virtue' was not forgotten: it could still reassert itself in individuals, even in Popes and saints. The barbarian societies of the West could aspire to it, and would ultimately attain it. But in Byzantium it had died. The proof of its death was in action, and in literature: no great men of action – not even 'the vigour of memorable crimes' – no great thinkers. The Byzantines possessed the intellectual and literary legacy of Greece and preserved and edited the texts. But they neither continued the tradition nor applied the philosophy. 'A degenerate people held in their lifeless hands the riches of their fathers without inheriting the spirit which had created and improved that sacred patrimony. They read, they praised, they compiled; but their languid souls seemed alike incapable of thought or action'; their political system 'checked the activity and progress of the human mind'; and it was left to the more virile 'barbarians' of the West to appropriate and apply the ideas which, in Byzantium, had been forgotten, or reduced to mere rhetoric.

As a statement of fact, this can hardly be denied and it conditioned Gibbon's judgement of Byzantium and his explanation of its 'decline'. No doubt, at times, it led him into misjudgements. But a great work can carry and absorb incidental errors. As the distinguished Russian byzantinist, George Ostrogorsky, has written, there is no need now for scholars 'indignantly to refute the assertions of Gibbon': Gibbon is 'a genuine historian', indeed 'a very great one'. His greatness lies in his erudition and his philosophy: his astonishing command over an immense range of evidence, and his use of it to pose and answer a great general problem. That problem is as relevant today as it was in his own time: perhaps even more relevant; and the very fact that his answers are still debated indicates the permanent interest of his work.

Besides, there is also the style, that inimitable style which reflects the quality of his mind and enlivens the whole work, even its learned footnotes: that 'grave and temperate irony' which he claimed to have learned from Pascal; those sallies of sometimes wicked wit; and that sharp eye for detail which has caused another modern scholar to write that 'thanks to his great erudition and to a native capacity for choosing what is picturesque, he is far more amusing than any other historian except Herodotus'.[1]

Hugh Trevor-Roper

[1] Arnaldo Momigliano, 'Gibbon's contribution to historical thought', in his *Studies in Historiography*, 1966.

THE HISTORY OF THE
DECLINE AND FALL
OF THE ROMAN
EMPIRE

CHAPTER XXXVII

Origin, Progress, and Effects of the Monastic Life – Conversion of the Barbarians to Christianity and Arianism – Persecution of the Vandals in Africa – Extinction of Arianism among the Barbarians.

THE indissoluble connection of civil and ecclesiastical affairs has compelled and encouraged me to relate the progress, the persecutions, the establishment, the divisions, the final triumph, and the gradual corruption of Christianity. I have purposely delayed the consideration of two religious events interesting in the study of human nature, and important in the decline and fall of the Roman empire. I. The institution of the monastic life;[1] and II. The conversion of the northern barbarians.

I. Prosperity and peace introduced the distinction of the *vulgar* and the *Ascetic Christians*.[2] The loose and imperfect practice of religion satisfied the conscience of the multitude. The prince or magistrate, the soldier or merchant, reconciled their fervent zeal and implicit faith with the exercise of their profession, the pursuit of their interest, and the indulgence of their passions: but the Ascetics, who obeyed and abused the rigid precepts of the Gospel, were inspired by the savage enthusiasm which represents man as a criminal, and God as a tyrant. They seriously renounced the business and the pleasures of the age; abjured the use of wine, of flesh, and of marriage; chastised their body, mortified their affections, and embraced a life of misery, as the price of eternal happines. In the reign of Constantine the Ascetics fled from a profane and degenerate world to perpetual solitude or religious society. Like the first Christians of

1 The origin of the monastic institution has been laboriously discussed by Thomassin (Discipline de l'Eglise, tom. i. p. 1419–1426) and Helyot (Hist. des Ordres Monastiques, tom. i. p. 1–66). These authors are very learned and tolerably honest, and their difference of opinion shows the subject in its full extent. Yet the cautious Protestant, who distrusts *any* Popish guides, may consult the seventh book of Bingham's Christian Antiquities.

2 See Euseb. Demonstrat. Evangel. (l. i. p. 20, 21, edit. Græc. Rob. Stephani, Paris, 1545). In his Ecclesiastical History, published twelve years after the Demonstration, Eusebius (l. ii. c. 17) asserts the Christianity of the Therapeutæ; but he appears ignorant that a similar institution was actually revived in Egypt.

Jerusalem,¹ they resigned the use or the property of their temporal possessions; established regular communities of the same sex and a similar disposition; and assumed the names of *Hermits, Monks,* and *Anachorets,* expressive of their lonely retreat in a natural or artificial desert. They soon acquired the respect of the world, which they despised; and the loudest applause was bestowed on this DIVINE PHILOSOPHY,² which surpassed, without the aid of science or reason, the laborious virtues of the Grecian schools. The monks might indeed contend with the Stoics in the contempt of fortune, of pain, and of death: the Pythagorean silence and submission were revived in their servile discipline; and they disdained as firmly as the Cynics themselves all the forms and decencies of civil society. But the votaries of this Divine Philosophy aspired to imitate a purer and more perfect model. They trod in the footsteps of the prophets, who had retired to the desert;³ and they restored the devout and contemplative life, which had been instituted by the Essenians in Palestine and Egypt. The philosophic eye of Pliny had surveyed with astonishment a solitary people, who dwelt among the palm-trees near the Dead Sea; who subsisted without money; who were propagated without women; and who derived from the disgust and repentance of mankind a perpetual supply of voluntary associates.⁴

1 Cassian (Collat. xviii. 5 [Max. Bibl. Patr. t. vii. p. 208]) claims this origin for the institution of the *Cænobites,* which gradually decayed till it was restored by Antony and his disciples.

2 Ὠφελιώτατον γάρ τι χρῆμα εἰς ἀνθρώπους ἐλθοῦσα παρὰ Θέου ἡ τοιαύτη φιλοσοφία. These are the expressive words of Sozomen, who copiously and agreeably describes (l. i. c. 12, 13, 14) the origin and progress of this monkish philosophy (see Suicer. Thesaur. Eccles. tom. ii. p. 1441). Some modern writers, Lipsius (tom. iv. p. 448; Manuduct. ad Philosoph. Stoic. iii. 13) and La Mothe de Vayer (tom. ix. de la Vertu des Payens, p. 228–262), have compared the Carmelites to the Pythagoreans, and the Cynics to the Capucins.

3 The Carmelites derive their pedigree in regular succession from the prophet Elijah (see the Theses of Beziers, A.D. 1682, in Bayle's Nouvelles de la République des Lettres, Œuvres, tom. i. p. 82, etc.; and the prolix irony of the Ordres Monastiques, an anonymous work, tom. i. p. 1–433; Berlin, 1751). Rome and the inquisition of Spain silenced the profane criticism of the Jesuits of Flanders (Helyot, Hist. des Ordres Monastiques, tom. i. p. 282–300), and the statue of Elijah the Carmelite has been erected in the church of St. Peter (Voyages du P. Labat, tom. iii. p. 87).

4 Plin. Hist. Natur. v. 15. Gens sola, et in toto orbe præter ceteras mira,

Egypt, the fruitful parent of superstition, afforded the first example of the monastic life. Antony,[1] an illiterate[2] youth of the lower parts of Thebais, distributed his patrimony,[3] deserted his family and native home, and executed his *monastic* penance with original and intrepid fanaticism. After a long and painful noviatiate among the tombs and in a ruined tower, he boldly advanced into the desert three days' journey to the eastward of the Nile; discovered a lonely spot, which possessed the advantages of shade and water; and fixed his last residence on Mount Colzim, near the Red Sea, where an ancient monastery still preserves the name and memory of the saint.[4] The curious devotion of the Christians pursued him to the desert; and when he was obliged

sine ullâ feminâ, omni venere abdicatâ, sine pecuniâ, socia palmarum. Ita per seculorum millia (incredibile dictu) gens æterna est in quâ nemo nascitur. Tam fecunda illis aliorum vitæ pœnitentia est. He places them just beyond the noxious influence of the lake, and names Engaddi and Masada as the nearest towns. The Laura and monastery of St. Sabas could not be far distant from this place. See Reland, Palestin. tom. i. p. 295; tom. ii. p. 763, 874, 880, 890.

1 See Athanas. Op. tom. ii. p. 450–505 [tom. i. p. 793–866, ed. Bened. 1698], and the Vit. Patrum, p. 26–74, with Rosweyde's Annotations. The former is the Greek original; the latter, a very ancient Latin version by Evagrius, the friend of St. Jerom.

2 Γράμματα μὲν μάθειν οὐκ ἠνέσχετο. Athanas. tom. ii. in Vit. St. Anton. p. 452 [p. 795, ed. Bened. 1698; cf. c. 72, p. 849], and the assertion of his total ignorance has been received by many of the ancients and moderns. But Tillemont (Mém. Ecclés. tom. vii. p. 666) shows, by some probable arguments, that Antony could read and write in the Coptic, his native tongue; and that he was only a stranger to the *Greek letters*. The philosopher Synesius (p. 51 [ed. Par. 1612]) acknowledges that the natural genius of Antony did not require the aid of learning.

[Athanasius, in his Life of Antony (chap. 47), boasts of the fact of the saint's holy horror of clean water, by which his feet at least had never been contaminated since his adoption of the holy rule, unless under the dire necessity of crossing a river or the like. – O.S.]

3 *Arura* autem erant ei trecentæ uberes, et valde optimæ (Vit. Patr. l. v. [l. i.] p. 36). If the *Arura* be a square measure of an hundred Egyptian cubits (Rosweyde, Onomasticon ad Vit. Patrum, p. 1014, 1015 [p. 1009]), and the Egyptian cubit of all ages be equal to twenty-two English inches (Greaves, vol. i. p. 233), the arura will consist of about three-quarters of an English acre.

4 The description of the monastery is given by Jerom (tom. i. p. 248, 249, in Vit. Hilarion [tom. ii. p. 31, ed. Vallars.]), and the P. Sicard (Missions du Levant, tom. v. p. 122–200). Their accounts cannot always be reconciled: the father painted from his fancy, and the Jesuit from his experience.

[For those desirous of studying the origin of monasticism, the earliest and perhaps, all things considered, the best authorities are Palladius, Rufinus, and

to appear at Alexandria, in the face of mankind, he supported his fame with discretion and dignity. He enjoyed the friendship of Athanasius, whose doctrine he approved; and the Egyptian peasant respectfully declined a respectful invitation from the emperor Constantine. The venerable patriarch (for Antony attained the age of one hundred and five years) beheld the numerous progeny which had been formed by his example and his lessons. The prolific colonies of monks multiplied with rapid increase on the sands of Libya, upon the rocks of Thebais, and in the cities of the Nile. To the south of Alexandria, the mountain, and adjacent desert, of Nitria was peopled by five thousand anachorets; and the traveller may still investigate the ruins of fifty monasteries, which were planted in that barren soil by the disciples of Antony.[1] In the Upper Thebais, the vacant island of Tabenne[2] was occupied by Pachomius and fourteen hundred of his

Sozomen. The monastic system began with the isolated individuals who, like Antony, went out into the desert to live the life of meditation and prayer. Then came the 'organised community,' evolved by Pachomius, who had become convinced that life in a society of recluses was more accordant to the mind of the Founder of Christianity than the solitary existence of an anchorite. He developed a rigid system or rule for the brethren thus living together. At first the church was opposed to the idea, and both the bishops and the clergy persecuted the monks. The church, however, soon discovered that, if it desired to retain its influence with the people, it must not only refrain from hindering, but must reconcile itself to and patronise a movement which was striking its roots deep into the spiritual imagination of the community at large. For a long time the church merely stood aloof, refraining from persecuting. Then by a tactful move on the part of the Patriarch Athanasius, the reconciliation between the church and monachism was accomplished. Grutzmacher has aptly said that Athanasius's Life of St. Antony is the seal which the church sets on its recognition of the new movement. Cf. Bury, vol. iv. Appendix 3, for a most valuable list of the authorities on monachism to which I am indebted; also, in German, Weingarten, Harnack, Mayer, and in French, Amelineau. – O. S.]

1 Jerom, tom. i. p. 146, and Eustochium [Ep. 22. p. 119, ed. Vall.]; Hist. Lausiac. c. 7, in Vit. Patrum, p. 712 [p. 982]. The P. Sicard (Missions du Levant, tom. ii. p. 29–79) visited and has described this desert, which now contains four monasteries, and twenty or thirty monks. See D'Anville, Description de l'Egypte, p. 74.

2 Tabenne is a small island in the Nile, in the diocese of Tentyra or Dendera, between the modern town of Girge and the ruins of ancient Thebes (D'Anville, p. 194). M. de Tillemont doubts whether it was an isle; but I may conclude, from his own facts, that the primitive name was afterwards transferred to the great monastery of Bau or Pabau (Mém. Ecclés. tom. vii. p. 678, 688).

brethren. That holy abbot successively founded nine monasteries of men, and one of women; and the festival of Easter sometimes collected fifty thousand religious persons, who followed his *angelic* rule of discipline.[1] The stately and populous city of Oxyrinchus, the seat of Christian orthodoxy, had devoted the temples, the public edifices, and even the ramparts, to pious and charitable uses; and the bishop, who might preach in twelve churches, computed ten thousand females, and twenty thousand males, of the monastic profession.[2] The Egyptians, who gloried in this marvellous revolution, were disposed to hope, and to believe, that the number of the monks was equal to the remainder of the people;[3] and posterity might repeat the saying which had formerly been applied to the sacred animals of the same country, that in Egypt it was less difficult to find a god than a man.

Athanasius introduced into Rome the knowledge and practice of the monastic life; and a school of this new philosophy was opened by the disciples of Antony, who accompanied their primate to the holy threshold of the Vatican. The strange and savage appearance of these Egyptians excited, at first, horror and contempt, and, at length, applause and zealous imitation. The senators, and more especially the matrons, transformed their palaces and villas into religious houses; and the narrow institution of *six* Vestals was eclipsed by the frequent monasteries, which were seated on the ruins of ancient temples and in the midst of the Roman forum.[4] Inflamed by the example of Antony, a Syrian youth, whose name was Hilarion,[5] fixed his dreary abode

1 See in the Codex Regularum (published by Lucas Holstenius, Rome, 1661) a preface of St. Jerom to his Latin version of the Rule of Pachomius, tom. i. p. 61 [tom. i. p. 25, ed. Augsb. 1759].

2 Rufin. c. 5, in Vit. Patrum, p. 459. He calls it civitas ampla valde et populosa, and reckons twelve churches. Strabo (l. xvii. p. 1166 [p. 812, ed. Casaub.]) and Ammianus (xxii. 16) have made honourable mention of Oxyrinchus, whose inhabitants adored a small fish in a magnificent temple.

3 Quanti populi habentur in urbibus, tantæ pene habentur in desertis multitudines monachorum. Rufin. c. 7, in Vit. Patrum, p. 461. He congratulates the fortunate change.

4 The introduction of the monastic life into Rome and Italy is occasionally mentioned by Jerom, tom. i. p. 119, 120, 199.

5 See the Life of Hilarion, by St. Jerom (tom. i. p. 241, 252 [tom. ii. p. 15, 24, ed. Vall.]). The stories of Paul, Hilarion, and Malchus, by the same author,

on a sandy beach between the sea and a morass, about seven miles from Gaza. The austere penance, in which he persisted forty-eight years, diffused a similar enthusiasm; and the holy man was followed by a train of two or three thousand anachorets, whenever he visited the innumerable monasteries of Palestine. The fame of Basil[1] is immortal in the monastic history of the East. With a mind that had tasted the learning and eloquence of Athens; with an ambition scarcely to be satisfied by the archbishopric of Cæsarea, Basil retired to a savage solitude in Pontus; and deigned, for a while, to give laws to the spiritual colonies which he profusely scattered along the coast of the Black Sea. In the West, Martin of Tours,[2] a soldier, a hermit, a bishop, and a saint, established the monasteries of Gaul; two thousand of his disciples followed him to the grave; and his eloquent historian challenges the deserts of Thebais to produce, in a more favourable climate, a champion of equal virtue. The progress of the monks was not less rapid or universal than that of Christianity itself. Every province, and, at last, every city, of the empire was filled with their increasing multitudes; and the bleak and barren isles, from Lerins to Lipari, that arise out of the Tuscan Sea, were chosen by the anachorets for the place of their voluntary exile. An easy and perpetual intercourse by sea and land connected the provinces of the Roman world; and the life of Hilarion displays the facility with which an indigent hermit of Palestine might traverse Egypt, embark for Sicily, escape to Epirus, and finally settle in the island of Cyprus.[3] The Latin

are admirably told; and the only defect of these pleasing compositions is the want of truth and common sense.

1 His original retreat was in a small village on the banks of the Iris, not far from Neo-Cæsarea. The ten or twelve years of his monastic life were disturbed by long and frequent avocations. Some critics have disputed the authenticity of his ascetic rules; but the external evidence is weighty, and they can only prove that it is the work of a real or affected enthusiast. See Tillemont, Mém. Ecclés. tom. ix. p. 636–644; Helyot, Hist. des Ordres Monastiques, tom. i. p. 175–181.

2 See his Life, and the three Dialogues by Sulpicius Severus, who asserts (Dialog. i. 16) that the booksellers of Rome were delighted with the quick and ready sale of his popular work.

3 When Hilarion sailed from Parætonium to Cape Pachynus, he offered to pay his passage with a book of the Gospels. Posthumian, a Gallic monk, who had visited Egypt, found a merchant-ship bound from Alexandria to Marseilles,

Christians embraced the religious institutions of Rome. The pilgrims who visited Jerusalem eagerly copied, in the most distant climates of the earth, the faithful model of the monastic life. The disciples of Antony spread themselves beyond the tropic, over the Christian empire of Æthiopia.[1] The monastery of Banchor,[2] in Flintshire, which contained above two thousand brethren, dispersed a numerous colony among the barbarians of Ireland;[3] and Iona, one of the Hebrides, which was planted by the Irish monks, diffused over the northern regions a doubtful ray of science and superstition.[4]

These unhappy exiles from social life were impelled by the dark and implacable genius of superstition. Their mutual resolution was supported by the example of millions, of either sex, of every age, and of every rank; and each proselyte who entered the gates of a monastery was persuaded that he trod the steep and thorny path of eternal happiness.[5] But the operation of these religious

and performed the voyage in thirty days (Sulp. Sever. Dialog. i. I). Athanasius, who addressed his Life of St. Antony to the foreign monks, was obliged to hasten the composition, that it might be ready for the sailing of the fleets (tom. ii. p. 451 [tom. i. p. 794, ed. Bened. 1698]).

1 See Jerom (tom. i. p. 126), Assemanni, Bibliot. Orient. tom. iv. p. 92, p. 857–919, and Geddes, Church History of Æthiopia, p. 29, 30, 31. The Abyssinian monks adhere very strictly to the primitive institution.

2 Camden's Britannia, vol. i. p. 666, 667.

3 All that learning can extract from the rubbish of the dark ages is copiously stated by Archbishop Usher in his Britannicarum Ecclesiarum Antiquitates, cap. xvi. p. 425–503.

4 This small though not barren spot, Iona, Hy, or Columbkill, only two miles in length and one mile in breadth, has been distinguished – 1. By the monastery of St. Columba, founded A.D. 566, whose abbot exercised an extraordinary jurisdiction over the bishops of Caledonia; 2. By a *classic* library, which afforded some hopes of an entire Livy; and, 3. By the tombs of sixty kings, Scots, Irish, and Norwegians, who reposed in holy ground. See Usher (p. 311, 360–370) and Buchanan (Rer. Scot. l. ii. p. 15, edit. Ruddiman).

5 Chrysostom (in the first tome of the Benedictine edition) has consecrated three books to the praise and defence of the monastic life. He is encouraged, by the example of the ark, to presume that none but the elect (the monks) can possibly be saved (l. i. p. 55, 56). Elsewhere, indeed, he becomes more merciful (l. iii. p. 83, 84), and allows different degrees of glory, like the sun, moon, and stars. In his lively comparison of a king and a monk (l. iii. p. 116–121), he supposes (what is hardly fair) that the king will be more sparingly rewarded, and more rigorously punished.

motives was variously determined by the temper and situation of mankind. Reason might subdue, or passion might suspend, their influence; but they acted most forcibly on the infirm minds of children and females; they were strengthened by secret remorse or accidental misfortune; and they might derive some aid from the temporal considerations of vanity or interest. It was naturally supposed that the pious and humble monks, who had renounced the world to accomplish the work of their salvation, were the best qualified for the spiritual government of the Christians. The reluctant hermit was torn from his cell, and seated, amidst the acclamations of the people, on the episcopal throne: the monasteries of Egypt, of Gaul, and of the East, supplied a regular succession of saints and bishops; and ambition soon discovered the secret road which led to the possession of wealth and honours.[1] The popular monks, whose reputation was connected with the fame and success of the order, assiduously laboured to multiply the number of their fellow-captives. They insinuated themselves into noble and opulent families; and the specious arts of flattery and seduction were employed to secure those proselytes who might bestow wealth or dignity on the monastic profession. The indignant father bewailed the loss, perhaps, of an only son;[2] the credulous maid was betrayed by vanity to violate the laws of nature; and the matron aspired to imaginary perfection by renouncing the virtues of domestic life. Paula yielded to the persuasive eloquence of Jerom;[3] and the profane title of mother-in-law of God[4] tempted that illustrious widow to consecrate the vir-

1 Thomassin (Discipline de l'Eglise, tom. i. p. 1426–1469) and Mabillon (Œuvres Posthumes, tom. ii. p. 115–158). The monks were gradually adopted as a part of the ecclesiastical hierarchy.

2 Dr. Middleton (vol. i. p. 110) liberally censures the conduct and writings of Chrysostom, one of the most eloquent and successful advocates for the monastic life.

3 Jerom's devout ladies form a very considerable portion of his works: the particular treatise, which he styles the Epitaph of Paula (tom. i. p. 169–192 [Ep. 108, tom. i. p. 684, ed. Vallars.]), is an elaborate and extravagant panegyric. The exordium is ridiculously turgid: – 'If all the members of my body were changed into tongues, and if all my limbs resounded with a human voice, yet should I be incapable,' etc.

4 Socrus Dei esse cœpisti (Jerom. tom. i. p. 140, ad Eustochium). Rufinus (in Hieronym. Op. tom. iv. p. 223), who was justly scandalised, asks his adversary, From what Pagan poet he had stolen an expression so impious and absurd?

ginity of her daughter Eustochium. By the advice, and in the company, of her spiritual guide, Paula abandoned Rome and her infant son; retired to the holy village of Bethlem; founded an hospital and four monasteries; and acquired, by her alms and penance, an eminent and conspicuous station in the catholic church. Such rare and illustrious penitents were celebrated as the glory and example of their age; but the monasteries were filled by a crowd of obscure and abject plebeians,[1] who gained in the cloister much more than they had sacrificed in the world. Peasants, slaves, and mechanics might escape from poverty and contempt to a safe and honourable profession, whose apparent hardships were mitigated by custom, by popular applause, and by the secret relaxation of discipline.[2] The subjects of Rome, whose persons and fortunes were made responsible for unequal and exorbitant tributes, retired from the oppression of the Imperial government; and the pusillanimous youth preferred the penance of a monastic, to the dangers of a military, life. The affrighted provincials of every rank, who fled before the barbarians, found shelter and subsistence; whole legions were buried in these religious sanctuaries; and the same cause which relieved the distress of individuals impaired the strength and fortitude of the empire.[3]

The monastic profession of the ancients[4] was an act of voluntary devotion. The inconstant fanatic was threatened with the

1 Nunc autem veniunt *plerumque* ad hanc professionem servitutis Dei, et ex conditione servili, vel etiam liberati, vel propter hoc a Dominis liberati sive liberandi; et ex vitâ rusticanâ, et ex opificum exercitatione, et plebeio labore. Augustin. de Oper. Monach. c. 22, ap. Thomassin, Discipline de l'Eglise, tom. iii. p. 1094. The Egyptian, who blamed Arsenius, owned that he led a more comfortable life as a monk than as a shepherd. See Tillemont, Mém. Ecclés. tom. xiv. p. 679.

2 A Dominican friar (Voyages du P. Labat, tom. i. p. 10), who lodged at Cadiz in a convent of his brethren, soon understood that their repose was never interrupted by nocturnal devotion; 'quoiqu'on ne laisse pas de sonner pour l'édification du peuple.'

3 See a very sensible preface of Lucas Holstenius to the Codex Regularum. The emperors attempted to support the obligation of public and private duties; but the feeble dykes were swept away by the torrent of superstition; and Justinian surpassed the most sanguine wishes of the monks (Thomassin, tom. i. p. 1782–1799, and Bingham, l. vii. c. 3, p. 253).

4 The monastic institutions, particularly those of Egypt, about the year 400, are described by four curious and devout travellers – Rufinus (Vit. Patrum, l. ii. iii. p. 424–536), Posthumian (Sulp. Sever. Dialog. i.), Palladius (Hist. Lausiac.

eternal vengeance of the God whom he deserted; but the doors
of the monastery were still open for repentance. Those monks
whose conscience was fortified by reason or passion were at
liberty to resume the character of men and citizens; and even the
spouses of Christ might accept the legal embraces of an earthly
lover.[1] The examples of scandal, and the progress of superstition,
suggested the propriety of more forcible restraints. After a sufficient trial, the fidelity of the novice was secured by a solemn
and perpetual vow; and his irrevocable engagement was ratified
by the laws of the church and state. A guilty fugitive was pursued, arrested, and restored to his perpetual prison; and the
interposition of the magistrate oppressed the freedom and merit
which had alleviated, in some degree, the abject slavery of the
monastic discipline.[2] The actions of a monk, his words, and even
his thoughts, were determined by an inflexible rule[3] or a capricious superior: the slightest offences were corrected by disgrace
or confinement, extraordinary fasts, or bloody flagellation; and
disobedience, murmur, or delay were ranked in the catalogue of
the most heinous sins.[4] A blind submission to the commands of

in Vit. Patrum, p. 709–863 [783]), and Cassian (see in tom. vii. Bibliothec. Max.
Patrum, his four first books of Institutes, and the twenty-four Collations or
Conferences).

1 The example of Malchus (Jerom. tom. i. p. 256 [tom. ii. p. 44, ed.
Vallars.]), and the design of Cassian and his friend (Collation xxiv. I), are
incontestable proofs of their freedom, which is elegantly described by Erasmus
in his Life of St. Jerom. See Chardon, Hist. des Sacremens, tom. vi. p. 279–300.

2 See the Laws of Justinian (Novell. cxxiii. No. 42 [Auth. Coll. ix. tit. vii.]),
and of Lewis the Pious (in the Historians of France, tom. vi. p. 427), and the
actual jurisprudence of France, in Denissart (Decisions, etc., tom. iv. p. 855, etc.).

3 The ancient Codex Regularum, collected by Benedict Anianinus, the reformer of the monks in the beginning of the ninth century, and published in
the seventeenth by Lucas Holstenius, contains thirty different rules for men and
women. Of these, seven were composed in Egypt, one in the East, one in
Cappadocia, one in Italy, one in Africa, four in Spain, eight in Gaul or France,
and one in England.

4 The rule of Columbanus, so prevalent in the West, inflicts one hundred
lashes for very slight offences (Cod. Reg. part ii. p. 174 [tom. i. p. 178, ed.
1759]). Before the time of Charlemagne the abbots indulged themselves in
mutilating their monks, or putting out their eyes – a punishment much less
cruel than the tremendous *vade in pace* (the subterraneous dungeon, or sepulchre), which was afterwards invented. See an admirable discourse of the
learned Mabillon (Œuvres Posthumes, tom. ii. p. 321–336), who, on this occa-

the abbot, however absurd, or even criminal, they might seem, was the ruling principle, the first virtue of the Egyptian monks; and their patience was frequently exercised by the most extravagant trials. They were directed to remove an enormous rock; assiduously to water a barren staff that was planted in the ground, till, at the end of three years, it should vegetate and blossom like a tree; to walk into a fiery furnace; or to cast their infant into a deep pond: and several saints, or madmen, have been immortalised in monastic story by their thoughtless and fearless obedience.[1] The freedom of the mind, the source of every generous and rational sentiment, was destroyed by the habits of credulity and submission; and the monk, contracting the vices of a slave, devoutly followed the faith and passions of his ecclesiastical tyrant. The peace of the Eastern church was invaded by a swarm of fanatics, incapable of fear, or reason, or humanity; and the Imperial troops acknowledged, without shame, that they were much less apprehensive of an encounter with the fiercest barbarians.[2]

Superstition has often framed and consecrated the fantastic garments of the monks:[3] but their apparent singularity sometimes proceeds from their uniform attachment to a simple and primitive model, which the revolutions of fashion have made ridiculous in the eyes of mankind. The father of the Benedictines expressly disclaims all idea of choice or merit; and soberly exhorts his disciples to adopt the coarse and convenient dress of the countries which they may inhabit.[4] The monastic habits of

sion, seems to be inspired by the genius of humanity. For such an effort, I can forgive his defence of the holy tear of Vendome (p. 361–399).

1 Sulp. Sever. Dialog. i. 12, 13, p. 532, etc. [ed. Lugd. B. 1647]; Cassian. Institut. l. iv. c. 26, 27. 'Præcipua ibi virtus et prima est obedientia.' Among the Verba seniorum (in Vit. Patrum, l. v. p. 617), the fourteenth libel or discourse is on the subject of obedience; and the Jesuit Rosweyde, who published that huge volume for the use of convents, has collected all the scattered passages in his two copious indexes.

2 Dr. Jortin (Remarks on Ecclesiastical History, vol. iv. p. 161) has observed the scandalous valour of the Cappadocian monks, which was exemplified in the banishment of Chrysostom.

3 Cassian has simply, though copiously, described the monastic habit of Egypt (Institut. l. i.), to which Sozomen (l. iii. c. 14) attributes such allegorical meaning and virtue.

4 Regul. Benedict. cap. 55, in Cod. Regul. Part ii. p. 51 [tom. i. p. 130, ed. Augsb. 1759].

the ancients varied with the climate and their mode of life; and they assumed, with the same indifference, the sheepskin of the Egyptian peasants or the cloak of the Grecian philosophers. They allowed themselves the use of linen in Egypt, where it was a cheap and domestic manufacture; but in the West they rejected such an expensive article of foreign luxury.[1] It was the practice of the monks either to cut or shave their hair; they wrapped their heads in a cowl, to escape the sight of profane objects; their legs and feet were naked, except in the extreme cold of winter; and their slow and feeble steps were supported by a long staff. The aspect of a genuine anachoret was horrid and disgusting: every sensation that is offensive to man was thought acceptable to God; and the angelic rule of Tabenne condemned the salutary custom of bathing the limbs in water and of anointing them with oil.[2] The austere monks slept on the ground, on a hard mat or a rough blanket; and the same bundle of palm-leaves served them as a seat in the day and a pillow in the night. Their original cells were low narrow huts, built of the slightest materials; which formed, by the regular distribution of the streets, a large and populous village, enclosing, within the common wall, a church, a hospital, perhaps a library, some necessary offices, a garden, and a fountain or reservoir of fresh water. Thirty or forty brethren composed a family of separate discipline and diet; and the great monasteries of Egypt consisted of thirty or forty families.

Pleasure and guilt are synonymous terms in the language of the monks, and they had discovered, by experience, that rigid fasts and abstemious diet are the most effectual preservatives against the impure desires of the flesh.[3] The rules of abstinence

1 See the Rule of Ferreolus, bishop of Usez (cap. 31, in Cod. Regul. part ii. p. 136 [tom. i. p. 162]), and of Isidore, bishop of Seville (cap. 13, in Cod. Regul. part ii. p. 214 [tom. i. p. 193]).

2 Some partial indulgences were granted for the hands and feet. 'Totum autem corpus nemo unguet nisi causâ infirmitatis, nec lavabitur aquâ nudo corpore, nisi languor perspicuus sit.' (Regul. Pachom. xcii. part. i. p. 78 [tom i. p. 31].)

3 St. Jerom, in strong but indiscreet language, expresses the most important use of fasting and abstinence: 'Non quod Deus universitatis Creator et Dominus, intestinorum nostrorum rugitû, et inanitate ventris, pulmonisque ardore delectetur, sed quod aliter pudicitia tuta esse non possit.' (Op. tom. i. p. 137, ad Eustochium [Ep. 22, tom. i. p. 94, ed. Vallars.].) See the twelfth and twenty-second Collations of Cassian, *de Castitate* and *de Illusionibus Nocturnis*.

which they imposed, or practised, were not uniform or perpetual:
the cheerful festival of the Pentecost was balanced by the extraordinary mortification of Lent; the fervour of new monasteries
was insensibly relaxed; and the voracious appetite of the Gauls
could not imitate the patient and temperate virtue of the Egyptians.[1] The disciples of Antony and Pachomius were satisfied
with their daily pittance[2] of twelve ounces of bread, or rather
biscuit,[3] which they divided into two frugal repasts, of the afternoon and of the evening. It was esteemed a merit, and almost a
duty, to abstain from the boiled vegetables which were provided
for the refectory; but the extraordinary bounty of the abbot
sometimes indulged them with the luxury of cheese, fruit, salad,
and the small dried fish of the Nile.[4] A more ample latitude of
sea and river fish was gradually allowed or assumed; but the use
of flesh was long confined to the sick or travellers: and when it
gradually prevailed in the less rigid monasteries of Europe, a
singular distinction was introduced; as if birds, whether wild or
domestic, had been less profane than the grosser animals of the
field. Water was the pure and innocent beverage of the primitive
monks; and the founder of the Benedictines regrets the daily
portion of half a pint of wine which had been extorted from him
by the intemperance of the age.[5] Such an allowance might be

1 Edacitas in Græcis gula est, in Gallis natura (Dialog. i. c. 4, p. 521).
Cassian fairly owns that the perfect model of abstinence cannot be imitated in
Gaul, on account of the aërum temperies, and the qualitas nostræ fragilitatis
(Institut. iv. II). Among the Western rules, that of Columbanus is the most
austere: he had been educated amidst the poverty of Ireland, as rigid, perhaps,
and inflexible as the abstemious virtue of Egypt. The rule of Isidore of Seville
is the mildest: on holidays he allows the use of flesh.

2 'Those who drink only water, and have no nutritious liquor, ought at least
to have a pound and a half (*twenty-four ounces*) of bread every day.' State of
Prisons, p. 40, by Mr. Howard.

3 See Cassian. Collat. ii. 19, 20, 21. The small loaves or biscuit of six ounces
each had obtained the name of *Paximacia* (Rosweyde, Onomasticon, p. 1045
[1033]). Pachomius, however, allowed his monks some latitude in the quantity
of their food; but he made them work in proportion as they ate (Pallad. in Hist.
Lausiac. c. 38, 39, in Vit. Patrum, l. viii. p. 736, 737).

4 See the banquet to which Cassian (Collation viii. I) was invited by Sere-
nus, an Egyptian abbot.

5 See the Rule of St. Benedict, cap. 39, 40 (in Cod. Reg. part ii. p. 41, 42
[tom. i. p. 129, ed. 1759]). Licet legamus vinum omnino monachorum non esse,
sed quia nostris temporibus id monachis persuaderi non potest; he allows them
a Roman *hemina*, a measure which may be ascertained from Arbuthnot's Tables.

easily supplied by the vineyards of Italy; and his victorious disciples, who passed the Alps, the Rhine, and the Baltic, required, in the place of wine, an adequate compensation of strong beer or cider.

The candidate who aspired to the virtue of evangelical poverty, abjured, at his first entrance into a regular community, the idea, and even the name, of all separate or exclusive possession.[1] The brethren were supported by their manual labour; and the duty of labour was strenuously recommended as a penance, as an exercise, and as the most laudable means of securing their daily subsistence.[2] The garden and fields, which the industry of the monks had often rescued from the forest or the morass, were diligently cultivated by their hands. They performed, without reluctance, the menial offices of slaves and domestics; and the several trades that were necessary to provide their habits, their utensils, and their lodging, were exercised within the precincts of the great monasteries. The monastic studies have tended, for the most part, to darken, rather than to dispel, the cloud of superstition. Yet the curiosity or zeal of some learned solitaries has cultivated the ecclesiastical and even the profane sciences: and posterity must gratefully acknowledge that the monuments of Greek and Roman literature have been preserved and multiplied by their indefatigable pens.[3] But the more humble industry of the monks, especially in Egypt, was contented with the silent,

1 Such expressions as *my* book, *my* cloak, *my* shoes (Cassian. Institut. l. iv. c. 13) were not less severely prohibited among the Western monks (Cod. Regul. part ii. p. 174 [tom. i. p. 178], 235, 288); and the Rule of Columbanus punished them with six lashes. The ironical author of the *Ordres Monastiques*, who laughs at the foolish nicety of modern convents, seems ignorant that the ancients were equally absurd.

2 Two great masters of ecclesiastical science, the P. Thomassin (Discipline de l'Eglise, tom. iii. p. 1090–1139) and the P. Mabillon (Etudes Monastiques, tom. i. p. 116–155), have seriously examined the manual labour of the monks, which the former considers as a *merit*, and the latter as a *duty*.

3 Mabillon (Etudes Monastiques, tom. i. p. 47–55) has collected many curious facts to justify the literary labours of his predecessors both in the East and West. Books were copied in the ancient monasteries of Egypt (Cassian. Institut. l. iv. c. 12), and by the disciples of St. Martin (Sulp. Sever. in Vit. Martin. c. 7, p. 473). Cassiodorus has allowed an ample scope for the studies of the monks; and *we* shall not be scandalised if their pen sometimes wandered from Chrysostom and Augustin to Homer and Virgil.

sedentary occupation of making wooden sandals, or of twisting
the leaves of the palm-tree into mats and baskets. The superfluous stock, which was not consumed in domestic use, supplied,
by trade, the wants of the community: the boats of Tabenne,
and the other monasteries of Thebais, descended the Nile as far
as Alexandria; and, in a Christian market, the sanctity of the
workmen might enhance the intrinsic value of the work.

But the necessity of manual labour was insensibly superseded.
The novice was tempted to bestow his fortune on the saints in
whose society he was resolved to spend the remainder of his life;
and the pernicious indulgence of the laws permitted him to receive, for their use, any future accessions of legacy or inheritance.[1] Melania contributed her plate, three hundred pounds'
weight of silver, and Paula contracted an immense debt for the
relief of their favourite monks, who kindly imparted the merits
of their prayers and penance to a rich and liberal sinner.[2] Time
continually increased, and accidents could seldom diminish, the
estates of the popular monasteries, which spread over the adjacent country and cities: and, in the first century of their institution, the infidel Zosimus has maliciously observed, that, for the
benefit of the poor, the Christian monks had reduced a great
part of mankind to a state of beggary.[3] As long as they maintained their original fervour, they approved themselves, however,
the faithful and benevolent stewards of the charity which was
intrusted to their care. But their discipline was corrupted by
prosperity: they gradually assumed the pride of wealth, and at
last indulged the luxury of expense. Their public luxury might

1 Thomassin (Discipline de l'Eglise, tom. iii. p. 118, 145, 146, 171–179) has
examined the revolution of the civil, canon, and common law. Modern France
confirms the death which monks have inflicted on themselves, and justly de-
prives them of all right of inheritance.

2 See Jerom (tom. i. p. 176, 183). The monk Pambo made a sublime answer
to Melania, who wished to specify the value of her gift: – 'Do you offer it to
me, or to God? If to God, HE who suspends the mountains in a balance need
not be informed of the weight of your plate.' (Pallad. Hist. Lausiac. c. 10, in
the Vit. Patrum, l. viii. p. 715.)

3 Τὸ πολὺ μέρος τῆς γῆς ᾠκειώσαντο, προφάσει τοῦ μεταδιδόναι πάντων
πτωχοῖς, πάντας (ὡς ειπεῖν) πτωχοὺς καταστήσαντες. Zosim. l. v. [c. 23] p. 325.
Yet the wealth of the Eastern monks was far surpassed by the princely greatness
of the Benedictines.

be excused by the magnificence of religious worship, and the decent motive of erecting durable habitations for an immortal society. But every age of the church has accused the licentiousness of the degenerate monks; who no longer remembered the object of their institution, embraced the vain and sensual pleasures of the world which they had renounced,[1] and scandalously abused the riches which had been acquired by the austere virtues of their founders.[2] Their natural descent, from such painful and dangerous virtue, to the common vices of humanity, will not, perhaps, excite much grief or indignation in the mind of a philosopher.

The lives of the primitive monks were consumed in penance and solitude, undisturbed by the various occupations which fill the time, and exercise the faculties, of reasonable, active, and social beings. Whenever they were permitted to step beyond the precincts of the monastery, two jealous companions were the mutual guards and spies of each other's actions; and, after their return, they were condemned to forget, or, at least, to suppress, whatever they had seen or heard in the world. Strangers, who professed the orthodox faith, were hospitably entertained in a separate apartment; but their dangerous conversation was restricted to some chosen elders of approved discretion and fidelity. Except in their presence, the monastic slave might not receive the visits of his friends or kindred; and it was deemed highly meritorious, if he afflicted a tender sister, or an aged parent, by the obstinate refusal of a word or look.[3] The monks themselves passed their lives, without personal attachments,

1 The sixth general council (the Quinisext in Trullo, Canon xlvii. in Beveridge, tom. i. p. 213) restrains women from passing the night in a male, or men in a female, monastery. The seventh general council (the second Nicene, Canon xx. in Beveridge, tom. i. p. 325) prohibits the erection of double or promiscuous monasteries of both sexes; but it appears from Balsamon that the prohibition was not effectual. On the irregular pleasures and expenses of the clergy and *monks*, see Thomassin, tom. iii. p. 1334–1368.

2 I have somewhere heard or read the frank confession of a Benedictine abbot: 'My vow of poverty has given me an hundred thousand crowns a year; my vow of obedience has raised me to the rank of a sovereign prince.' I forget the consequences of his vow of chastity.

3 Pior, an Egyptian monk, allowed his sister to see him; but he shut his eyes during the whole visit. See Vit. Patrum, l. iii. p. 504. Many such examples might be added.

among a crowd which had been formed by accident, and was detained, in the same prison, by force or prejudice. Recluse fanatics have few ideas or sentiments to communicate: a special licence of the abbot regulated the time and duration of their familiar visits; and, at their silent meals, they were enveloped in their cowls, inaccessible, and almost invisible, to each other.¹ Study is the resource of solitude; but education had not prepared and qualified for any liberal studies the mechanics and peasants who filled the monastic communities. They might work; but the vanity of spiritual perfection was tempted to disdain the exercise of manual labour; and the industry must be faint and languid which is not excited by the sense of personal interest.

According to their faith and zeal, they might employ the day, which they passed in their cells, either in vocal or mental prayer: they assembled in the evening, and they were awakened in the night, for the public worship of the monastery. The precise moment was determined by the stars, which are seldom clouded in the serene sky of Egypt; and a rustic horn, or trumpet, the signal of devotion, twice interrupted the vast silence of the desert.² Even sleep, the last refuge of the unhappy, was rigorously measured: the vacant hours of the monk heavily rolled along, without business or pleasure; and, before the close of each day, he had repeatedly accused the tedious progress of the sun.³ In this comfortless state, superstition still pursued and tormented her wretched votaries.⁴ The repose which they had sought in the cloister was disturbed by tardy repentance, profane doubts, and

1 The 7th, 8th, 29th, 30th, 31st, 34th, 57th, 60th, 86th, and 95th articles of the Rule of Pachomius, impose most intolerable *laws* of silence and mortification.

2 The diurnal and nocturnal prayers of the monks are copiously discussed by Cassian, in the third and fourth books of his Institutions; and he constantly prefers the liturgy which an angel had dictated to the monasteries of Tabennœ.

3 Cassian, from his own experience, describes the *acædia*, or listlessness of mind and body, to which a monk was exposed when he sighed to find himself alone. Sæpiusque egreditur et ingreditur cellam, et Solem velut ad occasum tardius properantem crebrius intuetur (Institut. x. 2).

4 The temptations and sufferings of Stagirius were communicated by that unfortunate youth to his friend St. Chrysostom. See Middleton's Works, vol. i. p. 107–110. Something similar introduces the life of every saint; and the famous Inigo, or Ignatius, the founder of the Jesuits (Vida d'Inigo de Guiposcoa, tom. i. p. 29–38) may serve as a memorable example.

guilty desires; and, while they considered each natural impulse as an unpardonable sin, they perpetually trembled on the edge of a flaming and bottomless abyss. From the painful struggles of disease and despair, these unhappy victims were sometimes relieved by madness or death; and, in the sixth century, a hospital was founded at Jerusalem for a small portion of the austere penitents who were deprived of their senses.[1] Their visions, before they attained this extreme and acknowledged term of frenzy, have afforded ample materials of supernatural history. It was their firm persuasion that the air which they breathed was peopled with invisible enemies; with innumerable demons, who watched every occasion, and assumed every form, to terrify, and above all to tempt, their unguarded virtue. The imagination, and even the senses, were deceived by the illusions of distempered fanaticism; and the hermit, whose midnight prayer was oppressed by involuntary slumber, might easily confound the phantoms of horror or delight which had occupied his sleeping and his waking dreams.[2]

The monks were divided into two classes: the *Cænobites*, who lived under a common and regular discipline; and the *Anachorets*, who indulged their unsocial, independent fanaticism.[3] The most devout, or the most ambitious, of the spiritual brethren renounced the convent, as they had renounced the world. The fervent monasteries of Egypt, Palestine, and Syria were surrounded by a *Laura*,[4] a distant circle of solitary cells; and the

1 Fleury, Hist. Ecclésiastique, tom. vii. p. 46. I have read somewhere in the Vitæ Patrum, but I cannot recover the place, that *several*, I believe *many*, of the monks, who did not reveal their temptations to the abbot, became guilty of suicide.

2 See the seventh and eighth Collations of Cassian, who gravely examines why the dæmons were grown less active and numerous since the time of St. Antony. Rosweyde's copious index to the Vitæ Patrum will point out a variety of infernal scenes. The devils were most formidable in a female shape.

3 For the distinction of the *Cænobites* and the *Hermits*, especially in Egypt, see Jerom (tom. i. p. 45, ad Rusticum [Ep. 125, tom. i. p. 932, ed. Vallars.]), the first Dialogue of Sulpicius Severus, Rufinus (c. 22, in Vit. Patrum, l. ii. p. 478), Palladius (c. 7, 69, in Vit. Patrum, l. viii. p. 712, 758), and, above all, the eighteenth and nineteenth Collations of Cassian. These writers, who compare the common and solitary life, reveal the abuse and danger of the latter.

4 Suicer. Thesaur. Ecclesiast. tom. ii. p. 205, 218. Thomassin (Discipline de l'Eglise, tom. i. p. 1501, 1502) gives a good account of these cells. When Gerasimus founded his monastery, in the wilderness of Jordan, it was accompanied by a Laura of seventy cells.

extravagant penance of the Hermits was stimulated by applause and emulation.[1] They sunk under the painful weight of crosses and chains; and their emaciated limbs were confined by collars, bracelets, gauntlets, and greaves of massy and rigid iron. All superfluous incumbrance of dress they contemptuously cast away; and some savage saints of both sexes have been admired, whose naked bodies were only covered by their long hair. They aspired to reduce themselves to the rude and miserable state in which the human brute is scarcely distinguished above his kindred animals; and the numerous sect of Anachorets derived their name from their humble practice of grazing in the fields of Mesopotamia with the common herd.[2] They often usurped the den of some wild beast whom they affected to resemble; they buried themselves in some gloomy cavern, which art or nature had scooped out of the rock; and the marble quarries of Thebais are still inscribed with the monuments of their penance.[3] The most perfect Hermits are supposed to have passed many days without food, many nights without sleep, and many years without speaking; and glorious was the *man* (I abuse that name) who contrived any cell, or seat, of a peculiar construction, which might expose him, in the most inconvenient posture, to the inclemency of the seasons.

Among these heroes of the monastic life, the name and genius of Simeon Stylites[4] have been immortalised by the singular invention of an aërial penance. At the age of thirteen the young Syrian deserted the profession of a shepherd, and threw himself into an austere monastery. After a long and painful novitiate, in which Simeon was repeatedly saved from pious suicide, he established his residence on a mountain, about thirty or forty miles

1 Theodoret, in a large volume (the Philotheus in Vit. Patrum, l. ix. p. 793–863) has collected the lives and miracles of thirty Anachorets. Evagrius (l. i. c. 21) more briefly celebrates the monks and hermits of Palestine.

2 Sozomen, l. vi. c. 33. The great St. Ephrem composed a panegyric on these βόσκοι, or grazing monks (Tillemont, Mém. Ecclés. tom. viii. p. 292).

3 The P. Sicard (Missions du Levant, tom. ii. p. 217–233) examined the caverns of the Lower Thebais with wonder and devotion. The inscriptions are in the old Syriac character, which was used by the Christians of Abyssinia.

4 See Theodoret (in Vit. Patrum, l. ix. p. 848–854), Antony (in Vit. Patrum, l. i. p. 170–177), Cosmas (in Asseman. Bibliot. Oriental. tom. i. p. 239–253), Evagrius (l. i. c. 13, 14), and Tillemont (Mém. Ecclés. tom. xv. p. 347–392).

to the east of Antioch. Within the space of a *mandra*, or circle
of stones, to which he had attached himself by a ponderous
chain, he ascended a column, which was successively raised from
the height of nine, to that of sixty, feet from the ground.[1] In this
last and lofty station, the Syrian Anachoret resisted the heat of
thirty summers, and the cold of as many winters. Habit and
exercise instructed him to maintain his dangerous situation without fear or giddiness, and successively to assume the different
postures of devotion. He sometimes prayed in an erect attitude,
with his outstretched arms in the figure of a cross; but his most
familiar practice was that of bending his meagre skeleton from
the forehead to the feet; and a curious spectator, after numbering
twelve hundred and forty-four repetitions, at length desisted
from the endless account. The progress of an ulcer in his thigh[2]
might shorten, but it could not disturb, this *celestial* life; and the
patient Hermit expired without descending from his column. A
prince, who should capriciously inflict such tortures, would be
deemed a tyrant; but it would surpass the power of a tyrant to
impose a long and miserable existence on the reluctant victims
of his cruelty. This voluntary martyrdom must have gradually
destroyed the sensibility both of the mind and body; nor can it
be presumed that the fanatics who torment themselves are susceptible of any lively affection for the rest of mankind. A cruel,
unfeeling temper has distinguished the monks of every age and
country: their stern indifference, which is seldom mollified by
personal friendship, is inflamed by religious hatred; and their
merciless zeal has strenuously administered the holy office of the
Inquisition.

The monastic saints, who excite only the contempt and pity
of a philosopher, were respected and almost adored by the prince
and people. Successive crowds of pilgrims from Gaul and India

1 The narrow circumference of two cubits, or three feet, which Evagrius
assigns for the summit of the column, is inconsistent with reason, with facts,
and with the rules of architecture. The people who saw it from below might
be easily deceived.

2 I must not conceal a piece of ancient scandal concerning the origin of
this ulcer. It has been reported that the Devil, assuming an angelic form, invited
him to ascend, like Elijah, into a fiery chariot. The saint too hastily raised his
foot, and Satan seized the moment of inflicting this chastisement on his vanity.

saluted the divine pillar of Simeon; the tribes of Saracens disputed in arms the honour of his benediction; the queens of
Arabia and Persia gratefully confessed his supernatural virtue;
and the angelic Hermit was consulted by the younger Theodosius
in the most important concerns of the church and state. His
remains were transported from the mountain of Telenissa, by a
solemn procession of the patriarch, the master-general of the
East, six bishops, twenty-one counts or tribunes, and six thousand soldiers; and Antioch revered his bones as her glorious
ornament and impregnable defence. The fame of the apostles
and martyrs was gradually eclipsed by these recent and popular
Anachorets; the Christian world fell prostrate before their
shrines; and the miracles ascribed to their relics exceeded, at least
in number and duration, the spiritual exploits of their lives. But
the golden legend of their lives[1] was embellished by the artful
credulity of their interested brethren; and a believing age was
easily persuaded that the slightest caprice of an Egyptian or a
Syrian monk had been sufficient to interrupt the eternal laws of
the universe. The favourites of Heaven were accustomed to cure
inveterate diseases with a touch, a word, or a distant message;
and to expel the most obstinate demons from the souls or bodies
which they possessed. They familiarly accosted, or imperiously
commanded, the lions and serpents of the desert; infused vegetation into a sapless trunk; suspended iron on the surface of the
water; passed the Nile on the back of a crocodile; and refreshed
themselves in a fiery furnace. These extravagant tales, which
display the fiction, without the genius, of poetry, have seriously
affected the reason, the faith, and the morals of the Christians.
Their credulity debased and vitiated the faculties of the mind:
they corrupted the evidence of history; and superstition gradually
extinguished the hostile light of philosophy and science. Every
mode of religious worship which had been practised by the
saints, every mysterious doctrine which they believed, was

1 I know not how to select or specify the miracles contained in the *Vitæ
Patrum* of Rosweyde, as the number very much exceeds the thousand pages of
that voluminous work. An elegant specimen may be found in the Dialogues of
Sulpicius Severus and his Life of St. Martin. He reveres the monks of Egypt;
yet he insults them with the remark that *they* never raised the dead; whereas the
bishop of Tours had restored *three* dead men to life.

fortified by the sanction of divine revelation, and all the manly virtues were oppressed by the servile and pusillanimous reign of the monks. If it be possible to measure the interval between the philosophic writings of Cicero and the sacred legend of Theodoret, between the character of Cato and that of Simeon, we may appreciate the memorable revolution which was accomplished in the Roman empire within a period of five hundred years.

II. The progress of Christianity has been marked by two glorious and decisive victories: over the learned and luxurious citizens of the Roman empire; and over the warlike barbarians of Scythia and Germany, who subverted the empire and embraced the religion of the Romans. The Goths were the foremost of these savage proselytes; and the nation was indebted for its conversion to a countryman, or at least to a subject, worthy to be ranked among the inventors of useful arts who have deserved the remembrance and gratitude of posterity. A great number of Roman provincials had been led away into captivity by the Gothic bands who ravaged Asia in the time of Gallienus; and of these captives many were Christians, and several belonged to the ecclesiastical order. Those involuntary missionaries, dispersed as slaves in the villages of Dacia, successively laboured for the salvation of their masters. The seeds which they planted of the evangelic doctrine were gradually propagated; and before the end of a century the pious work was achieved by the labours of Ulphilas, whose ancestors had been transported beyond the Danube from a small town of Cappadocia.

Ulphilas, the bishop and apostle of the Goths,[1] acquired their love and reverence by his blameless life and indefatigable zeal, and they received with implicit confidence the doctrines of truth

1 On the subject of Ulphilas and the conversion of the Goths, see Sozomen, l. vi. c. 37; Socrates, l. iv. c. 33; Theodoret, l. iv. c. 37; Philostorg. l. ii. c. 5. The heresy of Philostorgius appears to have given him superior means of information.

[The alphabet which Ulphilas or Ulfilas was obliged to construct is the Mœso-Gothic, of which many of the letters are evidently formed from the Greek and Roman. St. Martin contends that it is impossible that some written alphabet had not been known long before among the Goths. He supposes that their former letters were those inscribed on the runes, which being inseparably connected with the old idolatrous superstitions were proscribed by the Christian

and virtue which he preached and practised. He executed the arduous task of translating the Scriptures into their native tongue, a dialect of the German or Teutonic language; but he prudently suppressed the four books of Kings, as they might tend to irritate the fierce and sanguinary spirit of the barbarians. The rude, imperfect idiom of soldiers and shepherds, so ill qualified to communicate any spiritual ideas, was improved and modulated by his genius; and Ulphilas, before he could frame his version, was obliged to compose a new alphabet of twenty-four letters; four of which he invented to express the peculiar sounds that were unknown to the Greek and Latin pronunciation.[1] But the prosperous state of the Gothic church was soon afflicted by war and intestine discord, and the chieftains were divided by religion as well as by interest. Fritigern, the friend of the Romans, became the proselyte of Ulphilas; while the haughty soul of Athanaric disdained the yoke of the empire and of the Gospel. The

missionaries. Everywhere the runes, so common among all German tribes, disappear after the propagation of Christianity. On this point Bury says. 'The Goths before Ulfilas used the Runic alphabet, consisting of twenty-four signs. Ulfilas based his alphabet on the Greek, adopting the Greek order, and adapted it to the requirements of Gothic speech. But his alphabet has twenty-five letters, five of them being derived from the Runic, one from the Latin (S), and one is of uncertain origin. This uncertain letter has the value of Q, and corresponds in position in the alphabet to the Greek numeral sigma, between E and Z.' – O.S.]

1 A mutilated copy of the four Gospels in the Gothic version was published A.D. 1665, and is esteemed the most ancient monument of the Teutonic language, though Wetstein attempts, by some frivolous conjectures, to deprive Ulphilas of the honour of the work. Two of the four additional letters express the *W* and our own *Th*. See Simon, Hist. Critique du Nouveau Testament, tom. ii. p. 219–223. Mill. Prolegom. p. 151, edit. Kuster. Wetstein, Prolegom. tom. i. p. 114.

[This mutilated copy of the Gospels is contained in a MS. called the Codex Argenteus, found at Werden in Westphalia in the sixteenth century, and now preserved at Upsal. It contains more than half of the four Gospels. In 1762 Knettel discovered and published from a palimpsest MS. four chapters of the Epistle to the Romans. They were reprinted at Upsal, 1763. There can be little doubt that Ulfilas made such a version, but it is considered by many critics extremely doubtful whether it is contained in the MS. at Upsal, or whether the language of the MS. is genuine Old Gothic. These critics maintain that its language is a century and a half later than the time of Ulfilas. Cf. Aschbach, *Geschichte der Westgothen*, p. 35 *seq*. With regard to the accounts in Sozomen and Socrates, these are largely derived from Philostorgius. – O. S.]

faith of the new converts was tried by the persecution which he excited. A waggon, bearing aloft the shapeless image of Thor, perhaps, or of Woden, was conducted in solemn procession through the streets of the camp, and the rebels who refused to worship the god of their fathers were immediately burnt with their tents and families. The character of Ulphilas recommended him to the esteem of the Eastern court, where he twice appeared as the minister of peace; he pleaded the cause of the distressed Goths, who implored the protection of Valens; and the name of *Moses* was applied to this spiritual guide, who conducted his people through the deep waters of the Danube to the Land of Promise.[1] The devout shepherds, who were attached to his person and tractable to his voice, acquiesced in their settlement at the foot of the Mæsian mountains, in a country of woodlands and pastures, which supported their flocks and herds, and enabled them to purchase the corn and wine of the more plentiful provinces. These harmless barbarians multiplied in obscure peace and the profession of Christianity.[2]

Their fiercer brethren, the formidable Visigoths, universally adopted the religion of the Romans, with whom they maintained a perpetual intercourse of war, of friendship, or of conquest. In their long and victorious march from the Danube to the Atlantic Ocean they converted their allies; they educated the rising generation; and the devotion which reigned in the camp of Alaric, or the court of Toulouse, might edify or disgrace the palaces of Rome and Constantinople.[3] During the same period Christianity was embraced by almost all the barbarians who established their kingdoms on the ruins of the Western empire; the Burgundians in Gaul, the Suevi in Spain, the Vandals in Africa, the Ostrogoths in Pannonia, and the various bands of mercenaries that raised

1 Philostorgius erroneously places this passage under the reign of Constantine; but I am much inclined to believe that it preceded the great emigration.

2 We are obliged to Jornandes (de Reb. Get. c. 51, p. 688) for a short and lively picture of these lesser Goths. Gothi minores, populus immensus, cum suo Pontifice ipsoque primate Wulfila. The last words, if they are not mere tautology, imply some temporal jurisdiction.

3 At non ita Gothi non ita Vandali; malis licet doctoribus instituti, meliores tamen etiam in hâc parte quam nostri. Salvian de Gubern. Dei, l. vii. p. 243 [ed. Par. 1608].

Odoacer to the throne of Italy. The Franks and the Saxons still persevered in the errors of Paganism; but the Franks obtained the monarchy of Gaul by their submission to the example of Clovis; and the Saxon conquerors of Britain were reclaimed from their savage superstition by the missionaries of Rome. These barbarian proselytes displayed an ardent and successful zeal in the propagation of the faith. The Merovingian kings and their successors, Charlemagne and the Othos, extended by their laws and victories the dominion of the cross. England produced the apostle of Germany; and the evangelic light was gradually diffused from the neighbourhood of the Rhine to the nations of the Elbe, the Vistula, and the Baltic.[1]

The different motives which influenced the reason or the passions of the barbarian converts cannot easily be ascertained. They were often capricious and accidental; a dream, an omen, the report of a miracle, the example of some priest or hero, the charms of a believing wife, and, above all, the fortunate event of a prayer or vow which, in a moment of danger, they had addressed to the God of the Christians.[2] The early prejudices of education were insensibly erased by the habits of frequent and familiar society; the moral precepts of the Gospel were protected by the extravagant virtues of the monks; and a spiritual theology was supported by the visible power of relics, and the pomp of religious worship. But the rational and ingenious mode of persuasion which a Saxon bishop[3] suggested to a popular saint might sometimes be employed by the missionaries who laboured for the conversion of infidels. 'Admit,' says the sagacious disputant, 'whatever they are pleased to assert of the fabulous and carnal genealogy of their gods and goddesses, who are propagated from each other. From this principle deduce their imperfect nature

1 Mosheim has slightly sketched the progress of Christianity in the North, from the fourth to the fourteenth century. The subject would afford materials for an ecclesiastical and even philosophical history.

2 To such a cause has Socrates (l. vii. c. 30) ascribed the conversion of the Burgundians, whose Christian piety is celebrated by Orosius (l. vii. c. 19 [32]).

3 See an original and curious epistle from Daniel, the first bishop of Winchester (Beda, Hist. Eccles. Anglorum, l. v. c. 18, p. 203, edit. Smith), to St. Boniface, who preached the Gospel among the savages of Hesse and Thuringia. Epistol. Bonifacii, lxvii. in the Maxima Bibliotheca Patrum, tom. xiii. p. 93.

and human infirmities, the assurance they were *born*, and the probability that they will *die*. At what time, by what means, from what cause, were the eldest of the gods or goddesses produced? Do they still continue, or have they ceased, to propagate? If they have ceased, summon your antagonist to declare the reason of this strange alteration. If they still continue, the number of the gods must become infinite; and shall we not risk, by the indiscreet worship of some impotent deity, to excite the resentment of his jealous superior? The visible heavens and earth, the whole system of the universe, which may be conceived by the mind, is it created or eternal? If created, how or where could the gods themselves exist before the creation? If eternal, how could they assume the empire of an independent and pre-existing world? Urge these arguments with temper and moderation; insinuate, at seasonable intervals, the truth and beauty of the Christian revelation; and endeavour to make the unbelievers ashamed without making them angry.' This metaphysical reasoning, too refined perhaps for the barbarians of Germany, was fortified by the grosser weight of authority and popular consent. The advantage of temporal prosperity had deserted the Pagan cause and passed over to the service of Christianity. The Romans themselves, the most powerful and enlightened nation of the globe, had renounced their ancient superstition; and if the ruin of their empire seemed to accuse the efficacy of the new faith, the disgrace was already retrieved by the conversion of the victorious Goths. The valiant and fortunate barbarians who subdued the provinces of the West successively received and reflected the same edifying example. Before the age of Charlemagne, the Christian nations of Europe might exult in the exclusive possession of the temperate climates, of the fertile lands which produced corn, wine, and oil; while the savage idolaters and their helpless idols were confined to the extremities of the earth, the dark and frozen regions of the North.[1]

Christianity, which opened the gates of Heaven to the barbarians, introduced an important change in their moral and political

---

1 The sword of Charlemagne added weight to the argument; but when Daniel wrote this epistle (A.D. 723), the Mahometans, who reigned from India to Spain, might have retorted it against the Christians.

condition. They received, at the same time, the use of letters, so essential to a religion whose doctrines are contained in a sacred book; and while they studied the divine truth, their minds were insensibly enlarged by the distant view of history, of nature, of the arts, and of society. The version of the Scriptures into their native tongue, which had facilitated their conversion, must excite, among their clergy, some curiosity to read the original text, to understand the sacred liturgy of the church, and to examine, in the writings of the fathers, the chain of ecclesiastical tradition. These spiritual gifts were preserved in the Greek and Latin languages, which concealed the inestimable monuments of ancient learning. The immortal productions of Virgil, Cicero, and Livy, which were accessible to the Christian barbarians, maintained a silent intercourse between the reign of Augustus and the times of Clovis and Charlemange. The emulation of mankind was encouraged by the remembrance of a more perfect state; and the flame of science was secretly kept alive, to warm and enlighten the mature age of the Western world. In the most corrupt state of Christianity the barbarians might learn justice from the *law*, and mercy from the *gospel;* and if the knowledge of their duty was insufficient to guide their actions or to regulate their passions, they were sometimes restrained by conscience, and frequently punished by remorse. But the direct authority of religion was less effectual than the holy communion, which united them with their Christian brethren in spiritual friendship. The influence of these sentiments contributed to secure their fidelity in the service or the alliance of the Romans, to alleviate the horrors of war, to moderate the insolence of conquest, and to preserve, in the downfall of the empire, a permanent respect for the name and institutions of Rome. In the days of Paganism the priests of Gaul and Germany reigned over the people, and controlled the jurisdiction of the magistrates; and the zealous proselytes transferred an equal, or more ample, measure of devout obedience to the pontiffs of the Christian faith. The sacred character of the bishops was supported by their temporal possessions; they obtained an honourable seat in the legislative assemblies of soldiers and freemen; and it was their interest, as well as their duty, to mollify by peaceful counsels the fierce spirit of the barbarians. The perpetual correspondence of the Latin clergy, the frequent pilgrimages to Rome and Jerusalem, and the growing authority of the popes, cemented the union of the Christian republic, and gradually produced the similar manners and common jurisprudence which have distinguished from the rest of mankind the independent, and even hostile, nations of modern Europe.

But the operation of these causes was checked and retarded by the unfortunate accident which infused a deadly poison into the cup of salvation. Whatever might be the early sentiments of Ulphilas, his connections with the empire and the church were formed during the reign of Arianism. The apostle of the Goths subscribed the creed of Rimini; professed with freedom, and perhaps with sincerity, that the Son was not equal or consubstantial to the FATHER;[1] communicated these errors to the clergy and people; and infected the barbaric world with an heresy[2] which the great Theodosius proscribed and extinguished among the Romans. The temper and understanding of the new proselytes were not adapted to metaphysical subtleties; but they strenuously maintained what they had piously received as the pure and genuine doctrines of Christianity. The advantage of preaching and expounding the Scriptures in the Teutonic language promoted the apostolic labours of Ulphilas and his successors; and they ordained a competent number of bishops and presbyters for the instruction of the kindred tribes. The Ostrogoths, the Burgundians, the Suevi, and the Vandals, who had listened to the eloquence of the Latin clergy,[3] preferred the more intelligible lessons of their domestic teachers; and Arianism was adopted

1 The opinions of Ulphilas and the Goths inclined to semi-Arianism, since they would not say that the Son was a *creature*, though they held communion with those who maintained that heresy. Their apostle represented the whole controversy as a question of trifling moment which had been raised by the passions of the clergy. Theodoret, l. iv. c. 37.

2 The Arianism of the Goths has been imputed to the emperor Valens: 'Itaque justo Dei judicio ipsi eum vivum incenderunt, qui propter eum etiam mortui, vitio erroris arsuri sunt.' Orosius, l. vii. c. 33, p. 554. This cruel sentence is confirmed by Tillemont (Mém. Ecclés. tom. vi. p. 604–610), who coolly observes, 'un seul homme entraîna dans l'enfer un nombre infini de Septentrionaux,' etc. Salvian (de Gubern. Dei, l. v. p. 150, 151) pities and excuses their involuntary error.

3 Orosius affirms, in the year 416 (l. vii. c. 41, p. 580), that the churches of Christ (of the catholics) were filled with Huns, Suevi, Vandals, Burgundians.

as the national faith of the warlike converts who were seated on
the ruins of the Western empire. This irreconcilable difference
of religion was a perpetual source of jealousy and hatred; and
the reproach of *Barbarian* was embittered by the more odious
epithet of *Heretic*. The heroes of the North, who had submitted
with some reluctance to believe that all their ancestors were in
hell,[1] were astonished and exasperated to learn that they themselves had only changed the mode of their eternal condemnation. Instead of the smooth applause which Christian kings are
accustomed to expect from their loyal prelates, the orthodox
bishops and their clergy were in a state of opposition to the
Arian courts; and their indiscreet opposition frequently became
criminal, and might sometimes be dangerous.[2] The pulpit, that
safe and sacred organ of sedition, resounded with the names of
Pharaoh and Holofernes;[3] the public discontent was inflamed by
the hope or promise of a glorious deliverance; and the seditious
saints were tempted to promote the accomplishment of their
own predictions. Notwithstanding these provocations, the catholics of Gaul, Spain, and Italy enjoyed, under the reign of the
Arians, the free and peaceful exercise of their religion. Their
haughty masters respected the zeal of a numerous people, resolved to die at the foot of their altars, and the example of their
devout constancy was admired and imitated by the barbarians
themselves. The conquerors evaded, however, the disgraceful
reproach or confession of fear, by attributing their toleration to
the liberal motives of reason and humanity; and while they affected the language, they imperceptibly imbibed the spirit, of
genuine Christianity.

The peace of the church was sometimes interrupted. The
catholics were indiscreet, the barbarians were impatient; and the
partial acts of severity or injustice, which had been recommended

1 Radbod, king of the Frisons, was so much scandalised by this rash declaration of a missionary, that he drew back his foot after he had entered the
baptismal font. See Fleury, Hist. Ecclés. tom. ix. p. 167.

2 The epistles of Sidonius, bishop of Clermont under the Visigoths, and of
Avitus, bishop of Vienne under the Burgundians, explain, sometimes in dark
hints, the general dispositions of the catholics. The history of Clovis and Theodoric will suggest some particular facts.

3 Genseric confessed the resemblance by the severity with which he punished such indiscreet allusions. Victor Vitensis, i. 7, p. 10.

by the Arian clergy, were exaggerated by the orthodox writers.
The guilt of persecution may be imputed to Euric, king of the
Visigoths who suspended the exercise of ecclesiastical, or, at
least, of episcopal functions, and punished the popular bishops
of Aquitain with imprisonment, exile, and confiscation.[1] But the
cruel and absurd enterprise of subduing the minds of a whole
people was undertaken by the Vandals alone. Genseric himself,
in his early youth, had renounced the orthodox communion; and
the apostate could neither grant nor expect a sincere forgiveness.
He was exasperated to find that the Africans, who had fled
before him in the field, still presumed to dispute his will in
synods and churches; and his ferocious mind was incapable of
fear or of compassion. His catholic subjects were oppressed by
intolerant laws and arbitrary punishments. The language of
Genseric was furious and formidable; the knowledge of his intentions might justify the most unfavourable interpretation of his
actions; and the Arians were reproached with the frequent executions which stained the palace and the dominions of the
tyrant. Arms and ambition were, however, the ruling passions of
the monarch of the sea. But Hunneric, his inglorious son, who
seemed to inherit only his vices, tormented the catholics with
the same unrelenting fury which had been fatal to his brother,
his nephews, and the friends and favourites of his father; and
even to the Arian patriarch, who was inhumanly burnt alive in
the midst of Carthage. The religious war was preceded and prepared by an insidious truce; persecution was made the serious
and important business of the Vandal court; and the loathsome
disease which hastened the death of Hunneric revenged the injuries, without contributing to the deliverance, of the church.
The throne of Africa was successively filled by the two nephews
of Hunneric; by Gundamund, who reigned about twelve, and by
Thrasimund, who governed the nation above twenty-seven,
years. Their administration was hostile and oppressive to the
orthodox party. Gundamund appeared to emulate, or even to

1 Such are the contemporary complaints of Sidonius, bishop of Clermont
(l. vii. c. 6, p. 182, etc., edit. Sirmond). Gregory of Tours, who quotes this
Epistle (l. ii. c. 25, in tom. ii. p. 174), extorts an unwarrantable assertion, that,
of the nine vacancies in Aquitain, some had been produced by episcopal *mar-
tyrdoms.*

surpass, the cruelty of his uncle; and if at length he relented, if he recalled the bishops, and restored the freedom of Athanasian worship, a premature death intercepted the benefits of his tardy clemency. His brother, Thrasimund, was the greatest and most accomplished of the Vandal kings, whom he excelled in beauty, prudence, and magnanimity of soul. But this magnanimous character was degraded by his intolerant zeal and deceitful clemency. Instead of threats and tortures, he employed the gentle, but efficacious, powers of seduction. Wealth, dignity, and the royal favour were the liberal rewards of apostacy; the catholics who had violated the laws might purchase their pardon by the renunciation of their faith; and whenever Thrasimund meditated any rigorous measure, he patiently waited till the indiscretion of his adversaries furnished him with a specious opportunity. Bigotry was his last sentiment in the hour of death; and he exacted from his successor a solemn oath that he would never tolerate the sectaries of Athanasius. But his successor, Hilderic, the gentle son of the savage Hunneric, preferred the duties of humanity and justice to the vain obligation of an impious oath; and his accession was gloriously marked by the restoration of peace and universal freedom. The throne of that virtuous, though feeble, monarch was usurped by his cousin Gelimer, a zealous Arian: but the Vandal kingdom, before he could enjoy or abuse his power, was subverted by the arms of Belisarius; and the orthodox party retaliated the injuries which they had endured.[1]

The passionate declamations of the catholics, the sole historians of this persecution, cannot afford any distinct series of causes and events, any impartial view of characters or counsels; but the most remarkable circumstances that deserve either credit or notice may be referred to the following heads: I. In the

---

1 The original monuments of the Vandal persecution are preserved in the five books of the history of Victor Vitensis (de Persecutione Vandalicâ), a bishop who was exiled by Hunneric; in the Life of St. Fulgentius, who was distinguished in the persecution of Thrasimund (in Biblioth. Max. Patrum, tom. ix. p. 4–16); and in the first book of the Vandalic War, by the impartial Procopius (c. 7, 8, p. 196, 197, 198, 199 [ed. Paris; tom. i. p. 344 *sqq.*, ed. Bonn]). Dom Ruinart, the last editor of Victor, has illustrated the whole subject with a copious and learned apparatus of notes and supplement. (Paris, 1694.)

original law, which is still extant,[1] Hunneric expressly declares, and the declaration appears to be correct, that he had faithfully transcribed the regulations and penalties of the Imperial edicts against the heretical congregations, the clergy, and the people, who dissented from the established religion. If the rights of conscience had been understood, the catholics must have condemned their past conduct, or acquiesced in their actual sufferings. But they still persisted to refuse the indulgence which they claimed. While they trembled under the lash of persecution, they praised the *laudable* severity of Hunneric himself, who burnt or banished great numbers of Manichæans;[2] and they rejected with horror the ignominious compromise that the disciples of Arius and of Athanasius should enjoy a reciprocal and similar toleration in the territories of the Romans and in those of the Vandals.[3] II. The practice of a conference, which the catholics had so frequently used to insult and punish their obstinate antagonists, was retorted against themselves.[4] At the command of Hunneric, four hundred and sixty-six orthodox bishops assembled at Carthage; but when they were admitted into the hall of audience, they had the mortification of beholding the Arian Cyrila exalted on the patriarchal throne. The disputants were separated, after the mutual and ordinary reproaches of noise and silence, of delay and precipitation, of military force and of popular clamour. One martyr and one confessor were selected among the catholic bishops; twenty-eight escaped by flight, and eighty-eight by conformity; forty-six were sent into Corsica to cut timber for the royal navy; and three hundred and two were banished to the different parts of Africa, exposed to the insults of their enemies,

1 Victor, iv. 2, p. 65. Hunneric refuses the name of Catholics to the *Homoousians*. He describes, as the veri Divinæ Majestatis cultores, his own party, who professed the faith, confirmed by more than a thousand bishops, in the synods of Rimini and Seleucia.

2 Victor, ii. I, p. 21, 22, *Laudabilior* . . . videbatur. In the MSS. which omit this word, the passage is unintelligible. See Ruinart, Not. p. 164.

3 Victor, ii. 2, p. 22, 23 [21, 22]. The clergy of Carthage called these conditions *periculosæ;* and they seem, indeed, to have been proposed as a snare to entrap the catholic bishops.

4 See the narrative of this conference and the treatment of the bishops in Victor, ii. 13–18, p. 35–42, and the whole fourth book, p. 63–71. The third book, p. 42–62, is entirely filled by their apology or confession of faith.

and carefully deprived of all the temporal and spiritual comforts of life.[1] The hardships of ten years' exile must have reduced their numbers; and if they had complied with the law of Thrasimund, which prohibited any episcopal consecrations, the orthodox church of Africa must have expired with the lives of its actual members. They disobeyed; and their disobedience was punished by a second exile of two hundred and twenty bishops into Sardinia, where they languished fifteen years, till the accession of the gracious Hilderic.[2] The two islands were judiciously chosen by the malice of their Arian tyrants. Seneca, from his own experience, has deplored and exaggerated the miserable state of Corsica,[3] and the plenty of Sardinia was overbalanced by the unwholesome quality of the air.[4] III. The zeal of Genseric and his successors for the conversion of the catholics must have rendered them still more jealous to guard the purity of the Vandal faith. Before the churches were finally shut, it was a crime to appear in a barbarian dress; and those who presumed to neglect the royal mandate were rudely dragged backwards by their long hair.[5] The palatine officers, who refused to profess the religion of their prince, were ignominiously stripped of their honours and employments; banished to Sardinia and Sicily; or condemned to the servile labours of slaves and peasants in the

1 See the list of the African bishops, in Victor, p. 117–140, and Ruinart's notes, p. 215–397. The schismatic name of *Donatus* frequently occurs, and they appear to have adopted (like our fanatics of the last age) the pious appellations of *Deodatus, Deogratias, Quidvultdeus, Habetdeum*, etc.

2 Fulgent. Vit. c. 16–29. Thrasimund affected the praise of moderation and learning; and Fulgentius addressed three books of controversy to the Arian tyrant, whom he styles *piissime Rex*. Biblioth. Maxim. Patrum, tom. ix. p. 41. Only sixty bishops are mentioned as exiles in the Life of Fulgentius; they are increased to one hundred and twenty by Victor Tunnunensis and Isidore; but the number of two hundred and twenty is specified in the *Historia, Miscella* and a short authentic chronicle of the times. See Ruinart. p. 570, 571.

3 See the base and insipid epigrams of the Stoic, who could not support exile with more fortitude than Ovid. Corsica might not produce corn, wine, or oil; but it could not be destitute of grass, water, and even fire.

4 Si ob gravitatem cœli interissent, *vile* damnum. Tacit. Annal. ii. 85. In this application Thrasimund would have adopted the reading of some critics, *utile* damnum.

5 See these preludes of a *general* persecution, in Victor, ii. c. 3, 4, 7, and the two edicts of Hunneric, l. ii. p. 35, l. iv. p. 64.

fields of Utica. In the districts which had been peculiarly allotted to the Vandals, the exercise of the catholic worship was more strictly prohibited; and severe penalties were denounced against the guilt both of the missionary and the proselyte. By these arts the faith of the barbarians was preserved, and their zeal was inflamed: they discharged with devout fury the office of spies, informers, or executioners; and whenever their cavalry took the field, it was the favourite amusement of the march to defile the churches and to insult the clergy of the adverse faction.[1] IV. The citizens who had been educated in the luxury of the Roman province were delivered, with exquisite cruelty, to the Moors of the desert. A venerable train of bishops, presbyters, and deacons, with a faithful crowd of four thousand and ninety-six persons, whose guilt is not precisely ascertained, were torn from their native homes by the command of Hunneric. During the night they were confined, like a herd of cattle, amidst their own or-dure: during the day they pursued their march over the burning sands; and if they fainted under the heat and fatigue, they were goaded or dragged along till they expired in the hands of their tormentors.[2] These unhappy exiles, when they reached the Moor-ish huts, might excite the compassion of a people whose native humanity was neither improved by reason nor corrupted by fan-aticism: but if they escaped the dangers, they were condemned to share the distress, of a savage life. V. It is incumbent on the authors of persecution previously to reflect whether they are determined to support it in the last extreme. They excite the flame which they strive to extinguish; and it soon becomes necessary to chastise the contumacy, as well as the crime, of the offender. The fine, which is he unable or unwilling to discharge, exposes his person to the severity of the law; and his contempt of lighter penalties suggests the use and propriety of capital punishment. Through the veil of fiction and declamation we may clearly perceive that the catholics, more especially under the reign of Hunneric, endured the most cruel and ignominious

1 See Procopius de Bell. Vandal. l. i. c. 7 [c. 8], p. 197, 198 [tom. i. p. 344 sqq., ed. Bonn]. A Moorish prince endeavoured to propitiate the God of the Christians by his diligence to erase the marks of the Vandal sacrilege.

2 See this story in Victor, ii. 8–12, p. 30–34. Victor describes the distress of these confessors as an eye-witness.

treatment.[1] Respectable citizens, noble matrons, and consecrated virgins were stripped naked and raised in the air by pulleys, with a weight suspended at their feet. In this painful attitude their naked bodies were torn with scourges, or burnt in the most tender parts with red-hot plates of iron. The amputation of the ears, the nose, the tongue, and the right hand was inflicted by the Arians; and although the precise number cannot be defined, it is evident that many persons, among whom a bishop[2] and a proconsul[3] may be named, were entitled to the crown of martyrdom. The same honour has been ascribed to the memory of Count Sebastian, who professed the Nicene creed with unshaken constancy; and Genseric might detest as an heretic the brave and ambitious fugitive whom he dreaded as a rival.[4] VI. A new mode of conversion, which might subdue the feeble and alarm the timorous, was employed by the Arian ministers. They imposed, by fraud or violence, the rites of baptism; and punished the apostacy of the catholics, if they disclaimed this odious and profane ceremony, which scandalously violated the freedom of the will and the unity of the sacrament.[5] The hostile sects had formerly allowed the validity of each other's baptism; and the innovation, so fiercely maintained by the Vandals, can be imputed only to the example and advice of the Donatists. VII. The Arian clergy surpassed in religious cruelty the king and his Vandals; but they were incapable of cultivating the spiritual vineyard which they were so desirous to possess. A patriarch[6] might seat himself on the throne of Carthage; some bishops, in the principal

1 See the fifth book of Victor. His passionate complaints are confirmed by the sober testimony of Procopius and the public declaration of the emperor Justinian. Cod. l. i. tit. xxvii.

2 Victor, ii. 18, p. 41.

3 Victor, v. 4, p. 74, 75. His name was Victorianus, and he was a wealthy citizen of Adrumetum, who enjoyed the confidence of the king, by whose favour he had obtained the office, or at least the title, of proconsul of Africa.

4 Victor, i. 6, p. 8, 9. After relating the firm resistance and dexterous reply of Count Sebastian, he adds, quare alio [alîus] generis argumento postea bellicosum virum occidit.

5 Victor, v. 12, 13. Tillemont, Mém. Ecclés. tom. vi. p. 609.

6 *Primate* was more properly the title of the bishop of Carthage; but the name of *patriarch* was given by the sects and nations to their principal ecclesiastic. See Thomassin, Discipline de l'Eglise, tom. i. p. 155, 158.

cities, might usurp the place of their rivals; but the smallness of their numbers, and their ignorance of the Latin language,[1] disqualified the barbarians for the ecclesiastical ministry of a great church; and the Africans, after the loss of their orthodox pastors, were deprived of the public exercise of Christianity. VIII. The emperors were the natural protectors of the Homoousian doctrine; and the faithful people of Africa, both as Romans and as catholics, preferred their lawful sovereignty to the usurpation of the barbarous heretics. During an interval of peace and friendship Hunneric restored the cathedral of Carthage, at the intercession of Zeno, who reigned in the East, and of Placidia, the daughter and relict of emperors and the sister of the queen of the Vandals.[2] But this decent regard was of short duration; and the haughty tyrant displayed his contempt for the religion of the empire by studiously arranging the bloody images of persecution in all the principal streets through which the Roman ambassador must pass in his way to the palace.[3] An oath was required from the bishops who were assembled at Carthage, that they would support the succession of his son Hilderic, and that they would renounce all foreign or *transmarine* correspondence. This engagement, consistent, as it should seem, with their moral and religious duties, was refused by the more sagacious members[4] of the assembly. Their refusal, faintly coloured by the pretence that it is unlawful for a Christian to swear, must provoke the suspicions of a jealous tyrant.

The catholics, oppressed by royal and military force, were far superior to their adversaries in numbers and learning. With

---

1 The patriarch Cyrila himself publicly declared that he did not understand Latin (Victor, ii. 18, p. 41): Nescio Latine; and he might converse with tolerable ease, without being capable of disputing or preaching in that language. His vandal clergy were still more ignorant; and small confidence could be placed in the Africans who had conformed.

2 Victor, ii. 1, 2, p. 22.

3 Victor, v. 7, p. 77. He appeals to the ambassador himself, whose name was Uranius.

4 *Astutiores*, Victor, iv. 4, p. 70. He plainly intimates that their quotation of the Gospel, 'Non jurabitis in toto,' was only meant to elude the obligation of an inconvenient oath. The forty-six bishops who refused were banished to Corsica; the three hundred and two who swore were distributed through the provinces of Africa.

the same weapons which the Greek[1] and Latin fathers had already provided for the Arian controversy, they repeatedly silenced or vanquished the fierce and illiterate successors of Ulphilas. The consciousness of their own superiority might have raised them above the arts and passions of religious warfare. Yet, instead of assuming such honourable pride, the orthodox theologians were tempted, by the assurance of impunity, to compose fictions which must be stigmatised with the epithets of fraud and forgery. They ascribed their own polemical works to the most venerable names of Christian antiquity; the characters of Athanasius and Augustin were awkwardly personated by Vigilius and his disciples;[2] and the famous creed, which so clearly expounds the mysteries of the Trinity and the Incarnation, is deduced, with strong probability, from this African school.[3] Even the Scriptures themselves were profaned by their rash and sacrilegious hands. The memorable text which asserts the unity of the THREE who bear witness in heaven[4] is condemned by the universal silence of the orthodox fathers, ancient versions, and

1 Fulgentius, bishop of Ruspæ, in the Byzacene province, was of a senatorial family and had received a liberal education. He could repeat all Homer and Menander before he was allowed to study Latin, his native tongue (Vit. Fulgent. c. 1). Many African bishops might understand Greek, and many Greek theologians were translated into Latin.

2 Compare the two prefaces to the Dialogue of Vigilius of Thapsus (p. 118, 119, edit. Chiflet). He might amuse his learned reader with an innocent fiction; but the subject was too grave, and the Africans were too ignorant.

3 The P. Quesnel started this opinion, which has been favourably received. But the three following truths, however surprising they may seem, are *now* universally acknowledged (Gerard Vossius, tom. vi. p. 516–522; Tillemont, Mém. Ecclés. tom. viii. p. 667–671). 1. St. Athanasius is not the author of the creed which is so frequently read in our churches. 2. It does not appear to have existed within a century after his death. 3. It was originally composed in the Latin tongue, and, consequently, in the Western provinces. Gennadius, patriarch of Constantinople, was so much amazed by this extraordinary composition, that he frankly pronounced it to be the work of a drunken man. Petav. Dogmat. Theologica, tom. ii. l. vii. c. 8, p. 687.

4 I John v. 7. See Simon, Hist. Critique du Nouveau Testament, Part i. c. xviii. p. 203–218; and part ii. c. ix. p. 99–121; and the elaborate Prolegomena and Annotations of Dr. Mill and Wetstein to their editions of the Greek Testament. In 1689, the papist Simon strove to be free; in 1707, the Protestant Mill wished to be a slave; in 1751, the Arminian Wetstein used the liberty of his times and of his sect.

authentic manuscripts.[1] It was first alleged by the catholic bishops whom Hunneric summoned to the conference of Carthage.[2] An allegorical interpretation, in the form perhaps of a marginal note, invaded the text of the Latin Bibles which were renewed and corrected in a dark period of ten centuries.[3] After the invention of printing,[4] the editors of the Greek Testament yielded to their own prejudices, or those of the times;[5] and the pious fraud, which was embraced with equal zeal at Rome and at Geneva, has been infinitely multiplied in every country and every language of modern Europe.

The example of fraud must excite suspicion: and the specious miracles by which the African catholics have defended the truth and justice of their cause may be ascribed, with more reason, to their own industry than to the visible protection of Heaven. Yet the historian who views this religious conflict with an impartial eye may condescend to mention *one* preternatural event, which

1 Of *all* the MSS. now extant, above fourscore in number, some of which are more than 1200 years old (Wetstein ad loc.). The *orthodox* copies of the Vatican, of the Complutensian editors, of Robert Stephens, are become invisible; and the *two* MSS. of Dublin and Berlin are unworthy to form an exception. See Emyln's Works, vol. ii. p. 227–255, 269–299; and M. de Missy's four ingenious letters, in tom. viii. and ix. of the Journal Britannique.

2 Or, more properly, by the *four* bishops who composed and published the profession of faith in the name of their brethren. They styled this text luce clarius (Victor Vitensis de Persecut. Vandal. l. iii. c. 11, p. 54). It is quoted soon afterwards by the African polemics Vigilius and Fulgentius.

3 In the eleventh and twelfth centuries the Bibles were corrected by Lanfranc, archbishop of Canterbury, and by Nicolas, cardinal and librarian of the Roman church, secundum orthodoxam fidem (Wetstein, Prolegom. p. 84, 85). Notwithstanding these corrections, the passage is still wanting in twenty-five Latin MSS. (Wetstein ad loc.), the oldest and the fairest; two qualities seldom united, except in manuscripts.

4 The art which the Germans had invented was applied in Italy to the profane writers of Rome and Greece. The original Greek of the New Testament was published about the same time (A.D. 1514, 1516, 1520) by the industry of Erasmus and the munificence of Cardinal Ximenes. The Complutensian Polyglot cost the cardinal 50,000 ducats. See Mattaire, Annal. Typograph. tom. ii. p. 2–8, 125–133; and Wetstein, Prolegomena, p. 116–127.

5 The three witnesses have been established in our Greek Testaments by the prudence of Erasmus; the honest bigotry of the Complutensian editors; the typographical fraud or error of Robert Stephens in the placing a crotchet; and the deliberate falsehood or strange misapprehension of Theodore Beza.

will edify the devout and surprise the incredulous. Tipasa,[1] a
maritime colony of Mauritania, sixteen miles to the east of Cæsarea, had been distinguished in every age by the orthodox zeal
of its inhabitants. They had braved the fury of the Donatists;[2]
they resisted or eluded the tyranny of the Arians. The town was
deserted on the approach of an heretical bishop: most of the
inhabitants who could procure ships passed over to the coast of
Spain; and the unhappy remnant, refusing all communion with
the usurper, still presumed to hold their pious, but illegal, assemblies. Their disobedience exasperated the cruelty of Hunneric. A
military count was despatched from Carthage to Tipasa: he collected the catholics in the Forum, and, in the presence of the
whole province, deprived the guilty of their right hands and their
tongues. But the holy confessors continued to speak without
tongues; and this miracle is attested by Victor, an African bishop,
who published an history of the persecution within two years after
the event.[3] 'If any one,' says Victor, 'should doubt of the truth,
let him repair to Constantinople, and listen to the clear and
perfect language of Restitutus, the subdeacon, one of these glorious sufferers, who is now lodged in the palace of the emperor
Zeno, and is respected by the devout empress.' At Constantinople we are astonished to find a cool, a learned, and unexcep-
tionable witness, without interest, and without passion. Æneas
of Gaza, a Platonic philosopher, has accurately described his
own observations on these African sufferers. 'I saw them myself:
I heard them speak: I diligently inquired by what means such an
articulate voice could be formed without any organ of speech: I
used my eyes to examine the report of my ears: I opened their
mouth, and saw that the whole tongue had been completely torn
away by the roots; an operation which the physicians generally
suppose to be mortal.'[4] The testimony of Æneas of Gaza might

1 Plin. Hist. Natural. v. 1; Itinerar. Wesseling, p. 15; Cellarius, Geograph.
Antiq. tom. ii. part ii. p. 127. This Tipasa (which must not be confounded with
another in Numidia) was a town of some note, since Vespasian endowed it with
the right of Latium.

2 Optatus Milevitanus de Schism. Donatist. l. ii. p. 38.

3 Victor Vitensis, v. 6. p. 76. Ruinart, p. 483–487.

4 Æneas Gazæus in Theophrasto, in Biblioth. Patrum, tom. viii. p. 664, 665.
He was a Christian, and composed this Dialogue (the Theophrastus) on the

be confirmed by the superfluous evidence of the emperor Justinian, in a perpetual edict; of Count Marcellinus, in his Chronicle of the times; and of pope Gregory the First, who had resided at Constantinople as the minister of the Roman pontiff.[1] They all lived within the compass of a century; and they all appeal to their personal knowledge or the public notoriety for the truth of a miracle which was repeated in several instances, displayed on the greatest theatre of the world, and submitted during a series of years to the calm examination of the senses. This supernatural gift of the African confessors, who spoke without tongues, will command the assent of those, and of those only, who already believe that their language was pure and orthodox. But the stubborn mind of an infidel is guarded by secret, incurable suspicion; and the Arian, or Socinian, who has seriously rejected the doctrine of the Trinity, will not be shaken by the most plausible evidence of an Athanasian miracle.

The Vandals and the Ostrogoths persevered in the profession of Arianism till the final ruin of the kingdoms which they had founded in Africa and Italy. The barbarians of Gaul submitted to the orthodox dominion of the Franks; and Spain was restored to the catholic church by the voluntary conversion of the Visigoths.

This salutary revolution[2] was hastened by the example of a royal martyr, whom our calmer reason may style an ungrateful rebel. Leovigild, the Gothic monarch of Spain, deserved the respect of his enemies and the love of his subjects: the catholics

immortality of the soul and the resurrection of the body; besides twenty-five Epistles, still extant. See Cave (Hist. Litteraria, p. 297) and Fabricius (Biblioth. Græc. tom i. p. 422).

1 Justinian. Codex, l. i. tit. xxvii. [leg. 1]; Marcellin. in Chron. p. 45, in Thesaur. Temporum Scaliger; Procopius, de Bell. Vandal. l. i. c. 8, p. 196 [ed. Par.; tom. i. p. 345, ed. Bonn]; Gregor. Magnus, Dialog. iii. 32. None of these witnesses have specified the number of the confessors which is fixed at sixty in an old menology (apud Ruinart, p. 486). Two of them lost their speech by fornication; but the miracle is enhanced by the singular instance of a boy who had *never* spoken before his tongue was cut out.

2 See the two general historians of Spain, Mariana (Hist. de Rebus Hispaniæ, tom. i. l. v. c. 12–15, p. 182–194) and Ferreras (French translation, tom. ii. p. 206–247). Mariana almost forgets that he is a Jesuit, to assume the style and spirit of a Roman classic. Ferreras, an industrious compiler, reviews his facts and rectifies his chronology.

enjoyed a free toleration, and his Arian synods attempted, without much success, to reconcile their scruples by abolishing the unpopular rite of a *second* baptism. His eldest son Hermenegild, who was invested by his father with the royal diadem and the fair principality of Bætica, contracted an honourable and orthodox alliance with a Merovingian princess, the daughter of Sigebert, king of Austrasia, and of the famous Brunechild. The beauteous Ingundis, who was no more than thirteen years of age, was received, beloved, and persecuted in the Arian court of Toledo; and her religious constancy was alternately assaulted with blandishments and violence by Goisvintha, the Gothic queen, who abused the double claim of maternal authority.[1] Incensed by her resistance, Goisvintha seized the catholic princess by her long hair, inhumanly dashed her against the ground, kicked her till she was covered with blood, and at last gave orders that she should be stripped and thrown into a basin or fish-pond.[2] Love and honour might excite Hermenegild to resent this injurious treatment of his bride; and he was gradually persuaded that Ingundis suffered for the cause of divine truth. Her tender complaints, and the weighty arguments of Leander, archbishop of Seville, accomplished his conversion; and the heir of the Gothic monarchy was initiated in the Nicene faith by the solemn rites of confirmation.[3] The rash youth, inflamed by zeal, and perhaps by ambition, was tempted to violate the duties of a son and a subject; and the catholics of Spain, although they could not complain of persecution, applauded his pious rebellion against an heretical father. The civil war was protracted by the long and obstinate sieges of Merida, Cordova, and Seville, which had

1 Goisvintha successively married two kings of the Visigoths: Athanigild, to whom she bore Brunechild, the mother of Ingundis; and Leovigild, whose two sons, Hermeregild and Recared, were the issue of a former marriage.

2 Iracundiæ furore succensa, adprehensam per comam capitis puellam in terram conlidit, et diu calcibus verberatam, ac sanguine cruentatam, jussit exspoliari, et piscinæ immergi. Greg. Turon. l. v. c. 39, in tom. ii. p. 255. Gregory is one of our best originals for this portion of history.

3 The catholics, who admitted the baptism of heretics, repeated the rite, or, as it was afterwards styled, the sacrament, of confirmation, to which they ascribed many mystic and marvellous prerogatives, both visible and invisible. See Chardon, Hist. des Sacremens, tom. i. p. 405–552.

strenuously espoused the party of Hermenegild. He invited the orthodox barbarians, the Suevi and the Franks, to the destruction of his native land: he solicited the dangerous aid of the Romans, who possessed Africa and a part of the Spanish coast; and his holy ambassador, the archbishop Leander, effectually negotiated in person with the Byzantine court. But the hopes of the catholics were crushed by the active diligence of a monarch who commanded the troops and treasures of Spain; and the guilty Hermenegild, after his vain attempts to resist or to escape, was compelled to surrender himself into the hands of an incensed father. Leovigild was still mindful of that sacred character; and the rebel, despoiled of the regal ornaments, was still permitted, in a decent exile, to profess the catholic religion. His repeated and unsuccessful treasons at length provoked the indignation of the Gothic king; and the sentence of death, which he pronounced with apparent reluctance, was privately executed in the tower of Seville. The inflexible constancy with which he refused to accept the Arian communion, as the price of his safety, may excuse the honours that have been paid to the memory of St. Hermenegild. His wife and infant son were detained by the Romans in ignominious captivity; and this domestic misfortune tarnished the glories of Leovigild, and embittered the last moments of his life.

His son and successor, Recared, the first catholic king of Spain, had imbibed the faith of his unfortunate brother, which he supported with more prudence and success. Instead of revolting against his father, Recared patiently expected the hour of his death. Instead of condemning his memory, he piously supposed that the dying monarch had abjured the errors of Arianism, and recommended to his son the conversion of the Gothic nation. To accomplish that salutary end, Recared convened an assembly of the Arian clergy and nobles, declared himself a catholic, and exhorted them to imitate the example of their prince. The laborious interpretation of doubtful texts, or the curious pursuit of metaphysical arguments, would have excited an endless controversy; and the monarch discreetly proposed to his illiterate audience two substantial and visible arguments – the testimony of Earth and of Heaven. The *Earth* had submitted to the Nicene synod: the Romans, the barbarians, and the inhabitants of Spain unanimously professed the same orthodox creed; and the

Visigoths resisted, almost alone, the consent of the Christian world. A superstitious age was prepared to reverence, as the testimony of *Heaven*, the preternatural cures which were performed by the skill or virtue of the catholic clergy; the baptismal fonts of Osset in Bætica,[1] which were spontaneously replenished each year on the vigil of Easter;[2] and the miraculous shrine of St. Martin of Tours, which had already converted the Suevic prince and people of Gallicia.[3] The catholic king encountered some difficulties on this important change of the national religion. A conspiracy, secretly fomented by the queen-dowager, was formed against his life; and two counts excited a dangerous revolt in the Narbon-nese Gaul. But Recared disarmed the conspirators, defeated the rebels, and executed severe justice, which the Arians, in their turn, might brand with the reproach of persecution. Eight bishops, whose names betray their barbaric origin, abjured their errors; and all the books of Arian theology were reduced to ashes, with the house in which they had been purposely col-lected. The whole body of the Visigoths and Suevi were allured or driven into the pale of the catholic communion; the faith, at least of the rising generation, was fervent and sincere; and the devout liberality of the barbarians enriched the churches and monasteries of Spain. Seventy bishops, assembled in the council of Toledo, received the submission of their conquerors; and the zeal of the Spaniards improved the Nicene creed, by declaring the procession of the Holy Ghost from the Son, as well as from the Father; a weighty point of doctrine, which produced, long afterwards, the schism of the Greek and Latin churches.[4] The

1 Osset, or Julia Constantia, was opposite to Seville, on the northern side of the Bætis (Plin. Hist. Natur. iii. 3): and the authentic reference of Gregory of Tours (Hist. Francor. l. vi. c. 43, p. 288) deserves more credit than the name of Lusitania (de Gloriâ Martyr. c. 24), which has been eagerly embraced by the vain and superstitious Portuguese (Ferreras, Hist. d'Espagne, tom. ii. p. 166).

2 This miracle was skilfully performed. An Arian king sealed the doors and dug a deep trench round the church without being able to intercept the Easter supply of baptismal water.

3 Ferreras (tom. ii. p. 168–175, A.D. 550) has illustrated the difficulties which regard the time and circumstances of the conversion of the Suevi. They had been recently united by Leovigild to the Gothic monarchy of Spain.

4 This addition to the Nicene, or rather the Constantinopolitan creed, was first made in the eighth council of Toledo, A.D. 653; but it was expressive of the popular doctrine (Gerard Vossius, tom. vi. p. 527, de tribus Symbolis).

royal proselyte immediately saluted and consulted pope Gregory, surnamed the Great, a learned and holy prelate, whose reign was distinguished by the conversion of heretics and infidels. The ambassadors of Recared respectfully offered on the threshold of the Vatican his rich presents of gold and gems; they accepted, as a lucrative exchange, the hairs of St. John the Baptist; a cross which enclosed a small piece of the true wood; and a key that contained some particles of iron which had been scraped from the chains of St. Peter.[1]

The same Gregory, the spiritual conqueror of Britain, encouraged the pious Theodelinda, queen of the Lombards, to propagate the Nicene faith among the victorious savages, whose recent Christianity was polluted by the Arian heresy. Her devout labours still left room for the industry and success of future missionaries, and many cities of Italy were still disputed by hostile bishops. But the cause of Arianism was gradually suppressed by the weight of truth, of interest, and of example; and the controversy, which Egypt had derived from the Platonic school, was terminated, after a war of three hundred years, by the final conversion of the Lombards of Italy.[2]

The first missionaries who preached the Gospel to the barbarians appealed to the evidence of reason, and claimed the benefit of toleration.[3] But no sooner had they established their spiritual dominion than they exhorted the Christian kings to extirpate, without mercy, the remains of Roman or barbaric superstition. The successors of Clovis inflicted one hundred lashes on the peasants who refused to destroy their idols; the crime of sacrificing to the demons was punished by the Anglo-Saxon laws with the heavier penalties of imprisonment and

1 See Gregor. Magn. l. vii. Epist. 126, apud Baronium, Annal. Eccles. A.D. 599, No. 25, 26 [l. ix. Ep. 122, tom. ii. p. 1031, ed. Bened.].

2 Paul Warnefrid (de Gestis Langobard. l. iv. c. 44, p. 853, edit. Grot.) allows that Arianism still prevailed under the reign of Rotharis (A.D. 636–652). The pious *deacon* does not attempt to mark the precise era of the national conversion, which was accomplished, however, before the end of the seventh century.

3 Quorum fidei et conversioni ita congratulatus esse rex perhibetur, ut nullum tamen cogeret ad Christianismum. . . . Didicerat enim a doctoribus auctoribusque suæ salutis, servitium Christi voluntarium non coactitium esse debere. Bedæ Hist. Ecclesiastic. l. i. c. 26, p. 62, edit. Smith.

confiscation; and even the wise Alfred adopted, as an indispensable duty, the extreme rigour of the Mosaic institutions.[1] But the
punishment and the crime were gradually abolished among a
Christian people; the theological disputes of the schools were
suspended by propitious ignorance; and the intolerant spirit,
which could find neither idolaters nor heretics, was reduced to
the persecution of the Jews. That exiled nation had founded
some synagogues in the cities of Gaul; but Spain, since the time
of Hadrian, was filled with their numerous colonies.[2] The wealth
which they accumulated by trade and the management of the
finances invited the pious avarice of their masters; and they
might be oppressed without danger, as they had lost the use, and
even the remembrance, of arms. Sisebut, a Gothic king who
reigned in the beginning of the seventh century, proceeded at
once to the last extremes of persecution.[3] Ninety thousand Jews
were compelled to receive the sacrament of baptism; the fortunes of the obstinate infidels were confiscated, their bodies
were tortured, and it seems doubtful whether they were permitted to abandon their native country. The excessive zeal of the
catholic king was moderated even by the clergy of Spain, who
solemnly pronounced an inconsistent sentence: *that* the sacra-
ments should not be forcibly imposed; but *that* the Jews who
had been baptised should be constrained, for the honour of the
church, to persevere in the external practice of a religion which
they disbelieved and detested. Their frequent relapses provoked
one of the successors of Sisebut to banish the whole nation from
his dominions; and a council of Toledo published a decree that
every Gothic king should swear to maintain this salutary edict.

1 See the Historians of France, tom. iv. p. 114; and Wilkins, Leges Anglo-
Saxonicæ, p. 11, 31. Siquis sacrificium immolaverit præter Deo soli morte moriatur.

2 The Jews pretend that they were introduced into Spain by the fleets of
Solomon and the arms of Nebuchadnezzar; that Hadrian transported forty
thousand families of the tribe of Judah, and ten thousand of the tribe of
Benjamin, etc. Basnage, Hist. des Juifs, tom. vii. c. 9, p. 240–256.

3 Isidore, at that time archbishop of Seville, mentions, disapproves and
congratulates, the zeal of Sisebut (Chron. Goth. p. 728 [ed. Grot.]). Baronius
(A.D. 614, No. 41) assigns the number on the evidence of Aimoin (l. iv. c. 22):
but the evidence is weak, and I have not been able to verify the quotation
(Historians of France, tom. iii. p. 127).

But the tyrants were unwilling to dismiss the victims whom they delighted to torture, or to deprive themselves of the industrious slaves over whom they might exercise a lucrative oppression. The Jews still continued in Spain, under the weight of the civil and ecclesiastical laws, which in the same country have been faithfully transcribed in the Code of the Inquisition. The Gothic kings and bishops at length discovered that injuries will produce hatred, and that hatred will find the opportunity of revenge. A nation, the secret or professed enemies of Christianity, still multiplied in servitude and distress; and the intrigues of the Jews promoted the rapid success of the Arabian conquerors.[1]

As soon as the barbarians withdrew their powerful support, the unpopular heresy of Arius sunk into contempt and oblivion. But the Greeks still retained their subtle and loquacious disposition: the establishment of an obscure doctrine suggested new questions and new disputes; and it was always in the power of an ambitious prelate or a fanatic monk to violate the peace of the church, and perhaps of the empire. The historian of the empire may overlook those disputes which were confined to the obscurity of schools and synods. The Manichæans, who laboured to reconcile the religions of Christ and of Zoroaster, had secretly introduced themselves into the provinces: but these foreign sectaries were involved in the common disgrace of the Gnostics, and the Imperial laws were executed by the public hatred. The rational opinions of the Pelagians were propagated from Britain to Rome, Africa, and Palestine, and silently expired in a superstitious age. But the East was distracted by the Nestorian and Eutychian controversies, which attempted to explain the mystery of the incarnation, and hastened the ruin of Christianity in her native land. These controversies were first agitated under the reign of the younger Theodosius: but their important consequences extend far beyond the limits of the present volume. The metaphysical chain of argument, the contests of ecclesiastical ambition, and their political influence on the decline

---

1 Basnage (tom. viii. c. 13, p. 388–400) faithfully represents the state of the Jews: but he might have added, from the canons of the Spanish councils and the laws of the Visigoths, many curious circumstances essential to his subject, though they are foreign to mine.

of the Byzantine empire, may afford an interesting and instruct-
ive series of history, from the general councils of Ephesus and
Chalcedon to the conquest of the East by the successors of
Mahomet.

CHAPTER XXXVIII

Reign and Conversion of Clovis – His Victories over the Alemanni,
Burgundians, and Visigoths – Establishment of the French
Monarchy in Gaul – Laws of the Barbarians – State of the
Romans – The Visigoths of Spain – Conquest of Britain by
the Saxons

THE Gauls,[1] who impatiently supported the Roman yoke,
received a memorable lesson from one of the lieutenants of
Vespasian, whose weighty sense has been refined and expressed
by the genius of Tacitus.[2] 'The protection of the republic has
delivered Gaul from internal discord and foreign invasions. By
the loss of national independence you have acquired the name
and privileges of Roman citizens. You enjoy, in common with
ourselves, the permanent benefits of civil government; and your
remote situation is less exposed to the accidental mischiefs of
tyranny. Instead of exercising the rights of conquest, we have
been contented to impose such tributes as are requisite for your
own preservation. Peace cannot be secured without armies, and
armies must be supported at the expense of the people. It is for
your sake, not for our own, that we guard the barrier of the
Rhine against the ferocious Germans, who have so often attempted, and who will always desire, to exchange the solitude of

1 In this chapter I shall draw my quotations from the Recueil des Historiens
des Gaules et de la France, Paris, 1738–1767, in eleven volumes in folio. By the
labour of Dom Bouquet and the other Benedictines, all the original testimonies,
as far as A.D. 1060, are disposed in chronological order, and illustrated with
learned notes. Such a national work, which will be continued to the year 1500,
might provoke our emulation.

2 Tacit. Hist. iv. 73, 74, in tom. i. p. 445. To abridge Tacitus would indeed
be presumptuous; but I may select the general ideas which he applies to the
present state and future revolutions of Gaul.

their woods and morasses for the wealth and fertility of Gaul. The fall of Rome would be fatal to the provinces, and you would be buried in the ruins of that mighty fabric which has been raised by the valour and wisdom of eight hundred years. Your imaginary freedom would be insulted and oppressed by a savage master, and the expulsion of the Romans would be succeeded by the eternal hostilities of the barbarian conquerors."¹ This salutary advice was accepted, and this strange prediction was accomplished. In the space of four hundred years the hardy Gauls, who had encountered the arms of Cæsar, were imperceptibly melted into the general mass of citizens and subjects: the Western empire was dissolved; and the Germans who had passed the Rhine fiercely contended for the possession of Gaul, and excited the contempt or abhorrence of its peaceful and polished inhabitants. With that conscious pride which the pre-eminence of knowledge and luxury seldom fails to inspire, they derided the hairy and gigantic savages of the North; their rustic manners, dissonant joy, voracious appetite, and their horrid appearance, equally disgusting to the sight and to the smell. The liberal studies were still cultivated in the schools of Autun and Bordeaux, and the language of Cicero and Virgil was familiar to the Gallic youth. Their ears were astonished by the harsh and unknown sounds of the Germanic dialect, and they ingeniously lamented that the trembling muses fled from the harmony of a Burgundian lyre. The Gauls were endowed with all the advantages of art and nature, but, as they wanted courage to defend them, they were justly condemned to obey, and even to flatter, the victorious barbarians by whose clemency they held their precarious fortunes and their lives.²

As soon as Odoacer had extinguished the Western empire, he sought the friendship of the most powerful of the barbarians. The new sovereign of Italy resigned to Euric, king of the Visigoths, all the Roman conquests beyond the Alps, as far as the

1 Eadem semper causa Germanis transcendendi in Gallias, libido atque avaritia, et mutandæ sedis amor; ut relictis paludibus et solitudinibus suis, fecundissimum hoc solum vosque ipsos possiderent. . . . Nam pulsis Romanis quid aliud quam bella omnium interse gentium exsistent?

2 Sidonius Apollinaris ridicules, with affected wit and pleasantry, the hardship of his situation (Carm. xii. in tom. i. p. 811).

Rhine and the Ocean;[1] and the senate might confirm this liberal gift with some ostentation of power, and without any real loss of revenue or dominion. The lawful pretensions of Euric were justified by ambition and success, and the Gothic nation might aspire under his command to the monarchy of Spain and Gaul. Arles and Marseilles surrendered to his arms: he oppressed the freedom of Auvergne, and the bishop condescended to purchase his recall from exile by a tribute of just but reluctant praise. Sidonius waited before the gates of the palace among a crowd of ambassadors and suppliants, and their various business at the court of Bordeaux attested the power and the renown of the king of the Visigoths. The Heruli of the distant ocean, who painted their naked bodies with its cærulean colour, implored his protection; and the Saxons respected the maritime provinces of a prince who was destitute of any naval force. The tall Burgundians submitted to his authority; nor did he restore the captive Franks till he had imposed on that fierce nation the terms of an unequal peace. The Vandals of Africa cultivated his useful friendship, and the Ostrogoths of Pannonia were supported by his powerful aid against the oppression of the neighbouring Huns. The North (such are the lofty strains of the poet) was agitated or appeased by the nod of Euric, the great king of Persia consulted the oracle of the West, and the aged god of the Tiber was protected by the swelling genius of the Garonne.[2] The fortune of nations has often depended on accidents; and France may ascribe her greatness to the premature death of the Gothic king at a time when his son Alaric was a helpless infant, and his adversary Clovis[3] an ambitious and valiant youth.

While Childeric, the father of Clovis, lived an exile in Germany, he was hospitably entertained by the queen as well as by

1 See Procopius de Bell. Gothico, l. i. c. 12, in tom. ii. p. 31 [tom. ii. p. 64, ed. Bonn]. The character of Grotius inclines me to believe that he has not substituted the *Rhine* for the *Rhône* (Hist. Gothorum, p. 175) without the authority of some MS.

2 Sidonius, l. viii. Epist. 3, 9, in tom. i. p. 800. Jornandes de Rebus Geticis (c. 47, p. 680) justifies in some measure this portrait of the Gothic hero.

3 I use the familiar appellation of *Clovis*, from the Latin *Chlodovechus* or *Chlodovæus*. But the *Ch* expresses only the German aspiration; and the true name is not different from *Luduin* or *Lewis* (Mém. de l'Académie des Inscriptions, tom. xx. p. 68).

the king of the Thuringians. After his restoration Bafina escaped
from her husband's bed to the arms of her lover, freely declaring
that, if she had known a man wiser, stronger, or more beautiful
than Childeric, that man should have been the object of her
preference.[1] Clovis was the offspring of this voluntary union, and
when he was no more than fifteen years of age he succeeded, by
his father's death, to the command of the Salian tribe. The narrow limits of his kingdom[2] were confined to the island of the
Batavians, with the ancient dioceses of Tournay and Arras;[3] and
at the baptism of Clovis the number of his warriors could not
exceed five thousand. The kindred tribes of the Franks who had
seated themselves along the Belgic rivers, the Scheldt, the Meuse,
the Moselle, and the Rhine, were governed by their independent
kings of the Merovingian race – the equals, the allies, and sometimes the enemies, of the Salic prince. But the Germans, who
obeyed in peace the hereditary jurisdiction of their chiefs, were
free to follow the standard of a popular and victorious general;
and the superior merit of Clovis attracted the respect and allegiance of the national confederacy. When he first took the field,
he had neither gold and silver in his coffers, nor wine and corn
in his magazines;[4] but he imitated the example of Cæsar, who in
the same country had acquired wealth by the sword, and

1 Greg. Turon. l. ii. c. 12, in tom. ii. p. 168. Bafina speaks the language of
nature: the Franks, who had seen her in their youth, might converse with
Gregory in their old age; and the bishop of Tours could not wish to defame
the mother of the first Christian king.

2 The Abbé Dubos (Hist. Critique de l'Etablissement de la Monarchie Françoise dans les Gaules, tom. i. p. 630–650) has the merit of defining the primitive
kingdom of Clovis, and of ascertaining the genuine number of his subjects.

[The dominions of Clovis (or Chlodwig), Ragnachar, and Chararich, the
independent kings of the Merovingian race, over the tribes of Franks that had
seated themselves along the Belgian rivers, the Scheldt, Meuse, Moselle, and
Rhine, corresponded, according to Junghans, to Brabant, Hainault, and Flanders. – O. S.]

3 Ecclesiam incultam ac negligentiâ civium Paganorum prætermissam, ve-
prium densi tate oppletam, etc. Vit. St. Vedasti, in tom. iii. p. 372. This description supposes that Arras was possessed by the Pagans many years before the
baptism of Clovis.

4 Gregory of Tours (l. v. c. i. tom. ii. p. 232) contrasts the poverty of Clovis
with the wealth of his grandsons. Yet Remigius (in tom. iv. p. 52) mentions his
paternas opes, as sufficient for the redemption of captives.

purchased soldiers with the fruits of conquest. After each successful battle or expedition the spoils were accumulated in one common mass; every warrior received his proportionable share, and the royal prerogative submitted to the equal regulations of military law. The untamed spirit of the barbarians was taught to acknowledge the advantages of regular discipline.[1] At the annual review of the month of March their arms were diligently inspected, and when they traversed a peaceful territory they were prohibited from touching a blade of grass. The justice of Clovis was inexorable, and his careless or disobedient soldiers were punished with instant death. It would be superfluous to praise the valour of a Frank, but the valour of Clovis was directed by cool and consummate prudence.[2] In all his transactions with mankind he calculated the weight of interest, of passion, and of opinion; and his measures were sometimes adapted to the sanguinary manners of the Germans, and sometimes moderated by the milder genius of Rome and Christianity. He was intercepted in the career of victory, since he died in the forty-fifth year of his age: but he had already accomplished, in a reign of thirty years, the establishment of the French monarchy in Gaul.

The first exploit of Clovis was the defeat of Syagrius, the son of Ægidius, and the public quarrel might on this occasion be inflamed by private resentment. The glory of the father still insulted the Merovingian race; the power of the son might excite the jealous ambition of the king of the Franks. Syagrius inherited, as a patrimonial estate, the city and diocese of Soissons: the desolate remnant of the second Belgic, Rheims and Troyes, Beauvais and Amiens, would naturally submit to the count or patrician;[3] and after the dissolution of the Western empire he

1 See Gregory (l. ii. c. 27, 37, in tom. iii. p. 175, 181, 182). The famous story of the vase of Soissons explains both the power and the character of Clovis. As a point of controversy, it has been strangely tortured by Boulainvilliers, Dubos, and the other political antiquarians.

2 The Duke of Nivernois, a noble statesman, who has managed weighty and delicate negotiations, ingeniously illustrates (Mém. de l'Acad. des Inscriptions, tom. xx. p. 147–184) the political system of Clovis.

3 M. Biet (in a Dissertation which deserved the prize of the Academy of Soissons, p. 178–226) has accurately defined the nature and extent of the kingdom of Syagrius, and his father; but he too readily allows the slight evidence of Dubos (tom. ii. p. 54–57) to deprive him of Beauvais and Amiens.

might reign with the title, or at least with the authority, of king of the Romans.[1] As a Roman, he had been educated in the liberal studies of rhetoric and jurisprudence; but he was engaged by accident and policy in the familiar use of the Germanic idiom. The independent barbarians resorted to the tribunal of a stranger who possessed the singular talent of explaining, in their native tongue, the dictates of reason and equity. The diligence and affability of their judge rendered him popular, the impartial wisdom of his decrees obtained their voluntary obedience, and the reign of Syagrius over the Franks and Burgundians seemed to revive the original institution of civil society.[2] In the midst of these peaceful occupations Syagrius received, and boldly accepted, the hostile defiance of Clovis, who challenged his rival in the spirit, and almost in the language of chivalry, to appoint the day and the field[3] of battle. In the time of Cæsar, Soissons would have poured forth a body of fifty thousand horse; and such an army might have been plentifully supplied with shields, cuirasses, and military engines from the three arsenals or manufactures of the city.[4] But the courage and numbers of the Gallic youth were long since exhausted, and the loose bands of volunteers or mercenaries who marched under the standard of Syagrius were incapable of contending with the national valour of the

[The precise position of Syagrius in northern Gaul is thus succinctly stated by Bury: 'His kingdom was bounded by the Somme, beyond which was the Salian territory under Chlodwig; by the territory of the Ripuarian Franks on the Lower Mosel; by the Burgundian kingdom, Auxerre being probably near the frontier, and by the Seine.' – O. S.]

1 I may observe that Fredegarius, in his epitome of Gregory of Tours (tom. ii. p. 398 [c. 15]), has prudently substituted the name of *Patricius* for the incredible title of *Rex Romanorum*.

2 Sidonius (l. v. Epist. 5, in tom. i. p. 794), who styles him the Solon, the Amphion, of the barbarians, addresses this imaginary king in the tone of friendship and equality. From such offices of arbitration, the crafty Deioces had raised himself to the throne of the Medes (Herodot. l. i. c. 96–100).

3 Campum sibi præparari jussit. M. Biet (p. 226–251) has diligently ascertained this field of battle at Nogent, a Benedictine abbey, about ten miles to the north of Soissons. The ground was marked by a circle of Pagan sepulchres; and Clovis bestowed the adjacent lands of Leuilly and Coucy on the church of Rheims.

4 See Cæsar. Comment. de Bell. Gallic. ii. 4, in tom. i. p. 220, and the Notitiæ, tom. i. p. 126. The three *Fabricæ* of Soissons were, *Scutaria, Balistaria,* and *Clinabaria.* The last supplied the complete armour of the heavy cuirassiers.

Franks. It would be ungenerous, without some more accurate knowledge of his strength and resources, to condemn the rapid flight of Syagrius, who escaped after the loss of a battle to the distant court of Toulouse. The feeble minority of Alaric could not assist or protect an unfortunate fugitive; the pusillanimous[1] Goths were intimidated by the menaces of Clovis; and the Roman *king*, after a short confinement, was delivered into the hands of the executioner. The Belgic cities surrendered to the king of the Franks, and his dominions were enlarged towards the east by the ample diocese of Tongres,[2] which Clovis subdued in the tenth year of his reign.

The name of the Alemanni has been absurdly derived from their imaginary settlement on the banks of the *Leman* lake.[3] That fortunate district, from the lake to Avenche and Mount Jura, was occupied by the Burgundians.[4] The northern parts of Helvetia had indeed been subdued by the ferocious Alemanni, who destroyed with their own hands the fruits of their conquest. A province, improved and adorned by the arts of Rome, was again reduced to a savage wilderness, and some vestige of the stately Vindonissa may still be discovered in the fertile and populous

1 The epithet must be confined to the circumstances; and history cannot justify the French prejudice of Gregory (l. ii. c. 27, in tom. ii. p. 175), ut Gothorum pavere *mos* est.

2 Dubos has satisfied me (tom. i. p. 277–286) that Gregory of Tours, his transcribers or his readers, have repeatedly confounded the German kingdom of *Thuringia*, beyond the Rhine, and the Gallic *city* of *Tongria*, on the Meuse, which was more anciently the country of the Eburones, and more recently the diocese of Liege.

3 Populi habitantes juxta *Lemannum* lacum, *Alemanni* dicuntur. Servius, ad Virgil. Georgic. iv. 278. Dom Bouquet (tom. i. p. 817) has only alleged the more recent and corrupt text of Isidore of Seville.

4 Gregory of Tours sends St. Lupicinus inter illa Jurensis deserti secreta, quæ, inter Burgundiam Alamanniamque sita, Aventicæ adjacent civitati, in tom. i. p. 648. M. de Watteville (Hist. la Confédération Helvétique, tom. i. p. 9, 10) has accurately defined the Helvetian limits of the duchy of Alemannia, and the Transjurane and Avenche, or Lausanne, and are still discriminated in modern Switzerland by the use of the German or French language.

[I agree with Prof. Bury that the statement by Gibbon in this note is in all probability near the truth. The Alemanni were certainly defeated, and some of the tribes in all likelihood settled in Rhætia under the protection of Theodoric. – O. S.]

valley of the Aar.[1] From the source of the Rhine to its conflux
with the Main and the Moselle, the formidable swarms of the
Alemanni commanded either side of the river by the right of
ancient possession or recent victory. They had spread themselves
into Gaul over the modern provinces of Alsace and Lorraine;
and their bold invasion of the kingdom of Cologne summoned
the Salic prince to the defence of his Ripuarian allies. Clovis
encountered the invaders of Gaul in the plain of Tolbiac, about
twenty-four miles from Cologne, and the two fiercest nations of
Germany were mutually animated by the memory of past exploits and the prospect of future greatness. The Franks after an
obstinate struggle gave way, and the Alemanni, raising a shout
of victory, impetuously pressed their retreat. But the battle was
restored by the valour, the conduct, and perhaps by the piety, of
Clovis; and the event of the bloody day decided for ever the
alternative of empire or servitude. The last king of the Alemanni
was slain in the field, and his people were slaughtered and pursued till they threw down their arms and yielded to the mercy
of the conqueror. Without discipline it was impossible for them
to rally: they had contemptuously demolished the walls and fortifications which might have protected their distress; and they
were followed into the heart of their forests by an enemy not
less active or intrepid than themselves. The great Theodoric con-
gratulated the victory of Clovis, whose sister Albofleda the king
of Italy had lately married; but he mildly interceded with his
brother in favour of the suppliants and fugitives who had implored his protection. The Gallic territories which were possessed by the Alemanni became the prize of their conqueror;
and the haughty nation, invincible or rebellious to the arms of
Rome, acknowledged the sovereignty of the Merovingian kings,
who graciously permitted them to enjoy their peculiar manners
and institutions under the government of official, and, at
length, of hereditary dukes. After the conquest of the Western

1 See Guilliman de Rebus Helveticis, l. i. c. 3, p. 11, 12. Within the ancient
walls of Vindonissa, the castle of Hapsburg, the abbey of Königsfeld, and the
town of Bruck, have successively arisen. The philosophic traveller may compare
the monuments of Roman conquest, of feudal or Austrian tyranny, of monkish
superstition, and of industrious freedom. If he be truly a philosopher, he will
applaud the merit and happiness of his own times.

provinces, the Franks alone maintained their ancient habitations beyond the Rhine. They gradually subdued and civilised the exhausted countries as far as the Elbe and the mountains of Bohemia, and the peace of Europe was secured by the obedience of Germany.[1]

Till the thirtieth year of his age Clovis continued to worship the gods of his ancestors.[2] His disbelief, or rather disregard, of Christianity, might encourage him to pillage with less remorse the churches of an hostile territory: but his subjects of Gaul enjoyed the free exercise of religious worship, and the bishops entertained a more favourable hope of the idolater than of the heretics. The Merovingian prince had contracted a fortunate alliance with the fair Clotilda, the niece of the king of Burgundy, who in the midst of an Arian court was educated in the profession of the catholic faith. It was her interest as well as her duty to achieve the conversion[3] of a Pagan husband; and Clovis insensibly listened to the voice of love and religion. He consented (perhaps such terms had been previously stipulated) to the baptism of his eldest son; and though the sudden death of the infant excited some superstitious fears, he was persuaded a second time to repeat the dangerous experiment. In the distress of the battle of Tolbiac, Clovis loudly invoked the God of Clotilda and the Christians; and victory disposed him to hear with respectful

1 Gregory of Tours (l. ii. 30, 37, in tom. ii. p. 176, 177, 182), the Gesta Francorum (in tom. ii. p. 551), and the epistle of Theodoric (Cassiodor. Variar. l. ii. Ep. 41, in tom. iv. p. 4) represent the defeat of the Alemanni. Some of their tribes settled in Rhætia, under the protection of Theodoric, whose successors ceded the colony and their country to the grandson of Clovis. The state of the Alemanni under the Merovingian kings may be seen in Mascou (Hist. of the Ancient Germans, xi. 8, etc.; Annotation xxxvi.) and Guilliman (de Reb. Helvet. l. ii. c. 10–12, p. 72–80).

2 Clotilda, or rather Gregory, supposes that Clovis worshipped the gods of Greece and Rome. The fact is incredible, and the mistake only shows how completely, in less than a century, the national religion of the Franks had been abolished, and even forgotten.

3 Gregory of Tours relates the marriage and conversion of Clovis (l. ii. c. 28–31, in tom. ii. p. 175–178). Even Fredegarius, or the nameless Epitomiser (in tom. ii. p. 398–400), the author of the Gesta Francorum (in tom. ii. p. 548–552), and Aimoin himself (l. i. c. 13–16, in tom. iii. p. 37–40), may be heard without disdain. Tradition might long preserve some curious circumstances of these important transactions.

gratitude the eloquent[1] Remigius,[2] bishop of Rheims, who forcibly displayed the temporal and spiritual advantages of his conversion. The king declared himself satisfied of the truth of the
catholic faith; and the political reasons which might have suspended his public profession were removed by the devout or
loyal acclamations of the Franks, who showed themselves alike
prepared to follow their heroic leader to the field of battle or to
the baptismal font. The important ceremony was performed in
the cathedral of Rheims with every circumstance of magnificence
and solemnity that could impress an awful sense of religion on
the minds of its rude proselytes.[3] The new Constantine was immediately baptised with three thousand of his warlike subjects,
and their example was imitated by the remainder of the *gentle
barbarians*, who, in obedience to the victorious prelate, adored
the cross which they had burnt, and burnt the idols which they
had formerly adored.[4] The mind of Clovis was susceptible of
transient fervour: he was exasperated by the pathetic tale of the
passion and death of Christ; and instead of weighing the salutary
consequences of that mysterious sacrifice, he exclaimed with indiscreet fury, 'Had I been present at the head of my valiant

1 A traveller, who returned from Rheims to Auvergne, had stolen a copy
of his Declamations from the secretary or bookseller of the modest archbishop
(Sidonius Apollinar. l. ix. Epist. 7). Four epistles of Remigius, which are still
extant (in tom. iv. p. 51, 52, 53), do not correspond with the splendid praise of
Sidonius.

2 Hincmar, one of the successors of Remigius (A.D. 845–882), has composed his Life (in tom. iii. p. 373–380). The authority of ancient MSS. of the
church of Rheims might inspire some confidence, which is destroyed, however, by the selfish and audacious fictions of Hincmar. It is remarkable enough
that Remigius, who was consecrated at the age of twenty-two (A.D. 457), filled
the episcopal chair seventy-four years (Pagi Critica, in Baron. tom. ii. p. 384,
572).

3 A vial (the *Sainte Ampoulle*) of holy or rather celestial oil was brought
down by a white dove, for the baptism of Clovis; and it is still used and renewed
in the coronation of the kings of France. Hincmar (he aspired to the primacy
of Gaul) is the first author of this fable (in tom. iii. p. 377), whose slight
foundations the Abbé de Vertot (Mémoires de l'Académie des Inscriptions,
tom. ii. p. 619–633) has undermined with profound respect and consummate
dexterity.

4 Mitis depone colla, Sicamber: adora quod incendisti, incende quod ado-
rasti. Greg. Turon. l. ii. c. 31, in tom. ii. p. 177.

Franks, I would have revenged his injuries." But the savage conqueror of Gaul was incapable of examining the proofs of a religion which depends on the laborious investigation of historic evidence and speculative theology. He was still more incapable of feeling the mild influence of the Gospel, which persuades and purifies the heart of a genuine convert. His ambitious reign was a perpetual violation of moral and Christian duties: his hands were stained with blood in peace as well as in war; and, as soon as Clovis had dismissed a synod of the Gallican church, he calmly assassinated *all* the princes of the Merovingian race.² Yet the king of the Franks might sincerely worship the Christian God as a Being more excellent and powerful than his national deities; and the signal deliverance and victory of Tolbiac encouraged Clovis to confide in the future protection of the Lord of Hosts. Martin, the most popular of the saints, had filled the Western world with the fame of those miracles which were incessantly performed at his holy sepulchre of Tours. His visible or invisible aid promoted the cause of a liberal and orthodox prince; and the profane remark of Clovis himself, that St. Martin was an expensive friend,³ need not be interpreted as the symptom of any permanent or rational scepticism. But earth as well as heaven rejoiced in the conversion of the Franks. On the memorable day when Clovis ascended from the baptismal font, he alone in the Christian world deserved the name and prerogatives of a catholic king. The emperor Anastasius entertained some dangerous errors concerning the nature of the divine incarnation; and the barbarians

1 Si ego ibidem cum Francis meis fuissem, injurias ejus vindicassem. This rash expression, which Gregory has prudently concealed, is celebrated by Frede-garius (Epitom. c. 21, in tom. ii. p. 400), Aimoin (l. i. c. 16, in tom. iii. p. 40), and the Chroniques de St. Denys (l. i. c. 20, in tom. iii. p. 171), as an admirable effusion of Christian zeal.

2 Gregory (l. ii. c. 40–43, in tom. ii. p. 183–185), after coolly relating the repeated crimes and affected remorse of Clovis, concludes, perhaps undesigned-ly, with a lesson which ambition will never hear – 'His ita transactis . . . obiit.'

3 After the Gothic victory, Clovis made rich offerings to St. Martin of Tours. He wished to redeem his war-horse by the gift of one hundred pieces of gold, but the enchanted steed could not move from the stable till the price of his redemption had been doubled. This *miracle* provoked the king to exclaim, Vere B. Martinus est bonus in auxilio, sed carus in negotio. (Gesta Francorum, in tom. ii. p. 554, 555.)

of Italy, Africa, Spain, and Gaul were involved in the Arian heresy. The eldest, or rather the only son of the church, was acknowledged by the clergy as their lawful sovereign or glorious deliverer; and the arms of Clovis were strenuously supported by the zeal and favour of the catholic faction.[1]

Under the Roman empire the wealth and jurisdiction of the bishops, their sacred character and perpetual office, their numerous dependents, popular eloquence, and provincial assemblies, had rendered them always respectable, and sometimes dangerous. Their influence was augmented with the progress of superstition; and the establishment of the French monarchy may, in some degree, be ascribed to the firm alliance of an hundred prelates, who reigned in the discontented or independent cities of Gaul. The slight foundations of the *Armorican* republic had been repeatedly shaken or overthrown; but the same people still guarded their domestic freedom; asserted the dignity of the Roman name; and bravely resisted the predatory inroads and regular attacks of Clovis, who laboured to extend his conquests from the Seine to the Loire. Their successful opposition introduced an equal and honourable union. The Franks esteemed the valour of the Armoricans;[2] and the Armoricans were reconciled by the religion of the Franks. The military force which had been stationed for the defence of Gaul consisted of one hundred different bands of cavalry or infantry; and these troops, while they assumed the title and privileges of Roman soldiers, were renewed by an incessant supply of the barbarian youth. The extreme fortifications and scattered fragments of the empire were still defended by their hopeless courage. But their retreat was intercepted, and their communication was impracticable: they were abandoned by the Greek princes of Constantinople, and they piously disclaimed all connection with the Arian usurpers

1 See the epistle from Pope Anastasius to the royal convert (in tom. iv. p. 50, 51). Avitus, bishop of Vienne, addressed Clovis on the same subject (p. 49); and many of the Latin bishops would assure him of their joy and attachment.

2 Instead of the 'Αρβόρυχοι, an unknown people, who now appear in the text of Procopius [Bell, Goth. l. i. c. 12], Hadrian de Valois has restored the proper name of the 'Αρμόρυχοι; and this easy correction has been almost universally approved. Yet an unprejudiced reader would naturally suppose that Procopius means to describe a tribe of Germans in the alliance of Rome, and not a confederacy of Gallic cities which had revolted from the empire.

of Gaul. They accepted, without shame or reluctance, the generous capitulation which was proposed by a catholic hero; and this
spurious or legitimate progeny of the Roman legions was distinguished in the succeeding age by their arms, their ensigns, and
their peculiar dress and institutions. But the national strength
was increased by these powerful and voluntary accessions; and
the neighbouring kingdoms dreaded the numbers as well as the
spirit of the Franks. The reduction of the northern provinces of
Gaul, instead of being decided by the chance of a single battle,
appears to have been slowly effected by the gradual operation
of war and treaty; and Clovis acquired each object of his ambition by such efforts or such concessions as were adequate to its
real value. *His* savage character and the virtues of Henry IV
suggest the most opposite ideas of human nature; yet some resemblance may be found in the situation of two princes who
conquered France by their valour, their policy, and the merits of
a seasonable conversion.[1]

The kingdom of the Burgundians, which was defined by the
course of two Gallic rivers, the Saone and the Rhône, extended
from the forest of Vosges to the Alps and the sea of Marseilles.[2]
The sceptre was in the hands of Gundobald. That valiant and
ambitious prince had reduced the number of royal candidates by
the death of two brothers, one of whom was the father of Clotilda;[3]

1 This important digression of Procopius (de Bell. Gothic. l. i. c. 12, in
tom. ii. p. 29–36 [tom. ii. p. 62, *sqq.*, ed. Bonn]) illustrates the origin of the
French monarchy. Yet I must observe, 1. That the Greek historian betrays an
inexcusable ignorance of the geography of the West; 2. That these treaties
and privileges, which should leave some lasting traces, are totally invisible in
Gregory of Tours, the Salic laws, etc.

2 Regnum circa Rhodanum aut Ararim cum provinciâ Massiliensi retine-
bant. Greg. Turon. 1. ii. c. 32, in tom. ii. p. 178. The province of Marseilles, as
far as the Durance, was afterwards ceded to the Ostrogoths; and the signatures
of twenty-five bishops are supposed to represent the kingdom of Burgundy,
A.D. 519. (Concil. Epaon. in tom. iv. p. 104, 105.) Yet I would except Vindonissa.
The bishop, who lived under the pagan Alemanni, would naturally resort to the
synods of the next Christian kingdom. Mascou (in his four first annotations)
has explained many circumstances relative to the Burgundian monarchy.

3 Mascou (Hist. of the Germans, xi. 10), who very reasonably distrusts the
testimony of Gregory of Tours, has produced a passage from Avitus (Epist. v.)
to prove that Gundobald affected to deplore the tragic event which his subjects
affected to applaud.

but his imperfect prudence still permitted Godegesil, the young-est of his brothers, to possess the dependent principality of Geneva. The Arian monarch was justly alarmed by the satisfac-tion and the hopes which seemed to animate his clergy and people after the conversion of Clovis; and Gundobald convened at Lyons an assembly of his bishops, to reconcile, if it were possible, their religious and political discontents. A vain con-ference was agitated between the two factions. The Arians up-braided the catholics with the worship of three Gods: the catholics defended their cause by theological distinctions; and the usual arguments, objections, and replies were reverberated with obstinate clamour, till the king revealed his secret apprehen-sions by an abrupt but decisive question, which he addressed to the orthodox bishops: 'If you truly profess the Christian religion, why do you not restrain the king of the Franks? He has declared war against me, and forms alliances with my enemies for my destruction. A sanguinary and covetous mind is not the symptom of a sincere conversion: let him show his faith by his works.' The answer of Avitus, bishop of Vienne, who spoke in the name of his brethren, was delivered with the voice and countenance of an angel. 'We are ignorant of the motives and intentions of the king of the Franks: but we are taught by Scripture that the kingdoms which abandon the divine law are frequently subverted; and that enemies will arise on every side against those who have made God their enemy. Return, with thy people, to the law of God, and he will give peace and security to thy dominions.' The king of Burgundy, who was not prepared to accept the condition which the catholics considered as essential to the treaty, delayed and dismissed the ecclesiastical conference, after reproaching his bishops, that Clovis, their friend and proselyte, had privately tempted the allegiance of his brother.[1]

The allegiance of his brother was already seduced; and the obedience of Godegesil, who joined the royal standard with the troops of Geneva, more effectually promoted the success of the conspiracy. While the Franks and Burgundians contended

[1] See the original conference (in tom. iv. p. 99–102). Avitus, the principal actor, and probably the secretary of the meeting, was bishop of Vienne. A short account of his person and works may be found in Dupin (Bibliothèque Ecclé-siastique, tom. v. p. 5–10).

with equal valour, his seasonable desertion decided the event of
the battle; and as Gundobald was faintly supported by the disaffected Gauls, he yielded to the arms of Clovis, and hastily
retreated from the field, which appears to have been situate
between Langres and Dijon. He distrusted the strength of Dijon,
a quadrangular fortress, encompassed by two rivers and by a wall
thirty feet high and fifteen thick, with four gates and thirty-three
towers:[1] he abandoned to the pursuit of Clovis the important
cities of Lyons and Vienne; and Gundobald still fled with precipitation till he had reached Avignon, at the distance of two
hundred and fifty miles from the field of battle. A long siege and
an artful negotiation admonished the king of the Franks of the
danger and difficulty of his enterprise. He imposed a tribute on
the Burgundian prince, compelled him to pardon and reward his
brother's treachery, and proudly returned to his own dominions
with the spoils and captives of the southern provinces. This
splendid triumph was soon clouded by the intelligence that Gundobald had violated his recent obligations, and that the unfortunate Godegesil, who was left at Vienne with a garrison of five
thousand Franks,[2] had been besieged, surprised, and massacred
by his inhuman brother. Such an outrage might have exasperated
the patience of the most peaceful sovereign; yet the conqueror
of Gaul dissembled the injury, released the tribute, and accepted
the alliance and military service of the king of Burgundy. Clovis
no longer possessed those advantages which had assured the
success of the preceding war; and his rival, instructed by adversity, had found new resources in the affections of his people.
The Gauls or Romans applauded the mild and impartial laws of
Gundobald, which almost raised them to the same level with
their conquerors. The bishops were reconciled and flattered by

1 Gregory of Tours (1. iii. c. 19, in tom. ii. p. 197) indulges his genius, or
rather transcribes some more eloquent writer, in the description of Dijon – a
castle, which already deserved the title of a city. It depended on the bishops of
Langres till the twelfth century, and afterwards became the capital of the dukes
of Burgundy. Longuerue, Description de la France, part i. p. 280.

2 The Epitomiser of Gregory of Tours (in tom. ii. p. 401) has supplied this
number of Franks, but he rashly supposes that they were cut in pieces by
Gundobald. The prudent Burgundian spared the soldiers of Clovis, and sent
these captives to the king of the Visigoths, who settled them in the territory of
Toulouse.

the hopes which he artfully suggested of his approaching conversion; and though he eluded their accomplishment to the last
moment of his life, his moderation secured the peace and suspended the ruin of the kingdom of Burgundy.[1]

I am impatient to pursue the final ruin of that kingdom,
which was accomplished under the reign of Sigismond, the son
of Gundobald. The catholic Sigismond has acquired the honours
of a saint and martyr;[2] but the hands of the royal saint were
stained with the blood of his innocent son, whom he inhumanly
sacrificed to the pride and resentment of a stepmother. He soon
discovered his error, and bewailed the irreparable loss. While
Sigismond embraced the corpse of the unfortunate youth, he
received a severe admonition from one of his attendants: 'It is
not his situation, O king! it is thine which deserves pity and
lamentation.' The reproaches of a guilty conscience were alleviated, however, by his liberal donations to the monastery of
Agaunum, or St. Maurice, in Vallais; which he himself had
founded in honour of the imaginary martyrs of the Thebæan
legion.[3] A full chorus of perpetual psalmody was instituted by
the pious king; he assiduously practised the austere devotion of
the monks; and it was his humble prayer that Heaven would
inflict in this world the punishment of his sins. His prayer was
heard: the avengers were at hand; and the provinces of Burgundy
were overwhelmed by an army of victorious Franks. After the
event of an unsuccessful battle, Sigismond, who wished to

1 In this Burgundian war I have followed Gregory of Tours (l. ii. c. 32, 33,
in tom. ii. p. 178, 179), whose narrative *appears* so incompatible with that of
Procopius (de Bell. Goth. l. i. c. 12, in tom. ii. p. 31, 32 [tom, ii. p. 63, *sqq.* ed.
Bonn]), that some critics have supposed *two* different wars. The Abbé Dubos
(Hist. Critique, etc., tom. ii. p. 126–162) has distinctly represented the causes
and the events.

2 See his Life or legend (in tom. iii. p. 402). A martyr! how strangely has
that word been distorted from its original sense of a common witness! St.
Sigismond was remarkable for the cure of fevers.

3 Before the end of the fifth century, the church of St. Maurice, and his
Thebæan legion, had rendered Agaunum a place of devout pilgrimage. A promiscuous community of both sexes had introduced some deeds of darkness, which
were abolished (A.D. 515) by the regular monastery of Sigismond. Within fifty
years, his *angels of light* made a nocturnal sally to murder their bishop and his
clergy. See, in the Bibliothéque Raisonnée (tom. xxxvi. p. 435–438), the curious
remarks of a learned librarian of Geneva.

protract his life that he might prolong his penance, concealed himself in the desert in a religious habit till he was discovered and betrayed by his subjects, who solicited the favour of their new masters. The captive monarch, with his wife and two children, was transported to Orleans, and buried alive in a deep well by the stern command of the sons of Clovis, whose cruelty might derive some excuse from the maxims and examples of their barbarous age. Their ambition, which urged them to achieve the conquest of Burgundy, was inflamed or disguised by filial piety: and Clotilda, whose sanctity did not consist in the forgiveness of injuries, pressed them to revenge her father's death on the family of his assassin. The rebellious Burgundians, for they attempted to break their chains, were still permitted to enjoy their national laws under the obligation of tribute and military service; and the Merovingian princes peaceably reigned over a kingdom whose glory and greatness had been first overthrown by the arms of Clovis.[1]

The first victory of Clovis had insulted the honour of the Goths. They viewed his rapid progress with jealousy and terror; and the youthful fame of Alaric was oppressed by the more potent genius of his rival. Some disputes inevitably arose on the edge of their contiguous dominions; and after the delays of fruitless negotiation a personal interview of the two kings was proposed and accepted. This conference of Clovis and Alaric was held in a small island of the Loire, near Amboise. They embraced, familiarly conversed, and feasted together; and separated with the warmest professions of peace and brotherly love. But their apparent confidence concealed a dark suspicion of hostile and treacherous designs; and their mutual complaints solicited, eluded, and disclaimed a final arbitration. At Paris, which he already considered as his royal seat, Clovis declared to an assembly of the princes and warriors the pretence and the motive of a Gothic war. 'It grieves me to see that the Arians still possess the fairest portion of Gaul. Let us march against them with the

---

1 Marius, bishop of Avenche (Chron. in tom. ii. p. 15), has marked the authentic dates, and Gregory of Tours (l. iii. c. 5, 6, in tom. ii. p. 188, 189) has expressed the principal facts, of the life of Sigismond and the conquest of Burgundy. Procopius (in tom. ii. p. 34 [tom. ii. p. 65, ed. Bonn]) and Agathias (in tom. ii. p. 49) show their remote and imperfect knowledge.

aid of God; and, having vanquished the heretics, we will possess and divide their fertile provinces.'[1] The Franks, who were inspired by hereditary valour and recent zeal, applauded the generous design of their monarch; expressed their resolution to conquer or die, since death and conquest would be equally profitable; and solemnly protested that they would never shave their beards till victory should absolve them from that inconvenient vow. The enterprise was promoted by the public or private exhortations of Clotilda. She reminded her husband how effectually some pious foundation would propitiate the Deity and his servants: and the Christian hero, darting his battle-axe with a skilful and nervous hand, 'There (said he), on that spot where my *Francisca*[2] shall fall, will I erect a church in honour of the holy apostles.' This ostentatious piety confirmed and justified the attachment of the catholics, with whom he secretly corresponded; and their devout wishes were gradually ripened into a formidable conspiracy. The people of Aquitain was alarmed by the indiscreet reproaches of their Gothic tyrants, who justly accused them of preferring the dominion of the Franks; and their zealous adherent Quintianus, bishop of Rodez,[3] preached more forcibly in his exile than in his diocese. To resist these foreign and domestic enemies, who were fortified by the alliance of the Burgundians, Alaric collected his troops, far more numerous than the military powers of Clovis. The Visigoths resumed the exercise of arms, which they had neglected in a long and luxurious peace;[4] a select

1 Gregory of Tours (l. ii. c. 37, in tom. ii. p. 181) inserts the short but persuasive speech of Clovis. Valde moleste fero, quod hi Ariani partem teneant Galliarum (the author of the Gesta Francorum, in tom. ii. p. 553, adds the precious epithet of *optimam*), eamus cum Dei adjutorio, et, superatis eis, rediga-mus terram in ditionem nostram.

2 Tunc rex projecit a se in directum Bipennem suam quod est *Francisca*, etc. (Gesta Franc. in tom. ii. p. 554.) The form and use of this weapon are clearly described by Procopius (in tom. ii. p. 37 [Bell. Goth. l. ii. c. 25, tom. ii. p. 247, 248, ed. Bonn]). Examples of its *national* appellation in Latin and French may be found in the Glossary of Ducange and the large Dictionnaire de Trevoux.

3 It is singular enough that some important and authentic facts should be found in a Life of Quintianus, composed in rhyme in the old *patois* of Rouergue (Dubos, Hist. Critique, etc., tom. ii. p. 179).

4 Quamvis fortitudini vestræ confidentiam tribuat parentum vestrorum innumerabilis multitudo; quamvis Attilam potentem reminiscamini Visigotharum

band of valiant and robust slaves attended their masters to the field;[1] and the cities of Gaul were compelled to furnish their doubtful and reluctant aid. Theodoric, king of the Ostrogoths, who reigned in Italy, had laboured to maintain the tranquillity of Gaul; and he assumed, or affected, for that purpose the impartial character of a mediator. But the sagacious monarch dreaded the rising empire of Clovis, and he was firmly engaged to support the national and religious cause of the Goths.

The accidental or artificial prodigies which adorned the expedition of Clovis were accepted, by a superstitious age, as the manifest declaration of the Divine favour. He marched from Paris; and as he proceeded with decent reverence through the holy diocese of Tours, his anxiety tempted him to consult the shrine of St. Martin, the sanctuary, and the oracle of Gaul. His messengers were instructed to remark the words of the Psalm which should happen to be chanted at the precise moment when they entered the church. Those words most fortunately expressed the valour and victory of the champions of Heaven, and the application was easily transferred to the new Joshua, the new Gideon, who went forth to battle against the enemies of the Lord.[2] Orleans secured to the Franks a bridge on the Loire; but, at the distance of forty miles from Poitiers, their progress was intercepted by an extraordinary swell of the river Vigenna or Vienne; and the opposite banks were covered by the encampment of the Visigoths. Delay must be always dangerous to barbarians, who consume the country through which they march;

viribus inclinatum; tamen quia populorum ferocia corda longâ pace mollescunt, cavete subito in aleam mittere, quos constat tantis temporibus exercitia non habere. Such was the salutary but fruitless advice of peace, of reason, and of Theodoric (Cassiodor. l. iii. Ep. 2 [ed. Rotom. 1679]).

1 Montesquieu (Esprit des Loix, l. xv. c. 14) mentions and approves the law of the Visigoths (l. ix. tit. 2, in tom. iv. p. 425), which obliged all masters to arm and send or lead into the field a tenth of their slaves.

2 This mode of divination, by accepting as an omen the first sacred words which in particular circumstances should be presented to the eye or ear, was derived from the Pagans; and the Psalter or Bible was substituted to the poems of Homer and Virgil. From the fourth to the fourteenth century, these *sortes sanctorum*, as they are styled, were repeatedly condemned by the decrees of councils, and repeatedly practised by kings, bishops, and saints. See a curious dissertation of the Abbé du Resnel, in the Mémoires de l'Académie, tom. xix. p. 287–310.

and had Clovis possessed leisure and materials, it might have been impracticable to construct a bridge, or to force a passage, in the face of a superior enemy. But the affectionate peasants, who were impatient to welcome their deliverer, could easily betray some unknown or unguarded ford: the merit of the discovery was enhanced by the useful interposition of fraud or fiction; and a white hart, of singular size and beauty, appeared to guide and animate the march of the catholic army. The counsels of the Visigoths were irresolute and distracted. A crowd of impatient warriors, presumptuous in their strength, and disdaining to fly before the robbers of Germany, excited Alaric to assert in arms the name and blood of the conqueror of Rome. The advice of the graver chieftains pressed him to elude the first ardour of the Franks; and to expect, in the southern provinces of Gaul, the veteran and victorious Ostrogoths, whom the king of Italy had already sent to his assistance. The decisive moments were wasted in idle deliberation; the Goths too hastily abandoned, perhaps, an advantageous post; and the opportunity of a secure retreat was lost by their slow and disorderly motions. After Clovis had passed the ford, as it is still named, of the *Hart*, he advanced with bold and hasty steps to prevent the escape of the enemy. His nocturnal march was directed by a flaming meteor suspended in the air above the cathedral of Poitiers; and this signal, which might be previously concerted with the orthodox successor of St. Hilary, was compared to the column of fire that guided the Israelites in the desert. At the third hour of the day, about ten miles beyond Poitiers, Clovis overtook, and instantly attacked, the Gothic army, whose defeat was already prepared by terror and confusion. Yet they rallied in their extreme distress, and the martial youths, who had clamorously demanded the battle, refused to survive the ignominy of flight. The two kings encountered each other in single combat. Alaric fell by the hand of his rival; and the victorious Frank was saved, by the goodness of his cuirass and the vigour of his horse, from the spears of two desperate Goths, who furiously rode against him to revenge the death of their sovereign. The vague expression of a mountain of the slain serves to indicate a cruel, though indefinite, slaughter; but Gregory has carefully observed that his valiant countryman Apollinaris, the son of Sidonius, lost his life at the head of the nobles of Auvergne. Perhaps these suspected catholics had been maliciously exposed to the blind assault of the enemy; and perhaps the influence of religion was superseded by personal attachment or military honour.[1]

Such is the empire of Fortune (if we may still disguise our ignorance under that popular name), that it is almost equally difficult to foresee the events of war, or to explain their various consequences. A bloody and complete victory has sometimes yielded no more than the possession of the field; and the loss of ten thousand men has sometimes been sufficient to destroy, in a single day, the work of ages. The decisive battle of Poitiers was followed by the conquest of Aquitain. Alaric had left behind him an infant son, a bastard competitor, factious nobles, and a disloyal people; and the remaining forces of the Goths were oppressed by the general consternation, or opposed to each other in civil discord. The victorious king of the Franks proceeded without delay to the siege of Angoulême. At the sound of his trumpets the walls of the city imitated the example of Jericho, and instantly fell to the ground; a splendid miracle, which may be reduced to the supposition that some clerical engineers had secretly undermined the foundations of the rampart.[2] At Bordeaux, which had submitted without resistance, Clovis established his winter quarters; and his prudent economy transported from Toulouse the royal treasures, which were deposited in the capital of the monarchy. The conqueror penetrated as far as the confines of Spain;[3] restored the honours of the catholic church;

1 After correcting the text or excusing the mistake of Procopius, who places the defeat of Alaric near Carcassonne, we may conclude, from the evidence of Gregory, Fortunatus, and the author of the Gesta Francorum, that the battle was fought *in campo Vocladensi*, on the banks of the Clain, about ten miles to the south of Poitiers. Clovis overtook and attacked the Visigoths near Vivonne, and the victory was decided near a village still named Champagné St. Hilaire. See the Dissertations of the Abbé le Bœuf, tom. i. p. 304–331.

[This statement by Gibbon regarding the battle, that it was fought *in campo Vocladensi*, on the banks of the Clain, is scarcely correct. It should be at Vouille, which is more than ten miles from the river. – O.S.]

2 Angoulême is in the road from Poitiers to Bordeaux, and, although Gregory delays the siege, I can more readily believe that he confounded the order of history than that Clovis neglected the rules of war.

3 Pyrenæos montes usque Perpinianum subjecit, is the expression of Rorico, which betrays his recent date, since Perpignan did not exist before the tenth

fixed in Aquitain a colony of Franks;[1] and delegated to his lieutenants the easy task of subduing or extirpating the nation of the Visigoths. But the Visigoths were protected by the wise and powerful monarch of Italy. While the balance was still equal, Theodoric had perhaps delayed the march of the Ostrogoths; but their strenuous efforts successfully resisted the ambition of Clovis; and the army of the Franks, and their Burgundian allies, was compelled to raise the siege of Arles, with the loss, as it is said, of thirty thousand men. These vicissitudes inclined the fierce spirit of Clovis to acquiesce in an advantageous treaty of peace. The Visigoths were suffered to retain the possession of Septimania, a narrow tract of sea-coast, from the Rhône to the Pyrenees; but the ample province of Aquitain, from those mountains to the Loire, was indissolubly united to the kingdom of France.[2]

After the success of the Gothic war, Clovis accepted the honours of the Roman consulship. The emperor Anastasius ambitiously bestowed on the most powerful rival of Theodoric the title and ensigns of that eminent dignity; yet, from some unknown cause, the name of Clovis has not been inscribed in the *Fasti* either of the East or West.[3] On the solemn day, the

century (Marca Hispanica, p. 458). This florid and fabulous writer (perhaps a monk of Amiens – see the Abbé le Bœuf, Mém. de l'Académie, tom. xvii. p. 228–245) relates, in the *allegorical* character of a shepherd, the general history of his countrymen the Franks; but his narrative ends with the death of Clovis.

1 The author of the Gesta Francorum positively affirms that Clovis fixed a body of Franks in the Saintonge and Bourdelois; and he is not injudiciously followed by Rorico, electos milites, atque fortissimos, cum parvulis, atque mulieribus. Yet it should seem that they soon mingled with the Romans of Aquitain, till Charlemagne introduced a more numerous and powerful colony (Dubos, Hist. Critique, tom. ii. p. 215).

2 In the composition of the Gothic war I have used the following materials, with due regard to their unequal value: – Four epistles from Theodoric, king of Italy (Cassiodor. l. iii. Epist. 1–4, in tom. iv. p. 3–5), Procopius (de Bell. Goth. l. i. c. 12, in tom. ii. p. 32, 33), Gregory of Tours (l. ii. c. 35, 36, 37, in tom. ii. p. 181–183), Jornandes (de Reb. Geticis, c. 58, in tom. ii. p. 28), Fortunatus (in Vit. St. Hilarii, in tom. iii. p. 380), Isidore (in Chron. Goth. in tom. ii. p. 702), the Epitome of Gregory of Tours (in tom. ii. p. 401), the author of the Gesta Francorum (in tom. ii. p. 553–555), the Fragments of Fredegarius (in tom. ii. p. 463), Aimoin (l. i. c. 20, in tom. iii. p. 41, 42), and Rorico (l. iv. in tom. iii. p. 14–19).

3 The *Fasti* of Italy would naturally reject a consul, the enemy of their sovereign; but any ingenious hypothesis that might explain the silence of

monarch of Gaul, placing a diadem on his head, was invested, in the church of St. Martin, with a purple tunic and mantle. From thence he proceeded on horseback to the cathedral of Tours; and, as he passed through the streets, profusely scattered, with his own hand, a donative of gold and silver to the joyful multitude, who incessantly repeated their acclamations of *Consul* and *Augustus*. The actual or legal authority of Clovis could not receive any new accessions from the consular dignity. It was a name, a shadow, an empty pageant; and if the conqueror had been instructed to claim the ancient prerogatives of that high office, they must have expired with the period of its annual duration. But the Romans were disposed to revere, in the person of their master, that antique title which the emperors condescended to assume: the barbarian himself seemed to contract a sacred obligation to respect the majesty of the republic; and the successors of Theodosius, by soliciting his friendship, tacitly forgave, and almost ratified, the usurpation of Gaul.

Twenty-five years after the death of Clovis this important concession was more formally declared in a treaty between his

Constantinople and Egypt (the Chronicle of Marcellinus, and the Paschal) is overturned by the similar silence of Marius, bishop of Avenche, who composed his *Fasti* in the kingdom of Burgundy. If the evidence of Gregory of Tours were less weighty and positive (l. ii. c. 38, in tom. ii. p. 183), I could believe that Clovis, like Odoacer, received the lasting title and honours of *Patrician* (Pagi Critica, tom. ii. p. 474, 492).

[Dr. W. Smith in his edition says on the point whether or not Anastasius conferred the consulship on Clovis: 'It can scarcely admit of doubt that Anastasius conferred the consulship on Clovis, and this fact has been employed by Dubos and other writers to prove what may be called the Roman origin of the French monarchy, since they suppose that it was mainly by the recognition of Clovis as their emperor that he was recognised as their sovereign by the provincials of Gaul.' On the other side, Prof. Bury says: 'There is not the least probability in the theory supported by Valesius that Chlodwig was made a Patrician: nor was he a consul. The solution of the difficulty is supplied by his title in the Prologue to the Lex Salica "proconsolis regis Chlodovechi." Thus Clovis received the title of proconsul. Perhaps he asked for the consulship and was refused.' Gregory states 'that the Emperor sent him a letter about the consulate (codicillos de consulata). It may have offered the name proconsul instead of consul. At the same time the consular insignia were conferred. But what of Gregory's *aut Augustus*? It is difficult to believe that Anastasius would have granted to Chlodwig the highest title of all, or that if he had it should not have appeared in the Lex Salica.' See Note 2, p. 73. – O. S.]

sons and the emperor Justinian. The Ostrogoths of Italy, unable
to defend their distant acquisitions, had resigned to the Franks
the cities of Arles and Marseilles: of Arles, still adorned with the
seat of a Prætorian præfect, and of Marseilles, enriched by the
advantages of trade and navigation.¹ This transaction was confirmed by the Imperial authority; and Justinian, generously yielding to the Franks the sovereignty of the countries beyond the
Alps, which they already possessed, absolved the provincials from
their allegiance; and established on a more lawful, though not
more solid, foundation, the throne of the Merovingians.² From
that era they enjoyed the right of celebrating at Arles the games
of the circus; and by a singular privilege, which was denied even
to the Persian monarch, the *gold* coin, impressed with their name
and image, obtained a legal currency in the empire.³ A Greek
historian of that age has praised the private and public virtues

1 Under the Merovingian kings, Marseilles still imported from the East,
paper, wine, oil, linen, silk, precious stones, spices, etc. The Gauls or Franks
traded to Syria, and the Syrians were established in Gaul. See M. de Guignes,
Mém. de l'Académie, tom. xxxvii. p. 471–475.

2 Οὐ γάρ ποτε ᾦοντο Γαλλίας ξὺν τῷ ἀσφαλεῖ κεκτῆσθαι Φράγγοι, μὴ
τοῦ αὐτοκράτορος τὸ ἔργον ἐπισφραγίσαντος τουτό γε. This strong declaration
of Procopius (de Bell. Gothic. l. iii. cap. 33, in tom. ii. p. 41 [tom. ii. p. 417,
ed. Bonn]) would almost suffice to justify the Abbé Dubos.

[With regard to the remark by Gibbon in the above note, that the strong
declaration of Procopius there quoted would almost suffice to justify the Abbé
Dubos, it has been well observed by Hallam that it was merely a piece of Greek
vanity in Procopius to pretend that the Franks never thought themselves secure
of Gaul until they had obtained that sanction from the emperor. They had lately
put to flight the armies of Justinian in Italy, and they had held possession of
Gaul for the preceding sixty years. It may also be questioned whether Procopius
ever meant to say that Justinian confirmed to the Frank sovereign his rights
over the whole of Gaul. The word Γαλλίας should probably be understood
according to the general sense of the passage, which would limit its meaning
to Provence, the recent acquisition of the Franks. – O. S.]

3 The Franks, who probably used the mints of Trèves, Lyons, and Arles,
imitated the coinage of the Roman emperors, of seventy-two *solidi*, or pieces,
to the pound of gold. But as the Franks established only a decuple proportion
of gold and silver, ten shillings will be a sufficient valuation of their solidus of
gold. It was the common standard of the barbaric fines, and contained forty
denarii, or silver threepences. Twelve of these denarii made a *solidus*, or shilling,
the twentieth part of the ponderal and numeral *livre*, or pound of silver, which
has been so strangely reduced in modern France. See Le Blanc, Traité His-
torique des Monnoyes de France, p. 37–43, etc.

of the Franks, with a partial enthusiasm which cannot be sufficiently justified by their domestic annals.[1] He celebrates their
politeness and urbanity, their regular government, and orthodox
religion; and boldly asserts that these barbarians could be distinguished only by their dress and language from the subjects of
Rome. Perhaps the Franks already displayed the social disposition, and lively graces, which, in every age, have disguised their
vices, and sometimes concealed their intrinsic merit. Perhaps
Agathias, and the Greeks, were dazzled by the rapid progress of
their arms, and the splendour of their empire. Since the conquest
of Burgundy, Gaul, except the Gothic province of Septimania,
was subject, in its whole extent, to the sons of Clovis. They had
extinguished the German kingdom of Thuringia, and their vague
dominion penetrated beyond the Rhine, into the heart of their
native forests. The Alemanni and Bavarians, who had occupied
the Roman provinces of Rhætia and Noricum, to the south of
the Danube, confessed themselves the humble vassals of the
Franks; and the feeble barrier of the Alps was incapable of resisting their ambition. When the last survivor of the sons of
Clovis united the inheritance and conquests of the Merovingians,
his kingdom extended far beyond the limits of modern France.
Yet modern France, such has been the progress of arts and
policy, far surpasses, in wealth, populousness, and power, the
spacious but savage realms of Clotaire or Dagobert.[2]

The Franks, or French, are the only people of Europe who
can deduce a perpetual succession from the conquerors of the

[In criticising this statement, that the gold coin of the Merovingian kings,
which was denied to the Persian monarch, obtained a legal currency in the
empire, Hallam says that this legal currency was not distinctly mentioned by
Procopius, though he strongly asserts that it was not (οὐ θεμὶς) lawful for the
king of Persia to coin gold with his own effigy, as if the θεμὶς of Constantinople
were regarded at Seleucia. There is reason to believe that the Goths as well as
the Franks coined gold which might possibly circulate in the empire without
having, strictly speaking, a legal currency – O. S.]

1 Agathias, in tom. ii. p. 47 [p. 17, ed. Bonn]. Gregory of Tours exhibits a
very different picture. Perhaps it would not be easy, within the same historical
space, to find more vice and less virtue. We are continually shocked by the
union of savage and corrupt manners.

2 M. de Foncemagne has traced, in a correct and elegant dissertation (Mém.
de l'Académie, tom. viii. p. 505–528), the extent and limits of the French
monarchy.

Western empire. But their conquest of Gaul was followed by ten centuries of anarchy and ignorance. On the revival of learning, the students who had been formed in the schools of Athens and Rome disdained their barbarian ancestors; and a long period elapsed before patient labour could provide the requisite materials to satisfy, or rather to excite, the curiosity of more enlightened times.[1] At length the eye of criticism and philosophy was directed to the antiquities of France; but even philosophers have been tainted by the contagion of prejudice and passion. The most extreme and exclusive systems, of the personal servitude of the Gauls, or of their voluntary and equal alliance with the Franks, have been rashly conceived, and obstinately defended; and the intemperate disputants have accused each other of conspiring against the prerogative of the crown, the dignity of the nobles, or the freedom of the people. Yet the sharp conflict has usefully exercised the adverse powers of learning and genius; and each antagonist, alternately vanquished and victorious, has extirpated some ancient errors, and established some interesting truths. An impartial stranger, instructed by their discoveries, their disputes, and even their faults, may describe, from the same original materials, the state of the Roman provincials, after Gaul had submitted to the arms and laws of the Merovingian kings.[2]

The rudest, or the most servile, condition of human society, is regulated however by some fixed and general rules. When

---

1 The Abbé Dubos (Histoire Critique, tom. i. p. 29–36) has truly and agreeably represented the slow progress of these studies; and he observes that Gregory of Tours was only once printed before the year 1560. According to the complaint of Heineccius (Opera, tom. iii. Sylloge iii. p. 248, etc.), Germany received with indifference and contempt the codes of barbaric laws which were published by Heroldus, Lindebrogius, etc. At present those laws (as far as they relate to Gaul), the history of Gregory of Tours, and all the monuments of the Merovingian race, appear in a pure and perfect state, in the first four volumes of the Historians of France.

2 In the space of [about] thirty years (1728–1765) this interesting subject has been agitated by the free spirit of the Count de Boulainvilliers (Mémoires Historiques sur l'Etat de la France, particularly tom. i. p. 15–49), the learned ingenuity of the Abbé Dubos (Histoire Critique de l'Etablissement de la Monarchie Françoise dans les Gaules, 2 vols. in 4to.), the comprehensive genius of the President de Montesquieu (Esprit des Loix, particularly l. xxviii. xxx. xxxi.), and the good sense and diligence of the Abbé de Mably (Observations sur l'Histoire de France, 2 vols. 12mo.).

Tacitus surveyed the primitive simplicity of the Germans, he discovered some permanent maxims, or customs, of public and private life, which were preserved by faithful tradition till the introduction of the art of writing, and of the Latin tongue.[1] Before the election of the Merovingian kings, the most powerful tribe, or nation, of the Franks, appointed four venerable chieftains to compose the *Salic* laws;[2] and their labours were examined and approved in three successive assemblies of the people. After the baptism of Clovis, he reformed several articles that appeared incompatible with Christianity: the Salic law was again amended by his sons; and at length, under the reign of Dagobert, the code was revised and promulgated in its actual form, one hundred years after the establishment of the French monarchy. Within the same period, the customs of the *Ripuarians* were transcribed and published; and Charlemagne himself, the legislator of his age and country, had accurately studied the *two* national laws which still prevailed among the Franks.[3] The same care was extended

1 I have derived much instruction from two learned works of Heineccius – the *History* and the *Elements* of the Germanic law. In a judicious preface to the Elements, he considers, and tries to excuse, the defects of that barbarous jurisprudence.

2 Latin appears to have been the original language of the Salic law. It was probably composed in the beginning of the fifth century, before the era (A.D. 421) of the real or fabulous Pharamond. The preface mentions the four cantons which produced the four legislators; and many provinces – Franconia, Saxony, Hanover, Brabant, etc. – have claimed them as their own. See an excellent Dissertation of Heineccius, de Lege Salicâ, tom. iii. Sylloge iii. p. 247–267.

[With regard to the Salic law, Hallam says: 'The Salic law exists in two texts: one purely Latin, of which there are fifteen MSS.; the other mingled with German words, of which there are three. Most have considered the latter to be the original. The MSS. containing it are entitled, *Lex Salica antiquissima* or *vetustior*: the others generally run, *Lex Salica recentior* or *emendata*. This seems to create a presumption. But M. Wraida, who published a history of the Salic law in 1808, inclines to think the pure Latin older than the other, and M. Guizot adopts the same opinion. M. Wraida refers its original enactment to the period when the Franks were still on the left bank of the Rhine, *i.e.* before the reign of Clovis. . . . M. Guizot is of opinion that it bears marks of an age when the Franks had long been mingled with the Roman population.' Hallam's *Middle Ages*, vol. i. p. 276. – O. S.]

3 Eginhard, in Vit. Caroli Magni, c. 29, in tom. v. p. 100. By these two laws most critics understand the Salic and the Ripuarian. The former extended from the Carbonarian forest to the Loire (tom. iv. p. 151 [Lex Sal. tit. L.]), and the latter might be obeyed from the same forest to the Rhine (tom. iv. p. 232).

to their vassals; and the rude institutions of the *Alemanni* and *Bavarians* were diligently compiled and ratified by the supreme authority of the Merovingian kings. The *Visigoths* and *Burgundians*, whose conquests in Gaul preceded those of the Franks, showed less impatience to attain one of the principal benefits of civilised society. Euric was the first of the Gothic princes who expressed in writing the manners and customs of his people; and the composition of the Burgundian laws was a measure of policy rather than of justice, to alleviate the yoke and regain the affections of their Gallic subjects.[1] Thus, by a singular coincidence, the Germans framed their artless institutions at a time when the elaborate system of Roman jurisprudence was finally consummated. In the Salic laws, and the Pandects of Justinian, we may compare the first rudiments, and the full maturity, of civil wisdom; and whatever prejudices may be suggested in favour of barbarism, our calmer reflections will ascribe to the Romans the superior advantages, not only of science and reason, but of humanity and justice. Yet the laws of the barbarians were adapted to their wants and desires, their occupations and their capacity; and they all contributed to preserve the peace, and promote the improvements, of the society for whose use they were originally established. The Merovingians, instead of imposing a uniform rule of conduct on their various subjects, permitted each people, and each family, of their empire freely to enjoy their domestic institutions;[2] nor were the Romans excluded from the common benefits of this legal toleration.[3] The children embraced the *law*

1 Consult the ancient and modern prefaces of the several codes, in the fourth volume of the Historians of France. The original prologue to the Salic law expresses (though in a foreign dialect) the genuine spirit of the Franks more forcibly than the ten books of Gregory of Tours.

2 The Ripuarian law declares and defines this indulgence in favour of the plaintiff (tit. xxxi. in tom. iv. p. 240); and the same toleration is understood or expressed in all the codes except that of the Visigoths of Spain. Tanta diversitas legum (says Agobard in the ninth century) quanta non solum in [singulis] regionibus, aut civitatibus, sed etiam in multis domibus habetur. Nam plerumque contingit ut simul eant aut sedeant quinque homines, et nullus eorum communem legem cum altero habeat (in tom. vi. p. 356). He foolishly proposes to introduce an uniformity of law as well as of faith.

3 Inter Romanos negotia causarum Romanis legibus præcipimus terminari. Such are the words of a general constitution promulgated by Clotaire, the son of Clovis, and sole monarch of the Franks (in tom. iv. p. 116), about the year 560.

of their parents, the wife that of her husband, the freedman that of his patron; and in all causes where the parties were of different nations, the plaintiff or accuser was obliged to follow the tribunal of the defendant, who may always plead a judicial presumption of right or innocence. A more ample latitude was allowed, if every citizen, in the presence of the judge, might declare the law under which he desired to live, and the national society to which he chose to belong. Such an indulgence would abolish the partial distinctions of victory: and the Roman provincials might patiently acquiesce in the hardships of their condition, since it depended on themselves to assume the privilege, if they dared to assert the character, of free and warlike barbarians.[1]

When justice inexorably requires the death of a murderer, each private citizen is fortified by the assurance that the laws, the magistrate, and the whole community, are the guardians of his personal safety. But in the loose society of the Germans, revenge was always honourable, and often meritorious: the independent warrior chastised, or vindicated, with his own hand, the injuries which he had offered or received; and he had only to dread the resentment of the sons and kinsmen of the enemy whom he had sacrificed to his selfish or angry passions. The magistrate, conscious of his weakness, interposed, not to punish, but to reconcile; and he was satisfied if he could persuade or compel the contending parties to pay and to accept the moderate fine which had been ascertained as the price of blood.[2] The fierce

1 This liberty of choice has been aptly deduced (Esprit des Loix, l. xxviii. 2) from a constitution of Lothaire I. (Leg. Langobard. l. ii. tit. lvii. in Codex Lindebrog. p. 664), though the example is too recent and partial. From a various reading in the Salic law (tit. xliv. not. xlv.), the Abbé de Mably (tom. i. p. 290–293) has conjectured that at first a *barbarian* only, and afterwards any *man* (consequently a Roman), might live according to the law of the Franks. I am sorry to offend this ingenious conjecture by observing that the stricter sense (*barbarum*) is expressed in the reformed copy of Charlemagne, which is confirmed by the Royal and Wolfenbüttel MSS. The looser interpretation (*hominem*) is authorised only by the MS. of Fulda, from whence Heroldus published his edition. See the four original texts of the Salic law, in tom. iv. p. 147, 173, 196, 220.

2 In the heroic times of Greece, the guilt of murder was expiated by a pecuniary satisfaction to the family of the deceased (Feithius Antiquitat. Homer. l. ii. c. 8). Heineccius, in his preface to the Elements of Germanic Law, favourably suggests that at Rome and Athens homicide was only punished with exile. It is true; but exile was a *capital* punishment for a citizen of Rome or Athens.

spirit of the Franks would have opposed a more rigorous sentence; the same fierceness despised these ineffectual restraints; and, when their simple manners had been corrupted by the wealth of Gaul, the public peace was continually violated by acts of hasty or deliberate guilt. In every just government the same penalty is inflicted, or at least is imposed, for the murder of a peasant or a prince. But the national inequality established by the Franks in their criminal proceedings was the last insult and abuse of conquest.[1] In the calm moments of legislation they solemnly pronounced that the life of a Roman was of smaller value than that of a barbarian. The *Antrustion*,[2] a name expressive of the most illustrious birth or dignity among the Franks, was appreciated at the sum of six hundred pieces of gold; while the noble provincial, who was admitted to the king's table, might be legally murdered at the expense of three hundred pieces. Two hundred were deemed sufficient for a Frank of ordinary condition; but the meaner Romans were exposed to disgrace and danger by a trifling compensation of one hundred, or even fifty, pieces of gold. Had these laws been regulated by any principle of equity or reason, the public protection should have supplied, in just proportion, the want of personal strength. But the legislator had weighed in the scale, not of justice, but of policy, the loss of a soldier against that of a slave: the head of an insolent and rapacious barbarian was guarded by a heavy fine; and the slightest aid was afforded to the most defenceless subjects. Time insensibly abated the pride of the conquerors, and the patience of the vanquished; and the boldest citizen was taught by experience that he might suffer more injuries than he could inflict. As the manners of the Franks became less ferocious, their laws were rendered more severe; and the Merovingian kings attempted to

1 This proportion is fixed by the Salic (tit. xliv. in tom. iv. p. 147) and the Ripuarian (tit. vii. xi. xxxvi. in tom. iv. p. 237, 241) laws; but the latter does not distinguish any difference of Romans. Yet the orders of the clergy are placed above the Franks themselves, and the Burgundians and Alemanni between the Franks and the Romans.

2 The *Antrustiones, qui in truste Dominicâ sunt, leudi, fideles*, undoubtedly represent the first order of Franks; but it is a question whether their rank was personal or hereditary. The Abbé de Mably (tom. i. p. 334–347) is not displeased to mortify the pride of birth (Esprit, l. xxx. c. 25) by dating the *origin* of French nobility from the reign of Clotaire II. (A.D. 615).

imitate the impartial rigour of the Visigoths and Burgundians.[1] Under the empire of Charlemagne murder was universally pun- ished with death; and the use of capital punishments has been liberally multiplied in the jurisprudence of modern Europe.[2]

The civil and military professions, which had been separated by Constantine, were again united by the barbarians. The harsh sound of the Teutonic appellations was mollified into the Latin titles of Duke, of Count, or of Præfect; and the same officer assumed, within his district, the command of the troops and the administration of justice.[3] But the fierce and illiterate chieftain was seldom qualified to discharge the duties of a judge, which require all the faculties of a philosophic mind, laboriously cultivated by experience and study; and his rude ignorance was compelled to embrace some simple and visible methods of ascertaining the cause of justice. In every religion the Deity has been invoked to confirm the truth, or to punish the falsehood, of human testi- mony; but this powerful instrument was misapplied and abused by the simplicity of the German legislators. The party accused might justify his innocence, by producing before their tribunal a number of friendly witnesses, who solemnly declared their belief

1 See the Burgundian laws (tit. ii. in tom. iv. p. 257), the code of the Visigoths (l. vi. tit. v. in tom. iv. p. 383), and the constitution of *Childebert*, not of Paris, but most evidently of Austrasia (in tom. iv. p. 112). Their premature severity was sometimes rash and excessive. Childebert condemned not only murderers but robbers; quomodo sine lege involavit, sine lege moriatur; and even the negligent judge was involved in the same sentence. The Visigoths abandoned an unsuccessful surgeon to the family of his deceased patient, ut quod de eo facere voluerint habeant potestatem (l. xi. tit. i. in tom. iv. p. 435).

2 See in the sixth volume of the works of Heineccius, the Elementa Juris Germanici, l. ii. p. ii. No. 261, 262, 280–283. Yet some vestiges of these pecu- niary compositions for murder have been traced in Germany as late as the sixteenth century.

3 The whole subject of the Germanic judges, and their jurisdiction, is copiously treated by Heineccius (Element. Jur. Germ. l. iii. No. 1–72). I cannot find any proof that, under the Merovingian race, the *scabini*, or assessors, were chosen by the people.

[Gibbon, in his note on the Germanic judges, says he cannot find any proof that under the Merovingian race the *scabini*, or assessors, were chosen by the people. The whole question of the scabini is treated by Savigny, who questions the existence of the scabini before Charlemagne. Before that time the decision was by open court of the boni homines or freemen. In fact, as Bury says, 'the name does not appear until Carolingian times.' – O. S.]

or assurance that he was not guilty. According to the weight of
the charge this legal number of *compurgators* was multiplied:
seventy-two voices were required to absolve an incendiary or
assassin; and when the chastity of a queen of France was suspected, three hundred gallant nobles swore, without hesitation,
that the infant prince had been actually begotten by her deceased
husband.[1] The sin and scandal of manifest and frequent perjuries
engaged the magistrates to remove these dangerous temptations,
and to supply the defects of human testimony by the famous
experiments of fire and water. These extraordinary trials were so
capriciously contrived, that in some cases guilt, and innocence
in others, could not be proved without the interposition of a
miracle. Such miracles were readily provided by fraud and credulity; the most intricate causes were determined by this easy and
infallible method; and the turbulent barbarians, who might have
disdained the sentence of the magistrate, submissively acquiesced
in the judgment of God.[2]

But the trials by single combat gradually obtained superior
credit and authority among a warlike people, who could not
believe that a brave man deserved to suffer, or that a coward
deserved to live.[3] Both in civil and criminal proceedings, the
plaintiff, or accuser, the defendant, or even the witness, were
exposed to mortal challenge from the antagonist who was destitute of legal proofs; and it was incumbent on them either to
desert their cause or publicly to maintain their honour in the lists
of battle. They fought either on foot or on horseback, according

1 Gregor. Turon. l. viii. c. 9, in tom. ii. p. 316. Montesquieu observes
(Esprit des Loix, l. xxviii. c. 13) that the Salic law did not admit these *negative
proofs* so universally established in the barbaric codes. Yet this obscure concubine (Fredegundis), who became the wife of the grandson of Clovis, must
have followed the Salic law.

2 Muratori, in the Antiquities of Italy, has given two Dissertations (xxxviii.
xxxix.) on the *judgments of God.* It was expected that *fire* would not burn the
innocent, and that the pure element of *water* would not allow the guilty to sink
into its bosom.

3 Montesquieu (Esprit des Loix, l. xxviii. c. 17) has condescended to explain and excuse 'la manière de penser de nos pères' on the subject of judicial combats. He follows this strange institution from the age of Gundobald
to that of St. Lewis; and the philosopher is sometimes lost in the legal antiquarian.

to the custom of their nation;[1] and the decision of the sword or
lance was ratified by the sanction of Heaven, of the judge, and
of the people. This sanguinary law was introduced into Gaul by
the Burgundians; and their legislator Gundobald[2] condescended
to answer the complaints and objections of his subject Avitus.
'Is it not true,' said the king of Burgundy to the bishop, 'that the
event of national wars and private combats is directed by the
judgment of God; and that his providence awards the victory to
the juster cause?' By such prevailing arguments, the absurd and
cruel practice of judicial duels, which had been peculiar to some
tribes of Germany, was propagated and established in all the
monarchies of Europe, from Sicily to the Baltic. At the end of
ten centuries the reign of legal violence was not totally extinguished; and the ineffectual censures of saints, of popes, and of
synods, may seem to prove that the influence of superstition is
weakened by its unnatural alliance with reason and humanity.
The tribunals were stained with the blood, perhaps, of innocent
and respectable citizens; the law, which now favours the rich,
then yielded to the strong; and the old, the feeble, and the infirm,
were condemned either to renounce their fairest claims and possessions, to sustain the dangers of an unequal conflict,[3] or to
trust the doubtful aid of a mercenary champion. This oppressive
jurisprudence was imposed on the provincials of Gaul who complained of any injuries in their persons and property. Whatever
might be the strength or courage of individuals, the victorious

1 In a memorable duel at Aix-la-Chapelle (A.D. 820), before the emperor
Lewis the Pious, his biographer observes, secundum legem propriam, utpote
quia uterque Gothus erat, equestri pugnâ [prœlio] congressus est (Vit. Lud. Pii,
c. 33, in tom. vi. p. 103). Ermoldus Nigellus (l. iii. 543–628, in tom. vi. p. 48–50),
who describes the duel, admires the *ars nova* of fighting on horseback, which
was unknown to the Franks.

2 In his original edict, published at Lyons (A.D. 501), Gundobald establishes
and justifies the use of judicial combat. (Leg. Burgund. tit. xlv. in tom. iii. p. 267,
268.) Three hundred years afterwards, Agobard, bishop of Lyons, solicited
Lewis the Pious to abolish the law of an Arian tyrant (in tom. vi. p. 356–358).
He relates the conversation of Gundobald and Avitus.

3 'Accidit (says Agobard), ut non solum valentes viribus, sed etiam infirmi
et senes lacessantur ad [certamen et] pugnam, etiam pro vilissimis rebus. Quibus
feralibus certaminibus contingunt homicidia injusta, et crudeles ac perversi
eventus judiciorum' [tom. vi. p. 357]. Like a prudent rhetorician, he suppresses
the legal privilege of hiring champions.

barbarians excelled in the love and exercise of arms; and the vanquished Roman was unjustly summoned to repeat, in his own person, the bloody contest which had been already decided against his country.[1]

A devouring host of one hundred and twenty thousand Germans had formerly passed the Rhine under the command of Ariovistus. One-third part of the fertile lands of the Sequani was appropriated to their use; and the conqueror soon repeated his oppressive demand of another third, for the accommodation of a new colony of twenty-four thousand barbarians whom he had invited to share the rich harvest of Gaul.[2] At the distance of five hundred years the Visigoths and Burgundians, who revenged the defeat of Ariovistus, usurped the same unequal proportion of *two-thirds* of the subject lands. But this distribution, instead of spreading over the province, may be reasonably confined to the peculiar districts where the victorious people had been planted by their own choice or by the policy of their leader. In these districts each barbarian was connected by the ties of hospitality with some Roman provincial. To this unwelcome guest the proprietor was compelled to abandon two-thirds of his patrimony: but the German, a shepherd and a hunter, might sometimes content himself with a spacious range of wood and pasture, and resign the smallest, though most valuable, portion to the toil of the industrious husbandman.[3] The silence of ancient and

1 Montesquieu (Esprit des Loix, xxviii. c. 14), who understands *why* the judicial combat was admitted by the Burgundians, Ripuarians, Alemanni, Bavarians, Lombards, Thuringians, Frisons, and Saxons, is satisfied (and Agobard seems to countenance the assertion) that it was not allowed by the Salic law. Yet the same custom, at least in cases of treason, is mentioned by Ermoldus Nigellus (l. iii. 543, in tom. vi. p. 48) and the anonymous biographer of Lewis the Pious (c. 46, in tom. vi. p. 112), as the 'mos antiquus Francorum, more Francis solito,' etc., expressions too general to exclude the noblest of their tribes.

2 Cæsar de Bell. Gall. l. i. c. 31, in tom. i. p. 213.

3 The obscure hints of a division of lands occasionally scattered in the laws of the Burgundians (tit. liv. No. 1, 2, in tom. iv. p. 271, 272) and Visigoths (l. x. tit. i. No. 8, 9, 16, in tom. iv. p. 428, 429, 430) are skilfully explained by the President Montesquieu (Esprit des Loix, l. xxx. c. 7, 8, 9). I shall only add that, among the Goths, the division seems to have been ascertained by the judgment of the neighbourhood; that the barbarians frequently usurped the remaining *third;* and that the Romans might recover their right, unless they were barred by a prescription of fifty years.

authentic testimony has encouraged an opinion that the rapine of the *Franks* was not moderated or disguised by the forms of a legal division; that they dispersed themselves over the provinces of Gaul without order or control; and that each victorious robber, according to his wants, his avarice, and his strength, measured with his sword the extent of his new inheritance. At a distance from their sovereign the barbarians might indeed be tempted to exercise such arbitrary depredation; but the firm and artful policy of Clovis must curb a licentious spirit which would aggravate the misery of the vanquished whilst it corrupted the union and discipline of the conquerors.[1] The memorable vase of Soissons is a monument and a pledge of the regular distribution of the Gallic spoils. It was the duty and the interest of Clovis to provide rewards for a successful army, and settlements for a numerous people, without inflicting any wanton or superfluous injuries on the loyal catholics of Gaul. The ample fund which he might lawfully acquire of the Imperial patrimony, vacant lands, and Gothic usurpations, would diminish the cruel necessity of seizure and confiscation, and the humble provincials would more patiently acquiesce in the equal and regular distribution of their loss.[2]

The wealth of the Merovingian princes consisted in their extensive domain. After the conquest of Gaul they still delighted in the rustic simplicity of their ancestors; the cities were abandoned to solitude and decay; and their coins, their charters, and their synods, are still inscribed with the names of the villas or

1 [Sismondi notes upon this question that the Franks were not a conquering people who had emigrated with their families, like the Goths or Burgundians. The women, the children, and the old had not followed Clovis. They remained on their ancient possessions on the Waal and the Rhine. The adventurers alone had formed the invading force, and they always considered themselves as an army, not as a colony. Hence their laws retain no traces of the partition of the Roman properties. *Histoire des Français*, vol. i. p. 197. – O. S.]

2 It is singular enough that the President de Montesquieu (Esprit des Loix, l. xxx. c. 7) and the Abbé de Mably (Observations, tom. i. p. 21, 22) agree in this strange supposition of arbitrary and private rapine. The Count de Boulain-villiers (Etat de la France, tom. i. p. 22, 23) shows a strong understanding through a cloud of ignorance and prejudice.

[Sismondi supposes, regarding private rapine, that the barbarians, if a farm were conveniently situated, would show no great respect for the laws of property; but in general there would have been vacant land enough for the lots assigned to old and worn-out warriors. *Hist. des Français*, vol. i. p. 196. – O. S.]

rural palaces in which they successively resided. One hundred and sixty of these *palaces*, a title which need not excite any unseasonable ideas of art or luxury, were scattered through the provinces of their kingdom; and if some might claim the honours of a fortress, the far greater part could be esteemed only in the light of profitable farms. The mansion of the long-haired kings was surrounded with convenient yards and stables for the cattle and the poultry; the garden was planted with useful vegetables; the various trades, the labours of agriculture, and even the arts of hunting and fishing, were exercised by servile hands for the emolument of the sovereign; his magazines were filled with corn and wine, either for sale or consumption; and the whole administration was conducted by the strictest maxims of private economy.[1] This ample patrimony was appropriated to supply the hospitable plenty of Clovis and his successors, and to reward the fidelity of their brave companions, who, both in peace and war, were devoted to their personal service. Instead of a horse or a suit of armour, each companion, according to his rank, or merit, or favour, was invested with a *benefice*, the primitive name and most simple form of the feudal possessions. These gifts might be resumed at the pleasure of the sovereign; and his feeble prerogative derived some support from the influence of his liberality. But this dependent tenure was gradually abolished[2] by the independent and rapacious nobles of France, who established the perpetual property and hereditary succession of their benefices; a revolution salutary to the earth, which had been injured or neglected by its precarious masters.[3] Besides these royal and

1 See the rustic edict, or rather code, of Charlemagne, which contains seventy distinct and minute regulations of that great monarch (in tom. v. p. 652–657). He requires an account of the horns and skins of the goats, allows his fish to be sold, and carefully directs that the larger villas (*Capitaneæ*) shall maintain one hundred hens and thirty geese, and the smaller (*Mansionales*) fifty hens and twelve geese. Mabillon (de Re Diplomaticâ) has investigated the names, the number, and the situation of the Merovingian villas.

2 From a passage of the Burgundian law (tit. i. No. 4 [3] in tom. iv. p. 257) it is evident that a deserving son might expect to hold the lands which his father had received from the royal bounty of Gundobald. The Burgundians would firmly maintain their privilege, and their example might encourage the beneficiaries of France.

3 The revolutions of the benefices and fiefs are clearly fixed by the Abbé de Mably. His accurate distinction of *times* gives him a merit to which even Montesquieu is a stranger.

beneficiary estates, a large proportion had been assigned, in the division of Gaul, of *allodial* and *Salic* lands: they were exempt from tribute, and the Salic lands were equally shared among the male descendants of the Franks.[1]

In the bloody discord and silent decay of the Merovingian line a new order of tyrants arose in the provinces, who, under the appellation of *Seniors* or Lords, usurped a right to govern and a licence to oppress the subjects of their peculiar territory. Their ambition might be checked by the hostile resistance of an equal: but the laws were extinguished; and the sacrilegious barbarians, who dared to provoke the vengeance of a saint or bishop,[2] would seldom respect the landmarks of a profane and defenceless neighbour. The common or public rights of nature, such as they had always been deemed by the Roman jurisprudence,[3] were severely restrained by the German conquerors, whose amusement, or rather passion, was the exercise of hunting. The vague dominion which MAN has assumed over the wild inhabitants of the earth, the air, and the waters, was confined to some fortunate individuals of the human species. Gaul was again overspread with woods; and the animals, who were reserved for the use or pleasure of the lord, might ravage with impunity the fields of his industrious vassals. The chase was the sacred privilege of the nobles and their domestic servants. Plebeian transgressors were legally chastised with stripes and imprisonment;[4] but in an age

1 See the Salic law (tit. lxii. in tom. iv. p. 156). The origin and nature of these Salic lands, which in times of ignorance were perfectly understood, now perplex our most learned and sagacious critics.

[No solution seems more probable than that the ancient law-givers of the Salic Franks prohibited females from inheriting lands assigned to the nation, upon its conquest of Gaul, both in compliance with their ancient usages and in order to secure the military service of every proprietor. But lands subsequently acquired by purchase or otherwise, though equally bound to the public defence, were relieved from the severity of this rule, and presumed not to belong to the class of Salic. Hallam's *Middle Ages*, vol. i. p. 146; cf. Sismondi, vol. i. p. 196. – O. S.]

2 Many of the two hundred and six miracles of St. Martin (Greg. Turon. in Maximâ Bibliothecâ Patrum, tom. xi. p. 896–932) were repeatedly performed to punish sacrilege. Audite hæc omnes (exclaims the bishop of Tours) potestatem habentes, after relating how some horses ran mad that had been turned into a sacred meadow.

3 Heinec. Element. Jur. German. l. ii. p. 1, No. 8.

4 Jonas, bishop of Orleans (A.D. 821–826; Cave, Hist. Litteraria, p. 443), censures the *legal* tyranny of the nobles. Pro feris, quas cura hominum non aluit,

which admitted a slight composition for the life of a citizen, it
was a capital crime to destroy a stag or a wild bull within the
precincts of the royal forests.[1]

According to the maxims of ancient war, the conqueror became the lawful master of the enemy whom he had subdued and
spared:[2] and the fruitful cause of personal slavery, which had
been almost suppressed by the peaceful sovereignty of Rome,
was again revived and multiplied by the perpetual hostilities of
the independent barbarians. The Goth, the Burgundian, or the
Frank, who returned from a successful expedition, dragged after
him a long train of sheep, of oxen, and of human captives,
whom he treated with the same brutal contempt. The youths of
an elegant form and ingenuous aspect were set apart for the
domestic service; a doubtful situation, which alternately exposed
them to the favourable or cruel impulse of passion. The useful
mechanics and servants (smiths, carpenters, tailors, shoemakers,
cooks, gardeners, dyers, and workmen in gold and silver, etc.)
employed their skill for the use or profit of their master. But the
Roman captives who were destitute of art, but capable of labour,
were condemned, without regard to their former rank, to tend
the cattle and cultivate the lands of the barbarians. The number
of the hereditary bondsmen who were attached to the Gallic
estates was continually increased by new supplies; and the servile
people, according to the situation and temper of their lords, was
sometimes raised by precarious indulgence, and more frequently

sed Deus in commune mortalibus ad utendum concessit, pauperes a potentiori-
bus spoliantur, flagellantur, ergastulis detruduntur, et multa alia patiuntur.
Hoc enim qui faciunt, *lege mundi* se facere juste posse contendunt. De Institu-
tione Laicorum, l. ii. c. 23, apud Thomassin, Discipline de l'Eglise, tom. iii.
p. 1348.

1 On a mere suspicion, Chundo, a chamberlain of Gontran, king of Burgundy, was stoned to death (Greg. Turon. l. x. c. 10, in tom. ii. p. 369). John
of Salisbury (Policrat. l. i. c. 4) asserts the rights of nature, and exposes the
cruel practice of the twelfth century. See Heineccius, Elem. Jur. Germ. l. ii. p. 1,
No. 51–57.

2 The custom of enslaving prisoners of war was totally extinguished in the
thirteenth century by the prevailing influence of Christianity; but it might be
proved, from frequent passages of Gregory of Tours, etc., that it was practised
without censure under the Merovingian race; and even Grotius himself (de Jure
Belli et Pacis, l. iii. c. 7), as well as his commentator Barbeyrac, have laboured
to reconcile it with the laws of nature and reason.

depressed by capricious despotism.[1] An absolute power of life
and death was exercised by these lords; and when they married
their daughters, a train of useful servants, chained on the waggons to prevent their escape, was sent as a nuptial present into
a distant country.[2] The majesty of the Roman laws protected the
liberty of each citizen against the rash effects of his own distress
or despair. But the subjects of the Merovingian kings might
alienate their personal freedom; and this act of legal suicide,
which was familiarly practised, is expressed in terms most disgraceful and afflicting to the dignity of human nature.[3] The
example of the poor, who purchased life by the sacrifice of all
that can render life desirable, was gradually imitated by the feeble
and the devout, who, in times of public disorder, pusillanimously
crowded to shelter themselves under the battlements of a powerful chief and around the shrine of a popular saint. Their submission was accepted by these temporal or spiritual patrons; and
the hasty transaction irrecoverably fixed their own condition and
that of their latest posterity. From the reign of Clovis, during
five successive centuries, the laws and manners of Gaul uniformly tended to promote the increase, and to confirm the duration,
of personal servitude. Time and violence almost obliterated the
intermediate ranks of society, and left an obscure and narrow
interval between the noble and the slave. This arbitrary and
recent division has been transformed by pride and prejudice into
a *national* distinction, universally established by the arms and the
laws of the Merovingians. The nobles, who claimed their genuine
or fabulous descent from the independent and victorious Franks,

1 The state, professions, etc., of the German, Italian, and Gallic slaves,
during the middle ages, are explained by Heineccius (Element. Jur. Germ. l. i.
No. 28–47), Muratori (Dissertat. xiv. xv.), Ducange (Gloss. sub voce *Servi*), and
the Abbé de Mably (Observations, tom. ii. p. 3, etc., p. 237. etc.).

2 Gregory of Tours (l. vi. c. 45, in tom. ii. p. 289) relates a memorable
example, in which Chilperic only abused the private rights of a master. Many
families, which belonged to his *domus fiscales* in the neighbourhood of Paris, were
forcibly sent away into Spain.

3 Licentiam habeatis mihi qualemcunque volueritis disciplinam ponere; vel
venumdare, aut quod vobis placuerit de me facere. Marculf. Formul. l. ii. 28, in
tom. iv. p. 497. The *Formula* of Lindenbrogius (p. 559), and that of Anjou
(p. 565), are to the same effect. Gregory of Tours (l. vii. c. 45, in tom. ii. p. 311)
speaks of many persons who sold themselves for bread in a great famme.

have asserted and abused the indefeasible right of conquest over
a prostrate crowd of slaves and plebeians, to whom they imputed
the imaginary disgrace of a Gallic or Roman extraction.

The general state and revolutions of *France*, a name which was
imposed by the conquerors, may be illustrated by the particular
example of a province, a diocese, or a senatorial family. Auvergne had formerly maintained a just pre-eminence among the
independent states and cities of Gaul. The brave and numerous
inhabitants displayed a singular trophy – the sword of Cæsar
himself, which he had lost when he was repulsed before the walls
of Gergovia.[1] As the common offspring of Troy, they claimed a
fraternal alliance with the Romans;[2] and if each province had
imitated the courage and loyalty of Auvergne, the fall of the
Western empire might have been prevented or delayed. They
firmly maintained the fidelity which they had reluctantly sworn
to the Visigoths; but when their bravest nobles had fallen in the
battle of Poitiers, they accepted without resistance a victorious
and catholic sovereign. This easy and valuable conquest was
achieved and possessed by Theodoric, the eldest son of Clovis:
but the remote province was separated from his Austrasian
dominions by the intermediate kingdoms of Soissons, Paris, and
Orleans, which formed, after their father's death, the inheritance
of his three brothers. The king of Paris, Childebert, was tempted
by the neighbourhood and beauty of Auvergne.[3] The upper
country, which rises towards the south into the mountains of the
Cevennes, presented a rich and various prospect of woods and

1 When Cæsar saw it, he laughed (Plutarch. in Cæsar. [c. 26] in tom. i.
p. 409 [p. 720, ed. Frankf.]); yet he relates his unsuccessful siege of Gergovia
with less frankness than we might expect from a great man to whom victory
was familiar. He acknowledges, however, that in one attack he lost forty-six
centurions and seven hundred men (de Bell. Gallico, l. vi. [vii.] c. 44–53, in
tom. i. p. 270–272).

2 Audebant se quondam fratres Latio dicere, et sanguine ab Iliaco populos
computare (Sidon. Apollinar. l. vii. Epist. 7, in tom. i. p. 799). I am not informed
of the degrees and circumstances of this fabulous pedigree.

3 Either the first or second partition among the sons of Clovis had given
Berry to Childebert (Greg. Turon. l. iii. c. 12, in tom. ii. p. 192). Velim (said
he), Arvernam *Lemanem*, quæ tantæ jocunditatis gratiâ refulgere dicitur, oculis
cernere (l. iii. c. 9, p. 191). The face of the country was concealed by a thick
fog when the king of Paris made his entry into Clermont.

pastures; the sides of the hills were clothed with vines; and each eminence was crowned with a villa or castle. In the Lower Auvergne, the river Allier flows through the fair and spacious plain of Limagne; and the inexhaustible fertility of the soil supplied, and still supplies, without any interval of repose, the constant repetition of the same harvests.[1] On the false report that their lawful sovereign had been slain in Germany, the city and diocese of Auvergne were betrayed by the grandson of Sidonius Apollinaris. Childebert enjoyed this clandestine victory; and the free subjects of Theodoric threatened to desert his standard if he indulged his private resentment while the nation was engaged in the Burgundian war. But the Franks of Austrasia soon yielded to the persuasive eloquence of their king. 'Follow me,' said Theodoric, 'into Auvergne; I will lead you into a province where you may acquire gold, silver, slaves, cattle, and precious apparel, to the full extent of your wishes. I repeat my promise; I give you the people and their wealth as your prey; and you may transport them at pleasure into your own country.' By the execution of this promise Theodoric justly forfeited the allegiance of a people whom he devoted to destruction. His troops, reinforced by the fiercest barbarians of Germany,[2] spread desolation over the fruitful face of Auvergne; and two places only, a strong castle and a holy shrine, were saved or redeemed from their licentious fury. The castle of Meroliac[3] was seated on a lofty rock, which rose an hundred feet above the surface of the plain; and a large reservoir of fresh water was enclosed with some arable lands within the circle of its fortifications. The Franks beheld with

1 For the description of Auvergne, see Sidonius (l. iv. Epist. 21, in tom. i. p. 793), with the notes of Savaron and Sirmond (p. 279 and 51 of their respective editions). Boulainvilliers (Etat de la France, tom. ii. p. 242–268), and the Abbé de la Longuerue (Description de la France, part i. p. 132–139).

2 Furorem gentium, quæ de ulteriore Rheni amnis parte venerant, superare non poterat (Greg. Turon. l. iv. c. 50, in tom. ii. 229), was the excuse of another king of Austrasia (A.D. 574) for the ravages which his troops committed in the neighbourhood of Paris.

3 From the name and situation, the Benedictine editors of Gregory of Tours (in tom. ii. p. 192) have fixed this fortress at a place named *Chastel Merliac*, two miles from Mauriac, in the Upper Auvergne. In this description I translate *infra* as if I read *intra;* the two prepositions are perpetually confounded by Gregory or his transcribers, and the sense must always decide.

envy and despair this impregnable fortress: but they surprised a
party of fifty stragglers; and, as they were oppressed by the number of their captives, they fixed at a trifling ransom the alternative of life or death for these wretched victims, whom the cruel
barbarians were prepared to massacre on the refusal of the garrison. Another detachment penetrated as far as Brivas, or
Brioude, where the inhabitants, with their valuable effects, had
taken refuge in the sanctuary of St. Julian. The doors of the
church resisted the assault, but a daring soldier entered through
a window of the choir and opened a passage to his companions.
The clergy and people, the sacred and the profane spoils, were
rudely torn from the altar; and the sacrilegious division was made
at a small distance from the town of Brioude. But this act of
impiety was severely chastised by the devout son of Clovis. He
punished with death the most atrocious offenders; left their secret accomplices to the vengeance of St. Julian; released the
captives; restored the plunder; and extended the rights of sanctuary five miles round the sepulchre of the holy martyr.[1]

Before the Austrasian army retreated from Auvergne, Theodoric exacted some pledges of the future loyalty of a people
whose just hatred could be restrained only by their fear. A select
band of noble youths, the sons of the principal senators, was
delivered to the conqueror as the hostages of the faith of Childebert and of their countrymen. On the first rumour of war or
conspiracy these guiltless youths were reduced to a state of servitude; and one of them, Attalus,[2] whose adventures are more
particularly related, kept his master's horses in the diocese of
Trèves. After a painful search he was discovered, in this unworthy occupation, by the emissaries of his grandfather, Gregory
bishop of Langres; but his offers of ransom were sternly rejected

1 See these revolutions and wars of Auvergne in Gregory of Tours (l. ii.
c. 37, in tom. ii. p. 183, and l. iii. c. 9, 12, 13, p. 191, 192, de Miraculis St. Julian.
c. 13, in tom. ii. p. 466). He frequently betrays his extraordinary attention to
his native country.

2 The story of Attalus is related by Gregory of Tours (l. iii. c. 15, in tom. ii.
p. 193–195). His editor, the P. Ruinart, confounds this Attalus, who was a youth
(*puer*) in the year 532, with a friend of Sidonius of the same name, who was
count of Autun fifty or sixty years before. Such an error, which cannot be
imputed to ignorance, is excused in some degree by its own magnitude.

by the avarice of the barbarian, who required an exorbitant sum of ten pounds of gold for the freedom of his noble captive. His deliverance was effected by the hardy stratagem of Leo, a slave belonging to the kitchens of the bishop of Langres.[1] An unknown agent easily introduced him into the same family. The barbarian purchased Leo for the price of twelve pieces of gold; and was pleased to learn that he was deeply skilled in the luxury of an episcopal table: 'Next Sunday,' said the Frank, 'I shall invite my neighbours and kinsmen. Exert thy art, and force them to confess that they have never seen or tasted such an entertainment, even in the king's house.' Leo assured him that, if he would provide a sufficient quantity of poultry, his wishes should be satisfied. The master, who already aspired to the merit of elegant hospitality, assumed as his own the praise which the voracious guests unanimously bestowed on his cook; and the dexterous Leo insensibly acquired the trust and management of his household. After the patient expectation of a whole year, he cautiously whispered his design to Attalus, and exhorted him to prepare for flight in the ensuing night. At the hour of midnight the intemperate guests retired from table, and the Frank's son-in-law, whom Leo attended to his apartment with a nocturnal potation, condescended to jest on the facility with which he might betray his trust. The intrepid slave, after sustaining this dangerous raillery, entered his master's bed-chamber; removed his spear and shield; silently drew the fleetest horses from the stable; unbarred the ponderous gates; and excited Attalus to save his life and liberty by incessant diligence. Their apprehensions urged them to leave their horses on the banks of the Meuse;[2]

1 This Gregory, the great-grandfather of Gregory of Tours (in tom. ii. p. 197, 490), lived ninety-two years, of which he passed forty as count of Autun, and thirty-two as bishop of Langres. According to the poet Fortunatus, he displayed equal merit in these different stations: –

> Nobilis antiquâ decurrens prole parentum,
> Nobilior gestis, nunc super astra manet.
> Arbiter ante ferox, dein pius ipse sacerdos,
> Quos domuit judex, fovit amore patris.

2 As M. de Valois and the P. Ruinart are determined to change the *Mosella* of the text into *Mosa*, it becomes me to acquiesce in the alteration. Yet, after some examination of the topography, I could defend the common reading.

they swam the river, wandered three days in the adjacent forest, and subsisted only by the accidental discovery of a wild plum-tree. As they lay concealed in a dark thicket, they heard the noise of horses; they were terrified by the angry countenance of their master, and they anxiously listened to his declaration that, if he could seize the guilty fugitives, one of them he would cut in pieces with his sword, and would expose the other on a gibbet. At length Attalus and his faithful Leo reached the friendly habit-ation of a presbyter of Rheims, who recruited their fainting strength with bread and wine, concealed them from the search of their enemy, and safely conducted them beyond the limits of the Austrasian kingdom to the episcopal palace of Langres. Gregory embraced his grandson with tears of joy, gratefully de-livered Leo with his whole family from the yoke of servitude, and bestowed on him the property of a farm, where he might end his days in happiness and freedom. Perhaps this singular adventure, which is marked with so many circumstances of truth and nature, was related by Attalus himself to his cousin or nephew, the first historian of the Franks. Gregory of Tours[1] was born about sixty years after the death of Sidonius Apollinaris; and their situation was almost similar, since each of them was a native of Auvergne, a senator, and a bishop. The difference of their style and sentiments may, therefore, express the decay of Gaul; and clearly ascertain how much, in so short a space, the human mind had lost of its energy and refinement.[2]

We are now qualified to despise the opposite, and perhaps artful, misrepresentations which have softened or exaggerated

1 The parents of Gregory (Gregorius Florentius Georgius) were of noble extraction (*natalibus . . . illustres*), and they possessed large estates (*latifundia*) both in Auvergne and Burgundy. He was born in the year 539, was consecrated bishop of Tours in 573, and died in 593 or 595, soon after he had terminated his history. See his Life by Odo, abbot of Clugny (in tom. ii. p. 129–135), and a new Life in the Mémoires de l'Académie, etc., tom. xxvi. p. 598–637.

2 Decedente atque immo potius pereunte ab urbibus Gallicanis liberalium culturâ literarum, etc. (in præfat. in tom. ii. p. 137), is the complaint of Gregory himself, which he fully verifies by his own work. His style is equally devoid of elegance and simplicity. In a conspicuous station he still remained a stranger to his own age and country; and in a prolix work (the five last books contain ten years) he has omitted almost everything that posterity desires to learn. I have tediously acquired, by a painful perusal, the right of pronouncing this unfavour-able sentence.

the oppression of the Romans of Gaul under the reign of the
Merovingians. The conquerors never promulgated any *universal*-
edict of servitude or confiscation: but a degenerate people, who
excused their weakness by the specious names of politeness and
peace, was exposed to the arms and laws of the ferocious barbarians, who contemptuously insulted their possessions, their
freedom, and their safety. Their personal injuries were partial and
irregular; but the great body of the Romans survived the revolution, and still preserved the property and privileges of citizens.
A large portion of their lands was exacted for the use of the
Franks: but they enjoyed the remainder exempt from tribute;[1]
and the same irresistible violence which swept away the arts and
manufactures of Gaul destroyed the elaborate and expensive system of Imperial despotism. The provincials must frequently deplore the savage jurisprudence of the Salic or Ripuarian laws; but
their private life, in the important concerns of marriage, testaments, or inheritance, was still regulated by the Theodosian
Code; and a discontented Roman might freely aspire or descend
to the title and character of a barbarian. The honours of the state
were accessible to his ambition: the education and temper of the
Romans more peculiarly qualified them for offices of civil government; and as soon as emulation had rekindled their military
ardour, they were permitted to march in the ranks, or even at
the head, of the victorious Germans. I shall not attempt to
enumerate the generals and magistrates whose names[2] attest the
liberal policy of the Merovingians. The supreme command of
Burgundy, with the title of Patrician, was successively intrusted
to three Romans; and the last and most powerful, Mummolus,[3]

1 The Abbé de Mably (tom. i. p. 247–267) has diligently confirmed this
opinion of the President de Montesquieu (Esprit des Loix, l. xxx. c. 13).

2 See Dubos, Hist. Critique de la Monarchie Françoise, tom. ii. l. vi. c. 9,
10. The French antiquarians establish as a *principle* that the Romans and barbarians may be distinguished by their names. Their names undoubtedly form a
reasonable *presumption;* yet, in reading Gregory of Tours, I have observed Gon-
dulphus, of Senatorian or Roman extraction (l. vi. c. 11, in tom. ii. p. 273), and
Claudius, a barbarian (l. vii. c. 29, p. 303).

3 Eunius Mummolus is repeatedly mentioned by Gregory of Tours, from
the fourth (c. 42, p. 224) to the seventh (c. 40, p. 310) book. The computation
by talents is singular enough; but if Gregory attached any meaning to that obsolete word, the treasures of Mummolus must have exceeded £100,000 sterling.

who alternately saved and disturbed the monarchy, had supplanted his father in the station of count of Autun, and left a
treasure of thirty talents of gold and two hundred and fifty
talents of silver. The fierce and illiterate barbarians were excluded, during several generations, from the dignities, and even
from the orders, of the church.[1] The clergy of Gaul consisted
almost entirely of native provincials; the haughty Franks fell
prostrate at the feet of their subjects who were dignified with
the episcopal character; and the power and riches which had
been lost in war were insensibly recovered by superstition.[2] In
all temporal affairs the Theodosian Code was the universal law
of the clergy; but the barbaric jurisprudence had liberally provided for their personal safety: a sub-deacon was equivalent to
two Franks; the *antrustion* and priest were held in similar estimation; and the life of a bishop was appreciated far above the
common standard, at the price of nine hundred pieces of gold.[3]
The Romans communicated to their conquerors the use of the
Christian religion and Latin language;[4] but their language and
their religion had alike degenerated from the simple purity of the
Augustan and Apostolic age. The progress of superstition and
barbarism was rapid and universal: the worship of the saints
concealed from vulgar eyes the God of the Christians, and the
rustic dialect of peasants and soldiers was corrupted by a Teutonic idiom and pronunciation. Yet such intercourse of sacred
and social communion eradicated the distinctions of birth and

1 See Fleury, Discours iii. sur l'Histoire Ecclésiastique.

2 The bishop of Tours himself has recorded the complaint of Chilperic,
the grandson of Clovis. Ecce pauper remansit fiscus noster; ecce divitiæ nostræ
ad ecclesias sunt translatæ: nulli penitus nisi soli Episcopi regnant (l. vi. c. 46,
in tom. ii. p. 291).

3 See the Ripuarian Code (tit. xxxvi. in tom. iv. p. 241). The Salic law does
not provide for the safety of the clergy; and we might suppose, on the behalf
of the more civilised tribe, that they had not foreseen such an impious act as
the murder of a priest. Yet Prætextatus, archbishop of Rouen, was assassinated
by the order of queen Fredegundis before the altar (Greg. Turon. l. viii. c. 31,
in tom. ii. p. 326).

4 M. Bonamy (Mém. de l'Académie des Inscriptions, tom. xxiv. p. 582–670)
has ascertained the *Lingua Romana Rustica*, which, through the medium of the
Romance, has gradually been polished into the actual form of the French language. Under the Carlovingian race the kings and nobles of France still understood the dialect of their German ancestors.

victory; and the nations of Gaul were gradually confounded under the name and government of the Franks.

The Franks, after they mingled with their Gallic subjects, might have imparted the most valuable of human gifts, a spirit and system of constitutional liberty. Under a king, hereditary but limited, the chiefs and counsellors might have debated at Paris in the palace of the Cæsars: the adjacent field, where the emperors reviewed their mercenary legions, would have admitted the legislative assembly of freemen and warriors; and the rude model which had been sketched in the woods of Germany[1] might have been polished and improved by the civil wisdom of the Romans. But the careless barbarians, secure of their personal independence, disdained the labour of government: the annual assemblies of the month of March were silently abolished, and the nation was separated and almost dissolved by the conquest of Gaul.[2] The monarchy was left without any regular establishment of justice, of arms, or of revenue. The successors of Clovis wanted resolution to assume, or strength to exercise, the legislative and executive powers which the people had abdicated: the royal prerogative was distinguished only by a more ample privilege of rapine and murder; and the love of freedom, so often invigorated and disgraced by private ambition, was reduced among the licentious Franks to the contempt of order and the desire of impunity. Seventy-five years after the death of Clovis, his grandson Gontran, king of Burgundy, sent an army to invade the Gothic possessions of Septimania, or Languedoc. The troops of Burgundy, Berry, Auvergne, and the adjacent territories were excited by the hopes of spoil. They marched without discipline under the banners of German or Gallic counts: their attack was feeble and unsuccessful, but the friendly and hostile provinces were desolated with indiscriminate rage. The corn-fields, the villages, the churches themselves, were consumed by fire; the inhabitants were massacred or dragged into captivity; and, in the disorderly retreat, five thousand of these inhuman savages

1 Ce beau systême a été trouvé dans les bois. Montesquieu, Esprit des Loix, l. xi. c. 6.

2 See the Abbé de Mably, Observations, etc., tom. i. p. 34–56. It should seem that the institution of national assemblies, which are coeval with the French nation, has never been congenial to its temper.

were destroyed by hunger or intestine discord. When the pious Gontran reproached the guilt or neglect of their leaders, and threatened to inflict, not a legal sentence, but instant and arbitrary execution, they accused the universal and incurable corruption of the people. 'No one,' they said, 'any longer fears or respects his king, his duke, or his count. Each man loves to do evil, and freely indulges his criminal inclinations. The most gentle correction provokes an immediate tumult, and the rash magistrate who presumes to censure or restrain his seditious subjects seldom escapes alive from their revenge." It has been reserved for the same nation to expose, by their intemperate vices, the most odious abuse of freedom, and to supply its loss by the spirit of honour and humanity which now alleviates and dignifies their obedience to an absolute sovereign.

The Visigoths had resigned to Clovis the greatest part of their Gallic possessions; but their loss was amply compensated by the easy conquest and secure enjoyment of the provinces of Spain. From the monarchy of the Goths, which soon involved the Suevic kingdom of Gallicia, the modern Spaniards still derive some national vanity, but the historian of the Roman empire is neither invited nor compelled to pursue the obscure and barren series of their annals.² The Goths of Spain were separated from the rest of mankind by the lofty ridge of the Pyrenæan mountains: their manners and institutions, as far as they were common to the Germanic tribes, have been already explained. I have anticipated in the preceding chapter the most important of their ecclesiastical events – the fall of Arianism and the persecution of the Jews: and it only remains to observe some interesting circumstances which relate to the civil and ecclesiastical constitution of the Spanish kingdom.

1 Gregory of Tours (l. viii. c. 30, in tom. ii. p. 325, 326) relates, with much indifference, the crimes, the reproof, and the apology. Nullus Regem metuit, nullus Ducem, nullus Comitem reveretur; et si fortassis alicui ista displicent, et ea, pro longævitate vitæ vestræ, emendare conatur, statim seditio in populo, statim tumultus exoritur, et in tantum unusquisque contra seniorem, sævâ intentione grassatur, ut vix se credat evadere, si tandem silere nequiverit.

2 Spain in these dark ages has been peculiarly unfortunate. The Franks had a Gregory of Tours; the Saxons, or Angles, a Bede; the Lombards, a Paul Warnefrid, etc. But the history of the Visigoths is contained in the short and imperfect Chronicles of Isidore of Seville and John of Biclar.

After their conversion from idolatry or heresy, the Franks and the Visigoths were disposed to embrace, with equal submission, the inherent evils and the accidental benefits of superstition. But the prelates of France, long before the extinction of the Merovingian race, had degenerated into fighting and hunting barbarians. They disdained the use of synods, forgot the laws of temperance and chastity, and preferred the indulgence of private ambition and luxury to the general interest of the sacerdotal profession.[1] The bishops of Spain respected themselves, and were respected by the public: their indissoluble union disguised their vices, and confirmed their authority; and the regular discipline of the church introduced peace, order and stability into the government of the state. From the reign of Recared, the first catholic king, to that of Witiza, the immediate predecessor of the unfortunate Roderic, sixteen national councils were successively convened. The six metropolitans, Toledo, Seville, Merida, Braga, Tarragona, and Narbonne, presided according to their respective seniority; the assembly was composed of their suffragan bishops, who appeared in person or by their proxies, and a place was assigned to the most holy or opulent of the Spanish abbots. During the first three days of the convocation, as long as they agitated the ecclesiastical questions of doctrine and discipline, the profane laity was excluded from their debates, which were conducted, however, with decent solemnity. But on the morning of the fourth day the doors were thrown open for the entrance of the great officers of the palace, the dukes and counts of the provinces, the judges of the cities, and the Gothic nobles; and the decrees of Heaven were ratified by the consent of the people. The same rules were observed in the provincial assemblies, the annual synods, which were empowered to hear complaints and to redress grievances; and a legal government was supported by the prevailing influence of the Spanish clergy. The bishops, who in each revolution were prepared to flatter the victorious and to insult the prostrate, laboured with diligence and success to kindle the flames of persecution, and to exalt the mitre above the

[1] Such are the complaints of St. Boniface, the apostle of Germany and the reformer of Gaul (in tom. iv. p. 94). The fourscore years which he deplores of licence and corruption would seem to insinuate that the barbarians were admitted into the clergy about the year 660.

crown. Yet the national councils of Toledo, in which the free spirit of the barbarians was tempered and guided by episcopal policy, have established some prudent laws for the common benefit of the king and people. The vacancy of the throne was supplied by the choice of the bishops and palatines; and after the failure of the line of Alaric, the regal dignity was still limited to the pure and noble blood of the Goths. The clergy, who anointed their lawful prince, always recommended, and sometimes practised, the duty of allegiance: and the spiritual censures were denounced on the heads of the impious subjects who should resist his authority, conspire against his life, or violate by an indecent union the chastity even of his widow. But the monarch himself, when he ascended the throne, was bound by a reciprocal oath to God and his people that he would faithfully execute his important trust. The real or imaginary faults of his administration were subject to the control of a powerful aristocracy; and the bishops and palatines were guarded by a fundamental privilege that they should not be degraded, imprisoned, tortured, nor punished with death, exile, or confiscation, unless by the free and public judgment of their peers.[1]

One of these legislative councils of Toledo examined and ratified the code of laws which had been compiled by a succession of Gothic kings, from the fierce Euric to the devout Egica. As long as the Visigoths themselves were satisfied with the rude customs of their ancestors, they indulged their subjects of Aquitain and Spain in the enjoyment of the Roman law. Their gradual improvement in arts, in policy, and at length in religion, encouraged them to imitate and to supersede these foreign institutions, and to compose a code of civil and criminal jurisprudence for the use of a great and united people. The same obligations and the same privileges were communicated to the nations of the Spanish monarchy; and the conquerors, insensibly renouncing the Teutonic idiom, submitted to the restraints of equity, and

---

1 The acts of the councils of Toledo are still the most authentic records of the church and constitution of Spain. The following passages are particularly important: – iii. 17, 18; iv. 75; v. 2, 3, 4, 5, 8; vi. 11, 12, 13, 14, 17, 18; vii. 1; xiii. 2, 3, 6. I have found Mascou (Hist. of the Ancient Germans, xv. 29, and Annotations, xxvi. and xxxiii.) and Ferreras (Hist. Générale de l'Espagne, tom. ii.) very useful and accurate guides.

exalted the Romans to the participation of freedom. The merit of this impartial policy was enhanced by the situation of Spain under the reign of the Visigoths. The provincials were long separated from their Arian masters by the irreconcilable difference of religion. After the conversion of Recared had removed the prejudices of the catholics, the coasts both of the Ocean and Mediterranean were still possessed by the Eastern emperors, who secretly excited a discontented people to reject the yoke of the barbarians, and to assert the name and dignity of Roman citizens. The allegiance of doubtful subjects is indeed most effectually secured by their own persuasion that they hazard more in a revolt than they can hope to obtain by a revolution; but it has appeared so natural to oppress those whom we hate and fear, that the contrary system well deserves the praise of wisdom and moderation.[1]

While the kingdoms of the Franks and Visigoths were established in Gaul and Spain, the Saxons achieved the conquest of Britain, the third great diocese of the præfecture of the West. Since Britain was already separated from the Roman empire, I might without reproach decline a story familiar to the most illiterate, and obscure to the most learned, of my readers. The Saxons, who excelled in the use of the oar or the battle-axe, were ignorant of the art which could alone perpetuate the fame of their exploits; the provincials, relapsing into barbarism, neglected to describe the ruin of their country; and the doubtful tradition was almost extinguished before the missionaries of Rome restored the light of science and Christianity. The declamations of Gildas, the fragments or fables of Nennius, the obscure hints of the Saxon laws and chronicles, and the ecclesiastical tales of the venerable Bede,[2] have been illustrated by the diligence, and

1 The Code of the Visigoths, regularly divided into twelve books, has been correctly published by Dom Bouquet (in tom. iv. p. 283–460). It has been treated by the President de Montesquieu (Esprit des Loix, l. xxviii. c. 1) with excessive severity. I dislike the style; I detest the superstition; but I shall presume to think that the civil jurisprudence displays a more civilised and enlightened state of society than that of the Burgundians or even of the Lombards.

2 See Gildas de Excidio Britanniæ, c. 11–25, p. 4–9, edit. Gale; Nennius, Hist. Britonum, c. 28, 35–65, p. 105–115, edit. Gale; Bede, Hist. Ecclesiast. Gentis Anglorum, l. i. c. 12–16, p. 49–53, c. 22, p. 58, edit. Smith; Chron.

sometimes embellished by the fancy, of succeeding writers, whose works I am not ambitious either to censure or to transcribe.[1] Yet the historian of the empire may be tempted to pursue the revolutions of a Roman province till it vanishes from his sight; and an Englishman may curiously trace the establishment of the barbarians from whom he derives his name, his laws, and perhaps his origin.

About forty years after the dissolution of the Roman government Vortigern appears to have obtained the supreme, though precarious, command of the princes and cities of Britain. That unfortunate monarch has been almost unanimously condemned for the weak and mischievous policy of inviting[2] a formidable stranger to repel the vexatious inroads of a domestic foe. His ambassadors are despatched by the gravest historians to the coast of Germany: they address a pathetic oration to the general assembly of the Saxons, and those warlike barbarians resolve to assist with a fleet and army the suppliants of a distant and unknown island. If Britain had indeed been unknown to the Saxons, the measure of its calamities would have been less complete. But the strength of the Roman government could not always guard the maritime province against the pirates of Germany: the independent and divided states were exposed to their attacks, and the Saxons might sometimes join the Scots and the Picts in a tacit or express confederacy of rapine and destruction. Vortigern could only balance the various perils which assaulted on every side his throne and his people; and his policy may deserve

Saxonicum, p. 11–23, etc., edit. Gibson. The Anglo-Saxon laws were published by Wilkins, London, 1731, in folio; and the Leges Wallicæ, by Wotton and Clarke, London, 1730, in folio.

1 The laborious Mr. Carte and the ingenious Mr. Whitaker are the two modern writers to whom I am principally indebted. The particular historian of Manchester embraces, under that obscure title, a subject almost as extensive as the general history of England.

2 This *invitation*, which may derive some countenance from the loose expressions of Gildas and Bede, is framed into a regular story by Witikind, a Saxon monk of the tenth century (see Cousin, Hist. de l'Empire d'Occident, tom. ii. p. 356). Rapin, and even Hume, have too freely used this suspicious evidence without regarding the precise and probable testimony of Nennius: Interea venerunt tres Chiulæ à Germaniâ *in exilio pulsæ*, in quibus erant Hors et Hengist [c. 28].

either praise or excuse if he preferred the alliance of *those* barbarians whose naval power rendered them the most dangerous enemies, and the most serviceable allies. Hengist and Horsa, as they ranged along the eastern coast with three ships, were engaged by the promise of an ample stipend to embrace the defence of Britain, and their intrepid valour soon delivered the country from the Caledonian invaders. The Isle of Thanet, a secure and fertile district, was allotted for the residence of these German auxiliaries, and they were supplied according to the treaty with a plentiful allowance of clothing and provisions. This favourable reception encouraged five thousand warriors to embark with their families in seventeen vessels, and the infant power of Hengist was fortified by this strong and seasonable reinforcement. The crafty barbarian suggested to Vortigern the obvious advantage of fixing, in the neighbourhood of the Picts, a colony of faithful allies: a third fleet, of forty ships, under the command of his son and nephew, sailed from Germany, ravaged the Orkneys, and disembarked a new army on the coast of Northumberland or Lothian, at the opposite extremity of the devoted land. It was easy to foresee, but it was impossible to prevent, the impending evils. The two nations were soon divided and exasperated by mutual jealousies. The Saxons magnified all that they had done and suffered in the cause of an ungrateful people; while the Britons regretted the liberal rewards which could not satisfy the avarice of those haughty mercenaries. The causes of fear and hatred were inflamed into an irreconcilable quarrel. The Saxons flew to arms; and if they perpetrated a treacherous massacre during the security of a feast, they destroyed the reciprocal confidence which sustains the intercourse of peace and war.[1]

---

1 Nennius imputes to the Saxons the murder of three hundred British chiefs; a crime not unsuitable to their savage manners. But we are not obliged to believe (see Jeffrey of Monmouth, l. viii. c. 9–12) that Stonehenge is their monument, which the giants had formerly transported from Africa to Ireland, and which was removed to Britain by the order of Ambrosius and the art of Merlin.

[Macaulay remarks that 'Hengist and Horsa, Vortigern and Rowena, Arthur and Mordred, are mythical persons whose very existence may be questioned,

Hengist, who boldly aspired to the conquest of Britain, exhorted his countrymen to embrace the glorious opportunity: he painted in lively colours the fertility of the soil, the wealth of the cities, the pusillanimous temper of the natives, and the convenient situation of a spacious solitary island, accessible on all sides to the Saxon fleets. The successive colonies which issued in the period of a century from the mouths of the Elbe, the Weser, and the Rhine, were principally composed of three valiant tribes or nations of Germany; the *Jutes*, the *old Saxons*, and the *Angles*. The Jutes, who fought under the peculiar banner of Hengist, assumed the merit of leading their countrymen in the paths of glory, and of erecting in Kent the first independent kingdom. The fame of the enterprise was attributed to the primitive Saxons, and the common laws and language of the conquerors are described by the national appellation of a people which, at the end of four hundred years, produced the first monarchs of South Britain. The Angles were distinguished by their numbers and their success; and they claimed the honour of fixing a perpetual name on the country of which they occupied the most ample portion. The barbarians, who followed the hopes of rapine either on the land or sea, were insensibly blended with this triple

and whose adventures may be classed with those of Hercules and Romulus.' *History of England*, vol. i. p. 6.

The details of the Saxon conquest are very obscure, there being no reliable account by any contemporary writer, and rest wholly on tradition. Yet, as Freeman well says, there is no absurdity in the familiar story that a British prince took Teutonic mercenaries into his pay, and that these dangerous allies took advantage of the weakness of their hosts to establish themselves as permanent possessors of part of the island. If the story in question be rejected, the general narrative of the conquest is not affected. The conquest of England by the Saxons began somewhere about 449 A.D., but it is a mistake to set a hard and fast date, for there is evidence that there were Saxons in England before that date, because in the Notitia Imperii, which was drawn up about A.D. 400, there is mentioned as an officer of state 'Comes littoris Saxonici per Britannias,' whose government extended along the coast from the neighbourhood of Portsmouth to the Wash. The Saxons ravaged the coast of Britain in their piratical expeditions as early as A.D. 287, and it may reasonably be supposed that not long after that date they began to form isolated settlements in the island. 'The count of the Saxon shore' may either have taken his name from the shore exposed to the attacks of Saxon pirates, or from the shore peopled by Saxon colonists. See R. C. Collingwood and J. N. L. Myres, *Roman Britain and the English Settlements*, 1937; Sir F. Stenton, *Anglo-Saxon England*, 1937.

confederacy; the *Frisians*, who had been tempted by their vicinity to the British shores, might balance during a short space the strength and reputation of the native Saxons; the *Danes*, the *Prussians*, the *Rugians*, are faintly described; and some adventurous *Huns*, who had wandered as far as the Baltic, might embark on board the German vessels for the conquest of a new world.[1] But this arduous achievement was not prepared or executed by the union of national powers. Each intrepid chieftain, according to the measure of his fame and fortunes, assembled his followers; equipped a fleet of three, or perhaps of sixty, vessels; chose the place of the attack, and conducted his subsequent operations according to the events of the war and the dictates of his private interest. In the invasion of Britain many heroes vanquished and fell; but only seven victorious leaders assumed, or at least maintained, the title of kings. Seven independent thrones, the Saxon Heptarchy, were founded by the conquerors; and seven families, one of which has been continued, by female succession, to our present sovereign, derived their equal and sacred lineage from Woden, the god of war. It has been pretended that this republic of kings was moderated by a general council and a supreme magistrate. But such an artificial scheme of policy is repugnant to the rude and turbulent spirit of the Saxons: their laws are silent, and their imperfect annals afford only a dark and bloody prospect of intestine discord.[2]

A monk, who in the profound ignorance of human life has presumed to exercise the office of historian, strangely disfigures

1 All these tribes are expressly enumerated by Bede (l. i. c. 15, p. 52, l. v. c. 9, p. 190); and though I have considered Mr. Whitaker's remarks (Hist. of Manchester, vol. ii. p. 538–543), I do not perceive the absurdity of supposing that the Frisians, etc., were mingled with the Anglo-Saxons.

2 Bede has enumerated seven kings – two Saxons, a Jute, and four Angles – who successively acquired in the heptarchy an indefinite supremacy of power and renown. But their reign was the effect, not of law, but of conquest; and he observes, in similar terms, that one of them subdued the Isles of Man and Anglesey; and that another imposed a tribute on the Scots and Picts (Hist. Eccles. l. ii. c. 5, p. 83).

[The term Heptarchy no longer has any significance in fact, and must be rejected as conveying an idea radically erroneous. At no period were there ever in Saxon England seven kingdoms independent of each other. Mr. Sharon Turner was the first to confute the old-established doctrine that Saxon England was heptarchical in character. – O. S.]

the state of Britain at the time of its separation from the Western empire. Gildas[1] describes in florid language the improvements of agriculture, the foreign trade which flowed with every tide into the Thames and the Severn, the solid and lofty construction of public and private edifices: he accuses the sinful luxury of the British people; of a people, according to the same writer, ignorant of the most simple arts, and incapable, without the aid of the Romans, of providing walls of stone or weapons of iron for the defence of their native land.[2] Under the long dominion of the emperors, Britain had been insensibly moulded into the elegant and servile form of a Roman province, whose safety was intrusted to a foreign power. The subjects of Honorius contemplated their new freedom with surprise and terror; they were left destitute of any civil or military constitution; and their uncertain rulers wanted either skill, or courage, or authority to direct the public force against the common enemy. The introduction of the Saxons betrayed their internal weakness, and degraded the character both of the prince and people. Their consternation magnified the danger, the want of union diminished their resources, and the madness of civil factions was more solicitous to accuse than to remedy the evils which they imputed to the misconduct of their adversaries. Yet the Britons were not ignorant, they could not be ignorant, of the manufacture or the use of arms: the successive and disorderly attacks of the Saxons allowed them to recover from their amazement, and the prosperous or adverse events of the war added discipline and experience to their native valour.

While the continent of Europe and Africa yielded, without resistance, to the barbarians, the British island, alone and unaided, maintained a long, a vigorous, though an unsuccessful, struggle, against the formidable pirates who, almost at the same instant, assaulted the northern, the eastern, and the southern coasts. The cities, which had been fortified with skill, were defended with resolution; the advantages of ground, hills, forests, and morasses, were diligently improved by the inhabitants; the

1 See Gildas de Excidio Britanniæ, c. i. p. 1, edit. Gale.

2 Mr. Whitaker (History of Manchester, vol. ii. p. 503, 516) has smartly exposed this glaring absurdity, which had passed unnoticed by the general historians, as they were hastening to more interesting and important events.

conquest of each district was purchased with blood; and the defeats of the Saxons are strongly attested by the discreet silence of their annalist. Hengist might hope to achieve the conquest of Britain; but his ambition, in an active reign of thirty-five years, was confined to the possession of Kent; and the numerous colony which he had planted in the North was extirpated by the sword of the Britons. The monarchy of the West Saxons was laboriously founded by the persevering efforts of three martial generations. The life of Cerdic, one of the bravest of the children of Woden, was consumed in the conquest of Hampshire and the Isle of Wight; and the loss which he sustained in the battle of Mount Badon reduced him to a state of inglorious repose. Kenric, his valiant son, advanced into Wiltshire; besieged Salisbury, at that time seated on a commanding eminence; and vanquished an army which advanced to the relief of the city. In the subsequent battle of Marlborough,[1] his British enemies displayed their military science. Their troops were formed in three lines; each line consisted of three distinct bodies; and the cavalry, the archers, and the pikemen were distributed according to the principles of Roman tactics. The Saxons charged in one weighty column, boldly encountered with their short swords the long lances of the Britons, and maintained an equal conflict till the approach of night. Two decisive victories, the death of three British kings, and the reduction of Cirencester, Bath, and Gloucester, established the fame and power of Ceaulin, the grandson of Cerdic, who carried his victorious arms to the banks of the Severn.

After a war of an hundred years the independent Britons still occupied the whole extent of the western coast, from the wall of Antoninus to the extreme promontory of Cornwall; and the principal cities of the inland country still opposed the arms of the barbarians. Resistance became more languid, as the number and boldness of the assailants continually increased. Winning

1 At Beran-birig, or Barbury-castle, near Marlborough. The Saxon Chronicle assigns the name and date. Camden (Britannia, vol. i. p. 128) ascertains the place; and Henry of Huntingdon (Scriptores post Bedam, p. 314) relates the circumstances of this battle. They are probable and characteristic; and the historians of the twelfth century might consult some materials that no longer exist.

their way by slow and painful efforts, the Saxons, the Angles, and their various confederates, advanced from the North, from the East, and from the South, till their victorious banners were united in the centre of the island. Beyond the Severn the Britons still asserted their national freedom, which survived the heptarchy, and even the monarchy, of the Saxons. The bravest warriors, who preferred exile to slavery, found a secure refuge in the mountains of Wales: the reluctant submission of Cornwall was delayed for some ages;[1] and a band of fugitives acquired a settlement in Gaul, by their own valour, or the liberality of the Merovingian kings.[2] The western angle of Armorica acquired the new appellations of *Cornwall* and the *Lesser Britain;* and the vacant lands of the Osismii were filled by a strange people, who, under the authority of their counts and bishops, preserved the laws and language of their ancestors. To the feeble descendants of Clovis and Charlemagne, the Britons of Armorica refused the customary tribute, subdued the neighbouring dioceses of Vannes, Rennes, and Nantes, and formed a powerful, though vassal, state, which has been united to the crown of France.[3]

1 Cornwall was finally subdued by Athelstan (A.D. 927–941), who planted an English colony at Exeter, and confined the Britons beyond the river Tamar. See William of Malmesbury, l. ii. in the Scriptores post Bedam, p. 50. The spirit of the Cornish knights was degraded by servitude: and it should seem, from the romance of Sir Tristram, that their cowardice was almost proverbial.

2 The establishment of the Britons in Gaul is proved in the sixth century by Procopius [Bell. Goth. iv. 20], Gregory of Tours, the second council of Tours (A.D. 567), and the least suspicious of their chronicles and lives of saints. The subscription of a bishop of the Britons to the first council of Tours (A.D. 461, or rather 481), the army of Riothamus, and the loose declamation of Gildas (alii transmarinas petebant regiones, c. 25, p. 8), may countenance an emigration as early as the middle of the fifth century. Beyond that era the Britons of Armorica can be found only in romance; and I am surprised that Mr. Whitaker (Genuine History of the Britons, p. 214–221) should so faithfully transcribe the gross ignorance of Carte, whose venial errors he has so rigorously chastised.

[Lappenberg asserts that as early as the usurpation of Maximus in Britain, there was a settlement in Armorica of a Roman military colony (*milites limitanei*), consisting of British warriors, which has given name as well as a distinctive character to Bretagne. See accounts in Gildas, c. 10; Nennius, c. 23. Bæda also gives the words of Gildas. – O. S.]

3 The antiquities of *Bretagne*, which have been the subject even of political controversy, are illustrated by Hadrian Valesius (Notitia Galliarum, sub voce

In a century of perpetual, or at least implacable, war, much courage, and some skill, must have been exerted for the defence of Britain. Yet if the memory of its champions is almost buried in oblivion, we need not repine; since every age, however destitute of science or virtue, sufficiently abounds with acts of blood and military renown. The tomb of Vortimer, the son of Vortigern, was erected on the margin of the sea-shore, as a landmark formidable to the Saxons, whom he had thrice vanquished in the fields of Kent. Ambrosius Aurelian was descended from a noble family of Romans;[1] his modesty was equal to his valour, and his valour, till the last fatal action,[2] was crowned with splendid success. But every British name is effaced by the illustrious name of ARTHUR,[3] the hereditary prince of the Silures, in South

---

Britannia Cismarina, p. 98–100), M. d'Anville (Notice de l'Ancienne Gaule, *Corisopiti, Curiosolites, Osismii, Vorganium*, p. 248, 258, 508, 720, and Etats de l'Europe, p. 76–80), Longuerue (Description de la France, tom. i. p. 84–94), and the Abbé de Vertot (Hist. Critique de l'Etablissement des Bretons dans les Gaules, 2 vols. in 12mo. Paris, 1720). I may assume the merit of examining the original evidence which they have produced.

[Bretagne unquestionably had an existence of its own much earlier than is commonly supposed. Milman says that after careful study of Gallet (*Mémoires sur la Bretagne*) and Daru (*Histoire de Bretagne*), these writers appear to him to establish the point of the independence of Bretagne at the time that the insular Britons took refuge in their country, and that the greater part landed as fugitives rather than conquerors. – O. S.]

1 Bede, who in his chronicle (p. 28) places Ambrosius under the reign of Zeno (A.D. 474–491), observes that his parents had been 'purpurâ induti;' which he explains, in his ecclesiastical history, by 'regium nomen et insigne ferentibus' (l. i. c. 16, p. 53). The expression of Nennius (c. 44, p. 110, edit. Gale) is still more singular, 'Unus de *consulibus* gentis Romanicæ est pater meus.'

2 By the unanimous, though doubtful, conjecture of our antiquarians, Ambrosius is confounded with Natanleod, who (A.D. 508) lost his own life and five thousand of his subjects in a battle against Cerdic, the West Saxon (Chron. Saxon. p. 17, 18).

3 As I am a stranger to the Welsh bards, Myrdhin, Llomarch, and Taliessin, my faith in the existence and exploits of Arthur principally rests on the simple and circumstantial testimony of Nennius (Hist. Brit. c. 62, 63, p. 114). Mr. Whitaker (Hist. of Manchester, vol. ii. p. 31–71) has framed an interesting, and even probable, narrative of the wars of Arthur: though it is impossible to allow the reality of the round table.

[Gibbon quotes these names incorrectly. Myrdhin, Llomarch, and Taliessin are probably meant for Merlin, Llywarch Hen, or 'The Aged,' and Taliessin. See Sharon Turner's Essay on the Welsh Bards. – O. S.]

Wales, and the elective king or general of the nation. According to the most rational account, he defeated, in twelve successive battles, the Angles of the North and the Saxons of the West; but the declining age of the hero was embittered by popular ingratitude and domestic misfortunes. The events of his life are less interesting than the singular revolutions of his fame. During a period of five hundred years the tradition of his exploits was preserved, and rudely embellished, by the obscure bards of Wales and Armorica, who were odious to the Saxons, and unknown to the rest of mankind. The pride and curiosity of the Norman conquerors prompted them to inquire into the ancient history of Britain; they listened with fond credulity to the tale of Arthur, and eagerly applauded the merit of a prince who had triumphed over the Saxons, their common enemies. His romance, transcribed in the Latin of Jeffrey of Monmouth, and afterwards translated into the fashionable idiom of the times, was enriched with the various, though incoherent, ornaments which were familiar to the experience, the learning, or the fancy of the twelfth century. The progress of a Phrygian colony, from the Tiber to the Thames, was easily engrafted on the fable of the Æneid; and the royal ancestors of Arthur derived their origin from Troy, and claimed their alliance with the Cæsars. His trophies were decorated with captive provinces and Imperial titles; and his Danish victories avenged the recent injuries of his country. The gallantry and superstition of the British hero, his feasts and tournaments, and the memorable institution of his Knights of the *Round Table*, were faithfully copied from the reigning manners of chivalry; and the fabulous exploits of Uther's son appear less incredible than the adventures which were achieved by the enterprising valour of the Normans. Pilgrimage, and the holy wars, introduced into Europe the specious miracles of Arabian magic. Fairies and giants, flying dragons and enchanted palaces, were blended with the more simple fictions of the West; and the fate of Britain depended on the art, or the predictions, of Merlin. Every nation embraced and adorned the popular romance of Arthur and the Knights of the Round Table: their names were celebrated in Greece[1] and

1 [With reference to the Arthurian cycle of romance, as early as the twelfth century, a Greek epic poem, brought to light in the middle of the nineteenth

Italy; and the voluminous tales of Sir Lancelot and Sir Tristram[1] were devoutly studied by the princes and nobles who disregarded the genuine heroes and historians of antiquity. At length the light of science and reason was rekindled; the talisman was broken; the visionary fabric melted into air; and by a natural, though unjust, reverse of the public opinion, the severity of the present age is inclined to question the *existence* of Arthur.[2]

Resistance, if it cannot avert, must increase the miseries of conquest; and conquest has never appeared more dreadful and destructive than in the hands of the Saxons, who hated the valour of their enemies, disdained the faith of treaties, and violated, without remorse, the most sacred objects of the Christian worship. The fields of battle might be traced, almost in every district, by monuments of bones; the fragments of falling towers were stained with blood; the last of the Britons, without distinction of age or sex, was massacred,[3] in the ruins of Anderida;[4] and

century, was composed in celebration of Arthur and the Knights of the Round Table. It was first published by Von der Hagen in his *Denkmale des Mittelaters*, Berlin, 1824. It should be carefully studied. – O. S.]

1 [Regarding the poems, 'Tristram' and 'Lancelot du Laik,' the former may be said to have been brought to modern knowledge by Sir Walter Scott, whose edition, if now somewhat obsolete, is still full of interesting antiquarian information. 'Lancelot' has been immortalised by Tennyson in his 'Idylls of the King,' but the original poem was edited in 1865 by Dr. W. W. Skeat for the Early English Text Society, and is entitled 'Lancelot of the Laik,' a Scottish metrical romance about 1490–1500 re-edited from a MS. in Cambridge University Library. A former edition had been edited by Mr. Joseph Stevenson in 1839 for the Maitland Club, but was full of errors, consequent upon the state of etymological and philological scholarship at the time. These two poems were the great metrical romances of the Middle Ages. – O. S.]

2 The progress of romance and the state of learning in the middle ages are illustrated by Mr. Thomas Warton, with the taste of a poet and the minute diligence of an antiquarian. I have derived much instruction from the two learned dissertations prefixed to the first volume of his History of English Poetry.

3 Hoc anno (490) Ælla et Cissa obsederunt Andredes-Ceaster; et interfecerunt omnes qui id incolerent; adeo ut ne unus Brito ibi superstes fuerit (Chron. Saxon. p. 15); an expression more dreadful in its simplicity than all the vague and tedious lamentations of the British Jeremiah.

4 Andredes-Ceaster, or Anderida, is placed by Camden (Britannia, vol. i. p. 258) at Newenden, in the marshy grounds of Kent, which might be formerly covered by the sea, and on the edge of the great forest (Anderida) which overspread so large a portion of Hampshire and Sussex.

the repetition of such calamities was frequent and familiar under the Saxon heptarchy. The arts and religion, the laws and language, which the Romans had so carefully planted in Britain, were extirpated by their barbarous successors. After the destruction of the principal churches, the bishops who had declined the crown of martyrdom retired with the holy relics into Wales and Armorica; the remains of their flocks were left destitute of any spiritual food; the practice, and even the remembrance, of Christianity were abolished; and the British clergy might obtain some comfort from the damnation of the idolatrous strangers. The kings of France maintained the privileges of their Roman subjects; but the ferocious Saxons trampled on the laws of Rome and of the emperors. The proceedings of civil and criminal jurisdiction, the titles of honour, the forms of office, the ranks of society, and even the domestic rights of marriage, testament, and inheritance, were finally suppressed; and the indiscriminate crowd of noble and plebeian slaves was governed by the traditionary customs which had been coarsely framed for the shepherds and pirates of Germany. The language of science, of business, and of conversation, which had been introduced by the Romans, was lost in the general desolation. A sufficient number of Latin or Celtic words might be assumed by the Germans to express their new wants and ideas;[1] but those *illiterate* Pagans preserved and established the use of their national dialect.[2] Almost every name, conspicuous either in the church or state,

1 Dr. Johnson affirms that *few* English words are of British extraction. Mr. Whitaker, who understands the British language, has discovered more than *three thousand*, and actually produces a long and various catalogue (vol. ii. p. 235–329). It is possible, indeed, that many of these words may have been imported from the Latin or Saxon into the native idiom of Britain.

[Since Gibbon's time the science of philology has been completely revolutionised, and the Keltic family of languages has now taken its place as one of the branches of the great Indo-European group. It is now clear that the Anglo-Saxons adopted Keltic words to a far greater extent than was supposed. Many words denoting the daily processes of agriculture, domestic life, and generally those expressive of indoor and outdoor service, have been taken by us from the Keltic. Cf. Garnett, *Transactions Philological Society*, vol. i. p. 169; also *First Steps in English Accidence*, by Morris and Skeat. – O. S.]

2 In the beginning of the seventh century the Franks and the Anglo-Saxons mutually understood each other's language, which was derived from the same Teutonic root (Bede, l. i. c. 25, p. 60).

reveals its Teutonic origin;[1] and the geography of *England* was universally inscribed with foreign characters and appellations. The example of a revolution so rapid and so complete may not easily be found; but it will excite a probable suspicion that the arts of Rome were less deeply rooted in Britain than in Gaul or Spain; and that the native rudeness of the country and its inhabitants was covered by a thin varnish of Italian manners.

This strange alteration has persuaded historians, and even philosophers, that the provincials of Britain were totally exterminated; and that the vacant land was again peopled by the perpetual influx and rapid increase of the German colonies. Three hundred thousand Saxons are *said* to have obeyed the summons of Hengist;[2] the entire emigration of the Angles was attested, in the age of Bede, by the solitude of their native country;[3] and our experience has shown the free propagation of the human race, if they are cast on a fruitful wilderness, where their steps are unconfined, and their subsistence is plentiful. The Saxon kingdoms displayed the face of recent discovery and cultivation: the towns were small, the villages were distant; the husbandry was languid and unskilful; four sheep were equivalent to an acre of the best land;[4] an ample space of wood and morass was resigned to the vague dominion of nature; and the modern bishopric of Durham, the whole territory from the Tyne to the Tees, had returned to its primitive state of a savage and solitary forest.[5] Such imperfect population might have been supplied, in some generations, by the English colonies; but neither reason nor

1 After the first generation of Italian or Scottish missionaries, the dignities of the church were filled with Saxon proselytes.

2 Carte's History of England, vol. i. p. 195. He quotes the British historians; but I much fear that Jeffrey of Monmouth (l. vi. c. 15) is his only witness.

3 Bede, Hist. Ecclesiast. l. i. c. 15, p. 52. The fact is probable and well attested: yet such was the loose intermixture of the German tribes, that we find, in a subsequent period, the law of the Angli and Warini of Germany (Lindenbrog. Codex, p. 479–486).

4 See Dr. Henry's useful and laborious History of Great Britain, vol. ii. p. 388.

5 Quicquid (says John of Tinemouth) inter Tynam et Tesam fluvios extitit, sola eremi vastitudo tunc temporis fuit, et idcirco nullius ditioni servivit, eo quod sola indomitorum et silvestrium animalium spelunca et habitatio fuit (apud Carte, vol. i. p. 195). From Bishop Nicholson (English Historical Library, p. 65, 98) I understand that fair copies of John of Tinemouth's ample collections are preserved in the libraries of Oxford, Lambeth, etc.

facts can justify the unnatural supposition that the Saxons of Britain remained alone in the desert which they had subdued. After the sanguinary barbarians had secured their dominion and gratified their revenge, it was their interest to preserve the peasants, as well as the cattle, of the unresisting country. In each successive revolution the patient herd becomes the property of its new masters; and the salutary compact of food and labour is silently ratified by their mutual necessities. Wilfrid, the apostle of Sussex,[1] accepted from his royal convert the gift of the peninsula of Selsey, near Chichester, with the persons and property of its inhabitants, who then amounted to eighty-seven families. He released them at once from spiritual and temporal bondage; and two hundred and fifty slaves of both sexes were baptised by their indulgent master. The kingdom of Sussex, which spread from the sea to the Thames, contained seven thousand families: twelve hundred were ascribed to the Isle of Wight; and, if we multiply this vague computation, it may seem probable that England was cultivated by a million of servants, or *villains*, who were attached to the estates of their arbitrary landlords. The indigent barbarians were often tempted to sell their children or themselves into perpetual, and even foreign, bondage;[2] yet the special exemptions which were granted to *national* slaves[3] sufficiently declare that they were much less numerous than the strangers and captives who had lost their liberty, or changed their masters, by the accidents of war. When time and religion had mitigated the fierce spirit of the Anglo-Saxons, the laws encouraged the frequent practice of manumission; and their subjects, of Welsh or Cambrian extraction, assumed the respectable station of inferior freemen, possessed of lands, and entitled to the rights of civil society.[4] Such gentle treatment might secure the allegiance

1 See the mission of Wilfrid, etc., in Bede, Hist. Eccles. l. iv. c. 13, 16, p. 155, 156, 159.

2 From the concurrent testimony of Bede (l. ii. c. 1. p. 78) and William of Malmesbury (l. iii. p. 102), it appears that the Anglo-Saxons, from the first to the last age, persisted in this unnatural practice. Their youths were publicly sold in the market of Rome.

3 According to the laws of Ina they could not be lawfully sold beyond the seas.

4 The life of a *Wallus*, or *Cambricus, homo*, who possessed a hyde of land, is fixed at 120 shillings, by the same laws (of Ina, tit. xxxii. in Leg. Anglo-Saxon.

of a fierce people, who had been recently subdued on the confines of Wales and Cornwall. The sage Ina, the legislator of
Wessex, united the two nations in the bands of domestic alliance;
and four British lords of Somersetshire may be honourably distinguished in the court of a Saxon monarch.[1]

The independent Britons appear to have relapsed into the
state of original barbarism from whence they had been imperfectly reclaimed. Separated by their enemies from the rest of
mankind, they soon became an object of scandal and abhorrence
to the catholic world.[2] Christianity was still professed in the
mountains of Wales; but the rude schismatics, in the *form* of the
clerical tonsure, and in the *day* of the celebration of Easter,
obstinately resisted the imperious mandates of the Roman pontiffs. The use of the Latin language was insensibly abolished, and
the Britons were deprived of the arts and learning which Italy
communicated to her Saxon proselytes. In Wales and Armorica,
the Celtic tongue, the native idiom of the West, was preserved
and propagated; and the *Bards*, who had been the companions
of the Druids, were still protected, in the sixteenth century, by
the laws of Elizabeth. Their chief, a respectable officer of the
courts of Pengwern, or Aberfraw, or Caermarthen, accompanied
the king's servants to war: the monarchy of the Britons, which
he sung in the front of battle, excited their courage, and justified
their depredations; and the songster claimed for his legitimate
prize the fairest heifer of the spoil. His subordinate ministers,
the masters and disciples of vocal and instrumental music,
visited, in their respective circuits, the royal, the noble, and the
plebeian houses; and the public poverty, almost exhausted by the
clergy, was oppressed by the importunate demands of the bards.
Their rank and merit were ascertained by solemn trials, and the

p. 20) which allowed 200 shillings for a free Saxon, and 1200 for a Thane (see
likewise Leg. Anglo-Saxon. p. 71). We may observe that these legislators, the
West-Saxons and Mercians, continued their British conquests after they became
Christians. The laws of the four kings of Kent do not condescend to notice
the existence of any subject Britons.

1 See Carte's Hist. of England, vol. i. p. 278.

2 At the conclusion of his history (A.D. 731), Bede describes the ecclesiastical state of the island, and censures the implacable, though impotent, hatred
of the Britons against the English nation and the catholic church (l. v. c. 23,
p. 219).

strong belief of supernatural inspiration exalted the fancy of the poet and of his audience.[1] The last retreats of Celtic freedom, the extreme territories of Gaul and Britain, were less adapted to agriculture than to pasturage: the wealth of the Britons consisted in their flocks and herds; milk and flesh were their ordinary food; and bread was sometimes esteemed, or rejected, as a foreign luxury. Liberty had peopled the mountains of Wales and the morasses of Armorica: but their populousness has been maliciously ascribed to the loose practice of polygamy; and the houses of these licentious barbarians have been supposed to contain ten wives, and perhaps fifty children.[2] Their disposition was rash and choleric: they were bold in action and in speech;[3] and as they were ignorant of the arts of peace, they alternately indulged their passions in foreign and domestic war. The cavalry of Armorica, the spearmen of Gwent, and the archers of Merioneth, were equally formidable; but their poverty could seldom procure either shields or helmets; and the inconvenient weight would have retarded the speed and agility of their desultory operations. One of the greatest of the English monarchs was requested to satisfy the curiosity of a Greek emperor concerning the state of Britain; and Henry II. could assert, from his personal experience, that Wales was inhabited by a race of naked warriors, who encountered, without fear, the defensive armour of their enemies.[4]

1 Mr. Pennant's Tour in Wales (p. 426–449) has furnished me with a curious and interesting account of the Welsh bards. In the year 1568 a session was held at Caerwys by the special command of queen Elizabeth, and regular degrees in vocal and instrumental music were conferred on fifty-five minstrels. The prize (a silver harp) was adjudged by the Mostyn family.

2 Regio longe lateque diffusa, milite, magis quam credibile sit, referta. Partibus equidem in illis miles unus quinquaginta generat, sortitus more barbaro denas aut amplius uxores. This reproach of William of Poitiers (in the Historians of France, tom. xi. p. 88) is disclaimed by the Benedictine editors.

3 Giraldus Cambrensis confines this gift of bold and ready eloquence to the Romans, the French, and the Britons. The malicious Welshman insinuates that the English taciturnity might possibly be the effect of their servitude under the Normans.

4 The picture of Welsh and Armorican manners is drawn from Giraldus (Descript. Cambriæ, c. 6–15, inter Script. Camden. p. 886–891) and the authors quoted by the Abbé de Vertot (Hist. Critique, tom. ii. p. 259–266).

By the revolution of Britain the limits of science as well as of empire were contracted. The dark cloud which had been cleared by the Phœnician discoveries, and finally dispelled by the arms of Cæsar, again settled on the shores of the Atlantic, and a Roman province was again lost among the fabulous Islands of the Ocean. One hundred and fifty years after the reign of Honorius the gravest historian of the times[1] describes the wonders of a remote isle, whose eastern and western parts are divided by an antique wall, the boundary of life and death, or, more properly, of truth and fiction. The east is a fair country, inhabited by a civilised people: the air is healthy, the waters are pure and plentiful, and the earth yields her regular and fruitful increase. In the west, beyond the wall, the air is infectious and mortal; the ground is covered with serpents; and this dreary solitude is the region of departed spirits, who are transported from the opposite shores in substantial boats and by living rowers. Some families of fishermen, the subjects of the Franks, are excused from tribute, in consideration of the mysterious office which is performed by these Charons of the ocean. Each in his turn is summoned, at the hour of midnight, to hear the voices, and even the names, of the ghosts: he is sensible of their weight, and he feels himself impelled by an unknown, but irresistible, power. After this dream of fancy, we read with astonishment that the name of this island is *Brittia;* that it lies in the ocean, against the mouth of the Rhine, and less than thirty miles from the continent; that it is possessed by three nations, the Frisians, the Angles, and the Britons; and that some Angles had appeared at Constantinople in the train of the French ambassadors. From these ambassadors Procopius might be informed of a singular, though not improbable, adventure, which announces the spirit, rather than the delicacy, of an English heroine. She had been betrothed to Radiger, king of the Varni, a tribe of Germans who touched the ocean and the Rhine; but the perfidious lover was tempted, by motives of policy, to prefer his father's widow, the sister of Theodebert, king of the

1 See Procopius de Bell. Gothic. l. iv. c. 20, p. 620–625 [ed. Paris; tom. ii. p. 559 *sqq.*, ed. Bonn]. The Greek historian is himself so confounded by the wonders which he relates, that he weakly attempts to distinguish the islands of *Brittia* and *Britain*, which he has identified by so many inseparable circumstances.

Franks.¹ The forsaken princess of the Angles, instead of bewailing, revenged her disgrace. Her warlike subjects are *said* to have been ignorant of the use, and even of the form, of a horse; but she boldly sailed from Britain to the mouth of the Rhine, with a fleet of four hundred ships and an army of one hundred thousand men. After the loss of a battle the captive Radiger implored the mercy of his victorious bride, who generously pardoned his offence, dismissed her rival, and compelled the king of the Varni to discharge with honour and fidelity the duties of a husband.² This gallant exploit appears to be the last naval enterprise of the Anglo-Saxons. The arts of navigation, by which they had acquired the empire of Britain and of the sea, were soon neglected by the indolent barbarians, who supinely renounced all the commercial advantages of their insular situation. Seven independent kingdoms were agitated by perpetual discord; and the *British world* was seldom connected, either in peace or war, with the nations of the continent.³

I have now accomplished the laborious narrative of the decline and fall of the Roman empire, from the fortunate age of Trajan and the Antonines to its total extinction in the West, about five centuries after the Christian era. At that unhappy period the Saxons fiercely struggled with the natives for the possession of Britain: Gaul and Spain were divided between the

1 Theodebert, grandson of Clovis and king of Austrasia, was the most powerful and warlike prince of the age; and this remarkable adventure may be placed between the years 534 and 547, the extreme terms of his reign. His sister Theudechildis retired to Sens, where she founded monasteries and distributed alms (see the notes of the Benedictine editors, in tom. ii. p. 216). If we may credit the praises of Fortunatus (l. vi. carm. 5, in tom. ii. p. 507), Radiger was deprived of a most valuable wife.

2 Perhaps she was the sister of one of the princes or chiefs of the Angles who landed, in 527 and the following years, between the Humber and the Thames, and gradually founded the kingdoms of East Anglia and Mercia. The English writers are ignorant of her name and existence: but Procopius may have suggested to Mr. Rowe the character and situation of Rodogune in the tragedy of the Royal Convert.

3 In the copious history of Gregory of Tours we cannot find any traces of hostile or friendly intercourse between France and England, except in the marriage of the daughter of Caribert, king of Paris, quam in Cantia regis *cujusdam* filius matrimonio copulavit (l. ix. c. 26, in tom. ii. p. 348). The bishop of Tours ended his history and his life almost immediately before the conversion of Kent.

powerful monarchies of the Franks and Visigoths and the dependent kingdoms of the Suevi and Burgundians: Africa was exposed to the cruel persecution of the Vandals and the savage insults of the Moors: Rome and Italy, as far as the banks of the Danube, were afflicted by an army of barbarian mercenaries, whose lawless tyranny was succeeded by the reign of Theodoric the Ostrogoth. All the subjects of the empire, who, by the use of the Latin language, more particularly deserved the name and privileges of Romans, were oppressed by the disgrace and calamities of foreign conquest; and the victorious nations of Germany established a new system of manners and government in the western countries of Europe. The majesty of Rome was faintly represented by the princes of Constantinople, the feeble and imaginary successors of Augustus. Yet they continued to reign over the East, from the Danube to the Nile and Tigris; the Gothic and Vandal kingdoms of Italy and Africa were subverted by the arms of Justinian; and the history of the *Greek* emperors may still afford a long series of instructive lessons and interesting revolutions.

GENERAL OBSERVATIONS ON THE FALL OF THE ROMAN EMPIRE IN THE WEST

THE Greeks, after their country had been reduced into a province, imputed the triumphs of Rome, not to the merit, but to the FORTUNE, of the republic. The inconstant goddess, who so blindly distributes and resumes her favours, had *now* consented (such was the language of envious flattery) to resign her wings, to descend from her globe, and to fix her firm and immutable throne on the banks of the Tiber.[1] A wiser Greek, who has composed, with a philosophic spirit, the memorable history of his own times, deprived his countrymen of this vain

1 Such are the figurative expressions of Plutarch (Opera, tom. ii. p. 318, edit. Wechel [Frankf. 1620]), to whom, on the faith of his son Lamprias (Fabricius, Bibliot. Græc. tom. iii. p. 341), I shall boldly impute the malicious declamation περὶ τῆς Ῥωμαίων τύχης. The same opinions had prevailed among the Greeks two hundred and fifty years before Plutarch; and to confute them is the professed intention of Polybius (Hist. l. i. [c. 63] p. 90. edit. Gronov. Amstel. 1670).

and delusive comfort, by opening to their view the deep foundations of the greatness of Rome.¹ The fidelity of the citizens to
each other and to the state was confirmed by the habits of
education and the prejudices of religion. Honour, as well as
virtue, was the principle of the republic; the ambitious citizens
laboured to deserve the solemn glories of a triumph; and the
ardour of the Roman youth was kindled into active emulation as
often as they beheld the domestic images of their ancestors.² The
temperate struggles of the patricians and plebeians had finally
established the firm and equal balance of the constitution, which
united the freedom of popular assemblies with the authority and
wisdom of a senate and the executive powers of a regal magistrate. When the consul displayed the standard of the republic,
each citizen bound himself, by the obligation of an oath, to draw
his sword in the cause of his country till he had discharged the
sacred duty by a military service of ten years. This wise institution continually poured into the field the rising generations of
freemen and soldiers; and their numbers were reinforced by the
warlike and populous states of Italy, who, after a brave resistance, had yielded to the valour and embraced the alliance of
the Romans. The sage historian, who excited the virtue of the
younger Scipio and beheld the ruin of Carthage,³ has accurately
described their military system; their levies, arms, exercises, subordination, marches, encampments; and the invincible legion,
superior in active strength to the Macedonian phalanx of Philip
and Alexander. From these institutions of peace and war Polybius has deduced the spirit and success of a people incapable of
fear and impatient of repose. The ambitious design of conquest,

1 See the inestimable remains of the sixth book of Polybius, and many
other parts of his general history, particularly a digression in the seventeenth
book [l. xviii. c. 12–15], in which he compares the phalanx and the legion.

2 Sallust, de Bell. Jugurthin. c. 4. Such were the generous professions of
P. Scipio and Q. Maximus. The Latin historian had read, and most probably
transcribes, Polybius, their contemporary and friend.

3 While Carthage was in flames Scipio repeated two lines of the Iliad, which
express the destruction of Troy, acknowledging to Polybius, his friend and
preceptor (Polyb. [Fragm. l. xxxix. *sub fin*] in Excerpt. de Virtut. et Vit. tom. ii.
p. 1455–1465), that while he recollected the vicissitudes of human affairs he
inwardly applied them to the future calamities of Rome (Appian. in Libycis
[l. viii. c. 132], p. 136, edit. Toll.).

which might have been defeated by the seasonable conspiracy of mankind, was attempted and achieved; and the perpetual viol-ation of justice was maintained by the political virtues of prudence and courage. The arms of the republic, sometimes vanquished in battle, always victorious in war, advanced with rapid steps to the Euphrates, the Danube, the Rhine, and the Ocean; and the images of gold, or silver, or brass, that might serve to represent the nations and their kings, were successively broken by the *iron* monarchy of Rome.[1]

The rise of a city, which swelled into an empire, may deserve, as a singular prodigy, the reflection of a philosophic mind. But the decline of Rome was the natural and inevitable effect of immoderate greatness. Prosperity ripened the principle of decay; the causes of destruction multiplied with the extent of conquest; and as soon as time or accident had removed the artificial sup-ports, the stupendous fabric yielded to the pressure of its own weight. The story of its ruin is simple and obvious; and instead of inquiring *why* the Roman empire was destroyed, we should rather be surprised that it had subsisted so long. The victorious legions, who, in distant wars, acquired the vices of strangers and mercenaries, first oppressed the freedom of the republic, and afterwards violated the majesty of the purple. The emperors, anxious for their personal safety and the public peace, were reduced to the base expedient of corrupting the discipline which rendered them alike formidable to their sovereign and to the enemy; the vigour of the military government was relaxed and finally dissolved by the partial institutions of Constantine; and the Roman world was overwhelmed by a deluge of barbarians.

The decay of Rome has been frequently ascribed to the trans-lation of the seat of empire; but this history has already shown that the powers of government were *divided* rather than *removed*. The throne of Constantinople was erected in the East; while the

1 See Daniel ii. 31–40. 'And the fourth kingdom shall be strong as *iron*; forasmuch as iron breaketh in pieces and subdueth all things.' The remainder of the prophecy (the mixture of iron and *clay*) was accomplished, according to St. Jerom, in his own time. Sicut enim in principio nihil Romano Imperio fortius et durius, ita in fine rerum nihil imbecillius: quum et in bellis civilibus et adversus diversas nationes, aliarum gentium barbararum auxilio indigemus (Opera, tom. v. p. 572).

West was still possessed by a series of emperors who held their residence in Italy, and claimed their equal inheritance of the legions and provinces. This dangerous novelty impaired the strength and fomented the vices of a double reign: the instruments of an oppressive and arbitrary system were multiplied; and a vain emulation of luxury, not of merit, was introduced and supported between the degenerate successors of Theodosius. Extreme distress, which unites the virtue of a free people, embitters the factions of a declining monarchy. The hostile favourites of Arcadius and Honorius betrayed the republic to its common enemies; and the Byzantine court beheld with indifference, perhaps with pleasure, the disgrace of Rome, the misfortunes of Italy, and the loss of the West. Under the succeeding reigns the alliance of the two empires was restored; but the aid of the Oriental Romans was tardy, doubtful, and ineffectual; and the national schism of the Greeks and Latins was enlarged by the perpetual difference of language and manners, of interests, and even of religion. Yet the salutary event approved in some measure the judgment of Constantine. During a long period of decay his impregnable city repelled the victorious armies of barbarians, protected the wealth of Asia, and commanded, both in peace and war, the important straits which connect the Euxine and Mediterranean seas. The foundation of Constantinople more essentially contributed to the preservation of the East than to the ruin of the West.

As the happiness of a *future* life is the great object of religion, we may hear without surprise or scandal that the introduction, or at least the abuse of Christianity, had some influence on the decline and fall of the Roman empire. The clergy successfully preached the doctrines of patience and pusillanimity; the active virtues of society were discouraged; and the last remains of military spirit were buried in the cloister: a large portion of public and private wealth was consecrated to the specious demands of charity and devotion; and the soldiers' pay was lavished on the useless multitudes of both sexes who could only plead the merits of abstinence and chastity. Faith, zeal, curiosity, and the more earthly passions of malice and ambition, kindled the flame of theological discord; the church, and even the state, were distracted by religious factions, whose conflicts were sometimes bloody and always implacable; the attention of the emperors was diverted from camps to synods; the Roman world was oppressed by a new species of tyranny; and the persecuted sects became the secret enemies of their country. Yet party-spirit, however pernicious or absurd, is a principle of union as well as of dissension. The bishops, from eighteen hundred pulpits, inculcated the duty of passive obedience to a lawful and orthodox sovereign; their frequent assemblies and perpetual correspondence maintained the communion of distant churches; and the benevolent temper of the Gospel was strengthened, though confined, by the spiritual alliance of the catholics. The sacred indolence of the monks was devoutly embraced by a servile and effeminate age; but if superstition had not afforded a decent retreat, the same vices would have tempted the unworthy Romans to desert, from baser motives, the standard of the republic. Religious precepts are easily obeyed which indulge and sanctify the natural inclinations of their votaries; but the pure and genuine influence of Christianity may be traced in its beneficial, though imperfect, effects on the barbarian proselytes of the North. If the decline of the Roman empire was hastened by the conversion of Constantine, his victorious religion broke the violence of the fall, and mollified the ferocious temper of the conquerors.

This awful revolution may be usefully applied to the instruction of the present age. It is the duty of a patriot to prefer and promote the exclusive interest and glory of his native country: but a philosopher may be permitted to enlarge his views, and to consider Europe as one great republic, whose various inhabitants have attained almost the same level of politeness and cultivation. The balance of power will continue to fluctuate, and the prosperity of our own or the neighbouring kingdoms may be alternately exalted or depressed; but these partial events cannot essentially injure our general state of happiness, the system of arts, and laws, and manners, which so advantageously distinguish, above the rest of mankind, the Europeans and their colonies. The savage nations of the globe are the common enemies of civilised society; and we may inquire, with anxious curiosity, whether Europe is still threatened with a repetition of those calamities which formerly oppressed the arms and institutions of Rome. Perhaps the same reflections will illustrate the fall of that mighty empire, and explain the probable causes of our actual security.

I. The Romans were ignorant of the extent of their danger and the number of their enemies. Beyond the Rhine and Danube the northern countries of Europe and Asia were filled with innumerable tribes of hunters and shepherds, poor, voracious, and turbulent; bold in arms, and impatient to ravish the fruits of industry. The barbarian world was agitated by the rapid impulse of war; and the peace of Gaul or Italy was shaken by the distant revolutions of China. The Huns, who fled before a victorious enemy, directed their march towards the West; and the torrent was swelled by the gradual accession of captives and allies. The flying tribes who yielded to the Huns assumed in *their* turn the spirit of conquest; the endless column of barbarians pressed on the Roman empire with accumulated weight; and, if the foremost were destroyed, the vacant space was instantly replenished by new assailants. Such formidable emigrations no longer issue from the North; and the long repose, which has been imputed to the decrease of population, is the happy consequence of the progress of arts and agriculture. Instead of some rude villages thinly scattered among its woods and morasses, Germany now produces a list of two thousand three hundred walled towns: the Christian kingdoms of Denmark, Sweden, and Poland have been successively established; and the Hanse merchants, with the Teutonic knights, have extended their colonies along the coast of the Baltic as far as the Gulf of Finland. From the Gulf of Finland to the Eastern Ocean, Russia now assumes the form of a powerful and civilised empire. The plough, the loom, and the forge are introduced on the banks of the Volga, the Oby, and the Lena; and the fiercest of the Tartar hordes have been taught to tremble and obey. The reign of independent barbarism is now contracted to a narrow span; and the remnant of Calmucks or Uzbecks, whose forces may be almost numbered, cannot seriously excite the apprehensions of the great republic of Europe.[1] Yet this apparent security should not tempt us to forget that new enemies

1 The French and English editors of the Genealogical History of the Tartars have subjoined a curious, though imperfect, description of their present state. We might question the independence of the Calmucks, or Eluths, since they have been recently vanquished by the Chinese, who, in the year 1759,

and unknown dangers may *possibly* arise from some obscure people, scarcely visible in the map of the world. The Arabs or Saracens, who spread their conquests from India to Spain, had languished in poverty and contempt till Mahomet breathed into those savage bodies the soul of enthusiasm.

II. The empire of Rome was firmly established by the singular and perfect coalition of its members. The subject nations, resigning the hope and even the wish of independence, embraced the character of Roman citizens; and the provinces of the West were reluctantly torn by the barbarians from the bosom of their mother country.[1] But this union was purchased by the loss of national freedom and military spirit; and the servile provinces, destitute of life and motion, expected their safety from the mercenary troops and governors who were directed by the orders of a distant court. The happiness of an hundred millions depended on the personal merit of one or two men, perhaps children, whose minds were corrupted by education, luxury, and despotic power. The deepest wounds were inflicted on the empire during the minorities of the sons and grandsons of Theodosius; and, after those incapable princes seemed to attain the age of manhood, they abandoned the church to the bishops, the state to the eunuchs, and the provinces to the barbarians. Europe is now divided into twelve powerful, though unequal kingdoms, three respectable commonwealths, and a variety of smaller, though independent states: the chances of royal and ministerial talents are multiplied, at least, with the number of its rulers; and a Julian, or Semiramis, may reign in the North, while Arcadius and Honorius again slumber on the thrones of the South. The abuses of tyranny are restrained by the mutual influence of fear and shame; republics have acquired order and stability; monarchies have imbibed the principles of freedom, or, at least, of

subdued the lesser Bucharia, and advanced into the country of Badakshan, near the sources of the Oxus (Mémoires sur les Chinois. tom. i. p. 325–400). But these conquests are precarious, nor will I venture to ensure the safety of the Chinese empire.

1 The prudent reader will determine how far this general proposition is weakened by the revolt of the Isaurians, the independence of Britain and Armorica, the Moorish tribes, or the Bagaudæ of Gaul and Spain (vol. i. p. 310, vol. lii. pp. 322, 378, 465).

moderation; and some sense of honour and justice is introduced into the most defective constitutions by the general manners of the times. In peace, the progress of knowledge and industry is accelerated by the emulation of so many active rivals: in war, the European forces are exercised by temperate and undecisive contests. If a savage conqueror should issue from the deserts of Tartary, he must repeatedly vanquish the robust peasants of Russia, the numerous armies of Germany, the gallant nobles of France, and the intrepid freemen of Britain; who, perhaps, might confederate for their common defence. Should the victorious barbarians carry slavery and desolation as far as the Atlantic Ocean, ten thousand vessels would transport beyond their pursuit the remains of civilised society; and Europe would revive and flourish in the American world, which is already filled with her colonies and institutions.[1]

III. Cold, poverty, and a life of danger and fatigue fortify the strength and courage of barbarians. In every age they have oppressed the polite and peaceful nations of China, India, and Persia, who neglected, and still neglect, to counterbalance these natural powers by the resources of military art. The warlike states of antiquity, Greece, Macedonia, and Rome, educated a race of soldiers; exercised their bodies, disciplined their courage, multiplied their forces by regular evolutions, and converted the iron which they possessed into strong and serviceable weapons. But this superiority insensibly declined with their laws and manners: and the feeble policy of Constantine and his successors armed and instructed, for the ruin of the empire, the rude valour of the barbarian mercenaries. The military art has been changed by the invention of gunpowder; which enables man to command the two most powerful agents of nature, air and fire. Mathematics, chemistry, mechanics, architecture, have been applied to the service of war; and the adverse parties oppose to each other the most elaborate modes of attack and of defence. Historians may indignantly observe that the preparations of a siege would found

---

1 America now contains about six millions of European blood and descent; and their numbers, at least in the North, are continually increasing. Whatever may be the changes of their political situation, they must preserve the manners of Europe; and we may reflect with some pleasure that the English language will probably be diffused over an immense and populous continent.

and maintain a flourishing colony;[1] yet we cannot be displeased that the subversion of a city should be a work of cost and difficulty; or that an industrious people should be protected by those arts which survive and supply the decay of military virtue. Cannon and fortifications now form an impregnable barrier against the Tartar horse; and Europe is secure from any future irruption of barbarians; since, before they can conquer, they must cease to be barbarous. Their gradual advances in the science of war would always be accompanied, as we may learn from the example of Russia, with a proportionable improvement in the arts of peace and civil policy; and they themselves must deserve a place among the polished nations whom they subdue.

Should these speculations be found doubtful or fallacious, there still remains a more humble source of comfort and hope. The discoveries of ancient and modern navigators, and the domestic history or tradition of the most enlightened nations, represent the *human savage* naked both in mind and body, and destitute of laws, of arts, of ideas, and almost of language.[2] From this abject condition, perhaps the primitive and universal state of man, he has gradually arisen to command the animals, to fertilise the earth, to traverse the ocean, and to measure the heavens. His progress in the improvement and exercise of his

[1] On avoit fait venir (for the siege of Turin) 140 pièces de canon; et ill est à remarquer que chaque gros canon monté revient à environ 2000 écus: il y avoit 100,000 boulets; 106,000 cartouches d'une façon, et 300,000 d'une autre; 21,000 bombes; 27,700 grenades, 15,000 sacs à terre, 30,000 instruments pour la pionnage; 1,200,000 livres de poudre. Ajoutez à ces munitions le plomb, le fer, et le fer-blanc, les cordages, tout ce qui sert aux mineurs, le souphre, le salpêtre, les outils de toute espèce. Il est certain que les frais de tous ces préparatifs de destruction suffiroient pour fonder et pour faire fleurir la plus nombreuse colonie. Voltaire, Siècle de Louis XIV. c. xx. in his Works, tom. xi. p. 391.

[2] It would be an easy, though tedious, task to produce the authorities of poets, philosophers, and historians. I shall therefore content myself with appealing to the decisive and authentic testimony of Diodorus Siculus (tom. i. l. i. p. 11, 12, l. iii. [c. 14. *sqq.*] p. 184, etc., edit. Wesseling). The Ichthyophagi, who in his time wandered along the shores of the Red Sea, can only be compared to the natives of New Holland (Dampier's Voyages, vol. i. p. 464–469). Fancy, or perhaps reason, may still suppose an extreme and absolute state of nature far below the level of these savages, who had acquired some arts and instruments.

mental and corporeal faculties[1] has been irregular and various; infinitely slow in the beginning, and increasing by degrees with redoubled velocity: ages of laborious ascent have been followed by a moment of rapid downfall; and the several climates of the globe have felt the vicissitudes of light and darkness. Yet the experience of four thousand years should enlarge our hopes and diminish our apprehensions: we cannot determine to what height the human species may aspire in their advances towards perfection; but it may safely be presumed that no people, unless the face of nature is changed, will relapse into their original barbarism. The improvements of society may be viewed under a threefold aspect. 1. The poet or philosopher illustrates his age and country by the efforts of a *single* mind; but these superior powers of reason or fancy are rare and spontaneous productions; and the genius of Homer, or Cicero, or Newton, would excite less admiration if they could be created by the will of a prince or the lessons of a preceptor. 2. The benefits of law and policy, of trade and manufactures, of arts and sciences, are more solid and permanent; and *many* individuals may be qualified, by education and discipline, to promote, in their respective stations, the interest of the community. But this general order is the effect of skill and labour; and the complex machinery may be decayed by time, or injured by violence. 3. Fortunately for mankind, the more useful, or, at least, more necessary arts, can be performed without superior talents or national subordination; without the powers of *one*, or the union of *many*. Each village, each family, each individual, must always possess both ability and inclination to perpetuate the use of fire[2] and of metals; the propagation and service of domestic animals; the methods of hunting and fishing; the rudiments of navigation; the imperfect cultivation of corn or other nutritive grain; and the simple practice of the mechanic

1 See the learned and rational work of the President Goguet, de l'Origine des Loix, des Arts, et des Sciences. He traces from facts or conjectures (tom. i. p. 147–337, edit. 12mo.) the first and most difficult steps of human invention.

2 It is certain, however strange, that many nations have been ignorant of the use of fire. Even the ingenious natives of Otaheite, who are destitute of metals, have not invented any earthen vessels capable of sustaining the action of fire and of communicating the heat to the liquids which they contain.

trades. Private genius and public industry may be extirpated; but these hardy plants survive the tempest, and strike an everlasting root into the most unfavourable soil. The splendid days of Augustus and Trajan were eclipsed by a cloud of ignorance; and the barbarians subverted the laws and palaces of Rome. But the scythe, the invention or emblem of Saturn,[1] still continued annually to mow the harvests of Italy; and the human feasts of the Læstrigons[2] have never been renewed on the coast of Campania.

Since the first discovery of the arts, war, commerce, and religious zeal have diffused among the savages of the Old and New World these inestimable gifts: they have been successively propagated; they can never be lost. We may therefore acquiesce in the pleasing conclusion that every age of the world has increased and still increases the real wealth, the happiness, the knowledge, and perhaps the virtue, of the human race.[3]

CHAPTER XXXIX

Zeno and Anastasius, Emperors of the East – Birth, Education, and first Exploits of Theodoric the Ostrogoth – His Invasion and Conquest of Italy – The Gothic Kingdom of Italy – State of the West – Military and Civil Government – The Senator Boethius – Last Acts and Death of Theodoric

AFTER the fall of the Roman empire in the West, an interval of fifty years, till the memorable reign of Justinian, is faintly marked by the obscure names and imperfect annals of Zeno,

1 Plutarch. Quæst. Rom. in tom. ii. p. 275 [tom. vii. p. 112, ed. Reiske]. Macrob. Saturnal. l. i. c. 7, p. 152, edit. London. The arrival of Saturn (of his religious worship) in a ship may indicate that the savage coast of Latium was first discovered and civilised by the Phœnicians.

2 In the ninth and tenth books of the Odyssey, Homer has embellished the tales of fearful and credulous sailors who transformed the cannibals of Italy and Sicily into monstrous giants.

3 The merit of discovery has too often been stained with avarice, cruelty, and fanaticism; and the intercourse of nations has produced the communication of disease and prejudice. A singular exception is due to the virtue of our own times and country. The five great voyages, successively undertaken by the

Anastasius, and Justin, who successively ascended the throne of Constantinople. During the same period, Italy revived and flourished
under the government of a Gothic king who might have deserved
a status among the best and bravest of the ancient Romans.

Theodoric the Ostrogoth, the fourteenth in lineal descent of
the royal line of the Amali,[1] was born in the neighbourhood of
Vienna[2] two years after the death of Attila. A recent victory had
restored the independence of the Ostrogoths; and the three
brothers, Walamir, Theodemir, and Widimir, who ruled that warlike nation with united counsels, had separately pitched their
habitations in the fertile, though desolate, province of Pannonia.[3]
The Huns still threatened their revolted subjects, but their hasty
attack was repelled by the single forces of Walamir, and the news
of his victory reached the distant camp of his brother in the same
auspicious moment that the favourite concubine of Theodemir
was delivered of a son and heir.[4] In the eighth year of his age,
Theodoric was reluctantly yielded by his father to the public

command of his present Majesty, were inspired by the pure and generous love
of science and of mankind. The same prince, adapting his benefactions to the
different stages of society, has founded a school of painting in his capital, and
has introduced into the islands of the South Sea the vegetables and animals
most useful to human life.

1 Jornandes (de Rebus Geticis, c. 13, 14, p. 629, 630, edit. Grot.) has drawn
the pedigree of Theodoric from Gapt, one of the *Anses* or Demi-gods, who
lived about the time of Domitian. Cassiodorus, the first who celebrates the royal
race of the Amali (Variar. viii. 5, ix. 25, x. 2, xi. 1), reckons the grandson of
Theodoric as the xviith in descent. Peringsciold (the Swedish commentator of
Cochlœus, Vit. Theodoric. p. 271, etc., Stockholm, 1699) labours to connect
this genealogy with the legends or traditions of his native country.

[Amala was a name of peculiar respect and honour among the Ostrogoths.
It means 'strength,' and enters into many names. Amalaberg, Amalafred, Ama-
larich, etc. In the Nibelungen Lied the Ostrogoths are called the Amilungen.
– O. S.]

2 More correctly on the banks of the lake Pelso (Nieusiedler-see) near
Carnuntum, almost on the same spot where Marcus Antoninus composed his
Meditations (Jornandes, c. 52, p. 689. Severin. Pannonia Illustrata, p. 22. Cel-
larius, Geograph. Antiq. tom. i. p. 350).

3 [The division of the Gothic kingdom as given by Hodgkin, *Italy and Her
Invaders*, iii. p. 14. The portion of Walamer lay between the rivers Save and
Drave, that of Widimer between the Save and the Plattensee, Theodemir's
between the Plattensee and the Danube. – O. S.]

4 Genealogical table of the family of Theodoric:–

interest, as the pledge of an alliance which Leo, emperor of the East, had consented to purchase by an annual subsidy of three hundred pounds of gold. The royal hostage was educated at Constantinople with care and tenderness. His body was formed to all the exercises of war, his mind was expanded by the habits of liberal conversation; he frequented the schools of the most skilful masters, but he disdained or neglected the arts of Greece; and so ignorant did he always remain of the first elements of science, that a rude mark was contrived to represent the signature of the illiterate king of Italy.[1] As soon as he had attained the age of eighteen he was restored to the wishes of the Ostrogoths, whom the emperor aspired to gain by liberality and confidence. Walamir had fallen in battle; the youngest of the brothers, Widimir, had led away into Italy and Gaul an army of

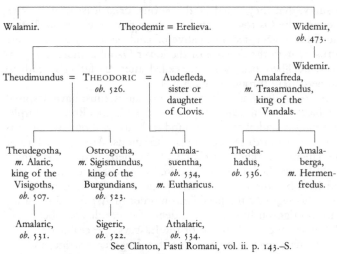

See Clinton, Fasti Romani, vol. ii. p. 143.–S.

1 The four first letters of his name (ΘΕΟΔ) were inscribed on a gold plate, and when it was fixed on the paper the king drew his pen through the intervals (Anonym. Valesian. ad calcem Amm. Marcellin. p. 722 [tom. ii. p. 313, ed. Bipon.]). This authentic fact, with the testimony of Procopius, or at least of the contemporary Goths (Gothic. l. i. c. 2. p. 312 [ed. Paris; tom. ii. p. 14, ed. Bonn]), far outweighs the vague praises of Ennodius (Sirmond. Opera, tom. i. p. 1596) and Theophanes (Chronograph. p. 112. [ed. Par.; p. 202, 203, ed. Bonn]).

barbarians; and the whole nation acknowledged for their king the father of Theodoric. His ferocious subjects admired the strength and stature of their young prince,[1] and he soon convinced them that he had not degenerated from the valour of his ancestors. At the head of six thousand volunteers he secretly left the camp in quest of adventures, descended the Danube as far as Singidunum or Belgrade, and soon returned to his father with the spoils of a Sarmatian king whom he had vanquished and slain. Such triumphs, however, were productive only of fame, and the invincible Ostrogoths were reduced to extreme distress by the want of clothing and food. They unanimously resolved to desert their Pannonian encampments, and boldly to advance into the warm and wealthy neighbourhood of the Byzantine court, which already maintained in pride and luxury so many bands of confederate Goths. After proving, by some acts of hostility, that they could be dangerous, or at least troublesome, enemies, the Ostrogoths sold at a high price their reconciliation and fidelity, accepted a donative of lands and money, and were intrusted with the defence of the lower Danube under the command of Theodoric, who succeeded after his father's death to the hereditary throne of the Amali.[2]

An hero, descended from a race of kings, must have despised the base Isaurian who was invested with the Roman purple, without any endowments of mind or body, without any advantages of royal birth or superior qualifications. After the failure of the Theodosian line, the choice of Pulcheria and of the senate might be justified in some measure by the characters of Marcian and Leo; but the latter of these princes confirmed and dishonoured his reign by the perfidious murder of Aspar and his sons, who too rigorously exacted the debt of gratitude and obedience. The inheritance of Leo and of the East was peaceably devolved on his infant grandson, the son of his daughter Ariadne; and her Isaurian husband, the fortunate Trascalisseus, exchanged that

1 Statura est quæ resignet proceritate regnantem (Ennodius, p. 1614). The bishop of Pavia (I mean the ecclesiastic who wished to be a bishop) then proceeds to celebrate the complexion, eyes, hands, etc., of his sovereign.

2 The state of the Ostrogoths and the first years of Theodoric are found in Jornandes (c. 52–56, p. 689–696) and Malchus (Excerpt. Legat. p. 78–80 [ed. Par.; p. 244–248, ed. Bonn]), who erroneously styles him the son of Walamir.

barbarous sound for the Grecian appellation of Zeno. After the decease of the elder Leo, he approached with unnatural respect the throne of his son, humbly received as a gift the second rank in the empire, and soon excited the public suspicion on the sudden and premature death of his young colleague, whose life could no longer promote the success of his ambition. But the palace of Constantinople was ruled by female influence, and agitated by female passions; and Verina, the widow of Leo, claiming his empire as her own, pronounced a sentence of deposition against the worthless and ungrateful servant on whom she alone had bestowed the sceptre of the East.[1] As soon as she sounded a revolt in the ears of Zeno, he fled with precipitation into the mountains of Isauria; and her brother Basiliscus, already infamous by his African expedition,[2] was unanimously proclaimed by the servile senate. But the reign of the usurper was short and turbulent. Basiliscus presumed to assassinate the lover of his sister; he dared to offend the lover of his wife, the vain and insolent Harmatius, who, in the midst of Asiatic luxury, affected the dress, the demeanour, and the surname of Achilles.[3] By the conspiracy of the malcontents, Zeno was recalled from exile; the armies, the capital, the person of Basiliscus, were betrayed; and his whole family was condemned to the long agony of cold and hunger by the inhuman conqueror, who wanted courage to encounter or to forgive his enemies. The haughty spirit of Verina was still incapable of submission or repose. She provoked the enmity of a favourite general, embraced his cause as soon as he was disgraced, created a new emperor in Syria and Egypt, raised an army of seventy thousand men, and persisted to the last moment of her life in a fruitless rebellion, which, according to the fashion of the age, had been predicted by Christian hermits and Pagan magicians. While the East was afflicted by the passions of Verina, her daughter Ariadne was distinguished by the female virtues of mildness and fidelity; she followed her

---

1 Theophanes (p. 111 [p. 200, ed. Bonn]) inserts a copy of her *sacred* letters to the provinces; ἵστε ὅτι τὸ βασίλειον ἡμέτερόν ἐστι ... καὶ ὅτι προχειρησάμεθα βασιλέα Τρασκαλλισαῖον, etc. Such female pretensions would have astonished the slaves of the *first* Cæsars.

2 Vol. iii. p. 501, *seq.*

3 Suidas, tom. i. p. 332, 333, edit. Kuster.

husband in his exile, and after his restoration she implored his clemency in favour of her mother. On the decease of Zeno, Ariadne, the daughter, the mother, and the widow of an emperor, gave her hand and the Imperial title to Anastasius, an aged domestic of the palace, who survived his elevation above twenty-seven years, and whose character is attested by the acclamation of the people, 'Reign as you have lived!'[1]

Whatever fear or affection could bestow was profusely lavished by Zeno on the king of the Ostrogoths; the rank of patrician and consul, the command of the Palatine troops, an equestrian statue, a treasure in gold and silver of many thousand pounds, the name of son, and the promise of a rich and honourable wife. As long as Theodoric condescended to serve, he supported with courage and fidelity the cause of his benefactor; his rapid march contributed to the restoration of Zeno; and in the second revolt, the *Walamirs*, as they were called, pursued and pressed the Asiatic rebels, till they left an easy victory to the Imperial troops.[2] But the faithful servant was suddenly converted into a formidable enemy, who spread the flames of war from Constantinople to the Hadriatic; many flourishing cities were reduced to ashes, and the agriculture of Thrace was almost extirpated by the wanton cruelty of the Goths, who deprived their captive peasants of the right hand that guided the plough.[3] On such occasions Theodoric sustained the loud and specious

1 The contemporary histories of Malchus and Candidus are lost; but some extracts or fragments have been saved by Photius (lxxviii. lxxix. p. 100–102 [p. 54–56, ed. Bekk.]), Constantine Porphyrogenitus (Excerpt. Leg. p. 78–97), and in various articles of the Lexicon of Suidas. The Chronicles of Marcellinus (Imago Historiæ) are originals for the reigns of Zeno and Anastasius; and I must acknowledge, almost for the last time, my obligations to the large and accurate collections of Tillemont (Hist. des Emp. tom. vi. p. 472–652).

2 In ipsis congressionis tuæ foribus cessit invasor, cum *profugo* per te sceptra redderentur de salute dubitanti. Ennodius then proceeds (p. 1596, 1597, tom. i. Sirmond) to transport his hero (on a flying dragon?) into Æthiopia, beyond the tropic of Cancer. The evidence of the Valesian Fragment (p. 717), Liberatus (Brev. Eutych. c. 25, p. 118), and Theophanes (p. 112 [p. 203, ed. Bonn]), is more sober and rational.

3 This cruel practice is specially imputed to the *Triarian* Goths, less barbarous, as it should seem, than the *Walamirs*; but the son of Theodemir is charged with the ruin of many Roman cities (Malchus, Excerpt. Leg. p. 95 [ed. Par.; p. 238, ed. Bonn]).

reproach of disloyalty, of ingratitude, and of insatiate avarice, which could be only excused by the hard necessity of his situation. He reigned, not as the monarch, but as the minister of a ferocious people, whose spirit was unbroken by slavery, and impatient of real or imaginary insults. Their poverty was incurable, since the most liberal donatives were soon dissipated in wasteful luxury, and the most fertile estates became barren in their hands; they despised, but they envied, the laborious provincials; and when their subsistence had failed, the Ostrogoths embraced the familiar resources of war and rapine. It had been the wish of Theodoric (such, at least, was his declaration) to lead a peaceful, obscure, obedient life, on the confines of Scythia, till the Byzantine court, by splendid and fallacious promises, seduced him to attack a confederate tribe of Goths, who had been engaged in the party of Basiliscus. He marched from his station in Mæsia, on the solemn assurance that before he reached Adrianople he should meet a plentiful convoy of provisions, and a reinforcement of eight thousand horse and thirty thousand foot, while the legions of Asia were encamped at Heraclea to second his operations. These measures were disappointed by mutual jealousy. As he advanced into Thrace, the son of Theodemir found an inhospitable solitude, and his Gothic followers, with an heavy train of horses, of mules, and of waggons, were betrayed by their guides among the rocks and precipices of Mount Sondis, where he was assaulted by the arms and invectives of Theodoric, the son of Triarius. From a neighbouring height his artful rival harangued the camp of the *Walamirs*, and branded their leader with the opprobrious names of child, of madman, of perjured traitor, the enemy of his blood and nation. 'Are you ignorant,' exclaimed the son of Triarius, 'that it is the constant policy of the Romans to destroy the Goths by each other's swords? Are you insensible that the victor in this unnatural contest will be exposed, and justly exposed, to their implacable revenge? Where are those warriors, my kinsmen and thy own, whose widows now lament that their lives were sacrificed to thy rash ambition? Where is the wealth which thy soldiers possessed when they were first allured from their native homes to enlist under thy standard? Each of them was then master of three or four horses; they now follow thee on foot like slaves, through the deserts of Thrace; those men who were tempted by the hope of measuring gold with a bushel, those brave men who are as free and as noble as thyself.' A language so well suited to the temper of the Goths excited clamour and discontent; and the son of Theodemir, apprehensive of being left alone, was com-pelled to embrace his brethren, and to imitate the example of Roman perfidy.[1]

In every state of his fortune the prudence and firmness of Theodoric were equally conspicuous: whether he threatened Constantinople at the head of the confederate Goths, or re-treated with a faithful band to the mountains and sea-coast of Epirus. At length the accidental death of the son of Triarius[2] destroyed the balance which the Romans had been so anxious to preserve, the whole nation acknowledged the supremacy of the Amali, and the Byzantine court subscribed an ignominious and oppressive treaty.[3] The senate had already declared that it was necessary to choose a party among the Goths, since the public was unequal to the support of their united forces. A subsidy of two thousand pounds of gold, with the ample pay of thirteen thousand men, were required for the least considerable of their armies;[4] and the Isaurians, who guarded not the empire but the emperor, enjoyed, besides the privilege of rapine, an annual pension of five thousand pounds. The sagacious mind of Theodoric soon perceived that he was odious to the Romans, and suspected by the barbarians; he understood the popular mur-mur, that his subjects were exposed in their frozen huts to in-tolerable hardships, while their king was dissolved in the luxury

1 Jornandes (c. 56, 57, p. 696) displays the services of Theodoric, confesses his rewards, but dissembles his revolt, of which such curious details have been preserved by Malchus (Excerpt. Legat. p. 78–97 [p. 244. *sqq.*, ed. Bonn]). Marcellinus, a domestic of Justinian, under whose ivth consulship (A.D. 534) he composed his Chronicle (Scaliger, Thesaurus Temporum, P. ii. p. 34–57), be-trays his prejudice and passion: in [apud] Græciam debacchantem ... Zenonis munificentiâ pene pacatus ... beneficiis nunquam satiatus, etc. [p. 368, 369, and 370, ed. Sirmond].

2 As he was riding in his own camp an unruly horse threw him against the point of a spear which hung before a tent, or was fixed on a waggon (Marcellin. in. Chron. Evagrius, l. iii. c. 25).

3 See Malchus (p. 91 [ed. Par.; p. 268, ed. Bonn]) and Evagrius (l. iii. c. 35).

4 Malchus, p. 85 [p. 256, ed. Bonn]. In a single action, which was decided by the skill and discipline of Sabinian, Theodoric could lose 5000 men.

of Greece; and he prevented the painful alternative of encountering the Goths as the champion, or of leading them to the field
as the enemy, of Zeno. Embracing an enterprise worthy of his
courage and ambition, Theodoric addressed the emperor in the
following words: — 'Although your servant is maintained in affluence by your liberality, graciously listen to the wishes of my
heart! Italy, the inheritance of your predecessors, and Rome itself, the head and mistress of the world, now fluctuate under the
violence and oppression of Odoacer the mercenary. Direct me,
with my national troops, to march against the tyrant. If I fall,
you will be relieved from an expensive and troublesome friend:
if, with the Divine permission, I succeed, I shall govern in your
name, and to your glory, the Roman senate, and the part of the
republic delivered from slavery by my victorious arms.' The proposal of Theodoric was accepted, and perhaps had been suggested, by the Byzantine court. But the forms of the commission
or grant appear to have been expressed with a prudent ambiguity, which might be explained by the event; and it was left
doubtful whether the conqueror of Italy should reign as the
lieutenant, the vassal, or the ally, of the emperor of the East.[1]

The reputation both of the leader and of the war diffused a
universal ardour; the *Walamirs* were multiplied by the Gothic
swarms already engaged in the service, or seated in the provinces,
of the empire; and each bold barbarian who had heard of the
wealth and beauty of Italy was impatient to seek, through the
most perilous adventures, the possession of such enchanting
objects. The march of Theodoric must be considered as the
emigration of an entire people; the wives and children of the
Goths, their aged parents, and most precious effects were carefully transported; and some idea may be formed of the heavy
baggage that now followed the camp by the loss of two thousand
waggons which had been sustained in a single action in the war
of Epirus. For their subsistence, the Goths depended on the
magazines of corn, which was ground in portable mills by the
hands of their women, on the milk and flesh of their flocks and

---

1 Jornandes (c. 57, p. 696, 697) has abridged the great history of Cassiodorus. See, compare, and reconcile, Procopius (Gothic. l. i. c. i), the Valesian
Fragment (p. 718 [ad calcem Amm. Marc. tom. ii. p. 306, ed. Bip.]), Theophanes
(p. 113 [p. 203, ed. Bonn]), and Marcellinus (in Chron.).

herds, on the casual produce of the chase, and upon the contributions which they might impose on all who should presume
to dispute the passage or to refuse their friendly assistance.[1]
Notwithstanding these precautions, they were exposed to the
danger, and almost to the distress, of famine, in a march of seven
hundred miles, which had been undertaken in the depth of a
rigorous winter. Since the fall of the Roman power, Dacia and
Pannonia no longer exhibited the rich prospect of populous
cities, well-cultivated fields, and convenient highways: the reign
of barbarism and desolation was restored; and the tribes of Bulgarians, Gepidæ, and Sarmatians, who had occupied the vacant
province, were prompted by their native fierceness, or the soli-
citations of Odoacer, to resist the progress of his enemy. In
many obscure though bloody battles, Theodoric fought and vanquished: till at length, surmounting every obstacle by skilful conduct and persevering courage, he descended from the Julian
Alps, and displayed his invincible banners on the confines of
Italy.[2]

Odoacer, a rival not unworthy of his arms, had already occupied the advantageous and well-known post of the river Sontius,
near the ruins of Aquileia, at the head of a powerful host, whose
independent *kings*[3] or leaders disdained the duties of subordination, and the prudence of delays. No sooner had Theodoric
granted a short repose and refreshment to his wearied cavalry,
then he boldly attacked the fortifications of the enemy; the Ostrogoths showed more ardour to acquire, than the mercenaries
to defend, the lands of Italy, and the reward of the first victory
was the possession of the Venetian province as far as the walls
of Verona. In the neighbourhood of that city, on the steep banks
of the rapid Adige, he was opposed by a new army, reinforced
in its numbers, and not impaired in its courage: the contest was

1 [Several attempts have been made to estimate the number of the fighting
men relatively to the nation. Hodgkin, in *Italy and its Invaders*, considers the
former to have been about 40,000, the latter 200,000. – O. S.]

2 Theodoric's march is supplied and illustrated by Ennodius (p. 1598–
1602), when the bombast of the oration is translated into the language of
common sense.

3 Tot reges, etc. (Ennodius, p. 1602). We must recollect how much the
royal title was multiplied and degraded, and that the mercenaries of Italy were
the fragments of many tribes and nations.

more obstinate, but the event was still more decisive; Odoacer fled to Ravenna, Theodoric advanced to Milan, and the vanquished troops saluted their conqueror with loud acclamations of respect and fidelity. But their want either of constancy or of faith soon exposed him to the most imminent danger; his vanguard, with several Gothic counts, which had been rashly intrusted to a deserter, was betrayed and destroyed near Faenza by his double treachery; Odoacer again appeared master of the field, and the invader, strongly entrenched in his camp of Pavia, was reduced to solicit the aid of a kindred nation, the Visigoths of Gaul. In the course of this history the most voracious appetite for war will be abundantly satiated; nor can I much lament that our dark and imperfect materials do not afford a more ample narrative of the distress of Italy, and of the fierce conflict which was finally decided by the abilities, experience, and valour of the Gothic king. Immediately before the battle of Verona he visited the tent of his mother[1] and sister, and requested that on a day, the most illustrious festival of his life, they would adorn him with the rich garments which they had worked with their own hands. 'Our glory,' said he, 'is mutual and inseparable. You are known to the world as the mother of Theodoric, and it becomes me to prove that I am the genuine offspring of those heroes from whom I claim my descent.' The wife or concubine of Theodemir was inspired with the spirit of the German matrons, who esteemed their sons' honour far above their safety; and it is reported that in a desperate action, when Theodoric himself was hurried along by the torrent of a flying crowd, she boldly met them at the entrance of the camp, and, by her generous reproaches, drove them back on the swords of the enemy.[2]

From the Alps to the extremity of Calabria, Theodoric reigned by the right of conquest: the Vandal ambassadors surrendered the island of Sicily as a lawful appendage of his kingdom,

---

1 See Ennodius, p. 1603, 1604. Since the orator, in the king's presence, could mention and praise his mother, we may conclude that the magnanimity of Theodoric was not hurt by the vulgar reproaches of concubine and bastard.

2 This anecdote is related on the modern but respectable authority of Sigonius (Op. tom. i. p. 580; De Occident. Imp. l. xv.): his words are curious:– 'Would you return?' etc. She presented and almost displayed the original recess.

and he was accepted as the deliverer of Rome by the senate and
people, who had shut their gates against the flying usurper.[1]
Ravenna alone, secure in the fortifications of art and nature, still
sustained a siege of almost three years, and the daring sallies of
Odoacer carried slaughter and dismay into the Gothic camp. At
length, destitute of provisions and hopeless of relief, that unfortunate monarch yielded to the groans of his subjects and the
clamours of his soldiers. A treaty of peace was negotiated by the
bishop of Ravenna; the Ostrogoths were admitted into the city;
and the hostile kings consented, under the sanction of an oath,
to rule with equal and undivided authority the provinces of Italy.
The event of such an agreement may be easily foreseen. After
some days had been devoted to the semblance of joy and friendship, Odoacer, in the midst of a solemn banquet, was stabbed
by the hand, or at least by the command, of his rival. Secret and
effectual orders had been previously despatched; the faithless
and rapacious mercenaries at the same moment, and without
resistance, were universally massacred; and the royalty of Theodoric was proclaimed by the Goths, with the tardy, reluctant,
ambiguous consent of the emperor of the East. The design of a
conspiracy was imputed, according to the usual forms, to the
prostrate tyrant, but his innocence and the guilt of his conquer-
or[2] are sufficiently proved by the advantageous treaty which *force*

1 Hist. Miscell. l. xv., a Roman history from Janus to the ninth century, an
Epitome of Eutropius, Paulus Diaconus, and Theophanes, which Muratori has
published from a MS. in the Ambrosian library (Script. Rerum Italicarum,
tom. i. p. 100).

[Prof. Bury cites the following account of the murder of Odoacer from a
fragment of John of Antioch. 'To a feast in the palace of the consul at the
south-east corner of Ravenna on March 5, 493, Theodoric invited Odoacer,
now 60 years of age. As the latter sat at table two men knelt before him with
a petition and clasped his hands. Then soldiers who had been hidden in recesses
on either side of the hall rushed out, but from some cause they could not bring
themselves to strike the king. Theodoric himself stepped forward and raised his
sword. "Where is God?" cried Odoacer. "Thus didst thou to my friends," said
Theodoric, and clave him from the collar bone to the loin. Surprised at his own
stroke he exclaimed, "The wretch can have had no bones in his body."' – O. S.]

2 Procopius (Gothic. l. i. c. i.) approves himself an impartial sceptic; φασὶ
. . . δολερῷ τρόπῳ ἔκτεινε [tom. ii. p. 10, ed. Bonn]. Cassiodorus (in Chron.)
and Ennodius (p. 1605) are loyal and credulous, and the testimony of the
Valesian Fragment (p. 718 [Amm. tom. ii. p. 307, ed. Bip.]) may justify their

would not sincerely have granted, nor *weakness* have rashly infringed. The jealousy of power, and the mischiefs of discord, may suggest a more decent apology, and a sentence less rigorous may be pronounced against a crime which was necessary to introduce into Italy a generation of public felicity. The living author of this felicity was audaciously praised in his own presence by sacred and profane orators;[1] but history (in his time she was mute and inglorious) has not left any just representation of the events which displayed, or of the defects which clouded, the virtues of Theodoric.[2] One record of his fame, the volume of public epistles composed by Cassiodorus in the royal name, is still extant, and has obtained more implicit credit than it seems to deserve.[3] They exhibit the forms, rather than the substance, of his government; and we should vainly search for the pure and spontaneous sentiments of the barbarian amidst the declamation and learning of a sophist, the wishes of a Roman senator, the precedents of office, and the vague professions which, in every court, and on every occasion, compose the language of discreet ministers. The reputation of Theodoric may repose with more confidence on the visible peace and prosperity of a reign of thirty-three years, the unanimous esteem of his own times, and the memory of his wisdom and courage, his justice and humanity, which was deeply impressed on the minds of the Goths and Italians.

belief. Marcellinus spits the venom of a Greek subject – perjuriis illectus, interfectusque est (in Chron. [anno 489]).

1 The sonorous and servile oration of Ennodius was pronounced at Milan or Ravenna in the years 507 or 508 (Sirmond, tom i. p. 1615). Two or three years afterwards the orator was rewarded with the bishopric of Pavia, which he held till his death in the year 521. (Dupin, Bibliot. Eccles. tom. v. p. 11–14. See Saxii Onomasticon, tom. ii. p. 12.)

2 Our best materials are occasional hints from Procopius and the Valesian Fragment, which was discovered by Sirmond and is published at the end of Ammianus Marcellinus. The author's name is unknown, and his style is barbarous; but in his various facts he exhibits the knowledge, without the passions, of a contemporary. The President Montesquieu had formed the plan of a history of Theodoric, which at a distance might appear a rich and interesting subject.

3 The best edition of the *Variarum Libri* xii. is that of Joh. Garretius (Rotomagi, 1679, in Opp. Cassiodor. 2 vols. in fol.); but they deserved and required such an editor as the Marquis Scipio Maffei, who thought of publishing them at Verona. The *Barbara Eleganza* (as it is ingeniously named by Tiraboschi) is never simple, and seldom perspicuous.

The partition of the lands of Italy, of which Theodoric assigned the third part to his soldiers, is *honourably* arraigned as the
sole injustice of his life. And even this act may be fairly justified
by the example of Odoacer, the rights of conquest, the true
interest of the Italians, and the sacred duty of subsisting a whole
people, who, on the faith of his promises, had transported themselves into a distant land.[1] Under the reign of Theodoric, and in
the happy climate of Italy, the Goths soon multiplied to a formidable host of two hundred thousand men,[2] and the whole
amount of their families may be computed by the ordinary addition of women and children. Their invasion of property, a part
of which must have been already vacant, was disguised by the
generous but improper name of *hospitality;* these unwelcome
guests were irregularly dispersed over the face of Italy, and the
lot of each barbarian was adequate to his birth and office, the
number of his followers, and the rustic wealth which he possessed in slaves and cattle. The distinctions of noble and plebeian
were acknowledged,[3] but the lands of every freeman were
exempt from taxes, and he enjoyed the inestimable privilege of
being subject only to the laws of his country.[4] Fashion, and even
convenience, soon persuaded the conquerors to assume the
more elegant dress of the natives, but they still persisted in the
use of their mother tongue; and their contempt for the Latin

1 Procopius, Gothic. l. i. c. i.; Variarum, ii. Maffei (Verona Illustrata, P. i.
p. 228) exaggerates the injustice of the Goths, whom he hated as an Italian
noble. The plebeian Muratori crouches under their oppression.

[With regard to the partition of the lands of Italy whereof Theodoric assigned a third part to his soldiers, Bury thinks that the process of distribution
may have been in the main a transferring of the thirds of the men of Odoacer
to the men of Theodoric. In this connection too (cf. Gibbon, vol. iii. p. 461)
it must be remembered that, as shown by Savigny, the Goths retained the land
tax and the capitation tax of the Roman emperors. *Geschichte des Römischen Rechts*,
vol. i. p. 332. – O. S.]

2 Procopius, Goth. l. iii. c. 4. and 21 [tom. ii. p. 295 and 366, ed. Bonn].
Ennodius describes (p. 1612, 1613) the military arts and increasing numbers of
the Goths.

3 When Theodoric gave his sister to the king of the Vandals, she sailed for
Africa with a guard of 1000 noble Goths, each of whom was attended by five
armed followers (Procop. Vandal. l. i. c. 8 [tom. i. p. 346, ed. Bonn]). The
Gothic nobility must have been as numerous as brave.

4 See the acknowledgment of Gothic liberty (Var. v. 30).

schools was applauded by Theodoric himself, who gratified their
prejudices, or his own, by declaring that the child who had trembled at a rod would never dare to look upon a sword.[1] Distress
might sometimes provoke the indigent Roman to assume the
ferocious manners which were insensibly relinquished by the rich
and luxurious barbarian;[2] but these mutual conversions were not
encouraged by the policy of a monarch who perpetuated the
separation of the Italians and Goths, reserving the former for
the arts of peace, and the latter for the service of war. To accomplish this design, he studied to protect his industrious subjects, and to moderate the violence, without enervating the
valour, of his soldiers, who were maintained for the public
defence. They held their lands and benefices as a military stipend:
at the sound of the trumpet they were prepared to march under
the conduct of their provincial officers, and the whole extent of
Italy was distributed into the several quarters of a well-regulated
camp. The service of the palace and of the frontiers was performed by choice or by rotation, and each extraordinary fatigue
was recompensed by an increase of pay and occasional donatives.
Theodoric had convinced his brave companions that empire
must be acquired and defended by the same arts. After his
example, they strove to excel in the use not only of the lance
and sword, the instruments of their victories, but of the missile
weapons, which they were too much inclined to neglect: and the
lively image of war was displayed in the daily exercise and annual
reviews of the Gothic cavalry. A firm though gentle discipline
imposed the habits of modesty, obedience, and temperance; and
the Goths were instructed to spare the people, to reverence the
laws, to understand the duties of civil society, and to disclaim
the barbarous licence of judicial combat and private revenge.[3]

1 Procopius, Goth. l. i. c. 2 [tom. ii. p. 14, ed. Bonn]. The Roman boys
learnt the language (Var. viii. 21) of the Goths. Their general ignorance is not
destroyed by the exceptions of Amalasuntha, a female, who might study without
shame, or of Theodatus, whose learning provoked the indignation and contempt of his countrymen.

2 A saying of Theodoric was founded on experience: 'Romanus miser imitatur Gothum; et utilis (*dives*) Gothus imitatur Romanum.' (See the Fragment
and Notes of Valesius, p. 719 [Amm. ii. p. 308, ed. Bip.]).

3 The view of the military establishment of the Goths in Italy is collected
from the Epistles of Cassiodorus (Var. i. 24, 40; iii. 3, 24, 48; iv. 13, 14; v. 26,

Among the barbarians of the West the victory of Theodoric had spread a general alarm. But as soon as it appeared that he was satisfied with conquest and desirous of peace, terror was changed into respect, and they submitted to a powerful mediation, which was uniformly employed for the best purposes of reconciling their quarrels and civilising their manners.[1] The ambassadors who resorted to Ravenna from the most distant countries of Europe admired his wisdom, magnificence,[2] and courtesy; and if he sometimes accepted either slaves or arms, white horses or strange animals, the gift of a sun-dial, a water-clock, or a musician, admonished even the princes of Gaul of the superior art and industry of his Italian subjects. His domestic alliances,[3] a wife, two daughters, a sister, and a niece, united the family of Theodoric with the kings of the Franks, the Burgundians, the Visigoths, the Vandals, and the Thuringians, and contributed to maintain the harmony, or at least the balance, of the great republic of the West.[4] It is difficult in the dark forests of Germany and Poland to pursue the emigrations of the Heruli, a fierce people who disdained the use of armour, and who condemned their widows and aged parents not to survive the loss of their husbands or the decay of their strength.[5] The king of these savage warriors solicited the friendship of Theodoric, and

27; viii. 3, 4, 25). They are illustrated by the learned Mascou (Hist. of the Germans, l. xi. 40–44; Annotation xiv.).

1 See the clearness and vigour of his negotiations in Ennodius (p. 1607) and Cassiodorus (Var. iii. 1, 2, 3, 4; iv. 13; v. 43, 44), who gives the different styles of friendship, counsel, expostulation, etc.

2 Even of his table (Var. vi. 9) and palace (vii. 5). The admiration of strangers is represented as the most rational motive to justify these vain expenses, and to stimulate the diligence of the officers to whom these provinces were intrusted.

3 See the public and private alliances of the Gothic monarch, with the Burgundians (Var. i. 45, 46), with the Franks (ii. 40), with the Thuringians (iv. 1), and with the Vandals (v. 1); each of these epistles affords some curious knowledge of the policy and manners of the barbarians.

4 His political system may be observed in Cassiodorus (Var. iv. 1, ix. 1), Jornandes (c. 58, p. 698, 699), and the Valesian Fragment (p. 720, 721 [Amm. tom. ii. p. 311, ed. Bip.]). Peace, honourable peace, was the constant aim of Theodoric.

5 The curious reader may contemplate the Heruli of Procopius (Goth. l. ii. c. 14), and the patient reader may plunge into the dark and minute researches of M. de Buat (Hist. des Peuples Anciens, tom. ix. p. 348–396).

was elevated to the rank of his son, according to the barbaric rites of a military adoption.[1] From the shores of the Baltic the Æstians or Livonians laid their offerings of native amber[2] at the feet of a prince whose fame had excited them to undertake an unknown and dangerous journey of fifteen hundred miles. With the country[3] from whence the Gothic nation derived their origin he maintained a frequent and friendly correspondence: the Italians were clothed in the rich sables[4] of Sweden; and one of its sovereigns, after a voluntary or reluctant abdication, found an hospitable retreat in the palace of Ravenna. He had reigned over one of the thirteen populous tribes who cultivated a small portion of the great island or peninsula of Scandinavia, to which the vague appellation of Thule has been sometimes applied. That northern region was peopled, or had been explored, as high as the sixty-eighth degree of latitude, where the natives of the polar circle enjoy and lose the presence of the sun at each summer and winter solstice during an equal period of forty days.[5] The

[The Heruli are first mentioned about the middle of the third century, when they accompany the Goths in their expeditions on the Euxine in the reigns of Claudius and Gallienus. Hence it has been supposed they were Germans. This is not conclusive, however, as Slavonic tribes appear to have taken part in these expeditions. Cf. Zeuss *Die Deutschen und die Nachbarstämme.* – O. S.]

1 Variarum, iv. 2. The spirit and forms of this martial institution are noticed by Cassiodorus; but he seems to have only translated the sentiments of the Gothic king into the language of Roman eloquence.

2 Cassiodorus, who quotes Tacitus to the Æstians, the unlettered savages of the Baltic (Var. v. 2), describes the amber for which their shores have ever been famous as the gum of a tree hardened by the sun and purified and wafted by the waves. When that singular substance is analysed by the chemists, it yields a vegetable oil and a mineral acid.

3 Scanzia, or Thule, is described by Jornandes (c. 3, p. 610–613) and Procopius (Goth. l. ii. c. 15). Neither the Goth nor the Greek had visited the country: both had conversed with the natives in their exile at Ravenna or Constantinople.

4 *Saphirinas pelles.* In the time of Jornandes they inhabited *Suethans*, the proper Sweden; but that beautiful race of animals has gradually been driven into the eastern parts of Siberia. See Buffon (Hist. Nat. tom. xiii. p. 309–313, quarto edition); Pennant (System of Quadrupeds, vol. i. p. 322–328); Gmelin (Hist. Gén. des Voyages, tom. xviii. p. 257, 258); and Levesque (Hist. de Russie, tom. v. p. 165, 166, 514, 515).

5 In the system or romance of M. Bailly (Lettres sur les Sciences et sur l'Atlantide, tom. i. p. 249–256, tom. ii. p. 114–139), the phœnix of the Edda,

long night of his absence or death was the mournful season of distress and anxiety, till the messengers, who had been sent to the mountain tops, descried the first rays of returning light, and proclaimed to the plain below the festival of his resurrection.[1]

The life of Theodoric represents the rare and meritorious example of a barbarian who sheathed his sword in the pride of victory and the vigour of his age. A reign of three and thirty years was consecrated to the duties of civil government, and the hostilities, in which he was sometimes involved, were speedily terminated by the conduct of his lieutenants, the discipline of his troops, the arms of his allies, and even by the terror of his name. He reduced, under a strong and regular government, the unprofitable countries of Rhætia, Noricum, Dalmatia, and Pannonia, from the source of the Danube and the territory of the Bavarians[2] to the petty kingdom erected by the Gepidæ on the ruins of Sirmium. His prudence could not safely intrust the bulwark of Italy to such feeble and turbulent neighbours; and his justice might claim the lands which they oppressed, either as a part of his kingdom, or as the inheritance of his father. The greatness of a servant, who was named perfidious because he was successful, awakened the jealousy of the emperor Anastasius; and a war was kindled on the Dacian frontier, by the protection which the Gothic king, in the vicissitude of human affairs, had granted to one of the descendants of Attila. Sabinian, a general illustrious by his own and father's merit, advanced at the head of ten thousand Romans; and the provisions and arms, which

and the annual death and revival of Adonis and Osiris, are the allegorical symbols of the absence and return of the sun in the Arctic regions. This ingenious writer is a worthy disciple of the great Buffon; nor is it easy for the coldest reason to withstand the magic of their philosophy.

1 Αὕτη τε Θουλίταις ἡ μεγίστη τῶν ἑορτῶν ἐστι, says Procopius [tom. ii. p. 207, ed. Bonn]. At present a rude Manicheism (generous enough) prevails among the Samoyedes in Greenland and in Lapland (Hist. des Voyages, tom. xviii. p. 508, 509, tom. xix. p. 105, 106, 527, 528); yet, according to Grotius, Samojutæ cœlum atque astra adorant, numina haud aliis iniquiora (de Rebus Belgicis, l. iv. p. 338, folio edition); a sentence which Tacitus would not have disowned.

2 See the Hist. des Peuples Anciens, etc., tom. ix. p. 255–273, 396–501. The Count de Buat was French minister at the court of Bavaria: a liberal curiosity prompted his inquiries into the antiquities of the country, and that curiosity was the *germ* of twelve respectable volumes.

filled a long train of waggons, were distributed to the fiercest of
the Bulgarian tribes. But in the fields of Margus the Eastern
powers were defeated by the inferior forces of the Goths and
Huns; the flower and even the hope of the Roman armies was
irretrievably destroyed; and such was the temperance with which
Theodoric had inspired his victorious troops, that, as their leader
had not given the signal of pillage, the rich spoils of the enemy
lay untouched at their feet.[1] Exasperated by this disgrace, the
Byzantine court despatched two hundred ships and eight thousand men to plunder the sea-coast of Calabria and Apulia: they
assaulted the ancient city of Tarentum, interrupted the trade and
agriculture of a happy country, and sailed back to the Hellespont,
proud of their piratical victory over a people whom they still
presumed to consider as their *Roman* brethren.[2] Their retreat was
possibly hastened by the activity of Theodoric; Italy was covered
by a fleet of a thousand light vessels,[3] which he constructed with
incredible despatch; and his firm moderation was soon rewarded
by a solid and honourable peace. He maintained with a powerful
hand the balance of the West, till it was at length overthrown
by the ambition of Clovis; and although unable to assist his rash
and unfortunate kinsman the king of the Visigoths, he saved the
remains of his family and people, and checked the Franks in the
midst of their victorious career. I am not desirous to prolong or
repeat[4] this narrative of military events, the least interesting of
the reign of Theodoric; and shall be content to add that the

1 See the Gothic transactions on the Danube and in Illyricum, in Jornandes
(c. 58, p. 699), Ennodius (p. 1607–1610), Marcellinus (in Chron. p. 44, 47, 48),
and Cassiodorus (in Chron. and Var. iii. 23, 50; iv. 13; vii. 4, 24; viii. 9, 10, 11,
21; ix. 8, 9).

2 I cannot forbear transcribing the liberal and classic style of Count
Marcellinus: Romanus comes domesticorum, et Rusticus comes scholariorum
cum centum armatis navibus, totidemque dromonibus, octo millia militum
armatorum secum ferentibus, ad devastanda Italiæ littora processerunt, et
usque ad Tarentum antiquissimam civitatem aggressi sunt; remensoque mari
inhonestam victoriam quam piratico ausu Romani ex Romanis rapuerunt,
Anastasio Cæsari reportarunt (in Chron. p. 48 [anno 508]). See Variar. i. 16,
ii. 38.

3 See the royal orders and instructions (Var. iv. 15; v. 16–20). These armed
boats should be still smaller than the thousand vessels of Agamemnon at the
siege of Troy [Manso, p. 121].

4 Above, p. 65, *seq.*

Alemanni were protected,[1] that an inroad of the Burgundians was severely chastised, and that the conquest of Arles and Marseilles opened a free communication with the Visigoths, who revered him both as their national protector, and as the guardian of his grandchild, the infant son of Alaric. Under this respectable character, the king of Italy restored the Prætorian præfecture of the Gauls, reformed some abuses in the civil government of Spain, and accepted the annual tribute and apparent submission of its military governor, who wisely refused to trust his person in the palace of Ravenna.[2] The Gothic sovereignty was established from Sicily to the Danube, from Sirmium or Belgrade to the Atlantic Ocean; and the Greeks themselves have acknowledged that Theodoric reigned over the fairest portion of the Western empire.[3]

The union of the Goths and Romans might have fixed for ages the transient happiness of Italy; and the first of nations, a new people of free subjects and enlightened soldiers, might have gradually arisen from the mutual emulation of their respective virtues. But the sublime merit of guiding or seconding such a revolution was not reserved for the reign of Theodoric: he wanted either the genius or the opportunities of a legislator;[4] and

1 Ennodius (p. 1610) and Cassiodorus, in the royal name (Var. ii. 41), record his salutary protection of the Alemanni.

2 The Gothic transactions in Gaul and Spain are represented with some perplexity in Cassiodorus (Var. iii. 32, 38, 41, 43, 44; v. 39), Jornandes (c. 58, p. 698, 699), and Procopius (Goth. l. i. c. 12). I will neither hear nor reconcile the long and contradictory arguments of the Abbé Dubos and the Count de Buat, about the wars of Burgundy.

3 Theophanes, p. 113 [p. 203, ed. Bonn].

4 Procopius affirms that no laws whatsoever were promulgated by Theodoric and the succeeding kings of Italy (Goth. l. ii. c. 6 [tom. ii. p. 170, ed. Bonn]). He must mean in the Gothic language. A Latin edict of Theodoric is still extant, in one hundred and fifty-four articles.

[This Latin edict of Theodoric was promulgated in 500 A.D., and its articles were intended to apply to cases in which either the Romans or the Goths and Romans were concerned. While the Goths retained the exclusive privilege of arms, it was the policy of Theodoric to unite them and the Romans in all their civil relations into one people. In this respect the Ostrogothic kingdom was distinct from all the other German states founded upon the downfall of the empire, since in the latter each nation preserved its separate laws. Cf. Savigny. In differences between Goth and Roman, a Roman jurisconsult acted as assessor to the Comes Gothorum, or the official dealing with the disputes between

while he indulged the Goths in the enjoyment of rude liberty, he servilely copied the institutions, and even the abuses, of the political system which had been framed by Constantine and his successors. From a tender regard to the expiring prejudices of Rome, the barbarian declined the name, the purple, and the diadem of the emperors; but he assumed, under the hereditary title of king, the whole substance and plenitude of Imperial prerogative.[1] His addresses to the Eastern throne were respectful and ambiguous: he celebrated in pompous style the harmony of the two republics, applauded his own government as the perfect similitude of a sole and undivided empire, and claimed above the kings of the earth the same pre-eminence which he modestly allowed to the person or rank of Anastasius. The alliance of the East and West was annually declared by the unanimous choice of two consuls; but it should seem that the Italian candidate, who was named by Theodoric, accepted a formal confirmation from the sovereign of Constantinople.[2] The Gothic palace of Ravenna reflected the image of the court of Theodosius or Valentinian. The Prætorian præfect, the præfect of Rome, the quæstor, the master of the offices, with the public and patrimonial treasurers, whose functions are painted in gaudy colours by the rhetoric of Cassiodorus, still continued to act as the ministers of state. And the subordinate care of justice and the revenue was delegated to seven consulars, three correctors, and five presidents, who governed the fifteen *regions* of Italy according to the principles, and even the forms, of Roman jurisprudence.[3] The violence of the conquerors was abated or eluded by the slow

Goths themselves. Of course there was a natural leaning at times to the side of the Goth. – O. S.]

1 The image of Theodoric is engraved on his coins: his modest successors were satisfied with adding their own name to the head of the reigning emperor (Muratori, Antiquitat. Italiæ Medii Ævi, tom. ii. dessert. xxvii. p. 577–579. Giannone, Istoria Civile di Napoli, tom. i. p. 166).

2 The alliance of the emperor and the king of Italy are represented by Cassiodorus (Var. i. 1; ii. 1, 2, 3; vi. 1) and Procopius (Goth. l. ii. c. 6; l. iii. c. 21 [tom. ii. p. 369, ed. Bonn]), who celebrate the friendship of Anastasius and Theodoric: but the figurative style of compliment was interpreted in a very different sense at Constantinople and Ravenna.

3 To the seventeen provinces of the Notitia, Paul Warnefrid the deacon (De Reb. Longobard. l. ii. c. 14–22) has subjoined an eighteenth, the Apennine

artifice of judicial proceedings; the civil administration, with its honours and emoluments, was confined to the Italians; and the people still preserved their dress and language, their laws and customs, their personal freedom, and two-thirds of their landed property. It had been the object of Augustus to conceal the introduction of monarchy; it was the policy of Theodoric to disguise the reign of a barbarian.[1] If his subjects were sometimes awakened from this pleasing vision of a Roman government, they derived more substantial comfort from the character of a Gothic prince who had penetration to discern, and firmness to pursue, his own and the public interest. Theodoric loved the virtues which he possessed, and the talents of which he was destitute. Liberius was promoted to the office of Prætorian præfect for his unshaken fidelity to the unfortunate cause of Odoacer. The ministers of Theodoric, Cassiodorus,[2] and Boethius, have reflected on his reign the lustre of their genius and learning. More prudent or more fortunate than his colleague, Cassiodorus

(Muratori, Script. Rerum Italicarum, tom. i. p. 431–433). But of these, Sardinia and Corsica were possessed by the Vandals, and the two Rhætias, as well as the Cottian Alps, seem to have been abandoned to a military government. The state of the four provinces that now form the kingdom of Naples is laboured by Giannone (tom. i. p. 172, 178) with patriotic diligence.

1 See the Gothic history of Procopius (l. i. c. 1, l. ii. c. 6), the Epistles of Cassiodorus (passim, but especially the fifth and sixth books [vi. and vii.], which contain the *formulæ*, or patents of offices), and the Civil History of Giannone (tom. i. l. ii. iii.). The Gothic counts, which he places in every Italian city, are annihilated, however, by Maffei (Verona Illustrata, P. i. l. viii. p. 227); for those of Syracuse and Naples (Var. vi. 22, 23) were special and temporary commissions.

2 Two Italians of the name of Cassiodorus, the father (Var. i. 24 [4], 40) and the son (ix. 24, 25), were successively employed in the administration of Theodoric. The son was born in the year 479: his various epistles as quæstor, master of the offices, and Prætorian præfect, extend from 509 to 539, and he lived as a monk about thirty years. (Tiraboschi, Storia della Letteratura Italiana, tom. iii. p. 7–24. Fabricius, Biblioth. Lat. Med. Ævi. tom. i. p. 357, 358, edit. Mansi.)

[Cassiodorus was of an ancient and honourable family. His grandfather had distinguished himself in the defence of Sicily against the ravages of Genseric, while his father held a high rank at the court of Valentinian III. Cassiodorus was first the treasurer of the private expenditure to Odoacer, afterwards 'Count of the Sacred Largesses.' Yielding with the rest of the Romans to the dominion of Theodoric, he was instrumental in securing the peaceful submission of Sicily. He was successively governor of his native provinces of Bruttium and Lucania, quæstor, magister palatii, Prætorian Præfect, patrician, consul, private secretary, and, in fact, first minister to the king. He died in 575 at the great age of 95. – O. S.]

preserved his own esteem without forfeiting the royal favour; and after passing thirty years in the honours of the world, he was blessed with an equal term of repose in the devout and studious solitude of Squillace.

As the patron of the republic, it was the interest and duty of the Gothic king to cultivate the affections of the senate[1] and people. The nobles of Rome were flattered by sonorous epithets and formal professions of respect, which had been more justly applied to the merit and authority of their ancestors. The people enjoyed, without fear or danger, the three blessings of a capital, order, plenty, and public amusements. A visible diminution of their numbers may be found even in the measure of liberality;[2] yet Apulia, Calabria, and Sicily poured their tribute of corn into the granaries of Rome; an allowance of bread and meat was distributed to the indigent citizens; and every office was deemed honourable which was consecrated to the care of their health and happiness. The public games, such as a Greek ambassador might politely applaud, exhibited a faint and feeble copy of the magnificence of the Cæsars: yet the musical, the gymnastic, and the pantomime arts, had not totally sunk in oblivion; the wild beasts of Africa still exercised in the amphitheatre the courage and dexterity of the hunters; and the indulgent Goth either patiently tolerated or gently restrained the blue and green factions, whose contest so often filled the circus with clamour, and even with blood.[3] In the seventh year of his peaceful reign, Theodoric visited the old capital of the world; the senate and people advanced in solemn procession to salute a second Trajan, a new Valentinian; and he nobly supported that character, by the assurance of a just and legal government,[4] in a discourse which he

1 See his regard for the senate in Cochlœus (Vit. Theod. viii. p. 72–80).

2 No more than 120,000 *modii*, or four thousand quarters (Anonym. Valesian, p. 721 [Amm. ii. p. 310, ed. Bip.], and Var. i. 35, vi. 18, xi. 5, 39).

3 See his regard and indulgence for the spectacles of the circus, the amphitheatre, and the theatre, in the Chronicle and Epistles of Cassiodorus (Var. i. 20, 27, 30, 31, 32, iii. 51, iv. 51, illustrated by the fourteenth Annotation of Mascou's History), who has contrived to sprinkle the subject with ostentatious, though agreeable, learning.

4 Anonym. Vales. p. 721 [l. c. ed. Bip.]. Marius Aventicensis in Chron. In the scale of public and personal merit, the Gothic conqueror is at least as much *above* Valentinian as he may seem *inferior* to Trajan.

was not afraid to pronounce in public and to inscribe on a tablet of brass. Rome, in this august ceremony, shot a last ray of declining glory; and a saint, the spectator of this pompous scene, could only hope, in his pious fancy, that it was excelled by the celestial splendour of the New Jerusalem.[1] During a residence of six months, the fame, the person, and the courteous demeanour of the Gothic king excited the admiration of the Romans, and he contemplated, with equal curiosity and surprise, the monuments that remained of their ancient greatness. He imprinted the footsteps of a conqueror on the Capitoline hill, and frankly confessed that each day he viewed with fresh wonder the forum of Trajan and his lofty column. The theatre of Pompey appeared, even in its decay, as a huge mountain, artificially hollowed and polished, and adorned by human industry; and he vaguely computed that a river of gold must have been drained to erect the colossal amphitheatre of Titus.[2] From the mouths of fourteen aqueducts a pure and copious stream was diffused into every part of the city; among these the Claudian water, which arose at the distance of thirty-eight miles in the Sabine mountains, was conveyed along a gentle though constant declivity of solid arches, till it descended on the summit of the Aventine hill. The long and spacious vaults which had been constructed for the purpose of common sewers subsisted after twelve centuries in their pristine strength; and these subterraneous channels have been preferred to all the visible wonders of Rome.[3] The Gothic kings, so injuriously accused of the ruin of antiquity, were anxious to preserve the monuments of the nation whom they had subdued.[4]

1 Vit. Fulgentii in Baron. Annal. Eccles. A.D. 500, No. 10.

2 Cassiodorus describes in his pompous style the Forum of Trajan (Var. vii. 6), the theatre of Marcellus (iv. 51), and the amphitheatre of Titus (v. 42); and his descriptions are not unworthy of the reader's perusal. According to the modern prices, the Abbé Barthelemy computes that the brickwork and masonry of the Coliseum would now cost twenty millions of French livres (Mém. de l'Académie des Inscriptions, tom. xxviii. p. 585, 586). How small a part of that stupendous fabric!

3 For the aqueducts and cloacæ see Strabo (l. v. p. 360 [p. 235, ed. Casaub.]), Pliny (Hist. Nat. xxxvi. 24 [§ 3]), Cassiodorus (Var. iii. 30, 31, vi. 6), Procopius (Goth. l. i. c. 19), and Nardini (Roma Antica, p. 514–522). How such works could be executed by a king of Rome is yet a problem.

4 For the Gothic care of the buildings and the statues, see Cassiodorus (Var. i. 21, 25, ii. 34, iv. 30, vii. 6, 13, 15), and the Valesian Fragment (p. 721 [Amm. tom. ii. p. 310, ed. Bip.]).

The royal edicts were framed to prevent the abuses, the neglect, or the depredations of the citizens themselves; and a professed architect, the annual sum of two hundred pounds of gold, twenty-five thousand tiles, and the receipt of customs from the Lucrine port, were assigned for the ordinary repairs of the walls and public edifices. A similar care was extended to the statues of metal or marble of men or animals. The spirit of the horses which have given a modern name to the Quirinal was applauded by the barbarians;[1] the brazen elephants of the *Via sacra* were diligently restored;[2] the famous heifer of Myron deceived the cattle, as they were driven through the forum of peace;[3] and an officer was created to protect those works of art, which Theodoric considered as the noblest ornament of his kingdom.

After the example of the last emperors, Theodoric preferred the residence of Ravenna, where he cultivated an orchard with his own hands.[4] As often as the peace of his kingdom was threatened (for it was never invaded) by the barbarians, he removed his court to Verona[5] on the northern frontier, and the image of his palace, still extant on a coin, represents the oldest and most authentic model of Gothic architecture. These two capitals, as well as Pavia, Spoleto, Naples, and the rest of the Italian cities, acquired under his reign the useful or splendid decorations of churches, aqueducts, baths, porticoes, and palaces.[6] But the

1 Var. vii. 15. These horses of Monte Cavallo had been transported from Alexandria to the baths of Constantine (Nardini, p. 188). Their sculpture is disdained by the Abbé Dubos (Réflexions sur la Poésie et sur la Peinture, tom. i. section 39), and admired by Winckelman (Hist. de l'Art, tom. ii. p. 159).

2 Var. x. 30. They were probably a fragment of some triumphal car (Cuper de Elephantis, ii. 10).

3 Procopius (Goth. l. iv. c. 21 [tom. ii. p. 571, ed. Bonn]) relates a foolish story of Myron's cow, which is celebrated by the false wit of thirty-six Greek epigrams (Antholog. l. iv. p. 302–306, edit. Hen. Steph.; Auson. Epigram. lviii.–lxviii.).

4 See an epigram of Ennodius (ii. 3, p. 1893, 1894) on this garden and the royal gardener.

5 His affection for that city is proved by the epithet of 'Verona tua,' and the legend of the hero; under the barbarous name of Dietrich of Bern (Peringsciold ad Cochlœum, p. 240), Maffei traces him with knowledge and pleasure in his native country (l. ix. p. 230–236).

6 See Maffei (Verona Illustrata, Part i. p. 231, 232, 308, etc.). He imputes Gothic architecture, like the corruption of language, writing, etc., not to the

happiness of the subject was more truly conspicuous in the busy scene of labour and luxury, in the rapid increase and bold enjoyment of national wealth. From the shades of Tibur and Præneste, the Roman senators still retired in the winter season to the warm sun and salubrious springs of Baiæ; and their villas, which advanced on solid moles into the bay of Naples, commanded the various prospect of the sky, the earth, and the water. On the eastern side of the Hadriatic a new Campania was formed in the fair and fruitful province of Istria, which communicated with the palace of Ravenna by an easy navigation of one hundred miles. The rich productions of Lucania and the adjacent provinces were exchanged at the Marcilian fountain, in a populous fair annually dedicated to trade, intemperance, and superstition. In the solitude of Comum, which had once been animated by the mild genius of Pliny, a transparent basin above sixty miles in length still reflected the rural seats which encompassed the margin of the Larian lake; and the gradual ascent of the hills was covered by a triple plantation of olives, of vines, and of chest-nut-trees.[1] Agriculture revived under the shadow of peace, and the number of husbandmen was multiplied by the redemption of captives.[2] The iron-mines of Dalmatia, a gold-mine in Bruttium, were carefully explored, and the Pomptine marshes, as well as those of Spoleto, were drained and cultivated by private

barbarians, but to the Italians themselves. Compare his sentiments with those of Tiraboschi (tom. iii. p. 61).

[With regard to Theodoric's architecture, Hallam states that the 'image' of it is represented in Maffei, not from a coin, but from a seal. There is also an engraving from a mosaic in the church of St. Apollinaris in Ravenna representing a building ascribed to Theodoric in that city. Neither of these, as Hallam says, in the least approximates to the Gothic style. They are evidently the degenerate Roman architecture, and, as Milman says, more resemble the attempts of our English architects to get back from our national Gothic into a classical Greek style. One of them, adds Milman, calls to mind Inigo Jones's inner quadrangle in St. John's College, Oxford. – O. S.]

1 The villas, climate, and landscape of Baiæ (Var. ix. 6; see Cluver. Italia Antiq. l. iv. c. 2, p. 1119, etc.), Istria (Var. xii. 22, 26), and Comum (Var. xi. 14, compare with Pliny's two villas, ix. 7), are agreeably painted in the epistles of Cassiodorus.

2 In Liguria numerosa agricolarum progenies (Ennodius, p. 1678, 1679, 1680). St. Epiphanius of Pavia redeemed by prayer or ransom 6000 captives from the Burgundians of Lyons and Savoy. Such deeds are the best of miracles.

undertakers, whose distant reward must depend on the continuance of the public prosperity.[1] Whenever the seasons were less
propitious, the doubtful precautions of forming magazines of
corn, fixing the price, and prohibiting the exportation, attested
at least the benevolence of the state; but such was the extraordinary plenty which an industrious people produced from a grateful
soil, that a gallon of wine was sometimes sold in Italy for less
than three farthings, and a quarter of wheat at about five shillings
and sixpence.[2] A country possessed of so many valuable objects
of exchange soon attracted the merchants of the world, whose
beneficial traffic was encouraged and protected by the liberal
spirit of Theodoric. The free intercourse of the provinces by land
and water was restored and extended; the city gates were never
shut either by day or by night; and the common saying, that a
purse of gold might be safely left in the fields, was expressive of
the conscious security of the inhabitants.

A difference of religion is always pernicious and often fatal
to the harmony of the prince and people: the Gothic conqueror
had been educated in the profession of Arianism, and Italy was
devoutly attached to the Nicene faith. But the persuasion of
Theodoric was not infected by zeal: and he piously adhered to
the heresy of his fathers, without condescending to balance the
subtile arguments of theological metaphysics. Satisfied with the
private toleration of his Arian sectaries, he justly conceived himself to be the guardian of the public worship, and his external
reverence for a superstition which he despised may have nourished
in his mind the salutary indifference of a statesman or philosopher. The catholics of his dominions acknowledged, perhaps
with reluctance, the peace of the church; their clergy, according

1 The political economy of Theodoric (see Anonym. Vales. p. 721 [Amm.
tom. ii. p. 311, ed. Bip.] and Cassiodorus, in Chron.) may be distinctly traced
under the following heads: iron-mine (Var. iii. 25); gold-mine (ix. 3); Pomptine
marshes (ii. 32, 33); Spoleto (ii. 21); corn (i. 34, x. 27, 28, xi. 11, 12); trade (vi.
7, vii. 9, 23); fair of Leucothoe or St. Cyprian in Lucania (viii. 33); plenty (xii.
4); the cursus, or public post (i. 29, ii. 31, iv. 47, v. 5, vi. 6, vii. 33); the Flaminian
way (xii. 18).

2 LX modii tritici in solidum ipsius tempore fuerunt, et vinum xxx ampho-
ras in solidum (Fragment. Vales. [p. 311, ed. Bip.]). Corn was distributed from
the granaries at xv or xxv modii for a piece of gold, and the price was still
moderate.

to the degrees of rank or merit, were honourably entertained in the palace of Theodoric; he esteemed the living sanctity of Cæsarius[1] and Epiphanius,[2] the orthodox bishops of Arles and Pavia; and presented a decent offering on the tomb of St. Peter, without any scrupulous inquiry into the creed of the apostle.[3] His favourite Goths, and even his mother, were permitted to retain or embrace the Athanasian faith, and his long reign could not afford the example of an Italian catholic who, either from choice or compulsion, had deviated into the religion of the conqueror.[4] The people, and the barbarians themselves, were edified by the pomp and order of religious worship; the magistrates were instructed to defend the just immunities of ecclesiastical persons and possessions; the bishops held their synods, the metropolitans exercised their jurisdiction, and the privileges of sanctuary were maintained or moderated according to the spirit of the Roman jurisprudence.[5] With the protection, Theodoric assumed the legal supremacy, of the church; and his firm administration restored or extended some useful prerogatives which had been neglected by the feeble emperors of the West. He was not ignorant of the dignity and importance of the Roman pontiff, to whom the venerable name of POPE was now appropriated. The peace or the revolt of Italy might depend on the character of a

1 See the Life of St. Cæsarius in Baronius (A.D. 508, No. 12, 13, 14). The king presented him with 300 gold solidi, and a discus of silver of the weight of sixty pounds.

2 Ennodius in Vit. St. Epiphanii, in Sirmond Op. tom. i. p. 1672–1690. Theodoric bestowed some important favours on this bishop, whom he used as a counsellor in peace and war.

3 Devotissimus ac si catholicus (Anonym. Vales. p. 720 [p. 310, ed. Bip.]); yet his offering was no more than two silver candlesticks (cerostrata) of the weight of seventy pounds, far inferior to the gold and gems of Constantinople and France (Anastasius in Vit. Pont. in Hormisda, p. 34, edit. Paris [tom. i. p. 93, ed. Rom. 1718]).

4 The tolerating system of his reign (Ennodius, p. 1612, Anonym. Vales. p. 719 [p. 308, ed. Bip.], Procop. Goth. l. i. c. 1, l. ii. c. 6) may be studied in the Epistles of Cassiodorus, under the following heads: bishops (Var. i. 9, viii. 15, 24, xi. 23); immunities (i. 26, ii. 29, 30); church lands (iv. 17, 20); sanctuaries (ii. 11, iii. 47); church plate (xii. 20); discipline (iv. 44); which prove at the same time that he was the head of the church as well as of the state.

5 We may reject a foolish tale of his beheading a catholic deacon who turned Arian (Theodor. Lector. No. 17). Why is Theodoric surnamed Afer? From Vafer? (Vales. ad loc.) A light conjecture.

wealthy and popular bishop, who claimed such ample dominion both in heaven and earth; who had been declared in a numerous synod to be pure from all sin, and exempt from all judgment.[1] When the chair of St. Peter was disputed by Symmachus and Laurence, they appeared at his summons before the tribunal of an Arian monarch, and he confirmed the election of the most worthy or the most obsequious candidate. At the end of his life, in a moment of jealousy and resentment, he prevented the choice of the Romans, by nominating a pope in the palace of Ravenna. The danger and furious contests of a schism were mildly restrained, and the last decree of the senate was enacted to extinguish, if it were possible, the scandalous venality of the papal elections.[2]

I have descanted with pleasure on the fortunate condition of Italy, but our fancy must not hastily conceive that the golden age of the poets, a race of men without vice or misery, was realised under the Gothic conquest. The fair prospect was sometimes overcast with clouds; the wisdom of Theodoric might be deceived, his power might be resisted, and the declining age of the monarch was sullied with popular hatred and patrician blood. In the first insolence of victory he had been tempted to deprive the whole party of Odoacer of the civil and even the natural rights of society;[3] a tax, unseasonably imposed after the calamities of war, would have crushed the rising agriculture of Liguria; a rigid pre-emption of corn, which was intended for the public relief, must have aggravated the distress of Campania. These dangerous projects were defeated by the virtue and eloquence of Epiphanius and Boethius, who, in the presence of Theodoric himself,

1 Ennodius, p. 1621, 1622, 1636, 1638. His *libel* was approved and registered (synodaliter) by a Roman council (Baronius, A.D. 503, No. 6. Franciscus Pagi in Breviar. Pont. Rom. tom. i. p. 242).

2 See Cassiodorus (Var. viii. 15, ix. 15, 16), Anastasius (in Symmacho, p. 31 [p. 84, ed. Rom.]), and the seventeenth Annotation of Mascou. Baronius, Pagi, and most of the catholic doctors, confess, with an angry growl, this Gothic usurpation.

3 He disabled them – a licentia testandi; and all Italy mourned – lamentabili justitio. I wish to believe that these penalties were enacted against the rebels who had violated their oath of allegiance; but the testimony of Ennodius (p. 1675–1678) is the more weighty, as he lived and died under the reign of Theodoric.

successfully pleaded the cause of the people:[1] but, if the royal ear was open to the voice of truth, a saint and a philosopher are not always to be found at the ear of kings. The privileges of rank, or office, or favour were too frequently abused by Italian fraud and Gothic violence, and the avarice of the King's nephew was publicly exposed, at first by the usurpation, and afterwards by the restitution, of the estates which he had unjustly extorted from his Tuscan neighbours. Two hundred thousand barbarians, formidable even to their master, were seated in the heart of Italy; they indignantly supported the restraints of peace and discipline; the disorders of their march were always felt and sometimes compensated; and where it was dangerous to punish, it might be prudent to dissemble, the sallies of their native fierceness. When the indulgence of Theodoric had remitted two-thirds of the Ligurian tribute, he condescended to explain the difficulties of his situation, and to lament the heavy though inevitable burdens which he imposed on his subjects for their own defence.[2] These ungrateful subjects could never be cordially reconciled to the origin, the religion, or even the virtues of the Gothic conqueror; past calamities were forgotten, and the sense or suspicion of injuries was rendered still more exquisite by the present felicity of the times.

Even the religious toleration which Theodoric had the glory of introducing into the Christian world was painful and offensive to the orthodox zeal of the Italians. They respected the armed heresy of the Goths; but their pious rage was safely pointed against the rich and defenceless Jews, who had formed their establishments at Naples, Rome, Ravenna, Milan, and Genoa, for the benefit of trade and under the sanction of the laws.[3] Their persons were insulted, their effects were pillaged, and their synagogues were burnt by the mad populace of Ravenna and Rome,

1 Ennodius, in Vit. Epiphan. p. 1689, 1690. Boethius de Consolatione Philosophiæ, l. i. pros. iv. p. 45, 46, 47 [ed. Callyus, Par. 1680]. Respect, but weigh, the passions of the saint and the senator; and fortify or alleviate their complaints by the various hints of Cassiodorus (ii. 8, iv. 36, viii. 5).

2 Immanium expensarum pondus ... pro ipsorum salute, etc.; yet these are no more than words.

3 The Jews were settled at Naples (Procopius, Goth. l. i. c. 8 [tom. ii. p. 44, ed. Bonn]), at Genoa (Var. ii. 27, iv. 33), Milan (v. 37), Rome (iv. 43). See likewise Basnage, Hist. des Juifs, tom. viii. c. 7, p. 254.

inflamed, as it should seem, by the most frivolous or extravagant pretences. The government which could neglect, would have deserved such an outrage. A legal inquiry was instantly directed; and, as the authors of the tumult had escaped in the crowd, the whole community was condemned to repair the damage, and the obstinate bigots, who refused their contributions, were whipped through the streets by the hand of the executioner. This simple act of justice exasperated the discontent of the catholics, who applauded the merit and patience of these holy confessors. Three hundred pulpits deplored the persecution of the church; and if the chapel of St. Stephen at Verona was demolished by the command of Theodoric, it is probable that some miracle hostile to his name and dignity had been performed on that sacred theatre. At the close of a glorious life, the king of Italy discovered that he had excited the hatred of a people whose happiness he had so assiduously laboured to promote; and his mind was soured by indignation, jealousy, and the bitterness of unrequited love. The Gothic conqueror condescended to disarm the unwarlike natives of Italy, interdicting all weapons of offence, and excepting only a small knife for domestic use. The deliverer of Rome was accused of conspiring with the vilest informers against the lives of senators whom he suspected of a secret and treasonable correspondence with the Byzantine court.[1] After the death of Anastasius, the diadem had been placed on the head of a feeble old man, but the powers of government were assumed by his nephew Justinian, who already meditated the extirpation of heresy and the conquest of Italy and Africa. A rigorous law, which was published at Constantinople, to reduce the Arians, by the dread of punishment, within the pale of the church, awakened the just resentment of Theodoric, who claimed for his distressed brethren of the East the same indulgence which he had so long granted to the catholics of his dominions. At his stern command the Roman pontiff, with four *illustrious* senators, embarked on an embassy of which he must have alike dreaded the failure or the success. The singular veneration shown to the first pope who

1 Rex avidus communis exitii, etc. (Boethius, l. i. p. 55): rex dolum Romanis tendebat (Anonym. Vales. p. 723). These are hard words: they speak the passions of the Italians, and those (I fear) of Theodoric himself.

had visited Constantinople was punished as a crime by this jealous monarch; the artful or peremptory refusal of the Byzantine court might excuse an equal, and would provoke a larger, measure of retaliation; and a mandate was prepared in Italy to prohibit, after a stated day, the exercise of the catholic worship. By the bigotry of his subjects and enemies the most tolerant of princes was driven to the brink of persecution, and the life of Theodoric was too long, since he lived to condemn the virtue of Boethius and Symmachus.[1]

The senator Boethius[2] is the last of the Romans whom Cato or Tully could have acknowledged for their countryman. As a wealthy orphan, he inherited the patrimony and honours of the Anician family, a name ambitiously assumed by the kings and emperors of the age, and the appellation of Manlius asserted his genuine or fabulous descent from a race of consuls and dictators who had repulsed the Gauls from the Capitol, and sacrificed their sons to the discipline of the republic. In the youth of Boethius the studies of Rome were not totally abandoned; a Virgil[3] is now extant corrected by the hand of a consul; and the professors of grammar, rhetoric, and jurisprudence were maintained in their privileges and pensions by the liberality of the Goths. But the erudition of the Latin language was insufficient to satiate his ardent curiosity; and Boethius is said to have employed eighteen laborious years in the schools of Athens,[4] which

1 I have laboured to extract a rational narrative from the dark, concise, and various hints of the Valesian Fragment (p. 722, 723, 724 [p. 313, *sqq.* ed. Bip.]), Theophanes (p. 145 [tom. i. p. 261, ed. Bonn]), Anastasius (in Johanne, p. 35 [p. 94, ed. Rom.]), and the Hist. Miscella (p. 103, edit. Muratori [Milan, 1723]). A gentle pressure and paraphrase of their words is no violence. Consult likewise Muratori (Annali d'Italia, tom. iv. p. 471–478), with the Annals and Breviary (tom. i. p. 259–263) of the two Pagis, the uncle and the nephew.

2 Le Clerc has composed a critical and philosophical Life of Anicius Manlius Severinus Boethius (Bibliot. Choisie, tom. xvi. p. 168–275); and both Tiraboschi (tom. iii.) and Fabricius (Bibliot. Latin.) may be usefully consulted. The date of his birth may be placed about the year 470, and his death in 524, in a premature old age (Consol. Phil. Metrica, i. p. 5).

3 For the age and value of this MS., now in the Medicean library at Florence, see the Cenotaphia Pisana (p. 430–447) of Cardinal Noris.

4 The Athenian studies of Boethius are doubtful (Baronius, A.D. 510, No. 3, from a spurious tract, De Disciplina Scholarum), and the term of eighteen years is doubtless too long: but the simple fact of a visit to Athens is justified by

were supported by the zeal, the learning, and the diligence of Proclus and his disciples. The reason and piety of their Roman pupil were fortunately saved from the contagion of mystery and magic which polluted the groves of the Academy; but he imbibed the spirit, and imitated the method, of his dead and living masters, who attempted to reconcile the strong and subtle sense of Aristotle with the devout contemplation and sublime fancy of Plato. After his return to Rome, and his marriage with the daughter of his friend the patrician Symmachus, Boethius still continued, in a palace of ivory and marble, to prosecute the same studies.[1] The church was edified by his profound defence of the orthodox creed against the Arian, the Eutychian, and the Nestorian heresies; and the catholic unity was explained or exposed in a formal treatise by the *indifference* of three distinct though consubstantial persons. For the benefit of his Latin readers, his genius submitted to teach the first elements of the arts and sciences of Greece. The geometry of Euclid, the music of Pythagoras, the arithmetic of Nicomachus, the mechanics of Archimedes, the astronomy of Ptolemy, the theology of Plato, and the logic of Aristotle, with the commentary of Porphyry, were translated and illustrated by the indefatigable pen of the Roman senator. And he alone was esteemed capable of describing the wonders of art, a sun-dial, a water-clock, or a sphere which represented the motions of the planets. From these abstruse speculations Boethius stooped – or, to speak more truly, he rose – to the social duties of public and private life; the indigent were relieved by his liberality, and his eloquence, which flattery might compare to the voice of Demosthenes or Cicero, was uniformly exerted in the cause of innocence and humanity. Such conspicuous merit was felt and rewarded by a discerning

much internal evidence (Brucker, Hist. Crit. Philosoph. tom. iii. p. 524–527), and by an expression (though vague and ambiguous) of his friend Cassiodorus (Var. i. 45), 'longè positas Athenas introisti.'

1 Bibliothecæ comptos ebore ac vitro parietes, etc. (Consol. Phil. l. i. pros. v. p. 74). The Epistles of Ennodius (vi. 6, vii. 13, viii. 1, 31, 37, 40) and Cassiodorus (Var. i. 39, iv. 6, ix. 21) afford many proofs of the high reputation which he enjoyed in his own times. It is true that the bishop of Pavia wanted to purchase of him an old house at Milan, and praise might be tendered and accepted in part of payment.

prince: the dignity of Boethius was adorned with the titles of consul and patrician, and his talents were usefully employed in the important station of master of the offices. Notwithstanding the equal claims of the East and West, his two sons were created, in their tender youth, the consuls of the same year.[1] On the memorable day of their inauguration they proceeded in solemn pomp from their palace to the forum amidst the applause of the senate and people; and their joyful father, the true consul of Rome, after pronouncing an oration in the praise of his royal benefactor, distributed a triumphal largess in the games of the circus. Prosperous in his fame and fortunes, in his public honours and private alliances, in the cultivation of science and the consciousness of virtue, Boethius might have been styled happy, if that precarious epithet could be safely applied before the last term of the life of man.

A philosopher, liberal of his wealth and parsimonious of his time, might be insensible to the common allurements of ambition, the thirst of gold and employment. And some credit may be due to the asseveration of Boethius, that he had reluctantly obeyed the divine Plato, who enjoins every virtuous citizen to rescue the state from the usurpation of vice and ignorance. For the integrity of his public conduct he appeals to the memory of his country. His authority had restrained the pride and oppression of the royal officers, and his eloquence had delivered Paulianus from the dogs of the palace. He had always pitied, and often relieved, the distress of the provincials, whose fortunes were exhausted by public and private rapine; and Boethius alone had courage to oppose the tyranny of the barbarians, elated by conquest, excited by avarice, and as he complains, encouraged by impunity. In these honourable contests his spirit soared above the consideration of danger, and perhaps of prudence; and we may learn from the example of Cato that a character of pure and inflexible virtue is the most apt to be misled by prejudice, to be heated by enthusiasm, and to confound private enmities with

1 Pagi, Muratori, etc., are agreed that Boethius himself was consul in the year 510, his two sons in 522, and in 487, perhaps, his father. A desire of ascribing the last of these consulships to the philosopher had perplexed the chronology of his life. In his honours, alliances, children, he celebrates his own felicity – his past felicity (p. 109, 110).

public justice. The disciple of Plato might exaggerate the infirmities of nature and the imperfections of society; and the mildest
form of a Gothic kingdom, even the weight of allegiance and
gratitude, must be insupportable to the free spirit of a Roman
patriot. But the favour and fidelity of Boethius declined in just
proportion with the public happiness, and an unworthy colleague
was imposed to divide and control the power of the master of
the offices. In the last gloomy season of Theodoric he indignantly felt that he was a slave; but as his master had only power over
his life, he stood, without arms and without fear, against the face
of an angry barbarian, who had been provoked to believe that
the safety of the senate was incompatible with his own. The
senator Albinus was accused and already convicted on the presumption of *hoping*, as it was said, the liberty of Rome. 'If Albinus
be criminal,' exclaimed the orator, 'the senate and myself are all
guilty of the same crime. If we are innocent, Albinus is equally
entitled to the protection of the laws.' These laws might not have
punished the simple and barren wish of an unattainable blessing;
but they would have shown less indulgence to the rash confession of Boethius, that, had he known of a conspiracy, the tyrant
never should.[1] The advocate of Albinus was soon involved in
the danger and perhaps the guilt of his client; their signature
(which they denied as a forgery) was affixed to the original address inviting the emperor to deliver Italy from the Goths; and
three witnesses of honourable rank, perhaps of infamous reputation, attested the treasonable designs of the Roman patrician.[2]
Yet his innocence must be presumed, since he was deprived by
Theodoric of the means of justification, and rigorously confined
in the tower of Pavia, while the senate, at the distance of five
hundred miles, pronounced a sentence of confiscation and death
against the most illustrious of its members. At the command
of the barbarians, the occult science of a philosopher was

1 Si ego scissem tu nescisses. Boethius adopts this answer (l. i. pros. 4,
p. 53) of Julius Canus, whose philosophic death is described by Seneca (De
Tranquillitate Animi, c. 14).
2 The characters of his two delators, Basilius (Var. ii. 10, 11, iv. 22) and
Opilio (v. 41, viii. 16), are illustrated, not much to their honour, in the Epistles
of Cassiodorus, which likewise mention Decoratus (v. 31), the worthless colleague of Boethius (l. iii. pros. 4, p. 193).

stigmatised with the names of sacrilege and magic.[1] A devout and dutiful attachment to the senate was condemned as criminal by the trembling voices of the senators themselves; and their ingratitude deserved the wish or prediction of Boethius, that, after him, none should be found guilty of the same offence.[2]

While Boethius, oppressed with fetters, expected each moment the sentence or the stroke of death, he composed in the tower of Pavia the *Consolation of Philosophy;* a golden volume not unworthy of the leisure of Plato or Tully, but which claims incomparable merit from the barbarism of the times and the situation of the author. The celestial guide whom he had so long invoked at Rome and Athens now condescended to illumine his dungeon, to revive his courage, and to pour into his wounds her salutary balm. She taught him to compare his long prosperity and his recent distress, and to conceive new hopes from the inconstancy of fortune. Reason had informed him of the precarious condition of her gifts; experience had satisfied him of their real value; he had enjoyed them without guilt, he might resign them without a sigh, and calmly disdain the impotent malice of his enemies, who had left him happiness, since they had left him virtue. From the earth Boethius ascended to heaven in search of the SUPREME GOOD; explored the metaphysical labyrinth of chance and destiny, of prescience and free-will, of time and eternity; and generously attempted to reconcile the perfect attributes of the Deity with the apparent disorders of his moral and physical government. Such topics of consolation, so obvious, so vague, or so abstruse, are ineffectual to subdue the feelings of human nature. Yet the sense of misfortune may be diverted by the labour of thought; and the sage who could artfully combine in the same work the various riches of philosophy,

1 A severe inquiry was instituted into the crime of magic (Var. iv. 22, 23, ix. 18); and it was believed that many necromancers had escaped by making their gaolers mad: for *mad*, I should read *drunk*.

2 Boethius had composed his own Apology (p. 53), perhaps more interesting than his Consolation. We must be content with the general view of his honours, principles, persecution, etc. (l. i. pros. 4, p. 42–62), which may be compared with the short and weighty words of the Valesian Fragment (p. 723 [Amm. tom. ii. p. 314, ed. Bip.]). An anonymous writer (Sinner, Catalog. MSS. Bibliot. Bern. tom. i. p. 287) charges him home with honourable and patriotic treason.

poetry, and eloquence, must already have possessed the intrepid calmness which he affected to seek. Suspense, the worst of evils, was at length determined by the ministers of death, who executed, and perhaps exceeded, the inhuman mandate of Theodoric. A strong cord was fastened round the head of Boethius, and forcibly tightened till his eyes almost started from their sockets; and some mercy may be discovered in the milder torture of beating him with clubs till he expired.[1] But his genius survived to diffuse a ray of knowledge over the darkest ages of the Latin world; the writings of the philosopher were translated by the most glorious of the English kings,[2] and the third emperor of the name of Otho removed to a more honourable tomb the bones of a catholic saint who, from his Arian persecutors, had acquired the honours of martyrdom and the fame of miracles.[3] In the last hours of Boethius he derived some comfort from the safety of his two sons, of his wife, and of his father-in-law, the venerable Symmachus. But the grief of Symmachus was indiscreet, and perhaps disrespectful: he had presumed to lament, he might dare to revenge, the death of an injured friend. He was dragged in chains from Rome to the palace of Ravenna, and the suspicions of Theodoric could only be appeased by the blood of an innocent and aged senator.[4]

1 He was executed in Agro Calventiano (Calvenzano, between Marignano and Pavia), Anonym. Vales. p. 723 [p. 315, ed. Bip.], by order of Eusebius count of Ticinum or Pavia. The place of his confinement is styled the *baptistery*, an edifice and name peculiar to cathedrals. It is claimed by the perpetual tradition of the church of Pavia. The tower of Boethius subsisted till the year 1584, and the draught is yet preserved (Tiraboschi, tom. iii. p. 47, 48).

2 See the Biographia Britannica, ALFRED, tom. i. p. 80, 2nd edition. The work is still more honourable if performed under the learned eye of Alfred by his foreign and domestic doctors. For the reputation of Boethius in the middle ages consult Brucker (Hist. Crit. Philosoph. tom. iii. p. 565, 566).

3 The inscription on his new tomb was composed by the preceptor of Otho the Third, the learned pope Silvester II., who, like Boethius himself, was styled a magician by the ignorance of the times. The catholic martyr had carried his head in his hands a considerable way (Baronius, A.D. 526, No. 17, 18); yet on a similar tale, a lady of my acquaintance once observed, 'La distance n'y fait rien; il n'y a que le premier pas qui coûte.'

4 Boethius applauds the virtues of his father-in-law (l. i. pros. 4, p. 59, l. ii. pros. 4, p. 118). Procopius (Goth. l. i. c. i. [tom. ii. p. 11, ed. Bonn]), the Valesian Fragment (p. 724 [p. 316, ed. Bip.]), and the Historia Miscella (l. xv.

Humanity will be disposed to encourage any report which testifies the jurisdiction of conscience and the remorse of kings; and philosophy is not ignorant that the most horrid spectres are sometimes created by the powers of a disordered fancy, and the weakness of a distempered body. After a life of virtue and glory, Theodoric was now descending with shame and guilt into the grave: his mind was humbled by the contrast of the past, and justly alarmed by the invisible terrors of futurity. One evening, as it is related, when the head of a large fish was served on the royal table,[1] he suddenly exclaimed that he beheld the angry countenance of Symmachus, his eyes glaring fury and revenge, and his mouth armed with long sharp teeth, which threatened to devour him. The monarch instantly retired to his chamber, and, as he lay trembling with aguish cold under a weight of bed-clothes, he expressed in broken murmurs to his physician Elpidius his deep repentance for the murders of Boethius and Symmachus.[2] His malady increased, and, after a dysentery which continued three days, he expired in the palace of Ravenna, in the thirty-third, or, if we compute from the invasion of Italy, in the thirty-seventh year of his reign. Conscious of his approaching end, he divided his treasures and provinces between his two grandsons, and fixed the Rhône as their common boundary.[3] Amalaric was restored to the throne of Spain. Italy, with all the conquests of the Ostrogoths, was bequeathed to Athalaric, whose age did not exceed ten years, but who was cherished as the last male offspring of the line of Amali, by the

p. 105 [103?]), agree in praising the superior innocence or sanctity of Symmachus; and in the estimation of the legend, the guilt of his murder is equal to the imprisonment of a pope.

1 In the fanciful eloquence of Cassiodorus, the variety of sea and river fish are an evidence of extensive dominion; and those of the Rhine, of Sicily, and of the Danube, were served on the table of Theodoric (Var. xii. 44). The monstrous turbot of Domitian (Juvenal, Satir. iv. 39) had been caught on the shores of the Hadriatic.

2 Procopius, Goth. l. i. c. 1 [tom. ii. p. 11, ed. Bonn]. But he might have informed us whether he had received this curious anecdote from common report, or from the mouth of the royal physician.

3 Procopius, Goth. l. i. c. 1, 2, 12, 13. This partition had been directed by Theodoric, though it was not executed till after his death. Regni hereditatem superstes reliquit (Isidor. Chron. p. 721, edit. Grot.).

short-lived marriage of his mother Amalasuntha with a royal
fugitive of the same blood.¹ In the presence of the dying monarch the Gothic chiefs and Italian magistrates mutually engaged
their faith and loyalty to the young prince and to his guardian
mother; and received, in the same awful moment, his last salutary advice to maintain the laws, to love the senate and people
of Rome, and to cultivate with decent reverence the friendship
of the emperor.² The monument of Theodoric was erected by
his daughter Amalasuntha in a conspicuous situation, which
commanded the city of Ravenna, the harbour, and the adjacent
coast. A chapel of a circular form, thirty feet in diameter, is
crowned by a dome of one entire piece of granite: from the
centre of the dome four columns arose, which supported in
a vase of porphyry the remains of the Gothic king, surrounded
by the brazen statues of the twelve apostles.³ His spirit, after
some previous expiation, might have been permitted to mingle
with the benefactors of mankind, if an Italian hermit had not
been witness in a vision to the damnation of Theodoric,⁴ whose
soul was plunged by the ministers of divine vengeance into the
volcano of Lipari, one of the flaming mouths of the infernal
world.⁵

1 Berimund, the third in descent from Hermanric, king of the Ostrogoths,
had retired into Spain, where he lived and died in obscurity (Jornandes, c. 33,
p. 202, edit. Muratori). See the discovery, nuptials, and death of his grandson
Eutharic (c. 58, p. 220). His Roman games might render him popular (Cassiodor. in Chron.), but Eutharic was asper in religione (Anonym. Vales. p. 722,
723 [p. 313, ed. Bip.]).
2 See the counsels of Theodoric, and the professions of his successor, in
Procopius (Goth. l. i. c. 1, 2), Jornandes (c. 59 [p. 700, 701, ed. Grot.]), and
Cassiodorus (Var. viii. 1–7). These epistles are the triumph of his ministerial
eloquence.
3 Anonym. Vales. p. 724 [p. 316, ed. Bip.]. Agnellus de Vitis Pont. Raven.
in Muratori Script. Rerum Ital. tom. ii. P. i. p. 67. Alberti Descrizione d'Italia,
p. 311.
4 This legend is related by Gregory I. (Dialog. iv. 30 [tom. ii. p. 420, ed.
Bened.]), and approved by Baronius (A.D. 526, No. 28); and both the pope and
cardinal are grave doctors, sufficient to establish a *probable* opinion.
5 Theodoric himself, or rather Cassiodorus, had described in tragic
strains the volcanos of Lipari (Cluver. Sicilia, p. 406–410), and Vesuvius ([Var.]
iv. 50).

CHAPTER XL

Elevation of Justin the Elder – Reign of Justinian – I. The Empress Theodora – II. Factions of the Circus, and Sedition of Constantinople – III. Trade and Manufacture of Silk – IV. Finances and Taxes – V. Edifices of Justinian – Church of St. Sophia – Fortifications and Frontiers of the Eastern Empire – Abolition of the Schools of Athens and the Consulship of Rome

THE emperor Justinian was born[1] near the ruins of Sardica (the modern Sophia), of an obscure race[2] of barbarians,[3] the inhabitants of a wild and desolate country, to which the names of Dardania, of Dacia, and of Bulgaria have been successively applied.[4] His elevation was prepared by the adventurous spirit of

1 There is some difficulty in the date of his birth (Ludewig in Vit. Justiniani, p. 125); none in the place – the district Bederiana – the village Tauresium, which he afterwards decorated with his name and splendour (D'Anville, Hist. de l'Acad. etc. tom. xxxi. p. 287–292).

[The father of Justinian was named Sabatius, and he was the brother of Justin: while his mother's name was Bigleniza. – O. S.]

2 The names of these Dardanian peasants are Gothic, and almost English: *Justinian* is a translation of *uprauda* (*upright*); his father *Sabatius* (in Græco-barbarous language *stipes*) was styled in his village *Istock* (*Stock*); his mother Bigleniza was softened into Vigilantia.

3 Ludewig (p. 127–135) attempts to justify the Anician name of Justinian and Theodora, and to connect them with a family from which the house of Austria has been derived.

4 The following table exhibits the most important persons of the family of Justinian:–

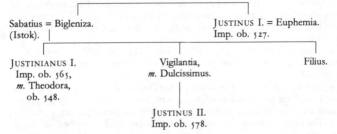

Sabatius = Bigleniza. (Istok).		JUSTINUS I. = Euphemia. Imp. ob. 527.	
JUSTINIANUS I. Imp. ob. 565, *m.* Theodora, ob. 548.	Vigilantia, *m.* Dulcissimus.		Filius.
	JUSTINUS II. Imp. ob. 578.		

Justinian had several other nephews besides Justin II., the children both of his

his uncle Justin, who, with two other peasants of the same village, deserted for the profession of arms the more useful employment of husbandmen or shepherds.[1] On foot, with a scanty
provision of biscuit in their knapsacks, the three youths followed
the high road of Constantinople, and were soon enrolled, for
their strength and stature, among the guards of the emperor Leo.
Under the two succeeding reigns, the fortunate peasant emerged
to wealth and honours; and his escape from some dangers which
threatened his life was afterwards ascribed to the guardian angel
who watches over the fate of kings. His long and laudable service
in the Isaurian and Persian wars would not have preserved from
oblivion the name of Justin; yet they might warrant the military
promotion which, in the course of fifty years, he gradually obtained – the rank of tribune, of count and of general, the dignity
of senator, and the command of the guards, who obeyed him as
their chief at the important crisis when the emperor Anastasius
was removed from the world. The powerful kinsmen whom he
had raised and enriched were excluded from the throne; and the
eunuch Amantius, who reigned in the palace, had secretly resolved to fix the diadem on the head of the most obsequious of
his creatures. A liberal donative, to conciliate the suffrage of the
guards, was intrusted for that purpose in the hands of their
commander. But these weighty arguments were treacherously
employed by Justin in his own favour; and as no competitor
presumed to appear, the Dacian peasant was invested with the
purple by the unanimous consent of the soldiers, who knew him
to be brave and gentle; of the clergy and people, who believed
him to be orthodox; and of the provincials, who yielded a blind
and implicit submission to the will of the capital. The elder
Justin, as he is distinguished from another emperor of the same
family and name, ascended the Byzantine throne at the age of
sixty-eight years; and, had he been left to his own guidance, every

sister Vigilantia, and of his brother, whose name is unknown. See the genealogical table by Alemannus (Procop. vol. iii. p. 417, ed. Bonn).

1 See the Anecdotes of Procopius (c. 6) with the notes of N. Alemannus.
The satirist would not have sunk, in the vague and decent appellation of
γέωργος, the βούκολος and σύφορβος of Zonaras. Yet why are those names
disgraceful? – and what German baron would not be proud to descend from
the Eumæus of the Odyssey?

moment of a nine-years' reign must have exposed to his subjects the impropriety of their choice. His ignorance was similar to that of Theodoric; and it is remarkable that, in an age not destitute of learning, two contemporary monarchs had never been instructed in the knowledge of the alphabet. But the genius of Justin was far inferior to that of the Gothic king: the experience of a soldier had not qualified him for the government of an empire; and though personally brave, the consciousness of his own weakness was naturally attended with doubt, distrust, and political apprehension. But the official business of the state was diligently and faithfully transacted by the quæstor Proclus;[1] and the aged emperor adopted the talents and ambition of his nephew Justinian, an aspiring youth, whom his uncle had drawn from the rustic solitude of Dacia, and educated at Constantinople as the heir of his private fortune, and at length of the Eastern empire.

Since the eunuch Amantius had been defrauded of his money, it became necessary to deprive him of his life. The task was easily accomplished by the charge of a real or fictitious conspiracy; and the judges were informed, as an accumulation of guilt, that he was secretly addicted to the Manichæan heresy.[2] Amantius lost his head; three of his companions, the first domestics of the palace, were punished either with death or exile; and their unfortunate candidate for the purple was cast into a deep dungeon, overwhelmed with stones, and ignominiously thrown without burial into the sea. The ruin of Vitalian was a work of more difficulty and danger. That Gothic chief had rendered himself popular by the civil war which he boldly waged against Anastasius for the defence of the orthodox faith; and after the conclusion of an advantageous treaty, he still remained in the neighbourhood of Constantinople at the head of a formidable

1 His virtues are praised by Procopius (Persic. l. i. c. 11 [tom. i. p. 52, ed. Bonn]). The quæstor Proclus was the friend of Justinian and the enemy of every other adoption.

2 Manichæan signifies Eutychian. Hear the furious acclamations of Constantinople and Tyre, the former no more than six days after the decease of Anastasius. They produced, the latter applauded, the eunuch's death (Baronius, A.D. 518, P. ii. No. 15; Fleury, Hist. Ecclés. tom. vii. p. 200, 205, from the Councils, tom. v. p. 182, 207).

and victorious army of barbarians. By the frail security of oaths he was tempted to relinquish this advantageous situation, and to trust his person within the walls of a city whose inhabitants, particularly the *blue* faction, were artfully incensed against him by the remembrance even of his pious hostilities. The emperor and his nephew embraced him as the faithful and worthy champion of the church and state, and gratefully adorned their favourite with the titles of consul and general; but in the seventh month of his consulship Vitalian was stabbed with seventeen wounds at the royal banquet,[1] and Justinian, who inherited the spoil, was accused as the assassin of a spiritual brother, to whom he had recently pledged his faith in the participation of the Christian mysteries.[2] After the fall of his rival, he was promoted, without any claim of military service, to the office of master-general of the Eastern armies, whom it was his duty to lead into the field against the public enemy. But, in the pursuit of fame, Justinian might have lost his present dominion over the age and weakness of his uncle; and instead of acquiring by Scythian or Persian trophies the applause of his countrymen,[3] the prudent warrior solicited their favour in the churches, the circus, and the senate of Constantinople. The catholics were attached to the nephew of Justin, who, between the Nestorian and Eutychian heresies, trod the narrow path of inflexible and intolerant orthodoxy.[4] In the first days of the new reign he prompted and gratified the popular enthusiasm against the memory of the deceased emperor.

1 His power, character, and intentions are perfectly explained by the Count de Buat (tom. ix. p. 54–81). He was great-grandson of Aspar, hereditary prince in the Lesser Scythia, and count of the Gothic *fœderati* of Thrace. The Bessi, whom he could influence, are the minor Goths of Jornandes (c. 51).

2 Justiniani patricii factione dicitur interfectus fuisse (Victor Tununensis Chron. in Thesaur. Temp. Scaliger, P. ii. p. 7). Procopius (Anecdot. c. 7 [c. 6, tom. iii. p. 46, ed. Bonn]) styles him a tyrant, but acknowledges the ἀδελφοπίστια, which is well explained by Alemannus.

3 In his earliest youth (plane adolescens) he had passed some time as a hostage with Theodoric. For this curious fact Alemannus (ad Procop. Anecdot. c. 9, p. 34 [tom. iii. p. 383, ed. Bonn] of the first edition) quotes a MS. history of Justinian, by his preceptor Theophilus. Ludewig (p. 143) wishes to make him a soldier.

4 The ecclesiastical history of Justinian will be shown hereafter. See Baronius, A.D. 518–521, and the copious article *Justinianus* in the index to the seventh volume of his Annals.

After a schism of thirty-four years, he reconciled the proud and angry spirit of the Roman pontiff, and spread among the Latins a favourable report of his pious respect for the apostolic see. The thrones of the East were filled with catholic bishops devoted to his interest, the clergy and the monks were gained by his liberality, and the people were taught to pray for their future sovereign, the hope and pillar of the true religion. The magnificence of Justinian was displayed in the superior pomp of his public spectacles, an object not less sacred and important in the eyes of the multitude than the creed of Nice or Chalcedon: the expense of his consulship was esteemed at two hundred and eighty-eight thousand pieces of gold; twenty lions and thirty leopards were produced at the same time in the amphitheatre; and a numerous train of horses, with their rich trappings, was bestowed as an extraordinary gift on the victorious charioteers of the circus. While he indulged the people of Constantinople, and received the addresses of foreign kings, the nephew of Justin assiduously cultivated the friendship of the senate. That venerable name seemed to qualify its members to declare the sense of the nation, and to regulate the succession of the Imperial throne. The feeble Anastasius had permitted the vigour of government to degenerate into the form or substance of an aristocracy, and the military officers who had obtained the senatorial rank were followed by their domestic guards, a band of veterans whose arms or acclamations might fix in a tumultuous moment the diadem of the East. The treasures of the state were lavished to procure the voices of the senators, and their unanimous wish that he would be pleased to adopt Justinian for his colleague was communicated to the emperor. But this request, which too clearly admonished him of his approaching end, was unwelcome to the jealous temper of an aged monarch desirous to retain the power which he was incapable of exercising; and Justin, holding his purple with both his hands, advised them to prefer, since an election was so profitable, some older candidate. Notwithstanding this reproach, the senate proceeded to decorate Justinian with the royal epithet of *nobilissimus;* and their decree was ratified by the affection or the fears of his uncle. After some time the languor of mind and body to which he was reduced by an incurable wound in his thigh indispensably required the aid of a guardian. He summoned the patriarch and senators, and in their presence solemnly placed the diadem on the head of his nephew, who was conducted from the palace to the circus, and saluted by the loud and joyful applause of the people. The life of Justin was prolonged about four months; but from the instant of this ceremony he was considered as dead to the empire, which acknowledged Justinian, in the forty-fifth year of his age, for the lawful sovereign of the East.[1]

From his elevation to his death, Justinian governed the Roman empire thirty-eight years, seven months, and thirteen days. The events of his reign, which excite our curious attention by their number, variety, and importance, are diligently related by the secretary of Belisarius, a rhetorician, whom eloquence had promoted to the rank of senator and præfect of Constantinople. According to the vicissitudes of courage or servitude, of favour or disgrace, Procopius[2] successively composed the *history*, the *panegyric*, and the *satire* of his own times. The eight books of the Persian, Vandalic, and Gothic wars,[3] which are continued in the five books of Agathias, deserve our esteem as a laborious and successful imitation of the Attic, or at least of the Asiatic, writers of ancient Greece. His facts are collected from the personal experience and free conversation of a soldier, a statesman, and a traveller; his style continually aspires, and often attains, to the

1 The reign of the elder Justin may be found in the three Chronicles of Marcellinus, Victor, and John Malala (tom. ii. p. 130–150 [ed. Oxon.; l. xvii. p. 410–424, ed. Bonn]), the last of whom (in spite of Hody, Prolegom. No. 14, 39, edit. Oxon.) lived soon after Justinian (Jortin's Remarks, etc., vol. iv. p. 383); in the Ecclesiastical History of Evagrius (l. iv. c. 1, 2, 3, 9), and the Excerpta of Theodorus Lector (No. 37 [l. ii]), and in Cedrenus (p. 363–366 [ed. Par.; tom. i. p. 636–642, ed. Bonn]) and Zonaras (l. xiv. p. 58–60), who may pass for an original.

2 See the characters of Procopius and Agathias in La Mothe le Vayer (tom. viii. p. 144–174), Vossius (de Historicis Græcis, l. ii. c. 22), and Fabricius (Bibliot. Græc. l. v. c. 5, tom. vi. p. 248–278). Their religion, an honourable problem, betrays occasional conformity, with a secret attachment to Paganism and Philosophy.

3 In the seven first books, two Persic, two Vandalic, and three Gothic, Procopius has borrowed from Appian the division of provinces and wars: the eighth book, though it bears the name of Gothic, is a miscellaneous and general supplement down to the spring of the year 553, from whence it is continued by Agathias till 559 (Pagi, Critica, A.D. 579, No. 5).

merit of strength and elegance; his reflections, more especially in the speeches, which he too frequently inserts, contain a rich fund of political knowledge; and the historian, excited by the generous ambition of pleasing and instructing posterity, appears to disdain the prejudices of the people and the flattery of courts. The writings of Procopius[1] were read and applauded by his contemporaries:[2] but, although he respectfully laid them at the foot of the throne, the pride of Justinian must have been wounded by the praise of a hero who perpetually eclipses the glory of his inactive sovereign. The conscious dignity of independence was subdued by the hopes and fears of a slave; and the secretary of Belisarius laboured for pardon and reward in the six books of the Imperial *edifices*. He had dexterously chosen a subject of apparent splendour, in which he could loudly celebrate the genius, the magnificence, and the piety of a prince who, both as a conqueror and legislator, had surpassed the puerile virtues of Themistocles and Cyrus.[3] Disappointment might urge the flatterer to secret revenge; and the first glance of favour might again tempt him to suspend and suppress a libel[4] in which the Roman Cyrus is degraded into an odious and contemptible tyrant, in which

1 The literary fate of Procopius has been somewhat unlucky. 1. His books de Bello Gothico were stolen by Leonard Aretin, and published (Fulginii, 1470; Venet. 1471, apud Janson. Mattaire, Annal. Typograph. tom. i. edit. posterior, p. 290, 304, 279, 299) in his own name (see Vossius de Hist. Lat. l. iii. c. 5, and the feeble defence of the Venice Giornale de' Letterati, tom. xix. p. 207). 2. His works were mutilated by the first Latin translators, Christopher Persona (Giornale, tom. xix. p. 340–348) and Raphael de Volaterra (Huet. de Claris Interpretibus, p. 166), who did not even consult the MS. of the Vatican library, of which they were præfects (Aleman. in Præfat. Anecdot.). 3. The Greek text was not printed till 1607, by Hoeschelius of Augsburg (Dictionnaire de Bayle, tom. ii. p. 782). 4. The Paris edition was imperfectly executed by Claude Maltret, a Jesuit of Toulouse (in 1663), far distant from the Louvre press and the Vatican MS, from which, however, he obtained some supplements. His promised commentaries, etc., have never appeared. The Agathias of Leyden (1594) has been wisely reprinted by the Paris editor, with the Latin version of Bonaventura Vulcanius, a learned interpreter (Huet, p. 176).

2 Agathias in Præfat. p. 7, 8, l. iv. p. 136 [ed. Par.; p. 11, 264, ed. Bonn]; Evagrius, l. iv. c. 12. See likewise Photius, cod. lxiii. p. 65 [p. 21, ed. Bekk.].

3 Κύρου παιδεία (says he, Præfat. ad l. de Ædificiis περὶ κτισμάτων) is no more than Κύρου παιδία – a pun! In these five books Procopius affects a Christian as well as a courtly style.

4 Procopius discloses himself (Præfat. ad Anecdot. c. 1, 2, 5), and the anecdotes are reckoned as the ninth book by Suidas (tom. iii. p. 186, ed. Kuster).

both the emperor and his consort Theodora are seriously represented as two dæmons who had assumed a human form for the
destruction of mankind.[1] Such base inconsistency must doubtless
sully the reputation, and detract from the credit, of Procopius:
yet, after the venom of his malignity has been suffered to exhale,
the residue of the *anecdotes*, even the most disgraceful facts, some
of which had been tenderly hinted in his public history, are
established by their internal evidence, or the authentic monuments of the times.[2] From these various materials I shall now
proceed to describe the reign of Justinian, which will deserve and
occupy an ample space. The present chapter will explain the
elevation and character of Theodora, the factions of the circus,
and the peaceful administration of the sovereign of the East. In
the three succeeding chapters I shall relate the wars of Justinian,
which achieved the conquest of Africa and Italy; and I shall
follow the victories of Belisarius and Narses, without disguising
the vanity of their triumphs, or the hostile virtue of the Persian
and Gothic heroes. The series of this volume will embrace the
jurisprudence and theology of the emperor; the controversies
and sects which still divide the Oriental church; the reformation
of the Roman law which is obeyed or respected by the nations
of modern Europe.

I. In the exercise of supreme power, the first act of Justinian
was to divide it with the woman whom he loved, the famous
Theodora,[3] whose strange elevation cannot be applauded as the

The silence of Evagrius is a poor objection. Baronius (A.D. 548, No. 24) regrets
the loss of this secret history: it was then in the Vatican library, in his own
custody, and was first published sixteen years after his death, with the learned
but partial notes of Nicholas Alemannus (Lugd. 1623).

1 Justinian an ass – the perfect likeness of Domitian – Anecdot. c. 8 –
Theodora's lovers driven from her bed by rival dæmons – her marriage foretold
with a great dæmon – a monk saw the prince of the dæmons, instead of
Justinian, on the throne – the servants who watched beheld a face without
features, a body walking without a head, etc. etc. Procopius declares his own
and his friends' belief in these diabolical stories (c. 12).

2 Montesquieu (Considérations sur la Grandeur et la Décadence des Romains, c. xx.) gives credit to these anecdotes, as connected, 1, with the weakness
of the empire, and, 2, with the instability of Justinian's laws.

3 For the life and manners of the empress Theodora see the Anecdotes;
more especially c. 1–5, 9, 10–15, 16, 17, with the learned notes of Alemannus
– a reference which is always implied.

triumph of female virtue. Under the reign of Anastasius, the care of the wild beasts maintained by the green faction at Constantinople was intrusted to Acacius, a native of the isle of Cyprus, who, from his employment, was surnamed the master of the bears. This honourable office was given after his death to another candidate, notwithstanding the diligence of his widow, who had already provided a husband and a successor. Acacius had left three daughters, Comito,[1] THEODORA, and Anastasia, the eldest of whom did not then exceed the age of seven years. On a solemn festival, these helpless orphans were sent by their distressed and indignant mother, in the garb of suppliants, into the midst of the theatre: the green faction received them with contempt, the blues with compassion; and this difference, which sunk deep into the mind of Theodora, was felt long afterwards in the administration of the empire. As they improved in age and beauty, the three sisters were successively devoted to the public and private pleasures of the Byzantine people; and Theodora, after following Comito on the stage, in the dress of a slave, with a stool on her head, was at length permitted to exercise her independent talents. She neither danced, nor sung, nor played on the flute; her skill was confined to the pantomime arts; she excelled in buffoon characters; and as often as the comedian swelled her cheeks, and complained with a ridiculous tone and gesture of the blows that were inflicted, the whole theatre of Constantinople resounded with laughter and applause. The beauty of Theodora[2] was the subject of more flattering praise, and the source of more exquisite delight. Her features were delicate and regular; her complexion, though somewhat pale, was tinged with a natural colour; every sensation was instantly expressed by the vivacity of her eyes; her easy motions displayed the graces of a small but elegant figure; and either love or adulation might proclaim that painting and poetry were incapable of

1 Comito was afterwards married to Sittas duke of Armenia, the father, perhaps, at least she might be the mother, of the empress Sophia. Two nephews of Theodora may be the sons of Anastasia (Aleman. p. 30, 31).

2 Her statue was raised at Constantinople on a porphyry column. See Procopius (de Ædif. l. i. c. 11), who gives her portrait in the Anecdotes (c. 10 [tom. iii. p. 69, ed. Bonn]). Aleman. (p. 47) produces one from a mosaic at Ravenna, loaded with pearls and jewels, and yet handsome.

delineating the matchless excellence of her form. But this form was degraded by the facility with which it was exposed to the public eye, and prostituted to licentious desire. Her venal charms were abandoned to a promiscuous crowd of citizens and strangers, of every rank and of every profession: the fortunate lover who had been promised a night of enjoyment was often driven from her bed by a stronger or more wealthy favourite; and when she passed through the streets, her presence was avoided by all who wished to escape either the scandal or the temptation. The satirical historian has not blushed[1] to describe the naked scenes which Theodora was not ashamed to exhibit in the theatre.[2] After exhausting the arts of sensual pleasure,[3] she most ungratefully murmured against the parsimony of Nature;[4] but her murmurs, her pleasures, and her arts, must be veiled in the obscurity of a learned language. After reigning for some time the delight and contempt of the capital, she condescended to accompany Ecebolus, a native of Tyre, who had obtained the government of the African Pentapolis. But this union was frail and transient: Ecebolus soon rejected an expensive or faithless concubine; she was reduced at Alexandria to extreme distress; and in her laborious

1 A fragment of the Anecdotes (c. 9), somewhat too naked, was suppressed by Alemannus, though extant in the Vatican MS.; nor has the defect been supplied in the Paris or Venice editions. La Mothe le Vayer (tom. viii. p. 155) gave the first hint of this curious and genuine passage (Jortin's Remarks, vol. iv. p. 366), which he had received from Rome, and it has been since published in the Menagiana (tom. iii. p. 254–259), with a Latin version.

2 After the mention of a narrow girdle (as none could appear stark naked in the theatre), Procopius thus proceeds: ἀναπεπτωκυῖά τε ἐν τῷ ἐδάφει ὑπτία ἔκειτο. Θῆτες δέ τινες... κριθὰς αὐτῇ ὕπερθεν τῶν αἰδοίων ἐρρίπτουν, ἅς δὴ οἱ χῆνες, οἵ ἐς τοῦτο παρεσκευασμένοι ἐτύγχανον, τοῖς στόμασιν ἐνθένδε κατὰ μίαν ἀνελόμενοι ἤσθιον. I have heard that a learned prelate, now deceased, was fond of quoting this passage in conversation.

3 Theodora surpassed the Crispa of Ausonius (Epigram lxxi.), who imitated the capitalis luxus of the females of Nola. See Quintilian Institut. viii. 6, and Torrentius ad Horat. Sermon. l. i. sat. 2, v. 101. At a memorable supper thirty slaves waited round the table; ten young men feasted with Theodora. Her charity was *universal*.

Et lassata viris, necdum satiata, recessit.

4 Ἡ δε κἀκ τῶν τριῶν τρυπημάτων ἐργαζομένη ἐνεκάλει τῇ φύσει, δυσφορουμένη ὅτι δὴ μὴ καὶ τοὺς τιτθοὺς αὐτῇ εὐρύτερον ἤ νῦν εἴσι τρυπῷη, ὅπως δυνατὴ εἴη καὶ ἐκείνῃ ἐργάζεσθαι. She wished for a *fourth* altar on which she might pour libations to the god of love.

return to Constantinople, every city of the East admired and enjoyed the fair Cyprian, whose merit appeared to justify her descent from the peculiar island of Venus. The vague commerce of Theodora, and the most detestable precautions, preserved her from the danger which she feared; yet once, and once only, she became a mother. The infant was saved and educated in Arabia by his father, who imparted to him on his death-bed that he was the son of an empress. Filled with ambitious hopes, the unsuspecting youth immediately hastened to the palace of Constantinople, and was admitted to the presence of his mother. As he was never more seen, even after the decease of Theodora, she deserves the foul imputation of extinguishing with his life a secret so offensive to her imperial virtue.

In the most abject state of her fortune and reputation, some vision, either of sleep or of fancy, had whispered to Theodora the pleasing assurance that she was destined to become the spouse of a potent monarch. Conscious of her approaching greatness, she returned from Paphlagonia to Constantinople; assumed, like a skilful actress, a more decent character; relieved her poverty by the laudable industry of spinning wool; and affected a life of chastity and solitude in a small house, which she afterwards changed into a magnificent temple.[1] Her beauty, assisted by art or accident, soon attracted, captivated, and fixed, the patrician Justinian, who already reigned with absolute sway under the name of his uncle. Perhaps she contrived to enhance the value of a gift which she had so often lavished on the meanest of mankind; perhaps she inflamed, at first by modest delays, and at last by sensual allurements, the desires of a lover who, from nature or devotion, was addicted to long vigils and abstemious diet. When his first transports had subsided, she still maintained the same ascendant over his mind by the more solid merit of temper and understanding. Justinian delighted to ennoble and enrich the object of his affection: the treasures of the East were poured at her feet, and the nephew of Justin was determined, perhaps by religious scruples, to bestow on his

1 Anonym. de Antiquitat. C. P. l. iii. 132, in Banduri Imperium Orient. tom. i. p. 47. Ludewig (p. 154) argues sensibly that Theodora would not have immortalised a brothel: but I apply this fact to her second and chaster residence at Constantinople.

concubine the sacred and legal character of a wife. But the laws
of Rome expressly prohibited the marriage of a senator with any
female who had been dishonoured by a servile origin or theatrical profession: the empress Lupicina or Euphemia, a barbarian
of rustic manners, but of irreproachable virtue, refused to accept
a prostitute for her niece; and even Vigilantia, the superstitious
mother of Justinian, though she acknowledged the wit and
beauty of Theodora, was seriously apprehensive lest the levity
and arrogance of that artful paramour might corrupt the piety
and happiness of her son. These obstacles were removed by the
inflexible constancy of Justinian. He patiently expected the death
of the empress; he despised the tears of his mother, who soon
sunk under the weight of her affliction; and a law was promulgated, in the name of the emperor Justin, which abolished the
rigid jurisprudence of antiquity. A glorious repentance (the
words of the edict) was left open for the unhappy females who
had prostituted their persons on the theatre, and they were permitted to contract a legal union with the most illustrious of the
Romans.[1] This indulgence was speedily followed by the solemn
nuptials of Justinian and Theodora; her dignity was gradually
exalted with that of her lover; and, as soon as Justin had invested
his nephew with the purple, the patriarch of Constantinople
placed the diadem on the heads of the emperor and empress of
the East. But the usual honours which the severity of Roman
manners had allowed to the wives of princes could not satisfy
either the ambition of Theodora or the fondness of Justinian.
He seated her on the throne as an equal and independent colleague
in the sovereignty of the empire, and an oath of allegiance was
imposed on the governors of the provinces in the joint names
of Justinian and Theodora.[2] The Eastern world fell prostrate

1 See the old law in Justinian's Code (l. v. tit. v. leg. 7, tit. xxvii. leg. 1)
under the years 336 and 454. The new edict (about the year 521 or 522, Aleman.
p. 38, 96) very awkwardly repeals no more than the clause of mulieres *scenicæ*,
libertinæ, tabernariæ. See the novels 89 and 117, and a Greek rescript from
Justinian to the bishops (Aleman. p. 41).

2 I swear by the Father, etc., by the Virgin Mary, by the four Gospels, quæ
in manibus teneo, and by the Holy Archangels Michael and Gabriel, puram con-
scientiam germanumque servitium me servaturum, sacratissimis DDNN. Justinia-
no et Theodoræ conjugi ejus (Novell. viii. tit. 3). Would the oath have been binding
in favour of the widow? Communes tituli et triumphi, etc. (Aleman. p. 47, 48).

before the genius and fortune of the daughter of Acacius. The prostitute who, in the presence of innumerable spectators, had polluted the theatre of Constantinople, was adored as a queen in the same city, by grave magistrates, orthodox bishops, victorious generals, and captive monarchs.[1]

Those who believe that the female mind is totally depraved by the loss of chastity will eagerly listen to all the invectives of private envy or popular resentment, which have dissembled the virtues of Theodora, exaggerated her vices, and condemned with rigour the venal or voluntary sins of the youthful harlot. From a motive of shame or contempt, she often declined the servile homage of the multitude, escaped from the odious light of the capital, and passed the greatest part of the year in the palaces and gardens which were pleasantly seated on the sea-coast of the Propontis and the Bosphorus. Her private hours were devoted to the prudent as well as grateful care of her beauty, the luxury of the bath and table, and the long slumber of the evening and the morning. Her secret apartments were occupied by the favourite women and eunuchs, whose interests and passions she indulged at the expense of justice: the most illustrious personages of the state were crowded into a dark and sultry antechamber; and when at last, after tedious attendance, they were admitted to kiss the feet of Theodora, they experienced, as her humour might suggest, the silent arrogance of an empress or the capricious levity of a comedian. Her rapacious avarice to accumulate an immense treasure may be excused by the apprehension of her husband's death, which could leave no alternative between ruin and the throne; and fear as well as ambition might exasperate Theodora against two generals who, during a malady of the emperor, had rashly declared that they were not disposed to acquiesce in the choice of the capital. But the reproach of cruelty, so repugnant even to her softer vices, has left an indelible stain on the memory of Theodora. Her numerous spies observed and zealously reported every action, or word, or look, injurious to their royal mistress. Whomsoever they accused were

---

1 'Let greatness own her, and she's mean no more,' etc.
Without Warburton's critical telescope I should never have seen, in this general picture of triumphant vice, any personal allusion to Theodora.

cast into her peculiar prisons,[1] inaccessible to the inquiries of justice; and it was rumoured that the torture of the rack or scourge had been inflicted in the presence of a female tyrant, insensible to the voice of prayer or of pity.[2] Some of these unhappy victims perished in deep unwholesome dungeons, while others were permitted, after the loss of their limbs, their reason, or their fortune, to appear in the world, the living monuments of her vengeance, which was commonly extended to the children of those whom she had suspected or injured. The senator or bishop whose death or exile Theodora had pronounced, was delivered to a trusty messenger, and his diligence was quickened by a menace from her own mouth. 'If you fail in the execution of my commands, I swear by him who liveth for ever that your skin shall be flayed from your body.'[3]

If the creed of Theodora had not been tainted with heresy, her exemplary devotion might have atoned, in the opinion of her contemporaries, for pride, avarice, and cruelty; but if she employed her influence to assuage the intolerant fury of the emperor, the present age will allow some merit to her religion, and much indulgence to her speculative errors.[4] The name of Theodora was introduced, with equal honour, in all the pious and charitable foundations of Justinian; and the most benevolent institution of his reign may be ascribed to the sympathy of the empress for her less fortunate sisters, who had been seduced or compelled to embrace the trade of prostitution. A palace, on the Asiatic side of the Bosphorus, was converted into a stately and spacious monastery, and a liberal maintenance was assigned to five hundred women who had been collected from the streets and brothels of Constantinople. In this safe and holy retreat they were devoted to perpetual confinement; and the despair of some,

1 Her prisons, a labyrinth, a Tartarus (Anecdot. c. 4), were under the palace. Darkness is propitious to cruelty, but it is likewise favourable to calumny and fiction.

2 A more jocular whipping was inflicted on Saturninus, for presuming to say that his wife, a favourite of the empress, had not been found ἄτρητος (Anecdot. c. 17 [tom. iii. p. 104, ed. Bonn]).

3 Per viventem in sæcula excoriari te faciam. Anastasius de Vitis Pont. Roman. in Vigilio, p. 40.

4 Ludewig, p. 161–166. I give him credit for the charitable attempt, although *he* hath not much charity in his temper.

who threw themselves headlong into the sea, was lost in the gratitude of the penitents who had been delivered from sin and misery by their generous benefactress.[1] The prudence of Theodora is celebrated by Justinian himself; and his laws are attributed to the sage counsels of his most reverend wife, whom he had received as the gift of the Deity.[2] Her courage was displayed amidst the tumult of the people and the terrors of the court. Her chastity, from the moment of her union with Justinian, is founded on the silence of her implacable enemies; and although the daughter of Acacius might be satiated with love, yet some applause is due to the firmness of a mind which could sacrifice pleasure and habit to the stronger sense either of duty or interest. The wishes and prayers of Theodora could never obtain the blessing of a lawful son, and she buried an infant daughter, the sole offspring of her marriage.[3] Notwithstanding this disappointment, her dominion was permanent and absolute; she preserved, by art or merit, the affections of Justinian; and their seeming dissensions were always fatal to the courtiers who believed them to be sincere. Perhaps her health had been impaired by the licentiousness of her youth; but it was always delicate, and she was directed by her physicians to use the Pythian warm-baths. In this journey the empress was followed by the Prætorian præfect, the great treasurer, several counts and patricians, and a splendid train of four thousand attendants: the highways were repaired at her approach; a palace was erected for her reception; and as she passed through Bithynia she distributed liberal alms to the churches, the monasteries, and the hospitals, that they might implore Heaven for the restoration of her health.[4] At length, in the twenty-fourth year of her marriage, and the

1 Compare the Anecdotes (c. 17) with the Edifices (l. i. c. 9). How differently may the same fact be stated! John Malala (tom. ii. p. 174, 175 [p. 440, 441, ed. Bonn]) observes, that on this, or a similar occasion, she released and clothed the girls whom she had purchased from the stews at five aurei apiece.

2 Novel viii. 1. An allusion to Theodora. Her enemies read the name Dæmonodora (Aleman. p. 66 [Procop. tom. iii. p. 415, ed. Bonn.])

3 St. Sabas refused to pray for a son of Theodora, lest he should prove a heretic worse than Anastasius himself (Cyril in Vit. St. Sabæ, apud Aleman. p. 70, 109 [Procop. tom. iii. p. 421, 462, ed. Bonn]).

4 See John Malala, tom. ii. p. 174 [p. 441, ed. Bonn]. Theophanes, p. 158 [tom. i. p. 286, ed. Bonn]. Procopius de Ædific. l. v. c. 3.

twenty-second of her reign, she was consumed by a cancer;[1] and the irreparable loss was deplored by her husband, who, in the room of a theatrical prostitute, might have selected the purest and most noble virgin of the East.[2]

II. A material difference may be observed in the games of antiquity: the most eminent of the Greeks were actors, the Romans were merely spectators. The Olympic stadium was open to wealth, merit, and ambition; and if the candidates could depend on their personal skill and activity, they might pursue the footsteps of Diomede and Menelaus, and conduct their own horses in the rapid career.[3] Ten, twenty, forty chariots, were allowed to start at the same instant; a crown of leaves was the reward of the victor, and his fame, with that of his family and country, was chanted in lyric strains more durable than monuments of brass and marble. But a senator, or even a citizen, conscious of his dignity, would have blushed to expose his person or his horses in the circus of Rome. The games were exhibited at the expense of the republic, the magistrates, or the emperors; but the reins were abandoned to servile hands; and if the profits of a favourite charioteer sometimes exceeded those of an advocate, they must be considered as the effects of popular extravagance, and the high wages of a disgraceful profession. The race, in its first institution, was a simple contest of two chariots, whose drivers were distinguished by *white* and *red* liveries: two additional colours, a light *green* and a cærulean *blue*, were afterwards introduced; and, as the races were repeated twenty-five times, one hundred

1 Theodora Chalcedonensis synodi inimica canceris plagâ toto corpore perfusa vitam prodigiose finivit (Victor Tununensis in Chron.). On such occasions an orthodox mind is steeled against pity. Alemannus (p. 12, 13) understands the εὐσεβῶς ἐκοιμήθη of Theophanes as civil language, which does not imply either piety or repentance; yet two years after her death St. Theodora is celebrated by Paul Silentiarius (in Proem. ver. 58–62).

2 As she persecuted the popes, and rejected a council, Baronius exhausts the names of Eve, Dalila, Herodias, etc.; after which he has recourse to his infernal dictionary: civis inferni – alumna dæmonum – satanico agitata spiritû – œstro percita diabolico, etc. etc. (A.D. 548, No. 24).

3 Read and feel the twenty-third book of the Iliad, a living picture of manners, passions, and the whole form and spirit of the chariot-race. West's Dissertation on the Olympic Games (sect. xii.–xvii.) affords much curious and authentic information.

chariots contributed in the same day to the pomp of the circus. The four *factions* soon acquired a legal establishment and a mysterious origin, and their fanciful colours were derived from the various appearances of nature in the four seasons of the year; the red dog-star of summer, the snows of winter, the deep shades of autumn, and the cheerful verdure of the spring.[1] Another interpretation preferred the elements to the seasons, and the struggle of the green and blue was supposed to represent the conflict of the earth and sea. Their respective victories announced either a plentiful harvest or a prosperous navigation, and the hostility of the husbandmen and mariners was somewhat less absurd than the blind ardour of the Roman people, who devoted their lives and fortunes to the colour which they had espoused. Such folly was disdained and indulged by the wisest princes; but the names of Caligula, Nero, Vitellius, Verus, Commodus, Caracalla, and Elagabalus, were enrolled in the blue or green factions of the circus: they frequented their stables, applauded their favourites, chastised their antagonists, and deserved the esteem of the populace by the natural or affected imitation of their manners. The bloody and tumultuous contest continued to disturb the public festivity till the last age of the spectacles of Rome; and Theodoric, from a motive of justice or affection, interposed his authority to protect the greens against the violence of a consul and a patrician who were passionately addicted to the blue faction of the circus.[2]

Constantinople adopted the follies, though not the virtues, of ancient Rome; and the same factions which had agitated the circus raged with redoubled fury in the hippodrome. Under the reign of Anastasius, this popular frenzy was inflamed by religious zeal; and the greens, who had treacherously concealed stones and daggers under baskets of fruit, massacred at a solemn festival

1 The four colours, *albati, russati, prasini, veneti*, represent the four seasons, according to Cassiodorus (Var. iii. 51), who lavishes much wit and eloquence on this theatrical mystery. Of these colours, the three first may be fairly translated, *white, red,* and *green. Venetus* is explained by *cæruleus*, a word various and vague: it is properly the sky reflected in the sea; but custom and convenience may allow *blue* as an equivalent. (Robert. Stephan. sub voce. Spence's Polymetis, p. 228.)

2 See Onuphrius Panvinius de Ludis Circensibus, l. i. c. 10, 11; the seventeenth Annotation on Mascou's History of the Germans; and Aleman. ad. c. vii.

three thousand of their blue adversaries.[1] From the capital this pestilence was diffused into the provinces and cities of the East, and the sportive distinction of two colours produced two strong and irreconcilable factions, which shook the foundations of a feeble government.[2] The popular dissensions, founded on the most serious interest or holy pretence, have scarcely equalled the obstinacy of this wanton discord, which invaded the peace of families, divided friends and brothers, and tempted the female sex, though seldom seen in the circus, to espouse the inclinations of their lovers, or to contradict the wishes of their husbands. Every law, either human or divine, was trampled under foot; and as long as the party was successful, its deluded followers appeared careless of private distress or public calamity. The licence, without the freedom, of democracy, was revived at Antioch and Constantinople, and the support of a faction became necessary to every candidate for civil or ecclesiastical honours. A secret attachment to the family or sect of Anastasius was imputed to the greens; the blues were zealously devoted to the cause of orthodoxy and Justinian,[3] and their grateful patron protected, above five years, the disorders of a faction whose seasonable tumults overawed the palace, the senate, and the capitals of the East. Insolent with royal favour, the blues affected to strike terror by a peculiar and barbaric dress – the long hair of the Huns, their close sleeves and ample garments, a lofty step, and a sonorous voice. In the day they concealed their two-edged poniards, but in the night they boldly assembled in arms and in numerous bands, prepared for every act of violence and rapine.

1 Marcellin in Chron. p. 47 [anno 501]. Instead of the vulgar word *veneta*, he uses the more exquisite terms of *cærulea* and *cærealis*. Baronius (A.D. 501, No. 4, 5, 6) is satisfied that the blues were orthodox; but Tillemont is angry at the supposition, and will not allow any martyrs in a playhouse (Hist. des Emp. tom. vi. p. 554).

2 See Procopius (Persic. l. i. c. 24). In describing the vices of the factions and of the government, the *public* is not more favourable than the *secret* historian. Aleman. (p. 26 [tom. iii. p. 373, ed. Bonn]) has quoted a fine passage from Gregory Nazianzen, which proves the inveteracy of the evil.

3 The partiality of Justinian for the blues (Anecdot. c. 7 [tom. iii. p. 53, ed. Bonn]) is attested by Evagrius (Hist. Eccles. l. iv. c. 32), John Malala (tom. ii. p. 138, 139 [p. 152, ed. Oxon.; lib. xviii. p. 425, ed. Bonn]), especially for Antioch, and Theophanes (p. 142 [p. 256, ed. Bonn]).

Their adversaries of the green faction, or even inoffensive citizens, were stripped and often murdered by these nocturnal robbers, and it became dangerous to wear any gold buttons or girdles, or to appear at a late hour in the streets of a peaceful capital. A daring spirit, rising with impunity, proceeded to violate the safeguard of private houses; and fire was employed to facilitate the attack, or to conceal the crimes, of these factious rioters. No place was safe or sacred from their depredations; to gratify either avarice or revenge they profusely spilt the blood of the innocent; churches and altars were polluted by atrocious murders, and it was the boast of the assassins that their dexterity could always inflict a mortal wound with a single stroke of their dagger. The dissolute youth of Constantinople adopted the blue livery of disorder; the laws were silent, and the bonds of society were relaxed; creditors were compelled to resign their obligations; judges to reverse their sentence; masters to enfranchise their slaves; fathers to supply the extravagance of their children; noble matrons were prostituted to the lust of their servants; beautiful boys were torn from the arms of their parents; and wives, unless they preferred a voluntary death, were ravished in the presence of their husbands.[1] The despair of the greens, who were persecuted by their enemies and deserted by the magistrate, assumed the privilege of defence, perhaps of retaliation; but those who survived the combat were dragged to execution, and the unhappy fugitives, escaping to woods and caverns, preyed without mercy on the society from whence they were expelled. Those ministers of justice who had courage to punish the crimes and to brave the resentment of the blues became the victims of their indiscreet zeal: a præfect of Constantinople fled for refuge to the holy sepulchre, a count of the East was ignominiously whipped, and a governor of Cilicia was hanged, by the order of Theodora, on the tomb of two assassins whom he had condemned for the murder of his groom, and a daring attack upon his own life.[2] An

1 A wife (says Procopius), who was seized and almost ravished by a blue-coat, threw herself into the Bosphorus. The bishops of the second Syria (Aleman. p. 26 [tom. iii. p. 374, ed. Bonn]) deplore a similar suicide, the guilt or glory of female chastity, and name the heroine.

2 The doubtful credit of Procopius (Anecdot. c. 17) is supported by the less partial Evagrius, who confirms the fact, and specifies the names. The tragic

aspiring candidate may be tempted to build his greatness on the public confusion, but it is the interest as well as duty of a sovereign to maintain the authority of the laws. The first edict of Justinian, which was often repeated and sometimes executed, announced his firm resolution to support the innocent, and to chastise the guilty, of every denomination and *colour.* Yet the balance of justice was still inclined in favour of the blue faction, by the secret affection, the habits, and the fears of the emperor; his equity, after an apparent struggle, submitted without reluctance to the implacable passions of Theodora, and the empress never forgot or forgave the injuries of the comedian. At the accession of the younger Justin, the proclamation of equal and rigorous justice indirectly condemned the partiality of the former reign. 'Ye blues, Justinian is no more! ye greens, he is still alive!'[1]

A sedition, which almost laid Constantinople in ashes, was excited by the mutual hatred and momentary reconciliation of the two factions. In the fifth year of his reign Justinian celebrated the festival of the ides of January: the games were incessantly disturbed by the clamorous discontent of the greens; till the twenty-second race the emperor maintained his silent gravity; at length, yielding to his impatience, he condescended to hold, in abrupt sentences, and by the voice of a crier, the most singular dialogue[2] that ever passed between a prince and his subjects. Their first complaints were respectful and modest; they accused the subordinate ministers of oppression, and proclaimed their wishes for the long life and victory of the emperor. 'Be patient and attentive, ye insolent railers!' exclaimed Justinian; 'be mute, ye Jews, Samaritans, and Manichæans!' The greens still attempted to awaken his compassion. 'We are poor, we are innocent, we are injured, we dare not pass through the streets: a general

fate of the præfect of Constantinople is related by John Malala (tom. ii. p. 139 [p. 416, ed. Bonn]).

1 See John Malala (tom. ii. p. 147 [p. 422, ed. Bonn]); yet he owns that Justinian was attached to the blues. The seeming discord of the emperor and Theodora is perhaps viewed with too much jealousy and refinement by Procopius (Anecdot. c. 10 [t. iii. p. 70, ed. Bonn]). See Aleman. Præfat. p. 6.

2 This dialogue, which Theophanes has preserved, exhibits the popular language, as well as the manners, of Constantinople in the sixth century. Their Greek is mingled with many strange and barbarous words, for which Ducange cannot always find a meaning or etymology.

persecution is exercised against our name and colour. Let us die, O emperor! but let us die by your command, and for your service!' But the repetition of partial and passionate invectives degraded, in their eyes, the majesty of the purple; they renounced allegiance to the prince who refused justice to his people, lamented that the father of Justinian had been born, and branded his son with the opprobrious names of a homicide, an ass, and a perjured tyrant. 'Do you despise your lives?' cried the indignant monarch. The blues rose with fury from their seats, their hostile clamours thundered in the hippodrome, and their adversaries, deserting the unequal contest, spread terror and despair through the streets of Constantinople. At this dangerous moment, seven notorious assassins of both factions, who had been condemned by the præfect, were carried round the city, and afterwards transported to the place of execution in the suburb of Pera. Four were immediately beheaded; a fifth was hanged; but, when the same punishment was inflicted on the remaining two, the rope broke, they fell alive to the ground, the populace applauded their es-cape, and the monks of St. Conon, issuing from the neighbour-ing convent, conveyed them in a boat to the sanctuary of the church.[1] As one of these criminals was of the blue, and the other of the green, livery, the two factions were equally provoked by the cruelty of their oppressor or the ingratitude of their patron, and a short truce was concluded till they had delivered their prisoners and satisfied their revenge. The palace of the præfect, who withstood the seditious torrent, was instantly burnt, his officers and guards were massacred, the prisons were forced open, and freedom was restored to those who could only use it for the public destruction. A military force which had been des-patched to the aid of the civil magistrate was fiercely en-countered by an armed multitude, whose numbers and boldness continually increased: and the Heruli, the wildest barbarians in the service of the empire, overturned the priests and their relics, which, from a pious motive, had been rashly interposed to sep-arate the bloody conflict. The tumult was exasperated by this sacrilege; the people fought with enthusiasm in the cause of God; the women, from the roofs and windows, showered stones

1 See this church and monastery in Ducange, C. P. Christiana, l. iv. p. 182.

on the heads of the soldiers, who darted firebrands against the houses; and the various flames, which had been kindled by the hands of citizens and strangers, spread without control over the face of the city. The conflagration involved the cathedral of St. Sophia, the baths of Zeuxippus, a part of the palace from the first entrance to the altar of Mars, and the long portico from the palace to the forum of Constantine: a large hospital, with the sick patients, was consumed; many churches and stately edifices were destroyed; and an immense treasure of gold and silver was either melted or lost. From such scenes of horror and distress the wise and wealthy citizens escaped over the Bosphorus to the Asiatic side, and during five days Constantinople was abandoned to the factions, whose watchword, NIKA, *vanquish!* has given a name to this memorable sedition.[1]

As long as the factions were divided, the triumphant blues and desponding greens appeared to behold with the same indifference the disorders of the state. They agreed to censure the corrupt management of justice and the finance; and the two responsible ministers, the artful Tribonian and the rapacious John of Cappadocia, were loudly arraigned as the authors of the public misery. The peaceful murmurs of the people would have been disregarded: they were heard with respect when the city was in flames; the quæstor and the præfect were instantly removed, and their offices were filled by two senators of blameless integrity. After this popular concession Justinian proceeded to the hippodrome to confess his own errors, and to accept the repentance of his grateful subjects; but they distrusted his assurances, though solemnly pronounced in the presence of the holy gospels; and the emperor, alarmed by their distrust, retreated with precipitation to the strong fortress of the palace. The obstinacy of the tumult was now imputed to a secret and ambitious conspiracy, and a suspicion was entertained that the insurgents, more especially the green faction, had been supplied with arms and money by Hypatius and Pompey, two patricians who could

1 The history of the *Nika* sedition is extracted from Marcellinus (in Chron. [an. 532]), Procopius (Persic. l. i. c. 26 [c. 24, tom. i. p. 119, ed. Bonn]), John Malala (tom. ii. p. 213–218 [ed. Ox.; p. 473–477, ed. Bonn]), Chron. Paschal. (p. 336–340, tom. i. p. 620 *sqq.*, ed. Bonn]), Theophanes (Chronograph. p. 154–158 [ed. Par. tom. i. p. 278–286, ed. Bonn]), and Zonaras (l. xiv. p. 61–63).

neither forget with honour, nor remember with safety, that they were the nephews of the emperor Anastasius. Capriciously trusted, disgraced, and pardoned by the jealous levity of the monarch, they had appeared as loyal servants before the throne, and, during five days of the tumult, they were detained as important hostages; till at length, the fears of Justinian prevailing over his prudence, he viewed the two brothers in the light of spies, perhaps of assassins, and sternly commanded them to depart from the palace. After a fruitless representation that obedience might lead to involuntary treason, they retired to their houses, and in the morning of the sixth day Hypatius was surrounded and seized by the people, who, regardless of his virtuous resistance and the tears of his wife, transported their favourite to the forum of Constantine, and, instead of a diadem, placed a rich collar on his head. If the usurper, who afterwards pleaded the merit of his delay, had complied with the advice of his senate, and urged the fury of the multitude, their first irresistible effort might have oppressed or expelled his trembling competitor. The Byzantine palace enjoyed a free communication with the sea, vessels lay ready at the garden-stairs, and a secret resolution was already formed to convey the emperor with his family and treasures to a safe retreat at some distance from the capital.

Justinian was lost, if the prostitute whom he raised from the theatre had not renounced the timidity as well as the virtues of her sex. In the midst of a council where Belisarius was present, Theodora alone displayed the spirit of a hero, and she alone, without apprehending his future hatred, could save the emperor from the imminent danger and his unworthy fears. 'If flight,' said the consort of Justinian, 'were the only means of safety, yet I should disdain to fly. Death is the condition of our birth, but they who have reigned should never survive the loss of dignity and dominion. I implore Heaven that I may never be seen, not a day, without my diadem and purple; that I may no longer behold the light when I cease to be saluted with the name of queen. If you resolve, O Cæsar! to fly, you have treasures; behold the sea, you have ships; but tremble lest the desire of life should expose you to wretched exile and ignominious death. For my own part, I adhere to the maxim of antiquity, that the throne is a glorious sepulchre.' The firmness of a woman restored the courage to deliberate and act, and courage soon discovers the resources of the most desperate situation. It was an easy and a decisive measure to revive the animosity of the factions; the blues were astonished at their own guilt and folly, that a trifling injury should provoke them to conspire with their implacable enemies against a gracious and liberal benefactor; they again proclaimed the majesty of Justinian; and the greens, with their upstart emperor, were left alone in the hippodrome. The fidelity of the guards was doubtful; but the military force of Justinian consisted in three thousand veterans, who had been trained to valour and discipline in the Persian and Illyrian wars. Under the command of Belisarius and Mundus, they silently marched in two divisions from the palace, forced their obscure way through narrow passages, expiring flames, and falling edifices, and burst open at the same moment the two opposite gates of the hippodrome. In this narrow space the disorderly and affrighted crowd was incapable of resisting on either side a firm and regular attack; the blues signalised the fury of their repentance, and it is computed that above thirty thousand persons were slain in the merciless and promiscuous carnage of the day. Hypatius was dragged from his throne, and conducted with his brother Pompey to the feet of the emperor; they implored his clemency, but their crime was manifest, their innocence uncertain, and Justinian had been too much terrified to forgive. The next morning the two nephews of Anastasius, with eighteen *illustrious* accomplices, of patrician or consular rank, were privately executed by the soldiers, their bodies were thrown into the sea, their palaces razed, and their fortunes confiscated. The hippodrome itself was condemned, during several years, to a mournful silence; with the restoration of the games the same disorders revived, and the blue and green factions continued to afflict the reign of Justinian, and to disturb the tranquillity of the Eastern empire.[1]

III. That empire, after Rome was barbarous, still embraced the nations whom she had conquered beyond the Hadriatic, and as

1 Marcellinus says, in general terms, innumeris populis in circo trucidatis. Procopius numbers 30,000 victims [tom. i. p.129, ed. Bonn]; and the 35,000 of Theophanes are swelled to 40,000 by the more recent Zonaras [tom. ii. p. 63]. Such is the usual progress of exaggeration.

far as the frontiers of Ethiopia and Persia. Justinian reigned over sixty-four provinces and nine hundred and thirty-five cities;[1] his dominions were blessed by nature with the advantages of soil, situation, and climate, and the improvements of human art had been perpetually diffused along the coast of the Mediterranean and the banks of the Nile from ancient Troy to the Egyptian Thebes. Abraham[2] had been relieved by the well-known plenty of Egypt; the same country, a small and populous tract, was still capable of exporting each year two hundred and sixty thousand quarters of wheat for the use of Constantinople;[3] and the capital of Justinian was supplied with the manufactures of Sidon fifteen centuries after they had been celebrated in the poems of Homer.[4] The annual powers of vegetation, instead of being exhausted by two thousand harvests, were renewed and invigorated by skilful husbandry, rich manure, and seasonable repose. The breed of domestic animals was infinitely multiplied. Plantations, buildings, and the instruments of labour and luxury, which are more durable than the term of human life, were accumulated by the care of successive generations. Tradition preserved, and experience simplified, the humble practice of the arts; society was enriched by the division of labour and the facility of exchange; and every Roman was lodged, clothed, and subsisted by the industry of a thousand hands. The invention of the loom and distaff has been piously ascribed to the gods. In every age a variety of animal and vegetable productions, hair, skins, wool, flax, cotton, and at

1 Hierocles, a contemporary of Justinian, composed his Συνέκδημος (Itineraria, p. 631), or review of the eastern provinces and cities, before the year 535 (Wesseling, in Præfat. and Not. ad p. 623, etc.).

2 See the Book of Genesis (xii. 10), and the administration of Joseph. The annals of the Greeks and Hebrews agree in the early arts and plenty of Egypt: but this antiquity supposes a long series of improvement; and Warburton, who is almost stifled by the Hebrew, calls aloud for the Samaritan, chronology (Divine Legation, vol. iii. p. 29, etc.).

3 Eight millions of Roman modii, besides a contribution of 80,000 aurei for the expenses of water-carriage, from which the subject was graciously excused. See the thirteenth Edict of Justinian [c. viii.]; the numbers are checked and verified by the agreement of the Greek and Latin texts.

4 Homer's Iliad, vi. 289. These veils, πέπλοι παμποίκιλοι, were the work of the Sidonian women. But this passage is more honourable to the manufactures than to the navigation of Phœnicia, from whence they had been imported to Troy in Phrygian bottoms.

length *silk*, have been skilfully manufactured to hide or adorn
the human body; they were stained with an infusion of permanent colours, and the pencil was successfully employed to im-
prove the labours of the loom. In the choice of those colours[1]
which imitate the beauties of nature, the freedom of taste and
fashion was indulged; but the deep purple[2] which the Phœnicians extracted from a shell-fish was restrained to the sacred
person and palace of the emperor, and the penalties of treason
were denounced against the ambitious subjects who dared to
usurp the prerogative of the throne.[3]

I need not explain that *silk*[4] is originally spun from the bowels
of a caterpillar, and that it composes the golden tomb from

1 See in Ovid (de Arte Amandi, iii. 269, etc.) a poetical list of twelve colours
borrowed from flowers, the elements, etc. But it is almost impossible to discriminate by words all the nice and various shades both of art and nature.

2 By the discovery of cochineal, etc., we far surpass the colours of antiquity.
Their royal purple had a strong smell, and a dark cast as deep as bull's blood –
obscuritas rubens (says Cassiodorus, Var. l. 1, c. 2) nigredo sanguinea. The
President Goguet (Origine des Loix et des Arts, part ii. l. ii. c. 2, p. 184–215)
will amuse and satisfy the reader. I doubt whether his book, especially in
England, is as well known as it deserves to be.

3 Historical proofs of this jealousy have been occasionally introduced, and
many more might have been added; but the arbitrary acts of despotism were
justified by the sober and general declarations of law (Codex Theodosian. l. x.
tit. 21, leg. 3; Codex Justinian. l. xi. tit. 8, leg. 5). An inglorious permission, and
necessary restriction, was applied to the *mimæ*, the female dancers (Cod. Theodos. l. xv. tit. 7, leg. 11).

4 In the history of insects (far more wonderful than Ovid's Metamor-
phoses) the silkworm holds a conspicuous place. The bombyx of the isle of
Ceos, as described by Pliny (Hist. Natur. xi. 26, 27, with the notes of the two
learned Jesuits, Hardouin and Brotier), may be illustrated by a similar species
in China (Mémories sur les Chinois, tom. ii. p. 575–598); but our silkworm, as
well as the white mulberry-tree, were unknown to Theophrastus and Pliny.

[The first ancient writer who gives any information respecting the use of
silk is Aristotle (*Hist. Anim.* v. c. 19), whose account has been adopted with
various modifications by Pliny, Clemens Alexandrinus, and Basil. Gibbon has
fallen into one or two mistakes here. He has confounded the island of Ceos,
near the coast of Attica, with the island of Cos, off the western coast of Asia
Minor, the latter, and not Ceos, being celebrated for its transparent garments;
and he has without authority supposed that a species of silkworm was bred in
this island. But Aristotle, after describing the silkworm of the East, only says,
'Pamphile, daughter of Plates, is reported to have first woven in Cos.' It is
therefore probable that the raw silk from the interior of Asia was brought to
Cos, and there manufactured, in the same way, as we learn from Procopius,

whence a worm emerges in the form of a butterfly. Till the reign of Justinian, the silkworms who feed on the leaves of the white mulberry-tree were confined to China; those of the pine, the oak, and the ash were common in the forests both of Asia and Europe; but as their education is more difficult, and their produce more uncertain, they were generally neglected, except in the little island of Ceos, near the coast of Attica. A thin gauze was procured from their webs, and this Cean manufacture, the invention of a woman, for female use, was long admired both in the East and at Rome. Whatever suspicions may be raised by the garments of the Medes and Assyrians, Virgil is the most ancient writer who expressly mentions the soft wool which was combed from the trees of the Seres or Chinese;[1] and this natural error, less marvellous than the truth, was slowly corrected by the knowledge of a valuable insect, the first artificer of the luxury of nations. That rare and elegant luxury was censured, in the reign of Tiberius, by the gravest of the Romans; and Pliny, in affected though forcible language, has condemned the thirst of gain, which explored the last confines of the earth for the pernicious purpose of exposing to the public eye naked draperies and transparent matrons.[2] A dress which showed the turn of the limbs and colour of the skin might gratify vanity or provoke desire; the silks which had been closely woven in China were sometimes unravelled by the Phœnician women, and the precious materials were multiplied by a looser texture, and the intermixture of linen threads.[3] Two hundred years after the age of Pliny the use of

that it was brought some centuries later to be woven in the Phœnician cities of Tyre and Berytus. – O. S.]

1 Georgic. ii. 121. Serica quando venerint in usum planissime non scio: suspicor tamen in Julii Cæsaris ævo, nam ante non invenio, says Justus Lipsius (Excursus i. ad Tacit. Annal. ii. 32). See Dion Cassius (l. xliii. [c. 24] p. 358, edit. Reimar) and Pausanias (l. vi. [c. 26, § 6–9] p. 519), the first who describes, however strangely, the Seric insect.

2 Tam longinquo orbe petitur, ut in publico matrona transluceat ... ut denudet fœminas vestis (Plin. vi. 20, xi. 26). Varro and Publius Syrus had already played on the Toga vitrea, ventus textilis, and nebula linea (Horat. Sermon. i. 2, 101, with the notes of Torrentius and Dacier).

3 On the texture, colours, names, and use of the silk, half-silk, and linen garments of antiquity, see the profound, diffuse, and obscure researches of the great Salmasius (in Hist. August. p. 127, 309, 310, 339, 341, 342, 344, 388–391, 395, 513), who was ignorant of the most common trades of Dijon or Leyden.

pure or even of mixed silks was confined to the female sex, till the opulent citizens of Rome and the provinces were insensibly familiarised with the example of Elagabalus, the first who, by this effeminate habit, had sullied the dignity of an emperor and a man. Aurelian complained that a pound of silk was sold at Rome for twelve ounces of gold; but the supply increased with the demand, and the price diminished with the supply. If accident or monopoly sometimes raised the value even above the standard of Aurelian, the manufacturers of Tyre and Berytus were sometimes compelled, by the operation of the same causes, to content themselves with a ninth part of that extravagant rate.[1] A law was thought necessary to discriminate the dress of comedians from that of senators, and of the silk exported from its native country the far greater part was consumed by the subjects of Justinian. They were still more intimately acquainted with a shell-fish of the Mediterranean, surnamed the silkworm of the sea: the fine wool or hair by which the mother-of-pearl affixes itself to the rock is now manufactured for curiosity rather than use; and a robe obtained from the same singular materials was the gift of the Roman emperor to the satraps of Armenia.[2]

A valuable merchandise of small bulk is capable of defraying the expense of land-carriage, and the caravans traversed the whole latitude of Asia in two hundred and forty-three days from the Chinese ocean to the sea-coast of Syria. Silk was immediately delivered to the Romans by the Persian merchants,[3] who frequented the fairs of Armenia and Nisibis; but this trade, which in the intervals of truce was oppressed by avarice and jealousy, was totally interrupted by the long wars of the rival monarchies.

1 Flavius Vopiscus in Aurelian. c. 45, in Hist. August. p. 224. See Salmasius ad Hist. Aug. p. 392, and Plinian. Exercitat. in Solinum, p. 694, 695. The Anecdotes of Procopius (c. 25) state a partial and imperfect rate of the price of silk in the time of Justinian.

2 Procopius de Ædif. l. iii. c. 1. These *pinnes de mer* are found near Smyrna, Sicily, Corsica, and Minorca; and a pair of gloves of their silk was presented to Pope Benedict XIV.

3 Procopius, Persic. l. i. c. 20; l. ii. c. 25; Gothic. l. iv. c. 17. Menander in Excerpt. Legat. p. 107 [ed. Par.; p. 296, ed. Bonn]. Of the Parthian or Persian empire, Isidore of Charax (in Stathmis Parthicis, p. 7, 8, in Hudson, Geograph, Minor. tom. ii.) has marked the roads, and Ammianus Marcellinus (l. xxiii. c. 6, p. 400) has enumerated the provinces.

The Great King might proudly number Sogdiana, and even *Serica*, among the provinces of his empire, but his real dominion was bounded by the Oxus, and his useful intercourse with the Sogdoites, beyond the river, depended on the pleasure of their conquerors, the white Huns and the Turks, who successively reigned over that industrious people. Yet the most savage dominion has not extirpated the seeds of agriculture and commerce in a region which is celebrated as one of the four gardens of Asia; the cities of Samarcand and Bochara are advantageously seated for the exchange of its various productions, and their merchants purchased from the Chinese[1] the raw or manufactured silk which they transported into Persia for the use of the Roman empire. In the vain capital of China the Sogdian caravans were entertained as the suppliant embassies of tributary kingdoms, and, if they returned in safety, the bold adventure was rewarded with exorbitant gain. But the difficult and perilous march from Samarcand to the first town of Shensi could not be performed in less than sixty, eighty, or one hundred days; as soon as they had passed the Jaxartes they entered the desert, and the wandering hordes, unless they are restrained by armies and garrisons, have always considered the citizen and the traveller as the objects of lawful rapine. To escape the Tartar robbers and the tyrants of Persia, the silk-caravans explored a more southern road: they traversed the mountains of Thibet, descended the streams of the Ganges or the Indus, and patiently expected, in the ports of Guzerat and Malabar, the annual fleets of the West.[2] But the

1 The blind admiration of the Jesuits confounds the different periods of the Chinese history. They are more critically distinguished by M. de Guignes (Hist. des Huns, tom. i. part i. in the Tables, part ii. in the Geography. Mémories de l'Académie des Inscriptions, tom. xxxii. xxxvi. xlii. xliii.), who discovers the gradual progress of the truth of the annals and the extent of the monarchy, till the Christian era. He has searched with a curious eye the connections of the Chinese with the nations of the West; but these connections are slight, casual, and obscure; nor did the Romans entertain a suspicion that the Seres or Sinæ possessed an empire not inferior to their own.

2 The roads from China to Persia and Hindostan may be investigated in the relations of Hackluyt and Thevenot (the ambassadors of Sharokh, Anthony Jenkinson, the Père Greuber, etc. See likewise Hanway's Travels, vol. i. p. 345–357). A communication through Thibet has been lately explored by the English sovereigns of Bengal.

dangers of the desert were found less intolerable than toil, hunger, and the loss of time; the attempt was seldom renewed, and the only European who has passed that unfrequented way applauds his own diligence that, in nine months after his departure from Pekin, he reached the mouth of the Indus. The ocean, however, was open to the free communication of mankind. From the great river to the tropic of Cancer the provinces of China were subdued and civilised by the emperors of the North; they were filled about the time of the Christian era with cities and men, mulberry-trees and their precious inhabitants; and if the Chinese, with the knowledge of the compass, had possessed the genius of the Greeks or Phœnicians, they might have spread their discoveries over the southern hemisphere. I am not qualified to examine, and I am not disposed to believe, their distant voyages to the Persian Gulf or the Cape of Good Hope; but their ancestors might equal the labours and success of the present race, and the sphere of their navigation might extend from the isles of Japan to the straits of Malacca, the Pillars, if we may apply that name, of an Oriental Hercules.[1] Without losing sight of land, they might sail along the coast to the extreme promontory of Achin, which is annually visited by ten or twelve ships laden with the productions, the manufactures, and even the artificers of China; the island of Sumatra and the opposite peninsula are faintly delineated[2] as the regions of gold and silver, and the trading cities named in the geography of Ptolemy may indicate that this wealth was not solely derived from the mines. The direct interval between Sumatra and Ceylon is about three hundred leagues; the Chinese and Indian navigators were conducted by the flight of birds and periodical winds, and the ocean might

1 For the Chinese navigation to Malacca and Achin, perhaps to Ceylon, see Renaudot (on the two Mahometan Travellers, p. 8–11, 13–17, 141–157), Dampier (vol. ii. p. 136), the Hist. Philosophique des deux Indes (tom. i. p. 98), and the Hist. Générale des Voyages (tom. vi. p. 201).

2 The knowledge, or rather ignorance, of Strabo, Pliny, Ptolemy, Arrian, Marcian, etc., of the countries eastward of Cape Comorin, is finely illustrated by D'Anville (Antiquité Géographique de l'Inde, especially p. 161–198). Our geography of India is improved by commerce and conquest; and has been illustrated by the excellent maps and memoirs of Major Rennell. If he extends the sphere of his inquiries with the same critical knowledge and sagacity, he will succeed, and may surpass, the first of modern geographers.

be securely traversed in square-built ships, which, instead of iron, were sewed together with the strong thread of the cocoanut. Ceylon, Serendib, or Taprobana was divided between two hostile princes, one of whom possessed the mountains, the elephants, and the luminous carbuncle, and the other enjoyed the more solid riches of domestic industry, foreign trade, and the capacious harbour of Trinquemale, which received and dismissed the fleets of the East and West. In this hospitable isle, at an equal distance (as it was computed) from their respective countries, the silk-merchants of China, who had collected in their voyages aloes, cloves, nutmeg, and sandal-wood, maintained a free and beneficial commerce with the inhabitants of the Persian Gulf. The subjects of the Great King exalted, without a rival, his power and magnificence; and the Roman, who confounded their vanity by comparing his paltry coin with a gold medal of the emperor Anastasius, had sailed to Ceylon, in an Æthiopian ship, as a simple passenger.[1]

As silk became of indispensable use, the emperor Justinian saw with concern that the Persians had occupied by land and sea the monopoly of this important supply, and that the wealth of his subjects was continually drained by a nation of enemies and idolators. An active government would have restored the trade of Egypt and the navigation of the Red Sea, which had decayed with the prosperity of the empire; and the Roman vessels might have sailed for the purchase of silk to the ports of Ceylon, of Malacca, or even of China. Justinian embraced a more humble expedient, and solicited the aid of his Christian allies, the Æthiopians of Abyssinia, who had recently acquired the arts of navigation, the spirit of trade, and the seaport of Adulis,[2] still decorated with the trophies of a Grecian conqueror. Along the

1 The Taprobane of Pliny (vi. 24), Solinus (c. 56), and Salmas. Plinianæ Exercitat. (p. 781, 782), and most of the ancients, who often confound the islands of Ceylon and Sumatra, is more clearly described by Cosmas Indicopleustes; yet even the Christian topographer has exaggerated its dimensions. His information on the Indian and Chinese trade is rare and curious (l. ii. p. 138, l. xi. p. 337, 338, edit. Montfaucon [Coll. Nova Patrum, tom. ii. Paris, 1706]).

2 See Procopius, Persic. (l. ii. c. 20 [l. i. c. 19]). Cosmas affords some interesting knowledge of the port and inscription of Adulis (Topograph. Christ. l. ii. p. 139, 140–143), and of the trade of the Axumites along the African coast of Barbaria or Zingi (p. 138, 139), and as far as Taprobane (l. xi. p. 339).

African coast they penetrated to the equator in search of gold, emeralds, and aromatics; but they wisely declined an unequal competition, in which they must be always prevented by the vicinity of the Persians to the markets of India: and the emperor submitted to the disappointment till his wishes were gratified by an unexpected event. The Gospel had been preached to the Indians: a bishop already governed the Christians of St. Thomas on the pepper-coast of Malabar; a church was planted in Ceylon, and the missionaries pursued the footsteps of commerce to the extremities of Asia.[1] Two Persian monks had long resided in China, perhaps in the royal city of Nankin, the seat of a monarch addicted to foreign superstitions, and who actually received an embassy from the isle of Ceylon. Amidst their pious occupations they viewed with a curious eye the common dress of the Chinese, the manufactures of silk, and the myriads of silkworms, whose education (either on trees or in houses) had once been considered as the labour of queens.[2] They soon discovered that it was impracticable to transport the short-lived insect, but that in the eggs a numerous progeny might be preserved and multiplied in a distant climate. Religion or interest had more power over the Persian monks than the love of their country: after a long journey they arrived at Constantinople, imparted their project to the emperor, and were liberally encouraged by the gifts and promises of Justinian. To the historians of that prince a campaign at the foot of Mount Caucasus has seemed more deserving of a minute relation than the labours of these missionaries of commerce, who again entered China, deceived a jealous people by concealing the eggs of the silkworm in a hollow cane, and returned in triumph with the spoils of the East. Under their direction the eggs were hatched at the proper season by the artificial heat of dung; the worms were fed with mulberry-leaves; they lived and laboured in a foreign climate; a sufficient number of butterflies was saved to propagate the race, and trees were planted to supply the nourishment of the rising generations.

1 See the Christian missions in India, in Cosmas (l. iii. p. 178, 179, l. xi. p. 337), and consult Asseman. Bibliot. Orient. (tom. iv. p. 413–548).

2 The invention, manufacture, and general use of silk in China, may be seen in Duhalde (Description Générale de la Chine, tom. ii. p. 165, 205–223). The province of Chekian is the most renowned both for quantity and quality.

Experience and reflection corrected the errors of a new attempt, and the Sogdoite ambassadors acknowledged in the succeeding reign that the Romans were not inferior to the natives of China in the education of the insects and the manufactures of silk,[1] in which both China and Constantinople have been surpassed by the industry of modern Europe. I am not insensible of the benefits of elegant luxury; yet I reflect with some pain that if the importers of silk had introduced the art of printing, already practised by the Chinese, the comedies of Menander and the entire decads of Livy would have been perpetuated in the editions of the sixth century. A larger view of the globe might at least have promoted the improvement of speculative science; but the Christian geography was forcibly extracted from texts of Scripture, and the study of nature was the surest symptom of an unbelieving mind. The orthodox faith confined the habitable world to *one* temperate zone, and represented the earth as an oblong surface, four hundred days' journey in length, two hundred in breadth, encompassed by the ocean and covered by the solid crystal of the firmament.[2]

1 Procopius, Bell. Gothic. iv. c. 17. Theophanes, Byzant. apud Phot. Cod. lxxxiv. [lxiv.] p. 38 [ed. Hoeschel.; p. 26 a, ed. Bekk.]. Zonaras (tom. ii. l. xiv. p. 69). Pagi (tom. ii. p. 602) assigns to the year 552 this memorable importation. Menander (in Excerpt. Legat. p. 107 [p. 295, 296, ed. Bonn.]) mentions the admiration of the Sogdoites; and Theophylact Simocatta (l. vii. c. 9) darkly represents the two rival kingdoms in (*China*) the country of silk.

2 Cosmas, surnamed Indicopleustes, or the Indian navigator, performed his voyage about the year 522, and composed at Alexandria, between 535 and 547, Christian Topography (Montfaucon, Præfat. c. i.), in which he refutes the impious opinion that the earth is a globe; and Photius had read this work (Cod. xxxvi. p. 9, 10 [p. 7, ed. Bekk.]), which displays the prejudices of a monk, with the knowledge of a merchant: the most valuable part has been given in French and in Greek by Melchisedec Thevenot (Relations Curieuses, part i.), and the whole is since published in a splendid edition by Père Montfaucon (Collectio Nova Patrum, Paris, 1706, 2 vols. in fol. tom. ii. p. 113–346). But the editor, a theologian, might blush at not discovering the Nestorian heresy of Cosmas, which has been detected by La Croze (Christianisme des Indes, tom. i. p. 40–56).

[See the character of Anastasius in Joannes Lydus de Magistratibus, lib. iii. c. 45, 46. His economy is there said to have degenerated into parsimony. He is accused of having taken away the levying of taxes and payment of the troops from the municipal authorities (the decurionate) in the Eastern cities, and entrusted it to an extortionate officer named Mannus. But he admits that the Imperial revenue was enormously increased by this measure. – O. S.]

IV. The subjects of Justinian were dissatisfied with the times and with the government. Europe was overrun by the barbarians and Asia by the monks: the poverty of the West discouraged the trade and manufactures of the East: the produce of labour was consumed by the unprofitable servants of the church, the state, and the army; and a rapid decrease was felt in the fixed and circulating capitals which constitute the national wealth. The public distress had been alleviated by the economy of Anastasius, and that prudent emperor accumulated an immense treasure while he delivered his people from the most odious or oppressive taxes. Their gratitude universally applauded the abolition of the *gold of affliction*, a personal tribute on the industry of the poor,[1] but more intolerable, as it should seem, in the form than in the substance, since the flourishing city of Edessa paid only one hundred and forty pounds of gold, which was collected in four years from ten thousand artificers.[2] Yet such was the parsimony which supported this liberal disposition, that, in a reign of twenty-seven years, Anastasius saved from his annual revenue the enormous sum of thirteen millions sterling, or three hundred and twenty thousand pounds of gold.[3] His example was neglected, and his treasure was abused, by the nephew of Justin. The riches of Justinian were speedily exhausted by alms and buildings, by ambitious wars and ignominious treaties. His revenues were found inadequate to his expenses. Every art was tried to extort from the people the gold and silver which he scattered with a lavish hand from Persia to France:[4] his reign was

1 Evagrius (l. iii. c. 39, 40) is minute and grateful, but angry with Zosimus for calumniating the great Constantine. In collecting all the bonds and records of the tax, the humanity of Anastasius was diligent and artful: fathers were sometimes compelled to prostitute their daughters (Zosim. Hist. l. ii. c. 38, p. 165, 166, Lipsiæ, 1784 [p. 104, ed. Bonn.]). Timotheus of Gaza chose such an event for the subject of a tragedy (Suidas, tom. iii. p. 475), which contributed to the abolition of the tax (Cedrenus, p. 357 [ed. Par.; tom. i. p. 627, ed. Bonn.]) – an happy instance (if it be true) of the use of the theatre.

2 See Josua Stylites, in the Bibliotheca Orientalis of Asseman (tom. i. p. 268). This capitation-tax is slightly mentioned in the Chronicle of Edessa.

3 Procopius (Anecdot. c. 19 [tom. iii. p. 113, ed. Bonn]) fixes this sum from the report of the treasurers themselves. Tiberius had *vicies ter millies*; but far different was his empire from that of Anastasius.

4 Evagrius (l. iv. c. 30), in the next generation, was moderate and well informed; and Zonaras (l. xiv. c. 61), in the twelfth century, had read with care,

marked by the vicissitudes, or rather by the combat, of rapa-
ciousness and avarice, of splendour and poverty; he lived with
the reputation of hidden treasures,[1] and bequeathed to his successor the payment of his debts.[2] Such a character has been justly
accused by the voice of the people and of posterity: but public
discontent is credulous; private malice is bold; and a lover of
truth will peruse with a suspicious eye the instructive anecdotes
of Procopius. The secret historian represents only the vices of
Justinian, and those vices are darkened by his malevolent pencil.
Ambiguous actions are imputed to the worst motives: error is
confounded with guilt, accident with design, and laws with
abuses; the partial injustice of a moment is dexterously applied
as the general maxim of a reign of thirty-two years: the emperor
alone is made responsible for the faults of his officers, the disorders of the times, and the corruption of his subjects; and even
the calamities of nature, plagues, earthquakes, and inundations,
are imputed to the prince of the dæmons, who had mischievously assumed the form of Justinian.[3]

After this precaution I shall briefly relate the anecdotes of
avarice and rapine under the following heads: I. Justinian was so
profuse that he could not be liberal. The civil and military officers, when they were admitted into the service of the palace,
obtained a humble rank and a moderate stipend; they ascended
by seniority to a station of affluence and repose; the annual
pensions, of which the most honourable class was abolished by
Justinian, amounted to four hundred thousand pounds; and this
domestic economy was deplored by the venal or indigent courtiers as the last outrage on the majesty of the empire. The posts,
the salaries of physicians, and the nocturnal illuminations were

and thought without prejudice: yet their colours are almost as black as those of
the Anecdotes.

1 Procopius (Anecdot. c. 30) relates the idle conjectures of the times. The
death of Justinian, says the secret historian, will expose his wealth or poverty.

2 See Corippus de Laudibus Justini Aug. l. ii. v. 260, etc., 389, etc.

'Plurima sunt vivo nimium neglecta parente,
Unde tot exhaustus contraxit debita fiscus.'

Centenaries of gold were brought by strong arms into the Hippodrome:

'Debita persolvit genitoris, cauta recepit.'

3 The Anecdotes (c. 11–14, 18, 20–30) supply many facts and more complaints.

objects of more general concern; and the cities might justly complain that he usurped the municipal revenues which had been
appropriated to these useful institutions. Even the soldiers were
injured; and such was the decay of military spirit, that they
were injured with impunity. The emperor refused at the return
of each fifth year the customary donative of five pieces of gold,
reduced his veterans to beg their bread, and suffered unpaid armies
to melt away in the wars of Italy and Persia. II. The humanity
of his predecessors had always remitted, in some auspicious circumstance of their reign, the arrears of the public tribute, and
they dexterously assumed the merit of resigning those claims
which it was impracticable to enforce. 'Justinian, in the space of
thirty-two years, has never granted a similar indulgence; and many
of his subjects have renounced the possession of those lands
whose value is insufficient to satisfy the demands of the treasury.
To the cities which had suffered by hostile inroads Anastasius
promised a general exemption of seven years: the provinces of
Justinian have been ravaged by the Persians and Arabs, the Huns
and Sclavonians; but his vain and ridiculous dispensation of a
single year has been confined to those places which were actually
taken by the enemy.' Such is the language of the secret historian,
who expressly denies that *any* indulgence was granted to Palestine after the revolt of the Samaritans; a false and odious charge,
confuted by the authentic record which attests a relief of thirteen
centenaries of gold (fifty-two thousand pounds) obtained for that
desolate province by the intercession of St. Sabas.[1] III. Procopius
has not condescended to explain the system of taxation, which
fell like a hail-storm upon the land, like a devouring pestilence
on its inhabitants: but we should become the accomplices of his
malignity if we imputed to Justinian alone the ancient, though
rigorous principle, that a whole district should be condemned to
sustain the partial loss of the persons or property of individuals.
The *Annona*, or supply of corn for the use of the army and
capital, was a grievous and arbitrary exaction, which exceeded,

1 One to Scythopolis, capital of the second Palestine, and twelve for the
rest of the province. Aleman. (p. 59 [Procop. tom. iii. p. 407, 408, ed. Bonn.])
honestly produces this fact from a MS. Life of St. Sabas, by his disciple Cyril,
in the Vatican library, and since published by Cotelerius.

perhaps in a tenfold proportion, the ability of the farmer; and his distress was aggravated by the partial injustice of weights and measures, and the expense and labour of distant carriage. In a time of scarcity an extraordinary requisition was made to the adjacent provinces of Thrace, Bithynia, and Phrygia: but the proprietors, after a wearisome journey and a perilous navigation, received so inadequate a compensation, that they would have chosen the alternative of delivering both the corn and price at the doors of their granaries. These precautions might indicate a tender solicitude for the welfare of the capital; yet Constantinople did not escape the rapacious despotism of Justinian. Till his reign the straits of the Bosphorus and Hellespont were open to the freedom of trade, and nothing was prohibited except the exportation of arms for the service of the barbarians. At each of these gates of the city a prætor was stationed, the minister of Imperial avarice; heavy customs were imposed on the vessels and their merchandise; the oppression was retaliated on the helpless consumer; the poor were afflicted by the artificial scarcity and exorbitant price of the market; and a people accustomed to depend on the liberality of their prince might sometimes complain of the deficiency of water and bread.[1] The *aërial* tribute, without a name, a law, or a definite object, was an annual gift of one hundred and twenty thousand pounds, which the emperor accepted from his Prætorian præfect; and the means of payment were abandoned to the discretion of that powerful magistrate. IV. Even such a tax was less intolerable than the privilege of monopolies, which checked the fair competition of industry, and, for the sake of a small and dishonest gain, imposed an arbitrary burden on the wants and luxury of the subject. 'As soon (I transcribe the Anecdotes) as the exclusive sale of silk was usurped by the Imperial treasurer, a whole people, the manufacturers of Tyre and Berytus, was reduced to extreme misery, and either perished with hunger or fled to the hostile dominions of Persia.' A province might suffer by the decay of its manufactures, but in this example of silk Procopius has partially overlooked

---

1 John Malala (tom. ii. p. 232 [p. 488, ed. Bonn]) mentions the want of bread, and Zonaras (l. xiv. p. 63) the leaden pipes, which Justinian, or his servants, stole from the aqueducts.

the inestimable and lasting benefit which the empire received from the curiosity of Justinian. His addition of one-seventh to the ordinary price of copper-money may be interpreted with the same candour; and the alteration, which might be wise, appears to have been innocent; since he neither alloyed the purity nor enhanced the value of the gold coin,[1] the legal measure of public and private payments. V. The ample jurisdiction required by the farmers of the revenue to accomplish their engagements might be placed in an odious light, as if they had purchased from the emperor the lives and fortunes of their fellow-citizens. And a more direct sale of honours and offices was transacted in the palace, with the permission, or at least with the connivance, of Justinian and Theodora. The claims of merit, even those of favour, were disregarded, and it was almost reasonable to expect that the bold adventurer who had undertaken the trade of a magistrate should find a rich compensation for infamy, labour, danger, the debts which he had contracted, and the heavy interest which he paid. A sense of the disgrace and mischief of this venal practice at length awakened the slumbering virtue of Justinian; and he attempted, by the sanction of oaths[2] and penalties, to guard the integrity of his government: but at the end of a year of perjury his rigorous edict was suspended, and corruption licentiously abused her triumph over the impotence of the laws. VI. The testament of Eulalius, count of the domestics, declared the emperor his sole heir, on condition, however, that he should discharge his debts and legacies, allow to his three daughters a decent maintenance, and bestow each of them in marriage, with a portion of ten pounds of gold. But the splendid fortune of Eulalius had been consumed by fire, and the inventory of his goods did not exceed the trifling sum of five hundred and

1 For an aureus, one-sixth of an ounce of gold, instead of 210, he gave no more than 180 folles or ounces of copper. A disproportion of the mint, below the market price, must have soon produced a scarcity of small money. In England, *twelve* pence in copper would sell for no more than *seven* pence (Smith's Inquiry into the Wealth of Nations, vol. i. p. 49). For Justinian's gold coin, see Evagrius (l. iv. c. 30).

2 The oath is conceived in the most formidable words (Novell. viii. tit. 3). The defaulters imprecate on themselves, quicquid habent telorum armamentaria cœli; the part of Judas, the leprosy of Giezi, the tremor of Cain, etc., besides all temporal pains.

sixty-four pieces of gold. A similar instance in Grecian history admonished the emperor of the honourable part prescribed for his imitation. He checked the selfish murmurs of the treasury, applauded the confidence of his friend, discharged the legacies and debts, educated the three virgins under the eye of the empress Theodora, and doubled the marriage-portion which had satisfied the tenderness of their father.[1] The humanity of a prince (for princes cannot be generous) is entitled to some praise; yet even in this act of virtue we may discover the inveterate custom of supplanting the legal or natural heirs which Procopius imputes to the reign of Justinian. His charge is supported by eminent names and scandalous examples; neither widows nor orphans were spared; and the art of soliciting, or extorting, or supposing testaments, was beneficially practised by the agents of the palace. This base and mischievous tyranny invades the security of private life; and the monarch who has indulged an appetite for gain will soon be tempted to anticipate the moment of succession, to interpret wealth as an evidence of guilt, and to proceed, from the claim of inheritance, to the power of confiscation. VII. Among the forms of rapine a philosopher may be permitted to name the conversion of Pagan or heretical riches to the use of the faithful; but in the time of Justinian this holy plunder was condemned by the sectaries alone, who became the victims of his orthodox avarice.[2]

Dishonour might be ultimately reflected on the character of Justinian; but much of the guilt, and still more of the profit, was intercepted by the ministers, who were seldom promoted for their virtues, and not always selected for their talents.[3] The merits of Tribonian the quæstor will hereafter be weighed in the reformation of the Roman law; but the economy of the East was

1 A similar or more generous act of friendship is related by Lucian of Eudamidas of Corinth (in Toxare, c. 22, 23, tom. ii. p. 530), and the story has produced an ingenious, though feeble, comedy of Fontenelle.

2 John Malala, tom. ii. p. 101, 102, 103 [p. 171–173, ed. Oxon.; 439, 440, ed. Bonn].

3 One of these, Anatolius, perished in an earthquake – doubtless a judgment! The complaints and clamours of the people in Agathias (l. v. p. 146, 147 [ed. Par.; p. 284 *sq.*, ed. Bonn]) are almost an echo of the anecdote. The aliena pecunia reddenda of Corippus (l. ii. 381, etc. [Laud. Just. Min.]) is not very honourable to Justinian's memory.

subordinate to the Prætorian præfect; and Procopius has justified his anecdotes by the portrait which he exposes, in his public history, of the notorious vices of John of Cappadocia.[1] His knowledge was not borrowed from the schools,[2] and his style was scarcely legible; but he excelled in the powers of native genius, to suggest the wisest counsels, and to find expedients in the most desperate situations. The corruption of his heart was equal to the vigour of his understanding. Although he was sus-pected of magic and Pagan superstition, he appeared insensible to the fear of God or the reproaches of man; and his aspiring fortune was raised on the death of thousands, the poverty of millions, the ruin of cities, and the desolation of provinces. From the dawn of light to the moment of dinner, be assiduously la-boured to enrich his master and himself at the expense of the Roman world; the remainder of the day was spent in sensual and obscene pleasures, and the silent hours of the night were inter-rupted by the perpetual dread of the justice of an assassin. His abilities, perhaps his vices, recommended him to the lasting friendship of Justinian: the emperor yielded with reluctance to the fury of the people; his victory was displayed by the immedi-ate restoration of their enemy; and they felt above ten years, under his oppressive administration, that he was stimulated by revenge rather than instructed by misfortune. Their murmurs served only to fortify the resolution of Justinian; but the præfect, in the insolence of favour, provoked the resentment of Theodo-ra, disdained a power before which every knee was bent, and attempted to sow the seeds of discord between the emperor and his beloved consort. Even Theodora herself was constrained to dissemble, to wait a favourable moment, and, by an artful con-spiracy, to render John of Cappadocia the accomplice of his own destruction. At a time when Belisarius, unless he had been a hero, must have shown himself a rebel, his wife Antonina, who enjoyed the secret confidence of the empress, communicated his feigned discontent to Euphemia, the daughter of the præfect; the

1 See the history and character of John of Cappadocia in Procopius (Persic. l. i. c. 24, 25, l. ii. c. 30. Vandal. l. i. c. 13. Anecdot. c. 2, 17, 22). The agreement of the history and anecdotes is a mortal wound to the reputation of the præfect.

2 Οὐ γὰρ ἄλλο οὐδὲν ἐς γραμματιστοῦ φοιτῶν ἔμαθεν, ὅτι μὴ γράμματα, καὶ ταῦτα κακὰ κακῶς γράψαι – a forcible expression [Pers. i. c. 24].

credulous virgin imparted to her father the dangerous project; and John, who might have known the value of oaths and promises, was tempted to accept a nocturnal, and almost treasonable, interview with the wife of Belisarius. An ambuscade of guards and eunuchs had been posted by the command of Theodora; they rushed with drawn swords to seize or to punish the guilty minister: he was saved by the fidelity of his attendants; but, instead of appealing to a gracious sovereign who had privately warned him of his danger, he pusillanimously fled to the sanctuary of the church. The favourite of Justinian was sacrificed to conjugal tenderness or domestic tranquillity; the conversion of a præfect into a priest extinguished his ambitious hopes; but the friendship of the emperor alleviated his disgrace, and he retained in the mild exile of Cyzicus an ample portion of his riches. Such imperfect revenge could not satisfy the unrelenting hatred of Theodora; the murder of his old enemy, the bishop of Cyzicus, afforded a decent pretence; and John of Cappadocia, whose actions had deserved a thousand deaths, was at last condemned for a crime of which he was innocent. A great minister, who had been invested with the honours of consul and patrician, was ignominiously scourged like the vilest of malefactors; a tattered cloak was the sole remnant of his fortunes; he was transported in a bark to the place of his banishment at Antinopolis in Upper Egypt, and the præfect of the East begged his bread through the cities which had trembled at his name. During an exile of seven years, his life was protracted and threatened by the ingenious cruelty of Theodora; and when her death permitted the emperor to recall a servant whom he had abandoned with regret, the ambition of John of Cappadocia was reduced to the humble duties of the sacerdotal profession. His successors convinced the subjects of Justinian that the arts of oppression might still be improved by experience and industry; the frauds of a Syrian banker were introduced into the administration of the finances; and the example of the præfect was diligently copied by the quæstor, the public and private treasurer, the governors of provinces, and the principal magistrates of the Eastern empire.[1]

1 The chronology of Procopius is loose and obscure; but with the aid of Pagi I can discern that John was appointed Prætorian præfect of the East in

V. The *edifices* of Justinian were cemented with the blood and treasure of his people; but those stately structures appeared to announce the prosperity of the empire, and actually displayed the skill of their architects. Both the theory and practice of the arts which depend on mathematical science and mechanical power were cultivated under the patronage of the emperors; the fame of Archimedes was rivalled by Proclus and Anthemius; and if their *miracles* had been related by intelligent spectators, they might now enlarge the speculations, instead of exciting the distrust, of philosophers. A tradition has prevailed that the Roman fleet was reduced to ashes in the port of Syracuse by the burning-glasses of Archimedes;[1] and it is asserted that a similar expedient was employed by Proclus to destroy the Gothic vessels in the harbour of Constantinople, and to protect his benefactor Anastasius against the bold enterprise of Vitalian.[2] A machine was fixed on the walls of the city, consisting of a hexagon mirror of polished brass, with many smaller and movable polygons to receive and reflect the rays of the meridian sun; and a consuming flame was darted to the distance, perhaps, of two hundred feet.[3] The truth of these two extraordinary facts is invalidated by the silence of the most authentic historians; and the use of burning-glasses was never adopted in the attack or defence of places.[4]

the year 530; that he was removed in January, 532 – restored before June, 533 – banished in 541 – and recalled between June, 548, and April 1, 549. Aleman. (p. 96, 97 [Procop. tom. iii. p. 449, 450, ed. Bonn]) gives the list of his ten successors – a rapid series in a part of a single reign.

1 This conflagration is hinted by Lucian (in Hippia, c. 2) and Galen (l. iii. de Temperamentis, tom. i. p. 81, edit. Basil) in the second century. A thousand years afterwards it is positively affirmed by Zonaras (l. ix. p. 424) on the faith of Dion Cassius, by Tzetzes (Chiliad ii. 119, etc.), Eustathius (ad Iliad, E. p. 338), and the scholiast of Lucian. See Fabricius (Biblioth. Græc. l. iii. c. 22, tom. ii. p. 551, 552 [ed. Hamb. 1716]), to whom I am more or less indebted for several of these quotations.

2 Zonaras (l. xiv. p. 55) affirms the fact, without quoting any evidence.

3 Tzetzes describes the artifice of these burning-glasses, which he had read, perhaps with no learned eyes, in a mathematical treatise of Anthemius. That treatise, περὶ παραδόξων μηχανημάτων, has been lately published, translated, and illustrated, by M. Dupuys, a scholar and a mathematician (Mémoires de l'Académie des Inscriptions, tom. xlii. p. 392–451).

4 In the siege of Syracuse, by the silence of Polybius, Plutarch, Livy; in the siege of Constantinople, by that of Marcellinus and all the contemporaries of the sixth century.

Yet the admirable experiments of a French philosopher[1] have demonstrated the possibility of such a mirror; and, since it is possible, I am more disposed to attribute the art to the greatest mathematicians of antiquity, than to give the merit of the fiction to the idle fancy of a monk or a sophist. According to another story, Proclus applied sulphur to the destruction of the Gothic fleet;[2] in a modern imagination, the name of sulphur is instantly connected with the suspicion of gunpowder, and that suspicion is propagated by the secret arts of his disciple Anthemius.[3] A citizen of Tralles in Asia had five sons, who were all distinguished in their respective professions by merit and success. Olympius excelled in the knowledge and practice of the Roman jurisprudence. Dioscorus and Alexander became learned physicians; but the skill of the former was exercised for the benefit of his fellow-citizens, while his more ambitious brother acquired wealth and reputation at Rome. The fame of Metrodorus the grammarian, and of Anthemius the mathematician and architect, reached the ears of the emperor Justinian, who invited them to Constantinople; and while the one instructed the rising generation in the schools of eloquence, the other filled the capital and provinces with more lasting monuments of his art. In a trifling dispute relative to the walls or windows of their contiguous houses, he had been vanquished by the eloquence of his neighbour Zeno; but the orator was defeated in his turn by the master of mechanics, whose malicious, though harmless, stratagems are darkly represented by the ignorance of Agathias. In a lower room, Anthemius arranged several vessels or caldrons of water, each of them covered by the wide bottom of a leathern tube, which rose to a narrow top, and was artificially conveyed among

1 Without any previous knowledge of Tzetzes or Anthemius, the immortal Buffon imagined and executed a set of burning-glasses, with which he could inflame planks at the distance of 200 feet (Supplément à l'Hist. Naturelle, tom. i. p. 399–483, quarto edition). What miracles would not his genius have performed for the public service, with royal expense, and in the strong sun of Constantinople or Syracuse!

2 John Malala (tom. ii. p. 120–124 [p. 403–406, ed. Bonn]) relates the fact; but he seems to confound the names or persons of Proclus and Marinus.

3 Agathias, l. v. p. 149–152 [ed. Par.; p. 289–294, ed. Bonn]. The merit of Anthemius as an architect is loudly praised by Procopius (de Ædif. l. i. c. 1 [tom. iii. p. 174, ed. Bonn]) and Paulus Silentiarius (part i. 134, etc. [p. 15, ed. Bonn]).

the joists and rafters of the adjacent building. A fire was kindled beneath the caldron; the steam of the boiling water ascended through the tubes; the house was shaken by the efforts of imprisoned air, and its trembling inhabitants might wonder that the city was unconscious of the earthquake which they had felt. At another time, the friends of Zeno, as they sat at table, were dazzled by the intolerable light which flashed in their eyes from the reflecting mirrors of Anthemius; they were astonished by the noise which he produced from the collision of certain minute and sonorous particles; and the orator declared in tragic style to the senate, that a mere mortal must yield to the power of an antagonist who shook the earth with the trident of Neptune, and imitated the thunder and lightning of Jove himself. The genius of Anthemius, and his colleague Isidore the Milesian, was excited and employed by a prince whose taste for architecture had degenerated into a mischievous and costly passion. His favourite architects submitted their designs and difficulties to Justinian, and discreetly confessed how much their laborious meditations were surpassed by the intuitive knowledge or celestial inspiration of an emperor whose views were always directed to the benefit of his people, the glory of his reign, and the salvation of his soul.[1]

The principal church, which was dedicated by the founder of Constantinople to Saint Sophia, or the eternal wisdom, had been twice destroyed by fire; after the exile of John Chrysostom and during the *Nika* of the blue and green factions. No sooner did the tumult subside than the Christian populace deplored their sacrilegious rashness; but they might have rejoiced in the calamity, had they foreseen the glory of the new temple, which at the end of forty days was strenuously undertaken by the piety of Justinian.[2] The ruins were cleared away, a more spacious plan

1 See Procopius (de Ædificiis, l. i. c. 1, 2, l. ii. c. 3). He relates a coincidence of dreams which supposes some fraud in Justinian or his architect. They both saw, in a vision, the same plan for stopping an inundation at Dara. A stone-quarry near Jerusalem was revealed to the emperor (l. v. c. 6 [tom. iii. p. 323, ed. Bonn]): an angel was tricked into the perpetual custody of St. Sophia (Anonym. de Antiq. C. P. l. iv. p. 70).

2 Among the crowd of ancients and moderns who have celebrated the edifice of St. Sophia, I shall distinguish and follow, 1. Four original spectators and historians: Procopius (de Ædific. l. i. c. 1), Agathias (l. v. p. 152, 153 [p. 296,

was described, and, as it required the consent of some proprietors of ground, they obtained the most exorbitant terms from
the eager desires and timorous conscience of the monarch. Anthemius formed the design, and his genius directed the hands of
ten thousand workmen, whose payment in pieces of fine silver
was never delayed beyond the evening. The emperor himself,
clad in a linen tunic, surveyed each day their rapid progress, and
encouraged their diligence by his familiarity, his zeal, and his
rewards. The new cathedral of St. Sophia was consecrated by the
patriarch, five years, eleven months, and ten days from the first
foundation; and in the midst of the solemn festival Justinian
exclaimed with devout vanity, 'Glory be to God, who hath
thought me worthy to accomplish so great a work: I have vanquished thee, O Solomon!'¹ But the pride of the Roman Solomon, before twenty years had elapsed, was humbled by an
earthquake, which overthrew the eastern part of the dome. Its
splendour was again restored by the perseverance of the same
prince; and in the thirty-sixth year of his reign Justinian celebrated the second dedication of a temple which remains, after
twelve centuries, a stately monument of his fame. The architecture of St. Sophia, which is now converted into the principal
mosque, has been imitated by the Turkish sultans, and that
venerable pile continues to excite the fond admiration of the

297, ed. Bonn]), Paul Silentiarius (in a poem of 1026 hexameters, ad calcem
Annæ Comnen. Alexiad.), and Evagrius (l. iv. c. 31). 2. Two legendary Greeks
of a later period: George Codinus (de Origin. C. P. p. 64–74 [ed. Par.; p. 130–148,
ed. Bonn]), and the anonymous writer of Banduri (Imp. Orient. tom. i. l. iv.
p. 65–80). 3. The great Byzantine antiquarian, Ducange (Comment. ad Paul
Silentiar. p. 525–598, and C. P. Christ. l. iii. p. 5–78). 4. Two French travellers
– the one, Peter Gyllius (de Topograph. C. P. l. ii. c. 3, 4) in the sixteenth; the
other, Grelot (Voyage de C. P. p. 95–164, Paris, 1680, in 4to): he has given
plans, prospects, and inside views of St. Sophia; and his plans, though on a
smaller scale, appear more correct than those of Ducange. I have adopted and
reduced the measures of Grelot: but as no Christian can now ascend the dome,
the height is borrowed from Evagrius, compared with Gyllius, Greaves, and the
Oriental Geographer.

1 Solomon's temple was surrounded with courts, porticoes, etc.; but the
proper structure of the house of God was no more (if we take the Egyptian or
Hebrew cubit at 22 inches) than 55 feet in height, $36\frac{2}{3}$ in breadth, and 110 in
length – a small parish church, says Prideaux (Connection, vol. i. p. 144, folio);
but few sanctuaries could be valued at four or five millions sterling!

Greeks, and the more rational curiosity of European travellers. The eye of the spectator is disappointed by an irregular prospect of half-domes and shelving roofs: the western front, the principal approach, is destitute of simplicity and magnificence; and the scale of dimensions has been much surpassed by several of the Latin cathedrals. But the architect who first erected an *aërial* cupola is entitled to the praise of bold design and skilful execution. The dome of St. Sophia, illuminated by four-and-twenty windows, is formed with so small a curve, that the depth is equal only to one-sixth of its diameter; the measure of that diameter is one hundred and fifteen feet, and the lofty centre, where a crescent has supplanted the cross, rises to the perpendicular height of one hundred and eighty feet above the pavement. The circle which encompasses the dome lightly reposes on four strong arches, and their weight is firmly supported by four massy piles, whose strength is assisted on the northern and southern sides by four columns of Egyptian granite. A Greek cross, inscribed in a quadrangle, represents the form of the edifice; the exact breadth is two hundred and forty-three feet, and two hundred and sixty-nine may be assigned for the extreme length, from the sanctuary in the east to the nine western doors which open into the vestibule, and from thence into the *narthex* or exterior portico. That portico was the humble station of the penitents. The nave or body of the church was filled by the congregation of the faithful; but the two sexes were prudently distinguished, and the upper and lower galleries were allotted for the more private devotion of the women. Beyond the northern and southern piles, a balustrade, terminated on either side by the thrones of the emperor and the patriarch, divided the nave from the choir; and the space, as far as the steps of the altar, was occupied by the clergy and singers. The altar itself, a name which insensibly became familiar to Christian ears, was placed in the eastern recess, artificially built in the form of a demicylinder; and this sanctuary communicated by several doors with the sacristy, the vestry, the baptistery, and the contiguous buildings, subservient either to the pomp of worship, or the private use of the ecclesiastical ministers. The memory of past calamities inspired Justinian with a wise resolution that no wood, except for the doors, should be admitted into the new edifice; and the choice of the

materials was applied to the strength, the lightness, or the splendour of the respective parts. The solid piles which sustained the
cupola were composed of huge blocks of freestone, hewn into
squares and triangles, fortified by circles of iron, and firmly
cemented by the infusion of lead and quicklime; but the weight
of the cupola was diminished by the levity of its substance, which
consists either of pumice-stone that floats in the water, or of
bricks, from the isle of Rhodes, five times less ponderous than
the ordinary sort. The whole frame of the edifice was constructed of brick; but those base materials were concealed by a
crust of marble; and the inside of St. Sophia, the cupola, the two
larger and the six smaller semidomes, the walls, the hundred
columns, and the pavement, delight even the eyes of barbarians
with a rich and variegated picture.

A poet,[1] who beheld the primitive lustre of St. Sophia, enumerates the colours, the shades, and the spots of ten or twelve
marbles, jaspers, and porphyries, which nature had profusely
diversified, and which were blended and contrasted as it were by
a skilful painter. The triumph of Christ was adorned with the
last spoils of Paganism, but the greater part of these costly stones
was extracted from the quarries of Asia Minor, the isles and
continent of Greece, Egypt, Africa, and Gaul. Eight columns of
porphyry, which Aurelian had placed in the Temple of the Sun,
were offered by the piety of a Roman matron; eight others of
green marble were presented by the ambitious zeal of the magistrates of Ephesus: both are admirable by their size and beauty,
but every order of architecture disclaims their fantastic capitals.
A variety of ornaments and figures was curiously expressed in
mosaic; and the images of Christ, of the Virgin, of saints, and
of angels, which have been defaced by Turkish fanaticism, were

1 Paul Silentiarius, in dark and poetic language, describes the various stones
and marbles that were employed in the edifice of St. Sophia (P. ii. ver. 129,
133, etc. etc. [p. 27 sqq., ed. Bonn]): 1. The *Carystian* – pale, with iron veins.
2. The *Phrygian* – of two sorts, both of a rosy hue; the one with a white shade,
the other purple, with silver flowers. 3. The *Porphyry of Egypt* – with small stars.
4. The *green marble of Laconia*. 5. The *Carian* – from Mount Iassis, with oblique
veins, white and red. 6. The *Lydian* – pale, with a red flower. 7. The *African*, or
Mauritanian – of a gold or saffron hue. 8. The *Celtic* – black, with white veins.
9. The *Bosphoric* – white, with black edges. Besides the *Proconnesian*, which formed
the pavement; the *Thessalian, Molossian*, etc., which are less distinctly painted.

dangerously exposed to the superstition of the Greeks. According to the sanctity of each object, the precious metals were distributed in thin leaves or in solid masses. The balustrade of the choir, the capitals of the pillars, the ornaments of the doors and galleries, were of gilt bronze. The spectator was dazzled by the glittering aspect of the cupola. The sanctuary contained forty thousand pound weight of silver, and the holy vases and vestments of the altar were of the purest gold, enriched with inestimable gems. Before the structure of the church had arisen two cubits above the ground, forty-five thousand two hundred pounds were already consumed, and the whole expense amounted to three hundred and twenty thousand. Each reader, according to the measure of his belief, may estimate their value either in gold or silver; but the sum of one million sterling is the result of the lowest computation. A magnificent temple is a laudable monument of national taste and religion, and the enthusiast who entered the dome of St. Sophia might be tempted to suppose that it was the residence, or even the workmanship, of the Deity. Yet how dull is the artifice, how insignificant is the labour, if it be compared with the formation of the vilest insect that crawls upon the surface of the temple!

So minute a description of an edifice which time has respected may attest the truth and excuse the relation of the innumerable works, both in the capital and provinces, which Justinian constructed on a smaller scale and less durable foundations.[1] In Constantinople alone, and the adjacent suburbs, he dedicated twenty-five churches to the honour of Christ, the Virgin, and the saints. Most of these churches were decorated with marble and gold; and their various situation was skilfully chosen in a populous square or a pleasant grove, on the margin of the sea-shore or on some lofty eminence which overlooked the continents of Europe and Asia. The church of the Holy Apostles at Constantinople, and that of St. John at Ephesus, appear to have

---

1 The six books of the Edifices of Procopius are thus distributed: the *first* is confined to Constantinople; the *second* includes Mesopotamia and Syria; the *third*, Armenia and the Euxine; the *fourth*, Europe; the *fifth*, Asia Minor and Palestine; the *sixth*, Egypt and Africa. Italy is forgot by the emperor or the historian, who published this work of adulation before the date (A.D. 555) of its final conquest.

been framed on the same model: their domes aspired to imitate
the cupolas of St. Sophia, but the altar was more judiciously
placed under the centre of the dome, at the junction of four
stately porticoes, which more accurately expressed the figure of
the Greek cross. The Virgin of Jerusalem might exult in the
temple erected by her imperial votary on a most ungrateful spot,
which afforded neither ground nor materials to the architect. A
level was formed by raising part of a deep valley to the height
of the mountain. The stones of a neighbouring quarry were hewn
into regular forms; each block was fixed on a peculiar carriage
drawn by forty of the strongest oxen, and the roads were widened
for the passage of such enormous weights. Lebanon furnished
her loftiest cedars for the timbers of the church; and the seasonable discovery of a vein of red marble supplied its beautiful
columns, two of which, the supporters of the exterior portico,
were esteemed the largest in the world. The pious munificence
of the emperor was diffused over the Holy Land; and if reason
should condemn the monasteries of both sexes which were built
or restored by Justinian, yet charity must applaud the wells which
he sunk, and the hospitals which he founded, for the relief of the
weary pilgrims. The schismatical temper of Egypt was ill entitled
to the royal bounty; but in Syria and Africa some remedies were
applied to the disasters of wars and earthquakes, and both Carthage and Antioch, emerging from their ruins, might revere the
name of their gracious benefactor.[1] Almost every saint in the
calendar acquired the honours of a temple – almost every city
of the empire obtained the solid advantages of bridges, hospitals, and aqueducts; but the severe liberality of the monarch disdained to indulge his subjects in the popular luxury of baths
and theatres. While Justinian laboured for the public service, he
was not unmindful of his own dignity and ease. The Byzantine
palace, which had been damaged by the conflagration, was restored with new magnificence; and some notion may be conceived of the whole edifice by the vestibule or hall, which, from
the doors perhaps, or the roof, was surnamed *chalce*, or the
brazen. The dome of a spacious quadrangle was supported by

1　Justinian once gave forty-five centenaries of gold (£180,000) for the repairs of Antioch after the earthquake (John Malala, tom. ii. p. 146–149 [p. 422–
424, ed. Bonn]).

massy pillars; the pavement and walls were incrusted with many-coloured marbles – the emerald green of Laconia, the fiery red, and the white Phrygian stone, intersected with veins of a sea-green hue. The mosaic paintings of the dome and sides represented the glories of the African and Italian triumphs. On the Asiatic shore of the Propontis, at a small distance to the east of Chalcedon, the costly palace and gardens of Heræum[1] were prepared for the summer residence of Justinian, and more especially of Theodora. The poets of the age have celebrated the rare alliance of nature and art, the harmony of the nymphs of the groves, the fountains and the waves; yet the crowd of attendants who followed the court complained of their inconvenient lodgings,[2] and the nymphs were too often alarmed by the famous Porphyrio, a whale of ten cubits in breadth and thirty in length, who was stranded at the mouth of the river Sangaris after he had infested more than half a century the seas of Constantinople.[3]

The fortifications of Europe and Asia were multiplied by Justinian; but the repetition of those timid and fruitless precautions exposes, to a philosophic eye, the debility of the empire.[4] From Belgrade to the Euxine, from the conflux of the Save to the mouth of the Danube, a chain of above fourscore fortified places was extended along the banks of the great river. Single watch-towers were changed into spacious citadels; vacant walls, which the engineers contracted or enlarged according to the

1 For the Heræum, the palace of Theodora, see Gyllius (de Bosphoro Thracio, l. iii. c. xi.), Aleman. (Not. ad Anec. p. 80, 81 [Procop. tom. iii. p. 431, 432, ed. Bonn], who quotes several epigrams of the Anthology) and Ducange (C. P. Christ. l. iv. c. 13, p. 175, 176).

2 Compare, in the Edifices (l. i. c. 11) and in the Anecdotes (c. 8, 15), the different styles of adulation and malevolence: stripped of the paint, or cleansed from the dirt, the object appears to be the same.

3 Procopius, Goth. iii. 29; most probably a stranger and wanderer, as the Mediterranean does not breed whales. Balænæ quoque in nostra maria penetrant (Plin. Hist. Natur. ix. 2 [5]). Between the polar circle and the tropic, the cetaceous animals of the ocean grow to the length of 50, 80, or 100 feet. (Hist. des Voyages, tom. xv. p. 289. Pennant's British Zoology, vol. iii. p. 35.)

4 Montesquieu observes (tom. iii. p. 503, Considérations sur la Grandeur et la Décadence des Romains, c. xx.) that Justinian's empire was like France in the time of the Norman inroads – never so weak as when every village was fortified.

nature of the ground, were filled with colonies or garrisons; a strong fortress defended the ruins of Trajan's bridge;[1] and several military stations affected to spread beyond the Danube the pride of the Roman name. But that name was divested of its terrors; the barbarians, in their annual inroads, passed and contemptuously repassed before these useless bulwarks; and the inhabitants of the frontier, instead of reposing under the shadow of the general defence, were compelled to guard with incessant vigilance their separate habitations. The solitude of ancient cities was replenished; the new foundations of Justinian acquired, perhaps too hastily, the epithets of impregnable and populous; and the auspicious place of his own nativity attracted the grateful reverence of the vainest of princes. Under the name of *Justiniana prima*, the obscure village of Tauresium became the seat of an archbishop and a præfect, whose jurisdiction extended over seven warlike provinces of Illyricum;[2] and the corrupt appellation of *Giustendil* still indicates, about twenty miles to the south of Sophia, the residence of a Turkish sanjak.[3] For the use of the emperor's countrymen, a cathedral, a palace, and an aqueduct were speedily constructed; the public and private edifices were adapted to the greatness of a royal city; and the strength of the walls resisted, during the lifetime of Justinian, the unskilful assaults of the Huns and Sclavonians. Their progress was sometimes retarded, and their hopes of rapine were disappointed, by

1 Procopius affirms (l. iv. c. 6 [tom. iii. p. 289, ed. Bonn]) that the Danube was stopped by the ruins of the bridge. Had Apollodorus, the architect, left a description of his own work, the fabulous wonders of Dion Cassius (l. lxviii. [c. 13] p. 1129) would have been corrected by the genuine picture. Trajan's bridge consisted of twenty or twenty-two stone piles with wooden arches; the river is shallow, the current gentle, and the whole interval no more than 443 (Reimar ad Dion, from Marsigli) or 515 *toises* (D'Anville, Géographie Ancienne, tom. i. p. 305).

2 Of the two Dacias, *Mediterranea* and *Ripensis*, Dardania, Prævalitana, the second Mæsia, and the second Macedonia. See Justinian (Novell. xi. [Præf.]), who speaks of his castles beyond the Danube, and of homines semper bellicis sudoribus inhærentes.

3 See D'Anville (Mémoires de l'Académie, etc. tom. xxxi. p. 289, 290). Rycaut (Present State of the Turkish Empire, p. 97, 316), Marsigli (Stato Militare del Imperio Ottomano, p. 130). The sanjak of Giustendil is one of the twenty under the beglerbeg of Rumelia, and his district maintains 48 *zaims* and 588 *timariots*.

the innumerable castles which, in the provinces of Dacia, Epirus, Thessaly, Macedonia, and Thrace, appeared to cover the whole face of the country. Six hundred of these forts were built or repaired by the emperor; but it seems reasonable to believe that the far greater part consisted only of a stone or brick tower in the midst of a square or circular area, which was surrounded by a wall and ditch, and afforded in a moment of danger some protection to the peasants and cattle of the neighbouring villages.[1] Yet these military works, which exhausted the public treasure, could not remove the just apprehensions of Justinian and his European subjects. The warm-baths of Anchialus, in Thrace, were rendered as safe as they were salutary; but the rich pastures of Thessalonica were foraged by the Scythian cavalry; the delicious vale of Tempe, three hundred miles from the Danube, was continually alarmed by the sound of war;[2] and no unfortified spot, however distant or solitary, could securely enjoy the blessings of peace. The straits of Thermopylæ, which seemed to protect, but which had so often betrayed, the safety of Greece, were diligently strengthened by the labours of Justinian. From the edge of the sea-shore, through the forests and valleys, and as far as the summit of the Thessalian mountains, a strong wall was continued which occupied every practicable entrance. Instead of a hasty crowd of peasants, a garrison of two thousand soldiers was stationed along the rampart, granaries of corn and reservoirs of water were provided for their use, and, by a precaution that inspired the cowardice which it foresaw, convenient fortresses were erected for their retreat. The walls of Corinth, overthrown by an earthquake, and the mouldering bulwarks of Athens and Platæa, were carefully restored; the barbarians were discouraged by the prospect of successive and painful sieges, and the naked cities of Peloponnesus were covered by the fortifications of the isthmus of Corinth. At the extremity of Europe, another peninsula, the Thracian Chersonesus, runs three days'

1 These fortifications may be compared to the castles in Mingrelia (Chardin, Voyages en Perse, tom. i. p. 60, 131) – a natural picture.

2 The valley of Tempe is situated along the river Peneus, between the hills of Ossa and Olympus: it is only five miles long, and in some places no more than 120 feet in breadth. Its verdant beauties are elegantly described by Pliny (Hist. Natur. l. iv. 15), and more diffusely by Ælian (Hist. Var. l. iii. c. i.).

journey into the sea, to form, with the adjacent shores of Asia, the straits of the Hellespont. The intervals between eleven populous towns were filled by lofty woods, fair pastures, and arable lands; and the isthmus, of thirty-seven stadia or furlongs, had been fortified by a Spartan general nine hundred years before the reign of Justinian.[1] In an age of freedom and valour the slightest rampart may prevent a surprise; and Procopius appears insensible of the superiority of ancient times, while he praises the solid construction and double parapet of a wall whose long arms stretched on either side into the sea, but whose strength was deemed insufficient to guard the Chersonesus, if each city, and particularly Gallipoli and Sestus, had not been secured by their peculiar fortifications. The *long* wall, as it was emphatically styled, was a work as disgraceful in the object as it was respectable in the execution. The riches of a capital diffuse themselves over the neighbouring country, and the territory of Constantinople, a paradise of nature, was adorned with the luxurious gardens and villas of the senators and opulent citizens. But their wealth served only to attract the bold and rapacious barbarians; the noblest of the Romans, in the bosom of peaceful indolence, were led away into Scythian captivity; and their sovereign might view from his palace the hostile flames which were insolently spread to the gates of the Imperial city. At the distance only of forty miles, Anastasius was constrained to establish a last frontier; his long wall of sixty miles, from the Propontis to the Euxine, proclaimed the impotence of his arms; and as the danger became more imminent, new fortifications were added by the indefatigable prudence of Justinian.[2]

Asia Minor, after the submission of the Isaurians,[3] remained without enemies and without fortifications. Those bold savages, who had disdained to be the subjects of Gallienus, persisted two

[1] Xenophon Hellenic. l. iii. c. 2. After a long and tedious conversation with the Byzantine declaimers, how refreshing is the truth, the simplicity, the elegance of an Attic writer!

[2] See the long wall in Evagrius (l. iv. [iii.] c. 38). This whole article is drawn from the fourth book of the Edifices, except Anchialus (l. iii. c. 7).

[3] Turn back to Vol. I. p. 311. In the course of this history I have sometimes mentioned, and much oftener slighted, the hasty inroads of the Isaurians, which were not attended with any consequences.

hundred and thirty years in a life of independence and rapine. The most successful princes respected the strength of the mountains and the despair of the natives: their fierce spirit was sometimes soothed with gifts, and sometimes restrained by terror; and a military count, with three legions, fixed his permanent and ignominious station in the heart of the Roman provinces.[1] But no sooner was the vigilance of power relaxed or diverted, than the light-armed squadrons descended from the hills, and invaded the peaceful plenty of Asia. Although the Isaurians were not remarkable for stature or bravery, want rendered them bold, and experience made them skilful in the exercise of predatory war. They advanced with secrecy and speed to the attack of villages and defenceless towns; their flying parties have sometimes touched the Hellespont, the Euxine, and the gates of Tarsus, Antioch, or Damascus;[2] and the spoil was lodged in their inaccessible mountains, before the Roman troops had received their orders, or the distant province had computed its loss. The guilt of rebellion and robbery excluded them from the rights of national enemies; and the magistrates were instructed by an edict, that the trial or punishment of an Isaurian, even on the festival of Easter, was a meritorious act of justice and piety.[3] If the captives were condemned to domestic slavery, they maintained, with their sword or dagger, the private quarrel of their masters; and it was found expedient for the public tranquillity to prohibit the service of such dangerous retainers. When their countryman Tarcalissæus or Zeno ascended the throne, he invited a faithful and formidable band of Isaurians, who insulted the court and city, and were rewarded by an annual tribute of five thousand pounds of gold. But the hopes of fortune depopulated the mountains, luxury enervated the hardiness of their minds and

---

1 Trebellius Pollio in Hist. August p. 197 [Triginta Tyr. 25], who lived under Diocletian, or Constantine. See likewise Pancirolus ad Notit. Imp. Orient. c. 115, 141. See Cod. Theodos. l. ix. tit. 35, leg. 37 [7], with a copious collective Annotation of Godefroy, tom. iii. p. 256, 257.

2 See the full and wide extent of their inroads in Philostorgius (Hist. Eccles. l. xi. c. 8), with Godefroy's learned Dissertations.

3 Cod. Justinian. l. ix. tit. 12, leg. 10. The punishments are severe – a fine of an hundred pounds of gold, degradation, and even death. The public peace might afford a pretence, but Zeno was desirous of monopolising the valour and service of the Isaurians.

bodies, and, in proportion as they mixed with mankind, they became less qualified for the enjoyment of poor and solitary freedom. After the death of Zeno, his successor Anastasius suppressed their pensions, exposed their persons to the revenge of the people, banished them from Constantinople, and prepared to sustain a war which left only the alternative of victory or servitude. A brother of the last emperor usurped the title of Augustus; his cause was powerfully supported by the arms, the treasures, and the magazines collected by Zeno; and the native Isaurians must have formed the smallest portion of the hundred and fifty thousand barbarians under his standard, which was sanctified for the first time by the presence of a fighting bishop. Their disorderly numbers were vanquished in the plains of Phrygia by the valour and discipline of the Goths, but a war of six years almost exhausted the courage of the emperor.[1] The Isaurians retired to their mountains, their fortresses were successively besieged and ruined, their communication with the sea was intercepted, the bravest of their leaders died in arms, the surviving chiefs before their execution were dragged in chains through the hippodrome, a colony of their youth was transplanted into Thrace, and the remnant of the people submitted to the Roman government. Yet some generations elapsed before their minds were reduced to the level of slavery. The populous villages of Mount Taurus were filled with horsemen and archers; they resisted the imposition of tributes, but they recruited the armies of Justinian; and his civil magistrates, the proconsul of Cappadocia, the count of Isauria, and the prætors of Lycaonia and Pisidia, were invested with military power to restrain the licentious practice of rapes and assassinations.[2]

1 The Isaurian war and the triumph of Anastasius are briefly and darkly represented by John Malala (tom. ii. p. 106, 107 [p. 393, 394, ed. Bonn], Evagrius (l. iii. c. 35), Theophanes (p. 118–120 [ed. Par.; tom. i. p. 212–215, ed. Bonn]), and the Chronicle of Marcellinus.

2 Fortes ea regio (says Justinian) viros habet, nec in ullo differt ab Isauriâ, though Procopius (Persic. l. i. c. 18 [tom. i. p. 96, ed. Bonn]) marks an essential difference between their military character; yet in former times the Lycaonians and Pisidians had defended their liberty against the Great King (Xenophon. Anabasis, l. iii. c. 2). Justinian introduces some false and ridiculous erudition of the ancient empire of the Pisidians, and of Lycaon, who, after visiting Rome (long before Æneas), gave a name and people to Lycaonia (Novell. 24, 25, 27, 30).

If we extend our view from the tropic to the mouth of the Tanais, we may observe, on one hand, the precautions of Justinian to curb the savages of Æthiopia,[1] and, on the other, the long walls which he constructed in Crimæa for the protection of his friendly Goths, a colony of three thousand shepherds and warriors.[2] From that peninsula to Trebizond the eastern curve of the Euxine was secured by forts, by alliance, or by religion; and the possession of *Lazica*, the Colchos of ancient, the Mingrelia of modern, geography, soon became the object of an important war. Trebizond, in after times the seat of a romantic empire, was indebted to the liberality of Justinian for a church, an aqueduct, and a castle, whose ditches are hewn in the solid rock. From that maritime city a frontier line of five hundred miles may be drawn to the fortress of Circesium, the last Roman station on the Euphrates.[3] Above Trebizond immediately, and five days' journey to the south, the country rises into dark forests and craggy mountains, as savage though not so lofty as the Alps and the Pyrenees. In this rigorous climate,[4] where the snows seldom melt, the fruits are tardy and tasteless; even honey is

1 See Procopius, Persic. l. i. c. 19. The altar of national concord, of annual sacrifice and oaths, which Diocletian had erected in the Isle of Elephantine, was demolished by Justinian with less policy than zeal.

2 Procopius de Ædificiis, l. iii. c. 7 [p. 262, ed. Bonn]; Bell. Goth. iv. c. 3, 4 [p. 469, *seq*., ed. Bonn]. These unambitious Goths had refused to follow the standard of Theodoric. As late as the fifteenth and sixteenth century the name and nation might be discovered between Caffa and the Straits of Azoph (D'Anville, Mémoires de l'Académie, tom. xxx. p. 240). They well deserved the curiosity of Busbequius (p. 321–326); but seem to have vanished in the more recent account of the Missions du Levant (tom. i.), Tott, Peysonnel, etc.

3 For the geography and architecture of this Armenian border see the Persian Wars and Edifices (l. ii. c. 4–7; l. iii. c. 2–7) of Procopius.

4 The country is described by Tournefort (Voyage au Levant, tom. iii. lettre xvii. xviii.). That skilful botanist soon discovered the plant that infects the honey (Plin. xxi. 44, 45): he observes that the soldiers of Lucullus might indeed be astonished at the cold, since, even in the plain of Erzerum, snow sometimes falls in June, and the harvest is seldom finished before September. The hills of Armenia are below the fortieth degree of latitude; but in the mountainous country which I inhabit it is well known that an ascent of some hours carries the traveller from the climate of Languedoc to that of Norway; and a general theory has been introduced that, under the line, an elevation of 2400 *toises* is equivalent to the cold of the polar circle (Remond, Observations sur les Voyages de Coxe dans la Suisse, tom. ii. p. 104).

poisonous: the most industrious tillage would be confined to some pleasant valleys, and the pastoral tribes obtained a scanty sustenance from the flesh and milk of their cattle. The *Chaly-bians*¹ derived their name and temper from the iron quality of the soil; and, since the days of Cyrus, they might produce, under the various appellations of Chaldæans and Zanians, an uninterrupted prescription of war and rapine. Under the reign of Justinian they acknowledged the god and the emperor of the Romans, and seven fortresses were built in the most accessible passes to exclude the ambition of the Persian monarch.² The principal source of the Euphrates descends from the Chalybian mountains, and seems to flow towards the west and the Euxine: bending to the south-west, the river passes under the walls of Satala and Melitene (which were restored by Justinian as the bulwarks of the lesser Armenia), and gradually approaches the Mediterranean Sea, till at length, repelled by Mount Taurus,³ the Euphrates inclines his long and flexible course to the south-east and the Gulf of Persia. Among the Roman cities beyond the Euphrates we distinguish two recent foundations, which were named from Theodosius and the relics of the martyrs, and two capitals, Amida and Edessa, which are celebrated in the history of every age. Their strength was proportioned by Justinian to the danger of their situation. A ditch and palisade might be sufficient to resist the artless force of the cavalry of Scythia, but more elaborate works were required to sustain a regular siege against the arms and treasures of the Great King. His skilful engineers understood the methods of conducting deep mines, and of raising platforms to the level of the rampart. He shook the strongest battlements with his military engines, and sometimes advanced to the assault with a line of movable turrets on the backs of

1 The identity or proximity of the Chalybians, or Chaldæans, may be investigated in Strabo (l. xii. p. 825, 826 [p. 548, 549, ed. Casaub.]), Cellarius (Geograph. Antiq. tom. ii. p. 202–204), and Fréret (Mém. de l'Académie, tom. iv. p. 594). Xenophon supposes, in his romance (Cyropæd. l. iii. [c. 2]), the same barbarians against whom he had fought in his retreat (Anabasis, l. iv. [c. 3]).

2 Procopius, Persic. l. i. c. 15; De Ædific. l. iii. c. 6.

3 Ni Taurus obstet in nostra maria venturus (Pomponius Mela, iii. 8). Pliny, a poet as well as a naturalist (v. 20), personifies the river and mountain and describes their combat. See the course of the Tigris and Euphrates in the excellent treatise of D'Anville.

elephants. In the great cities of the East the disadvantage of space, perhaps of position, was compensated by the zeal of the people, who seconded the garrison in the defence of their country and religion; and the fabulous promise of the Son of God, that Edessa should never be taken, filled the citizens with valiant confidence and chilled the besiegers with doubt and dismay.[1] The subordinate towns of Armenia and Mesopotamia were diligently strengthened, and the posts which appeared to have any command of ground or water were occupied by numerous forts substantially built of stone, or more hastily erected with the obvious materials of earth and brick. The eye of Justinian investigated every spot, and his cruel precautions might attract the war into some lonely vale, whose peaceful natives, connected by trade and marriage, were ignorant of national discord and the quarrels of princes. Westward of the Euphrates a sandy desert extends above six hundred miles to the Red Sea. Nature had interposed a vacant solitude between the ambition of two rival empires; the Arabians, till Mahomet arose, were formidable only as robbers; and in the proud security of peace the fortifications of Syria were neglected on the most vulnerable side.

But the national enmity, at least the effects of that enmity, had been suspended by a truce which continued above fourscore years. An ambassador from the emperor Zeno accompanied the rash and unfortunate Perozes in his expedition against the Nephthalites, or White Huns, whose conquests had been stretched from the Caspian to the heart of India, whose throne was enriched with emeralds,[2] and whose cavalry was supported

1 Procopius (Persic. l. ii. c. 12 [tom. i. p. 208, ed. Bonn]) tells the story with the tone, half sceptical, half superstitious, of Herodotus. The promise was not in the primitive lie of Eusebius, but dates at least from the year 400; and a third lie, the *Veronica*, was soon raised on the two former (Evagrius, l. iv. c. 27). As Edessa *has* been taken, Tillemont *must* disclaim the promise (Mém. Ecclés. tom. i. p. 362, 383, 617).

2 They were purchased from the merchants of Adulis who traded to India (Cosmas, Topograph. Christ. l. xi. p. 339); yet, in the estimate of precious stones, the Scythian emerald was the first, the Bactrian the second, the Æthiopian only the third (Hill's Theophrastus, p. 61, etc., 92). The production, mines, etc., of emeralds, are involved in darkness; and it is doubtful whether we possess any of the twelve sorts known to the ancients (Goguet, Origine des Loix, etc., part ii. l. ii. c. 2, art. 3). In this war the Huns got, or at least Perozes lost, the finest pearl in the world, of which Procopius relates a ridiculous fable.

by a line of two thousand elephants.¹ The Persians were twice
circumvented, in a situation which made valour useless and flight
impossible, and the double victory of the Huns was achieved by
military stratagem. They dismissed their royal captive after he
had submitted to adore the majesty of a barbarian, and the humiliation was poorly evaded by the casuistical subtlety of the
Magi, who instructed Perozes to direct his attention to the rising
sun. The indignant successor of Cyrus forgot his danger and his
gratitude; he renewed the attack with headstrong fury, and lost
both his army and his life.² The death of Perozes abandoned
Persia to her foreign and domestic enemies, and twelve years of
confusion elapsed before his son Cabades or Kobad could embrace any designs of ambition or revenge. The unkind parsimony
of Anastasius was the motive or pretence of a Roman war;³ the
Huns and Arabs marched under the Persian standard, and the
fortifications of Armenia and Mesopotamia were at that time in
a ruinous or imperfect condition. The emperor returned his
thanks to the governor and people of Martyropolis for the
prompt surrender of a city which could not be successfully
defended, and the conflagration of Theodosiopolis might justify
the conduct of their prudent neighbours. Amida sustained a long
and destructive siege: at the end of three months the loss of fifty
thousand of the soldiers of Cabades was not balanced by any
prospect of success, and it was in vain that the Magi deduced a
flattering prediction from the indecency of the women on the
ramparts, who had revealed their most secret charms to the eyes

1 The Indo-Scythæ continued to reign from the time of Augustus (Dionys.
Perieget. 1088, with the Commentary of Eustathius, in Hudson, Geograph.
Minor. tom. iv.) to that of the elder Justin (Cosmas, Topograph. Christ. l. xi.
p. 338, 339). On their origin and conquests see D'Anville (sur l'Inde, p. 18, 45,
etc., 69, 85, 89). In the second century they were masters of Larice or Guzerat.

2 See the fate of Phirouz or Perozes and its consequences, in Procopius
(Persic. l. i. c. 3–6), who may be compared with the fragments of Oriental
history (D'Herbelot, Bibliot. Orient. p. 351, and Texeira, History of Persia,
translated or abridged by Stephens, l. i. c. 32, p. 132–138). The chronology is
ably ascertained by Asseman (Bibliot. Orient. tom. iii. p. 396–427).

3 The Persian war, under the reigns of Anastasius and Justin, may be
collected from Procopius (Persic. l. i. c. 7, 8, 9), Theophanes (in Chronograph.
p. 124–127 [ed. Par.; tom. i. p. 222–229, ed. Bonn]), Evagrius (l. iii. c. 37),
Marcellinus (in Chron. p. 47 [p. 372, sq., ed. Sirmond.]), and Josua Stylites (apud
Asseman. tom. i. p. 272–281).

of the assailants. At length, in a silent night, they ascended the most accessible tower, which was guarded only by some monks, oppressed, after the duties of a festival, with sleep and wine. Scaling-ladders were applied at the dawn of day; the presence of Cabades, his stern command, and his drawn sword, compelled the Persians to vanquish, and, before it was sheathed, fourscore thousand of the inhabitants had expiated the blood of their companions. After the siege of Amida the war continued three years, and the unhappy frontier tasted the full measure of its calamities. The gold of Anastasius was offered too late, the number of his troops was defeated by the number of their generals, the country was stripped of its inhabitants, and both the living and the dead were abandoned to the wild beasts of the desert. The resistance of Edessa and the deficiency of spoil inclined the mind of Cabades to peace; he sold his conquests for an exorbitant price; and the same line, though marked with slaughter and devastation, still separated the two empires. To avert the repetition of the same evils, Anastasius resolved to found a new colony, so strong that it should defy the power of the Persian, so far advanced towards Assyria that its stationary troops might defend the province by the menace or operation of offensive war. For this purpose the town of Dara,[1] fourteen miles from Nisibis, and four days' journey from the Tigris, was peopled and adorned: the hasty works of Anastasius were improved by the persevance of Justinian, and, without insisting on places less important, the fortifications of Dara may represent the military architecture of the age. The city was surrounded with two walls, and the interval between them, of fifty paces, afforded a retreat to the cattle of the besieged. The inner wall was a monument of strength and beauty: it measured sixty feet from the ground, and the height of the towers was one hundred feet; the loopholes, from whence an enemy might be annoyed with missile weapons, were small, but numerous; the soldiers were planted along the rampart, under the shelter of double galleries; and a third platform, spacious and secure, was raised on the summit of the

1 The description of Dara is amply and correctly given by Procopius (Persic. l. i. c. 10, l. ii. c. 13; De Ædific. l. ii. c. 1, 2, 3; l. iii. c. 5). See the situation in D'Anville (l'Euphrate et le Tigre, p. 53, 54, 55), though he seems to double the interval between Dara and Nisibis.

towers. The exterior wall appears to have been less lofty, but more solid, and each tower was protected by a quadrangular bulwark. A hard rocky soil resisted the tools of the miners, and on the south-east, where the ground was more tractable, their approach was retarded by a new work, which advanced in the shape of a half-moon. The double and treble ditches were filled with a stream of water, and in the management of the river the most skilful labour was employed to supply the inhabitants, to distress the besiegers, and to prevent the mischiefs of a natural or artificial inundation. Dara continued more than sixty years to fulfil the wishes of its founders and to provoke the jealousy of the Persians, who incessantly complained that this impregnable fortress had been constructed in manifest violation of the treaty of peace between the two empires.

Between the Euxine and the Caspian the countries of Colchos, Iberia, and Albania are intersected in every direction by the branches of Mount Caucasus, and the two principal *gates*, or passes, from north to south, have been frequently confounded in the geography both of the ancients and moderns. The name of *Caspian* or *Albanian* gates is properly applied to Derbend,[1] which occupies a short declivity between the mountains and the sea; the city, if we give credit to local tradition, had been founded by the Greeks, and this dangerous entrance was fortified by the kings of Persia with a mole, double walls, and doors of iron. The *Iberian* gates[2] are formed by a narrow passage of six miles in Mount Caucasus, which opens from the northern side of Iberia or Georgia into the plain that reaches to the Tanais and the Volga. A fortress, designed by Alexander perhaps, or one of his successors, to command that important pass, had descended by right of conquest or inheritance to a prince of the Huns, who offered it for a moderate price to the emperor; but while

1 For the city and pass of Derbend see D'Herbelot (Bibliot. Orient. p. 157, 291, 807), Petit de la Croix (Hist. de Gengiscan, l. iv. c. 9), Historie Généalogique des Tatars (tom. i. p. 120), Olearius (Voyage en Perse, p. 1039–1041), and Corneille le Bruyn (Voyages, tom. i. p. 146, 147): his view may be compared with the plan of Olearius, who judges the wall to be of shells and gravel hardened by time.

2 Procopius, though with some confusion, always denominates them Caspian (Persic. l. i. c. 10). The pass is now styled Tatar-topa, the Tartar-gates (D'Anville, Géographie Ancienne, tom. ii. p. 119, 120).

Anastasius paused, while he timorously computed the cost and the distance, a more vigilant rival interposed, and Cabades forcibly occupied the straits of Caucasus. The Albanian and Iberian gates excluded the horsemen of Scythia from the shortest and most practicable roads, and the whole front of the mountains was covered by the rampart of Gog and Magog, the long wall which has excited the curiosity of an Arabian caliph[1] and a Russian conqueror.[2] According to a recent description, huge stones, seven feet thick, twenty-one feet in length or height, are artificially joined, without iron or cement, to compose a wall which runs above three hundred miles from the shores of Derbend, over the hills and through the valleys of Daghestan and Georgia. Without a vision such a work might be undertaken by the policy of Cabades; without a miracle it might be accomplished by his son, so formidable to the Romans under the name of Chosroes, so dear to the Orientals under the appellation of Nushirvan. The Persian monarch held in his hand the keys both of peace and war; but he stipulated in every treaty that Justinian should contribute to the expense of a common barrier which equally protected the two empires from the inroads of the Scythians.[3]

VI. Justinian suppressed the schools of Athens and the consulship of Rome, which had given so many sages and heroes to mankind. Both these institutions had long since degenerated from their primitive glory, yet some reproach may be justly inflicted on the avarice and jealousy of a prince by whose hand such venerable ruins were destroyed.

Athens, after her Persian triumphs, adopted the philosophy of Ionia and the rhetoric of Sicily; and these studies became the patrimony of a city whose inhabitants, about thirty thousand

1 The imaginary rampart of Gog and Magog, which was seriously explored and believed by a caliph of the ninth century, appears to be derived from the gates of Mount Caucasus, and a vague report of the wall of China (Geograph. Nubiensis, p. 267–270; Mémoires de l'Académie, tom. xxxi. p. 210–219).

2 See a learned dissertation of Baier, *de muro Caucaseo*, in Comment. Acad. Petropol. ann. 1726, tom. i. p. 425–463; but it is destitute of a map or plan. When the Czar Peter I. became master of Derbend in the year 1722, the measure of the wall was found to be 3285 Russian *orgygiæ*, or fathom, each of seven feet English; in the whole somewhat more than four miles in length.

3 See the fortifications and treaties of Chosroes or Nushirwan, in Procopius (Persic. l. i. c. 16, 22, l. ii.) and D'Herbelot (p. 682).

males, condensed, within the period of a single life, the genius of ages and millions. Our sense of the dignity of human nature is exalted by the simple recollection that Isocrates[1] was the companion of Plato and Xenophon; that he assisted, perhaps with the historian Thucydides, at the first representations of the Œdipus of Sophocles and the Iphigenia of Euripides; and that his pupils Æschines and Demosthenes contended for the crown of patriotism in the presence of Aristotle, the master of Theophrastus, who taught at Athens with the founders of the Stoic and Epicurean sects.[2] The ingenuous youth of Attica enjoyed the benefits of their domestic education, which was communicated without envy to the rival cities. Two thousand disciples heard the lessons of Theophrastus;[3] the schools of rhetoric must have been still more populous than those of philosophy; and a rapid succession of students diffused the fame of their teachers as far as the utmost limits of the Grecian language and name. Those limits were enlarged by the victories of Alexander; the arts of Athens survived her freedom and dominion; and the Greek colonies which the Macedonians planted in Egypt, and scattered over Asia, undertook long and frequent pilgrimages to worship the Muses in their favourite temple on the banks of the Ilissus. The Latin conquerors respectfully listened to the instructions of their subjects and captives; the names of Cicero and Horace were enrolled in the schools of Athens; and after the perfect settlement of the Roman empire, the natives of Italy, of Africa, and of Britain, conversed in the groves of the Academy with their fellow-students of the East. The studies of philosophy and eloquence are congenial to a popular state, which encourages the freedom of inquiry, and submits only to the force of persuasion. In the republics of Greece and Rome the art of speaking was

1 The life of Isocrates extends from Olymp. lxxxvi. 1, to cx. 3 (ante Christ. 436–338). See Dionys. Halicarn. tom. ii. p. 149, 150, edit. Hudson. Plutarch (sive anonymus), in Vit. X. Oratorum, p. 1538–1543, edit. H. Steph. Phot. cod. cclix. p. 1453 [p. 486 b, ed. Bekk.].

2 The schools of Athens are copiously though concisely represented in the Fortuna Attica of Meursius (c. viii. p. 59–73, in tom. i. Opp.). For the state and arts of the city, see the first book of Pausanias, and a small tract of Dicæarchus (in the second volume of Hudson's Geographers), who wrote about Olymp. cxvii. (Dodwell's Dissertat. sect. 4).

3 Diogen. Laert. de Vit. Philosoph. l. v. [c. 2] segm. 37, p. 289.

the powerful engine of patriotism or ambition; and the schools
of rhetoric poured forth a colony of statesmen and legislators.
When the liberty of public debate was suppressed, the orator, in
the honourable profession of an advocate, might plead the cause
of innocence and justice; he might abuse his talents in the more
profitable trade of panegyric; and the same precepts continued
to dictate the fanciful declamations of the sophist, and the chaster beauties of historical composition. The systems which professed to unfold the nature of God, of man, and of the universe,
entertained the curiosity of the philosophic student; and according to the temper of his mind, he might doubt with the Sceptics,
or decide with the Stoics, sublimely speculate with Plato, or
severely argue with Aristotle. The pride of the adverse sects had
fixed an unattainable term of moral happiness and perfection:
but the race was glorious and salutary; the disciples of Zeno, and
even those of Epicurus, were taught both to act and to suffer;
and the death of Petronius was not less effectual than that of
Seneca to humble a tyrant by the discovery of his impotence.
The light of science could not indeed be confined within the
walls of Athens. Her incomparable writers address themselves to
the human race; the living masters emigrated to Italy and Asia;
Berytus, in later times, was devoted to the study of the law;
astronomy and physic were cultivated in the museum of Alexandria; but the Attic schools of rhetoric and philosophy maintained their superior reputation from the Peloponnesian war to
the reign of Justinian. Athens, though situate in a barren soil,
possessed a pure air, a free navigation, and the monuments of
ancient art. That sacred retirement was seldom disturbed by the
business of trade or government; and the last of the Athenians
were distinguished by their lively wit, the purity of their taste and
language, their social manners, and some traces, at least in discourse, of the magnanimity of their fathers. In the suburbs of
the city, the *Academy* of the Platonists, the *Lyceum* of the Peripatetics, the *Portico* of the Stoics, and the *Garden* of the Epicureans, were planted with trees and decorated with statues; and
the philosophers, instead of being immured in a cloister, delivered their instructions in spacious and pleasant walks, which
at different hours were consecrated to the exercises of the mind
and body. The genius of the founders still lived in those venerable

seats; the ambition of succeeding to the masters of human reason excited a generous emulation; and the merit of the candidates was determined, on each vacancy, by the free voices of
an enlightened people. The Athenian professors were paid by
their disciples: according to their mutual wants and abilities, the
price appears to have varied from a mina to a talent; and Isocrates himself, who derides the avarice of the sophists, required,
in his school of rhetoric, about thirty pounds from each of his
hundred pupils. The wages of industry are just and honourable,
yet the same Isocrates shed tears at the first receipt of a stipend:
the Stoic might blush when he was hired to preach the contempt
of money; and I should be sorry to discover that Aristotle or
Plato so far degenerated from the example of Socrates as to
exchange knowledge for gold. But some property of lands and
houses was settled, by the permission of the laws, and the legacies of deceased friends, on the philosophic chairs of Athens.
Epicurus bequeathed to his disciples the gardens which he had
purchased for eighty minæ or two hundred and fifty pounds,
with a fund sufficient for their frugal subsistence and monthly
festivals;[1] and the patrimony of Plato afforded an annual rent,
which, in eight centuries, was gradually increased from three to
one thousand pieces of gold.[2] The schools of Athens were protected by the wisest and most virtuous of the Roman princes.
The library, which Hadrian founded, was placed in a portico
adorned with pictures, statues, and a roof of alabaster, and supported by one hundred columns of Phrygian marble. The public
salaries were assigned by the generous spirit of the Antonines;
and each professor, of politics, of rhetoric, of the Platonic, the
Peripatetic, the Stoic, and the Epicurean philosophy, received an
annual stipend of ten thousand drachmæ, or more than three
hundred pounds sterling.[3] After the death of Marcus, these

1 See the Testament of Epicurus in Diogen. Laert. l. x. [c. 1] segm. 16–20,
p. 611, 612. A single epistle (ad Familiares, xiii. 1) displays the injustice of the
Areopagus, the fidelity of the Epicureans, the dexterous politeness of Cicero,
and the mixture of contempt and esteem with which the Roman senators
considered the philosophy and philosophers of Greece.

2 Damascius, in Vit. Isidor. apud Photium, cod. ccxlii. p. 1057 [p. 346 a,
ed. Bekk.].

3 See Lucian (in Eunuch. tom. ii. [c. 3, *sqq.*] p. 350–359, edit Reitz), Philostratus (in Vit. Sophist. l. ii. c. 2), and Dion Cassius, or Xiphilin (l. lxxi. [c. 31]

liberal donations, and the privileges attached to the *thrones* of science, were abolished and revived, diminished and enlarged; but some vestige of royal bounty may be found under the successors of Constantine; and their arbitrary choice of an unworthy candidate might tempt the philosophers of Athens to regret the days of independence and poverty.[1] It is remarkable that the impartial favour of the Antonines was bestowed on the four adverse sects of philosophy, which they considered as equally useful, or at least as equally innocent. Socrates had formerly been the glory and the reproach of his country; and the first lessons of Epicurus so strangely scandalised the pious ears of the Athenians, that by his exile, and that of his antagonists, they silenced all vain disputes concerning the nature of the gods. But in the ensuing year they recalled the hasty decree, restored the liberty of the schools, and were convinced by the experience of ages that the moral character of philosophers is not affected by the diversity of their theological speculations.[2]

The Gothic arms were less fatal to the schools of Athens than the establishment of a new religion, whose ministers superseded the exercise of reason, resolved every question by an article of faith, and condemned the infidel or sceptic to eternal flames. In many a volume of laborious controversy they exposed the weakness of the understanding and the corruption of the heart, insulted human nature in the sages of antiquity, and proscribed the spirit of philosophical inquiry, so repugnant to the doctrine, or at least to the temper, of a humble believer. The surviving sect of the Platonists, whom Plato would have blushed to acknowledge, extravagantly mingled a sublime theory with the practice of superstition and magic; and as they remained alone in the midst of a Christian world, they indulged a secret rancour against the government of the church and state, whose severity was still suspended over their heads. About a century after the reign of

---

p. 1195), with their editors Du Soul, Olearius, and Reimar, and, above all, Salmasius (ad Hist. August. p. 72). A judicious philosopher (Smith's Wealth of Nations, vol. ii. p. 340–374) prefers the free contributions of the students to a fixed stipend for the professor.

1 Brucker, Hist. Crit. Philosoph. tom. ii. p. 310, etc.

2 The birth of Epicurus is fixed to the year 342 before Christ (Bayle), Olympiad cix. 3; and he opened his school at Athens, Olymp. cxviii. 3, 306

Julian,[1] Proclus[2] was permitted to teach in the philosophic chair of the Academy; and such was his industry, that he frequently, in the same day, pronounced five lessons, and composed seven hundred lines. His sagacious mind explored the deepest questions of morals and metaphysics, and he ventured to urge eighteen arguments against the Christian doctrine of the creation of the world. But in the intervals of study he *personally* conversed with Pan, Æsculapius, and Minerva, in whose mysteries he was secretly initiated, and whose prostrate statues he adored; in the devout persuasion that the philosopher, who is a citizen of the universe, should be the priest of its various deities. An eclipse of the sun announced his approaching end; and his Life, with that of his scholar Isidore,[3] compiled by two of their most learned disciples, exhibits a deplorable picture of the second childhood of human reason. Yet the golden chain, as it was fondly styled, of the Platonic succession, continued forty-four years from the death of Proclus to the edict of Justinian,[4] which imposed a perpetual silence on the schools of Athens, and excited the grief and indignation of the few remaining votaries of Grecian science and superstition. Seven friends and philosophers, Diogenes and Hermias, Eulalius and Priscian, Damascius, Isidore, and Simplicius, who dissented from the religion of their

years before the same era. This intolerant law (Athenæus, l. xiii. p. 610; Diogen. Laertius, l. v. [c. 2] s. 38, p. 290; Julius Pollux, ix. 5) was enacted in the same or the succeeding year (Sigonius, Opp. tom. v. p. 62; Menagius, ad Diogen. Laert. p. 204; Corsini, Fasti Attici, tom. iv. p. 67, 68). Theophrastus, chief of the Peripatetics, and disciple of Aristotle, was involved in the same exile.

1 This is no fanciful era: the Pagans reckoned their calamities from the reign of their hero. Proclus, whose nativity is marked by his horoscope (A.D. 412, February 8, at C. P.), died 124 years ἀπὸ 'Ιουλιανοῦ βασιλέως, A.D. 485 (Marin. in Vitâ Procli, c. 36).

2 The Life of Proclus, by Marinus, was published by Fabricius (Hamburg, 1700, et ad calcem Biblioth. Latin. Lond. 1703). See Suidas (tom. iii. p. 185, 186), Fabricius (Biblioth. Græc. l. v. c. 26, p. 449–552), and Brucker (Hist. Crit. Philosoph. tom. ii. p. 319–326).

3 The Life of Isidore was composed by Damascius (apud Photium, cod. ccxlii. p. 1028–1076 [p. 335–353, ed. Bekk.]). See the last age of the Pagan philosophers in Brucker (tom. ii. p. 341–351).

4 The suppression of the schools of Athens is recorded by John Malala (tom. ii. p. 187 [p. 451, ed. Bonn], sub Decio Cos. Sol.), and an anonymous Chronicle in the Vatican library (apud Aleman. p. 106 [Procop. tom. iii. p. 459, ed. Bonn]).

sovereign, embraced the resolution of seeking in a foreign land
the freedom which was denied in their native country. They had
heard, and they credulously believed, that the republic of Plato
was realised in the despotic government of Persia, and that a
patriot king reigned over the happiest and most virtuous of
nations. They were soon astonished by the natural discovery that
Persia resembled the other countries of the globe; that Chosroes,
who affected the name of a philosopher, was vain, cruel, and
ambitious; that bigotry, and a spirit of intolerance, prevailed
among the Magi; that the nobles were haughty, the courtiers
servile, and the magistrates unjust; that the guilty sometimes
escaped, and that the innocent were often oppressed. The disappointment of the philosophers provoked them to overlook the
real virtues of the Persians; and they were scandalised, more
deeply perhaps than became their profession, with the plurality
of wives and concubines, the incestuous marriages, and the custom of exposing dead bodies to the dogs and vultures, instead
of hiding them in the earth, or consuming them with fire. Their
repentance was expressed by a precipitate return, and they loudly
declared that they had rather die on the borders of the empire
than enjoy the wealth and favour of the barbarian. From this
journey, however, they derived a benefit which reflects the purest
lustre on the character of Chosroes. He required that the seven
sages who had visited the court of Persia should be exempted
from the penal laws which Justinian enacted against his Pagan
subjects; and this privilege, expressly stipulated in a treaty of
peace, was guarded by the vigilance of a powerful mediator.[1]
Simplicius and his companions ended their lives in peace and
obscurity; and as they left no disciples, they terminate the long
list of Grecian philosophers, who may be justly praised, notwithstanding their defects, as the wisest and most virtuous of their
contemporaries. The writings of Simplicius are now extant. His
physical and metaphysical commentaries on Aristotle have passed
away with the fashion of the times; but his moral interpretation

---

1 Agathias (l. ii. p. 69, 70, 71 [ed. Par.; p. 130–136, ed. Bonn]) relates this
curious story. Chosroes ascended the throne in the year 531, and made his first
peace with the Romans in the beginning of 533, a date not compatible with
his *young* fame and the *old* age of Isidore (Asseman. Biblioth. Orient. tom. iii.
p. 404; Pagi, tom. ii. p. 543, 550).

of Epictetus is preserved in the library of nations, as a classic book, most excellently adapted to direct the will, to purify the heart, and to confirm the understanding, by a just confidence in the nature both of God and man.

About the same time that Pythagoras first invented the appellation of philosopher, liberty and the consulship were founded at Rome by the elder Brutus. The revolutions of the consular office, which may be viewed in the successive lights of a substance, a shadow, and a name, have been occasionally mentioned in the present history. The first magistrates of the republic had been chosen by the people, to exercise, in the senate and in the camp, the powers of peace and war, which were afterwards translated to the emperors. But the tradition of ancient dignity was long revered by the Romans and barbarians. A Gothic historian applauds the consulship of Theodoric as the height of all temporal glory and greatness;[1] the king of Italy himself congratulates those annual favourites of fortune who, without the cares, enjoyed the splendour of the throne; and at the end of a thousand years two consuls were created by the sovereigns of Rome and Constantinople for the sole purpose of giving a date to the year and a festival to the people. But the expenses of this festival, in which the wealthy and the vain aspired to surpass their predecessors, insensibly arose to the enormous sum of fourscore thousand pounds; the wisest senators declined a useless honour which involved the certain ruin of their families, and to this reluctance I should impute the frequent chasms in the last age of the consular *Fasti*. The predecessors of Justinian had assisted from the public treasures the dignity of the less opulent candidates; the avarice of that prince preferred the cheaper and more convenient method of advice and regulation.[2] Seven *processions* or spectacles were the number to which his edict confined the horse and chariot races, the athletic sports, the music and pantomimes of the theatre, and the hunting of wild beasts; and small pieces of silver were discreetly substituted to the gold medals, which had always excited tumult and drunkenness when they were

1 Cassiodor. Variarum Epist. vi. 1. Jornandes, c. 57, p. 696, edit. Grot. Quod summum bonum primumque in mundo decus edicitur.

2 See the regulations of Justinian (Novell. cv.), dated at Constantinople, July 5, and addressed to Strategius, treasurer of the empire.

scattered with a profuse hand among the populace. Notwithstanding these precautions and his own example, the succession of
consuls finally ceased in the thirteenth year of Justinian, whose
despotic temper might be gratified by the silent extinction of a
title which admonished the Romans of their ancient freedom.[1]
Yet the annual consulship still lived in the minds of the people;
they fondly expected its speedy restoration; they applauded the
gracious condescension of successive princes, by whom it was
assumed in the first year of their reign; and three centuries elapsed,
after the death of Justinian, before that obsolete dignity, which
had been suppressed by custom, could be abolished by law.[2] The
imperfect mode of distinguishing each year by the name of a
magistrate was usefully supplied by the date of a permanent era:
the creation of the world, according to the Septuagint version,
was adopted by the Greeks;[3] and the Latins, since the age of
Charlemagne, have computed their time from the birth of Christ.[4]

1 Procopius, in Anecdot. c. 26 [tom. iii. p. 144, ed. Bonn]. Aleman, p. 106
[p. 459, ed. Bonn]. In the eighteenth year after the consulship of Basilius, according
to the reckoning of Marcellinus, Victor, Marius, etc., the secret history was composed, and, in the eyes of Procopius, the consulship was finally abolished.

2 By Leo, the philosopher (Novell. xciv. A.D. 886–911). See Pagi (Dissertat.
Hypatica, p. 325–362) and Ducange (Gloss. Græc. p. 1635, 1636). Even the title
was vilified: consulatus codicilli . . . vilescunt, says the emperor himself.

3 According to Julius Africanus, etc., the world was created the first of
September, 5508 years, three months, and twenty-five days before the birth of
Christ (see Pezron, Antiquité des Tems défendue, p. 20–28); and this era has
been used by the Greeks, the Oriental Christians, and even by the Russians, till
the reign of Peter I. The period, however arbitrary, is clear and convenient. Of
the 7296 years which are supposed to elapse since the creation, we shall find
3000 of ignorance and darkness; 2000 either fabulous or doubtful; 1000 of
ancient history, commencing with the Persian empire and the republics of Rome
and Athens; 1000 from the fall of the Roman empire in the West to the
discovery of America; and the remaining 296 will almost complete three centuries of the modern state of Europe and mankind. I regret this chronology,
so far preferable to our double and perplexed method of counting backwards
and forwards the years before and after the Christian era.

4 The era of the world has prevailed in the East since the sixth general
council (A.D. 681). In the West the Christian era was first invented in the sixth
century: it was propagated in the eighth by the authority and writings of venerable Bede; but it was not till the tenth that the use became legal and popular.
See l'Art de vérifier les Dates Dissert. Préliminaire, p. iii. xii.; Dictionnaire
Diplomatique, tom. i. p. 329–337: the works of a laborious society of Benedictine monks.

CHAPTER XLI

Conquests of Justinian in the West – Character and first Campaigns of Belisarius – He invades and subdues the Vandal Kingdom of Africa – His Triumph – The Gothic War – He recovers Sicily, Naples, and Rome – Siege of Rome by the Goths – Their Retreat and Losses – Surrender of Ravenna – Glory of Belisarius – His domestic Shame and Misfortunes

WHEN Justinian ascended the throne, about fifty years after the fall of the Western Empire, the kingdoms of the Goths and Vandals had obtained a solid, and, as it might seem, a legal establishment both in Europe and Africa. The titles which Roman victory had inscribed were erased with equal justice by the sword of the barbarians; and their successful rapine derived a more venerable sanction from time, from treaties, and from the oaths of fidelity, already repeated by a second or third generation of obedient subjects. Experience and Christianity had refuted the superstitious hope that Rome was founded by the gods to reign for ever over the nations of the earth. But the proud claim of perpetual and indefeasible dominion, which her soldiers could no longer maintain, was firmly asserted by her statesmen and lawyers, whose opinions have been sometimes revived and propagated in the modern schools of jurisprudence. After Rome herself had been stripped of the Imperial purple, the princes of Constantinople assumed the sole and sacred sceptre of the monarchy; demanded, as their rightful inheritance, the provinces which had been subdued by the consuls or possessed by the Cæsars; and feebly aspired to deliver their faithful subjects of the West from the usurpation of heretics and barbarians. The execution of this splendid design was in some degree reserved for Justinian. During the five first years of his reign he reluctantly waged a costly and unprofitable war against the Persians, till his pride submitted to his ambition, and he purchased, at the price of four hundred and forty thousand pounds sterling, the benefit of a precarious truce, which, in the language of both nations, was dignified with the appellation of the *endless* peace. The safety of the East enabled the emperor to employ his forces against the

Vandals; and the internal state of Africa afforded an honourable motive, and promised a powerful support, to the Roman arms.[1]

According to the testament of the founder, the African kingdom had lineally descended to Hilderic, the eldest of the Vandal princes. A mild disposition inclined the son of a tyrant, the grandson of a conqueror, to prefer the counsels of clemency and peace, and his accession was marked by the salutary edict which restored two hundred bishops to their churches, and allowed the free profession of the Athanasian creed.[2] But the catholics accepted with cold and transient gratitude a favour so inadequate to their pretensions, and the virtues of Hilderic offended the prejudices of his countrymen. The Arian clergy presumed to insinuate that he had renounced the faith, and the soldiers more loudly complained that he had degenerated from the courage, of his ancestors. His ambassadors were suspected of a secret and disgraceful negotiation in the Byzantine court; and his general, the Achilles,[3] as he was named, of the Vandals, lost a battle against the naked and disorderly Moors. The public discontent was exasperated by Gelimer, whose age, descent, and military fame gave him an apparent title to the succession: he assumed, with the consent of the nation, the reins of government, and his unfortunate sovereign sunk without a struggle from the throne to a dungeon, where he was strictly guarded with a faithful counsellor, and his unpopular nephew the Achilles of the Vandals.

1 The complete series of the Vandal war is related by Procopius in a regular and elegant narrative (l. i. c. 9–25, l. ii. c. 1–13); and happy would be my lot, could I always tread in the footsteps of such a guide. From the entire and diligent perusal of the Greek text I have a right to pronounce that the Latin and French versions of Grotius and Cousin may not be implicitly trusted; yet the President Cousin has been often praised, and Hugo Grotius was the first scholar of a learned age.

2 See Ruinart, Hist. Persecut. Vandal. c. xii. p. 589 [ed. Par. 1694]. His best evidence is drawn from the Life of St. Fulgentius, composed by one of his disciples, transcribed in a great measure in the Annals of Baronius, and printed in several great collections (Catalog. Bibliot. Bunavianæ, tom. i. vol. ii. p. 1258).

3 For what quality of the mind or body? For speed, or beauty, or valour? – In what language did the Vandals read Homer? – Did he speak German? – The Latins had four versions (Fabric. tom. i. l. ii. c. 3, p. 297): yet, in spite of the praises of Seneca (Consol. [ad Polyb.] c. 26), they appear to have been more successful in imitating than in translating the Greek poets. But the name of Achilles might be famous and popular, even among the illiterate barbarians.

But the indulgence which Hilderic had shown to his catholic subjects had powerfully recommended him to the favour of Justinian, who, for the benefit of his own sect, could acknowledge the use and justice of religious toleration: their alliance, while the nephew of Justin remained in a private station, was cemented by the mutual exchange of gifts and letters, and the emperor Justinian asserted the cause of royalty and friendship. In two successive embassies he admonished the usurper to repent of his treason, or to abstain, at least, from any further violence which might provoke the displeasure of God and of the Romans, to reverence the laws of kindred and succession, and to suffer an infirm old man peaceably to end his days either on the throne of Carthage or in the palace of Constantinople. The passions or even the prudence of Gelimer compelled him to reject these requests, which were urged in the haughty tone of menace and command; and he justified his ambition in a language rarely spoken in the Byzantine court, by alleging the right of a free people to remove or punish their chief magistrate who had failed in the execution of the kingly office. After this fruitless expostulation, the captive monarch was more rigorously treated, his nephew was deprived of his eyes, and the cruel Vandal, confident in his strength and distance, derided the vain threats and slow preparations of the emperor of the East. Justinian resolved to deliver or revenge his friend, Gelimer to maintain his usurpation; and the war was preceded, according to the practice of civilised nations, by the most solemn protestations that each party was sincerely desirous of peace.

The report of an African war was grateful only to the vain and idle populace of Constantinople, whose poverty exempted them from tribute, and whose cowardice was seldom exposed to military service. But the wiser citizens, who judged of the future by the past, revolved in their memory the immense loss, both of men and money, which the empire had sustained in the expedition of Basiliscus. The troops, which, after five laborious campaigns, had been recalled from the Persian frontier, dreaded the sea, the climate, and the arms of an unknown enemy. The ministers of the finances computed, as far as they might compute, the demands of an African war, the taxes which must be found and levied to supply those insatiate demands, and the danger lest their own lives, or at least their lucrative employments, should be made responsible for the deficiency of the supply. Inspired by such selfish motives (for we may not suspect him of any zeal for the public good), John of Cappadocia ventured to oppose in full council the inclinations of his master. He confessed that a victory of such importance could not be too dearly purchased; but he represented in a grave discourse the certain difficulties and the uncertain event. 'You undertake,' said the præfect, 'to besiege Carthage: by land the distance is not less than one hundred and forty days' journey; on the sea, a whole year[1] must elapse before you can receive any intelligence from your fleet. If Africa should be reduced, it cannot be preserved without the additional conquest of Sicily and Italy. Success will impose the obligation of new labours; a single misfortune will attract the barbarians into the heart of your exhausted empire.' Justinian felt the weight of his salutary advice; he was confounded by the unwonted freedom of an obsequious servant; and the design of the war would perhaps have been relinquished, if his courage had not been revived by a voice which silenced the doubts of profane reason. 'I have seen a vision,' cried an artful or fanatic bishop of the East. 'It is the will of Heaven, O emperor! that you should not abandon your holy enterprise for the deliverance of the African church. The God of battles will march before your standard, and disperse your enemies, who are the enemies of his Son.' The emperor might be tempted, and his counsellors were constrained, to give credit to this seasonable revelation; but they derived more rational hope from the revolt which the adherents of Hilderic or Athanasius had already excited on the borders of the Vandal monarchy. Pudentius, an African subject, had privately signified his loyal intentions, and a small military aid restored the province of Tripoli to the obedience of the Romans. The government of Sardinia had been intrusted to Godas, a valiant barbarian: he suspended the payment of tribute, disclaimed his allegiance to the usurper, and gave audience to

---

1 *A year* – absurd exaggeration! The conquest of Africa may be dated A.D. 533, September 14. It is celebrated by Justinian in the preface to his Institutes, which were published November 21 of the same year. Including the voyage and return, such a computation might be truly applied to *our* Indian empire.

the emissaries of Justinian, who found him master of that fruitful island, at the head of his guards, and proudly invested with the ensigns of royalty. The forces of the Vandals were diminished by discord and suspicion; the Roman armies were animated by the spirit of Belisarius, one of those heroic names which are familiar to every age and to every nation.[1]

The Africanus of new Rome was born, and perhaps educated, among the Thracian peasants,[2] without any of those advantages which had formed the virtues of the elder and younger Scipio – a noble origin, liberal studies, and the emulation of a free state. The silence of a loquacious secretary may be admitted to prove that the youth of Belisarius could not afford any subject of praise: he served, most assuredly with valour and reputation, among the private guards of Justinian; and when his patron became emperor, the domestic was promoted to military command. After a bold inroad into Persarmenia, in which his glory was shared by a colleague, and his progress was checked by an enemy, Belisarius repaired to the important station of Dara, where he first accepted the service of Procopius, the faithful companion, and diligent historian, of his exploits.[3] The Mirranes

1 [Stilicho, Aëtius, Boniface, Belisarius, were the quartette of great soldiers who hurled back the hordes of barbarians, and of these unquestionably the first and the last were the greatest and best. See Lord Mahon's *Life of Belisarius* (London, 1848, second ed.). – O. S.]

2 Ὥρμητο δὲ ὁ Βελισάριος ἐκ Γερμανίας, ἥ Θρᾳκῶντε καὶ Ἰλλυριῶν μεταξὺ κεῖται (Procop. Vandal. l. i. c. 11 [tom. i. p. 361, ed. Bonn]). Aleman. (Not. ad Anecdot. p. 5), an Italian, could easily reject the German vanity of Giphanius and Velserus, who wished to claim the hero; but his Germania, a metropolis of Thrace, I cannot find in any civil or ecclesiastical lists of the provinces and cities.

[Lord Mahon expresses surprise that Gibbon cannot find the town of Germania in any civil or ecclesiastical lists, and says that it is mentioned by Procopius (de Ædific. lib. iv. c. 1) as near Sardica. In that passage it is called Γερμάνη. It is also mentioned by Constant. Porphyrog. de Themat. l. ii. under Δυρραχιον θέμα 9, Banduri Imp. Orient. i. p. 26, where it is placed in the eparchia of Dacia; and by the grammarian Hierocles in the same work (p. 36), where it is called Γερμαη. Von Hammer, in a review of Lord Mahon's book in the *Jahrbücher der Literatur* of Vienna, in 1832, observes that Germania may be identified with the present Tschirmien or Tschermen, a town near the line of road between Constantinople and Adrianople, and about one day's journey from the latter. – O. S.]

3 The two first Persian campaigns of Belisarius are fairly and copiously related by his secretary (Persic. l. i. c. 12–18).

of Persia advanced with forty thousand of her best troops, to
raze the fortifications of Dara; and signified the day and the hour
on which the citizens should prepare a bath for his refreshment
after the toils of victory. He encountered an adversary equal to
himself, by the new title of General of the East; his superior in
the science of war, but much inferior in the number and quality
of his troops, which amounted only to twenty-five thousand
Romans and strangers, relaxed in their discipline, and humbled
by recent disasters. As the level plain of Dara refused all shelter
to stratagem and ambush, Belisarius protected his front with a
deep trench, which was prolonged at first in perpendicular, and
afterwards in parallel, lines, to cover the wings of cavalry advantageously posted to command the flanks and rear of the enemy.
When the Roman centre was shaken, their well-timed and rapid
charge decided the conflict: the standard of Persia fell; the *im-
mortals* fled; the infantry threw away their bucklers, and eight
thousand of the vanquished were left on the field of battle. In
the next campaign Syria was invaded on the side of the desert;
and Belisarius, with twenty thousand men, hastened from Dara
to the relief of the province. During the whole summer the designs
of the enemy were baffled by his skilful dispositions:[1] he pressed
their retreat, occupied each night their camp of the preceding
day, and would have secured a bloodless victory, if he could have
resisted the impatience of his own troops. Their valiant promise
was faintly supported in the hour of battle; the right wing was
exposed by the treacherous or cowardly desertion of the Christian Arabs; the Huns, a veteran band of eight hundred warriors,
were oppressed by superior numbers; the flight of the Isaurians
was intercepted; but the Roman infantry stood firm on the left;
for Belisarius himself, dismounting from his horse, showed them
that intrepid despair was their only safety. They turned their
backs to the Euphrates, and their faces to the enemy: innumerable arrows glanced without effect from the compact and shelving order of their bucklers; an impenetrable line of pikes was
opposed to the repeated assaults of the Persian cavalry; and after

1 [The statement that during the whole summer the designs of the Persians
were baffled by the skilful dispositions of Belisarius is also incorrect, because,
as Lord Mahon says, the decisive battle of Callinicum was fought on Easter
Sunday (April 19). – O. S.]

a resistance of many hours, the remaining troops were skilfully embarked under the shadow of the night. The Persian commander retired with disorder and disgrace, to answer a strict account of the lives of so many soldiers which he had consumed in a barren victory. But the fame of Belisarius was not sullied by a defeat in which he alone had saved his army from the consequences of their own rashness: the approach of peace relieved him from the guard of the eastern frontier, and his conduct in the sedition of Constantinople amply discharged his obligations to the emperor. When the African war became the topic of popular discourse and secret deliberation, each of the Roman generals was apprehensive, rather than ambitious, of the dangerous honour; but as soon as Justinian had declared his preference of superior merit, their envy was rekindled by the unanimous applause which was given to the choice of Belisarius. The temper of the Byzantine court may encourage a suspicion that the hero was darkly assisted by the intrigues of his wife, the fair and subtle Antonina, who alternately enjoyed the confidence, and incurred the hatred, of the empress Theodora. The birth of Antonina was ignoble; she descended from a family of charioteers; and her chastity has been stained with the foulest reproach. Yet she reigned with long and absolute power over the mind of her illustrious husband; and if Antonina disdained the merit of conjugal fidelity, she expressed a manly friendship to Belisarius, whom she accompanied with undaunted resolution in all the hardships and dangers of a military life.[1]

The preparations for the African war were not unworthy of the last contest between Rome and Carthage. The pride and flower of the army consisted of the guards of Belisarius, who, according to the pernicious indulgence of the times, devoted themselves, by a particular oath of fidelity, to the service of their patrons. Their strength and stature, for which they had been curiously selected, the goodness of their horses and armour, and the assiduous practice of all the exercises of war, enabled them to act whatever their courage might prompt; and their courage was exalted by the social honour of their rank, and the personal

---

1 See the birth and character of Antonina, in the Anecdotes, c. 1, and the notes of Alemannus, p. 3.

ambition of favour and fortune. Four hundred of the bravest of
the Heruli marched under the banner of the faithful and active
Pharas; their untractable valour was more highly prized than the
tame submission of the Greeks and Syrians; and of such importance was it deemed to procure a reinforcement of six hundred
Massagetæ, or Huns, that they were allured by fraud and deceit
to engage in a naval expedition. Five thousand horse and ten
thousand foot were embarked at Constantinople for the conquest of Africa; but the infantry, for the most part levied in
Thrace and Isauria, yielded to the more prevailing use and reputation of the cavalry; and the Scythian bow was the weapon on
which the armies of Rome were now reduced to place their
principal dependence. From a laudable desire to assert the dignity of his theme, Procopius defends the soldiers of his own time
against the morose critics, who confined that respectable name
to the heavy-armed warriors of antiquity, and maliciously observed that the word *archer* is introduced by Homer[1] as a term
of contempt. 'Such contempt might perhaps be due to the naked
youths who appeared on foot in the fields of Troy, and, lurking
behind a tombstone, or the shield of a friend, drew the bow-
string to their breast,[2] and dismissed a feeble and lifeless arrow.
But our archers (pursues the historian) are mounted on horses,
which they manage with admirable skill; their head and shoulders
are protected by a casque or buckler; they wear greaves of iron
on their legs, and their bodies are guarded by a coat of mail. On
their right side hangs a quiver, a sword on their left, and their
hand is accustomed to wield a lance or javelin in closer combat.
Their bows are strong and weighty; they shoot in every possible
direction, advancing, retreating, to the front, to the rear, or to
either flank; and as they are taught to draw the bowstring not to

1 See the preface of Procopius [Bell. Pers. c. 1]. The enemies of archery
might quote the reproaches of Diomede (Iliad, Λ, 385, etc.) and the permittere
vulnera ventis of Lucan (viii. 383): yet the Romans could not despise the arrows
of the Parthians; and in the siege of Troy, Pandarus, Paris, and Teucer pierced
those haughty warriors who insulted them as women or children.

2 Νευρὴν μὲν μαζῷ πέλασεν, τόξῳ δὲ σίδηρον (Iliad. Δ, 123). How concise – how just – how beautiful is the whole picture! I see the attitudes of the
archer – I hear the twanging of the bow: –

    Λίγξε βιὸς, νευρὴ δὲ μέγ' ἴαχεν, ἆλτο δ' ὀϊστός.

the breast, but to the right ear, firm indeed must be the armour that can resist the rapid violence of their shaft.' Five hundred transports, navigated by twenty thousand mariners of Egypt, Cilicia, and Ionia, were collected in the harbour of Constantinople. The smallest of these vessels may be computed at thirty, the largest at five hundred, tons; and the fair average will supply an allowance, liberal, but not profuse, of about one hundred thousand tons,¹ for the reception of thirty-five thousand soldiers and sailors, of five thousand horses, of arms, engines, and military stores, and of a sufficient stock of water and provisions for a voyage, perhaps, of three months. The proud galleys which in former ages swept the Mediterranean with so many hundred oars had long since disappeared; and the fleet of Justinian was escorted only by ninety-two light brigantines, covered from the missile weapons of the enemy, and rowed by two thousand of the brave and robust youth of Constantinople. Twenty-two generals are named, most of whom were afterwards distinguished in the wars of Africa and Italy; but the supreme command, both by land and sea, was delegated to Belisarius alone, with a boundless power of acting according to his discretion, as if the emperor himself were present. The separation of the naval and military professions is at once the effect and the cause of the modern improvements in the science of navigation and maritime war.

In the seventh year of the reign of Justinian, and about the time of the summer solstice, the whole fleet of six hundred ships was ranged in martial pomp before the gardens of the palace. The patriarch pronounced his benediction, the emperor signified his last commands, the general's trumpet gave the signal of departure, and every heart, according to its fears or wishes, explored with anxious curiosity the omens of misfortune and success. The first halt was made at Perinthus or Heraclea, where

1 The text appears to allow for the largest vessels 50,000 medimni, or 3000 tons (since the *medimnus* weighed 160 Roman, or 120 avoirdupois, pounds). I have given a more rational interpretation, by supposing that the Attic style of Procopius conceals the legal and popular *modius*, a sixth part of the *medimnus* (Hooper's Ancient Measures, p. 152, etc.). A contrary, and indeed a stranger, mistake has crept into an oration of Dinarchus (contra Demosthenem, in Reiske Orator. Græc. tom. iv. P. ii. p. 34). By reducing the *number* of ships from 500 to 50, and translating μεδίμνοι by *mines*, or pounds, Cousin has generously allowed 500 tons for the whole of the Imperial fleet? – Did he never think?

Belisarius waited five days to receive some Thracian horses, a
military gift of his sovereign. From thence the fleet pursued their
course through the midst of the Propontis; but as they struggled
to pass the Straits of the Hellespont, an unfavourable wind detained them four days at Abydus, where the general exhibited a
memorable lesson of firmness and severity. Two of the Huns,
who in a drunken quarrel had slain one of their fellow-soldiers,
were instantly shown to the army suspended on a lofty gibbet.
The national indignity was resented by their countrymen, who
disclaimed the servile laws of the empire, and asserted the free
privilege of Scythia, where a small fine was allowed to expiate
the hasty sallies of intemperance and anger. Their complaints
were specious, their clamours were loud, and the Romans were
not averse to the example of disorder and impunity. But the
rising sedition was appeased by the authority and eloquence of
the general, and he represented to the assembled troops the
obligation of justice, the importance of discipline, the rewards
of piety and virtue, and the unpardonable guilt of murder, which,
in his apprehension, was aggravated rather than excused by the
vice of intoxication.[1] In the navigation from the Hellespont to
Peloponnesus, which the Greeks after the siege of Troy had
performed in four days,[2] the fleet of Belisarius was guided in
their course by his master-galley, conspicuous in the day by the
redness of the sails, and in the night by the torches blazing from
the mast-head. It was the duty of the pilots, as they steered
between the islands and turned the capes of Malea and Tæna-
rium, to preserve the just order and regular intervals of such a
multitude of ships; as the wind was fair and moderate, their
labours were not unsuccessful, and the troops were safely disembarked at Methone on the Messenian coast, to repose themselves for awhile after the fatigues of the sea. In this place they

1 I have read of a Greek legislator who inflicted a *double* penalty on the
crimes committed in a state of intoxication; but it seems agreed that this was
rather a political than a moral law.

2 Or even in three days, since they anchored the first evening in the neighbouring isle of Tenedos: the second day they sailed to Lesbos, the third to the
promontory of Eubæa, and on the fourth they reached Argos (Homer. Odyss.
Γ 130–183; Wood's Essay on Homer, p. 40–46). A pirate sailed from the
Hellespont to the seaport of Sparta in three days (Xenophon. Hellen. l. ii. c. 1).

experienced how avarice, invested with authority, may sport with
the lives of thousands which are bravely exposed for the public
service. According to military practice, the bread or biscuit of
the Romans was twice prepared in the oven, and the diminution
of one-fourth was cheerfully allowed for the loss of weight. To
gain this miserable profit, and to save the expense of wood, the
præfect, John of Cappadocia, had given orders that the flour
should be slightly baked by the same fire which warmed the
baths of Constantinople; and when the sacks were opened, a soft
and mouldy paste was distributed to the army. Such unwholesome food, assisted by the heat of the climate and season, soon
produced an epidemical disease which swept away five hundred
soldiers. Their health was restored by the diligence of Belisarius,
who provided fresh bread at Methone, and boldly expressed his
just and humane indignation: the emperor heard his complaint;
the general was praised, but the minister was not punished. From
the port of Methone the pilots steered along the western coast
of Peloponnesus, as far as the isle of Zacynthus or Zante, before
they undertook the voyage (in their eyes a most arduous voyage)
of one hundred leagues over the Ionian Sea. As the fleet was
surprised by a calm, sixteen days were consumed in the slow
navigation; and even the general would have suffered the intolerable hardship of thirst, if the ingenuity of Antonina had not
preserved the water in glass bottles, which she buried deep in
the sand in a part of the ship impervious to the rays of the sun.
At length the harbour of Caucana,[1] on the southern side of Sicily,
afforded a secure and hospitable shelter. The Gothic officers,
who governed the island in the name of the daughter and grandson of Theodoric, obeyed their imprudent orders to receive the
troops of Justinian like friends and allies; provisions were liberally supplied, the cavalry was remounted,[2] and Procopius soon
returned from Syracuse with correct information of the state and
designs of the Vandals. His intelligence determined Belisarius to

1 Caucana, near Camarina, is at least 50 miles (350 or 400 stadia) from
Syracuse (Cluver. Sicilia Antiqua, p. 191).

2 Procopius, Gothic. l. i. c. 3. Tibi tollit hinnitum apta quadrigis equa, in
the Sicilian pastures of Grosphus (Horat. Carm. ii. 16). Acragas ... magnani-
mûm quondam generator equorum (Virg. Æneid. iii. 704). Thero's horses,
whose victories are immortalised by Pindar, were bred in this country.

hasten his operations, and his wise impatience was seconded by the winds. The fleet lost sight of Sicily, passed before the isle of Malta, discovered the capes of Africa, ran along the coast with a strong gale from the north-east, and finally cast anchor at the promontory of Caput Vada, about five day's journey to the south of Carthage.[1]

If Gelimer had been informed of the approach of the enemy, he must have delayed the conquest of Sardinia for the immediate defence of his person and kingdom.[2] A detachment of five thousand soldiers and one hundred and twenty galleys would have joined the remaining forces of the Vandals; and the descendant of Genseric might have surprised and oppressed a fleet of deep-laden transports incapable of action, and of light brigantines that seem only qualified for flight.[3] Belisarius had secretly trembled when he overheard his soldiers in the passage emboldening each other to confess their apprehensions. If they were once on shore, they hoped to maintain the honour of their arms; but if they should be attacked at sea, they did not blush to acknowledge that they wanted courage to contend at the same time with the winds, the waves, and the barbarians.[4] The knowledge of their sentiments decided Belisarius to seize the first opportunity of landing them on the coast of Africa; and he prudently rejected, in a council of war, the proposal of sailing with the fleet and army into the port of Carthage. Three months after their departure

1 The Caput Vada of Procopius (where Justinian afterwards founded a city – De Ædific. l. vi. c. 6) is the promontory of Ammon in Strabo, the Brachodes of Ptolemy, the Capaudia of the moderns, a long narrow slip that runs into the sea (Shaw's Travels, p. 111).

[Procopius suggests that the reason why Belisarius chose Caput Vada as the place for disembarking his troops was doubtless because the province of Tripolitana had revolted against the Vandals (Procop. Bell. Vandal. l. i. c. 10, p. 337). In case of a reverse by land or by sea, Belisarius would be able to retreat to the imperial provinces of Cyrenaïca and Egypt. – O. S.]

2 [Lord Mahon, in his *Life of Belisarius*, suggests that in place of 'Caucana' we should read 'Catana,' the ancient name of Catania. – O. S.]

3 [Lord Mahon, in his *Life of Belisarius*, says that the proposal, rejected by Belisarius, was not to sail into the port of Carthage, but into a haven 40 stadia from Carthage, viz., the present Lake of Tunis. – O. S.]

4 A centurion of Mark Antony expressed, though in a more manly strain, the same dislike to the sea and to naval combats (Plutarch in Antonio, p. 1730, edit. Hen. Steph.).

from Constantinople, the men and horses, the arms and military stores, were safely disembarked; and five soldiers were left as a guard on board each of the ships, which were disposed in the form of a semicircle. The remainder of the troops occupied a camp on the sea-shore, which they fortified, according to ancient discipline, with a ditch and rampart; and the discovery of a source of fresh water, while it allayed the thirst, excited the superstitious confidence of the Romans. The next morning some of the neighbouring gardens were pillaged; and Belisarius, after chastising the offenders, embraced the slight occasion, but the decisive moment, of inculcating the maxims of justice, moderation, and genuine policy. 'When I first accepted the commission of subduing Africa, I depended much less,' said the general, 'on the numbers, or even the bravery of my troops, than upon the friendly disposition of the natives, and their immortal hatred to the Vandals. You alone can deprive me of this hope: if you continue to extort by rapine what might be purchased for a little money, such acts of violence will reconcile these implacable enemies, and unite them in a just and holy league against the invaders of their country.' These exhortations were enforced by a rigid discipline, of which the soldiers themselves soon felt and praised the salutary effects. The inhabitants, instead of deserting their houses or hiding their corn, supplied the Romans with a fair and liberal market, the civil officers of the province continued to exercise their functions in the name of Justinian, and the clergy, from motives of conscience and interest, assiduously laboured to promote the cause of a catholic emperor. The small town of Sullecte,[1] one day's journey from the camp, had the honour of being foremost to open her gates and to resume her ancient allegiance; the larger cities of Leptis and Adrumetum imitated the example of loyalty as soon as Belisarius appeared;

1 Sullecte is perhaps the Turris Hannibalis, an old building, now as large as the Tower of London. The march of Belisarius to Leptis, Adrumetum, etc., is illustrated by the campaign of Cæsar (Hirtius de Bello Africano, with the Analyse of Guichardt), and Shaw's Travels (p. 105–113) in the same country.

[The name of Sullecte is still preserved in that of Salekto, a small town on the coast, situate about eight French leagues from Capaudia (Caput Vada). Leptis is now called Lenta, also Lamba, Adrumetum is Soussa, and Grasse is conjectured to be the town previously called Aphrodisium, now Faradise. – O. S.]

and he advanced without opposition as far as Grasse, a palace of the Vandal kings, at the distance of fifty miles from Carthage. The weary Romans indulged themselves in the refreshment of shady groves, cool fountains, and delicious fruits; and the preference which Procopius allows to these gardens over any that he had seen, either in the East or West, may be ascribed either to the taste or the fatigue of the historian. In three generations prosperity and a warm climate had dissolved the hardy virtue of the Vandals, who insensibly became the most luxurious of mankind. In their villas and gardens, which might deserve the Persian name of *Paradise*,[1] they enjoyed a cool and elegant repose; and, after the daily use of the bath, the barbarians were seated at a table profusely spread with the delicacies of the land and sea. Their silken robes, loosely flowing after the fashion of the Medes, were embroidered with gold; love and hunting were the labours of their life, and their vacant hours were amused by pantomimes, chariot-races, and the music and dances of the theatre.

In a march of ten or twelve days the vigilance of Belisarius was constantly awake and active against his unseen enemies, by whom, in every place and at every hour, he might be suddenly attacked. An officer of confidence and merit, John the Armenian, led the vanguard of three hundred horse, six hundred Massagetæ covered at a certain distance the left flank, and the whole fleet, steering along the coast, seldom lost sight of the army, which moved each day about twelve miles, and lodged in the evening in strong camps or in friendly towns. The near approach of the Romans to Carthage filled the mind of Gelimer with anxiety and terror. He prudently wished to protract the war till his brother, with his veteran troops, should return from the conquest of Sardinia; and he now lamented the rash policy of his ancestors, who, by destroying the fortifications of Africa, had left him only the dangerous resource of risking a battle in the neighbourhood of his capital. The Vandal conquerors, from their original number of fifty thousand, were multiplied, without including their women and children, to one hundred and sixty

---

1 Παράδεισος κάλλιστος ἁπάντων ὧν ἡμεῖς ἴσμεν. The paradises, a name and fashion adopted from Persia, may be represented by the royal garden of Ispahan (Voyage d'Olearius, p. 774). See, in the Greek romances, their most perfect model (Longus, Pastoral. l. iv. p. 99–101; Achilles Tatius, l. i. p. 22, 23.)

thousand fighting men; and such forces, animated with valour
and union, might have crushed at their first landing the feeble
and exhausted bands of the Roman general. But the friends of
the captive king were more inclined to accept the invitations than
to resist the progress of Belisarius; and many a proud barbarian
disguised his aversion to war under the more specious name of
his hatred to the usurper. Yet the authority and promises of
Gelimer collected a formidable army, and his plans were concerted with some degree of military skill. An order was despatched to his brother Ammatas to collect all the forces of
Carthage, and to encounter the van of the Roman army at the
distance of ten miles from the city: his nephew Gibamund with
two thousand horse was destined to attack their left, when the
monarch himself, who silently followed, should charge their rear
in a situation which excluded them from the aid or even the
view of their fleet. But the rashness of Ammatas was fatal to
himself and his country. He anticipated the hour of the attack,
outstripped his tardy followers, and was pierced with a mortal
wound after he had slain with his own hand twelve of his boldest
antagonists. His Vandals fled to Carthage; the highway, almost
ten miles, was strewed with dead bodies; and it seemed incredible
that such multitudes could be slaughtered by the swords of three
hundred Romans. The nephew of Gelimer was defeated, after a
slight combat, by the six hundred Massagetæ: they did not equal
the third part of his numbers, but each Scythian was fired by the
example of his chief, who gloriously exercised the privilege of
his family by riding foremost and alone to shoot the first arrow
against the enemy. In the meanwhile Gelimer himself, ignorant
of the event, and misguided by the windings of the hills, inadvertently passed the Roman army, and reached the scene of action where Ammatas had fallen. He wept the fate of his brother
and of Carthage, charged with irresistible fury the advancing
squadrons, and might have pursued, and perhaps decided the
victory, if he had not wasted those inestimable moments in the
discharge of a vain though pious duty to the dead. While his spirit
was broken by this mournful office, he heard the trumpet of
Belisarius, who, leaving Antonina and his infantry in the camp,
pressed forwards with his guards and the remainder of the cavalry to rally his flying troops, and to restore the fortune of the

day. Much room could not be found in this disorderly battle for
the talents of a general; but the king fled before the hero, and the
Vandals, accustomed only to a Moorish enemy, were incapable
of withstanding the arms and discipline of the Romans. Gelimer
retired with hasty steps towards the desert of Numidia; but he
had soon the consolation of learning that his private orders for
the execution of Hilderic and his captive friends had been faithfully obeyed. The tyrant's revenge was useful only to his enemies.
The death of a lawful prince excited the compassion of his
people; his life might have perplexed the victorious Romans; and
the lieutenant of Justinian, by a crime of which he was innocent,
was relieved from the painful alternative of forfeiting his honour
or relinquishing his conquests.

As soon as the tumult had subsided, the several parts of the
army informed each other of the accidents of the day; and Belisarius pitched his camp on the field of victory, to which the tenth
mile-stone from Carthage had applied the Latin appellation of
Decimus. From a wise suspicion of the stratagems and resources
of the Vandals, he marched the next day in order of battle, halted
in the evening before the gates of Carthage, and allowed a night
of repose, that he might not in darkness and disorder expose the
city to the licence of the soldiers, or the soldiers themselves to
the secret ambush of the city. But as the fears of Belisarius were
the result of calm and intrepid reason, he was soon satisfied that
he might confide, without danger, in the peaceful and friendly
aspect of the capital. Carthage blazed, with innumerable torches,
the signals of the public joy; the chain was removed that guarded
the entrance of the port, the gates were thrown open, and the
people with acclamations of gratitude hailed and invited their
Roman deliverers. The defeat of the Vandals and the freedom
of Africa were announced to the city on the eve of St. Cyprian,
when the churches were already adorned and illuminated for the
festival of the martyr, whom three centuries of superstition had
almost raised to a local deity. The Arians, conscious that their
reign had expired, resigned the temple to the catholics, who
rescued their saint from profane hands, performed the holy rites,
and loudly proclaimed the creed of Athanasius and Justinian.
One awful hour reversed the fortunes of the contending parties.
The suppliant Vandals, who had so lately indulged the vices of

conquerors, sought an humble refuge in the sanctuary of the church; while the merchants of the East were delivered from the deepest dungeon of the palace by their affrighted keeper, who implored the protection of his captives, and showed them, through an aperture in the wall, the sails of the Roman fleet. After their separation from the army, the naval commanders had proceeded with slow caution along the coast till they reached the Hermæan promontory, and obtained the first intelligence of the victory of Belisarius. Faithful to his instructions, they would have cast anchor about twenty miles from Carthage, if the more skilful seamen had not represented the perils of the shore and the signs of an impending tempest. Still ignorant of the revolution, they declined, however, the rash attempt of forcing the chain of the port; and the adjacent harbour and suburb of Mandracium were insulted only by the rapine of a private officer who disobeyed and deserted his leaders. But the imperial fleet, advancing with a fair wind, steered through the narrow entrance of the Goletta, and occupied in the deep and capacious lake of Tunis a secure station about five miles from the capital.[1] No sooner was Belisarius informed of their arrival than he despatched orders that the greatest part of the mariners should be immediately landed, to join the triumph, and to swell the apparent numbers of the Romans. Before he allowed them to enter the gates of Carthage, he exhorted them, in a discourse worthy of himself and the occasion, not to disgrace the glory of their arms; and to remember that the Vandals had been the tyrants, but that *they* were the deliverers, of the Africans, who must now be respected as the voluntary and affectionate subjects of their common sovereign. The Romans marched through the streets in close ranks, prepared for battle if an enemy had appeared: the strict order maintained by the general imprinted on their minds the duty of obedience; and in an age in which custom and impunity almost

1 The neighbourhood of Carthage, the sea, the land, and the rivers, are changed almost as much as the works of man. The isthmus, or neck, of the city is now confounded with the continent; the harbour is a dry plain; and the lake, or stagnum, no more than a morass, with six or seven feet of water in the mid-channel. See D'Anville (Géographie Ancienne, tom. iii. p. 82), Shaw (Travels, p. 77–84), Marmol (Description de l'Afrique, tom. ii. p. 465), and Thuanus (lviii. 12. tom. iii. p. 334).

sanctified the abuse of conquest, the genius of one man repressed the passions of a victorious army. The voice of menace
and complaint was silent; the trade of Carthage was not interrupted; while Africa changed her master and her government,
the shops continued open and busy; and the soldiers, after sufficient guards had been posted, modestly departed to the houses
which were allotted for their reception. Belisarius fixed his
residence in the palace, seated himself on the throne of Genseric,
accepted and distributed the barbaric spoil, granted their lives to
the suppliant Vandals, and laboured to repair the damage which
the suburb of Mandracium had sustained in the preceding night.
At supper he entertained his principal officers with the form and
magnificence of a royal banquet.[1] The victor was respectfully
served by the captive officers of the household; and in the moments of festivity, when the impartial spectators applauded the
fortune and merit of Belisarius, his envious flatterers secretly
shed their venom on every word and gesture which might alarm
the suspicions of a jealous monarch. One day was given to these
pompous scenes, which may not be despised as useless if they
attracted the popular veneration; but the active mind of Belisarius, which in the pride of victory could suppose a defeat, had
already resolved that the Roman empire in Africa should not
depend on the chance of arms or the favour of the people. The
fortifications of Carthage had alone been exempted from the
general proscription; but in the reign of ninety-five years they
were suffered to decay by the thoughtless and indolent Vandals.
A wiser conqueror restored, with incredible despatch, the walls
and ditches of the city. His liberality encouraged the workmen;
the soldiers, the mariners, and the citizens vied with each other
in the salutary labour; and Gelimer, who had feared to trust his
person in an open town, beheld with astonishment and despair
the rising strength of an impregnable fortress.

That unfortunate monarch, after the loss of his capital, applied himself to collect the remains of an army scattered, rather
than destroyed, by the preceding battle, and the hopes of pillage

1 From Delphi, the name of Delphicum was given, both in Greek and Latin,
to a tripod; and, by an easy analogy, the same appellation was extended at
Rome, Constantinople, and Carthage to the royal banqueting-room. (Procopius.
Vandal. l. i. c. 21. Ducange, Gloss. Græc. p. 277. Δέλφικον, ad Alexiad. 412.)

attracted some Moorish bands to the standard of Gelimer. He encamped in the fields of Bulla, four days' journey from Carthage; insulted the capital, which he deprived of the use of an aqueduct; proposed a high reward for the head of every Roman; affected to spare the persons and property of his African subjects; and secretly negotiated with the Arian sectaries and the confederate Huns. Under these circumstances the conquest of Sardinia served only to aggravate his distress: he reflected, with the deepest anguish, that he had wasted in that useless enterprise five thousand of his bravest troops, and he read, with grief and shame, the victorious letters of his brother Zano, who expressed a sanguine confidence that the king, after the example of their ancestors, had already chastised the rashness of the Roman invader. 'Alas! my brother,' replied Gelimer, 'Heaven has declared against our unhappy nation. While you have subdued Sardinia, we have lost Africa. No sooner did Belisarius appear with a handful of soldiers, than courage and prosperity deserted the cause of the Vandals. Your nephew Gibamund, your brother Ammatas, have been betrayed to death by the cowardice of their followers. Our horses, our ships, Carthage itself, and all Africa, are in the power of the enemy. Yet the Vandals still prefer an ignominious repose, at the expense of their wives and children, their wealth and liberty. Nothing now remains except the field of Bulla, and the hope of your valour. Abandon Sardinia; fly to our relief; restore our empire, or perish by our side.' On the receipt of this epistle Zano imparted his grief to the principal Vandals, but the intelligence was prudently concealed from the natives of the island. The troops embarked in one hundred and twenty galleys at the port of Cagliari, cast anchor the third day on the confines of Mauritania, and hastily pursued their march to join the royal standard in the camp of Bulla. Mournful was the interview: the two brothers embraced; they wept in silence; no questions were asked of the Sardinian victory; no inquiries were made of the African misfortunes: they saw before their eyes the whole extent of their calamities, and the absence of their wives and children afforded a melancholy proof that either death or captivity had been their lot. The languid spirit of the Vandals was at length awakened and united by the entreaties of their king, the example of Zano, and the instant danger which threatened their monarchy and religion. The military strength of the nation advanced to battle, and such was the rapid increase, that, before their army reached Tricameron, about twenty miles from Carthage, they might boast, perhaps with some exaggeration, that they surpassed, in a tenfold proportion, the diminutive powers of the Romans. But these powers were under the command of Belisarius, and, as he was conscious of their superior merit, he permitted the barbarians to surprise him at an unseasonable hour. The Romans were instantly under arms; a rivulet covered their front; the cavalry formed the first line, which Belisarius supported in the centre at the head of five hundred guards; the infantry, at some distance, was posted in the second line; and the vigilance of the general watched the separate station and ambiguous faith of the Massagetæ, who secretly reserved their aid for the conquerors. The historian has inserted, and the reader may easily supply, the speeches[1] of the commanders, who, by arguments the most apposite to their situation, inculcated the importance of victory and the contempt of life. Zano, with the troops which had followed him to the conquest of Sardinia, was placed in the centre, and the throne of Genseric might have stood, if the multitude of Vandals had imitated their intrepid resolution. Casting away their lances and missile weapons, they drew their swords and expected the charge; the Roman cavalry thrice passed the rivulet, they were thrice repulsed, and the conflict was firmly maintained till Zano fell and the standard of Belisarius was displayed. Gelimer retreated to his camp, the Huns joined the pursuit, and the victors despoiled the bodies of the slain. Yet no more than fifty Romans and eight hundred Vandals were found on the field of battle; so inconsiderable was the carnage of a day which extinguished a nation and transferred the empire of Africa. In the evening Belisarius led his infantry to the attack of the camp, and the pusillanimous flight of Gelimer exposed the vanity of his recent declarations, that to the vanquished death was a relief, life a burden, and infamy the only object of terror. His departure was secret, but, as soon as the Vandals discovered that their king had deserted them, they hastily

---

1 These orations always express the sense of the times, and sometimes of the actors. I have condensed that sense, and thrown away declamation.

dispersed, anxious only for their personal safety, and careless of every object that is dear or valuable to mankind. The Romans entered the camp without resistance, and the wildest scenes of disorder were veiled in the darkness and confusion of the night. Every barbarian who met their swords was inhumanly massacred: their widows and daughters, as rich heirs or beautiful concubines, were embraced by the licentious soldiers; and avarice itself was almost satiated with the treasures of gold and silver, the accumulated fruits of conquest or economy in a long period of prosperity and peace. In this frantic search the troops, even of Belisarius, forgot their caution and respect. Intoxicated with lust and rapine, they explored, in small parties or alone, the adjacent fields, the woods, the rocks, and the caverns that might possibly conceal any desirable prize; laden with booty, they deserted their ranks, and wandered, without a guide, on the high road to Carthage, and, if the flying enemies had dared to return, very few of the conquerors would have escaped. Deeply sensible of the disgrace and danger, Belisarius passed an apprehensive night on the field of victory; at the dawn of day he planted his standard on a hill, recalled his guards and veterans, and gradually restored the modesty and obedience of the camp. It was equally the concern of the Roman general to subdue the hostile, and to save the prostrate, barbarian; and the suppliant Vandals, who could be found only in churches, were protected by his authority, disarmed, and separately confined, that they might neither disturb the public peace nor become the victims of popular revenge. After despatching a light detachment to tread the footsteps of Gelimer, he advanced, with his whole army, about ten days' march, as far as Hippo Regius, which no longer possessed the relics of St. Augustin.[1] The season, and the certain

---

1 The relics of St. Augustin were carried by the African bishops to their Sardinian exile (A.D. 500); and it was believed, in the eighth century, that Liutprand, king of the Lombards, transported them (A.D. 721) from Sardinia to Pavia. In the year 1695 the Augustin friars of that city *found* a brick arch, marble coffin, silver case, silk wrapper, bones, blood, etc., and perhaps an inscription of Agostino in Gothic letters. But this useful discovery has been disputed by reason and jealousy. (Baronius, Annal. A.D. 725, No. 2–9. Tillemont, Mém. Ecclés. tom. xiii. p. 944. Montfaucon, Diarium Ital. p. 26–30. Muratori, Antiq. Ital. Medii Ævi. tom. v. dissert. lviii. p. 9, who had composed a separate treatise before the decree of the bishop of Pavia, and pope Benedict XIII.)

intelligence that the Vandal had fled to the inaccessible country of the Moors, determined Belisarius to relinquish the vain pursuit, and to fix his winter quarters at Carthage. From thence he despatched his principal lieutenant to inform the emperor that in the space of three months he had achieved the conquest of Africa.

Belisarius spoke the language of truth. The surviving Vandals yielded, without resistance, their arms and their freedom; the neighbourhood of Carthage submitted to his presence, and the more distant provinces were successively subdued by the report of his victory. Tripoli was confirmed in her voluntary allegiance; Sardinia and Corsica surrendered to an officer who carried instead of a sword the head of the valiant Zano; and the isles of Majorca, Minorca, and Yvica consented to remain an humble appendage of the African kingdom. Cæsarea, a royal city, which in looser geography may be confounded with the modern Algiers, was situate thirty days' march to the westward of Carthage; by land the road was infested by the Moors, but the sea was open, and the Romans were now masters of the sea. An active and discreet tribune sailed as far as the Straits, where he occupied Septem or Ceuta,[1] which rises opposite to Gibraltar on the African coast; that remote place was afterwards adorned and fortified by Justinian, and he seems to have indulged the vain ambition of extending his empire to the Columns of Hercules. He received the messengers of victory at the time when he was preparing to publish the Pandects of the Roman law, and the devout or jealous emperor celebrated the divine goodness, and confessed in silence the merit of his successful general.[2] Impatient to abolish the temporal and spiritual tyranny of the Vandals, he proceeded without delay to the full establishment of the catholic church. Her jurisdiction, wealth, and immunities, perhaps the most

---

1 Τὰ τῆς πολιτείας προοίμια, is the expression of Procopius (de Ædific. l. vi. c. 7). Ceuta, which has been defaced by the Portuguese, flourished in nobles and palaces, in agriculture and manufactures, under the more prosperous reign of the Arabs (l'Afrique de Marmol, tom. ii. p. 236).

2 See the second and third preambles to the Digest, or Pandects, promulgated A.D. 533, December 16. To the titles of *Vandalicus* and *Africanus*, Justinian, or rather Belisarius, had acquired a just claim; *Gothicus* was premature, and *Francicus* false, and offensive to a great nation.

essential part of episcopal religion, were restored and amplified
with a liberal hand; the Arian worship was suppressed, the Donatist meetings were proscribed,[1] and the synod of Carthage, by
the voice of two hundred and seventeen bishops,[2] applauded the
just measure of pious retaliation. On such an occasion it may
not be presumed that many orthodox prelates were absent; but
the comparative smallness of their number, which in ancient
councils had been twice or even thrice multiplied, most clearly
indicates the decay both of the church and state. While Justinian approved himself the defender of the faith, he entertained
an ambitious hope that his victorious lieutenant would speedily
enlarge the narrow limits of his dominion to the space which
they occupied before the invasion of the Moors and Vandals;
and Belisarius was instructed to establish five *dukes* or commanders in the convenient stations of Tripoli, Leptis, Cirta, Cæsarea,
and Sardinia, and to compute the military force of *palatines* or
borderers that might be sufficient for the defence of Africa. The
kingdom of the Vandals was not unworthy of the presence of a
Prætorian præfect; and four consulars, three presidents, were
appointed to administer the seven provinces under his civil jurisdiction. The number of their subordinate officers, clerks, messengers, or assistants, was minutely expressed: three hundred and
ninety-six for the præfect himself, fifty for each of his viceger-
ents; and the rigid definition of their fees and salaries was
more effectual to confirm the right than to prevent the abuse.
These magistrates might be oppressive, but they were not idle,
and the subtle questions of justice and revenue were infinitely
propagated under the new government, which professed to revive the freedom and equity of the Roman republic. The conqueror was solicitous to extract a prompt and plentiful supply
from his African subjects, and he allowed them to claim, even
in the third degree and from the collateral line, the houses and
lands of which their families had been unjustly despoiled by

1 See the original acts in Baronius (A.D. 535, No. 21–54). The emperor
applauds his own clemency to the heretics, cum sufficiat eis vivere.

2 Dupin (Geograph. Sacra Africana, p. lix. ad Optat. Milev.) observes and
bewails this episcopal decay. In the more prosperous age of the church, he had
noticed 690 bishoprics; but however minute were the dioceses, it is not probable
that they all existed at the same time.

the Vandals. After the departure of Belisarius, who acted by a
high and special commission, no ordinary provision was made
for a master-general of the forces; but the office of Prætorian
præfect was intrusted to a soldier; the civil and military powers
were united, according to the practice of Justinian, in the chief
governor; and the representative of the emperor in Africa, as
well as in Italy, was soon distinguished by the appellation of
Exarch.[1]

Yet the conquest of Africa was imperfect till her former
sovereign was delivered, either alive or dead, into the hands of
the Romans. Doubtful of the event, Gelimer had given secret
orders that a part of his treasure should be transported to Spain,
where he hoped to find a secure refuge at the court of the king
of the Visigoths. But these intentions were disappointed by accident, treachery, and the indefatigable pursuit of his enemies,
who intercepted his flight from the sea-shore, and chased the
unfortunate monarch, with some faithful followers, to the inaccessible mountain of Papua,[2] in the inland country of Numidia.
He was immediately besieged by Pharas, an officer whose truth
and sobriety were the more applauded, as such qualities could
seldom be found among the Heruli, the most corrupt of the
barbarian tribes. To his vigilance Belisarius had intrusted this
important charge; and, after a bold attempt to scale the mountain, in which he lost an hundred and ten soldiers, Pharas expected,
during a winter siege, the operation of distress and famine on
the mind of the Vandal king. From the softest habits of pleasure,
from the unbounded command of industry and wealth, he was
reduced to share the poverty of the Moors,[3] supportable only to
themselves by their ignorance of a happier condition. In their
rude hovels of mud and hurdles, which confined the smoke and

1 The African laws of Justinian are illustrated by his German biographer
(Cod. l. i. tit. 27. Novell. 36, 37, 131. Vit. Justinian. p. 349–377).

2 Mount Papua is placed by D'Anville (tom. iii. p. 92, and Tabul. Imp.
Rom. Occident.) near Hippo Regius and the sea; yet this situation ill agrees with
the long pursuit beyond Hippo, and the words of Procopius (l. ii. c. 4 [tom. i.
p. 427, ed. Bonn]), ἐν τοῖς Νουμιδίας ἐσχάτοις.

3 Shaw (Travels, p. 220) most accurately represents the manners of the
Bedoweens and Kabyles, the last of whom, by their language, are the remnant
of the Moors; yet how changed – how civilised are these modern savages! –
provisions are plenty among them, and bread is common.

excluded the light, they promiscuously slept on the ground, perhaps on a sheepskin, with their wives, their children, and their
cattle. Sordid and scanty were their garments; the use of bread
and wine was unknown, and their oaten or barley cakes, imperfectly baked in the ashes, were devoured almost in a crude state
by the hungry savages. The health of Gelimer must have sunk
under these strange and unwonted hardships, from whatsoever
cause they had been endured; but his actual misery was embittered by the recollection of past greatness, the daily insolence of
his protectors, and the just apprehension that the light and venal
Moors might be tempted to betray the rights of hospitality. The
knowledge of his situation dictated the humane and friendly
epistle of Pharas. 'Like yourself,' said the chief of the Heruli, 'I
am an illiterate barbarian, but I speak the language of plain sense
and an honest heart. Why will you persist in hopeless obstinacy?
Why will you ruin yourself, your family, and nation? The love of
freedom and abhorrence of slavery? Alas! my dearest Gelimer,
are you not already the worst of slaves, the slave of the vile
nation of the Moors? Would it not be preferable to sustain at
Constantinople a life of poverty and servitude, rather than to
reign the undoubted monarch of the mountain of Papua? Do
you think it a disgrace to be the subject of Justinian? Belisarius
is his subject, and we ourselves, whose birth is not inferior to
your own, are not ashamed of our obedience to the Roman
emperor. That generous prince will grant you a rich inheritance
of lands, a place in the senate, and the dignity of patrician: such
are his gracious intentions, and you may depend with full assurance on the word of Belisarius. So long as Heaven has condemned us to suffer, patience is a virtue; but, if we reject the
proffered deliverance, it degenerates into blind and stupid despair.' 'I am not insensible,' replied the king of the Vandals, 'how
kind and rational is your advice. But I cannot persuade myself
to become the slave of an unjust enemy, who has deserved my
implacable hatred. *Him* I had never injured either by word or
deed; yet he has sent against me, I know not from whence, a
certain Belisarius, who has cast me headlong from the throne
into this abyss of misery. Justinian is a man; he is a prince; does
he not dread for himself a similar reverse of fortune? I can write
no more; my grief oppresses me. Send me, I beseech you, my

dear Pharas, send me a lyre,[1] a sponge, and a loaf of bread.' From
the Vandal messenger, Pharas was informed of the motives of
this singular request. It was long since the king of Africa had
tasted bread, a defluxion had fallen on his eyes, the effect of
fatigue or incessant weeping, and he wished to solace the melancholy hours by singing to the lyre the sad story of his own
misfortunes. The humanity of Pharas was moved: he sent the
three extraordinary gifts; but even his humanity prompted him
to redouble the vigilance of his guard, that he might sooner
compel his prisoner to embrace a resolution advantageous to the
Romans, but salutary to himself. The obstinacy of Gelimer at
length yielded to reason and necessity; the solemn assurances of
safety and honourable treatment were ratified in the emperor's
name by the ambassador of Belisarius, and the king of the Vandals descended from the mountain. The first public interview
was in one of the suburbs of Carthage; and when the royal
captive accosted his conqueror, he burst into a fit of laughter.
The crowd might naturally believe that extreme grief had deprived Gelimer of his senses; but in this mournful state unseasonable mirth insinuated to more intelligent observers that the
vain and transitory scenes of human greatness are unworthy of
a serious thought.[2]

Their contempt was soon justified by a new example of a
vulgar truth – that flattery adheres to power, and envy to superior merit. The chiefs of the Roman army presumed to think
themselves the rivals of an hero. Their private despatches maliciously affirmed that the conqueror of Africa, strong in his reputation and the public love, conspired to seat himself on the throne
of the Vandals. Justinian listened with too patient an ear; and
his silence was the result of jealousy rather than of confidence.

---

1 By Procopius it is styled a *lyre*; perhaps *harp* would have been more
national. The instruments of music are thus distinguished by Venantius Fortunatus: –

> Romanusque *lyrâ* tibi plaudat, Barbarus *harpâ*.

2 Herodotus elegantly describes the strange effects of grief in another royal
captive, Psammetichus [Psammenitus] of Egypt, who wept at the lesser and
was silent at the greatest of his calamities (l. iii. c. 14). In the interview of Paulus
Æmilius and Perses, Belisarius might study his part: but it is probable that he
never read either Livy or Plutarch; and it is certain that his generosity did not
need a tutor.

An honourable alternative, of remaining in the province or of returning to the capital, was indeed submitted to the discretion of Belisarius; but he wisely concluded, from intercepted letters and the knowledge of his sovereign's temper, that he must either resign his head, erect his standard, or confound his enemies by his presence and submission. Innocence and courage decided his choice: his guards, captives, and treasures were diligently embarked; and so prosperous was the navigation, that his arrival at Constantinople preceded any certain account of his departure from the port of Carthage. Such unsuspecting loyalty removed the apprehensions of Justinian: envy was silenced and inflamed by the public gratitude; and the third Africanus obtained the honours of a triumph, a ceremony which the city of Constantine had never seen, and which ancient Rome, since the reign of Tiberius, had reserved for the *auspicious* arms of the Cæsars.[1] From the palace of Belisarius the procession was conducted through the principal streets to the hippodrome; and this memorable day seemed to avenge the injuries of Genseric and to expiate the shame of the Romans. The wealth of nations was displayed, the trophies of martial or effeminate luxury; rich armour, golden thrones, and the chariots of state which had been used by the Vandal queen; the massy furniture of the royal banquet, the splendour of precious stones, the elegant forms of statues and vases, the more substantial treasure of gold, and the holy vessels of the Jewish temple, which, after their long peregrination, were respectfully deposited in the Christian church of Jerusalem. A long train of the noblest Vandals reluctantly exposed their lofty stature and manly countenance. Gelimer slowly advanced: he was clad in a purple robe, and still maintained the majesty of a king. Not a tear escaped from his eyes, not a sigh was heard; but his pride or piety derived some secret consolation from the words of Solomon,[2] which he repeatedly pronounced,

1 After the title of *imperator* had lost the old military sense, and the Roman *auspices* were abolished by Christianity (see La Bléterie, Mém. de l'Académie, tom. xxi. p. 302–332), a triumph might be given with less inconsistency to a private general.

2 If the Ecclesiastes be truly a work of Solomon, and not, like Prior's poem, a pious and moral composition of more recent times, in his name, and on the subject of his repentance. The latter is the opinion of the learned and free-

VANITY! VANITY! ALL IS VANITY! Instead of ascending a triumphal car drawn by four horses or elephants, the modest conqueror marched on foot at the head of his brave companions: his prudence might decline an honour too conspicuous for a subject; and his magnanimity might justly disdain what had been so often sullied by the vilest of tyrants. The glorious procession entered the gate of the hippodrome; was saluted by the acclamations of the senate and people; and halted before the throne where Justinian and Theodora were seated to receive the homage of the captive monarch and the victorious hero. They both performed the customary adoration; and falling prostrate on the ground, respectfully touched the footstool of a prince who had not unsheathed his sword, and of a prostitute who had danced on the theatre: some gentle violence was used to bend the stubborn spirit of the grandson of Genseric; and however trained to servitude, the genius of Belisarius must have secretly rebelled. He was immediately declared consul for the ensuing year, and the day of his inauguration resembled the pomp of a second triumph: his curule chair was borne aloft on the shoulders of captive Vandals; and the spoils of war, gold cups, and rich girdles, were profusely scattered among the populace.

But the purest reward of Belisarius was in the faithful execution of a treaty for which his honour had been pledged to the king of the Vandals. The religious scruples of Gelimer, who adhered to the Arian heresy, were incompatible with the dignity of senator or patrician: but he received from the emperor an ample estate in the province of Galatia, where the abdicated monarch retired, with his family and friends, to a life of peace, of affluence, and perhaps of content.[1] The daughters of Hilderic were entertained with the respectful tenderness due to their age and misfortune; and Justinian and Theodora accepted the honour of educating and enriching the female descendants of the

spirited Grotius (Opp. Theolog. tom. i. p. 258); and indeed the Ecclesiastes and Proverbs display a larger compass of thought and experience than seem to belong either to a Jew or a king.

1 In the Bélisaire of Marmontel the king and the conqueror of Africa meet, sup, and converse, without recollecting each other. It is surely a fault of that romance, that not only the hero, but all to whom he had been so conspicuously known, appear to have lost their eyes or their memory.

great Theodosius. The bravest of the Vandal youth were distributed into five squadrons of cavalry, which adopted the name
of their benefactor, and supported in the Persian wars the glory of
their ancestors. But these rare exceptions, the reward of birth or
valour, are insufficient to explain the fate of a nation whose
numbers, before a short and bloodless war, amounted to more
than six hundred thousand persons. After the exile of their king
and nobles, the servile crowd might purchase their safety by
adjuring their character, religion, and language; and their degenerate posterity would be insensibly mingled with the common
herd of African subjects. Yet even in the present age, and in the
heart of the Moorish tribes, a curious traveller has discovered
the white complexion and long flaxen hair of a northern race;[1]
and it was formerly believed that the boldest of the Vandals fled
beyond the power, or even the knowledge, of the Romans, to
enjoy their solitary freedom on the shores of the Atlantic ocean.[2]
Africa had been their empire, it became their prison; nor could
they entertain a hope, or even a wish, of returning to the banks
of the Elbe, where their brethren, of a spirit less adventurous,
still wandered in their native forests. It was impossible for cow-
ards to surmount the barriers of unknown seas and hostile barbarians; it was impossible for brave men to expose their
nakedness and defeat before the eyes of their countrymen, to
describe the kingdoms which they had lost, and to claim a share
of the humble inheritance which, in a happier hour, they had
almost unanimously renounced.[3] In the country between the
Elbe and the Oder several populous villages of Lusatia are inhabited by the Vandals: they still preserve their language, their
customs, and the purity of their blood; support, with some

1 Shaw, p. 59. Yet since Procopius (l. ii. c. 13 [tom. i. p. 466, ed. Bonn])
speaks of a people of Mount Atlas, as already distinguished by white bodies
and yellow hair, the phenomenon (which is likewise visible in the Andes of
Peru, Buffon, tom. iii. p. 504) may naturally be ascribed to the elevation of the
ground and the temperature of the air.

2 The geographer of Ravenna (l. iii. c. xi. p. 129, 130, 131; Paris, 1688)
describes the Mauritania *Gaditana* (opposite to Cadiz), ubi gens Vandalorum, a
Belisario devicta in Africâ, fugit, et nunquam comparuit.

3 A single voice had protested, and Genseric dismissed, without a formal
answer, the Vandals of Germany: but those of Africa derided his prudence, and
affected to despise the poverty of their forests (Procopius, Vandal. l. i. c. 22).

impatience, the Saxon or Prussian yoke; and serve, with secret and voluntary allegiance, the descendant of their ancient kings, who in his garb and present fortune is confounded with the meanest of his vassals.[1] The name and situation of this unhappy people might indicate their descent from one common stock with the conquerors of Africa. But the use of a Sclavonian dialect more clearly represents them as the last remnant of the new colonies who succeeded to the genuine Vandals, already scattered or destroyed in the age of Procopius.[2]

If Belisarius had been tempted to hesitate in his allegiance, he might have urged, even against the emperor himself, the indispensable duty of saving Africa from an enemy more barbarous than the Vandals. The origin of the Moors is involved in darkness: they were ignorant of the use of letters.[3] Their limits cannot be precisely defined; a boundless continent was open to the Libyan shepherds; the change of seasons and pastures regulated their motions; and their rude huts and slender furniture were transported with the same ease as their arms, their families, and their cattle, which consisted of sheep, oxen, and camels.[4] During the vigour of the Roman power they observed a respectful distance from Carthage and the sea-shore; under the feeble reign of the Vandals they invaded the cities of Numidia, occupied the sea-coast from Tangier to Cæsarea, and pitched their

1 From the mouth of the Great Elector (in 1687) Tollius describes the secret royalty and rebellious spirit of the Vandals of Brandenburgh, who could muster five or six thousand soldiers, who had procured some cannon, etc. (Itinerar. Hungar. p. 42, apud Dubos, Hist. de la Monarchie Françoise, tom. i. p. 182, 183). The veracity, not of the elector, but of Tollius himself, may justly be suspected.

2 Procopius (l. i. c. 22 [tom. i. p. 400, ed. Bonn]) was in total darkness – οὔτε μνήμη τις οὔτε ὄνομα ἐς ἐμὲ σώζεται. Under the reign of Dagobert (A.D. 630) the Sclavonian tribes of the Sorbi and Venedi already bordered on Thuringia (Mascou, Hist. of the Germans, xv. 3, 4, 5).

3 Sallust represents the Moors as a remnant of the army of Heracles (de Bell. Jugurth. c. 21 [18]), and Procopius (Vandal. l. ii. c. 10 [tom. ii. p. 450, ed. Bonn]) as the posterity of the Cananæans who fled from the robber Joshua (λῃστής). He quotes two columns, with a Phœnician inscription. I believe in the columns – I doubt the inscription – and I reject the pedigree.

4 Virgil (Georgic. iii. 339) and Pomponius Mela (i. 8) describe the wandering life of the African shepherds, similar to that of the Arabs and Tartars; and Shaw (p. 222) is the best commentator on the poet and the geographer.

camps, with impunity, in the fertile province of Byzacium. The formidable strength and artful conduct of Belisarius secured the neutrality of the Moorish princes, whose vanity aspired to receive in the emperor's name the ensigns of their regal dignity.¹ They were astonished by the rapid event, and trembled in the presence of their conqueror. But his approaching departure soon relieved the apprehensions of a savage and superstitious people; the number of their wives allowed them to disregard the safety of their infant hostages; and when the Roman general hoisted sail in the port of Carthage, he heard the cries and almost beheld the flames of the desolated province. Yet he persisted in his resolution; and leaving only a part of his guards to reinforce the feeble garrisons, he intrusted the command of Africa to the eunuch Solomon,² who proved himself not unworthy to be the successor of Belisarius. In the first invasion some detachments, with two officers of merit, were surprised and intercepted; but Solomon speedily assembled his troops, marched from Carthage into the heart of the country, and in two great battles destroyed sixty thousand of the barbarians. The Moors depended on their multitude, their swiftness, and their inaccessible mountains; and the aspect and smell of their camels are said to have produced some confusion in the Roman cavalry.³ But as soon as they were commanded to dismount, they derided this contemptible obstacle: as soon as the columns ascended the hills, the naked and disorderly crowd was dazzled by glittering arms and regular evolutions; and the menace of their female prophets was repeatedly fulfilled, that the Moors should be discomfited by a *beardless* antagonist. The victorious

1 The customary gifts were a sceptre, a crown or cap, a white cloak, a figured tunic, and shoes, all adorned with gold and silver; nor were these precious metals less acceptable in the shape of coin (Procop. Vandal. l. i. c. 25).

2 See the African government and warfare of Solomon in Procopius (Vandal. l. ii. c. 10, 11, 12, 13, 19, 20). He was recalled and again restored; and his last victory dates in the thirteenth year of Justinian (A.D. 539). An accident in his childhood had rendered him an eunuch (l. i. c. 11): the other Roman generals were amply furnished with beards, πώγωνος ἐμπιπλάμενοι (l. ii. c. 8).

3 This natural antipathy of the horse for the camel is affirmed by the ancients (Xenophon. Cyropæd. l. vi. [c. 2] p. 438; l. vii. [c. 1] p. 483, 492, edit. Hutchinson; Polyæn. Stratagem. vii. 6 [§ 6]; Plin. Hist. Nat. viii. 26; Ælian de Natur. Animal. l. iii. c. 7); but it is disproved by daily experience, and derided by the best judges, the Orientals (Voyage d'Olearius, p. 553).

eunuch advanced thirteen days' journey from Carthage to besiege Mount Aurasius,[1] the citadel, and at the same time the garden, of Numidia. That range of hills, a branch of the great Atlas, contains, within a circumference of one hundred and twenty miles, a rare variety of soil and climate; the intermediate valleys and elevated plains abound with rich pastures, perpetual streams, and fruits of a delicious taste and uncommon magnitude. This fair solitude is decorated with the ruins of Lambesa, a Roman city, once the seat of a legion, and the residence of forty thousand inhabitants. The Ionic temple of Æsculapius is encompassed with Moorish huts; and the cattle now graze in the midst of an amphitheatre, under the shade of Corinthian columns. A sharp perpendicular rock rises above the level of the mountain, where the African princes deposited their wives and treasure; and a proverb is familiar to the Arabs, that the man may eat fire who dares to attack the craggy cliffs and inhospitable natives of Mount Aurasius. This hardy enterprise was twice attempted by the eunuch Solomon: from the first, he retreated with some disgrace; and in the second, his patience and provisions were almost exhausted; and he must again have retired, if he had not yielded to the impetuous courage of his troops, who audaciously scaled, to the astonishment of the Moors, the mountain, the hostile camp, and the summit of the Geminian rock. A citadel was erected to secure this important conquest, and to remind the barbarians of their defeat; and as Solomon pursued his march to the west, the long-lost province of Mauritanian Sitifi was again annexed to the Roman empire. The Moorish war continued several years after the departure of Belisarius; but the laurels which he resigned to a faithful lieutenant may be justly ascribed to his own triumph.

The experience of past faults, which may sometimes correct the mature age of an individual, is seldom profitable to the successive generations of mankind. The nations of antiquity, careless of each other's safety, were separately vanquished and enslaved by the Romans. This awful lesson might have instructed the

---

1 Procopius is the first who describes Mount Aurasius (Vandal. l. ii. c. 13; De Ædific. l. vi. c. 7). He may be compared with Leo Africanus (dell' Africa, parte v. in Ramusio, tom. i. fol. 77, recto), Marmol (tom. ii. p. 430), and Shaw (p. 56–59).

barbarians of the West to oppose, with timely counsels and confederate arms, the unbounded ambition of Justinian. Yet the
same error was repeated, the same consequences were felt, and
the Goths, both of Italy and Spain, insensible of their approaching danger, beheld with indifference, and even with joy, the rapid
downfall of the Vandals. After the failure of the royal line,
Theudes, a valiant and powerful chief, ascended the throne of
Spain, which he had formerly administered in the name of Theodoric and his infant grandson. Under his command the Visigoths besieged the fortress of Ceuta, on the African coast; but,
while they spent the Sabbath-day in peace and devotion, the
pious security of their camp was invaded by a sally from the
town, and the king himself, with some difficulty and danger,
escaped from the hands of a sacrilegious enemy.[1] It was not long
before his pride and resentment were gratified by a suppliant
embassy from the unfortunate Gelimer, who implored, in his
distress, the aid of the Spanish monarch. But instead of sacrificing these unworthy passions to the dictates of generosity and
prudence, Theudes amused the ambassadors till he was secretly
informed of the loss of Carthage, and then dismissed them, with
obscure and contemptuous advice, to seek in their native country
a true knowledge of the state of the Vandals.[2] The long continuance of the Italian war delayed the punishment of the Visigoths, and the eyes of Theudes were closed before they tasted
the fruits of his mistaken policy. After his death the sceptre of
Spain was disputed by a civil war. The weaker candidate solicited
the protection of Justinian, and ambitiously subscribed a treaty
of alliance which deeply wounded the independence and happiness of his country. Several cities, both on the ocean and the
Mediterranean, were ceded to the Roman troops, who afterwards
refused to evacuate those pledges, as it should seem, either of
safety or payment; and as they were fortified by perpetual supplies from Africa, they maintained their impregnable stations for
the mischievous purpose of inflaming the civil and religious

1 Isidor. Chron. p. 722, edit. Grot. Mariana, Hist. Hispan. l. v. c. 8, p. 173.
Yet, according to Isidore, the siege of Ceuta and the death of Theudes hap-
pened, A. Æ. H. 586–A.D. 548; and the place was defended, not by the Vandals,
but by the Romans.
2 Procopius, Vandal. l. i. c. 24.

factions of the barbarians. Seventy years elapsed before this painful thorn could be extirpated from the bosom of the monarchy;
and as long as the emperors retained any share of these remote
and useless possessions, their vanity might number Spain in the
list of their provinces, and the successors of Alaric in the rank
of their vassals.[1]

The error of the Goths who reigned in Italy was less excus-
able than that of their Spanish brethren, and their punishment
was still more immediate and terrible. From a motive of private
revenge, they enabled their most dangerous enemy to destroy
their most valuable ally. A sister of the great Theodoric had been
given in marriage to Thrasimond the African king:[2] on this occasion the fortress of Lilybæum,[3] in Sicily, was resigned to the
Vandals, and the princess Amalafrida was attended by a martial
train of one thousand nobles and five thousand Gothic soldiers,
who signalised their valour in the Moorish wars. Their merit was
over-rated by themselves, and perhaps neglected by the Vandals:
they viewed the country with envy, and the conquerors with
disdain; but their real or fictitious conspiracy was prevented by
a massacre; the Goths were oppressed, and the captivity of Amalafrida was soon followed by her secret and suspicious death.
The eloquent pen of Cassiodorus was employed to reproach the
Vandal court with the cruel violation of every social and public
duty; but the vengeance which he threatened in the name of his
sovereign might be derided with impunity as long as Africa was
protected by the sea, and the Goths were destitute of a navy. In
the blind impotence of grief and indignation they joyfully saluted
the approach of the Romans, entertained the fleet of Belisarius
in the ports of Sicily, and were speedily delighted or alarmed by
the surprising intelligence that their revenge was executed beyond the measure of their hopes, or perhaps of their wishes. To

1 See the original Chronicle of Isidore and the fifth and sixth books of the
History of Spain by Mariana. The Romans were finally expelled by Suintila king
of the Visigoths (A.D. 621–626), after their re-union to the catholic church.

2 See the marriage and fate of Amalafrida in Procopius (Vandal. l. i. c. 8,
9), and in Cassiodorus (Var. ix. 1) the expostulation of her royal brother.
Compare likewise the Chronicle of Victor Tunnunensis.

3 Lilybæum was built by the Carthaginians, Olymp. xcv. 4; and in the first
Punic war a strong situation and excellent harbour rendered that place an
important object to both nations.

their friendship the emperor was indebted for the kingdom of
Africa, and the Goths might reasonably think that they were
entitled to resume the possession of a barren rock, so recently
separated as a nuptial gift from the island of Sicily. They were
soon undeceived by the haughty mandate of Belisarius, which
excited their tardy and unavailing repentance. 'The city and promontory of Lilybæum,' said the Roman general, 'belonged to the
Vandals, and I claim them by the right of conquest. Your submission may deserve the favour of the emperor; your obstinacy
will provoke his displeasure, and must kindle a war that can
terminate only in your utter ruin. If you compel us to take up
arms, we shall contend, not to regain the possession of a single
city, but to deprive you of all the provinces which you unjustly
withhold from their lawful sovereign.' A nation of two hundred
thousand soldiers might have smiled at the vain menace of Justinian and his lieutenant; but a spirit of discord and disaffection
prevailed in Italy, and the Goths supported with reluctance the
indignity of a female reign.[1]

The birth of Amalasontha, the regent and queen of Italy,[2]
united the two most illustrious families of the barbarians. Her
mother, the sister of Clovis, was descended from the long-haired
kings of the *Merovingian* race,[3] and the regal succession of the
Amali was illustrated in the eleventh generation by her father,
the great Theodoric, whose merit might have ennobled a plebeian origin. The sex of his daughter excluded her from the
Gothic throne; but his vigilant tenderness for his family and his
people discovered the last heir of the royal line, whose ancestors
had taken refuge in Spain, and the fortunate Eutharic was suddenly exalted to the rank of a consul and a prince. He enjoyed
only a short time the charms of Amalasontha and the hopes of

1 Compare the different passages of Procopius (Vandal. l. ii. c. 5; Gothic.
l. i. c. 3).

2 For the reign and character of Amalasontha see Procopius (Gothic. l. i.
c. 2, 3, 4, and Anecdot. c. 16, with the Notes of Alemannus), Cassiodorus (Var.
viii. ix. x. and xi. 1), and Jornandes (de Rebus Geticis, c. 59, and De Successione
Regnorum, in Muratori, tom. i. p. 241).

3 The marriage of Theodoric with Audefleda, the sister of Clovis, may be
placed in the year 495, soon after the conquest of Italy (De Buat, Hist. des
Peuples, tom. ix. p. 213). The nuptials of Eutharic and Amalasontha were
celebrated in 515 (Cassiodor. in Chron. p. 453 [tom. i. p. 395, ed. Rotom.]).

the succession; and his widow, after the death of her husband
and father, was left the guardian of her son Athalaric and the
kingdom of Italy. At the age of about twenty-eight years, the
endowments of her mind and person had attained their perfect
maturity. Her beauty, which, in the apprehension of Theodora
herself, might have disputed the conquest of an emperor, was
animated by manly sense, activity, and resolution. Education and
experience had cultivated her talents; her philosophic studies
were exempt from vanity; and, though she expressed herself with
equal elegance and ease in the Greek, the Latin, and the Gothic
tongue, the daughter of Theodoric maintained in her counsels a
discreet and impenetrable silence. By a faithful imitation of the
virtues, she revived the prosperity of his reign; while she strove,
with pious care, to expiate the faults and to obliterate the darker
memory of his declining age. The children of Boethius and Symmachus were restored to their paternal inheritance; her extreme
lenity never consented to inflict any corporal or pecuniary penalties on her Roman subjects; and she generously despised the
clamours of the Goths, who, at the end of forty years, still
considered the people of Italy as their slaves or their enemies.
Her salutary measures were directed by the wisdom and celebrated by the eloquence of Cassiodorus; she solicited and
deserved the friendship of the emperor; and the kingdoms of
Europe respected, both in peace and war, the majesty of the
Gothic throne. But the future happiness of the queen of Italy
depended on the education of her son, who was destined, by his
birth, to support the different and almost incompatible characters of the chief of a barbarian camp and the first magistrate of
a civilised nation. From the age of ten years[1] Athalaric was diligently instructed in the arts and sciences either useful or or-
namental for a Roman prince, and three venerable Goths were
chosen to instil the principles of honour and virtue into the mind
of their young king. But the pupil who is insensible of the benefits must abhor the restraints of education; and the solicitude of
the queen, which affection rendered anxious and severe, offended

---

1 At the death of Theodoric his grandson Athalaric is described by Procopius as a boy about eight years old – ὀκτὼ γεγονὼς ἔτη. Cassiodorus,
with authority and reason, adds two years to his age – infantulum adhuc vix
decennem.

the untractable nature of her son and his subjects. On a solemn festival, when the Goths were assembled in the palace of Ravenna, the royal youth escaped from his mother's apartment, and, with tears of pride and anger, complained of a blow which his stubborn disobedience had provoked her to inflict. The barbarians resented the indignity which had been offered to their king, accused the regent of conspiring against his life and crown, and imperiously demanded that the grandson of Theodoric should be rescued from the dastardly discipline of women and pedants, and educated, like a valiant Goth, in the society of his equals and the glorious ignorance of his ancestors. To this rude clamour, importunately urged as the voice of the nation, Amalasontha was compelled to yield her reason and the dearest wishes of her heart. The king of Italy was abandoned to wine, to women, and to rustic sports; and the indiscreet contempt of the ungrateful youth betrayed the mischievous designs of his favourites and her enemies. Encompassed with domestic foes, she entered into a secret negotiation with the emperor Justinian, obtained the assurance of a friendly reception, and had actually deposited at Dyrrachium, in Epirus, a treasure of forty thousand pounds of gold. Happy would it have been for her fame and safety if she had calmly retired from barbarous faction to the peace and splendour of Constantinople. But the mind of Amalasontha was inflamed by ambition and revenge; and while her ships lay at anchor in the port, she waited for the success of a crime which her passions excused or applauded as an act of justice. Three of the most dangerous malcontents had been separately removed, under the pretence of trust and command, to the frontiers of Italy: they were assassinated by her private emissaries; and the blood of these noble Goths rendered the queen-mother absolute in the court of Ravenna, and justly odious to a free people. But if she had lamented the disorders of her son, she soon wept his irreparable loss; and the death of Athalaric, who, at the age of sixteen, was consumed by premature intemperance, left her destitute of any firm support or legal authority. Instead of submitting to the laws of her country, which held as a fundamental maxim that the succession could never pass from the lance to the distaff, the daughter of Theodoric conceived the impracticable design of sharing, with one of her cousins, the regal title, and of reserving in her own hands the substance of supreme power. He received the proposal with profound respect and affected gratitude; and the eloquent Cassiodorus announced to the senate and the emperor that Amalasontha and Theodatus had ascended the throne of Italy. His birth (for his mother was the sister of Theodoric) might be considered as an imperfect title; and the choice of Amalasontha was more strongly directed by her contempt of his avarice and pusillanimity, which had deprived him of the love of the Italians and the esteem of the barbarians. But Theodatus was exasperated by the contempt which he deserved: her justice had repressed and reproached the oppression which he exercised against his Tuscan neighbours; and the principal Goths, united by common guilt and resentment, conspired to instigate his slow and timid disposition. The letters of congratulation were scarcely despatched before the queen of Italy was imprisoned in a small island of the lake of Bolsena,¹ where, after a short confinement, she was strangled in the bath, by the order or with the connivance of the new king, who instructed his turbulent subjects to shed the blood of their sovereigns.

Justinian beheld with joy the dissensions of the Goths, and the mediation of an ally concealed and promoted the ambitious views of the conqueror. His ambassadors, in their public audience, demanded the fortress of Lilybæum, ten barbarian fugitives, and a just compensation for the pillage of a small town on the Illyrian borders; but they secretly negotiated with Theodatus to betray the province of Tuscany, and tempted Amalasontha to extricate herself from danger and perplexity by a free surrender of the kingdom of Italy. A false and servile epistle was subscribed by the reluctant hand of the captive queen; but the confession of the Roman senators who were sent to Constantinople revealed the truth of her deplorable situation, and Justinian, by the voice of a new ambassador, most powerfully interceded for

---

1 The lake, from the neighbouring towns of Etruria, was styled either Vulsiniensis (now of Bolsena) or Tarquiniensis. It is surrounded with white rocks, and stored with fish and wild-fowl. The younger Pliny (Epist. ii. 96 [95]) celebrates two woody islands that floated on its waters: if a fable, how credulous the ancients! if a fact, how careless the moderns! Yet, since Pliny, the island may have been fixed by new and gradual accessions.

her life and liberty. Yet the secret instructions of the same minister were adapted to serve the cruel jealousy of Theodora, who
dreaded the presence and superior charms of a rival: he
prompted, with artful and ambiguous hints, the execution of a
crime so useful to the Romans,[1] received the intelligence of her
death with grief and indignation, and denounced, in his master's
name, immortal war against the perfidious assassin. In Italy, as
well as in Africa, the guilt of a usurper appeared to justify the
arms of Justinian; but the forces which he prepared were insufficient for the subversion of a mighty kingdom, if their feeble
numbers had not been multiplied by the name, the spirit, and
the conduct of a hero. A chosen troop of guards, who served
on horseback and were armed with lances and bucklers, attended
the person of Belisarius; his cavalry was composed of two hundred Huns, three hundred Moors, and four thousand *confederates*,
and the infantry consisted only of three thousand Isaurians.
Steering the same course as in his former expedition, the Roman
consul cast anchor before Catana, in Sicily, to survey the strength
of the island, and to decide whether he should attempt the conquest or peaceably pursue his voyage for the African coast. He
found a fruitful land and a friendly people. Notwithstanding the
decay of agriculture, Sicily still supplied the granaries of Rome;
the farmers were graciously exempted from the oppression of
military quarters; and the Goths, who trusted the defence of the
island to the inhabitants, had some reason to complain that their
confidence was ungratefully betrayed. Instead of soliciting and
expecting the aid of the king of Italy, they yielded to the first
summons a cheerful obedience; and this province, the first fruits
of the Punic wars, was again, after a long separation, united to
the Roman empire.[2] The Gothic garrison of Palermo, which
alone attempted to resist, was reduced, after a short siege, by a

---

1 Yet Procopius discredits his own evidence (Anecdot. c. 16), by confessing
that in his public history he had not spoken the truth. See the Epistles from
queen Gundelina to the empress Theodora (Var. x. 20, 21, 23, and observe a
suspicious word, de illâ personâ, etc.), with the elaborate Commentary of Buat
(tom. x. p. 177–185).

2 For the conquest of Sicily compare the narrative of Procopius with the
complaints of Totila (Gothic. l. i. c. 5; l. iii. c. 16). The Gothic queen had lately
relieved that thankless island (Var. ix. 10, 11).

singular stratagem. Belisarius introduced his ships into the deepest recess of the harbour; their boats were laboriously hoisted with ropes and pulleys to the top-mast head, and he filled them with archers, who, from that superior station, commanded the ramparts of the city. After this easy though successful campaign, the conqueror entered Syracuse in triumph, at the head of his victorious bands, distributing gold medals to the people, on the day which so gloriously terminated the year of the consulship. He passed the winter season in the palace of ancient kings, amidst the ruins of a Grecian colony which once extended to a circumference of two-and-twenty miles;[1] but in the spring, about the festival of Easter, the prosecution of his designs was interrupted by a dangerous revolt of the African forces. Carthage was saved by the presence of Belisarius, who suddenly landed with a thousand guards. Two thousand soldiers of doubtful faith returned to the standard of their old commander, and he marched, without hesitation, above fifty miles, to seek an enemy whom he affected to pity and despise. Eight thousand rebels trembled at his approach; they were routed at the first onset by the dexterity of their master, and this ignoble victory would have restored the peace of Africa, if the conqueror had not been hastily recalled to Sicily to appease a sedition which was kindled during his absence in his own camp.[2] Disorder and disobedience were the common malady of the times: the genius to command and the virtue to obey resided only in the mind of Belisarius.

Although Theodatus descended from a race of heroes, he was ignorant of the art and averse to the dangers of war. Although he had studied the writings of Plato and Tully, philosophy was incapable of purifying his mind from the basest passions, avarice and fear. He had purchased a sceptre by ingratitude and murder: at the first menace of an enemy he degraded his own majesty,

1 The ancient magnitude and splendour of the five quarters of Syracuse are delineated by Cicero (in Varrem, actio ii. l. iv. c. 52, 53), Strabo (l. vi. p. 415 [p. 270, ed. Casaub.]), and D'Orville Sicula (tom. ii. p. 174–202). The new city, restored by Augustus, shrunk towards the island.

2 Procopius (Vandal. l. ii. c. 14, 15) so clearly relates the return of Belisarius into Sicily (p. 146, edit. Hœschelii [tom. i. p. 481, ed. Bonn]), that I am astonished at the strange misapprehension and reproaches of a learned critic (Œuvres de la Mothe le Vayer, tom. viii. p. 162, 163).

and that of a nation which already disdained their unworthy
sovereign. Astonished by the recent example of Gelimer, he saw
himself dragged in chains through the streets of Constantinople:
the terrors which Belisarius inspired were heightened by the eloquence of Peter, the Byzantine ambassador; and that bold and
subtle advocate persuaded him to sign a treaty too ignominious
to become the foundation of a lasting peace. It was stipulated
that in the acclamations of the Roman people the name of the
emperor should be always proclaimed before that of the Gothic
king; and that, as often as the statue of Theodatus was erected
in brass or marble, the divine image of Justinian should be placed
on its right hand. Instead of conferring, the king of Italy was
reduced to solicit, the honours of the senate; and the consent of
the emperor was made indispensable before he could execute,
against a priest or senator, the sentence either of death or confiscation. The feeble monarch resigned the possession of Sicily;
offered, as the annual mark of his dependence, a crown of gold
of the weight of three hundred pounds; and promised to supply,
at the requisition of his sovereign, three thousand Gothic auxiliaries for the service of the empire. Satisfied with these extraordinary concessions, the successful agent of Justinian hastened his
journey to Constantinople; but no sooner had he reached the
Alban villa¹ than he was recalled by the anxiety of Theodatus;
and the dialogue which passed between the king and the ambassador deserves to be represented in its original simplicity. 'Are
you of opinion that the emperor will ratify this treaty? *Perhaps.*
If he refuses, what consequence will ensue? *War.* Will such a war
be just or reasonable? *Most assuredly: every one should act according to
his character.* What is your meaning? *You are a philosopher – Justinian
is emperor of the Romans: it would ill become the disciple of Plato to shed
the blood of thousands in his private quarrel: the successor of Augustus
should vindicate his rights, and recover by arms the ancient provinces of his
empire.*' This reasoning might not convince, but it was sufficient
to alarm and subdue the weakness of Theodatus; and he soon
descended to his last offer, that for the poor equivalent of a

1 The ancient Alba was ruined in the first age of Rome. On the same spot,
or at least in the neighbourhood, successively arose, 1. The villa of Pompey, etc.
2. A camp of the Prætorian cohorts. 3. The modern episcopal city of Albanum
of Albano (Procop. Goth. l. ii. c. 4. Cluver. Ital. Antiq. tom. ii. p. 914).

pension of forty-eight thousand pounds sterling he would resign
the kingdom of the Goths and Italians, and spend the remainder
of his days in the innocent pleasures of philosophy and agriculture. Both treaties were intrusted to the hands of the ambassador, on the frail security of an oath not to produce the second
till the first had been positively rejected. The event may be easily
foreseen: Justinian required and accepted the abdication of the
Gothic king. His indefatigable agent returned from Constantinople to Ravenna with ample instructions, and a fair epistle,
which praised the wisdom and generosity of the royal philosopher, granted his pension, with the assurance of such honours
as a subject and a catholic might enjoy, and wisely referred the
final execution of the treaty to the presence and authority of
Belisarius. But in the interval of suspense two Roman generals,
who had entered the province of Dalmatia, were defeated and
slain by the Gothic troops. From blind and abject despair, Theodatus capriciously rose to groundless and fatal presumption,[1]
and dared to receive, with menace and contempt, the ambassador of Justinian, who claimed his promise, solicited the allegiance
of his subjects, and boldly asserted the inviolable privilege of his
own character. The march of Belisarius dispelled this visionary
pride; and as the first campaign[2] was employed in the reduction
of Sicily, the invasion of Italy is applied by Procopius to the
second year of the GOTHIC WAR.[3]

After Belisarius had left sufficient garrisons in Palermo and
Syracuse, he embarked his troops at Messina, and landed them,

1 A Sibylline oracle was ready to pronounce – Africâ captâ *mundus* cum
nato peribit; a sentence of portentous ambiguity (Gothic. l. i. c. 7), which has
been published in unknown characters by Opsopæus, an editor of the oracles.
The Père Maltret has promised a commentary; but all his promises have been
vain and fruitless.

2 In his chronology, imitated in some degree from Thucydides, Procopius
begins each spring the years of Justinian and of the Gothic war; and his first
era coincides with the first of April, 535, and not 536, according to the Annals
of Baronius (Pagi Crit. tom. ii. p. 555, who is followed by Muratori and the
editors of Sigonius). Yet in some passages we are at a loss to reconcile the dates
of Procopius with himself, and with the Chronicle of Marcellinus.

3 The series of the first Gothic war is represented by Procopius (l. i.
c. 5–29, l. ii. c. 1–30, l. iii. c. 1) till the captivity of Vitiges. With the aid of
Sigonius (Opp. tom. i. de Imp. Occident. l. xvii., xviii.) and Muratori (Annali
d'Italia, tom. v.), I have gleaned some few additional facts.

without resistance, on the opposite shores of Rhegium. A Gothic prince, who had married the daughter of Theodatus, was stationed with an army to guard the entrance of Italy; but he imitated without scruple the example of a sovereign faithless to his public and private duties. The perfidious Ebermor deserted with his followers to the Roman camp, and was dismissed to enjoy the servile honours of the Byzantine court.[1] From Rhegium to Naples the fleet and army of Belisarius, almost always in view of each other, advanced near three hundred miles along the sea-coast. The people of Bruttium, Lucania, and Campania, who abhorred the name and religion of the Goths, embraced the specious excuse that their ruined walls were incapable of defence: the soldiers paid a just equivalent for a plentiful market; and curiosity alone interrupted the peaceful occupations of the husbandman or artificer. Naples, which has swelled to a great and populous capital, long cherished the language and manners of a Grecian colony;[2] and the choice of Virgil had ennobled this elegant retreat, which attracted the lovers of repose and study from the noise, the smoke, and the laborious opulence of Rome.[3] As soon as the place was invested by sea and land, Belisarius gave audience to the deputies of the people, who exhorted him to disregard a conquest unworthy of his arms, to seek the Gothic king in a field of battle, and, after his victory, to claim, as the sovereign of Rome, the allegiance of the dependent cities. 'When I treat with my enemies,' replied the Roman chief with a haughty smile, 'I am more accustomed to give than to receive counsel; but I hold in one hand inevitable ruin, and in the other peace and freedom, such as Sicily now enjoys.' The impatience of delay urged him to grant the most liberal terms; his honour secured

1 Jornandes, de Rebus Geticis, c. 60, p. 702, edit. Grot., and tom. i. p. 221, Muratori. de Success. Regn. [ib.] p. 241.

2 Nero (says Tacitus, Annal. xv. 33) Neapolim quasi Græcam urbem delegit. One hundred and fifty years afterwards, in the time of Septimius Severus, the *Hellenism* of the Neapolitans is praised by Philostratus: γένος ''Ελληνες καὶ ἀστυκοὶ, ὅθεν καὶ τὰς σπουδὰς τῶν λόγων 'Ελληνικοὶ εἰσι (Icon. l. i. p. 763, edit. Olear.).

3 The otium of Naples is praised by the Roman poets, by Virgil, Horace, Silius Italicus, and Statius (Cluver. Ital. Ant. l. iv. p. 1149, 1150). In an elegant epistle (Silv. l. iii. 5. p. 94–98, edit. Markland) Statius undertakes the difficult task of drawing his wife from the pleasures of Rome to that calm retreat.

their performance: but Naples was divided into two factions; and the Greek democracy was inflamed by their orators, who with much spirit and some truth represented to the multitude that the Goths would punish their defection, and that Belisarius himself must esteem their loyalty and valour. Their deliberations, however, were not perfectly free: the city was commanded by eight hundred barbarians, whose wives and children were detained at Ravenna as the pledge of their fidelity; and even the Jews, who were rich and numerous, resisted, with desperate enthusiasm, the intolerant laws of Justinian. In a much later period the circumference of Naples[1] measured only two thousand three hundred and sixty-three paces:[2] the fortifications were defended by precipices or the sea; when the aqueducts were intercepted, a supply of water might be drawn from wells and fountains; and the stock of provisions was sufficient to consume the patience of the besiegers. At the end of twenty days that of Belisarius was almost exhausted, and he had reconciled himself to the disgrace of abandoning the siege, that he might march, before the winter season, against Rome and the Gothic king. But his anxiety was relieved by the bold curiosity of an Isaurian, who explored the dry channel of an aqueduct, and secretly reported that a passage might be perforated to introduce a file of armed soldiers into the heart of the city. When the work had been silently executed, the humane general risked the discovery of his secret by a last and fruitless admonition of the impending danger. In the darkness of the night four hundred Romans entered the aqueduct, raised themselves by a rope, which they fastened to an olive-tree, into the house or garden of a solitary matron, sounded their trumpets, surprised the sentinels, and gave admittance to their companions, who on all sides scaled the walls and burst open the gates of the city. Every crime which is punished by social justice was

1 This measure was taken by Roger I. after the conquest of Naples (A.D. 1139), which he made the capital of his new kingdom (Giannone, Istoria Civile, tom. ii. p. 169). That city, the third in Christian Europe, is now at least twelve miles in circumference (Jul. Cæsar. Capaccii Hist. Neapol. l. i. p. 47), and contains more inhabitants (350,000) in a given space than any other spot in the known world.

2 Not geometrical, but common, paces or steps, of 22 French inches (D'Anville, Mesures Itinéraires, p. 7, 8): the 2363 do not make an English mile.

practised as the rights of war: the Huns were distinguished by cruelty and sacrilege, and Belisarius alone appeared in the streets and churches of Naples to moderate the calamities which he predicted. 'The gold and silver,' he repeatedly exclaimed, 'are the just rewards of your valour. But spare the inhabitants; they are Christians, they are suppliants, they are now your fellow-subjects. Restore the children to their parents, the wives to their husbands; and show them by your generosity of what friends they have obstinately deprived themselves.' The city was saved by the virtue and authority of its conqueror;[1] and when the Neapolitans returned to their houses, they found some consolation in the secret enjoyment of their hidden treasures. The barbarian garrison enlisted in the service of the emperor; Apulia and Calabria, delivered from the odious presence of the Goths, acknowledged his dominion; and the tusks of the Calydonian boar, which were still shown at Beneventum, are curiously described by the historian of Belisarius.[2]

The faithful soldiers and citizens of Naples had expected their deliverence from a prince who remained the inactive and almost indifferent spectator of their ruin. Theodatus secured his person within the walls of Rome, while his cavalry advanced forty miles on the Appian way, and encamped in the Pomptine marshes; which, by a canal of nineteen miles in length, had been recently drained and converted into excellent pastures.[3] But the principal forces of the Goths were dispersed in Dalmatia, Venetia, and Gaul; and the feeble mind of their king was confounded by the unsuccessful event of a divination which seemed to presage the

---

1 Belisarius was reproved by pope Sylverius for the massacre. He re-peopled Naples, and imported colonies of African captives into Sicily, Calabria, and Apulia (Hist. Miscell. l. xvi. in Muratori, tom. i. p. 106, 107).

2 Beneventum was built by Diomede, the nephew of Meleager (Cluver tom. ii. p. 1195, 1196). The Calydonian hunt is a picture of savage life (Ovid, Metamorph. l. viii.). Thirty or forty heroes were leagued against a hog: the brutes (not the hog) quarrelled with a lady for the head.

3 The *Decennovium* is strangely confounded by Cluverius (tom. ii. p. 1007) with the river Ufens. It was in truth a canal of nineteen miles, from Forum Appii to Terracina, on which Horace embarked in the night. The Decennovium which is mentioned by Lucan, Dion Cassius, and Cassiodorus, has been suc-cessively ruined, restored, and obliterated (D'Anville, Analyse de l'Italie, p. 185, etc.).

downfall of his empire.[1] The most abject slaves have arraigned
the guilt or weakness of an unfortunate master. The character of
Theodatus was rigorously scrutinised by a free and idle camp of
barbarians, conscious of their privilege and power: he was declared unworthy of his race, his nation, and his throne; and their
general Vitiges, whose valour had been signalised in the Illyrian
war, was raised with unanimous applause on the bucklers of his
companions. On the first rumour the abdicated monarch fled
from the justice of his country, but he was pursued by private
revenge. A Goth, whom he had injured in his love, overtook
Theodatus on the Flaminian way, and, regardless of his unmanly
cries, slaughtered him as he lay prostrate on the ground, like a
victim (says the historian) at the foot of the altar. The choice of
the people is the best and purest title to reign over them: yet
such is the prejudice of every age, that Vitiges impatiently wished
to return to Ravenna, where he might seize, with the reluctant
hand of the daughter of Amalasontha, some faint shadow of
hereditary right. A national council was immediately held, and
the new monarch reconciled the impatient spirit of the barbarians to a measure of disgrace which the misconduct of his
predecessor rendered wise and indispensable. The Goths consented to retreat in the presence of a victorious enemy, to delay
till the next spring the operations of offensive war, to summon
their scattered forces, to relinquish their distant possessions, and
to trust even Rome itself to the faith of its inhabitants. Leuderis,
an aged warrior, was left in the capital with four thousand soldiers; a feeble garrison, which might have seconded the zeal,
though it was incapable of opposing the wishes, of the Romans.
But a momentary enthusiasm of religion and patriotism was kindled
in their minds. They furiously exclaimed that the apostolic throne
should no longer be profaned by the triumph or toleration of
Arianism; that the tombs of the Cæsars should no longer be trampled by the savages of the North; and, without reflecting that
Italy must sink into a province of Constantinople, they fondly

1 A Jew gratified his contempt and hatred for *all* the Christians, by enclosing three bands, each of ten hogs, and discriminated by the names of Goths,
Greeks, and Romans. Of the first, almost all were found dead – almost all of
the second were alive – of the third, half died, and the rest lost their bristles.
No unsuitable emblem of the event.

hailed the restoration of a Roman emperor as a new era of freedom and prosperity. The deputies of the pope and clergy, of the senate and people, invited the lieutenant of Justinian to accept their voluntary allegiance, and to enter the city, whose gates would be thrown open for his reception. As soon as Belisarius had fortified his new conquests, Naples and Cumæ, he advanced about twenty miles to the banks of the Vulturnus, contemplated the decayed grandeur of Capua, and halted at the separation of the Latin and Appian ways. The work of the censor, after the incessant use of nine centuries, still preserved its primæval beauty, and not a flaw could be discovered in the large polished stones of which that solid though narrow road was so firmly compacted.[1] Belisarius, however, preferred the Latin way, which, at a distance from the sea and the marshes, skirted in a space of one hundred and twenty miles along the foot of the mountains. His enemies had disappeared: when he made his entrance through the Asinarian gate the garrison departed without molestation along the Flaminian way; and the city, after sixty years' servitude, was delivered from the yoke of the barbarians. Leuderis alone, from a motive of pride or discontent, refused to accompany the fugitives; and the Gothic chief, himself a trophy of the victory, was sent with the keys of Rome to the throne of the emperor Justinian.[2]

The first days, which coincided with the old Saturnalia, were devoted to mutual congratulations and the public joy; and the catholics prepared to celebrate without a rival the approaching festival of the nativity of Christ. In the familiar conversation of a hero the Romans acquired some notion of the virtues which history ascribed to their ancestors; they were edified by the apparent respect of Belisarius for the successor of St. Peter, and his rigid discipline secured in the midst of war the blessings of tranquillity and justice. They applauded the rapid success of his

1 Bergier (Hist. des Grands Chemins des Romains, tom. i. p. 221–228, 440–444) examines the structure and materials, while D'Anville (Analyse de l'Italie, p. 200–213) defines the geographical line.

2 Of the first recovery of Rome, the *year* (536) is certain, from the series of events, rather than from the corrupt, or interpolated, text of Procopius: the *month* (December) is ascertained by Evagrius (l. iv. c. 19); and the *day* (the *tenth*) may be admitted on the slight evidence of Nicephorus Callistus (l. xvii. c. 13). For this accurate chronology we are indebted to the diligence and judgment of Pagi (tom. ii. p. 559, 560).

arms, which overran the adjacent country as far as Narni, Perusia, and Spoleto; but they trembled, the senate, the clergy, and
the unwarlike people, as soon as they understood that he had
resolved, and would speedily be reduced, to sustain a siege against
the powers of the Gothic monarchy. The designs of Vitiges were
executed during the winter season with diligence and effect. From
their rustic habitations, from their distant garrisons, the Goths
assembled at Ravenna for the defence of their country; and such
were their numbers, that, after an army had been detached for
the relief of Dalmatia, one hundred and fifty thousand fighting
men marched under the royal standard. According to the degrees
of rank or merit, the Gothic king distributed arms and horses,
rich gifts, and liberal promises: he moved along the Flaminian
way, declined the useless sieges of Perusia and Spoleto, respected
the impregnable rock of Narni, and arrived within two miles of
Rome at the foot of the Milvian bridge. The narrow passage was
fortified with a tower, and Belisarius had computed the value of
the twenty days which must be lost in the construction of another bridge. But the consternation of the soldiers of the tower,
who either fled or deserted, disappointed his hopes, and betrayed
his person into the most imminent danger. At the head of one
thousand horse the Roman general sallied from the Flaminian
gate to mark the ground of an advantageous position, and to
survey the camp of the barbarians; but while he still believed
them on the other side of the Tiber, he was suddenly encompassed and assaulted by their innumerable squadrons. The fate
of Italy depended on his life; and the deserters pointed to the
conspicuous horse, a bay[1] with a white face, which he rode on
that memorable day. 'Aim at the bay horse,' was the universal
cry. Every bow was bent, every javelin was directed, against that
fatal object, and the command was repeated and obeyed by thousands who were ignorant of its real motive. The bolder barbarians advanced to the more honourable combat of swords and
spears; and the praise of an enemy has graced the fall of Visandus,

---

1 A horse of a bay or red colour was styled φάλιος by the Greeks, balan
by the barbarians, and spadix by the Romans. Honesti spadices, says Virgil
(Georgic. l. iii. 81, with the Observations of Martin and Heyne). Σπαδὶξ, or
βαίον, signifies a branch of the palm-tree, whose name, φοινὶξ, is synonymous
to *red* (Aulus Gellius, ii. 26).

the standard-bearer,[1] who maintained his foremost station, till he was pierced with thirteen wounds, perhaps by the hand of Belisarius himself. The Roman general was strong, active, and dexterous: on every side he discharged his weighty and mortal strokes: his faithful guards imitated his valour and defended his person; and the Goths, after the loss of a thousand men, fled before the arms of a hero. They were rashly pursued to their camp; and the Romans, oppressed by multitudes, made a gradual and at length a precipitate retreat to the gates of the city: the gates were shut against the fugitives; and the public terror was increased by the report that Belisarius was slain. His countenance was indeed disfigured by sweat, dust, and blood; his voice was hoarse, his strength was almost exhausted; but his unconquerable spirit still remained; he imparted that spirit to his desponding companions; and their last desperate charge was felt by the flying barbarians as if a new army, vigorous and entire, had been poured from the city. The Flaminian gate was thrown open to a *real* triumph; but it was not before Belisarius had visited every post and provided for the public safety that he could be persuaded by his wife and friends to taste the needful refreshments of food and sleep. In the more improved state of the art of war a general is seldom required, or even permitted, to display the personal prowess of a soldier, and the example of Belisarius may be added to the rare examples of Henry IV., of Pyrrhus, and of Alexander.

After this first and unsuccessful trial of their enemies, the whole army of the Goths passed the Tiber, and formed the siege of the city, which continued above a year, till their final departure. Whatever fancy may conceive, the severe compass of the geographer defines the circumference of Rome within a line of twelve miles and three hundred and forty-five paces; and that circumference, except in the Vatican, has invariably been the same from the triumph of Aurelian to the peaceful but obscure reign of the modern popes.[2] But in the day of her greatness the

1 I interpret βανδαλάριος, not as a proper name, but an office, standard bearer, from *bandum* (vexillum), a barbaric word adopted by the Greeks and Romans (Paul Diacon. l. i. c. 20, p. 760). Grot. Nomina Gothica, p. 575. (Ducange, Gloss. Latin. tom. i. p. 539, 540.)

2 M. D'Anville has given, in the Memoirs of the Academy for the year 1756 (tom. xxx. p. 198–236), a plan of Rome on a smaller scale, but far more accurate,

space within her walls was crowded with habitations and inhabitants, and the populous suburbs, that stretched along the public
roads, were darted like so many rays from one common centre.
Adversity swept away these extraneous ornaments, and left naked
and desolate a considerable part even of the seven hills. Yet
Rome in its present state could send into the field above thirty
thousand males of a military age;[1] and, notwithstanding the want
of discipline and exercise, the far greater part, inured to the
hardships of poverty, might be capable of bearing arms for the
defence of their country and religion. The prudence of Belisarius
did not neglect this important resource. His soldiers were relieved by the zeal and diligence of the people, who watched while
they slept, and laboured while *they* reposed: he accepted the voluntary service of the bravest and most indigent of the Roman
youth; and the companies of townsmen sometimes represented
in a vacant post the presence of the troops which had been
drawn away to more essential duties. But his just confidence was
placed in the veterans who had fought under his banner in the
Persian and African wars; and although that gallant band was
reduced to five thousand men, he undertook, with such contemptible numbers, to defend a circle of twelve miles against an
army of one hundred and fifty thousand barbarians. In the walls
of Rome, which Belisarius constructed or restored, the materials
of ancient architecture may be discerned;[2] and the whole fortifi-
cation was completed, except in a chasm still extant between
the Pincian and Flaminian gates, which the prejudices of the
Goths and Romans left under the effectual guard of St. Peter
the apostle.[3]

than that which he had delineated in 1738 for Rollin's history. Experience had
improved his knowledge; and instead of Rossi's topography he used the new
and excellent map of Nolli. Pliny's old measure of xiii must be reduced to viii
miles. It is easier to alter a text than to remove hills or buildings.

1 In the year 1709 Labat (Voyages en Italie, tom. iii. p. 218) reckoned
138,568 Christian souls, besides 8000 or 10,000 Jews – without souls? – In the
year 1763 the numbers exceeded 160,000.

2 The accurate eye of Nardini (Roma Antica, l. i. c. viii. p. 31) could
distinguish the tumultuarie opere di Belisario.

3 The fissure and leaning in the upper part of the wall, which Procopius
observed (Goth. l. i. c. 14 [tom. ii. p. 76, ed. Bonn]), is visible to the present
hour (Donat. Roma Vetus, l. i. c. 17, p. 53, 54).

The battlements or bastions were shaped in sharp angles; a ditch, broad and deep, protected the foot of the rampart; and the archers on the rampart were assisted by military engines; the *balista*, a powerful cross-bow, which darted short but massy arrows; the *onagri*, or wild asses, which, on the principle of a sling, threw stones and bullets of an enormous size.[1] A chain was drawn across the Tiber; the arches of the aqueducts were made impervious, and the mole or sepulchre of Hadrian[2] was converted, for the first time, to the uses of a citadel. That venerable structure, which contained the ashes of the Antonines, was a circular turret rising from a quadrangular basis: it was covered with the white marble of Paros, and decorated by the statues of gods and heroes; and the lover of the arts must read with a sigh that the works of Praxiteles or Lysippus were torn from their lofty pedestals, and hurled into the ditch on the heads of the besiegers.[3] To each of his lieutenants Belisarius assigned the defence of a gate, with the wise and peremptory instruction that, whatever might be the alarm, they should steadily adhere to their respective posts, and trust their general for the safety of Rome. The formidable host of the Goths was insufficient to embrace the ample measure of the city: of the fourteen gates, seven only were invested from the Prænestine to the Flaminian way; and Vitiges divided his troops into six camps, each of which was fortified with a ditch and rampart. On the Tuscan side of the river a seventh encampment was formed in the field or circus of the Vatican, for the important purpose of commanding the

1 Lipsius (Opp. tom. iii. Poliorcet. l. iii.) was ignorant of this clear and conspicuous passage of Procopius (Goth. l. i. c. 21 [p. 104, ed. Bonn]). The engine was named ὄναγρος, the wild ass, a calcitrando (Hen. Steph. Thesaur. Linguæ Græc. tom. ii. p. 1340, 1341, tom. iii. p. 877). I have seen an ingenious model, contrived and executed by General Melville, which imitates or surpasses the art of antiquity.

2 The description of this mausoleum, or mole, in Procopius (l. i. c. 22 [tom. i. p. 106, ed. Bonn]), is the first and best. The height above the walls σχεδόν τι ἐς λίθου βολὴν. On Nolli's great plan, the sides measure 260 English feet.

3 Praxiteles excelled in Fauns, and that of Athens was his own masterpiece. Rome now contains above thirty of the same character. When the ditch of St. Angelo was cleansed under Urban VIII. the workmen found the sleeping Faun of the Barberini palace; but a leg, a thigh, and the right arm had been broken from that beautiful statue (Winckelman, Hist. de l'Art, tom. ii. p. 52, 53, tom. iii. p. 265).

Milvian bridge and the course of the Tiber; but they approached with devotion the adjacent church of St. Peter; and the threshold of the holy apostles was respected during the siege by a Christian enemy. In the ages of victory, as often as the senate decreed some distant conquest, the consul denounced hostilities by un-barring, in solemn pomp, the gates of the temple of Janus.[1] Domestic war now rendered the admonition superfluous, and the ceremony was superseded by the establishment of a new religion. But the brazen temple of Janus was left standing in the forum; of a size sufficient only to contain the statue of the god, five cubits in height, of a human form, but with two faces di-rected to the east and west. The double gates were likewise of brass; and a fruitless effort to turn them on their rusty hinges revealed the scandalous secret that some Romans were still at-tached to the superstition of their ancestors.

Eighteen days were employed by the besiegers to provide all the instruments of attack which antiquity had invented. Fascines were prepared to fill the ditches, scaling-ladders to ascend the walls. The largest trees of the forest supplied the timbers of four battering-rams: their heads were armed with iron; they were sus-pended by ropes, and each of them was worked by the labour of fifty men. The lofty wooden turrets moved on wheels or rollers, and formed a spacious platform of the level of the ram-part. On the morning of the nineteenth day a general attack was made from the Prænestine gate to the Vatican: seven Gothic columns, with their military engines, advanced to the assault; and the Romans, who lined the ramparts, listened with doubt and anxiety to the cheerful assurances of their commander. As soon as the enemy approached the ditch, Belisarius himself drew the first arrow; and such was his strength and dexterity, that he transfixed the foremost of the barbarian leaders.

A shout of applause and victory was re-echoed along the wall. He drew a second arrow, and the stroke was followed with the same success and the same acclamation. The Roman general then gave the word that the archers should aim at the teams of

1 Procopius has given the best description of the temple of Janus [Goth. l. i. c. 25], a national deity of Latium (Heyne, Excurs. v. ad l vii. Æneid). It was once a gate in the primitive city of Romulus and Numa (Nardini, p. 13, 256, 329). Virgil has described the ancient rite like a poet and an antiquarian.

oxen; they were instantly covered with mortal wounds; the towers which they drew remained useless and immovable, and a
single moment disconcerted the laborious projects of the king
of the Goths. After this disappointment Vitiges still continued,
or feigned to continue, the assault of the Salarian gate, that he
might divert the attention of his adversary, while his principal
forces more strenuously attacked the Prænestine gate and the
sepulchre of Hadrian, at the distance of three miles from each
other. Near the former, the double walls of the Vivarium¹ were
low or broken; the fortifications of the latter were feebly guarded:
the vigour of the Goths was excited by the hope of victory and
spoil; and if a single post had given way, the Romans, and Rome
itself, were irrecoverably lost. This perilous day was the most
glorious in the life of Belisarius. Amidst tumult and dismay, the
whole plan of the attack and defence was distinctly present to
his mind; he observed the changes of each instant, weighed every
possible advantage, transported his person to the scenes of
danger, and communicated his spirit in calm and decisive orders.
The contest was fiercely maintained from the morning to the
evening; the Goths were repulsed on all sides; and each Roman
might boast that he had vanquished thirty barbarians, if the
strange disproportion of numbers were not counterbalanced by
the merit of one man. Thirty thousand Goths, according to the
confession of their own chiefs, perished in this bloody action;
and the multitude of the wounded was equal to that of the slain.
When they advanced to the assault, their close disorder suffered
not a javelin to fall without effect; and as they retired, the populace of the city joined the pursuit, and slaughtered, with impunity,
the backs of their flying enemies. Belisarius instantly sallied from
the gates; and while the soldiers chanted his name and victory, the
hostile engines of war were reduced to ashes. Such was the loss
and consternation of the Goths, that from this day the siege of
Rome degenerated into a tedious and indolent blockade; and
they were incessantly harassed by the Roman general, who, in
frequent skirmishes, destroyed above five thousand of their

---

1 *Vivarium* was an angle in the new wall enclosed for wild beasts (Procopius, Goth. l. i. c. 23 [tom. ii. p. 111, ed. Bonn]). The spot is still visible in
Nardini (l. iv. c. 2, p. 159, 160) and Nolli's great plan of Rome.

bravest troops. Their cavalry was unpractised in the use of the bow; their archers served on foot; and this divided force was incapable of contending with their adversaries, whose lances and arrows, at a distance or at hand, were alike formidable. The consummate skill of Belisarius embraced the favourable opportunities; and as he chose the ground and the moment, as he pressed the charge or sounded the retreat,[1] the squadrons which he detached were seldom unsuccessful. These partial advantages diffused an impatient ardour among the soldiers and people, who began to feel the hardships of a siege, and to disregard the dangers of a general engagement. Each plebeian conceived himself to be a hero, and the infantry, who, since the decay of discipline, were rejected from the line of battle, aspired to the ancient honours of the Roman legion. Belisarius praised the spirit of his troops, condemned their presumption, yielded to their clamours, and prepared the remedies of a defeat, the possibility of which he alone had courage to suspect. In the quarter of the Vatican the Romans prevailed; and if the irreparable moments had not been wasted in the pillage of the camp, they might have occupied the Milvian bridge, and charged in the rear of the Gothic host. On the other side of the Tiber, Belisarius advanced from the Pincian and Salarian gates. But his army, four thousand soldiers perhaps, was lost in a spacious plain; they were encompassed and oppressed by fresh multitudes, who continually relieved the broken ranks of the barbarians. The valiant leaders of the infantry were unskilled to conquer; they died: the retreat (a hasty retreat) was covered by the prudence of the general, and the victors started back with affright from the formidable aspect of an armed rampart. The reputation of Belisarius was unsullied by a defeat; and the vain confidence of the Goths was not less serviceable to his designs than the repentance and modesty of the Roman troops.

From the moment that Belisarius had determined to sustain a siege, his assiduous care provided Rome against the danger of famine, more dreadful than the Gothic arms. An extraordinary

---

1 For the Roman trumpet and its various notes, consult Lipsius, de Militiâ Romanâ (Opp. tom. iii. l. iv. dialog. x. p. 125–129). A mode of distinguishing the *charge* by the horse-trumpet of solid brass, and the *retreat* by the foot-trumpet of leather and light wood, was recommended by Procopius, and adopted by Belisarius (Goth. l. ii. c. 23 [tom. ii. p. 241, ed. Bonn]).

supply of corn was imported from Sicily: the harvests of Campania and Tuscany were forcibly swept for the use of the city; and the rights of private property were infringed by the strong plea of the public safety. It might easily be foreseen that the enemy would intercept the aqueducts; and the cessation of the water-mills was the first inconvenience, which was speedily removed by mooring large vessels, and fixing mill-stones in the current of the river. The stream was soon embarrassed by the trunks of trees, and polluted with dead bodies; yet so effectual were the precautions of the Roman general, that the waters of the Tiber still continued to give motion to the mills and drink to the inhabitants: the more distant quarters were supplied from domestic wells; and a besieged city might support, without impatience, the privation of her public baths. A large portion of Rome, from the Prænestine gate to the church of St. Paul, was never invested by the Goths; their excursions were restrained by the activity of the Moorish troops: the navigation of the Tiber, and the Latin, Appian, and Ostian ways, were left free and unmolested for the introduction of corn and cattle, or the retreat of the inhabitants who sought a refuge in Campania or Sicily. Anxious to relieve himself from a useless and devouring multitude, Belisarius issued his peremptory orders for the instant departure of the women, the children, and slaves; required his soldiers to dismiss their male and female attendants; and regulated their allowance that one moiety should be given in provisions and the other in money. His foresight was justified by the increase of the public distress as soon as the Goths had occupied two important posts in the neighbourhood of Rome. By the loss of the port, or, as it is now called, the city of Porto, he was deprived of the country on the right of the Tiber and the best communication with the sea; and he reflected with grief and anger that three hundred men, could he have spared such a feeble band, might have defended its impregnable works. Seven miles from the capital, between the Appian and the Latin ways, two principal aqueducts crossing, and again crossing each other, enclosed within their solid and lofty arches a fortified space,[1] where Vitiges

---

[1] Procopius (Goth. l. ii. c. 3 [p. 154, ed. Bonn]) has forgot to name these aqueducts; nor can such a double intersection, at such a distance from Rome,

established a camp of seven thousand Goths to intercept the convoys of Sicily and Campania. The granaries of Rome were insensibly exhausted; the adjacent country had been wasted with fire and sword; such scanty supplies as might yet be obtained by hasty excursions were the reward of valour and the purchase of wealth; the forage of the horses and the bread of the soldiers never failed; but in the last months of the siege the people was exposed to the miseries of scarcity, unwholesome food,[1] and contagious disorders. Belisarius saw and pitied their sufferings; but he had foreseen, and he watched, the decay of their loyalty and the progress of their discontent. Adversity had awakened the Romans from the dreams of grandeur and freedom, and taught them the humiliating lesson that it was of small moment to their real happiness whether the name of their master was derived from the Gothic or the Latin language. The lieutenant of Justinian listened to their just complaints, but he rejected with disdain the idea of flight or capitulation; repressed their clamorous impatience for battle; amused them with the prospect of sure and speedy relief; and secured himself and the city from the effects of their despair or treachery. Twice in each month he changed the station of the officers to whom the custody of the gates was committed: the various precautions of patrols, watch-words, lights, and music, were repeatedly employed to discover whatever passed on the ramparts; out-guards were posted beyond the ditch, and the trusty vigilance of dogs supplied the more doubtful fidelity of mankind. A letter was intercepted which assured the king of the Goths that the Asinarian gate, adjoining to the Lateran church, should be secretly opened to his troops. On the proof or suspicion of treason several senators were banished, and the pope Sylverius was summoned to attend the representative of his sovereign at his headquarters in the Pincian

be clearly ascertained from the writings of Frontinus, Fabretti, and Eschinard, de Aquis and de Agro Romano, or from the local maps of Lameti and Cingolani. Seven or eight miles from the city (50 stadia), on the road to Albano, between the Latin and Appian ways, I discern the remains of an aqueduct (probably the Septimian), a series (630 paces) of arches twenty-five feet high (ὑψηλὼ ἐς ἄγαν).

1 They made sausages, ἀλλᾶντας, of mule's flesh: unwholesome, if the animals had died of the plague. Otherwise the famous Bologna sausages are said to be made of ass-flesh (Voyages de Labat, tom. ii. p. 218).

palace.[1] The ecclesiastics, who followed their bishop, were detained in the first or second apartment,[2] and he alone was admitted to the presence of Belisarius. The conqueror of Rome and Carthage was modestly seated at the feet of Antonina, who reclined on a stately couch: the general was silent, but the voice of reproach and menace issued from the mouth of his imperious wife. Accused by credible witnesses, and the evidence of his own subscription, the successor of St. Peter was despoiled of his pontifical ornaments, clad in the mean habit of a monk, and embarked, without delay, for a distant exile in the East. At the emperor's command, the clergy of Rome proceeded to the choice of a new bishop, and, after a solemn invocation of the Holy Ghost, elected the deacon Vigilius, who had purchased the papal throne by a bribe of two hundred pounds of gold. The profit, and consequently the guilt, of this simony was imputed to Belisarius: but the hero obeyed the orders of his wife; Antonina served the passions of the empress; and Theodora lavished her treasures in the vain hope of obtaining a pontiff hostile or indifferent to the council of Chalcedon.[3]

The epistle of Belisarius to the emperor announced his victory, his danger, and his resolution. 'According to your commands, we have entered the dominions of the Goths, and reduced to your obedience Sicily, Campania, and the city of Rome; but the loss of these conquests will be more disgraceful than their acquisition was glorious. Hitherto we have successfully fought against the multitudes of the barbarians, but their multitudes may

1 The name of the palace, the hill, and the adjoining gate were all derived from the senator Pincius. Some recent vestiges of temples and churches are now smoothed in the garden of the Minims of the Trinità del Monte (Nardini, l. iv. c. 7, p. 196; Eschinard, p. 209, 210; the old plan of Buffalino; and the great plan of Nolli). Belisarius had fixed his station between the *Pincian* and Salarian gates (Procop. Goth. l. i. c. 19 [tom. ii. p. 97, ed. Bonn]).

2 From the mention of the primum et secundum velum, it should seem that Belisarius, even in a siege, represented the emperor, and maintained the proud ceremonial of the Byzantine palace.

3 Of this act of sacrilege, Procopius (Goth. l. i. c. 25 [tom. ii. p. 121, ed. Bonn]) is a dry and reluctant witness. The narratives of Liberatus (Breviarium, c. 22), and Anastasius (de Vit. Pont. p. 39 [ap. Murat. tom. iii. p. 130]) are characteristic, but passionate. Hear the execrations of Cardinal Baronius (A.D. 536, No. 123; A.D. 538, No. 4–20): portentum, facinus omni execratione dignum.

finally prevail. Victory is the gift of Providence, but the reputation of kings and generals depends on the success or the failure
of their designs. Permit me to speak with freedom: if you wish
that we should live, send us subsistence; if you desire that we
should conquer, send us arms, horses, and men. The Romans
have received us as friends and deliverers: but in our present
distress, *they* will be either betrayed by their confidence, or we
shall be oppressed by *their* treachery and hatred. For myself, my
life is consecrated to your service: it is yours to reflect whether
my death in this situation will contribute to the glory and prosperity of your reign.' Perhaps that reign would have been equally
prosperous if the peaceful master of the East had abstained from
the conquest of Africa and Italy: but as Justinian was ambitious
of fame, he made some efforts, they were feeble and languid, to
support and rescue his victorious general. A reinforcement of
sixteen hundred Sclavonians and Huns was led by Martin and
Valerian; and as they had reposed during the winter season in
the harbours of Greece, the strength of the men and horses was
not impaired by the fatigues of a sea-voyage; and they distinguished their valour in the first sally against the besiegers. About
the time of the summer solstice, Euthalius landed at Terracina
with large sums of money for the payment of the troops: he
cautiously proceeded along the Appian way, and this convoy
entered Rome through the gate Capena,[1] while Belisarius, on the
other side, diverted the attention of the Goths by a vigorous and
successful skirmish. These seasonable aids, the use and reputation of which were dexterously managed by the Roman general,
revived the courage, or at least the hopes, of the soldiers and
people. The historian Procopius was despatched with an important commission to collect the troops and provisions which Campania could furnish or Constantinople had sent; and the secretary
of Belisarius was soon followed by Antonina herself,[2] who boldly

1 The old Capena was removed by Aurelian to, or near, the modern gate
of St. Sebastian (see Nolli's plan). That memorable spot has been consecrated
by the Egerian grove, the memory of Numa, triumphal arches, the sepulchres
of the Scipios, Metelli, etc.

2 The expression of Procopius has an invidious cast – τύχην ἐκ τοῦ
ἀσφηλοῦς τὴν σφίσι ξυμβησομένην καραδοκεῖν (Goth. l. ii. c. 4 [tom. ii. p. 160,
ed. Bonn]). Yet he is speaking of a woman.

traversed the posts of the enemy, and returned with the Oriental succours to the relief of her husband and the besieged city. A fleet of three thousand Isaurians cast anchor in the bay of Naples, and afterwards at Ostia. Above two thousand horse, of whom a part were Thracians, landed at Tarentum; and, after the junction of five hundred soldiers of Campania, and a train of waggons laden with wine and flour, they directed their march on the Appian way from Capua to the neighbourhood of Rome. The forces that arrived by land and sea were united at the mouth of the Tiber. Antonina convened a council of war: it was resolved to surmount, with sails and oars, the adverse stream of the river; and the Goths were apprehensive of disturbing, by any rash hostilities, the negotiation to which Belisarius had craftily listened. They credulously believed that they saw no more than the vanguard of a fleet and army which already covered the Ionian Sea and the plains of Campania; and the illusion was supported by the haughty language of the Roman general when he gave audience to the ambassadors of Vitiges. After a specious discourse to vindicate the justice of his cause, they declared that, for the sake of peace, they were disposed to renounce the possession of Sicily. 'The emperor is not less generous,' replied his lieutenant, with a disdainful smile; 'in return for a gift which you no longer possess, he presents you with an ancient province of the empire; he resigns to the Goths the sovereignty of the British island.' Belisarius rejected with equal firmness and contempt the offer of a tribute; but he allowed the Gothic ambassadors to seek their fate from the mouth of Justinian himself, and consented, with seeming reluctance, to a truce of three months, from the winter solstice to the equinox of spring. Prudence might not safely trust either the oaths or hostages of the barbarians, but the conscious superiority of the Roman chief was expressed in the distribution of his troops. As soon as fear or hunger compelled the Goths to evacuate Alba, Porto, and Centumcellæ, their place was instantly supplied; the garrisons of Narni, Spoleto, and Perusia were reinforced, and the seven camps of the besiegers were gradually encompassed with the calamities of a siege. The prayers and pilgrimage of Datius, bishop of Milan, were not without effect; and he obtained one thousand Thracians and Isaurians to assist the revolt of Liguria against her Arian tyrant.

At the same time, John the Sanguinary,[1] the nephew of Vitalian, was detached with two thousand chosen horse, first to Alba on the Fucine lake, and afterwards to the frontiers of Picenum on the Hadriatic Sea. 'In that province,' said Belisarius, 'the Goths have deposited their families and treasures, without a guard or the suspicion of danger. Doubtless they will violate the truce: let them feel your presence before they hear of your motions. Spare the Italians; suffer not any fortified places to remain hostile in your rear; and faithfully reserve the spoil for an equal and common partition. It would not be reasonable,' he added, with a laugh, 'that, whilst we are toiling to the destruction of the drones, our more fortunate brethren should rifle and enjoy the honey.'

The whole nation of the Ostrogoths had been assembled for the attack, and was almost entirely consumed in the siege of Rome. If any credit be due to an intelligent spectator, one-third at least of their enormous host was destroyed in frequent and bloody combats under the walls of the city. The bad fame and pernicious qualities of the summer air might already be imputed to the decay of agriculture and population, and the evils of famine and pestilence were aggravated by their own licentiousness and the unfriendly disposition of the country. While Vitiges struggled with his fortune, while he hesitated between shame and ruin, his retreat was hastened by domestic alarms. The king of the Goths was informed by trembling messengers that John the Sanguinary spread the devastations of war from the Apennine to the Hadriatic; that the rich spoils and innumerable captives of Picenum were lodged in the fortifications of Rimini; and that this formidable chief had defeated his uncle, insulted his capital, and seduced, by secret correspondence, the fidelity of his wife, the imperious daughter of Amalasontha. Yet, before he retired, Vitiges made a last effort either to storm or to surprise the city. A secret passage was discovered in one of the aqueducts; two citizens of the Vatican were tempted by bribes to intoxicate the guards of the Aurelian gate; an attack was meditated on the walls beyond the Tiber, in a place which was not fortified with towers; and the barbarians advanced, with torches and scaling-ladders,

1 Anastasius (p. 40 [tom. iii. p. 130, ed. Murat.]) has preserved this epithet of *Sanguinarius*, which might do honour to a tiger.

to the assault of the Pincian gate. But every attempt was defeated by the intrepid vigilance of Belisarius and his band of veterans, who, in the most perilous moments, did not regret the absence of their companions; and the Goths, alike destitute of hope and subsistence, clamorously urged their departure before the truce should expire, and the Roman cavalry should again be united. One year and nine days after the commencement of the siege, an army so lately strong and triumphant burnt their tents, and tumultuously repassed the Milvian bridge. They repassed not with impunity; their thronging multitudes, oppressed in a narrow passage, were driven headlong into the Tiber by their own fears and the pursuit of the enemy, and the Roman general, sallying from the Pincian gate, inflicted a severe and disgraceful wound on their retreat. The slow length of a sickly and desponding host was heavily dragged along the Flaminian way, from whence the barbarians were sometimes compelled to deviate, lest they should encounter the hostile garrisons that guarded the high road to Rimini and Ravenna. Yet so powerful was this flying army, that Vitiges spared ten thousand men for the defence of the cities which he was most solicitous to preserve, and detached his nephew Uraias, with an adequate force, for the chastisement of rebellious Milan. At the head of his principal army he besieged Rimini, only thirty-three miles distant from the Gothic capital. A feeble rampart and a shallow ditch were maintained by the skill and valour of John the Sanguinary, who shared the danger and fatigue of the meanest soldier, and emulated, on a theatre less illustrious, the military virtues of his great commander. The towers and battering-engines of the barbarians were rendered useless, their attacks were repulsed, and the tedious blockade, which reduced the garrison to the last extremity of hunger, afforded time for the union and march of the Roman forces. A fleet, which had surprised Ancona, sailed along the coast of the Hadriatic to the relief of the besieged city. The eunuch Narses landed in Picenum with two thousand Heruli and five thousand of the bravest troops of the East. The rock of the Apennine was forced, ten thousand veterans moved round the foot of the mountains, under the command of Belisarius himself, and a new army, whose encampment blazed with innumerable lights, *appeared* to advance along the Flaminian way. Overwhelmed with astonishment and despair, the Goths abandoned the siege of Rimini, their tents, their standards, and their leaders; and Vitiges, who gave or followed the example of flight, never halted till he found a shelter within the walls and morasses of Ravenna.

To these walls, and to some fortresses destitute of any mutual support, the Gothic monarchy was now reduced. The provinces of Italy had embraced the party of the emperor, and his army, gradually recruited to the number of twenty thousand men, must have achieved an easy and rapid conquest if their invincible powers had not been weakened by the discord of the Roman chiefs. Before the end of the siege, an act of blood, ambiguous and indiscreet, sullied the fair fame of Belisarius. Presidius, a loyal Italian, as he fled from Ravenna to Rome, was rudely stopped by Constantine, the military governor of Spoleto, and despoiled, even in a church, of two daggers, richly inlaid with gold and precious stones. As soon as the public danger had subsided, Presidius complained of the loss and injury; his complaint was heard, but the order of restitution was disobeyed by the pride and avarice of the offender. Exasperated by the delay, Presidius boldly arrested the general's horse as he passed through the forum, and, with the spirit of a citizen, demanded the common benefit of the Roman laws. The honour of Belisarius was engaged: he summoned a council, claimed the obedience of his subordinate officer, and was provoked, by an insolent reply, to call hastily for the presence of his guards. Constantine, viewing their entrance as the signal of death, drew his sword, and rushed on the general, who nimbly eluded the stroke and was protected by his friends, while the desperate assassin was disarmed, dragged into a neighbouring chamber, and executed, or rather murdered, by the guards, at the arbitrary command of Belisarius.[1] In this hasty act of violence the guilt of Constantine was no longer remembered; the despair and death of that valiant officer were

1 This transaction is related in the public history (Goth. l. ii. c. 8 [p. 180, ed. Bonn]) with candour or caution; in the Anecdotes (c. 7 [c. i. p. 16, ed. Bonn]) with malevolence or freedom; but Marcellinus, or rather his continuator (in Chron.), casts a shade of premeditated assassination over the death of Constantine. He had performed good service at Rome and Spoleto (Procop. Goth. l. i. c. 7, 16 [tom. ii. p. 81, ed. Bonn]); but Alemannus confounds him with a Constantianus comes stabuli.

secretly imputed to the revenge of Antonina; and each of his colleagues, conscious of the same rapine, was apprehensive of the same fate. The fear of a common enemy suspended the effects of their envy and discontent, but, in the confidence of approaching victory, they instigated a powerful rival to oppose the conqueror of Rome and Africa. From the domestic service of the palace and the administration of the private revenue, Narses the eunuch was suddenly exalted to the head of an army, and the spirit of a hero, who afterwards equalled the merit and glory of Belisarius, served only to perplex the operations of the Gothic war. To his prudent counsels the relief of Rimini was ascribed by the leaders of the discontented faction, who exhorted Narses to assume an independent and separate command. The epistle of Justinian had indeed enjoined his obedience to the general, but the dangerous exception, 'as far as may be advantageous to the public service,' reserved some freedom of judgment to the discreet favourite, who had so lately departed from the *sacred* and familiar conversation of his sovereign. In the exercise of this doubtful right the eunuch perpetually dissented from the opinions of Belisarius, and, after yielding with reluctance to the siege of Urbino, he deserted his colleague in the night, and marched away to the conquest of the Æmilian province. The fierce and formidable bands of the Heruli were attached to the person of Narses;[1] ten thousand Romans and confederates were persuaded to march under his banners; every malcontent embraced the fair opportunity of revenging his private or imaginary wrongs; and the remaining troops of Belisarius were divided and dispersed from the garrisons of Sicily to the shores of the Hadriatic. His skill and perseverance overcame every obstacle: Urbino was taken, the sieges of Fæsulæ, Orvieto, and Auximum were undertaken, and vigorously prosecuted, and the eunuch Narses was at length recalled to the domestic cares of the palace. All dissensions were healed, and all opposition was subdued, by the temperate authority of the Roman general, to whom his enemies could not refuse their esteem; and Belisarius inculcated

1 They refused to serve after his departure; sold their captives and cattle to the Goths; and swore never to fight against them. Procopius introduces a curious digression on the manners and adventures of this wandering nation, a part of whom finally emigrated to Thule or Scandinavia (Goth. l. ii. c. 14, 15).

the salutary lesson that the forces of the state should compose
one body and be animated by one soul. But in the interval of
discord the Goths were permitted to breathe; an important season was lost, Milan was destroyed, and the northern provinces
of Italy were afflicted by an inundation of the Franks.

When Justinian first meditated the conquest of Italy, he sent
ambassadors to the kings of the Franks, and adjured them, by
the common ties of alliance and religion, to join in the holy
enterprise against the Arians. The Goths, as their wants were
more urgent, employed a more effectual mode of persuasion,
and vainly strove, by the gift of lands and money, to purchase
the friendship, or at least the neutrality, of a light and perfidious
nation.[1] But the arms of Belisarius and the revolt of the Italians
had no sooner shaken the Gothic monarchy, than Theodebert
of Austrasia, the most powerful and warlike of the Merovingian
kings, was persuaded to succour their distress by an indirect and
seasonable aid. Without expecting the consent of their sovereign,
ten thousand Burgundians, his recent subjects, descended from
the Alps, and joined the troops which Vitiges had sent to chastise the revolt of Milan. After an obstinate siege the capital of
Liguria was reduced by famine, but no capitulation could be
obtained, except for the safe retreat of the Roman garrison.
Datius, the orthodox bishop, who had seduced his countrymen
to rebellion[2] and ruin, escaped to the luxury and honours of the
Byzantine court;[3] but the clergy, perhaps the Arian clergy, were
slaughtered at the foot of their own altars by the defenders of
the catholic faith. Three hundred thousand males were *reported*
to be slain;[4] the female sex and the more precious spoil was

1 This national reproach of perfidy (Procop. Goth. l. ii. c. 25 [tom. ii.
p. 247, ed. Bonn]) offends the ear of La Mothe le Vayer (tom. viii. p. 163–165),
who criticises, as if he had not read, the Greek historian.

2 Baronius applauds his treason, and justifies the catholic bishops – quine
sub heretico principe degant omnem lapidem movent – a useful caution. The
more rational Muratori (Annali d'Italia, tom. v. p. 54) hints at the guilt of
perjury, and blames at least the *imprudence* of Datius.

3 St. Datius was more successful against devils than against barbarians. He
travelled with a numerous retinue, and occupied at Corinth a large house (Baronius, A.D. 538, No. 89; A.D. 539, No. 20).

4 Μυριάδες τριάκοντα (compare Procopius, Goth. l. ii. c. 7, 21 [tom. ii.
p. 234, ed. Bonn]). Yet such population is incredible; and the second or third

resigned to the Burgundians; and the houses, or at least the walls, of Milan were levelled with the ground. The Goths, in their last moments, were revenged by the destruction of a city second only to Rome in size and opulence, in the splendour of its buildings, or the number of its inhabitants, and Belisarius sympathised alone in the fate of his deserted and devoted friends. Encouraged by this successful inroad, Theodebert himself, in the ensuing spring, invaded the plains of Italy with an army of one hundred thousand barbarians.[1] The king and some chosen followers were mounted on horseback and armed with lances; the infantry, without bows or spears, were satisfied with a shield, a sword, and a double-edged battle-axe, which in their hands became a deadly and unerring weapon. Italy trembled at the march of the Franks, and both the Gothic prince and the Roman general, alike ignorant of their designs, solicited with hope and terror the friendship of these dangerous allies. Till he had secured the passage of the Po on the bridge of Pavia, the grandson of Clovis dissembled his intentions, which he at length declared by assaulting, almost at the same instant, the hostile camps of the Romans and Goths. Instead of uniting their arms, they fled with equal precipitation, and the fertile though desolate provinces of Liguria and Æmilia were abandoned to a licentious host of barbarians, whose rage was not mitigated by any thoughts of settlement or conquest. Among the cities which they ruined, Genoa, not yet constructed of marble, is particularly enumerated; and the deaths of thousands, according to the regular practice of war, appear to have excited less horror than some idolatrous sacrifices of women and children which were performed with impunity in the camp of the most Christian king. If it were not a melancholy truth that the first and most cruel sufferings must be the lot of the innocent and helpless, history might exult in the misery of

city of Italy need not repine if we only decimate the numbers of the present text. Both Milan and Genoa revived in less than thirty years (Paul Diacon. de Gestis Langobard. l. ii. c. 38 [16 or 22?]).

1 Besides Procopius, perhaps too Roman, see the Chronicles of Marius and Marcellinus, Jornandes (in Success. Regn. in Muratori, tom. i. p. 241), and Gregory of Tours (l. iii. c. 32, in tom. ii. of the Historians of France). Gregory supposes a defeat of Belisarius, who, in Aimoin (de Gestis Franc. l. ii. c. 23, in tom. iii. p. 59), is slain by the Franks.

the conquerors, who, in the midst of riches, were left destitude of bread or wine, reduced to drink the waters of the Po, and to feed on the flesh of distempered cattle. The dysentery swept away one-third of their army, and the clamours of his subjects, who were impatient to pass the Alps, disposed Theodebert to listen with respect to the mild exhortations of Belisarius. The memory of this inglorious and destructive warfare was perpetuated on the medals of Gaul, and Justinian, without unsheathing his sword, assumed the title of conqueror of the Franks. The Merovingian prince was offended by the vanity of the emperor; he affected to pity the fallen fortunes of the Goths; and his insidious offer of a fœderal union was fortified by the promise or menace of descending from the Alps at the head of five hundred thousand men. His plans of conquest were boundless, and perhaps chimerical. The king of Austrasia threatened to chastise Justinian, and to march to the gates of Constantinople;[1] he was overthrown and slain[2] by a wild bull,[3] as he hunted in the Belgic or German forests.

As soon as Belisarius was delivered from his foreign and domestic enemies, he seriously applied his forces to the final reduction of Italy. In the siege of Osimo the general was nearly transpierced with an arrow, if the mortal stroke had not been intercepted by one of his guards, who lost in that pious office the use of his hand. The Goths of Osimo, four thousand warriors, with those of Fæsulæ and the Cottian Alps, were among the last who maintained their independence; and their gallant resistance, which almost tired the patience, deserved the esteem, of the conqueror. His prudence refused to subscribe the safe-conduct which they asked to join their brethren of Ravenna: but

1 Agathias, l. i. [c. 4], p. 14, 15 [ed. Par.; p. 20, 21, ed. Bonn]. Could he have seduced or subdued the Gepidæ or Lombards of Pannonia, the Greek historian is confident that he must have been destroyed in Thrace.

2 The king pointed his spear – the bull overturned a tree on his head – he expired the same day. Such is the story of Agathias; but the original historians of France (tom. ii. p. 202, 403, 558, 667) impute his death to a fever.

3 Without losing myself in a labyrinth of species and names – the aurochs, urus, bisons, bubalus, bonasus, buffalo, etc. (Buffon. Hist. Nat. tom. xi. and Supplement, tom. iii. vi.), it is certain that in the sixth century a large wild species of horned cattle was hunted in the great forests of the Vosges in Lorraine, and the Ardennes (Greg. Turon. tom. ii. l. x. c. 10, p. 369).

they saved, by an honourable capitulation, one moiety at least of their wealth, with the free alternative of retiring peaceably to their estates or enlisting to serve the emperor in his Persian wars. The multitudes which yet adhered to the standard of Vitiges far surpassed the number of the Roman troops, but neither prayers nor defiance, nor the extreme danger of his most faithful subjects, could tempt the Gothic king beyond the fortifications of Ravenna. These fortifications were indeed impregnable to the assaults of art or violence, and when Belisarius invested the capital he was soon convinced that famine only could tame the stubborn spirit of the barbarians. The sea, the land, and the channels of the Po were guarded by the vigilance of the Roman general; and his morality extended the rights of war to the practice of poisoning the waters[1] and secretly firing the granaries[2] of a besieged city.[3] While he pressed the blockade of Ravenna, he was surprised by the arrival of two ambassadors from Constantinople, with a treaty of peace, which Justinian had imprudently signed without deigning to consult the author of his victory. By this disgraceful and precarious agreement, Italy and the Gothic treasure were divided, and the provinces beyond the Po were left with the regal title to the successor of Theodoric. The ambassadors were eager to accomplish their salutary commission; the captive Vitiges accepted with transport the unexpected offer of a crown; honour was less prevalent among the Goths than the

---

1 In the siege of Auximum, he first laboured to demolish an old aqueduct, and then cast into the stream, 1. dead bodies; 2. mischievous herbs; and 3. quick lime, which is named (says Procopius, l. ii. c. 27) τίτανος by the ancients; by the moderns ἄσβεστος. Yet both words are used as synonymous in Galen, Dioscorides, and Lucian (Hen. Steph. Thesaur. Ling. Græc. tom. iii. p. 748).

2 The Goths suspected Mathasuenta as an accomplice in the mischief, which perhaps was occasioned by accidental lightning.

3 In strict philosophy, a limitation of the rights of war seems to imply nonsense and contradiction. Grotius himself is lost in an idle distinction between the jus naturæ and the jus gentium, between poison and infection. He balances in one scale the passages of Homer (Odyss. A, 259, etc.) and Florus (l. ii. c. 20, No. 7, ult.); and in the other, the examples of Solon (Pausanias, l. x. c. 37) and Belisarius. See his great work De Jure Belli et Pacis (l. iii. c. 4, s. 15, 16, 17, and in Barbeyrac's version, tom. ii. p. 257, etc.). Yet I can understand the benefit and validity of an agreement, tacit or express, mutually to abstain from certain modes of hostility. See the Amphictyonic oath in Æschines, de Falsâ Legatione.

want and appetite of food; and the Roman chiefs, who murmured at the continuance of the war, professed implicit submission to the commands of the emperor. If Belisarius had
possessed only the courage of a soldier, the laurel would have
been snatched from his hand by timid and envious counsels; but
in this decisive moment he resolved, with the magnanimity of a
statesman, to sustain alone the danger and merit of generous
disobedience. Each of his officers gave a written opinion that
the siege of Ravenna was impracticable and hopeless; the general
then rejected the treaty of partition, and declared his own resolution of leading Vitiges in chains to the feet of Justinian. The
Goths retired with doubt and dismay; this peremptory refusal
deprived them of the only signature which they could trust, and
filled their minds with a just apprehension that a sagacious enemy
had discovered the full extent of their deplorable state. They
compared the fame and fortune of Belisarius with the weakness
of their ill-fated king, and the comparison suggested an extraordinary project, to which Vitiges, with apparent resignation, was
compelled to acquiesce. Partition would ruin the strength, exile
would disgrace the honour, of the nation; but they offered their
arms, their treasures, and the fortifications of Ravenna, if Belisarius would disclaim the authority of a master, accept the choice
of the Goths, and assume, as he had deserved, the kingdom of
Italy. If the false lustre of a diadem could have tempted the
loyalty of a faithful subject, his prudence must have foreseen the
inconstancy of the barbarians, and his rational ambition would
prefer the safe and honourable station of a Roman general. Even
the patience and seeming satisfaction with which he entertained
a proposal of treason might be susceptible of a malignant interpretation. But the lieutenant of Justinian was conscious of his
own rectitude; he entered into a dark and crooked path, as it
might lead to the voluntary submission of the Goths; and his
dexterous policy persuaded them that he was disposed to comply
with their wishes, without engaging an oath or a promise for the
performance of a treaty which he secretly abhorred. The day of
the surrender of Ravenna was stipulated by the Gothic ambassadors; a fleet, laden with provisions, sailed as a welcome guest
into the deepest recess of the harbour, the gates were opened to
the fancied king of Italy, and Belisarius, without meeting an

enemy, triumphantly marched through the streets of an impregnable city.¹ The Romans were astonished by their success; the
multitudes of tall and robust barbarians were confounded by the
image of their own patience; and the masculine females, spitting
in the faces of their sons and husbands, most bitterly reproached
them for betraying their dominion and freedom to these pigmies
of the south, contemptible in their numbers, diminutive in their
stature. Before the Goths could recover from the first surprise
and claim the accomplishment of their doubtful hopes, the victor
established his power in Ravenna beyond the danger of repentance and revolt. Vitiges, who perhaps had attempted to escape,
was honourably guarded in his palace;² the flower of the Gothic
youth was selected for the service of the emperor; the remainder
of the people was dismissed to their peaceful habitations in the
southern provinces, and a colony of Italians was invited to replenish the depopulated city. The submission of the capital was
imitated in the towns and villages of Italy which had not been
subdued or even visited by the Romans; and the independent
Goths, who remained in arms at Pavia and Verona, were ambitious only to become the subjects of Belisarius. But his inflexible
loyalty rejected, except as the substitute of Justinian, their oaths
of allegiance, and he was not offended by the reproach of their
deputies that he rather chose to be a slave than a king.

After the second victory of Belisarius, envy again whispered,
Justinian listened, and the hero was recalled. 'The remnant of
the Gothic war was no longer worthy of his presence: a gracious
sovereign was impatient to reward his services and to consult his
wisdom; and he alone was capable of defending the East against

1 Ravenna was taken, not in the year 540, but in the latter end of 539; and
Pagi (tom. ii. p. 569) is rectified by Muratori (Annali d'Italia, tom. v. p. 62), who
proves, from an original act on papyrus (Antiquit. Italiæ Medii Ævi, tom. ii.
dissert. xxxii. p. 999–1007; Maffei, Istoria Diplomat. p. 155–160), that before
the third of January, 540, peace and free correspondence were restored between
Ravenna and Faenza.

2 He was seized by John the Sanguinary, but an oath or sacrament was
pledged for his safety in the Basilica Julii (Hist. Miscell. l. xvi. in Muratori,
tom. i. p. 107). Anastasius (in Vit. Pont. p. 40 [t. iii. p. 130, ed. Murat.]) gives
a dark but probable account. Montfaucon is quoted by Mascou (Hist. of the
Germans, xii. 21) for a votive shield representing the captivity of Vitiges, and
now in the collection of Signor Landi at Rome.

the innumerable armies of Persia.' Belisarius understood the suspicion, accepted the excuse, embarked at Ravenna his spoils and trophies, and proved by his ready obedience that such an abrupt removal from the government of Italy was not less unjust than it might have been indiscreet. The emperor received with honourable courtesy both Vitiges and his more noble consort; and as the king of the Goths conformed to the Athanasian faith, he obtained, with a rich inheritance of lands in Asia, the rank of senator and patrician.[1] Every spectator admired, without peril, the strength and stature of the young barbarians: they adored the majesty of the throne, and promised to shed their blood in the service of their benefactor. Justinian deposited in the Byzantine palace the treasures of the Gothic monarchy. A flattering senate was sometimes admitted to gaze on the magnificent spectacle, but it was enviously secluded from the public view; and the conqueror of Italy renounced without a murmur, perhaps without a sigh, the well-earned honours of a second triumph. His glory was, indeed, exalted above all external pomp; and the faint and hollow praises of the court were supplied, even in a servile age, by the respect and admiration of his country. Whenever he appeared in the streets and public places of Constantinople, Belisarius attracted and satisfied the eyes of the people. His lofty stature and majestic countenance fulfilled their expectations of a hero, the meanest of his fellow-citizens were emboldened by his gentle and gracious demeanour, and the martial train which attended his footsteps left his person more accessible than in a day of battle. Seven thousand horsemen, matchless for beauty and valour, were maintained in the service, and at the private expense, of the general.[2] Their prowess was always conspicuous in single combats or in the foremost ranks, and both parties confessed

---

1 Vitiges lived two years at Constantinople, and imperatoris in affectû *convictus* (or conjunctus) rebus excessit humanis. His widow, *Mathasuenta*, the wife and mother of the patricians, the elder and younger Germanus, united the streams of Anician and Amali blood. (Jornandes, c. 60, p. 221, in Muratori, tom. i.).

2 Procopius, Goth. l. iii. c. 1 [p. 283, ed. Bonn]. Aimoin, a French monk of the eleventh century, who had obtained, and has disfigured, some authentic information of Belisarius, mentions, in his name, 12,000 *pueri* or slaves – quos propriis alimus stipendiis – besides 18,000 soldiers (Historians of France, tom. iii. De Gestis Franc. l. ii. c. 6, p. 48).

that in the siege of Rome the guards of Belisarius had alone vanquished the barbarian host. Their numbers were continually augmented by the bravest and most faithful of the enemy; and his fortunate captives, the Vandals, the Moors, and the Goths, emulated the attachment of his domestic followers. By the union of liberality and justice he acquired the love of the soldiers, without alienating the affections of the people. The sick and wounded were relieved with medicines and money, and still more efficaciously by the healing visits and smiles of their commander. The loss of a weapon or a horse was instantly repaired, and each deed of valour was rewarded by the rich and honourable gifts of a bracelet or a collar, which were rendered more precious by the judgment of Belisarius. He was endeared to the husbandmen by the peace and plenty which they enjoyed under the shadow of his standard. Instead of being injured, the country was enriched by the march of the Roman armies; and such was the rigid discipline of their camp, that not an apple was gathered from the tree, not a path could be traced in the fields of corn. Belisarius was chaste and sober. In the licence of a military life, none could boast that they had seen him intoxicated with wine; the most beautiful captives of Gothic or Vandal race were offered to his embraces, but he turned aside from their charms, and the husband of Antonina was never suspected of violating the laws of conjugal fidelity. The spectator and historian of his exploits has observed that amidst the perils of war he was daring without rashness, prudent without fear, slow or rapid according to the exigencies of the moment; that in the deepest distress he was animated by real or apparent hope, but that he was modest and humble in the most prosperous fortune. By these virtues he equalled or excelled the ancient masters of the military art. Victory, by sea and land, attended his arms. He subdued Africa, Italy, and the adjacent islands; led away captives the successors of Genseric and Theodoric; filled Constantinople with the spoils of their palaces; and in the space of six years recovered half the provinces of the Western empire. In his fame and merit, in wealth and power, he remained without a rival, the first of the Roman subjects; the voice of envy could only magnify his dangerous importance, and the emperor might applaud his own discerning spirit, which had discovered and raised the genius of Belisarius.

It was the custom of the Roman triumphs that a slave should be placed behind the chariot, to remind the conqueror of the instability of fortune and the infirmities of human nature. Procopius, in his Anecdotes, has assumed that servile and ungrateful office. The generous reader may cast away the libel, but the evidence of facts will adhere to his memory; and he will reluctantly confess that the fame and even the virtue of Belisarius were polluted by the lust and cruelty of his wife, and that the hero deserved an appellation which may not drop from the pen of the decent historian. The mother of Antonina[1] was a theatrical prostitute, and both her father and grandfather exercised, at Thessalonica and Constantinople, the vile though lucrative profession of charioteers. In the various situations of their fortune she became the companion, the enemy, the servant, and the favourite of the empress Theodora: these loose and ambitious females had been connected by similar pleasures; they were separated by the jealousy of vice, and at length reconciled by the partnership of guilt. Before her marriage with Belisarius, Antonina had one husband and many lovers; Photius, the son of her former nuptials, was of an age to distinguish himself at the siege of Naples; and it was not till the autumn of her age and beauty[2] that she indulged a scandalous attachment to a Thracian youth. Theodosius had been educated in the Eunomian heresy; the African voyage was consecrated by the baptism and auspicious name of the first soldier who embarked, and the proselyte was adopted into the family of his spiritual parents,[3] Belisarius and Antonina. Before they touched the shores of Africa, this holy kindred degenerated into sensual love; and as Antonina soon

1 The diligence of Alemannus could add but little to the four first and most curious chapters of the Anecdotes. Of these strange Anecdotes, a part may be true, because probable; and a part true, because improbable. Procopius must have *known* the former, and the latter he could scarcely *invent*.

2 Procopius insinuates (Anecdot. c. 4 [tom. iii. p. 35, ed. Bonn]), that, when Belisarius returned to Italy (A.D. 543), Antonina was sixty years of age. A forced, but more polite construction, which refers that date to the moment when he was writing (A.D. 559), would be compatible with the manhood of Photius (Gothic. l. i. c. 10) in 536.

3 Compare the Vandalic War (l. i. c. 12) with the Anecdotes (c. i. [tom. iii. p. 14, ed. Bonn]) and Alemannus (p. 2, 3). This mode of baptismal adoption was revived by Leo the philosopher.

overleaped the bounds of modesty and caution, the Roman general was alone ignorant of his own dishonour. During their residence at Carthage he surprised the two lovers in a subterraneous chamber, solitary, warm, and almost naked. Anger flashed from his eyes. 'With the help of this young man,' said the unblushing Antonina, 'I was secreting our most precious effects from the knowledge of Justinian.' The youth resumed his garments, and the pious husband consented to disbelieve the evidence of his own senses. From this pleasing and perhaps voluntary delusion, Belisarius was awakened at Syracuse by the officious information of Macedonia; and that female attendant, after requiring an oath for her security, produced two chamberlains who like herself had often beheld the adulteries of Antonina. A hasty flight into Asia saved Theodosius from the justice of an injured husband, who had signified to one of his guards the order of his death; but the tears of Antonina and her artful seductions assured the credulous hero of her innocence, and he stooped, against his faith and judgment, to abandon those imprudent friends who had presumed to accuse or doubt the chastity of his wife. The revenge of a guilty woman is implacable and bloody: the unfortunate Macedonia, with the two witnesses, were secretly arrested by the minister of her cruelty; their tongues were cut out, their bodies were hacked into small pieces, and their remains were cast into the sea of Syracuse. A rash though judicious saying of Constantine, 'I would sooner have punished the adulteress than the boy,' was deeply remembered by Antonina; and two years afterwards, when despair had armed that officer against his general, her sanguinary advice decided and hastened his execution. Even the indignation of Photius was not forgiven by his mother; the exile of her son prepared the recall of her lover, and Theodosius condescended to accept the pressing and humble invitation of the conqueror of Italy. In the absolute direction of his household, and in the important commissions of peace and war,[1] the favourite youth most rapidly acquired a fortune of four hundred thousand pounds sterling; and after

1 In November, 537, Photius arrested the pope (Liberat. Brev. c. 22, Pagi, tom. ii. p. 562). About the end of 539 Belisarius sent Theodosius – τὸν τῇ οἰκίᾳ τῇ αὐτοῦ ἐφέστωτα – on an important and lucrative commission to Ravenna (Goth. l. ii. c. 28 [tom. ii. p. 261, ed. Bonn]).

their return to Constantinople the passion of Antonina at least continued ardent and unabated. But fear, devotion, and lassitude perhaps, inspired Theodosius with more serious thoughts. He dreaded the busy scandal of the capital, and the indiscret fondness of the wife of Belisarius, escaped from her embraces, and, retiring to Ephesus, shaved his head and took refuge in the sanctuary of a monastic life. The despair of the new Ariadne could scarcely have been excused by the death of her husband. She wept, she tore her hair, she filled the palace with her cries; 'she had lost the dearest of friends, a tender, a faithful, a laborious friend!' But her warm entreaties, fortified by the prayers of Belisarius, were insufficient to draw the holy monk from the solitude of Ephesus. It was not till the general moved forward for the Persian war that Theodosius could be tempted to return to Constantinople, and the short interval before the departure of Antonina herself was boldly devoted to love and pleasure.

A philosopher may pity and forgive the infirmities of female nature from which he receives no real injury; but contemptible is the husband who feels, and yet endures, his own infamy in that of his wife. Antonina pursued her son with implacable hatred, and the gallant Photius[1] was exposed to her secret persecutions in the camp beyond the Tigris. Enraged by his own wrongs and by the dishonour of his blood, he cast away in his turn the sentiments of nature, and revealed to Belisarius the turpitude of a woman who had violated all the duties of a mother and a wife. From the surprise and indignation of the Roman general, his former credulity appears to have been sincere: he embraced the knees of the son of Antonina, adjured him to remember his obligations rather than his birth, and confirmed at the altar their holy vows of revenge and mutual defence. The dominion of Antonina was impaired by absence; and when she met her husband on his return from the Persian confines, Belisarius, in his first and transient emotions, confined her person and threatened her life. Photius was more resolved to punish, and less prompt to pardon; he flew to Ephesus, extorted from a trusty eunuch of his mother the full confession of her guilt,

1 Theophanes (Chronograph. p. 204 [ed. Par.; tom. i. p. 373, ed. Bonn]) styles him *Photinus*, the son-in-law of Belisarius; and he is copied by the Historia Miscella and Anastasius.

arrested Theodosius and his treasures in the church of St. John the Apostle, and concealed his captives, whose execution was only delayed, in a secure and sequestered fortress of Cilicia. Such a daring outrage against public justice could not pass with impunity, and the cause of Antonina was espoused by the empress, whose favour she had deserved by the recent services of the disgrace of a præfect, and the exile and murder of a pope. At the end of the campaign Belisarius was recalled; he complied as usual with the Imperial mandate. His mind was not prepared for rebellion: his obedience, however adverse to the dictates of honour, was consonant to the wishes of his heart; and when he embraced his wife, at the command and perhaps in the presence of the empress, the tender husband was disposed to forgive or to be forgiven. The bounty of Theodora reserved for her companion a more precious favour. 'I have found,' she said, 'my dearest patrician, a pearl of inestimable value; it has not yet been viewed by any mortal eye, but the sight and the possession of this jewel are destined for my friend.' As soon as the curiosity and impatience of Antonina were kindled, the door of a bedchamber was thrown open, and she beheld her lover, whom the diligence of the eunuchs had discovered in his secret prison. Her silent wonder burst into passionate exclamations of gratitude and joy, and she named Theodora her queen, her benefactress, and her saviour. The monk of Ephesus was nourished in the palace with luxury and ambition; but instead of assuming, as he was promised, the command of the Roman armies, Theodosius expired in the first fatigues of an amorous interview. The grief of Antonina could only be assuaged by the sufferings of her son. A youth of consular rank and a sickly constitution was punished without a trial, like a malefactor and a slave; yet such was the constancy of his mind, that Photius sustained the tortures of the scourge and the rack without violating the faith which he had sworn to Belisarius. After this fruitless cruelty the son of Antonina, while his mother feasted with the empress, was buried in her subterraneous prisons, which admitted not the distinction of night and day. He twice escaped to the most venerable sanctuaries of Constantinople, the churches of St. Sophia and of the Virgin; but his tyrants were insensible of religion as of pity, and the helpless youth, amidst the clamours of the clergy and people, was twice dragged from the altar to the dungeon. His third attempt was more successful. At the end of three years the prophet Zachariah, or some mortal friend, indicated the means of an escape: he eluded the spies and guards of the empress, reached the holy sepulchre of Jerusalem, embraced the profession of a monk, and the abbot Photius was employed, after the death of Justinian, to reconcile and regulate the churches of Egypt. The son of Antonina suffered all that an enemy can inflict; her patient husband imposed on himself the more exquisite misery of violating his promise and deserting his friend.

In the succeeding campaign Belisarius was again sent against the Persians: he saved the East, but he offended Theodora, and perhaps the emperor himself. The malady of Justinian had countenanced the rumour of his death; and the Roman general, on the supposition of that probable event, spoke the free language of a citizen and a soldier. His colleague Buzes, who concurred in the same sentiments, lost his rank, his liberty, and his health by the persecution of the empress; but the disgrace of Belisarius was alleviated by the dignity of his own character and the influence of his wife, who might wish to humble, but could not desire to ruin, the partner of her fortunes. Even his removal was coloured by the assurance that the sinking state of Italy would be retrieved by the single presence of its conqueror. But no sooner had he returned, alone and defenceless, than a hostile commission was sent to the East to seize his treasures and criminate his actions; the guards and veterans who followed his private banner were distributed among the chiefs of the army, and even the eunuchs presumed to cast lots for the partition of his martial domestics. When he passed with a small and sordid retinue through the streets of Constantinople, his forlorn appearance excited the amazement and compassion of the people. Justinian and Theodora received him with cold ingratitude, the servile crowd with insolence and contempt; and in the evening he retired with trembling steps to his deserted palace. An indisposition, feigned or real, had confined Antonina to her apartment; and she walked disdainfully silent in the adjacent portico, while Belisarius threw himself on his bed, and expected, in an agony of grief and terror, the death which he had so often braved under the walls of Rome. Long after sunset a messenger was announced from the empress: he opened with anxious curiosity the letter which contained the sentence of his fate. 'You cannot be ignorant how much you have deserved my displeasure. I am not insensible of the services of Antonina. To her merits and intercession I have granted your life, and permit you to retain a part of your treasures, which might be justly forfeited to the state. Let your gratitude where it is due be displayed, not in words, but in your future behaviour.' I know not how to believe or to relate the transports with which the hero is said to have received this ignominious pardon. He fell prostrate before his wife, he kissed the feet of his saviour, and he devoutly promised to live the grateful and submissive slave of Antonina. A fine of one hundred and twenty thousand pounds sterling was levied on the fortunes of Belisarius; and with the office of count, or master of the royal stables, he accepted the conduct of the Italian war. At his departure from Constantinople, his friends, and even the public, were persuaded that as soon as he regained his freedom he would renounce his dissimulation; and that his wife, Theodora, and perhaps the emperor himself, would be sacrificed to the just revenge of a virtuous rebel. Their hopes were deceived; and the unconquerable patience and loyalty of Belisarius appear either *below* or *above* the character of a MAN.[1]

CHAPTER XLII

State of the Barbaric World – Establishment of the Lombards on the Danube – Tribes and Inroads of the Sclavonians – Origin, Empire, and Embassies of the Turks – The Flight of the Avars – Chosroes I., or Nushirvan, King of Persia – His prosperous Reign and Wars with the Romans – The Colchian or Lazic War – The Æthiopians

OUR estimate of personal merit is relative to the common faculties of mankind. The aspiring efforts of genius or virtue, either in active or speculative life, are measured not so much by their real elevation as by the height to which they ascend above the level of their age or country; and the same

---

1 The continuator of the Chronicle of Marcellinus gives, in a few decent words, the substance of the Anecdotes: Belisarius de Oriente evocatus, in

stature which in a people of giants would pass unnoticed, must appear conspicuous in a race of pigmies. Leonidas and his three hundred companions devoted their lives at Thermopylæ; but the education of the infant, the boy, and the man, had prepared and almost ensured this memorable sacrifice; and each Spartan would approve, rather than admire, an act of duty, of which himself and eight thousand of his fellow-citizens were equally capable.[1] The great Pompey might inscribe on his trophies that he had defeated in battle two millions of enemies, and reduced fifteen hundred cities from the lake Mæotis to the Red Sea;[2] but the fortune of Rome flew before his eagles; the nations were oppressed by their own fears; and the invincible legions which he commanded had been formed by the habits of conquest and the discipline of ages. In this view the character of Belisarius may be deservedly placed above the heroes of the ancient republics. His imperfections flowed from the contagion of the times; his virtues were his own, the free gift of nature or reflection; he raised himself without a master or a rival; and so inadequate were the arms committed to his hand, that his sole advantage was derived from the pride and presumption of his adversaries. Under his command, the subjects of Justinian often deserved to be called Romans; but the unwarlike appellation of Greeks was imposed as a term of reproach by the haughty Goths, who affected to blush that they must dispute the kingdom of Italy with a nation of tragedians, pantomimes, and pirates.[3] The climate of Asia has indeed been found less congenial than that of Europe

offensam periculumque incurrens grave, et invidiæ subjacens rursus remittitur in Italiam (p. 54).

1 It will be a pleasure, not a task, to read Herodotus (l. vii. c. 104, 134, p. 550, 615). The conversation of Xerxes and Demaratus at Thermopylæ is one of the most interesting and moral scenes in history. It was the torture of the royal Spartan to behold, with anguish and remorse, the virtue of his country.

2 See this proud inscription in Pliny (Hist. Natur. vii. 27). Few men have more exquisitely tasted of glory and disgrace; nor could Juvenal (Satir. x.) produce a more striking example of the vicissitudes of fortune, and the vanity of human wishes.

3 Γραικοὺς... ἐξ ὧν τὰ πρότερα οὐδένα ἐς Ἰταλίαν ἥκοντα εἶδον, ὅτι μὴ τραγῳδοὺς, καὶ ναύτας λωποδύτας [Goth. i. 18, tom. ii. p. 93, ed. Bonn]. This last epithet of Procopius is too nobly translated by pirates; naval thieves is the proper word: strippers of garments, either for injury or insult (Demosthenes contra Conon. in Reiske, Orator. Græc. tom. ii. p. 1264).

to military spirit: those populous countries were enervated by
luxury, despotism, and superstition, and the monks were more
expensive and more numerous than the soldiers of the East. The
regular force of the empire had once amounted to six hundred
and forty-five thousand men: it was reduced, in the time of
Justinian, to one hundred and fifty thousand; and this number,
large as it may seem, was thinly scattered over the sea and land –
in Spain and Italy, in Africa and Egypt, on the banks of the
Danube, the coast of the Euxine, and the frontiers of Persia. The
citizen was exhausted, yet the soldier was unpaid; his poverty
was mischievously soothed by the privilege of rapine and indolence, and the tardy payments were detained and intercepted
by the fraud of those agents who usurp, without courage or
danger, the emoluments of war. Public and private distress recruited the armies of the state; but in the field, and still more in
the presence of the enemy, their numbers were always defective.
The want of national spirit was supplied by the precarious faith
and disorderly service of barbarian mercenaries. Even military
honour, which has often survived the loss of virtue and freedom,
was almost totally extinct. The generals, who were multiplied
beyond the example of former times, laboured only to prevent
the success or to sully the reputation of their colleagues; and they
had been taught by experience that, if merit sometimes provoked
the jealousy, error, or even guilt, would obtain the indulgence,
of a gracious emperor.[1] In such an age the triumphs of Belisarius,
and afterwards of Narses, shine with incomparable lustre; but
they are encompassed with the darkest shades of disgrace and
calamity. While the lieutenant of Justinian subdued the kingdoms
of the Goths and Vandals, the emperor,[2] timid, though ambitious, balanced the forces of the barbarians, fomented their divisions by flattery and falsehood, and invited by his patience and
liberality the repetition of injuries.[3] The keys of Carthage, Rome,

1 See the third and fourth books of the Gothic War: the writer of the
Anecdotes cannot aggravate these abuses.

2 Agathias. l. v. [c. 14] p. 157, 158 [p. 306, ed. Bonn]. He confines this
weakness of the emperor and the empire to the old age of Justinian; but, alas!
he was never young.

3 This mischievous policy, which Procopius (Anecdot. c. 19 [tom. iii.
p. 113, ed. Bonn]) imputes to the emperor, is revealed in his epistle to a

and Ravenna were presented to their conqueror, while Antioch was destroyed by the Persians, and Justinian trembled for the safety of Constantinople.

Even the Gothic victories of Belisarius were prejudicial to the state, since they abolished the important barrier of the Upper Danube, which had been so faithfully guarded by Theodoric and his daughter. For the defence of Italy, the Goths evacuated Pannonia and Noricum, which they left in a peaceful and flourishing condition: the sovereignty was claimed by the emperor of the Romans; the actual possession was abandoned to the boldness of the first invader. On the opposite banks of the Danube, the plains of Upper Hungary and the Transylvanian hills were possessed, since the death of Attila, by the tribes of the Gepidæ, who respected the Gothic arms, and despised, not indeed the gold of the Romans, but the secret motive of their annual subsidies. The vacant fortifications of the river were instantly occupied by these barbarians; their standards were planted on the walls of Sirmium and Belgrade; and the ironical tone of their apology aggravated this insult on the majesty of the empire: 'So extensive, O Cæsar, are your dominions, so numerous are your cities, that you are continually seeking for nations to whom, either in peace or war, you may relinquish these useless possessions. The Gepidæ are your brave and faithful allies, and, if they have anticipated your gifts, they have shown a just confidence in your bounty.' Their presumption was excused by the mode of revenge which Justinian embraced. Instead of asserting the rights of a sovereign for the protection of his subjects, the emperor invited a strange people to invade and possess the Roman provinces between the Danube and the Alps; and the ambition of the Gepidæ was checked by the rising power and fame of the LOMBARDS.[1] This corrupt appellation has been diffused in the

Scythian prince who was capable of understanding it. Ἄγαν προμηθῆ καὶ ἀγχινούστατον says Agathias (l. v. [c. 5] p. 170, 171 [p. 331, ed. Bonn]).

1 Gens Germanâ feritate ferocior, says Velleius Paterculus of the Lombards (ii. 106). Langobardos paucitas nobilitat. Plurimis ac valentissimis nationibus cincti non per obsequium, sed prœliis et periclitando, tuti sunt (Tacit. de Moribus German. c. 40). See likewise Strabo (l. vii. p. 446 [p. 290, 291, ed. Casaub.]). The best geographers place them beyond the Elbe, in the bishopric of Magdeburg and the middle march of Brandenburg; and their situation will agree with the patriotic remark of the Count de Hertzberg, that most of the barbarian

thirteenth century by the merchants and bankers, the Italian posterity of these savage warriors; but the original name of *Lango-bards* is expressive only of the peculiar length and fashion of their beards. I am not disposed either to question or to justify their Scandinavian origin,[1] nor to pursue the migrations of the Lombards through unknown regions and marvellous adventures. About the time of Augustus and Trajan, a ray of historic light breaks on the darkness of their antiquities, and they are discovered, for the first time, between the Elbe and the Oder. Fierce, beyond the example of the Germans, they delighted to propagate the tremendous belief that their heads were formed like the heads of dogs, and that they drank the blood of their enemies whom they vanquished in battle. The smallness of their numbers was recruited by the adoption of their bravest slaves; and alone, amidst their powerful neighbours, they defended by arms their high-spirited independence. In the tempests of the north, which overwhelmed so many names and nations, this little bark of the Lombards still floated on the surface; they gradually descended towards the south and the Danube, and at the end of four hundred years they again appear with their ancient valour and renown. Their manners were not less ferocious. The assassination of a royal guest was executed in the presence and by the command of the king's daughter, who had been provoked by some words of insult, and disappointed by his diminutive stature; and a tribute, the price of blood, was imposed on the Lombards by his brother, the king of the Heruli. Adversity revived a sense

conquerors issued from the same countries which still produce the armies of Prussia.

[The etymology of the word Lombards, from Langobards, so called from the peculiar length and fashion of their beards, has been called in question, and it is now believed that the name Langobardi should be derived from the district they inhabited on the banks of the Elbe, where Börde (or Bord) still signifies a fertile plain by the side of a river, and a district near Magdeburg is still called the 'lange börde.' According to this view langobardi would mean 'inhabitants of the long bord of the river;' and traces of their name are still supposed to occur in such words as Bardengau and Bardewick in the neighbourhood of the Elbe. – O. S.]

1 The Scandinavian origin of the Goths and Lombards, as stated by Paul Warnefrid [l. i. c. 2], surnamed the Deacon, is attacked by Cluverius (Germania Antiq. l. iii. c. 26, p. 102, etc.), a native of Prussia, and defended by Grotius (Prolegom. ad Hist. Goth. p. 28, etc.), the Swedish ambassador.

of moderation and justice, and the insolence of conquest was chastised by the signal defeat and irreparable dispersion of the Heruli, who were seated in the southern provinces of Poland.[1] The victories of the Lombards recommended them to the friendship of the emperors; and, at the solicitation of Justinian, they passed the Danube to reduce, according to their treaty, the cities of Noricum and the fortresses of Pannonia. But the spirit of rapine soon tempted them beyond these ample limits; they wandered along the coast of the Hadriatic as far as Dyrrachium, and presumed, with familiar rudeness, to enter the towns and houses of their Roman allies, and to seize the captives who had escaped from their audacious hands. These acts of hostility, the sallies, as it might be pretended, of some loose adventurers, were disowned by the nation, and excused by the emperor; but the arms of the Lombards were more seriously engaged by a contest of thirty years, which was terminated only by the extirpation of the Gepidæ. The hostile nations often pleaded their cause before the throne of Constantinople; and the crafty Justinian, to whom the barbarians were almost equally odious, pronounced a partial and ambiguous sentence, and dexterously protracted the war by slow and ineffectual succours. Their strength was formidable, since the Lombards, who sent into the field several *myriads* of soldiers, still claimed, as the weaker side, the protection of the Romans. Their spirit was intrepid; yet such is the uncertainty of courage, that the two armies were suddenly struck with a panic: they fled from each other, and the rival kings remained with their guards in the midst of an empty plain. A short truce was obtained; but their mutual resentment again kindled, and the remembrance of their shame rendered the next encounter more desperate and bloody. Forty thousand of the barbarians perished in the decisive battle which broke the power of the Gepidæ, transferred the fears and wishes of Justinian, and first displayed the character of Alboin, the youthful prince of the Lombards, and the future conqueror of Italy.[2]

1 Two facts in the narrative of Paul Diaconius (l. i. c. 20) are expressive of national manners: 1. Dum *ad tabulam* luderet – while he played at draughts. 2. Camporum viridantia *lina*. The cultivation of flax supposes property, commerce, agriculture, and manufactures.

2 I have used, without undertaking to reconcile, the facts in Procopius (Goth. l. ii. c. 14, l. iii. c. 33, 34, l. iv. c. 18, 25), Paul Diaconus (de Gestis

The wild people who dwelt or wandered in the plains of Russia, Lithuania, and Poland, might be reduced, in the age of Justinian, under the two great families of the BULGARIANS[1] and the SCLAVONIANS. According to the Greek writers, the former, who touched the Euxine and the lake Mæotis, derived from the Huns their name or descent; and it is needless to renew the simple and well-known picture of Tartar manners. They were bold and dexterous archers, who drank the milk and feasted on the flesh of their fleet and indefatigable horses; whose flocks and herds followed, or rather guided, the motions of their roving camps; to whose inroads no country was remote or impervious, and who were practised in flight, though incapable of fear. The nation was divided into two powerful and hostile tribes, who pursued each other with fraternal hatred. They eagerly disputed the friendship or rather the gifts of the emperor; and the

Langobard. l. i. c. 1–23, in Muratori, Script. Rerum Italicarum, tom. i. p. 405–419), and Jornandes (de Success. Regnorum, p. 242). The patient reader may draw some light from Mascou (Hist. of the Germans, and Annotat. xxiii.) and De Buat (Hist. des Peuples, etc., tom. ix. x. xi.).

1 I adopt the appellation of Bulgarians from Ennodius (in Panegyr. Theodorici, Opp. Sirmond, tom. i. p. 1598, 1599), Jornandes (de Rebus Geticis, c. 5, p. 194, et de Regn. Successione, p. 242), Theophanes (p. 185 [tom. i. p. 338, ed. Bonn]), and the Chronicles of Cassiodorus and Marcellinus. The name of Huns is too vague: the tribes of the Cutturgurians and Utturgurians are too minute and too harsh.

[The Bulgarians unquestionably derived their descent from a Hunnish source. Procopius and Agathias explain that the Kotrigurs inhabiting 'this side of the Mæotic Lake,' and the Uturgurs or Utigurs beyond that on the east of the Cimmerian Bosphorus, the river Don dividing their territories, were also of Hunnish extraction. Therefore Kotrigurs, Uturgurs, and Bulgarians were all closely allied to the Huns of Attila and spoke a cognate language. But the modern Bulgarian exhibits far more features of affinity to the Slav than to the Hun. The Slavonians or Sarmatians are believed to be the ancestors of the various modern Slav families of nations. For convenience sake it may be stated briefly that the ancient Sarmatians or Slavonians inhabited that part of modern Europe which lies between the Vistula, the Carpathian Mountains, the Volga, and the Black Sea. They were akin to the ancient Scythians, and were therefore Iranians, probably of Median descent. The Sarmatians almost exterminated the Scythians, and were in turn conquered by the Goths, to become in time the ancestors of the modern Slavs. These are divided into an Eastern and a Western branch, the Eastern including the various types of Russians, including the Red and White Russians, some of the modern Bulgarians, the Serbo-Croats, the Montenegrins and Slovenzi; while the Western branch comprehended the Poles, the Czechs, the Moravians, the Slovaks, and the Lusatian Wends. – O. S.]

distinction which nature had fixed between the faithful dog and
the rapacious wolf was applied by an ambassador who received
only verbal instructions from the mouth of his illiterate prince.[1]
The Bulgarians, of whatsoever species, were equally attracted by
Roman wealth: they assumed a vague dominion over the Sclavonian name, and their rapid marches could only be stopped by
the Baltic Sea, or the extreme cold and poverty of the north. But
the same race of Sclavonians appears to have maintained, in
every age, the possession of the same countries. Their numerous
tribes, however distant or adverse, used one common language
(it was harsh and irregular), and were known by the resemblance
of their form, which deviated from the swarthy Tartar, and approached without attaining the lofty stature and fair complexion
of the German. Four thousand six hundred villages[2] were scattered over the provinces of Russia and Poland, and their huts
were hastily built of rough timber, in a country deficient both in
stone and iron. Erected, or rather concealed, in the depth of
forests, on the banks of rivers, or the edge of morasses, we may
not perhaps, without flattery, compare them to the architecture
of the beaver, which they resembled in a double issue, to the
land and water, for the escape of the savage inhabitant, an animal
less cleanly, less diligent, and less social, than that marvellous
quadruped. The fertility of the soil, rather than the labour of the
natives, supplied the rustic plenty of the Sclavonians. Their sheep
and horned cattle were large and numerous, and the fields which
they sowed with millet and panic[3] afforded, in the place of bread,
a coarse and less nutritive food. The incessant rapine of their
neighbours compelled them to bury this treasure in the earth;

1 Procopius (Goth. l. iv. c. 19 [tom. ii. p. 556, ed. Bonn]). His verbal
message (he owns himself an illiterate barbarian) is delivered as an epistle. The
style is savage, figurative, and original.

2 This sum is the result of a particular list, in a curious MS. fragment of
the year 550, found in the library of Milan. The obscure geography of the times
provokes and exercises the patience of the Count de Buat (tom. xi. p. 69–189).
The French minister often loses himself in a wilderness which requires a Saxon
and Polish guide.

3 *Panicum, milium*. See Columella, l. ii. c. 9, p. 430, edit. Gesner. Plin. Hist.
Natur. xviii. 24, 25. The Sarmatians made a pap of millet, mingled with mare's
milk or blood. In the wealth of modern husbandry, our millet feeds poultry,
and not heroes. See the dictionaries of Bomare and Miller.

but on the appearance of a stranger it was freely imparted by a people whose unfavourable character is qualified by the epithets of chaste, patient, and hospitable. As their supreme god, they adored an invisible master of the thunder. The rivers and the nymphs obtained their subordinate honours, and the popular worship was expressed in vows and sacrifice. The Sclavonians disdained to obey a despot, a prince, or even a magistrate; but their experience was too narrow, their passions too headstrong, to compose a system of equal law or general defence. Some voluntary respect was yielded to age and valour; but each tribe or village existed as a separate republic, and all must be per-suaded where none could be compelled. They fought on foot, almost naked, and, except an unwieldy shield, without any de-fensive armour: their weapons of offence were a bow, a quiver of small poisoned arrows, and a long rope, which they dexter-ously threw from a distance, and entangled their enemy in a running noose. In the field, the Sclavonian infantry was danger-ous by their speed, agility, and hardiness: they swam, they dived, they remained under water, drawing their breath through a hol-low cane; and a river or lake was often the scene of their unsus-pected ambuscade. But these were the achievements of spies or stragglers: the military art was unknown to the Sclavonians; their name was obscure, and their conquests were inglorious.[1]

I have marked the faint and general outline of the Sclavonians and Bulgarians, without attempting to define their intermediate boundaries, which were not accurately known or respected by the barbarians themselves. Their importance was measured by their vicinity to the empire; and the level country of Moldavia and Wallachia was occupied by the Antes,[2] a Sclavonian tribe,

1 For the name and nation, the situation and manners, of the Sclavonians, see the original evidence of the sixth century, in Procopius (Goth. l. ii. c. 26, l. iii. c. 14), and the emperor Mauritius or Maurice (Stratagemat. l. xi. c. 5, apud Mascou, Annotat. xxxi.). The Stratagems of Maurice have been printed only, as I understand, at the end of Scheffer's edition of Arrian's Tactics, at Upsal, 1664 (Fabric. Bibliot. Græc. l. iv. c. 8, tom. iii. p. 278), a scarce, and hitherto, to me, an inaccessible book.

[The *Stategikon* (or the Stratagems) is a scarce work of the sixth century, but it is not by Maurice. – O. S.]

2 Antes eorum fortissimi ... Taysis [Tausis] qui rapidus et verticosus in Histri fluenta furens devolvitur (Jornandes, c. 5, p. 194, edit. Murator.

which swelled the titles of Justinian with an epithet of conquest.[1]
Against the Antes he erected the fortifications of the Lower
Danube, and laboured to secure the alliance of a people seated
in the direct channel of northern inundation, an interval of two
hundred miles between the mountains of Transylvania and the
Euxine Sea. But the Antes wanted power and inclination to stem
the fury of the torrent: and the light-armed Sclavonians from a
hundred tribes pursued with almost equal speed the footsteps of
the Bulgarian horse. The payment of one piece of gold for each
soldier procured a safe and easy retreat through the country of
the Gepidæ, who commanded the passage of the Upper Danube.[2] The hopes or fears of the barbarians, their intestine union
or discord, the accident of a frozen or shallow stream, the prospect of harvest or vintage, the prosperity or distress of the Romans, were the causes which produced the uniform repetition of
annual visits,[3] tedious in the narrative, and destructive in the
event. The same year, and possibly the same month, in which
Ravenna surrendered, was marked by an invasion of the Huns
or Bulgarians, so dreadful that it almost effaced the memory of
their past inroads. They spread from the suburbs of Constantinople to the Ionian Gulf, destroyed thirty-two cities or castles,
erased Potidæa, which Athens had built and Philip had besieged,
and repassed the Danube, dragging at their horses' heels one
hundred and twenty thousand of the subjects of Justinian. In a
subsequent inroad they pierced the wall of the Thracian Chersonesus, extirpated the habitations and the inhabitants, boldly
traversed the Hellespont, and returned to their companions
laden with the spoils of Asia. Another party, which seemed a
multitude in the eyes of the Romans, penetrated without opposition from the straits of Thermopylæ to the isthmus of Corinth;

Procopius, Goth. l. iii. c. 14, et de Ædific. l. iv. c. 7). Yet the same Procopius
mentions the Goths and Huns as neighbours, γειτονοῦντα, to the Danube
(de Ædific. l. iv. c. 1).

1 The national title of *Anticus*, in the laws and inscriptions of Justinian, was
adopted by his successors, and is justified by the pious Ludewig (in Vit. Justinian. p. 515). It had strangely puzzled the civilians of the middle age.

2 Procopius, Goth. l. iv. c. 25 [tom. ii. p. 592, ed. Bonn].

3 An inroad of the Huns is connected by Procopius with a comet; perhaps
that of 531 (Persic. l. ii. c. 4). Agathias (l. v. [c. 11] p. 154, 155 [p. 300, ed.
Bonn]) borrows from his predecessor some early facts.

and the last ruin of Greece has appeared an object too minute for the attention of history. The works which the emperor raised for the protection, but at the expense of his subjects, served only to disclose the weakness of some neglected part; and the walls, which by flattery had been deemed impregnable, were either deserted by the garrison or scaled by the barbarians. Three thousand Sclavonians, who insolently divided themselves into two bands, discovered the weakness and misery of a triumphant reign. They passed the Danube and the Hebrus, vanquished the Roman generals who dared to oppose their progress, and plundered with impunity the cities of Illyricum and Thrace, each of which had arms and numbers to overwhelm their contemptible assailants. Whatever praise the boldness of the Sclavonians may deserve, it is sullied by the wanton and deliberate cruelty which they are accused of exercising on their prisoners. Without distinction of rank or age or sex, the captives were impaled or flayed alive, or suspended between four posts and beaten with clubs till they expired, or enclosed in some spacious building and left to perish in the flames with the spoil and cattle which might impede the march of these savage victors.[1] Perhaps a more impartial narrative would reduce the number and qualify the nature of these horrid acts, and they might sometimes be excused by the cruel laws of retaliation. In the siege of Topirus,[2] whose obstinate defence had enraged the Sclavonians, they massacred fifteen thousand males, but they spared the women and children; the most valuable captives were always reserved for labour or ransom; the servitude was not rigorous, and the terms of their deliverance were speedy and moderate. But the subject, or the historian of Justinian, exhaled his just indignation in the language of complaint and reproach; and Procopius has confidently affirmed that in a reign of thirty-two years each *annual* inroad of the barbarians consumed two hundred thousand of the

1 The cruelties of the Sclavonians are related or magnified by Procopius (Goth. l. iii. c. 29, 38). For their mild and liberal behaviour to their prisoners we may appeal to the authority, somewhat more recent, of the emperor Maurice (Stratagem. l. xi. c. 5 [p. 272, *sqq.*]).

2 Topirus was situate near Philippi in Thrace, or Macedonia, opposite to the isle of Thasos, twelve days' journey from Constantinople (Cellarius, tom. i. p. 676, 840).

inhabitants of the Roman empire. The entire population of Turkish Europe, which nearly corresponds with the provinces of Justinian, would perhaps be incapable of supplying six millions of persons, the result of this incredible estimate.[1]

In the midst of these obscure calamities, Europe felt the shock of a revolution, which first revealed to the world the name and nation of the TURKS. Like Romulus, the founder of that martial people was suckled by a she-wolf, who afterwards made him the father of a numerous progeny; and the representation of that animal in the banners of the Turks preserved the memory, or rather suggested the idea, of a fable which was invented, without any mutual intercourse, by the shepherds of Latium and those of Scythia. At the equal distance of two thousand miles from the Caspian, the Icy, the Chinese, and the Bengal seas, a ridge of mountains is conspicuous, the centre, and perhaps the summit, of Asia, which, in the language of different nations, has been styled Imaus, and Caf,[2] and Altai, and the Golden

---

1 According to the malevolent testimony of the Anecdotes (c. 18 [tom. iii. p. 108, ed. Bonn] these inroads had reduced the provinces south of the Danube to the state of a Scythian wilderness.

[The Turks were essentially an Eastern Asiatic race, coming from the neighbourhood of Lake Baikal (see Note, vol. iii. p. 15, for divisions thereof). A branch of these dwelling on Mount Altai were styled Thu-Kiu by Chinese writers, and are regarded as the same people as the Hiongnu of earlier times. The name of Thu-kiu first appears at the beginning of the fifth century in the Chinese writers, who relate that 500 families of the Hiongnu, under their leader Assena, when the major part of their tribe was crushed by the Tungusic Tartars, fled west from their abodes in Pe-leang to the territory of the Geougen, settling at the foot of a helmet-shaped mountain 'terk,' whence they derived their name. They were employed by the Geougen or Jeugen as iron workers. The seat of the Turkish power, about the sixth century was near the eastern frontier of the Chinese province of to-day Kansuh. This, in fact, was where they had been working for over 200 years for the Geougen. The Turks became very powerful under their leader Tumere, who, after conquering the Geougen, invited under his sway all the Turkish tribes in Central and Northern Asia, and assumed the title of Chagan or Khan, A.D. 546. – O. S.]

2 From Caf to Caf; which a more rational geography would interpret, from Imaus, perhaps, to Mount Atlas. According to the religious philosophy of the Mahometans the basis of Mount Caf is an emerald, whose reflection produces the azure of the sky. The mountain is endowed with a sensitive action in its roots or nerves; and their vibration, at the command of God, is the cause of earthquakes (D'Herbelot, p. 230, 231).

Mountains, and the Girdle of the Earth. The sides of the hills were productive of minerals; and the iron-forges,[1] for the purpose of war, were exercised by the Turks, the most despised portion of the slaves of the great khan of the Geougen. But their servitude could only last till a leader, bold and eloquent, should arise to persuade his countrymen that the same arms which they forged for their masters might become in their own hands the instruments of freedom and victory. They sallied from the mountain;[2] a sceptre was the reward of his advice; and the annual ceremony, in which a piece of iron was heated in the fire, and a smith's hammer was successively handled, by the prince and his nobles, recorded for ages the humble profession and rational pride of the Turkish nation. Bertezena, their first leader, signalised their valour and his own in successful combats against the neighbouring tribes; but when he presumed to ask in marriage the daughter of the great khan, the insolent demand of a slave and a mechanic was contemptuously rejected. The disgrace was expiated by a more noble alliance with a princess of China; and the decisive battle which almost extirpated the nation of the Geougen established in Tartary the new and more powerful empire of the Turks. They reigned over the north; but they confessed the vanity of conquest by their faithful attachment to the mountain of their fathers. The royal encampment seldom lost sight of Mount Altai, from whence the river Irtish descends to water the rich pastures of the Calmucks,[3] which nourish the largest sheep

1 The Siberian iron is the best and most plentiful in the world: and in the southern parts above sixty mines are now worked by the industry of the Russians (Strahlenberg, Hist. of Siberia, p. 342, 387; Voyage en Sibérie, par l'Abbé Chappe d'Auteroche, p. 603–608, edit. in 12mo. Amsterdam, 1770). The Turks offered iron for sale; yet the Roman ambassadors, with strange obstinacy, persisted in believing that it was all a trick, and that their country produced none (Menander in Excerpt. Leg. p. 152 [ed. Par.; p. 380, ed. Bonn]).

2 Of Irgana-kon (Abulghazi Khan, Hist. Généalogique des Tatars, P. ii. c. 5, p. 71–77, c. 15, p. 155). The tradition of the Moguls, of the 450 years which they passed in the mountains, agrees with the Chinese periods of the history of the Huns and Turks (De Guignes, tom. i. part ii. p. 376), and the twenty generations from their restoration to Zingis.

3 The country of the Turks, now of the Calmucks, is well described in the Genealogical History, p. 521–562. The curious notes of the French translator are enlarged and digested in the second volume of the English version.

and oxen in the world. The soil is fruitful, and the climate mild and temperate: the happy region was ignorant of earthquake and pestilence; the emperor's throne was turned towards the east, and a golden wolf on the top of a spear seemed to guard the entrance of his tent. One of the successors of Bertezena was tempted by the luxury and superstition of China; but his design of building cities and temples was defeated by the simple wisdom of a barbarian counsellor. 'The Turks,' he said, 'are not equal in number to one hundredth part of the inhabitants of China. If we balance their power, and elude their armies, it is because we wander without any fixed habitations in the exercise of war and hunting. Are we strong? we advance and conquer: are we feeble? we retire and are concealed. Should the Turks confine themselves within the walls of cities, the loss of a battle would be the destruction of their empire. The bonzes preach only patience, humility, and the renunciation of the world. Such, O king! is not the religion of heroes.' They entertained with less reluctance the doctrines of Zoroaster; but the greatest part of the nation acquiesced without inquiry in the opinions, or rather in the practice, of their ancestors. The honours of sacrifice were reserved for the supreme deity; they acknowledged in rude hymns their obligations to the air, the fire, the water, and the earth; and their priests derived some profit from the art of divination. Their unwritten laws were rigorous and impartial: theft was punished by a tenfold restitution; adultery, treason, and murder with death; and no chastisement could be inflicted too severe for the rare and inexpiable guilt of cowardice. As the subject nations marched under the standard of the Turks, their cavalry, both men and horses, were proudly computed by millions; one of their effective armies consisted of four hundred thousand soldiers, and in less than fifty years they were connected in peace and war with the Romans, the Persians, and the Chinese. In their northern limits some vestige may be discovered of the form and situation of Kamtchatka, of a people of hunters and fishermen, whose sledges were drawn by dogs, and whose habitations were buried in the earth. The Turks were ignorant of astronomy; but the observation taken by some learned Chinese, with a gnomon of eight feet, fixes the royal camp in the latitude of forty-nine degrees, and marks their extreme progress within three, or at

least ten degrees of the polar circle.¹ Among their southern conquests the most splendid was that of the Nephthalites or White
Huns, a polite and warlike people, who possessed the commercial cities of Bochara and Samarcand, who had vanquished the
Persian monarch, and carried their victorious arms along the
banks and perhaps to the mouth of the Indus. On the side of
the west the Turkish cavalry advanced to the lake Mæotis. They
passed that lake on the ice. The khan, who dwelt at the foot of
Mount Altai, issued his commands for the siege of Bosphorus,²
a city the voluntary subject of Rome, and whose princes had
formerly been the friends of Athens.³ To the east the Turks
invaded China, as often as the vigour of the government was
relaxed: and I am taught to read in the history of the times that
they mowed down their patient enemies like hemp or grass, and
that the mandarins applauded the wisdom of an emperor who
repulsed these barbarians with golden lances. This extent of savage empire compelled the Turkish monarch to establish three
subordinate princes of his own blood, who soon forgot their
gratitude and allegiance. The conquerors were enervated by luxury, which is always fatal except to an industrious people; the
policy of China solicited the vanquished nations to resume their
independence; and the power of the Turks was limited to a
period of two hundred years. The revival of their name and
dominion in the southern countries of Asia are the events of a
later age; and the dynasties which succeeded to their native realms
may sleep in oblivion, since *their* history bears no relation to the
decline and fall of the Roman empire.⁴

In the rapid career of conquest the Turks attacked and subdued the nation of the Ogors or Varchonites on the banks of

1 Visdelou, p. 141, 151. The fact, though it strictly belongs to a subordinate
and successive tribe, may be introduced here.

2 Procopius (Persic. l. i. c. 12, l. ii. c. 3; Peyssonel, Observations sur les
Peuples Barbares, p. 99, 100) defines the distance between Caffa and the old
Bosphorus at xvi long Tartar leagues.

3 See, in a Mémoire of M. de Boze (Mém. de l'Académie des Inscriptions,
tom. vi. p. 549–565), the ancient kings and medals of the Cimmerian Bosphorus;
and the gratitude of Athens, in the Oration of Demosthenes against Leptines
(in Reiske, Orator. Græc. tom. i. p. 466, 467).

4 For the origin and revolutions of the first Turkish empire, the Chinese
details are borrowed from De Guignes (Hist. des Huns, tom. i. P. ii. p. 367–462)

the river Til, which derived the epithet of Black from its dark water or gloomy forests.[1] The khan of the Ogors was slain with three hundred thousand of his subjects, and their bodies were scattered over the space of four days' journey: their surviving countrymen acknowledged the strength and mercy of the Turks; and a small portion, about twenty thousand warriors, preferred exile to servitude. They followed the well-known road of the Volga, cherished the error of the nations who confounded them with the AVARS, and spread the terror of that false, though famous appellation, which had not, however, saved its lawful proprietors from the yoke of the Turks.[2] After a long and victorious march the new Avars arrived at the foot of Mount Caucasus, in the country of the Alani[3] and Circassians, where they first heard of the splendour and weakness of the Roman empire. They humbly requested their confederate, the prince of the Alani, to lead them to this source of riches; and their ambassador, with the permission of the governor of Lazica, was transported by the Euxine Sea to Constantinople. The whole city was poured forth to behold with curiosity and terror the aspect of a

and Visdelou (Supplément à la Bibliothèque Orient. d'Herbelot, p. 82–114). The Greek or Roman hints are gathered in Menander (p. 108–164 [p. 298, 404, ed. Bonn]), and Theophylact Simocatta (l. vii. c. 7, 8).

1 The river Til, or Tula, according to the geography of De Guignes (tom. i. part ii. p. lviii. and 352), is a small, though grateful, stream of the desert, that falls into the Orhon, Selinga, etc. See Bell, Journey from Petersburg to Pekin (vol. ii. p. 124); yet his own description of the Keat, down which he sailed into the Oby, represents the name and attributes of the *black river* (p. 139).

[The river is supposed to be an eastern affluent of the Volga, the Kama, which, from the colour of its waters, may be called black. The Volga, however, is called Atel or Etel by all the Turkish tribes. – O. S.]

2 Theophylact, l. vii. c. 7, 8. And yet his *true* Avars are invisible even to the eyes of M. de Guignes; and what can be more illustrious than the *false?* The right of the fugitive Ogors to that national appellation is confessed by the Turks themselves (Menander, p. 108).

[The Avars, like the Huns, belonged to the Turkish stock. Their chiefs bear the Turkish or Mongolian titles of Chagan or Khan. They are first mentioned after the downfall of the empire of the Huns, between 461–465, as devastating the lands of the tribes on the Mæotic Lake and Caspian Sea. – O. S.]

3 The Alani are still found in the Genealogical History of the Tartars (p. 617), and in D'Anville's maps. They opposed the march of the generals of Zingis round the Caspian Sea, and were overthrown in a great battle (Hist. de Gengiscan, l. iv. c. 9, p. 447).

strange people; their long hair, which hung in tresses down their backs, was gracefully bound with ribands, but the rest of their habit appeared to imitate the fashion of the Huns. When they were admitted to the audience of Justinian, Candish, the first of the ambassadors, addressed the Roman emperor in these terms: 'You see before you, O mighty prince, the representatives of the strongest and most populous of nations, the invincible, the irresistible Avars. We are willing to devote ourselves to your service: we are able to vanquish and destroy all the enemies who now disturb your repose. But we expect, as the price of our alliance, as the reward of our valour, precious gifts, annual subsidies, and fruitful possessions.' At the time of this embassy Justinian had reigned above thirty, he had lived above seventy-five years: his mind, as well as his body, was feeble and languid; and the conqueror of Africa and Italy, careless of the permanent interest of his people, aspired only to end his days in the bosom even of inglorious peace. In a studied oration, he imparted to the senate his resolution to dissemble the insult and to purchase the friendship of the Avars; and the whole senate, like the mandarins of China, applauded the incomparable wisdom and foresight of their sovereign. The instruments of luxury were immediately prepared to captivate the barbarians; silken garments, soft and splendid beds, and chains and collars incrusted with gold. The ambassadors, content with such liberal reception, departed from Constantinople, and Valentin, one of the emperor's guards, was sent with a similar character to their camp at the foot of Mount Caucasus. As their destruction or their success must be alike advantageous to the empire, he persuaded them to invade the enemies of Rome; and they were easily tempted, by gifts and promises, to gratify their ruling inclinations. These fugitives, who fled before the Turkish arms, passed the Tanais and Borysthenes, and boldly advanced into the heart of Poland and Germany, violating the law of nations and abusing the rights of victory. Before ten years had elapsed their camps were seated on the Danube and the Elbe, many Bulgarian and Sclavonian names were obliterated from the earth, and the remainder of their tribes are found, as tributaries and vassals, under the standard of the Avars. The chagan, the peculiar title of their king, still affected to cultivate the friendship of the emperor; and Justinian entertained some thoughts of fixing them in Pannonia, to balance the prevailing power of the Lombards. But the virtue or treachery of an Avar betrayed the secret enmity and ambitious designs of their countrymen; and they loudly complained of the timid, though jealous policy, of detaining their ambassadors and denying the arms which they had been allowed to purchase in the capital of the empire.[1]

Perhaps the apparent change in the dispositions of the emperors may be ascribed to the embassy which was received from the conquerors of the Avars.[2] The immense distance which eluded their arms could not extinguish their resentment: the Turkish ambassadors pursued the footsteps of the vanquished to the Jaik, the Volga, Mount Caucasus, the Euxine, and Constantinople, to request that he would not espouse the cause of rebels and fugitives. Even commerce had some share in this remarkable negotiation: and the Sogdoites, who were now the tributaries of the Turks, embraced the fair occasion of opening, by the north of the Caspian, a new road for the importation of Chinese silk into the Roman empire. The Persian, who preferred the navigation of Ceylon, had stopped the caravans of Bochara and Samarcand: their silk was contemptuously burnt: some Turkish ambassadors died in Persia, with a suspicion of poison; and the great khan permitted his faithful vassal Maniach, the prince of the Sogdoites, to propose, at the Byzantine court, a treaty of alliance against their common enemies. Their splendid apparel and rich presents, the fruit of Oriental luxury, distinguished Maniach and his colleagues from the rude savages of the North: their letters, in the Scythian character and language, announced a people who had attained the rudiments of science:[3] they

1 The embassies and first conquests of the Avars may be read in Menander (Excerpt. Legat. p. 99, 100, 101, 154, 155 [p. 282–287, 385–388, ed. Bonn]), Theophanes (p. 196 [tom. i. p. 359, ed. Bonn]), the Historia Miscella (l. xvi. p. 109), and Gregory of Tours (l. iv. c. 23, 29, in the Historians of France, tom. ii. p. 214, 217).

2 Theophanes (Chron. p. 204) and the Hist. Miscella (l. xvi. p. 110), as understood by De Guignes (tom. i. part ii. p. 354), *appear* to speak of a Turkish embassy to Justinian himself; but that of Maniach, in the fourth year of his successor Justin, is positively the first that reached Constantinople (Menander, p. 108).

3 The Russians have found characters, rude hieroglyphics, on the Irtish and Yenisei, on medals, tombs, idols, rocks, obelisks, etc. (Strahlenberg, Hist. of

enumerated the conquests, they offered the friendship and military aid, of the Turks; and their sincerity was attested by direful
imprecations (if they were guilty of falsehood) against their own
head and the head of Disabul their master. The Greek prince
entertained with hospitable regard the ambassadors of a remote
and powerful monarch: the sight of silkworms and looms disappointed the hopes of the Sogdoites; the emperor renounced, or
seemed to renounce, the fugitive Avars, but he accepted the
alliance of the Turks; and the ratification of the treaty was carried
by a Roman minister to the foot of Mount Altai. Under the
successors of Justinian the friendship of the two nations was
cultivated by frequent and cordial intercourse; the most favoured
vassals were permitted to imitate the example of the great khan;
and one hundred and six Turks, who on various occasions had
visited Constantinople, departed at the same time for their native
country. The duration and length of the journey from the Byzantine court to Mount Altai are not specified: it might have
been difficult to mark a road through the nameless deserts, the
mountains, rivers, and morasses of Tartary; but a curious account has been preserved of the reception of the Roman ambassadors at the royal camp. After they had been purified with fire
and incense, according to a rite still practised under the sons of
Zingis, they were introduced to the presence of Disabul. In a
valley of the Golden Mountain they found the great khan in his
tent, seated in a chair with wheels, to which a horse might be
occasionally harnessed. As soon as they had delivered their presents, which were received by the proper officers, they exposed
in a florid oration the wishes of the Roman emperor that victory
might attend the arms of the Turks, that their reign might be
long and prosperous, and that a strict alliance, without envy or
deceit, might for ever be maintained between the two most
powerful nations of the earth. The answer of Disabul corresponded with these friendly professions, and the ambassadors
were seated by his side at a banquet which lasted the greatest
part of the day: the tent was surrounded with silk hangings, and

Siberia, p. 324, 346, 406, 429). Dr. Hyde (de Religione Veterum Persarum,
p. 521, etc.) has given two alphabets of Thibet and of the Eygours. I have long
harboured a suspicion that *all* the Scythian, and *some*, perhaps *much*, of the Indian
science, was derived from the Greeks of Bactriana.

a Tartar liquor was served on the table which possessed at least
the intoxicating qualities of wine. The entertainment of the succeeding day was more sumptuous; the silk hangings of the second tent were embroidered in various figures; and the royal seat,
the cups, and the vases were of gold. A third pavilion was supported by columns of gilt wood; a bed of pure and massy gold
was raised on four peacocks of the same metal: and before the
entrance of the tent, dishes, basins, and statues of solid silver
and admirable art were ostentatiously piled in waggons, the
monuments of valour rather than of industry. When Disabul led
his armies against the frontiers of Persia, his Roman allies followed many days the march of the Turkish camp, nor were they
dismissed till they had enjoyed their precedency over the envoy
of the Great King, whose loud and intemperate clamours interrupted the silence of the royal banquet. The power and ambition
of Chosroes cemented the union of the Turks and Romans, who
touched his dominions on either side: but those distant nations,
regardless of each other, consulted the dictates of interest, without recollecting the obligations of oaths and treaties. While the
successor of Disabul celebrated his father's obsequies, he was
saluted by the ambassadors of the emperor Tiberius, who proposed an invasion of Persia, and sustained with firmness the
angry and perhaps the just reproaches of that haughty barbarian.
'You see my ten fingers,' said the great khan, and he applied
them to his mouth. 'You Romans speak with as many tongues,
but they are tongues of deceit and perjury. To me you hold one
language, to my subjects another; and the nations are successively deluded by your perfidious eloquence. You precipitate your
allies into war and danger, you enjoy their labours, and you
neglect your benefactors. Hasten your return, inform your master that a Turk is incapable of uttering or forgiving falsehood,
and that he shall speedily meet the punishment which he deserves. While he solicits my friendship with flattering and hollow
words, he is sunk to a confederate of my fugitive Varchonites.
If I condescend to march against those contemptible slaves, they
will tremble at the sound of our whips; they will be trampled,
like a nest of ants, under the feet of my innumerable cavalry. I
am not ignorant of the road which they have followed to invade
your empire; nor can I be deceived by the vain pretence that

Mount Caucasus is the impregnable barrier of the Romans. I know the course of the Dniester, the Danube, and the Hebrus; the most warlike nations have yielded to the arms of the Turks; and from the rising to the setting sun the earth is my inheritance.' Notwithstanding this menace, a sense of mutual advantage soon renewed the alliance of the Turks and Romans: but the pride of the great khan survived his resentment; and when he announced an important conquest to his friend the emperor Maurice, he styled himself the master of the seven races and the lord of the seven climates of the world.[1]

Disputes have often arisen between the sovereigns of Asia for the title of king of the world, while the contest has proved that it could not belong to either of the competitors. The kingdom of the Turks was bounded by the Oxus or Gihon; and *Touran* was separated by that great river from the rival monarchy of *Iran*, or Persia, which in a smaller compass contained perhaps a larger measure of power and population. The Persians, who alternately invaded and repulsed the Turks and the Romans, were still ruled by the house of Sassan, which ascended the throne three hundred years before the accession of Justinian. His contemporary, Cabades, or Kobad, had been successful in war against the emperor Anastasius; but the reign of that prince was distracted by civil and religious troubles. A prisoner in the hands of his subjects, an exile among the enemies of Persia, he recovered his liberty by prostituting the honour of his wife, and regained his kingdom with the dangerous and mercenary aid of the barbarians who had slain his father. His nobles were suspicious that Kobad never forgave the authors of his expulsion, or even those of his restoration. The people was deluded and inflamed by the fanaticism of Mazdak,[2] who asserted the

1 All the details of these Turkish and Roman embassies, so curious in the history of human manners, are drawn from the Extracts of Menander (p. 106–110, 151–154, 161–164 [295–303, 380–385, 397–405, ed. Bonn]), in which we often regret the want of order and connection.

2 See D'Herbelot (Bibliot. Orient. p. 568, 929); Hyde (de Religione Vet. Persarum, c. 21, p. 290, 291); Pocock (Specimen Hist. Arab. p. 70, 71); Eutychius (Annal. tom. ii. p. 176); Texeira (in Stevens, Hist. of Persia, l. i. c. 34).

[Mazdak was an Archimagus born at Nischapour in Khorassan. His father's name was Bamdadan. He announced himself as a reformer of Zoroastrianism, and carried the doctrine of the two principles to a much greater height. He

community of women[1] and the equality of mankind, whilst he appropriated the richest lands and most beautiful females to the use of his sectaries. The view of these disorders, which had been fomented by his laws and example,[2] embittered the declining age of the Persian monarch; and his fears were increased by the consciousness of his design to reverse the natural and customary order of succession in favour of his third and most favoured son, so famous under the names of Chosroes and Nushirvan. To render the youth more illustrious in the eyes of the nations, Kobad was desirous that he should be adopted by the emperor Justin: the hope of peace inclined the Byzantine court to accept this singular proposal; and Chosroes might have acquired a specious claim to the inheritance of his Roman parent. But the future mischief was diverted by the advice of the quæstor Proclus: a difficulty was started, whether the adoption should be performed as a civil or military rite;[3] the treaty was abruptly dissolved; and the sense of this indignity sunk deep into the mind of Chosroes, who had already advanced to the Tigris on his road to Constantinople. His father did not long survive the disappointment of his wishes: the testament of their deceased sovereign was read in the assembly of the nobles; and a powerful faction, prepared for the event, and regardless of the priority of

taught the absolute indifference of human action, perfect equality of rank, community of property and women, marriages between the nearest kindred, but he interdicted animal food and enforced a vegetable diet. Prof. Bury says, 'Its religious character distinguished Mazdakism from all modern socialistic theories. His doctrines were embraced by the ancient Gnostics, and Mazdak was enrolled by them with Thoth, Saturn, Zoroaster, Pythagoras, Epicurus, John, and Christ as the teachers of the true Gnostic doctrines.' – O. S.]

1 The fame of the new law for the community of women was soon propagated in Syria (Asseman. Biblioth. Orient. tom. iii. p. 402) and Greece (Procop. Persic. l. i. c. 5).

2 He offered his own wife and sister to the prophet; but the prayers of Nushirvan saved his mother, and the indignant monarch never forgave the humiliation to which his filial piety had stooped: pedes tuos deosculatus (said he to Mazdak) cujus fœtor adhuc nares occupat (Pocock, Specimen Hist. Arab. p. 71).

3 Procopius, Persic. l. i. c. 11. Was not Proclus over-wise? Was not the danger imaginary? – The excuse, at least, was injurious to a nation not ignorant of letters: οὐ γράμμασιν οἱ βάρβαροι τοὺς παῖδας ποιοῦνται ἀλλ' ὅπλων σκευῇ. Whether any mode of adoption was practised in Persia I much doubt.

age, exalted Chosroes to the throne of Persia. He filled that throne during a prosperous period of forty-eight years;[1] and the JUSTICE of Nushirvan is celebrated as the theme of immortal praise by the nations of the East.

But the justice of kings is understood by themselves, and even by their subjects, with an ample indulgence for gratification of passion and interest. The virtue of Chosroes was that of a conqueror who, in the measures of peace and war, is excited by ambition and restrained by prudence; who confounds the greatness with the happiness of a nation, and calmly devotes the lives of thousands to the fame, or even the amusement, of a single man. In his domestic administration the just Nushirvan would merit in our feelings the appellation of a tyrant. His two elder brothers had been deprived of their fair expectations of the diadem: their future life, between the supreme rank and the condition of subjects, was anxious to themselves and formidable to their master: fear, as well as revenge, might tempt them to rebel; the slightest evidence of a conspiracy satisfied the author of their wrongs; and the repose of Chosroes was secured by the death of these unhappy princes, with their families and adherents. One guiltless youth was saved and dismissed by the compassion of a veteran general; and this act of humanity, which was revealed by his son, overbalanced the merit of reducing twelve nations to the obedience of Persia. The zeal and prudence of Mebodes had fixed the diadem on the head of Chosroes himself; but he delayed to attend the royal summons till he had performed the duties of a military review: he was instantly commanded to repair to the iron tripod which stood before the gate of the palace,[2]

1 From Procopius and Agathias, Pagi (tom. ii. p. 543, 626) has proved that Chosroes Nushirvan ascended the throne in the fifth year of Justinian (A.D. 531, April 1–A.D. 532, April 1). But the true chronology, which harmonises with the Greeks and Orientals, is ascertained by John Malala (tom. ii. 211 [ed. Oxon.; p. 471, ed. Bonn]). Cabades, or Kobad, after a reign of forty-three years and two months, sickened the 8th, and died the 13th of September, A.D. 531, aged eighty-two years. According to the Annals of Eutychius, Nushirvan reigned forty-seven years and six months; and his death must consequently be placed in March, A.D. 579.

2 Procopius, Persic. l. i. c. 23 [tom. i. p. 118, ed. Bonn]. Brisson de Regn. Pers. p. 494. The gate of the palace of Ispahan is, or was, the fatal scene of disgrace or death (Chardin, Voyage en Perse, tom. iv. p. 312, 313).

where it was death to relieve or approach the victim; and Mebodes languished several days before his sentence was pronounced by the inflexible pride and calm ingratitude of the son of Kobad. But the people, more especially in the East, is disposed to forgive, and even to applaud, the cruelty which strikes at the loftiest heads – at the slaves of ambition, whose voluntary choice has exposed them to live in the smiles, and to perish by the frown, of a capricious monarch. In the execution of the laws which he had no temptation to violate; in the punishment of crimes which attacked his own dignity, as well as the happiness of individuals; Nushirvan, or Chosroes, deserved the appellation of *just*. His government was firm, rigorous, and impartial. It was the first labour of his reign to abolish the dangerous theory of common or equal possessions: the lands and women which the sectaries of Mazdak had usurped were restored to their lawful owners; and the temperate chastisement of the fanatics or impostors confirmed the domestic rights of society. Instead of listening with blind confidence to a favourite minister, he established four viziers over the four great provinces of his empire – Assyria, Media, Persia, and Bactriana. In the choice of judges, præfects, and counsellors, he strove to remove the mask which is always worn in the presence of kings: he wished to substitute the natural order of talents for the accidental distinctions of birth and fortune; he professed, in specious language, his intention to prefer those men who carried the poor in their bosoms, and to banish corruption from the seat of justice, as dogs were excluded from the temples of the Magi. The code of laws of the first Artaxerxes was revived and published as the rule of the magistrates; but the assurance of speedy punishment was the best security of their virtue. Their behaviour was inspected by a thousand eyes, their words were overheard by a thousand ears, the secret or public agents of the throne; and the provinces, from the Indian to the Arabian confines, were enlightened by the frequent visits of a sovereign who affected to emulate his celestial brother in his rapid and salutary career. Education and agriculture he viewed as the two objects most deserving of his care. In every city of Persia, orphans and the children of the poor were maintained and instructed at the public expense; the daughters were given in marriage to the richest citizens of their own rank, and the sons, according to their different talents, were employed in mechanic trades or promoted to more honourable service. The deserted villages were relieved by his bounty; to the peasants and farmers who were found incapable of cultivating their lands he distributed cattle, seed, and the instruments of husbandry; and the rare and inestimable treasure of fresh water was parsimoniously managed, and skilfully dispersed over the arid territory of Persia.[1] The prosperity of that kingdom was the effect and the evidence of his virtues; his vices are those of Oriental despotism; but in the long competition between Chosroes and Justinian, the advantage, both of merit and fortune, is almost always on the side of the barbarian.[2]

To the praise of justice Nushirvan united the reputation of knowledge; and the seven Greek philosophers who visited his court were invited and deceived by the strange assurance that a disciple of Plato was seated on the Persian throne. Did they expect that a prince, strenuously exercised in the toils of war and government, should agitate, with dexterity like their own, the abstruse and profound questions which amused the leisure of the schools of Athens? Could they hope that the precepts of philosophy should direct the life and control the passions of a despot whose infancy had been taught to consider *his* absolute and fluctuating will as the only rule of moral obligation?[3] The studies of Chosroes were ostentatious and superficial; but his example awakened the curiosity of an ingenious people, and the

1 In Persia the prince of the waters is an officer of state. The number of wells and subterraneous channels is much diminished, and with it the fertility of the soil: 400 wells have been recently lost near Tauris, and 42,000 were once reckoned in the province of Khorasan (Chardin, tom. iii. p. 99, 100; Tavernier, tom. i. p. 416).

2 The character and government of Nushirvan is represented sometimes in the words of D'Herbelot (Bibliot. Orient. p. 680, etc., from Khondemir), Eutychius (Annal. tom. ii. p. 179, 180 – very rich), Abulpharagius (Dynast. vii. p. 94, 95 – very poor), Tarikh Schikard (p. 144–150), Texeira (in Stevens, l. i. c. 35), Asseman (Bibliot. Orient. tom. iii. p. 404–410), and the Abbé Fourmont (Hist. de l'Acad. des Inscriptions, tom. vii p. 325–334), who has translated a spurious or geniune testament of Nushirvan.

3 A thousand years before his birth, the judges of Persia had given a solemn opinion – τῷ βασιλεύοντι Περσέων ἐξεῖναι ποιέειν τὸ ἄν βούληται (Herodot. l. iii. c. 31, p. 210, edit. Wesseling). Nor had this constitutional maxim been neglected as a useless and barren theory.

light of science was diffused over the dominions of Persia.[1] At Gondi Sapor, in the neighbourhood of the royal city of Susa, an academy of physic was founded, which insensibly became a liberal school of poetry, philosophy, and rhetoric.[2] The annals of the monarchy[3] were composed; and while recent and authentic history might afford some useful lessons both to the prince and people, the darkness of the first ages was embellished by the giants, the dragons, and the fabulous heroes of Oriental romance.[4] Every learned or confident stranger was enriched by the bounty and flattered by the conversation of the monarch: he nobly rewarded a Greek physician[5] by the deliverance of three thousand captives; and the sophists, who contended for his favour, were exasperated by the wealth and insolence of Uranius, their more successful rival. Nushirvan believed, or at least respected, the religion of the Magi; and some traces of persecution may be discovered in his reign.[6] Yet he allowed himself freely to compare the tenets of the various sects; and the theological disputes, in which he frequently presided, diminished the authority of the

1 On the literary state of Persia, the Greek versions, philosophers, sophists, the learning or ignorance of Chosroes, Agathias (l. ii. [c. 28 *sq.*] p. 66–71 [p. 126 *sqq.*, ed. Bonn]) displays much information and strong prejudices.

2 Asseman. Bibliot. Orient. tom. iv. p. DCCXLV. vi. vii.

3 The Shah Nameh, or Book of Kings, is perhaps the original record of history which was translated into Greek by the interpreter Sergius (Agathias, l. iv. [c. 30] p. 141 [p. 273, ed. Bonn]), preserved after the Mahometan conquest, and versified, in the year 994, by the national poet Ferdoussi. See D'Anquetil (Mém. de l'Académie, tom. xxxi. p. 379) and Sir William Jones (Hist. of Nadir Shah, p. 161).

4 In the fifth century, the name of Restom, or Rostam, a hero who equalled the strength of twelve [one hundred and twenty – S.] elephants, was familiar to the Armenians (Moses Chorenensis, Hist. Armen. l. ii. c. 7, p. 96, edit. Whiston). In the beginning of the seventh, the Persian romance of Rostam and Isfendiar was applauded at Mecca (Sale's Koran, c. xxxi. p. 335). Yet this exposition of ludicrum novæ historiæ is not given by Maracci (Refutat. Alcoran. p. 544–548).

5 Procop. (Goth. l. iv. c. 10 [tom. ii. p. 505, ed. Bonn]). Kobad had a favourite Greek physician, Stephen of Edessa (Persic. l. ii. c. 26 [tom. i. p. 271, ed. Bonn]). The practice was ancient; and Herodotus relates the adventures of Democedes of Crotona (l. iii. c. 125–137).

6 See Pagi, tom. ii. p. 626. In one of the treaties an honourable article was inserted for the toleration and burial of the catholics (Menander, in Excerpt. Legat. p. 142 [p. 363 *sq.*, ed. Bonn]). Nushizad, a son of Nushirvan, was a Christian, a rebel, and – a martyr? (D'Herbelot, p. 681.)

priest and enlightened the minds of the people. At his command
the most celebrated writers of Greece and India were translated
into the Persian language – a smooth and elegant idiom, recommended by Mahomet to the use of paradise, though it is branded
with the epithets of savage and unmusical by the ignorance and
presumption of Agathias.[1] Yet the Greek historian might reasonably wonder that it should be found possible to execute an entire
version of Plato and Aristotle in a foreign dialect, which had not
been framed to express the spirit of freedom and the subtleties
of philosophic disquisition. And, if the reason of the Stagyrite
might be equally dark or equally intelligible in every tongue, the
dramatic art and verbal argumentation of the disciple of Socrates[2] appear to be indissolubly mingled with the grace and
perfection of his Attic style. In the search of universal knowledge, Nushirvan was informed that the moral and political fables
of Pilpay, an ancient Brahman, were preserved with jealous reverence among the treasures of the kings of India. The physician
Perozes was secretly despatched to the banks of the Ganges,
with instructions to procure, at any price, the communication
of this valuable work. His dexterity obtained a transcript, his
learned diligence accomplished the translation; and the fables of
Pilpay[3] were read and admired in the assembly of Nushirvan and

1 On the Persian language, and its three dialects, consult D'Anquetil
(p. 339–343) and Jones (p. 153–185): ἀγρίᾳ τινὶ γλώττῃ καὶ ἀμουσοτάτῃ, is the
character which Agathias (l. ii. [c. 28] p. 67 [p. 126, ed. Bonn]) ascribes to an
idiom renowned in the East for poetical softness.

2 Agathias [l. c.] specifies the Gorgias, Phædon, Parmenides, and Timæus.
Renaudot (Fabricius, Biblioth. Græc. tom. xii. p. 246–261) does not mention
this barbaric version of Aristotle.

3 Of these fables I have seen three copies in three different languages: 1. In
Greek, translated by Simeon Seth [A.D. 1100] from the Arabic, and published by
Starck at Berlin in 1697, in 12mo. 2. In Latin, a version from the Greek,
Sapientia Indorum, inserted by Père Poussin at the end of his edition of Pa-
chymer (p. 547–620, edit. Roman.). 3. In French, from the Turkish, dedicated,
in 1540, to Sultan Soliman. Contes et Fables Indiennes de Bidpai et de Lokman,
par MM. Galland et Cardonne, Paris, 1778, 3 vols. in 12mo. Mr. Warton (History of English Poetry, vol. i. p. 129–131) takes a larger scope.

[The oldest Indian collection is the Panchatantra – literally, the five collections – which were translated into Pehlevi in the reign of Nushirvan, from
which the Arabic translation, executed by Abdolla Ibn Mokaffa in the eighth
century, and styled 'Kalila and Dimnah, or the Fables of Pilpay (or Bidpai),'

his nobles. The Indian original and the Persian copy have long since disappeared; but this venerable monument has been saved by the curiosity of the Arabian caliphs, revived in the modern Persic, the Turkish, the Syriac, the Hebrew, and the Greek idioms, and transfused through successive versions into the modern languages of Europe. In their present form, the peculiar character, the manners and religion of the Hindoos, are completely obliterated; and the intrinsic merit of the fables of Pilpay is far inferior to the concise elegance of Phædrus and the native graces of La Fontaine. Fifteen moral and political sentences are illustrated in a series of apologues; but the composition is intricate, the narrative prolix, and the precept obvious and barren. Yet the Brahman may assume the merit of *inventing* a pleasing fiction, which adorns the nakedness of truth, and alleviates, perhaps, to a royal ear, the harshness of instruction. With a similar design, to admonish kings that they are strong only in the strength of their subjects, the same Indians invented the game of chess, which was likewise introduced into Persia under the reign of Nushirvan.[1]

The son of Kobad found his kingdom involved in a war with the successor of Constantine; and the anxiety of his domestic situation inclined him to grant the suspension of arms which Justinian was impatient to purchase. Chosroes saw the Roman ambassadors at his feet. He accepted eleven thousand pounds of gold as the price of an *endless* or indefinite peace;[2] some mutual exchanges were regulated; the Persian assumed the guard of the gates of Caucasus, and the demolition of Dara was suspended on condition that it should never be made the residence of the general of the East. This interval of repose had been solicited and was diligently improved by the ambition of the emperor: his

was taken. They were rendered from Sanscrit into German in 1859 by Theodore Benfey, whose masterly introduction to the first volume of his 'Pantschatantra' is the source whence much of our knowledge regarding this specific branch of Indian literature is drawn. – O. S.]

1 See the Historia Shahiludii of Dr. Hyde (Syntagm. Dissertat. tom. ii. p. 61–69).

2 The endless peace (Procopius, Persic. l. i. c. 22 [tem. i. p. 114, ed. Bonn]) was concluded or ratified in the sixth year, and third consulship, of Justinian (A.D. 533, between January 1 and April 1; Pagi, tom. ii. p. 550). Marcellinus, in his Chronicle, uses the style of Medes and Persians.

African conquests were the first fruits of the Persian treaty; and the avarice of Chosroes was soothed by a large portion of the spoils of Carthage, which his ambassadors required in a tone of pleasantry and under the colour of friendship.[1] But the trophies of Belisarius disturbed the slumbers of the Great King; and he heard with astonishment, envy, and fear that Sicily, Italy, and Rome itself had been reduced in three rapid campaigns to the obedience of Justinian. Unpractised in the art of violating treaties, he secretly excited his bold and subtle vassal Almondar. That prince of the Saracens, who resided at Hira,[2] had not been included in the general peace, and still waged an obscure war against his rival Arethas, the chief of the tribe of Gassan, and confederate of the empire. The subject of their dispute was an extensive sheep-walk in the desert to the south of Palmyra. An immemorial tribute for the licence of pasture appeared to attest the rights of Almondar, while the Gassanite appealed to the Latin name of strata, a paved road, as an unquestionable evidence of the sovereignty and labours of the Romans.[3] The two monarchs supported the cause of their respective vassals; and the Persian Arab, without expecting the event of a slow and doubtful arbitration, enriched his flying camp with the spoil and captives of Syria. Instead of repelling the arms, Justinian attempted to seduce the fidelity of Almondar, while he called from the extremities of the earth the nations of Æthiopia and Scythia to invade the dominions of his rival. But the aid of such allies was distant and precarious, and the discovery of this hostile correspondence justified the complaints of the Goths and Armenians, who implored, almost at the same time, the protection of Chosroes. The descendants of Arsaces, who were still numerous in Armenia, had been provoked to assert the last relics of

1 Procopius, Persic. l. i. c. 26 [p. 137, ed. Bonn].

2 Almondar, king of Hira, was deposed by Kobad, and restored by Nushirvan. His mother, from her beauty, was surnamed *Celestial Water*, an appellation which became hereditary, and was extended for a more noble cause (liberality in famine) to the Arab princes of Syria (Pocock, Specimen Hist. Arab. p. 69, 70).

3 Procopius, Persic. l. ii. c. 1. [tom. i. p. 154. ed. Bonn]. We are ignorant of the origin and object of this *strata*, a paved road of ten days' journey from Auranitis to Babylonia. (See a Latin note in Delisle's Map Imp. Orient.) Wesseling and D'Anville are silent.

national freedom and hereditary rank; and the ambassadors of Vitiges had secretly traversed the empire to expose the instant, and almost inevitable, danger of the kingdom of Italy. Their representations were uniform, weighty, and effectual. 'We stand before your throne, the advocates of your interest as well as of our own. The ambitious and faithless Justinian aspires to be the sole master of the world. Since the endless peace, which betrayed the common freedom of mankind, that prince, your ally in words, your enemy in actions, has alike insulted his friends and foes, and has filled the earth with blood and confusion. Has he not violated the privileges of Armenia, the independence of Colchis, and the wild liberty of the Tzanian mountains? Has he not usurped, with equal avidity, the city of Bosphorus on the frozen Mæotis, and the vale of palm-trees on the shores of the Red Sea? The Moors, the Vandals, the Goths, have been successively oppressed, and each nation has calmly remained the spectator of their neighbour's ruin. Embrace, O king! the favourable moment; the East is left without defence, while the armies of Justinian and his renowned general are detained in the distant regions of the West. If you hesitate and delay, Belisarius and his victorious troops will soon return from the Tiber to the Tigris, and Persia may enjoy the wretched consolation of being the last devoured." By such arguments, Chosroes was easily persuaded to imitate the example which he condemned; but the Persian, ambitious of military fame, disdained the inactive warfare of a rival who issued his sanguinary commands from the secure station of the Byzantine palace.

Whatever might be the provocations of Chosroes, he abused the confidence of treaties; and the just reproaches of dissimulation and falsehood could only be concealed by the lustre of his victories.[2]

1 I have blended, in a short speech, the two orations of the Arsacides of Armenia and the Gothic ambassadors. Procopius, in his public history, feels, and makes us feel, that Justinian was the true author of the war (Persic. l. ii. c. 2, 3).

2 The invasion of Syria, the ruin of Antioch, etc., are related in a full and regular series by Procopius (Persic. l. ii. c. 5–14). Small collateral aid can be drawn from the Orientals: yet not they, but D'Herbelot himself (p. 680), should blush, when he blames them for making Justinian and Nushirvan contemporaries. On the geography of the seat of war, D'Anville (l'Euphrate et le Tigre) is sufficient and satisfactory.

The Persian army, which had been assembled in the plains of Babylon, prudently declined the strong cities of Mesopotamia, and followed the western bank of the Euphrates, till the small though populous town of Dura presumed to arrest the progress of the Great King. The gates of Dura, by treachery and surprise, were burst open; and as soon as Chosroes had stained his scimitar with the blood of the inhabitants, he dismissed the ambassador of Justinian to inform his master in what place he had left the enemy of the Romans. The conqueror still affected the praise of humanity and justice; and as he beheld a noble matron with her infant rudely dragged along the ground, he sighed, he wept, and implored the divine justice to punish the author of these calamities. Yet the herd of twelve thousand captives was ransomed for two hundred pounds of gold; the neighbouring bishop of Sergiopolis pledged his faith for the payment, and in the subsequent year the unfeeling avarice of Chosroes exacted the penalty of an obligation which it was generous to contract and impossible to discharge. He advanced into the heart of Syria; but a feeble enemy, who vanished at his approach, disappointed him of the honour of victory; and as he could not hope to establish his dominion, the Persian king displayed in this inroad the mean and rapacious vices of a robber. Hierapolis, Berrhœa or Aleppo, Apamea and Chalcis, were successively besieged: they redeemed their safety by a ransom of gold or silver proportioned to their respective strength and opulence, and their new master enforced without observing the terms of capitulation. Educated in the religion of the Magi, he exercised, without remorse, the lucrative trade of sacrilege; and, after stripping of its gold and gems a piece of the true cross, he generously restored the naked relic to the devotion of the Christians of Apamea. No more than fourteen years had elapsed since Antioch was ruined by an earthquake; but the queen of the East, the new Theopolis, had been raised from the ground by the liberality of Justinian; and the increasing greatness of the buildings and the people already erased the memory of this recent disaster. On one side the city was defended by the mountain, on the other by the river Orontes; but the most accessible part was commanded by a superior eminence: the proper remedies were rejected, from the despicable fear of discovering its weakness to the enemy; and

Germanus, the emperor's nephew, refused to trust his person and dignity within the walls of a besieged city. The people of Antioch had inherited the vain and satirical genius of their ancestors: they were elated by a sudden reinforcement of six thousand soldiers; they disdained the offers of an easy capitulation, and their intemperate clamours insulted from the ramparts the majesty of the Great King. Under his eye the Persian myriads mounted with scaling-ladders to the assault; the Roman mercenaries fled through the opposite gate of Daphne; and the generous assistance of the youth of Antioch served only to aggravate the miseries of their country. As Chosroes, attended by the ambassadors of Justinian, was descending from the mountain, he affected, in a plaintive voice, to deplore the obstinacy and ruin of that unhappy people; but the slaughter still raged with unrelenting fury, and the city, at the command of a barbarian, was delivered to the flames. The cathedral of Antioch was indeed preserved by the avarice, not the piety, of the conqueror: a more honourable exemption was granted to the church of St. Julian and the quarter of the town where the ambassadors resided; some distant streets were saved by the shifting of the wind, and the walls still subsisted to protect, and soon to betray, their new inhabitants. Fanaticism had defaced the ornaments of Daphne; but Chosroes breathed a purer air amidst her groves and fountains, and some idolaters in his train might sacrifice with impunity to the nymphs of that elegant retreat. Eighteen miles below Antioch the river Orontes falls into the Mediterranean. The haughty Persian visited the term of his conquests, and, after bathing alone in the sea, he offered a solemn sacrifice of thanksgiving to the sun, or rather to the Creator of the sun, whom the Magi adored. If this act of superstition offended the prejudices of the Syrians, they were pleased by the courteous and even eager attention with which he assisted at the games of the circus; and as Chosroes had heard that the *blue* faction was espoused by the emperor, his peremptory command secured the victory of the *green* charioteer. From the discipline of his camp the people derived more solid consolation, and they interceded in vain for the life of a soldier who had too faithfully copied the rapine of the just Nushirvan. At length, fatigued though unsatiated with the spoil of Syria, he slowly moved to the Euphrates, formed a temporary bridge in the neighbourhood of Barbalissus, and defined the space of three days for the entire passage of his numerous host. After his return he founded, at the distance of one day's journey from the palace of Ctesiphon, a new city, which perpetuated the joint names of Chosroes and of Antioch. The Syrian captives recognised the form and situation of their native abodes; baths and a stately circus were constructed for their use; and a colony of musicians and charioteers revived in Assyria the pleasures of a Greek capital. By the munificence of the royal founder, a liberal allowance was assigned to these fortunate exiles, and they enjoyed the singular privilege of bestowing freedom on the slaves whom they acknowledged as their kinsmen. Palestine and the holy wealth of Jerusalem were the next objects that attracted the ambition, or rather the avarice, of Chosroes. Constantinople and the palace of the Cæsars no longer appeared impregnable or remote; and his aspiring fancy already covered Asia Minor with the troops, and the Black Sea with the navies, of Persia.

These hopes might have been realised, if the conqueror of Italy had not been seasonably recalled to the defence of the East.[1] While Chosroes pursued his ambitious designs on the coast of the Euxine, Belisarius, at the head of an army without pay or discipline, encamped beyond the Euphrates, within six miles of Nisibis. He meditated, by a skilful operation, to draw the Persians from their impregnable citadel, and, improving his advantage in the field, either to intercept their retreat, or perhaps to enter the gates with the flying barbarians. He advanced one day's journey on the territories of Persia, reduced the fortress of Sisaurane, and sent the governor, with eight hundred chosen horsemen, to serve the emperor in his Italian wars. He detached Arethas and his Arabs, supported by twelve hundred Romans, to pass the Tigris, and to ravage the harvests of Assyria, a fruitful province, long exempt from the calamities of war. But the plans of Belisarius were disconcerted by the untractable spirit of Arethas, who neither returned to the camp, nor sent any intelligence

1 In the public history of Procopius (Persic. l. ii. c. 16, 18, 19, 20, 21, 24, 25, 26, 27, 28); and with some slight exceptions, we may reasonably shut our ears against the malevolent whisper of the Anecdotes (c. 2, 3, with the Notes, as usual, of Alemannus).

of his motions. The Roman general was fixed in anxious expectation to the same spot; the time of action elapsed; the ardent
sun of Mesopotamia inflamed with fevers the blood of his European soldiers; and the stationary troops and officers of Syria
affected to tremble for the safety of their defenceless cities. Yet
this diversion had already succeeded in forcing Chosroes to return with loss and precipitation; and if the skill of Belisarius had
been seconded by discipline and valour, his success might have
satisfied the sanguine wishes of the public, who required at his
hands the conquest of Ctesiphon and the deliverance of the
captives of Antioch. At the end of the campaign, he was recalled
to Constantinople by an ungrateful court, but the dangers of the
ensuing spring restored his confidence and command; and the
hero, almost alone, was despatched, with the speed of post-horses,
to repel, by his name and presence, the invasion of Syria. He
found the Roman generals, among whom was a nephew of Justinian, imprisoned by their fears in the fortifications of Hierapolis. But instead of listening to their timid counsels, Belisarius
commanded them to follow him to Europus, where he had resolved to collect his forces, and to execute whatever God should
inspire him to achieve against the enemy. His firm attitude on
the banks of the Euphrates restrained Chosroes from advancing
towards Palestine; and he received with art and dignity the ambassadors, or rather spies, of the Persian monarch. The plain
between Hierapolis and the river was covered with the squadrons
of cavalry, six thousand hunters, tall and robust, who pursued
their game without the apprehension of an enemy. On the opposite bank the ambassadors descried a thousand Armenian
horse, who appeared to guard the passage of the Euphrates. The
tent of Belisarius was of the coarsest linen, the simple equipage
of a warrior who disdained the luxury of the East. Around his
tent the nations who marched under his standard were arranged
with skilful confusion. The Thracians and Illyrians were posted
in the front, the Heruli and Goths in the centre; the prospect
was closed by the Moors and Vandals, and their loose array
seemed to multiply their numbers. Their dress was light and
active; one soldier carried a whip, another a sword, a third a bow,
a fourth, perhaps, a battle-axe, and the whole picture exhibited
the intrepidity of the troops and the vigilance of the general.

Chosroes was deluded by the address, and awed by the genius, of the lieutenant of Justinian. Conscious of the merit, and ignorant of the force, of his antagonist, he dreaded a decisive battle in a distant country, from whence not a Persian might return to relate the melancholy tale. The Great King hastened to repass the Euphrates; and Belisarius pressed his retreat, by affecting to oppose a measure so salutary to the empire, and which could scarcely have been prevented by an army of a hundred thousand men. Envy might suggest to ignorance and pride that the public enemy had been suffered to escape; but the African and Gothic triumphs are less glorious than this safe and bloodless victory, in which neither fortune, nor the valour of the soldiers, can subtract any part of the general's renown. The second removal of Belisarius from the Persian to the Italian war revealed the extent of his personal merit, which had corrected or supplied the want of discipline and courage. Fifteen generals, without concert or skill, led through the mountains of Armenia an army of thirty thousand Romans, inattentive to their signals, their ranks, and their ensigns. Four thousand Persians, entrenched in the camp of Dubis, vanquished, almost without a combat, this disorderly multitude; their useless arms were scattered along the road, and their horses sunk under the fatigue of their rapid flight. But the Arabs of the Roman party prevailed over their brethren; the Armenians returned to their allegiance; the cities of Dara and Edessa resisted a sudden assault and a regular siege, and the calamities of war were suspended by those of pestilence. A tacit or formal agreement between the two sovereigns protected the tranquillity of the Eastern frontier; and the arms of Chosroes were confined to the Colchian or Lazic war, which has been too minutely described by the historians of the times.[1]

The extreme length of the Euxine Sea,[2] from Constantinople to the mouth of the Phasis, may be computed as a voyage of nine days, and a measure of seven hundred miles. From the

[1] The Lazic war, the contest of Rome and Persia on the Phasis, is tediously spun through many a page of Procopius (Persic. l. ii. c. 15, 17, 28, 29, 30; Gothic. l. iv. c. 7–16) and Agathias (l. ii., iii., and iv., p. 55–132, 141).

[2] The *Periplus*, or circumnavigation of the Euxine Sea, was described in Latin by Sallust, and in Greek by Arrian: 1. The former work, which no longer exists, has been restored by the *singular* diligence of M. de Brosses, first

Iberian Caucasus, the most lofty and craggy mountains of Asia, that river descends with such oblique vehemence, that in a short space it is traversed by one hundred and twenty bridges. Nor does the stream become placid and navigable till it reaches the town of Sarapana, five days' journey from the Cyrus, which flows from the same hills, but in a contrary direction to the Caspian lake. The proximity of these rivers has suggested the practice, or at least the idea, of wafting the precious merchandise of India down the Oxus, over the Caspian, up the Cyrus, and with the current of the Phasis into the Euxine and Mediterranean seas. As it successively collects the streams of the plain of Colchis, the Phasis moves with diminished speed, though accumulated weight. At the mouth it is sixty fathoms deep and half a league broad, but a small woody island is interposed in the midst of the channel: the water, so soon as it has deposited an earthy or metallic sediment, floats on the surface of the waves, and is no longer susceptible of corruption. In a course of one hundred miles, forty of which are navigable for large vessels, the Phasis divides the celebrated region of Colchis,[1] or Mingrelia,[2] which,

president of the parliament of Dijon (Hist. de la République Romaine, tom. ii. l. iii. p. 199–298), who ventures to assume the character of the Roman historian. His description of the Euxine is ingeniously formed of *all* the fragments of the original, and of *all* the Greeks and Latins whom Sallust might copy, or by whom he might be copied; and the merit of the execution atones for the whimsical design. 2. The Periplus of Arrian is addressed to the emperor Hadrian (in Geograph. Minor. Hudson, tom. i.), and contains whatever the governor of Pontus had seen from Trebizond to Dioscurias; whatever he had heard from Dioscurias to the Danube; and whatever he knew from the Danube to Trebizond.

1 Besides the many occasional hints from the poets, historians, etc., of antiquity, we may consult the geographical descriptions of Colchis by Strabo (l. xi. p. 760–765 [p. 497–501, ed. Casaub.]) and Pliny (Hist. Natur. vi. 5, 19, etc.).

2 I shall quote, and have used, three modern descriptions of Mingrelia and the adjacent countries. 1. Of the Père Archangeli Lamberti (Relations de Thevenot, part i. p. 31–52, with a map), who has all the knowledge and prejudices of a missionary. 2. Of Chardin (Voyages en Perse, tom. i. p. 54, 68–168): his observations are judicious; and his own adventures in the country are still more instructive than his observations. 3. Of Peyssonel (Observations sur les Peuples Barbares, p. 49, 50, 51, 58, 62, 64, 65, 71, etc., and a more recent treatise, Sur le Commerce de la Mer Noire, tom. ii. p. 1–53): he had long resided at Caffa, as consul of France; and his erudition is less valuable than his experience.

on three sides, is fortified by the Iberian and Armenian mountains, and whose maritime coast extends about two hundred
miles from the neighbourhood of Trebizond to Dioscurias and
the confines of Circassia. Both the soil and climate are relaxed
by excessive moisture: twenty-eight rivers, besides the Phasis and
his dependent streams, convey their waters to the sea; and the
hollowness of the ground appears to indicate the subterraneous
channels between the Euxine and the Caspian. In the fields
where wheat or barley is sown, the earth is too soft to sustain
the action of the plough; but the *gom*, a small grain, not unlike
the millet or coriander seed, supplies the ordinary food of the
people; and the use of bread is confined to the prince and his
nobles. Yet the vintage is more plentiful than the harvest; and
the bulk of the stems, as well as the quality of the wine, display the unassisted powers of nature. The same powers continually tend to overshadow the face of the country with thick
forests: the timber of the hills, and the flax of the plains, contribute to the abundance of naval stores; the wild and tame
animals, the horse, the ox, and the hog, are remarkably prolific,
and the name of the pheasant is expressive of his native habita-
tion on the banks of the Phasis. The gold-mines to the south of
Trebizond, which are still worked with sufficient profit, were a
subject of national dispute between Justinian and Chosroes; and
it is not unreasonable to believe that a vein of precious metal
may be equally diffused through the circle of the hills, although
these secret treasures are neglected by the laziness, or concealed
by the prudence, of the Mingrelians. The waters, impregnated
with particles of gold, are carefully strained through sheepskins
or fleeces; but this expedient, the groundwork perhaps of a marvellous fable, affords a faint image of the wealth extracted from
a virgin earth by the power and industry of ancient kings. Their
silver palaces and golden chambers surpass our belief; but the
fame of their riches is said to have excited the enterprising
avarice of the Argonauts.[1] Tradition has affirmed, with some

1 Pliny, Hist. Natur. l. xxxiii. 15. The gold and silver mines of Colchis
attracted the Argonauts (Strab. l. i. p. 77 [p. 45, ed. Casaub.]). The sagacious
Chardin could find no gold in mines, rivers, or elsewhere. Yet a Mingrelian lost
his hand and foot for showing some specimens at Constantinople of native
gold.

colour of reason, that Egypt planted on the Phasis a learned and
polite colony,[1] which manufactured linen, built navies, and invented geographical maps. The ingenuity of the moderns has
peopled with flourishing cities and nations the isthmus between
the Euxine and the Caspian;[2] and a lively writer, observing the
resemblance of climate, and, in his apprehension, of trade, has
not hesitated to pronounce Colchis the Holland of antiquity.[3]

But the riches of Colchis shine only through the darkness of
conjecture or tradition; and its genuine history presents a uniform scene of rudeness and poverty. If one hundred and thirty
languages were spoken in the market of Dioscurias,[4] they were
the imperfect idioms of so many savage tribes or families, sequestered from each other in the valleys of Mount Caucasus; and
their separation, which diminished the importance, must have
multiplied the number, of their rustic capitals. In the present
state of Mingrelia, a village is an assemblage of huts within a
wooden fence; the fortresses are seated in the depth of forests;
the princely town of Cyta, or Cotatis, consists of two hundred
houses, and a stone edifice appertains only to the magnificence
of kings. Twelve ships from Constantinople, and about sixty
barks, laden with the fruits of industry, annually cast anchor on
the coast; and the list of Colchian exports is much increased,
since the natives had only slaves and hides to offer in exchange
for the corn and salt which they purchased from the subjects of
Justinian. Not a vestige can be found of the art, the knowledge,
or the navigation of the ancient Colchians: few Greeks desired
or dared to pursue the footsteps of the Argonauts; and even the
marks of an Egyptian colony are lost on a nearer approach. The
rite of circumcision is practised only by the Mahometans of

1 Herodot. l. ii. c. 104, 105, p. 150, 151; Diodor. Sicul. l. i. [c. 28] p. 33,
edit. Wesseling; Dionys. Perieget. 689; and Eustath. ad loc Scholiast. ad Apol-
lonium Argonaut. l. iv. 282–291.

2 Montesquieu, Esprit des Loix, l. xxi. c. 6. L'Isthme ... couvert de villes
et nations qui ne sont plus.

3 Bougainville, Mémoires de l'Académie des Inscriptions, tom. xxvi. p. 33,
on the African voyage of Hanno and the commerce of antiquity.

4 A Greek historian, Timosthenes, had affirmed, in eam ccc nationes dissi-
milibus linguis descendere; and the modest Pliny is content to add, et postea a
nostris cxxx interpretibus negotia ibi gesta (vi. 5): but the words nunc deserta
cover a multitude of past fictions.

the Euxine; and the curled hair and swarthy complexion of Africa no longer disfigure the most perfect of the human race. It is in the adjacent climates of Georgia, Mingrelia, and Circassia, that nature has placed, at least to our eyes, the model of beauty, in the shape of the limbs, the colour of the skin, the symmetry of the features, and the expression of the countenance.[1] According to the destination of the two sexes, the men seem formed for action, the women for love; and the perpetual supply of females from Mount Caucasus has purified the blood, and improved the breed, of the southern nations of Asia. The proper district of Mingrelia, a portion only of the ancient Colchis, has long sustained an exportation of twelve thousand slaves. The number of prisoners or criminals would be inadequate to the annual demand; but the common people are in a state of servitude to their lords; the exercise of fraud or rapine is unpunished in a lawless community; and the market is continually replenished by the abuse of civil and paternal authority. Such a trade,[2] which reduces the human species to the level of cattle, may tend to encourage marriage and population, since the multitude of children enriches their sordid and inhuman parent. But this source of impure wealth must inevitably poison the national manners, obliterate the sense of honour and virtue, and almost extinguish the instincts of nature: the *Christians* of Georgia and Mingrelia are the most dissolute of mankind; and their children, who, in a tender age, are sold into foreign slavery, have already learned to imitate the rapine of the father and the prostitution of the mother. Yet, amidst the rudest ignorance, the untaught natives discover a singular dexterity both of mind and hand; and although the want of union and discipline exposes them to their more powerful neighbours, a bold and intrepid spirit has animated the Colchians of every age. In the host of Xerxes they

1 Buffon (Hist. Nat. tom. iii. p. 433–437) collects the unanimous suffrage of naturalists and travellers. If, in the time of Herodotus, they were in truth μελάγχροες and οὐλότριχες (and he had observed them with care), this precious fact is an example of the influence of climate on a foreign colony.

2 The Mingrelian ambassador arrived at Constantinople with two hundred persons; but he ate (*sold*) them day by day, till his retinue was diminished to a secretary and two valets (Tavernier, tom. i. p. 365). To purchase his mistress, a Mingrelian gentleman sold twelve priests and his wife to the Turks (Chardin, tom. i. p. 66).

served on foot; and their arms were a dagger or a javelin, a
wooden casque, and a buckler or raw hides. But in their own
country the use of cavalry has more generally prevailed: the
meanest of the peasants disdain to walk; the martial nobles are
possessed, perhaps, of two hundred horses; and above five thousand are numbered in the train of the prince of Mingrelia. The
Colchian government has been always a pure and hereditary
kingdom; and the authority of the sovereign is only restrained
by the turbulence of his subjects. Whenever they were obedient,
he could lead a numerous army into the field; but some faith is
requisite to believe that the single tribe of the Suanians was
composed of two hundred thousand soldiers, or that the population of Mingrelia now amounts to four millions of inhabitants.[1]

It was the boast of the Colchians that their ancestors had
checked the victories of Sesostris; and the defeat of the Egyptian
is less incredible than his successful progress as far as the foot
of Mount Caucasus. They sunk without any memorable effort
under the arms of Cyrus, followed in distant wars the standard
of the Great King, and presented him every fifth year with one
hundred boys and as many virgins, the fairest produce of the
land.[2] Yet he accepted this *gift* like the gold and ebony of India,
the frankincense of the Arabs, or the negroes and ivory of
Æthiopia: the Colchians were not subject to the dominion of a
satrap, and they continued to enjoy the name as well as substance
of national independence.[3] After the fall of the Persian empire,
Mithridates, king of Pontus, added Colchis to the wide circle of
his dominions on the Euxine; and when the natives presumed
to request that his son might reign over them, he bound the

1 Strabo, l. xi. p. 763 [p. 499, ed. Casaub.]. Lamberti, Relation de la Min-
grelie. Yet we must avoid the contrary extreme of Chardin, who allows no more
than 20,000 inhabitants to supply an annual exportation of 12,000 slaves; an
absurdity unworthy of that judicious traveller.

2 Herodot. l. iii. c. 97. See, in l. vii. c. 79, their arms and service in the
expedition of Xerxes against Greece.

3 Xenophon, who had encountered the Colchians in his retreat (Anabasis,
l. iv. [c. 8] p. 320, 343, 348, edit. Hutchinson; and Foster's Dissertation, p. liii–
lviii., in Spelman's English version, vol. ii.), styles them αὐτόνομοι. Before the
conquest of Mithridates they are named by Appian ἔθνος ἀρειμανὲς (de Bell.
Mithridatico, c. 15, tom. i. p. 661, of the last and best edition, by John Schweig-
hæuser, Lipsiæ, 1785, 3 vols. large octavo).

ambitious youth in chains of gold, and delegated a servant in his place. In pursuit of Mithridates, the Romans advanced to the banks of the Phasis, and their galleys ascended the river till they reached the camp of Pompey and his legions.[1] But the senate, and afterwards the emperors, disdained to reduce that distant and useless conquest into the form of a province. The family of a Greek rhetorician was permitted to reign in Colchis and the adjacent kingdoms from the time of Mark Antony to that of Nero; and after the race of Polemo[2] was extinct, the eastern Pontus, which preserved his name, extended no farther than the neighbourhood of Trebizond. Beyond these limits the fortifications of Hyssus, of Apsarus, of the Phasis, of Dioscurias or Sebastopolis, and of Pityus, were guarded by sufficient detachments of horse and foot; and six princes of Colchis received their diadems from the lieutenants of Cæsar. One of these lieutenants, the eloquent and philosophic Arrian, surveyed and has described the Euxine coast under the reign of Hadrian. The garrison which he reviewed at the mouth of the Phasis consisted of four hundred chosen legionaries; the brick walls and towers, the double ditch, and the military engines on the rampart, rendered this place inaccessible to the barbarians; but the new suburbs which had been built by the merchants and veterans required in the opinion of Arrian some external defence.[3] As the strength of the empire was gradually impaired, the Romans stationed on the Phasis were either withdrawn or expelled; and the tribe of the Lazi,[4] whose posterity speak a foreign dialect and inhabit the sea-coast of Trebizond, imposed their name and dominion on

1 The conquest of Colchis by Mithridates and Pompey is marked by Appian (de Bell. Mithridat. [l. c.]) and Plutarch (in Vit. Pomp. [c. 30, 34]).

2 We may trace the rise and fall of the family of Polemo, in Strabo (l. xi. p. 755; l. xii. p. 867 [p. 493 and 578, ed. Casaub.]), Dion Cassius or Xiphilin (p. 588, 593, 601, 719, 754, 915, 946, edit. Reimar [l. xlix. c. 25, 33, 44; l. liii. c. 25; l. liv. c. 24; l. lix. c. 12; l. lx. c. 8]), Suetonius (in Neron. c. 18, in Vespasian. c. 8), Eutropius (vii. 14 [9], Josephus (Antiq. Judiac. l. xx. c. 6, p. 970, edit. Havercamp), and Eusebius (Chron. with Scaliger, Animadvers. p. 196).

3 In the time of Procopius there were no Roman forts on the Phasis. Pityus and Sebastopolis were evacuated on the rumour of the Persians (Goth. l. iv. c. 4); but the latter was afterwards restored by Justinian (de Ædif. l. iii. c. 7 [tom. iii. p. 261, ed. Bonn]).

4 In the time of Pliny, Arrian, and Ptolemy, the Lazi were a particular tribe on the northern skirts of Colchis (Cellarius, Geograph. Antiq. tom. ii. p. 222).

the ancient kingdom of Colchis. Their independence was soon invaded by a formidable neighbour, who had acquired by arms and treaties the sovereignty of Iberia. The dependent king of Lazica received his sceptre at the hands of the Persian monarch, and the successors of Constantine acquiesced in this injurious claim, which was proudly urged as a right of immemorial prescription. In the beginning of the sixth century their influence was restored by the introduction of Christianity, which the Mingrelians still profess with becoming zeal, without understanding the doctrines or observing the precepts of their religion. After the decease of his father, Zathus was exalted to the regal dignity by the favour of the Great King; but the pious youth abhorred the ceremonies of the Magi, and sought in the palace of Constantinople an orthodox baptism, a noble wife, and the alliance of the emperor Justin. The king of Lazica was solemnly invested with the diadem, and his cloak and tunic of white silk, with a gold border, displayed in rich embroidery the figure of his new patron, who soothed the jealousy of the Persian court, and excused the revolt of Colchis, by the venerable names of hospitality and religion. The common interest of both empires imposed on the Colchians the duty of guarding the passes of Mount Caucasus, where a wall of sixty miles is now defended by the monthly service of the musketeers of Mingrelia.[1]

But this honourable connection was soon corrupted by the avarice and ambition of the Romans. Degraded from the rank of allies, the Lazi were incessantly reminded by words and actions of their dependent state. At the distance of a day's journey beyond the Apsarus they beheld the rising fortress of Petra,[2]

In the age of Justinian they spread, or at least reigned, over the whole country. At present they have migrated along the coast towards Trebizond, and compose a rude seafaring people, with a peculiar language (Chardin, p. 149; Peyssonel, p. 64).

1 John Malala, Chron. tom. ii. p. 134–137 [ed. Oxon.; p. 412–414, ed Bonn]; Theophanes, p. 144 [tom. l. p. 259, ed. Bonn]; Hist. Miscell. l. xv. p. 103. The fact is authentic, but the date seems too recent. In speaking of their Persian alliance, the Lazi contemporaries of Justinian employ the most obsolete words – ἐν γράμμασι μνημεῖα, πρόγονοι, etc. Could they belong to a connection which had not been dissolved above twenty years?

2 The sole vestige of Petra subsists in the writings of Procopius and Agathias. Most of the towns and castles of Lazica may be found by comparing their names and position with the map of Mingrelia, in Lamberti.

which commanded the maritime country to the south of the Phasis. Instead of being protected by the valour, Colchis was insulted by the licentiousness, of foreign mercenaries; the benefits of commerce were converted into base and vexatious monopoly; and Gubazes, the native prince, was reduced to a pageant of royalty by the superior influence of the officers of Justinian. Disappointed in their expectations of Christian virtue, the indignant Lazi reposed some confidence in the justice of an unbeliever. After a private assurance that their ambassadors should not be delivered to the Romans, they publicly solicited the friendship and aid of Chosroes. The sagacious monarch instantly discerned the use and importance of Colchis, and meditated a plan of conquest which was renewed at the end of a thousand years by Shah Abbas, the wisest and most powerful of his successors.[1] His ambition was fired by the hope of launching a Persian navy from the Phasis, of commanding the trade and navigation of the Euxine Sea, of desolating the coast of Pontus and Bithynia, of distressing, perhaps of attacking, Constantinople, and of persuading the barbarians of Europe to second his arms and counsels against the common enemy of mankind. Under the pretence of a Scythian war he silently led his troops to the frontiers of Iberia; the Colchian guides were prepared to conduct them through the woods and along the precipices of Mount Caucasus, and a narrow path was laboriously formed into a safe and spacious highway for the march of cavalry, and even of elephants. Gubazes laid his person and diadem at the feet of the king of Persia, his Colchians imitated the submission of their prince; and after the walls of Petra had been shaken, the Roman garrison prevented by a capitulation the impending fury of the last assault. But the Lazi soon discovered that their impatience had urged them to choose an evil more intolerable than the calamities which they strove to escape. The monopoly of salt and corn was effectually removed by the loss of those valuable commodities. The authority of a Roman legislator was succeeded by the pride

1 See the amusing letters of Pietro della Valle, the Roman traveller (Viaggi, tom. ii. 207, 209, 213, 215, 266, 286, 300; tom. iii. p. 54, 127). In the years 1618, 1619, and 1620, he conversed with Shah Abbas, and strongly encouraged a design which might have united Persia and Europe against their common enemy the Turk.

of an Oriental despot, who beheld with equal disdain the slaves whom he had exalted, and the kings whom he had humbled before the footstool of his throne. The adoration of fire was introduced into Colchis by the zeal of the Magi, their intolerant spirit provoked the fervour of a Christian people, and the prejudice of nature or education was wounded by the impious practice of exposing the dead bodies of their parents on the summit of a lofty tower to the crows and vultures of the air.[1] Conscious of the increasing hatred which retarded the execution of his great designs, the just Nushirvan had secretly given orders to assassinate the king of the Lazi, to transplant the people into some distant land, and to fix a faithful and warlike colony on the banks of the Phasis. The watchful jealousy of the Colchians foresaw and averted the approaching ruin. Their repentance was accepted at Constantinople by the prudence, rather than the clemency, of Justinian; and he commanded Dagisteus, with seven thousand Romans and one thousand of the Zani, to expel the Persians from the coast of the Euxine.

The siege of Petra, which the Roman general with the aid of the Lazi immediately undertook, is one of the most remarkable actions of the age. The city was seated on a craggy rock, which hung over the sea, and communicated by a steep and narrow path with the land. Since the approach was difficult, the attack might be deemed impossible; the Persian conqueror had strengthened the fortifications of Justinian, and the places least inaccessible were covered by additional bulwarks. In this important fortress the vigilance of Chosroes had deposited a magazine of offensive and defensive arms sufficient for five times the number, not only of the garrison, but of the besiegers themselves. The stock of flour and salt provisions was adequate to the consumption of five years; the want of wine was supplied by vinegar, and grain from whence a strong liquor was extracted; and a triple

---

1 See Herodotus (l. i. c. 140, p. 69), who speaks with diffidence, Larcher (tom. i. p. 399–401; Notes sur Herodote), Procopius (Persic. l. i. c. 11 [tom. i. p. 56, ed. Bonn]), and Agathias (l. ii. p. 61, 62 [ed. Par.; p. 113 sq., ed. Bonn]). This practice, agreeable to the Zendavesta (Hyde, de Relig. Pers. c. 34, p. 414–421), demonstrates that the burial of the Persian kings (Xenophon, Cyropæd. l. viii. [c. 7] p. 658), τί γὰρ τούτου μακαρίωτερον τοῦ τῇ γῇ μιχθῆναι, is a Greek fiction, and that their tombs could be no more than cenotaphs.

aqueduct eluded the diligence and even the suspicions of the enemy. But the firmest defence of Petra was placed in the valour of fifteen hundred Persians, who resisted the assaults of the Romans, whilst in a softer vein of earth a mine was secretly perforated. The wall, supported by slender and temporary props, hung tottering in the air; but Dagisteus delayed the attack till he had secured a specific recompense, and the town was relieved before the return of his messenger from Constantinople. The Persian garrison was reduced to four hundred men, of whom no more than fifty were exempt from sickness or wounds; yet such had been their inflexible perseverance, that they concealed their losses from the enemy by enduring without a murmur the sight and putrefying stench of the dead bodies of their eleven hundred companions. After their deliverance the breaches were hastily stopped with sandbags, the mine was replenished with earth, a new wall was erected on a frame of substantial timber, and a fresh garrison of three thousand men was stationed at Petra to sustain the labours of a second siege. The operations, both of the attack and defence, were conducted with skilful obstinacy; and each party derived useful lessons from the experience of their past faults. A battering-ram was invented, of light construction and powerful effect; it was transported and worked by the hands of forty soldiers; and as the stones were loosened by its repeated strokes, they were torn with long iron hooks from the wall. From those walls a shower of darts was incessantly poured on the heads of the assailants, but they were most dangerously annoyed by a fiery composition of sulphur and bitumen, which in Colchis might with some propriety be named the oil of Medea. Of six thousand Romans who mounted the scaling-ladders, their general Besas was first, a gallant veteran of seventy years of age: the courage of their leader, his fall, and extreme danger, animated the irresistible effort of his troops, and their prevailing numbers oppressed the strength, without subduing the spirit, of the Persian garrison. The fate of these valiant men deserves to be more distinctly noticed. Seven hundred had perished in the siege, two thousand three hundred survived to defend the breach. One thousand and seventy were destroyed with fire and sword in the last assault; and if seven hundred and thirty were made prisoners, only eighteen among them were found without the marks of honourable wounds. The remaining five hundred escaped into the citadel, which they maintained without any hopes of relief, rejecting the fairest terms of capitulation and service till they were lost in the flames. They died in obedience to the commands of their prince, and such examples of loyalty and valour might excite their countrymen to deeds of equal despair and more prosperous event. The instant demolition of the works of Petra confessed the astonishment and apprehension of the conqueror.

A Spartan would have praised and pitied the virtue of these heroic slaves; but the tedious warfare and alternate success of the Roman and Persian arms cannot detain the attention of posterity at the foot of Mount Caucasus. The advantages obtained by the troops of Justinian were more frequent and splendid; but the forces of the Great King were continually supplied till they amounted to eight elephants and seventy thousand men, including twelve thousand Scythian allies and above three thousand Dilemites, who descended by their free choice from the hills of Hyrcania, and were equally formidable in close or in distant combat. The siege of Archæopolis, a name imposed or corrupted by the Greeks, was raised with some loss and precipitation, but the Persians occupied the passes of Iberia. Colchis was enslaved by their forts and garrisons, they devoured the scanty sustenance of the people, and the prince of the Lazi fled into the mountains. In the Roman camp faith and discipline were unknown, and the independent leaders, who were invested with equal power, disputed with each other the pre-eminence of vice and corruption. The Persians followed without a murmur the commands of a single chief, who implicitly obeyed the instructions of their supreme lord. Their general was distinguished among the heroes of the East by his wisdom in council and his valour in the field. The advanced age of Mermeroes, and the lameness of both his feet, could not diminish the activity of his mind or even of his body; and, whilst he was carried in a litter in the front of battle, he inspired terror to the enemy, and a just confidence to the troops, who under his banners were always successful. After his death the command devolved to Nacoragan, a proud satrap who, in a conference with the Imperial chiefs, had presumed to declare that he disposed of victory as absolutely as of the ring on his finger. Such presumption was the natural cause and forerunner of a shameful defeat. The Romans had been gradually repulsed to the edge of the sea-shore; and their last camp, on the ruins of the Grecian colony of Phasis, was defended on all sides by strong entrenchments, the river, the Euxine, and a fleet of galleys. Despair united their counsels and invigorated their arms; they withstood the assault of the Persians, and the flight of Nacoragan preceded or followed the slaughter of ten thousand of his bravest soldiers. He escaped from the Romans to fall into the hands of an unforgiving master, who severely chastised the error of his own choice: the unfortunate general was flayed alive, and his skin, stuffed into the human form, was exposed on a mountain – a dreadful warning to those who might hereafter be intrusted with the fame and fortune of Persia.[1] Yet the prudence of Chosroes insensibly relinquished the prosecution of the Colchian war, in the just persuasion that it is impossible to reduce, or at least to hold, a distant country against the wishes and efforts of its inhabitants. The fidelity of Gubazes sustained the most rigorous trials. He patiently endured the hardships of a savage life, and rejected with disdain the specious temptations of the Persian court. The king of the Lazi had been educated in the Christian religion; his mother was the daughter of a senator; during his youth he had served ten years a silentiary of the Byzantine palace,[2] and the arrears of an unpaid salary were a motive of attachment as well as of complaint. But the long continuance of his sufferings extorted from him a naked representation of the truth, and truth was an unpardonable libel on the lieutenants of Justinian, who, amidst the delays of a ruinous war, had spared his enemies and trampled on his allies. Their malicious information persuaded the emperor that his faithless vassal already meditated a second defection: an order was surprised to send him prisoner to Constantinople; a treacherous

---

1 The punishment of flaying alive could not be introduced into Persia by Sapor (Brisson, de Regn. Pers. l. ii. p. 578), nor could it be copied from the foolish tale of Marsyas the Phrygian piper, most foolishly quoted as a precedent by Agathias (l. iv. p. 132, 133).

2 In the palace of Constantinople there were thirty silentiaries, who are styled hastati ante fores cubiculi, τῆς [ἀμφὶ τὸν βασιλέα] σιγῆς ἐπιστάται, an honourable title which conferred the rank, without imposing the duties, of a senator (Cod. Theodos. l. vi. tit. 23; Gothofred. Comment. tom. ii. p. 129).

clause was inserted that he might be lawfully killed in case of resistance; and Gubazes, without arms or suspicion of danger, was stabbed in the security of a friendly interview. In the first moments of rage and despair, the Colchians would have sacrificed their country and religion to the gratification of revenge. But the authority and eloquence of the wiser few obtained a salutary pause: the victory of the Phasis restored the terror of the Roman arms, and the emperor was solicitous to absolve his own name from the imputation of so foul a murder. A judge of senatorial rank was commissioned to inquire into the conduct and death of the king of the Lazi. He ascended a stately tribunal, encompassed by the ministers of justice and punishment: in the presence of both nations this extraordinary cause was pleaded according to the forms of civil jurisprudence, and some satisfaction was granted to an injured people by the sentence and execution of the meaner criminals.[1]

In peace the king of Persia continually sought the pretences of a rupture, but no sooner had he taken up arms than he expressed his desire of a safe and honourable treaty. During the fiercest hostilities the two monarchs entertained a deceitful negotiation: and such was the superiority of Chosroes, that, whilst he treated the Roman ministers with insolence and contempt, he obtained the most unprecedented honours for his own ambassadors at the Imperial court. The successor of Cyrus assumed the majesty of the Eastern sun, and graciously permitted his younger brother Justinian to reign over the West with the pale and reflected splendour of the moon. This gigantic style was supported by the pomp and eloquence of Isdigune, one of the royal chamberlains. His wife and daughters, with a train of eunuchs and camels, attended the march of the ambassador; two satraps with golden diadems were numbered among his followers; he was guarded by five hundred horse, the most valiant of the Persians, and the Roman governor of Dara wisely refused to admit more than twenty of this martial and hostile caravan. When Isdigune had saluted the emperor and delivered his presents,

1 On these judicial orations Agathias (l. iii. p. 81–89; l. iv. p. 108–119 [p. 155–170, 206–230, ed. Bonn]) lavishes eighteen or twenty pages of false and florid rhetoric. His ignorance or carelessness overlooks the strongest argument against the king of Lazica – his former revolt.

he passed ten months at Constantinople without discussing any serious affairs. Instead of being confined in his palace, and receiving food and water from the hands of his keepers, the Persian ambassador, without spies or guards, was allowed to visit the capital, and the freedom of conversation and trade enjoyed by his domestics offended the prejudices of an age which rigorously practised the law of nations without confidence or courtesy.[1] By an unexampled indulgence, his interpreter, a servant below the notice of a Roman magistrate, was seated at the table of Justinian by the side of his master, and one thousand pounds of gold might be assigned for the expense of his journey and entertainment. Yet the repeated labours of Isdigune could procure only a partial and imperfect truce, which was always purchased with the treasures, and renewed at the solicitation, of the Byzantine court. Many years of fruitless desolation elapsed before Justinian and Chosroes were compelled by mutual lassitude to consult the repose of their declining age. At a conference held on the frontier, each party, without expecting to gain credit, displayed the power, the justice, and the pacific intentions of their respective sovereigns; but necessity and interest dictated the treaty of peace, which was concluded for a term of fifty years, diligently composed in the Greek and Persian languages, and attested by the seals of twelve interpreters. The liberty of commerce and religion was fixed and defined, the allies of the emperor and the Great King were included in the same benefits and obligations, and the most scrupulous precautions were provided to prevent or determine the accidental disputes that might arise on the confines of two hostile nations. After twenty years of destructive though feeble war, the limits still remained without alteration, and Chosroes was persuaded to renounce his dangerous claim to the possession or sovereignty of Colchis and its dependent states. Rich in the accumulated treasures of the East, he extorted from the Romans an annual payment of thirty thousand pieces of gold; and the smallness of the sum revealed the

---

1 Procopius represents the practice of the Gothic court of Ravenna (Goth. l. i. c. 7 [tom. ii. p. 34, ed. Bonn]); and foreign ambassadors have been treated with the same jealousy and rigour in Turkey (Busbequius, Epist. iii. p. 149, 242, etc.), Russia (Voyage d'Olearius), and China (Narrative of M. de Lange, in Bell's Travels, vol. ii. p. 189–311).

disgrace of a tribute in its naked deformity. In a previous debate, the chariot of Sesostris and the wheel of fortune were applied by one of the ministers of Justinian, who observed that the reduction of Antioch and some Syrian cities had elevated beyond measure the vain and ambitious spirit of the barbarian. 'You are mistaken,' replied the modest Persian; 'the king of kings, the lord of mankind, looks down with contempt on such petty acquisitions; and of the ten nations vanquished by his invincible arms, he esteems the Romans as the least formidable.'[1] According to the Orientals, the empire of Nushirvan extended from Ferganah, in Transoxiana, to Yemen, or Arabia Felix. He subdued the rebels of Hyrcania, reduced the provinces of Cabul and Zablestan on the banks of the Indus, broke the power of the Euthalites, terminated by an honourable treaty the Turkish war, and admitted the daughter of the great khan into the number of his lawful wives. Victorious and respected among the princes of Asia, he gave audience, in his palace of Madain or Ctesiphon, to the ambassadors of the world. Their gifts or tributes, arms, rich garments, gems, slaves, or aromatics, were humbly presented at the foot of his throne; and he condescended to accept from the king of India ten quintals of the wood of aloes, a maid seven cubits in height, and a carpet softer than silk, the skin, as it was reported, of an extraordinary serpent.[2]

Justinian had been reproached for his alliance with the Æthiopians, as if he attempted to introduce a people of savage negroes into the system of civilised society. But the friends of the Roman empire, the Axumites or Abyssinians, may be always distinguished from the original natives of Africa.[3] The hand of nature has flattened the noses of the negroes, covered their heads

1 The negotiations and treaties between Justinian and Chosroes are copiously explained by Procopius (Persic. l. ii. c. 10, 13, 26, 27, 28; Gothic. l. ii. c. 11, 15; Agathias, l. iv. p. 141, 142 [ed. Par.; p. 274 *sq.*, ed. Bonn]), and Menander (in Excerpt. Legat. p. 132–147 [p. 346 *sqq.*, ed. Bonn]). Consult Barbeyrac, Hist. des Anciens Traités, tom. ii. p. 154, 181–184, 193–200.

2 D'Herbelot, Biblioth. Orient. p. 680, 681, 294, 295.

3 See Buffon, Hist. Naturelle, tom. iii. p. 449. This Arab cast of features and complexion, which has continued 3400 years (Ludolph. Hist. et Comment. Æthiopic. l. i. c. 4) in the colony of Abyssinia, will justify the suspicion that race, as well as climate, must have contributed to form the negroes of the adjacent and similar regions.

with shaggy wool, and tinged their skin with inherent and indelible blackness. But the olive complexion of the Abyssinians, their hair, shape, and features, distinctly mark them as a colony of Arabs, and this descent is confirmed by the resemblance of language and manners, the report of an ancient emigration, and the narrow interval between the shores of the Red Sea. Christianity had raised that nation above the level of African barbarism;[1] their intercourse with Egypt and the successors of Constantine[2] had communicated the rudiments of the arts and sciences: their vessels traded to the isle of Ceylon,[3] and seven kingdoms obeyed the Negus or supreme prince of Abyssinia. The independence of the Homerites,[4] who reigned in the rich and happy Arabia, was first violated by an Æthiopian conqueror: he drew his hereditary

1 The Portuguese missionaries, Alvarez (Ramusio, tom. i. fol. 204, rect. 274, vers.), Bermudez (Purchas's Pilgrims, vol. ii. l. v. c. 7, p. 1149–1188), Lobo (Relation, etc., par M. le Grand, with xv Dissertations, Paris, 1728), and Tellez (Relations de Thevenot, part iv.), could only relate of modern Abyssinia what they had seen or invented. The erudition of Ludolphus (Hist. Æthiopica, Francofurt. 1681; Commentarius, 1691; Appendix, 1694), in twenty-five languages, could add little concerning its ancient history. Yet the fame of Caled, or Ellisthæus, the conqueror of Yemen, is celebrated in national songs and legends.

2 The negotiations of Justinian with the Axumites, or Æthiopians, are recorded by Procopius (Persic. l. i. c. 19, 20) and John Malala (tom. ii. p. 163–165, 193–196 [p. 433, 434–457, 459, ed. Bonn]). The historian of Antioch quotes the original narrative of the ambassador Nonnosus, of which Photius (Biblioth. Cod. iii.) has preserved a curious extract.

3 The trade of the Axumites to the coast of India and Africa and the isle of Ceylon is curiously represented by Cosmas Indicopleustes (Topograph. Christian. l. ii. p. 132, 138, 139, 140; l. xi. p. 338, 339).

4 [The Axumites and the Hemyarites or Homerites were closely allied peoples. The Homerites hailed from Yemen in Arabia, and were largely engaged in the overland carrying trade between East and West, before the sea-route by the Cape of Good Hope was discovered by Vasco da Gama. These Homerites had crossed the Red Sea to Abyssinia, on the western side. The chief city of that state was called Axum, and the people were often termed Axumites. The Homerites succeeded in overcoming the Axumites at first, but eventually both states remained watchful rivals of each other until, in the fourth century, we find that the king of Axum had brought the Homerites under his authority. Both nations were originally adherents of the old Sabæan faith, but about the middle of the fourth century Christianity was introduced into Abyssinia, while the conversion of the Homerites was begun in the reign of the emperor Constantius, but it was not until about the beginning of the sixth century that the faith of Christ began to spread in both districts. But later in the same century

claim from the Queen of Sheba,[1] and his ambition was sanctified by religious zeal. The Jews, powerful and active in exile, had seduced the mind of Dunaan, prince of the Homerites. They urged him to retaliate the persecution inflicted by the Imperial laws on their unfortunate brethren; some Roman merchants were injuriously treated, and several Christians of Negra[2] were honoured with the crown of martyrdom.[3] The churches of Arabia implored the protection of the Abyssinian monarch. The Negus passed the Red Sea with a fleet and army, deprived the Jewish proselyte of his kingdom and life, and extinguished a race of princes who had ruled above two thousand years the seques-tered region of myrrh and frankincense. The conqueror imme-diately announced the victory of the Gospel, requested an orthodox patriarch, and so warmly professed his friendship to the Roman empire, that Justinian was flattered by the hope of diverting the silk trade through the channel of Abyssinia, and of exciting the forces of Arabia against the Persian king. Nonnosus, descended from a family of ambassadors, was named by the emperor to execute this important commission. He wisely de-clined the shorter but more dangerous road through the sandy deserts of Nubia, ascended the Nile, embarked on the Red Sea, and safely landed at the African port of Adulis. From Adulis to the royal city of Axume is no more than fifty leagues in a direct line, but the winding passes of the mountains detained the am-bassador fifteen days, and as he traversed the forests he saw, and

the Homerites and Axumites were at war, and religious matters suffered some-what until peace was restored. Those interested in this subject should read Bury's *Later Roman Empire* or Appendix 17, vol. iv. of his edition of Gibbon. – O. S.]

1 Ludolph. Hist. et Comment. Æthiop. l. ii. c. 3.

2 The city of Negra, or Nag'ran, in Yemen, is surrounded with palm-trees, and stands in the high road between Saana, the capital, and Mecca: from the former ten, from the latter twenty days' journey of a caravan of camels (Abul-feda, Descript. Arabiæ, p. 52).

3 The martyrdom of St. Arethas, prince of Negra, and his three hundred and forty companions, is embellished in the legends of Metaphrastes and Nice-phorus Callistus, copied by Baronius (A.D. 522, No. 22–66; A.D. 523, No. 16–29), and refuted, with obscure diligence, by Basnage (Hist. des Juifs, tom. xii. l. viii. c. ii. p. 333–348), who investigates the state of the Jews in Arabia and Æthiopia.

vaguely computed, about five thousand wild elephants. The capital, according to his report, was large and populous; and the *village* of Axume is still conspicuous by the regal coronations, by the ruins of a Christian temple, and by sixteen or seventeen obelisks inscribed with Grecian characters.[1] But the Negus gave audience in the open field, seated on a lofty chariot, which was drawn by four elephants superbly caparisoned, and surrounded by his nobles and musicians. He was clad in a linen garment and cap, holding in his hand two javelins and a light shield; and, although his nakedness was imperfectly covered, he displayed the barbaric pomp of gold chains, collars, and bracelets, richly adorned with pearls and precious stones. The ambassador of Justinian knelt: the Negus raised him from the ground, embraced Nonnosus, kissed the seal, perused the letter, accepted the Roman alliance, and, brandishing his weapons, denounced implacable war against the worshippers of fire. But the proposal of the silk-trade was eluded; and notwithstanding the assurances, and perhaps the wishes, of the Abyssinians, these hostile menaces evaporated without effect. The Homerites were unwilling to abandon their aromatic groves, to explore a sandy desert, and to encounter, after all their fatigues, a formidable nation from whom they had never received any personal injuries. Instead of enlarging his conquests, the king of Æthiopia was incapable of defending his possessions. Abrahah, the slave of a Roman merchant of Adulis, assumed the sceptre of the Homerites; the troops of Africa were seduced by the luxury of the climate; and Justinian solicited the friendship of the usurper, who honoured with a slight tribute the supremacy of his prince. After a long series of prosperity the power of Abrahah was overthrown before the gates of Mecca, his children were despoiled by the Persian conqueror, and the Æthiopians were finally expelled from the continent of Asia. This narrative of obscure and remote events is not foreign to the decline and fall of the Roman empire. If a Christian power had been maintained in Arabia, Mahomet

---

1 Alvarez (in Ramusio, tom. i. fol. 219, vers. 221, vers.) saw the flourishing state of Axume in the year 1520 — luogo molto buono e grande. It was ruined in the same century by the Turkish invasion. No more than one hundred houses remain; but the memory of its past greatness is preserved by the regal coronation (Ludolph. Hist. et Comment. l. ii. c. 11).

must have been crushed in his cradle, and Abyssinia would have prevented a revolution which has changed the civil and religious state of the world.[1]

CHAPTER XLIII

Rebellions of Africa – Restoration of the Gothic Kingdom by Totila – Loss and Recovery of Rome – Final Conquest of Italy by Narses – Extinction of the Ostrogoths – Defeat of the Franks and Alemanni – Last Victory, Disgrace, and Death of Belisarius – Death and Character of Justinian – Comet, Earthquakes, and Plague

THE review of the nations from the Danube to the Nile has exposed, on every side, the weakness of the Romans; and our wonder is reasonably excited that they should presume to enlarge an empire whose ancient limits they were incapable of defending. But the wars, the conquests, and the triumphs of Justinian, are the feeble and pernicious efforts of old age, which exhaust the remains of strength and accelerate the decay of the powers of life. He exulted in the glorious act of restoring Africa and Italy to the republic; but the calamities which followed the departure of Belisarius betrayed the impotence of the conqueror, and accomplished the ruin of those unfortunate countries.

From his new acquisitions Justinian expected that his avarice, as well as his pride, should be richly gratified. A rapacious minister of the finances closely pursued the footsteps of Belisarius; and, as the old registers of tribute had been burnt by the Vandals, he indulged his fancy in a liberal calculation and arbitrary

---

1 The revolutions of Yemen in the sixth century must be collected from Procopius (Persic. l. i. c. 19, 20), Theophanes Byzant. (apud Phot. cod. lxiv. p. 80 [p. 26, ed. Bekk.]), St. Theophanes (in Chronograph. p 144, 145, 188, 189, 206, 207 [tom. i. p. 259, 260, 377, 378, ed. Bonn], who is full of strange blunders), Pocock (Specimen Hist. Arab. p. 62, 65). D'Herbelot (Bibliot. Orientale, p. 12, 477), and Sale's Preliminary Discourse and Koran (c. 105). The revolt of Abrahah is mentioned by Procopius; and his fall, though clouded with miracles, is an historical fact.

assessment of the wealth of Africa.[1] The increase of taxes, which were drawn away by a distant sovereign, and a general resumption of the patrimony of crown lands, soon dispelled the intoxication of the public joy: but the emperor was insensible to the modest complaints of the people till he was awakened and alarmed by the clamours of military discontent. Many of the Roman soldiers had married the widows and daughters of the Vandals. As their own, by the double right of conquest and inheritance, they claimed the estates which Genseric had assigned to his victorious troops. They heard with disdain the cold and selfish representations of their officers, that the liberality of Justinian had raised them from a savage or servile condition; that they were already enriched by the spoils of Africa, the treasure, the slaves, and the movables of the vanquished barbarians; and that the ancient and lawful patrimony of the emperors would be applied only to the support of that government on which their own safety and reward must ultimately depend. The mutiny was secretly inflamed by a thousand soldiers, for the most part Heruli, who had imbibed the doctrines, and were instigated by the clergy, of the Arian sect; and the cause of perjury and rebellion was sanctified by the dispensing powers of fanaticism. The Arians deplored the ruin of their church, triumphant above a century in Africa; and they were justly provoked by the laws of the conqueror which interdicted the baptism of their children and the exercise of all religious worship. Of the Vandals chosen by Belisarius, the far greater part, in the honours of the Eastern service, forgot their country and religion. But a generous band of four hundred obliged the mariners, when they were in sight of the isle of Lesbos, to alter their course: they touched on Peloponnesus, ran ashore on a desert coast of Africa, and boldly erected on Mount Aurasius the standard of independence and

1 For the troubles of Africa I neither have nor desire another guide than Procopius, whose eye contemplated the image, and whose ear collected the reports, of the memorable events of his own times. In the second book of the Vandalic War he relates the revolt of Stoza (c. 14–24), the return of Belisarius (c. 15), the victory of Germanus (c. 16, 17, 18), the second administration of Solomon (c. 19, 20, 21), the government of Sergius (c. 22, 23), of Areobindus (c. 24), the tyranny and death of Gontharis (c. 25, 26, 27, 28); nor can I discern any symptoms of flattery or malevolence in his various portraits.

revolt. While the troops of the province disclaimed the commands of their superiors, a conspiracy was formed at Carthage against the life of Solomon, who filled with honour the place of Belisarius; and the Arians had piously resolved to sacrifice the tyrant at the foot of the altar during the awful mysteries of the festival of Easter. Fear or remorse restrained the daggers of the assassins, but the patience of Solomon emboldened their discontent, and at the end of ten days a furious sedition was kindled in the circus, which desolated Africa above ten years. The pillage of the city, and the indiscriminate slaughter of its inhabitants, were suspended only by darkness, sleep, and intoxication. The governor, with seven companions, among whom was the historian Procopius, escaped to Sicily. Two-thirds of the army were involved in the guilt of treason; and eight thousand insurgents, assembling in the field of Bulla, elected Stoza for their chief, a private soldier, who possessed in a superior degree the virtues of a rebel. Under the mask of freedom, his eloquence could lead, or at least impel, the passions of his equals. He raised himself to a level with Belisarius and the nephew of the emperor, by daring to encounter them in the field; and the victorious generals were compelled to acknowledge that Stoza deserved a purer cause and a more legitimate command. Vanquished in battle, he dexterously employed the arts of negotiation; a Roman army was seduced from their allegiance, and the chiefs who had trusted to his faithless promise were murdered by his order in a church of Numidia. When every resource, either of force or perfidy, was exhausted, Stoza, with some desperate Vandals, retired to the wilds of Mauritania, obtained the daughter of a barbarian prince, and eluded the pursuit of his enemies by the report of his death. The personal weight of Belisarius, the rank, the spirit, and the temper of Germanus, the emperor's nephew, and the vigour and success of the second administration of the eunuch Solomon, restored the modesty of the camp, and maintained for a while the tranquillity of Africa. But the vices of the Byzantine court were felt in that distant province; the troops complained that they were neither paid nor relieved; and as soon as the public disorders were sufficiently mature, Stoza was again alive, in arms, and at the gates of Carthage. He fell in a single combat, but he smiled in the agonies of death when he was

informed that his own javelin had reached the heart of his antagonist.[1] The example of Stoza, and the assurance that a fortunate
soldier had been the first king, encouraged the ambition of Gontharis, and he promised, by a private treaty, to divide Africa with
the Moors, if, with their dangerous aid, he should ascend the
throne of Carthage. The feeble Areobindus, unskilled in the affairs of peace and war, was raised by his marriage with the niece
of Justinian to the office of exarch. He was suddenly oppressed
by a sedition of the guards, and his abject supplications, which
provoked the contempt, could not move the pity, of the inexorable tyrant. After a reign of thirty days, Gontharis himself was
stabbed at a banquet by the hand of Artaban; and it is singular
enough that an Armenian prince of the royal family of Arsaces
should re-establish at Carthage the authority of the Roman empire.
In the conspiracy which unsheathed the dagger of Brutus against
the life of Cæsar, every circumstance is curious and important
to the eyes of posterity; but the guilt or merit of these loyal or
rebellious assassins could interest only the contemporaries of
Procopius, who, by their hopes and fears, their friendship or
resentment, were personally engaged in the revolutions of Africa.[2]

That country was rapidly sinking into the state of barbarism
from whence it had been raised by the Phœnician colonies and
Roman laws; and every step of intestine discord was marked by
some deplorable victory of savage man over civilised society.
The Moors,[3] though ignorant of justice, were impatient of oppression: their vagrant life and boundless wilderness disappointed

1 [Corippus relates the death of Stoza as occurring somewhat differently.
He was transfixed by an arrow from the hand of John, the son of Sisiniolus –
not the hero of his poem (the Johannidos, book iv. l. 211). All the other
authorities confirm Gibbon's account of the death of John by the hand of
Stoza. Stoza repented (says the poet) of his treasonous rebellion before his
death, but anticipated eternal torments as his punishment. Cf. Corippus, *Johannidos*, iv. 211. – O. S.]

2 Yet I must not refuse him the merit of painting, in lively colours, the
murder of Gontharis. One of the assassins uttered a sentiment not unworthy
of a Roman patriot: 'If I fail,' said Artasires, 'in the first stroke, kill me on the
spot, lest the rack should extort a discovery of my accomplices.' [Vand. ii. 28,
tom. i. p. 529, ed. Bonn.]

3 The Moorish wars are occasionally introduced into the narrative of Procopius (Vandal. l. ii. c. 19–23, 25, 27, 28; Gothic. l. iv. c. 17); and Theophanes
adds some prosperous and adverse events in the last years of Justinian.

the arms and eluded the chains of a conqueror; and experience had shown that neither oaths nor obligations could secure the fidelity of their attachment. The victory of Mount Auras had awed them into momentary submission; but if they respected the character of Solomon, they hated and despised the pride and luxury of his two nephews, Cyrus and Sergius, on whom their uncle had imprudently bestowed the provincial governments of Tripoli and Pentapolis. A Moorish tribe encamped under the walls of Leptis, to renew their alliance and receive from the governor the customary gifts. Fourscore of their deputies were introduced as friends into the city; but, on the dark suspicion of a conspiracy, they were massacred at the table of Sergius, and the clamour of arms and revenge was re-echoed through the valleys of Mount Atlas from both the Syrtes to the Atlantic Ocean. A personal injury, the unjust execution or murder of his brother, rendered Antalas the enemy of the Romans. The defeat of the Vandals had formerly signalised his valour; the rudiments of justice and prudence were still more conspicuous in a Moor; and, while he laid Adrumetum in ashes, he calmly admonished the emperor that the peace of Africa might be secured by the recall of Solomon and his unworthy nephews. The exarch led forth his troops from Carthage; but, at the distance of six days' journey, in the neighbourhood of Tebeste,[1] he was astonished by the superior numbers and fierce aspect of the barbarians. He proposed a treaty, solicited a reconciliation, and offered to bind himself by the most solemn oaths. 'By what oaths can he bind himself?' interrupted the indignant Moors. 'Will he swear by the Gospels, the divine books of the Christians? It was on those books that the faith of his nephew Sergius was pledged to eighty of our innocent and unfortunate brethren. Before we trust them a second time, let us try their efficacy in the chastisement of perjury and the vindication of their own honour.' Their honour

---

1 Now Tibesh, in the kingdom of Algiers. It is watered by a river, the Sujerass, which falls into the Mejerda (*Bagradas*). Tibesh is still remarkable for its walls of large stones (like the Coliseum of Rome), a fountain, and a grove of walnut-trees: the country is fruitful, and the neighbouring Bereberes are warlike. It appears from an inscription, that, under the reign of Hadrian, the road from Carthage to Tebeste was constructed by the third legion (Marmol, Description de l'Afrique, tom. ii. p. 442, 443; Shaw's Travels, p. 64, 65, 66).

was vindicated in the field of Tebeste by the death of Solomon and the total loss of his army.[1] The arrival of fresh troops and more skilful commanders soon checked the insolence of the Moors; seventeen of their princes were slain in the same battle; and the doubtful and transient submission of their tribes was celebrated with lavish applause by the people of Constantinople. Successive inroads had reduced the province of Africa to one-third of the measure of Italy; yet the Roman emperors continued to reign above a century over Carthage and the fruitful coast of the Mediterranean. But the victories and the losses of Justinian were alike pernicious to mankind; and such was the desolation of Africa, that in many parts a stranger might wander whole days without meeting the face either of a friend or an enemy. The nation of the Vandals had disappeared: they once amounted to a hundred and sixty thousand warriors, without including the children, the women, or the slaves. Their numbers were infinitely surpassed by the number of the Moorish families extirpated in a relentless war; and the same destruction was retaliated on the Romans and their allies, who perished by the climate, their mutual quarrels, and the rage of the barbarians. When Procopius first landed, he admired the populousness of the cities and country, strenuously exercised in the labours of commerce and agriculture. In less than twenty years that busy scene was converted into a silent solitude; the wealthy citizens escaped to Sicily and Constantinople; and the secret historian has confidently affirmed that five millions of Africans were consumed by the wars and government of the emperor Justinian.[2]

The jealousy of the Byzantine court had not permitted Belisarius to achieve the conquest of Italy; and his abrupt departure revived the courage of the Goths,[3] who respected his genius, his

1 [The defeat and death of Solomon are described at length in Corippus (*Johannidos*, book iii. 417–441) with historic fidelity. – O. S.]

2 Procopius, Anecdot. c. 18 [tom. iii. p. 107, ed. Bonn]. The series of the African history attests this melancholy truth.

3 In the second (c. 30) and third books (c. 1–40), Procopius continues the history of the Gothic war from the fifth to the fifteenth year of Justinian. As the events are less interesting than in the former period, he allots only half the space to double the time. Jornandes, and the Chronicle of Marcellinus, afford some collateral hints. Sigonius, Pagi, Muratori, Mascou, and De Buat are useful, and have been used.

virtue, and even the laudable motive which had urged the servant of Justinian to deceive and reject them. They had lost their king (an inconsiderable loss), their capital, their treasures, the provinces from Sicily to the Alps, and the military force of two hundred thousand barbarians, magnificently equipped with horses and arms. Yet all was not lost as long as Pavia was defended by one thousand Goths, inspired by a sense of honour, the love of freedom, and the memory of their past greatness. The supreme command was unanimously offered to the brave Uraias; and it was in his eyes alone that the disgrace of his uncle Vitiges could appear as a reason of exclusion. His voice inclined the election in favour of Hildibald, whose personal merit was recommended by the vain hope that his kinsman Theudes, the Spanish monarch, would support the common interest of the Gothic nation. The success of his arms in Liguria and Venetia seemed to justify their choice; but he soon declared to the world that he was incapable of forgiving or commanding his benefactor. The consort of Hildibald was deeply wounded by the beauty, the riches, and the pride of the wife of Uraias; and the death of that virtuous patriot excited the indignation of a free people. A bold assassin executed their sentence by striking off the head of Hildibald in the midst of a banquet; the Rugians, a foreign tribe, assumed the privilege of election; and Totila, the nephew of the late king, was tempted by revenge to deliver himself and the garrison of Trevigo into the hands of the Romans. But the gallant and accomplished youth was easily persuaded to prefer the Gothic throne before the service of Justinian; and, as soon as the palace of Pavia had been purified from the Rugian usurper, he reviewed the national force of five thousand soldiers, and generously undertook the restoration of the kingdom of Italy.

The successors of Belisarius, eleven generals of equal rank, neglected to crush the feeble and disunited Goths, till they were roused to action by the progress of Totila and the reproaches of Justinian. The gates of Verona were secretly opened to Artabazus, at the head of one hundred Persians in the service of the empire.[1] The Goths fled from the city. At the distance of sixty

1 ['At the head of one hundred Persians' – this did not imply that 'one hundred' was the total number of the army, but that he had 'one hundred picked men from the army.' – O. S.]

furlongs the Roman generals halted to regulate the division of the spoil. While they disputed, the enemy discovered the real number of the victors: the Persians were instantly overpowered, and it was by leaping from the wall that Artabazus preserved a life which he lost in a few days by the lance of a barbarian who had defied him to single combat. Twenty thousand Romans encountered the forces of Totila near Faenza, and on the hills of Mugello of the Florentine territory. The ardour of freedmen who fought to regain their country was opposed to the languid temper of mercenary troops, who were even destitute of the merits of strong and well-disciplined servitude. On the first attack they abandoned their ensigns, threw down their arms, and dispersed on all sides with an active speed which abated the loss, whilst it aggravated the shame, of their defeat. The king of the Goths, who blushed for the baseness of his enemies, pursued with rapid steps the path of honour and victory. Totila passed the Po, traversed the Apennine, suspended the important conquest of Ravenna, Florence, and Rome, and marched through the heart of Italy to form the siege, or rather the blockade, of Naples. The Roman chiefs, imprisoned in their respective cities and accusing each other of the common disgrace, did not presume to disturb his enterprise. But the emperor, alarmed by the distress and danger of his Italian conquests, despatched to the relief of Naples a fleet of galleys and a body of Thracian and Armenian soldiers. They landed in Sicily, which yielded its copious stores of provisions; but the delays of the new commander, an unwarlike magistrate, protracted the sufferings of the besieged; and the succours which he dropped with a timid and tardy hand were successively intercepted by the armed vessels stationed by Totila in the Bay of Naples. The principal officer of the Romans was dragged, with a rope round his neck, to the foot of the wall, from whence, with a trembling voice, he exhorted the citizens to implore, like himself, the mercy of the conqueror. They requested a truce, with a promise of surrendering the city if no effectual relief should appear at the end of thirty days. Instead of *one* month, the audacious barbarian granted them *three*, in the just confidence that famine would anticipate the term of their capitulation. After the reduction of Naples and Cumæ, the provinces of Lucania, Apulia, and Calabria submitted to the king of the Goths. Totila led his army to the gates of Rome, pitched his camp at Tibur or Tivoli, within twenty miles of the capital, and calmly exhorted the senate and people to compare the tyranny of the Greeks with the blessings of the Gothic reign.

The rapid success of Totila may be partly ascribed to the revolution which three years' experience had produced in the sentiments of the Italians. At the command, or at least in the name, of a catholic emperor, the pope,[1] their spiritual father, had been torn from the Roman church, and either starved or murdered on a desolate island.[2] The virtues of Belisarius were replaced by the various or uniform vices of eleven chiefs at Rome, Ravenna, Florence, Perugia, Spoleto, etc., who abused their authority for the indulgence of lust or avarice. The improvement of the revenue was committed to Alexander, a subtle scribe, long practised in the fraud and oppression of the Byzantine schools, and whose name of *Psalliction*, the *scissars*,[3] was drawn from the dexterous artifice with which he reduced the size, without defacing the figure, of the gold coin. Instead of expecting the restoration of peace and industry, he imposed a heavy assessment on the fortunes of the Italians. Yet his present or future demands were less odious than a prosecution of arbitrary rigour against the persons and property of all those who, under the Gothic kings, had been concerned in the receipt and expenditure of the public money. The subjects of Justinian who escaped these partial vexations were oppressed by the irregular maintenance of the soldiers, whom Alexander defrauded and despised, and their hasty sallies in quest of wealth or subsistence provoked the inhabitants of the country to await or implore their deliverance from the

1 Sylverius, bishop of Rome, was first transported to Patara, in Lycia, and at length starved (sub eorum custodiâ inedia confectus) in the isle of Palmaria, A.D. 538, June 20 (Liberat. in Breviar. c. 22; Anastasius, in Sylverio: Baronius, A.D. 540, No. 2. 3; Pagi, in Vit. Pont. tom. i. p. 285, 286). Procopius (Anecdot. c. 1) accuses only the empress and Antonina.

2 Palmaria, a small island, opposite to Terracina and the coast of the Volsci (Cluver. Ital. Antiq. l. iii. c. 7, p. 1014).

3 As the Logothete Alexander, and most of his civil and military colleagues, were either disgraced or despised, the ink of the Anecdotes (c. 4, 5, 18) is scarcely blacker than that of the Gothic History (l. iii. c. 1, 3, 4, 9, 20, 21, etc.)

virtues of a barbarian. Totila[1] was chaste and temperate, and none were deceived, either friends or enemies, who depended on his faith or his clemency. To the husbandmen of Italy the Gothic king issued a welcome proclamation, enjoining them to pursue their important labours, and to rest assured that, on the payment of the ordinary taxes, they should be defended by his valour and discipline from the injuries of war. The strong towns he successively attacked, and, as soon as they had yielded to his arms, he demolished the fortifications, to save the people from the calamities of a future siege, to deprive the Romans of the arts of defence, and to decide the tedious quarrel of the two nations by an equal and honourable conflict in the field of battle. The Roman captives and deserters were tempted to enlist in the service of a liberal and courteous adversary, the slaves were attracted by the firm and faithful promise that they should never be delivered to their masters; and from the thousand warriors of Pavia a new people, under the same appellation of Goths, was insensibly formed in the camp of Totila. He sincerely accomplished the articles of capitulation, without seeking or accepting any sinister advantage from ambiguous expressions or unforeseen events: the garrison of Naples had stipulated that they should be transported by sea; the obstinacy of the winds prevented their voyage, but they were generously supplied with horses, provisions, and a safe-conduct to the gates of Rome. The wives of the senators who had been surprised in the villas of Campania were restored without a ransom to their husbands; the violation of female chastity was inexorably chastised with death; and in the salutary regulation of the diet of the famished Neapolitans, the conqueror assumed the office of a humane and attentive physician. The virtues of Totila are equally laudable, whether they proceeded from true policy, religious principle, or the instinct of humanity. He often harangued his troops; and it was his constant theme that national vice and ruin are inseparably connected; that victory is the fruit of moral as well as military virtue; and that the prince, and even the people, are responsible for the crimes which they neglect to punish.

1 Procopius (l. iii. c. 2, 8, etc.) does ample and willing justice to the merit of Totila. The Roman historians, from Sallust and Tacitus, were happy to forget the vices of their countrymen in the contemplation of barbaric virtue.

The return of Belisarius to save the country which he had subdued was pressed with equal vehemence by his friends and enemies, and the Gothic war was imposed as a trust or an exile on the veteran commander. A hero on the banks of the Euphrates, a slave in the palace of Constantinople, he accepted with reluctance the painful task of supporting his own reputation and retrieving the faults of his successors. The sea was open to the Romans; the ships and soldiers were assembled at Salona, near the palace of Diocletian; he refreshed and reviewed his troops at Pola in Istria, coasted round the head of the Hadriatic, entered the port of Ravenna, and despatched orders rather than supplies to the subordinate cities. His first public oration was addressed to the Goths and Romans, in the name of the emperor, who had suspended for a while the conquest of Persia and listened to the prayers of his Italian subjects. He gently touched on the causes and the authors of the recent disasters, striving to remove the fear of punishment for the past, and the hope of impunity for the future, and labouring with more zeal than success to unite all the members of his government in a firm league of affection and obedience. Justinian, his gracious master, was inclined to pardon and reward, and it was their interest, as well as duty, to reclaim their deluded brethren, who had been seduced by the arts of the usurper. Not a man was tempted to desert the standard of the Gothic king. Belisarius soon discovered that he was sent to remain the idle and impotent spectator of the glory of a young barbarian, and his own epistle exhibits a genuine and lively picture of the distress of a noble mind. 'Most excellent prince, we are arrived in Italy, destitute of all the necessary implements of war – men, horses, arms, and money. In our late circuit through the villages of Thrace and Illyricum, we have collected with extreme difficulty about four thousand recruits, naked and unskilled in the use of weapons and the exercises of the camp. The soldiers already stationed in the province are discontented, fearful, and dismayed; at the sound of an enemy they dismiss their horses, and cast their arms on the ground. No taxes can be raised, since Italy is in the hands of the barbarians: the failure of payment has deprived us of the right of command, or even of admonition. Be assured, dread Sir, that the greater part of your troops have already deserted to the Goths. If the war could be

achieved by the presence of Belisarius alone, your wishes are
satisfied; Belisarius is in the midst of Italy. But if you desire to
conquer, far other preparations are requisite: without a military
force the title of general is an empty name. It would be expedient
to restore to my service my own veterans and domestic guards.
Before I can take the field I must receive an adequate supply of
light and heavy armed troops, and it is only with ready money
that you can procure the indispensable aid of a powerful body
of the cavalry of the Huns." An officer in whom Belisarius
confided was sent from Ravenna to hasten and conduct the
succours, but the message was neglected, and the messenger was
detained at Constantinople by an advantageous marriage. After
his patience had been exhausted by delay and disappointment,
the Roman general repassed the Hadriatic, and expected at
Dyrrachium the arrival of the troops, which were slowly assembled among the subjects and allies of the empire. His powers
were still inadequate to the deliverance of Rome, which was
closely besieged by the Gothic king. The Appian way, a march
of forty days, was covered by the barbarians; and as the prudence
of Belisarius declined a battle, he preferred the safe and speedy
navigation of five days from the coast of Epirus to the mouth
of the Tiber.

After reducing, by force or treaty, the towns of inferior note
in the midland provinces of Italy, Totila proceeded, not to assault, but to encompass and starve, the ancient capital. Rome
was afflicted by the avarice, and guarded by the valour, of Bessas,
a veteran chief of Gothic extraction, who filled, with a garrison
of three thousand soldiers, the spacious circle of her venerable
walls. From the distress of the people he extracted a profitable
trade, and secretly rejoiced in the continuance of the siege. It
was for his use that the granaries had been replenished; the
charity of Pope Vigilius had purchased and embarked an ample
supply of Sicilian corn, but the vessels which escaped the barbarians were seized by a rapacious governor, who imparted a scanty
sustenance to the soldiers, and sold the remainder to the wealthy

---

1 Procopius, l. iii. c. 12. The soul of a hero is deeply impressed on the
letter; nor can we confound such genuine and original acts with the elaborate
and often empty speeches of the Byzantine historians.

Romans. The medimnus, or fifth part of the quarter of wheat, was exchanged for seven pieces of gold; fifty pieces were given for an ox, a rare and accidental prize; the progress of famine enhanced this exorbitant value, and the mercenaries were tempted to deprive themselves of the allowance which was scarcely sufficient for the support of life. A tasteless and unwholesome mixture, in which the bran thrice exceeded the quantity of flour, appeased the hunger of the poor; they were gradually reduced to feed on dead horses, dogs, cats, and mice, and eagerly to snatch the grass and even the nettles which grew among the ruins of the city. A crowd of spectres, pale and emaciated, their bodies oppressed with disease and their minds with despair, surrounded the palace of the governor, urged, with unavailing truth, that it was the duty of a master to maintain his slaves, and humbly requested that he would provide for their subsistence, permit their flight, or command their immediate execution. Bessas replied, with unfeeling tranquillity, that it was impossible to feed, unsafe to dismiss, and unlawful to kill, the subjects of the emperor. Yet the example of a private citizen might have shown his countrymen that a tyrant cannot withhold the privilege of death. Pierced by the cries of five children, who vainly called on their father for bread, he ordered them to follow his steps, advanced with calm and silent despair to one of the bridges of the Tiber, and, covering his face, threw himself headlong into the stream, in the presence of his family and the Roman people. To the rich and pusillanimous, Bessas sold the permission of departure; but the greatest part of the fugitives expired on the public highways, or were intercepted by the flying parties of barbarians.[1] In the meanwhile the artful governor soothed the discontent, and revived the hopes, of the Romans, by the vague reports of the fleets and armies which were hastening to their relief from the extremities of the East. They derived more rational comfort from the assurance that Belisarius had landed at the *port*; and,

---

1 The avarice of Bessas is not dissembled by Procopius (l. iii. c. 17, 20). He expiated the loss of Rome by the glorious conquest of Petræa (Goth. l. iv. c. 12); but the same vices followed him from the Tiber to the Phasis (c. 13); and the historian is equally true to the merits and defects of his character. The chastisement which the author of the romance of *Belisaire* has inflicted on the oppressor of Rome is more agreeable to justice than to history.

without numbering his forces, they firmly relied on the humanity, the courage, and the skill of their great deliverer.

The foresight of Totila had raised obstacles worthy of such an antagonist. Ninety furlongs below the city, in the narrowest part of the river, he joined the two banks by strong and solid timbers in the form of a bridge, on which he erected two lofty towers, manned by the bravest of his Goths, and profusely stored with missile weapons and engines of offence. The approach of the bridge and towers was covered by a strong and massy chain of iron, and the chain, at either end, on the opposite sides of the Tiber, was defended by a numerous and chosen detachment of archers. But the enterprise of forcing these barriers and relieving the capital displays a shining example of the boldness and conduct of Belisarius. His cavalry advanced from the port along the public road to awe the motions and distract the attention of the enemy. His infantry and provisions were distributed in two hundred large boats, and each boat was shielded by a high rampart of thick planks, pierced with many small holes for the discharge of missile weapons. In the front, two large vessels were linked together to sustain a floating castle, which commanded the towers of the bridge, and contained a magazine of fire, sulphur, and bitumen. The whole fleet, which the general led in person, was laboriously moved against the current of the river. The chain yielded to their weight, and the enemies who guarded the banks were either slain or scattered. As soon as they touched the principal barrier, the fireship was instantly grappled to the bridge; one of the towers, with two hundred Goths, was consumed by the flames, the assailants shouted victory, and Rome was saved, if the wisdom of Belisarius had not been defeated by the misconduct of his officers. He had previously sent orders to Bessas to second his operations by a timely sally from the town, and he had fixed his lieutenant, Isaac, by a peremptory command, to the station of the port. But avarice rendered Bessas immovable, while the youthful ardour of Isaac delivered him into the hands of a superior enemy. The exaggerated rumour of his defeat was hastily carried to the ears of Belisarius: he paused, betrayed in that single moment of his life some emotions of surprise and perplexity, and reluctantly sounded a retreat to save his wife Antonina, his treasures, and the only harbour which he

possessed on the Tuscan coast. The vexation of his mind produced an ardent and almost mortal fever, and Rome was left
without protection to the mercy or indignation of Totila. The
continuance of hostilities had embittered the national hatred;
the Arian clergy was ignominiously driven from Rome; Pelagius,
the archdeacon, returned without success from an embassy to
the Gothic camp; and a Sicilian bishop, the envoy or nuncio of the
pope, was deprived of both his hands for daring to utter false-
hoods in the service of the church and state.

Famine had relaxed the strength and discipline of the garrison
of Rome. They could derive no effectual service from a dying
people; and the inhuman avarice of the merchant at length ab-
sorbed the vigilance of the governor. Four Isaurian sentinels,
while their companions slept and their officers were absent, descended by a rope from the wall, and secretly proposed to the
Gothic king to introduce his troops into the city. The offer was
entertained with coldness and suspicion; they returned in safety;
they twice repeated their visit: the place was twice examined; the
conspiracy was known and disregarded; and no sooner had Totila
consented to the attempt, than they unbarred the Asinarian gate
and gave admittance to the Goths. Till the dawn of day they halted
in order of battle, apprehensive of treachery or ambush; but the
troops of Bessas, with their leader, had already escaped; and
when the king was pressed to disturb their retreat, he prudently
replied that no sight could be more grateful than that of a flying
enemy. The patricians who were still possessed of horses, Decius, Basilius, etc., accompanied the governor; their brethren,
among whom Olybrius, Orestes, and Maximus are named by the
historian, took refuge in the church of St. Peter: but the assertion
that only five hundred persons remained in the capital inspires
some doubt of the fidelity either of his narrative or of his text.
As soon as daylight had displayed the entire victory of the Goths,
their monarch devoutly visited the tomb of the prince of the
apostles; but while he prayed at the altar, twenty-five soldiers and
sixty citizens were put to the sword in the vestibule of the temple.
The archdeacon Pelagius[1] stood before him, with the Gospels in

---

[1] During the long exile, and after the death of Vigilius, the Roman church
was governed, at first by the archdeacon, and at length (A.D. 555) by the pope
Pelagius, who was not thought guiltless of the sufferings of his predecessor.

his hand. 'O Lord, be merciful to your servant.' 'Pelagius,' said
Totila with an insulting smile, 'your pride now condescends to
become a suppliant.' 'I *am* a suppliant,' replied the prudent archdeacon; 'God has now made us your subjects, and, as your subjects, we are entitled to your clemency.' At his humble prayer the
lives of the Romans were spared; and the chastity of the maids
and matrons was preserved inviolate from the passions of the
hungry soldiers. But they were rewarded by the freedom of pillage, after the most precious spoils had been reserved for the
royal treasury. The houses of the senators were plentifully stored
with gold and silver; and the avarice of Bessas had laboured with
so much guilt and shame for the benefit of the conqueror. In
this revolution the sons and daughters of Roman consuls tasted
the misery which they had spurned or relieved, wandered in
tattered garments through the streets of the city, and begged
their bread, perhaps without success, before the gates of their
hereditary mansions. The riches of Rusticiana, the daughter of
Symmachus and widow of Boethius, had been generously devoted
to alleviate the calamities of famine. But the barbarians were
exasperated by the report that she had prompted the people to
overthrow the statues of the great Theodoric; and the life of that
venerable matron would have been sacrificed to his memory, if
Totila had not respected her birth, her virtues, and even the
pious motive of her revenge. The next day he pronounced two
orations, to congratulate and admonish his victorious Goths, and
to reproach the senate, as the vilest of slaves, with their perjury,
folly, and ingratitude; sternly declaring that their estates and honours were justly forfeited to the companions of his arms. Yet he
consented to forgive their revolt; and the senators repaid his
clemency by despatching circular letters to their tenants and vassals in the provinces of Italy, strictly to enjoin them to desert
the standard of the Greeks, to cultivate their lands in peace, and
to learn from their masters the duty of obedience to a Gothic
sovereign. Against the city which had so long delayed the course
of his victories he appeared inexorable: one-third of the walls,
in different parts, were demolished by his command; fire and

See the original Lives of the popes under the name of Anastasius (Muratori,
Script. Rer. Italicarum, tom. iii. P. i. p. 130, 131), who relates several curious
incidents of the sieges of Rome and the wars of Italy.

engines prepared to consume or subvert the most stately works of antiquity; and the world was astonished by the fatal decree that Rome should be changed into a pasture for cattle. The firm and temperate remonstrance of Belisarius suspended the execution; he warned the barbarian not to sully his fame by the destruction of those monuments which were the glory of the dead and the delight of the living; and Totila was persuaded, by the advice of an enemy, to preserve Rome as the ornament of his kingdom, or the fairest pledge of peace and reconciliation. When he had signified to the ambassadors of Belisarius his intention of sparing the city, he stationed an army at the distance of one hundred and twenty furlongs, to observe the motions of the Roman general. With the remainder of his forces he marched into Lucania and Apulia, and occupied on the summit of Mount Garganus[1] one of the camps of Hannibal.[2] The senators were dragged in his train, and afterwards confined in the fortresses of Campania; the citizens, with their wives and children, were dispersed in exile; and during forty days Rome was abandoned to desolate and dreary solitude.[3]

The loss of Rome was speedily retrieved by an action to which, according to the event, the public opinion would apply the names of rashness or heroism. After the departure of Totila, the Roman general sallied from the port at the head of a thousand horse, cut in pieces the enemy who opposed his progress, and visited with pity and reverence the vacant space of the *eternal* city. Resolved to maintain a station so conspicuous in the eyes of mankind, he summoned the greatest part of his troops to the

1 Mount Garganus, now Monte St. Angelo, in the kingdom of Naples, runs three hundred stadia into the Hadriatic Sea (Strab. l. vi. p. 436 [p. 284, ed. Casaub.]), and in the darker ages was illustrated by the apparition, miracles, and church of St. Michæl the archangel. Horace, a native of Apulia or Lucania, had seen the elms and oaks of Garganus labouring and bellowing with the north wind that blew on that lofty coast (Carm. ii. 9; Epist. ii. i. 202).

2 I cannot ascertain this particular camp of Hannibal; but the Punic quarters were long and often in the neighbourhood of Arpi (T. Liv. xxii. 9, 12; xxiv. 3, etc).

3 Totila ... Romam ingreditur ... ac evertit muros, domos aliquantas igni comburens, ac omnes Romanorum res in prædam accepit, hos ipsos Romanos in Campaniam captivos abduxit. Post quam devastationem, xl aut amplius dies, Roma fuit ita desolata, ut nemo ibi hominum, nisi (*nullae?*) bestiæ morarentur (Marcellin. in Chron. p. 54).

standard which he erected on the Capitol: the old inhabitants were recalled by the love of their country and the hopes of food; and the keys of Rome were sent a second time to the emperor Justinian. The walls, as far as they had been demolished by the Goths, were repaired with rude and dissimilar materials; the ditch was restored; iron spikes[1] were profusely scattered in the highways to annoy the feet of the horses; and as new gates could not suddenly be procured, the entrance was guarded by a Spartan rampart of his bravest soldiers. At the expiration of twenty-five days Totila returned by hasty marches from Apulia to avenge the injury and disgrace. Belisarius expected his approach. The Goths were thrice repulsed in three general assaults; they lost the flower of their troops; the royal standard had almost fallen into the hands of the enemy, and the fame of Totila sunk, as it had risen, with the fortune of his arms. Whatever skill and courage could achieve had been performed by the Roman general: it remained only that Justinian should terminate, by a strong and seasonable effort, the war which he had ambitiously undertaken. The indolence, perhaps the impotence, of a prince who despised his enemies and envied his servants, protracted the calamities of Italy. After a long silence Belisarius was commanded to leave a sufficient garrison at Rome, and to transport himself into the province of Lucania, whose inhabitants, inflamed by catholic zeal, had cast away the yoke of their Arian conquerors. In this ignoble warfare the hero, invincible against the power of the barbarians, was basely vanquished by the delay, the disobedience, and the cowardice of his own officers. He reposed in his winter quarters of Crotona, in the full assurance that the two passes of the Lucanian hills were guarded by his cavalry. They were betrayed by treachery or weakness; and the rapid march of the Goths scarcely allowed time for the escape of Belisarius to the coast of Sicily. At length a fleet and army were assembled for the relief of Ruscianum, or Rossano,[2]

---

1 The *tribuli* are small engines with four spikes, one fixed in the ground, the three others erect or adverse (Procopius, Gothic. l. iii. c. 24 [tom. ii. p. 379, ed. Bonn]; Just. Lipsius, Poliorcetῶν, l. v. c. 3). The metaphor was borrowed from the tribuli (*land-caltrops*), an herb with a prickly fruit, common in Italy (Martin, ad Virgil. Georgic. i. 153, vol. ii. p. 33).

2 Ruscia, the *navale Thuriorum*, was transferred to the distance of sixty stadia to Ruscianum, Rossano, an archbishopric without suffragans. The republic of

a fortress sixty furlongs from the ruins of Sybaris, where the nobles of Lucania had taken refuge. In the first attempt the Roman forces were dissipated by a storm. In the second, they approached the shore; but they saw the hills covered with archers, the landing-place defended by a line of spears, and the king of the Goths impatient for battle. The conqueror of Italy retired with a sigh, and continued to languish, inglorious and inactive, till Antonina, who had been sent to Constantinople to solicit succours, obtained, after the death of the empress, the permission of his return.

The five last campaigns of Belisarius might abate the envy of his competitors, whose eyes had been dazzled and wounded by the blaze of his former glory. Instead of delivering Italy from the Goths, he had wandered like a fugitive along the coast, without daring to march into the country, or to accept the bold and repeated challenge of Totila. Yet in the judgment of the few who could discriminate counsels from events, and compare the instruments with the execution, he appeared a more consummate master of the art of war than in the season of his prosperity, when he presented two captive kings before the throne of Justinian. The valour of Belisarius was not chilled by age: his prudence was matured by experience; but the moral virtues of humanity and justice seem to have yielded to the hard necessity of the times. The parsimony or poverty of the emperor compelled him to deviate from the rule of conduct which had deserved the love and confidence of the Italians. The war was maintained by the oppression of Ravenna, Sicily, and all the faithful subjects of the empire; and the rigorous prosecution of Herodian provoked that injured or guilty officer to deliver Spoleto into the hands of the enemy. The avarice of Antonina, which had been sometimes diverted by love, now reigned without a rival in her breast. Belisarius himself had always understood that riches, in a corrupt age, are the support and ornament of personal merit. And it cannot be presumed that he should stain his honour for the public service, without applying a part of the spoil to his private emolument. The hero had escaped the sword

Sybaris is now the estate of the Duke of Corigliano (Riedesel, Travels into Magna Græcia and Sicily, p. 166–171).

of the barbarians, but the dagger of conspiracy[1] awaited his return. In the midst of wealth and honours, Artaban, who had
chastised the African tyrant, complained of the ingratitude of
courts. He aspired to Præjecta, the emperor's niece, who wished
to reward her deliverer; but the impediment of his previous
marriage was asserted by the piety of Theodora. The pride of
royal descent was irritated by flattery; and the service in which
he gloried had proved him capable of bold and sanguinary deeds.
The death of Justinian was resolved, but the conspirators delayed
the execution till they could surprise Belisarius, disarmed and
naked, in the palace of Constantinople. Not a hope could be
entertained of shaking his long-tried fidelity; and they justly
dreaded the revenge, or rather justice, of the veteran general,
who might speedily assemble an army in Thrace to punish the
assassins, and perhaps to enjoy the fruits of their crime. Delay
afforded time for rash communications and honest confessions:
Artaban and his accomplices were condemned by the senate, but
the extreme clemency of Justinian detained them in the gentle
confinement of the palace, till he pardoned their flagitious attempt against his throne and life. If the emperor forgave his
enemies, he must cordially embrace a friend whose victories were
alone remembered, and who was endeared to his prince by the
recent circumstance of their common danger. Belisarius reposed
from his toils, in the high station of general of the East and
count of the domestics; and the older consuls and patricians
respectfully yielded the precedency of rank to the peerless merit
of the first of the Romans.[2] The first of the Romans still submitted to be the slave of his wife; but the servitude of habit and
affection became less disgraceful when the death of Theodora

1 This conspiracy is related by Procopius (Gothic. l. iii. c. 31, 32) with such
freedom and candour that the liberty of the Anecdotes gives him nothing to
add.

[Spoleto was betrayed by Herodian in 545 A.D. It was recovered by the
empire in 547; was lost once more about 549 A.D., and was recovered finally in
552. – O. S.]

2 The honours of Belisarius are gladly commemorated by his secretary
(Procop. Goth. l. iii. c. 35; l. iv. c. 21). The title of Στράτηγος is ill translated,
at least in this instance, by præfectus prætorio; and to a military character,
magister militum is more proper and applicable (Ducange, Gloss. Græc. p. 1458,
1459).

had removed the baser influence of fear. Joannina their daughter, and the sole heiress of their fortunes, was betrothed to Anastasius, the grandson, or rather the nephew, of the empress,[1] whose kind interposition forwarded the consummation of their youthful loves. But the power of Theodora expired, the parents of Joannina returned, and her honour, perhaps her happiness, were sacrificed to the revenge of an unfeeling mother, who dissolved the imperfect nuptials before they had been ratified by the ceremonies of the church.[2]

Before the departure of Belisarius, Perusia was besieged, and few cities were impregnable to the Gothic arms. Ravenna, Ancona, and Crotona still resisted the barbarians; and when Totila asked in marriage one of the daughters of France, he was stung by the just reproach that the king of Italy was unworthy of his title till it was acknowledged by the Roman people. Three thousand of the bravest soldiers had been left to defend the capital. On the suspicion of a monopoly, they massacred the governor, and announced to Justinian, by a deputation of the clergy, that, unless their offence was pardoned, and their arrears were satisfied, they should instantly accept the tempting offers of Totila. But the officer who succeeded to the command (his name was Diogenes) deserved their esteem and confidence; and the Goths, instead of finding an easy conquest, encountered a vigorous resistance from the soldiers and people, who patiently endured the loss of the port and of all maritime supplies. The siege of Rome would perhaps have been raised, if the liberality of Totila to the

1 Alemannus (ad Hist. Arcanam, p. 68 [tom. iii. p. 418, ed. Bonn]), Ducange (Familiæ Byzant. p. 98), and Heineccius (Hist. Juris Civilis, p. 434), all three represent Anastasius as the son of the daughter of Theodora; and their opinion firmly reposes on the unambiguous testimony of Procopius (Anecdot. c. 4, 5 – θυγατρίδῳ twice repeated). And yet I will remark, 1. That in the year 547 Theodora could scarcely have a grandson of the age of puberty; 2. That we are totally ignorant of this daughter and her husband; and, 3. That Theodora concealed her bastards, and that her grandson by Justinian would have been heir-apparent of the empire.

2 The ἁμαρτήματα, or sins, of the hero in Italy and after his return, are manifested ἀπαρακαλύπτως, and most probably swelled, by the author of the Anecdotes (c. 4, 5). The designs of Antonina were favoured by the fluctuating jurisprudence of Justinian. On the law of marriage and divorce, that emperor was trocho versatilior (Heineccius, Element. Juris Civil. ad Ordinem Pandect. P. iv. No. 233).

Isaurians had not encouraged some of their venal countrymen to copy the example of treason. In a dark night, while the Gothic trumpets sounded on another side, they silently opened the gate of St. Paul: the barbarians rushed into the city; and the flying garrison was intercepted before they could reach the harbour of Centumcellæ. A soldier trained in the school of Belisarius, Paul of Cilicia, retired with four hundred men to the mole of Hadrian. They repelled the Goths; but they felt the approach of famine; and their aversion to the taste of horse-flesh confirmed their resolution to risk the event of a desperate and decisive sally. But their spirit insensibly stooped to the offers of capitulation: they retrieved their arrears of pay, and preserved their arms and horses, by enlisting in the service of Totila; their chiefs, who pleaded a laudable attachment to their wives and children in the East, were dismissed with honour; and above four hundred enemies, who had taken refuge in the sanctuaries, were saved by the clemency of the victor. He no longer entertained a wish of destroying the edifices of Rome,[1] which he now respected as the seat of the Gothic kingdom: the senate and people were restored to their country; the means of subsistence were liberally provided; and Totila, in the robe of peace, exhibited the equestrian games of the circus. Whilst he amused the eyes of the multitude, four hundred vessels were prepared for the embarkation of his troops. The cities of Rhegium and Tarentum were reduced; he passed into Sicily, the object of his implacable resentment; and the island was stripped of its gold and silver, of the fruits of the earth, and of an infinite number of horses, sheep, and oxen. Sardinia and Corsica obeyed the fortune of Italy; and the seacoast of Greece was visited by a fleet of three hundred galleys.[2]

1 The Romans were still attached to the monuments of their ancestors; and according to Procopius (Goth. l. iv. c. 22 [tom. ii. p. 573, ed. Bonn]), the galley of Æneas, of a single rank of oars, 25 feet in breadth, 120 in length, was preserved entire in the *navalia*, near Monte Testaceo, at the foot of the Aventine (Nardini, Roma Antica, l. vii. c. 9, p. 466; Donatus, Roma Antiqua, l. iv. c. 13, p. 334). But all antiquity is ignorant of this relic.

2 In these seas Procopius searched without success for the isle of Calypso. He was shown, at Phæacia or Corcyra, the petrified ship of Ulysses (Odyss. xiii. 163); but he found it a recent fabric of many stones, dedicated by a merchant to Jupiter Casius (l. iv. c. 22 [tom. ii. p. 575, ed. Bonn]). Eustathius had supposed it to be the fanciful likeness of a rock.

The Goths were landed in Corcyra and the ancient continent of Epirus; they advanced as far as Nicopolis, the trophy of Augustus, and Dodona,[1] once famous by the oracle of Jove. In every step of his victories the wise barbarian repeated to Justinian his desire of peace, applauded the concord of their predecessors, and offered to employ the Gothic arms in the service of the empire.

Justinian was deaf to the voice of peace, but he neglected the prosecution of war; and the indolence of his temper disappointed, in some degree, the obstinacy of his passions. From this salutary slumber the emperor was awakened by the pope Vigilius and the patrician Cethegus, who appeared before his throne, and adjured him, in the name of God and the people, to resume the conquest and deliverance of Italy. In the choice of the generals, caprice, as well as judgment, was shown. A fleet and army sailed for the relief of Sicily, under the conduct of Liberius; but his want of youth and experience were afterwards discovered, and before he touched the shores of the island he was overtaken by his successor. In the place of Liberius the conspirator Artaban was raised from a prison to military honours, in the pious presumption that gratitude would animate his valour and fortify his allegiance. Belisarius reposed in the shade of his laurels, but the command of the principal army was reserved for Germanus,[2] the emperor's nephew, whose rank and merit had been long depressed by the jealousy of the court. Theodora had injured him in the rights of a private citizen, the marriage of his children, and the testament of his brother; and although his conduct was

1 M. D'Anville (Mémoires de l'Acad. tom. xxxii. p. 513–528) illustrates the gulf of Ambracia; but he cannot ascertain the situation of Dodona. A country in sight of Italy is less known than the wilds of America.

['Dodona once famous by the oracle of Jove.' The site of this once famous place cannot now be fixed with accuracy, though strong presumption exists that the fertile valley of Joannina was the territory of Dodona, and that the ruins upon the hill of Kastritza at the southen end of the lake of Joannina are those of the ancient city. – O. S.]

2 See the acts of Germanus in the public (Vandal. l. ii. c. 16, 17, 18; Goth. l. iii. c. 31, 32) and private history (Anecdot. c. 5), and those of his son Justin, in Agathias (l. iv. p. 130, 131 [p. 250 sq., ed. Bonn]). Notwithstanding an ambiguous expression of Jornandes, fratri suo, Alemannus has proved that he was the son of the emperor's brother.

pure and blameless, Justinian was displeased that he should be thought worthy of the confidence of the malcontents. The life of Germanus was a lesson of implicit obedience: he nobly refused to prostitute his name and character in the factions of the circus; the gravity of his manners was tempered by innocent cheerfulness; and his riches were lent without interest to indigent or deserving friends. His valour had formerly triumphed over the Sclavonians of the Danube and the rebels of Africa: the first report of his promotion revived the hopes of the Italians; and he was privately assured that a crowd of Roman deserters would abandon, on his approach, the standard of Totila. His second marriage with Malasontha, the grand-daughter of Theodoric, endeared Germanus to the Goths themselves; and they marched with reluctance against the father of a royal infant, the last offspring of the line of Amali.¹ A splendid allowance was assigned by the emperor: the general contributed his private fortune; his two sons were popular and active; and he surpassed, in the promptitude and success of his levies, the expectation of mankind. He was permitted to select some squadrons of Thracian cavalry: the veterans, as well as the youth of Constantinople and Europe, engaged their voluntary service; and as far as the heart of Germany, his fame and liberality attracted the aid of the barbarians. The Romans advanced to Sardica; an army of Sclavonians fled before their march; but within two days of their final departure the designs of Germanus were terminated by his malady and death. Yet the impulse which he had given to the Italian war still continued to act with energy and effect. The maritime towns, Ancona, Crotona, Centumcellæ, resisted the assaults of Totila. Sicily was reduced by the zeal of Artaban, and the Gothic navy was defeated near the coast of the Hadriatic. The two fleets were almost equal, forty-seven to fifty galleys: the victory was decided by the knowledge and dexterity of the Greeks; but the ships were so closely grappled that only twelve of the Goths escaped from this unfortunate conflict. They affected to depreciate an element in which they were unskilled; but their own experience confirmed the truth of a maxim, that

---

1 Conjuncta Aniciorum gens cum Amalâ stirpe spem adhuc utriusque generis promittit (Jornandes, c. 60, p. 703). He wrote at Ravenna before the death of Totila.

the master of the sea will always acquire the dominion of the land.[1]

After the loss of Germanus, the nations were provoked to smile by the strange intelligence that the command of the Roman armies was given to a eunuch. But the eunuch Narses[2] is ranked among the few who have rescued that unhappy name from the contempt and hatred of mankind. A feeble, diminutive body concealed the soul of a statesman and a warrior. His youth had been employed in the management of the loom and distaff, in the cares of the household, and the service of female luxury; but while his hands were busy, he secretly exercised the faculties of a vigorous and discerning mind. A stranger to the schools and the camp, he studied in the palace to dissemble, to flatter, and to persuade; and as soon as he approached the person of the emperor, Justinian listened with surprise and pleasure to the manly counsels of his chamberlain and private treasurer.[3] The talents of Narses were tried and improved in frequent embassies: he led an army into Italy, acquired a practical knowledge of the war and the country, and presumed to strive with the genius of Belisarius. Twelve years after his return the eunuch was chosen to achieve the conquest which had been left imperfect by the first of the Roman generals. Instead of being dazzled by vanity

1 The third book of Procopius is terminated by the death of Germanus (Add. l. iv. c. 23, 24, 25, 26).

2 Procopius relates the whole series of this second Gothic war and the victory of Narses (l. iv. c. 21, 26–35). A splendid scene! Among the six subjects of epic poetry which Tasso revolved in his mind, he hesitated between the conquests of Italy by Belisarius and by Narses (Hayley's Works, vol. iv. p. 70).

3 The country of Narses is unknown, since he must not be confounded with the Persarmenian. Procopius styles him (Goth. l. ii. c. 13 [tom. ii. p. 199, ed. Bonn]) βασιλικῶν χρημάτων ταμίας; Paul Warnefrid (l. ii. c. 3, p. 776), Chartularius: Marcellinus adds the name of Cubicularius. In an inscription on the Salarian bridge he is entitled Ex-consul, Ex-præpositus, Cubiculi Patricius (Mascou, Hist. of the Germans, l. xiii. c. 25). The law of Theodosius against eunuchs was obsolete or abolished (Annotation xx.), but the foolish prophecy of the Romans subsisted in full vigour (Procop. l. iv. c. 21 [tom. ii. p. 571, ed. Bonn]).

[There were two Persarmenians of the name of Narses, of whom one deserted to the Romans and the other received the deserter. The latter, who is called ὁ βασιλέως ταμίας, the imperial treasurer, is, as Procopius says, the individual in whom we are interested. – O. S.]

or emulation, he seriously declared that, unless he were armed with an adequate force, he would never consent to risk his own glory and that of his sovereign. Justinian granted to the favourite what he might have denied to the hero: the Gothic war was rekindled from its ashes, and the preparations were not unworthy of the ancient majesty of the empire. The key of the public treasure was put into his hand to collect magazines, to levy soldiers, to purchase arms and horses, to discharge the arrears of pay, and to tempt the fidelity of the fugitives and deserters. The troops of Germanus were still in arms; they halted at Salona in the expectation of a new leader, and legions of subjects and allies were created by the well-known liberality of the eunuch Narses. The king of the Lombards[1] satisfied or surpassed the obligations of a treaty, by lending two thousand two hundred of his bravest warriors, who were followed by three thousand of their martial attendants. Three thousand Heruli fought on horseback under Philemuth, their native chief; and the noble Aratus, who adopted the manners and discipline of Rome, conducted a band of veterans of the same nation. Dagistheus was released from prison to command the Huns; and Kobad, the grandson and nephew of the Great King, was conspicuous by the regal tiara at the head of his faithful Persians, who had devoted themselves to the fortunes of their prince.[2] Absolute in the exercise of his authority, more absolute in the affection of his troops, Narses led a numerous and gallant army from Philippopolis to Salona, from whence he coasted the eastern side of the Hadriatic as far as the confines of Italy. His progress was checked. The East could not supply vessels capable of transporting such

1 Paul Warnefrid, the Lombard, records with complacency the succour, service, and honourable dismission of his countrymen – Romanæ reipublicæ adversum æmulos adjutores fuerunt (l. ii. c. i. p. 774, edit. Grot.). I am surprised that Alboin, their martial king, did not lead his subjects in person.

[Gibbon here is in error. He has followed translators in place of the Greek of the original. Πεντακοσίους τε καὶ δισχιλίους reads Procopius (*Goth. Bell.* lib. iv. c. 26), but Gibbon prefers to follow the Latin translation of Maltretus, which by some unaccountable oversight translates the above phrase bis mille ducentos, or, in other words, two thousand two hundred. – O. S.]

2 He was, if not an impostor, the son of the blind Zames, saved by compassion and educated in the Byzantine court by the various motives of policy, pride, and generosity (Procop. Persic. l. i. c. 23 [tom. i. p. 115, ed. Bonn]).

multitudes of men and horses. The Franks, who in the general confusion had usurped the greater part of the Venetian province, refused a free passage to the friends of the Lombards. The station of Verona was occupied by Teias with the flower of the Gothic forces; and that skilful commander had overspread the adjacent country with the fall of woods and the inundation of waters.[1] In this perplexity an officer of experience proposed a measure, secure by the appearance of rashness, that the Roman army should cautiously advance along the sea-shore, while the fleet preceded their march, and successively cast a bridge of boats over the mouths of the rivers, the Timavus, the Brenta, the Adige, and the Po, that fall into the Hadriatic to the north of Ravenna. Nine days he reposed in the city, collected the fragments of the Italian army, and marched towards Rimini to meet the defiance of an insulting enemy.

The prudence of Narses impelled him to speedy and decisive action. His powers were the last effort of the state; the cost of each day accumulated the enormous account, and the nations, untrained to discipline or fatigue, might be rashly provoked to turn their arms against each other, or against their benefactor. The same considerations might have tempered the ardour of Totila. But he was conscious that the clergy and people of Italy aspired to a second revolution: he felt or suspected the rapid progress of treason, and he resolved to risk the Gothic kingdom on the chance of a day, in which the valiant would be animated by instant danger, and the disaffected might be awed by mutual ignorance. In his march from Ravenna the Roman general chastised the garrison of Rimini, traversed in a direct line the hills of Urbino, and re-entered the Flaminian way, nine miles beyond the perforated rock, an obstacle of art and nature which might have stopped or retarded his progress.[2] The Goths were assembled in

1 In the time of Augustus and in the middle ages the whole waste from Aquileia to Ravenna was covered with woods, lakes, and morasses. Man has subdued nature, and the land has been cultivated, since the waters are confined and embanked. See the learned researches of Muratori (Antiquitat. Italiæ Medii Ævi, tom. i. dissert. xxi. p. 253, 254), from Vitruvius, Strabo, Herodian, old charters, and local knowledge.

2 The Flaminian way, as it is corrected from the Itineraries, and the best modern maps, by D'Anville (Analyse de l'Italie, p. 147–162), may be thus stated:

the neighbourhood of Rome, they advanced without delay to seek a superior enemy, and the two armies approached each other at the distance of one hundred furlongs, between Tagina[1] and the sepulchres of the Gauls.[2] The haughty message of Narses was an offer not of peace, but of pardon. The answer of the Gothic king declared his resolution to die or conquer. 'What day,' said the messenger, 'will you fix for the combat?' 'The eighth day,' replied Totila; but early the next morning he attempted to surprise a foe suspicious of deceit and prepared for battle. Ten thousand Heruli and Lombards, of approved valour and doubtful faith, were placed in the centre. Each of the wings was composed of eight thousand Romans; the right was guarded by the cavalry of the Huns, the left was covered by fifteen hundred chosen horse, destined, according to the emergencies of action, to sustain the retreat of their friends, or to encompass the flank of the enemy. From his proper station at the head of the right wing, the eunuch rode along the line, expressing by his voice and countenance the assurance of victory, exciting the soldiers of the emperor to punish the guilt and madness of a band of robbers, and exposing to their view gold chains, collars, and bracelets, the rewards of military virtue. From the event of a single combat they drew an omen of success; and they beheld with pleasure the courage of fifty archers, who maintained a

ROME to Narni, 51 Roman miles; Terni, 57; Spoleto, 75; Foligno, 88; Nocera, 103; Cagli, 142; Intercisa, 157; Fossombrone, 160; Fano, 176; Pesaro, 184; RIMINI, 208 – about 189 English miles. He takes no notice of the death of Totila; but Wesseling (Itinerar. p. 614) exchanges, for the field of *Taginas*, the unknown appellation of *Ptanias*, eight miles from Nocera.

1 Taginæ, or rather Tadinæ, is mentioned by Pliny [iii. 19]; but the bishopric of that obscure town, a mile from Gualdo, in the plain, was united, in the year 1007, with that of Nocera. The signs of antiquity are preserved in the local appellations, *Fossato*, the camp; *Capraia*, Caprea; *Bastia*, Busta Gallorum. See Cluverius (Italia Antiqua. l. ii. c. 6, p. 615, 616, 617), Lucas Holstenius (Annotat. ad Cluver. p. 85, 86), Guazzesi (Dissertat. p. 177–217, a professed inquiry), and the maps of the ecclesiastical state and the march of Ancona, by Le Maire and Magini.

2 The battle was fought in the year of Rome 458; and consul Decius, by devoting his own life, assured the triumph of his country and his colleague Fabius (T. Liv. x. 28, 29). Procopius ascribes to Camillus the victory of the *Busta Gallorum* [tom. ii. p. 610, ed. Bonn]; and his error is branded by Cluverius with the national reproach of Græcorum nugamenta.

small eminence against three successive attacks of the Gothic cavalry. At the distance only of two bow-shots the armies spent the morning in dreadful suspense, and the Romans tasted some necessary food without unloosening the cuirass from their breast or the bridle from their horses. Narses awaited the charge; and it was delayed by Totila till he had received his last succours of two thousand Goths. While he consumed the hours in fruitless treaty, the king exhibited in a narrow space the strength and agility of a warrior. His armour was enchased with gold; his purple banner floated with the wind: he cast his lance into the air, caught it with the right hand, shifted it to the left, threw himself backwards, recovered his seat, and managed a fiery steed in all the paces and evolutions of the equestrian school. As soon as the succours had arrived, he retired to his tent, assumed the dress and arms of a private soldier, and gave the signal of battle. The first line of cavalry advanced with more courage than discretion, and left behind them the infantry of the second line. They were soon engaged between the horns of a crescent, into which the adverse wings had been insensibly curved, and were saluted from either side by the volleys of four thousand archers. Their ardour, and even their distress, drove them forwards to a close and unequal conflict, in which they could only use their lances against an enemy equally skilled in all the instruments of war. A generous emulation inspired the Romans and their barbarian allies; and Narses, who calmly viewed and directed their efforts, doubted to whom he should adjudge the prize of superior bravery. The Gothic cavalry was astonished and disordered, pressed and broken; and the line of infantry, instead of presenting their spears or opening their intervals, were trampled under the feet of the flying horse. Six thousand of the Goths were slaughtered without mercy in the field of Tagina. Their prince, with five attendants, was overtaken by Asbad, of the race of the Gepidæ: 'Spare the king of Italy,' cried a loyal voice, and Asbad struck his lance through the body of Totila. The blow was instantly revenged by the faithful Goths: they transported their dying monarch seven miles beyond the scene of his disgrace, and his last moments were not embittered by the presence of an enemy. Compassion afforded him the shelter of an obscure tomb; but the Romans were not satisfied of their victory till they beheld the corpse of the Gothic king. His hat, enriched with gems, and his bloody robe, were presented to Justinian by the messengers of triumph.[1]

As soon as Narses had paid his devotions to the Author of victory and the blessed Virgin, his peculiar patroness,[2] he praised, rewarded, and dismissed the Lombards. The villages had been reduced to ashes by these valiant savages: they ravished matrons and virgins on the altar; their retreat was diligently watched by a strong detachment of regular forces, who prevented a repetition of the like disorders. The victorious eunuch pursued his march through Tuscany, accepted the submission of the Goths, heard the acclamations and often the complaints of the Italians, and encompassed the walls of Rome with the remainder of his formidable host. Round the wide circumference Narses assigned to himself and to each of his lieutenants a real or a feigned attack, while he silently marked the place of easy and unguarded entrance. Neither the fortifications of Hadrian's mole, nor of the port, could long delay the progress of the conqueror; and Justinian once more received the keys of Rome, which, under his reign, had been *five* times taken and recovered.[3] But the deliverance of Rome was the last calamity of the Roman people. The barbarian allies of Narses too frequently confounded the privileges of peace and war. The despair of the flying Goths found some consolation in sanguinary revenge; and three hundred youths of the noblest families, who had been sent as hostages beyond the Po, were inhumanly slain by the successor of Totila. The fate of the senate suggests an awful lesson of the vicissitude of human affairs. Of the senators whom Totila had banished from their country, some were rescued by an officer of Belisarius and transported from Campania to Sicily, while others were too

1 Theophanes, Chron. p. 193 [tom. i. p. 354, ed. Bonn]. Hist. Miscell. xvi. p. 108.

2 Evagrius, l. iv. c. 24. The inspiration of the Virgin revealed to Narses the day, and the word, of battle (Paul Diacon. l. ii. c. 3, p. 776).

3 Ἐπὶ τούτου βασιλεύοντος τὸ πέμπτον ἑάλω. [Procop. Goth. lib. iv. c. 33; tom. ii. p. 632, ed. Bonn.] In the year 536 by Belisarius, in 546 by Totila, in 547 by Belisarius, in 549 by Totila, and in 552 by Narses. Maltretus had inadvertently translated *sextum*; a mistake which he afterwards retracts: but the mischief was done; and Cousin, with a train of French and Latin readers, have fallen into the snare.

guilty to confide in the clemency of Justinian, or too poor to provide horses for their escape to the sea-shore. Their brethren languished five years in a state of indigence and exile: the victory of Narses revived their hopes; but their premature return to the metropolis was prevented by the furious Goths, and all the fortresses of Campania were stained with patrician[1] blood. After a period of thirteen centuries the institution of Romulus expired; and if the nobles of Rome still assumed the title of senators, few subsequent traces can be discovered of a public council or constitutional order. Ascend six hundred years, and contemplate the kings of the earth soliciting an audience, as the slaves or freedmen of the Roman senate![2]

The Gothic war was yet alive. The bravest of the nation retired beyond the Po, and Teias was unanimously chosen to succeed and revenge their departed hero. The new king immediately sent ambassadors to implore, or rather to purchase, the aid of the Franks, and nobly lavished for the public safety the riches which had been deposited in the palace of Pavia. The residue of the royal treasure was guarded by his brother Aligern, at Cumæ in Campania; but the strong castle which Totila had fortified was closely besieged by the arms of Narses. From the Alps to the foot of Mount Vesuvius, the Gothic king by rapid and secret marches advanced to the relief of his brother, eluded the vigilance of the Roman chiefs, and pitched his camp on the banks of the Sarnus or *Draco*,[3] which flows from Nuceria into the bay of Naples. The river separated the two armies; sixty days were consumed in distant and fruitless combats, and Teias maintained this important post till he was deserted by his fleet and the hope of subsistence. With reluctant steps he ascended the *Lactarian* mount, where the physicians of Rome since the time of Galen

1 Compare two passages of Procopius (l. iii. c. 26, l. iv. c. 34 [tom. ii. p. 389 and 633, ed. Bonn]), which, with some collateral hints from Marcellinus and Jornandes, illustrate the state of the expiring senate.

2 See, in the example of Prusias, as it is delivered in the fragments of Polybius (Excerpt. Legat. xcvii. p. 927, 928), a curious picture of a royal slave.

3 The Δράκων of Procopius (Goth. l. iv. c. 35) is evidently the Sarnus. The text is accused or altered by the rash violence of Cluverius (l. iv. c. 3, p. 1156): but Camillo Pellegrini of Naples (Discorsi sopra la Campania Felice, p. 330, 331) has proved from old records that as early as the year 822 that river was called the Dracontio, or Draconcello.

had sent their patients for the benefit of the air and the milk.[1] But the Goths soon embraced a more generous resolution – to descend the hill, to dismiss their horses, and to die in arms and in the possession of freedom. The king marched at their head, bearing in his right hand a lance, and an ample buckler in his left: with the one he struck dead the foremost of the assailants, with the other he received the weapons which every hand was ambitious to aim against his life. After a combat of many hours, his left arm was fatigued by the weight of twelve javelins which hung from his shield. Without moving from his ground or suspending his blows, the hero called aloud on his attendants for a fresh buckler, but in the moment while his side was uncovered, it was pierced by a mortal dart. He fell; and his head, exalted on a spear, proclaimed to the nations that the Gothic kingdom was no more. But the example of his death served only to animate the companions who had sworn to perish with their leader. They fought till darkness descended on the earth. They reposed on their arms. The combat was renewed with the return of light, and maintained with unabated vigour till the evening of the second day. The repose of a second night, the want of water, and the loss of their bravest champions, determined the surviving Goths to accept the fair capitulation which the prudence of Narses was inclined to propose. They embraced the alternative of residing in Italy as the subjects and soldiers of Justinian, or departing with a portion of their private wealth in search of some independent country.[2] Yet the oath of fidelity or exile was alike rejected by one thousand Goths, who broke away before the treaty was signed, and boldly effected their retreat to the walls of Pavia. The spirit as well as the situation of Aligern prompted him to imitate rather than to bewail his brother: a strong and dexterous archer, he transpierced with a single arrow the armour

1 Galen (de Method. Medendi, l. v. apud Cluver. l. iv. c. 3, p. 1159, 1160) describes the lofty site, pure air, and rich milk of Mount Lactarius, whose medicinal benefits were equally known and sought in the time of Symmachus (l. vi. Epist. 18 [17?]), and Cassiodorus (Var. xi. 10). Nothing is now left except the name of the town of *Lettere*.

2 Buat (tom. xi. p. 2, etc.) conveys to his favourite Bavaria this remnant of Goths, who by others are buried in the mountains of Uri, or restored to their native isle of Gothland (Mascou, Annot. xxi.).

and breast of his antagonist, and his military conduct defended Cumæ[1] above a year against the forces of the Romans. Their industry had scooped the Sibyl's cave[2] into a prodigious mine; combustible materials were introduced to consume the temporary props: the wall and the gate of Cumæ sunk into the cavern, but the ruins formed a deep and inaccessible precipice. On the fragment of a rock Aligern stood alone and unshaken, till he calmly surveyed the hopeless condition of his country, and judged it more honourable to be the friend of Narses than the slave of the Franks. After the death of Teias the Roman general separated his troops to reduce the cities of Italy; Lucca sustained a long and vigorous siege, and such was the humanity or the prudence of Narses, that the repeated perfidy of the inhabitants could not provoke him to exact the forfeit lives of their hostages. These hostages were dismissed in safety, and their grateful zeal at length subdued the obstinacy of their countrymen.[3]

Before Lucca had surrendered, Italy was overwhelmed by a new deluge of barbarians. A feeble youth, the grandson of Clovis, reigned over the Austrasians or Oriental Franks. The guardians of Theodebald entertained with coldness and reluctance the magnificent promises of the Gothic ambassadors. But the spirit of a martial people outstripped the timid counsels of the court: two brothers, Lothaire and Buccelin,[4] the dukes of the Alemanni,

1 I leave Scaliger (Animadvers. in Euseb. p. 59) and Salmasius (Exercitat. Plinian. p. 51, 52) to quarrel about the origin of Cumæ, the oldest of the Greek colonies in Italy (Strab. l. v. p. 372 [p. 243, ed. Casaub.]; Velleius Paterculus, l. i. c. 4), already vacant in Juvenal's time (Satir. iii. [v. 2]), and now in ruins.

2 Agathias (l. i. p. 21 [c. 10, p. 34, ed. Bonn]) settles the Sibyl's cave under the wall of Cumæ: he agrees with Servius (ad l. vi. Æneid.); nor can I perceive why their opinion should be rejected by Heyne, the excellent editor of Virgil (tom. ii. p. 650, 651). In urbe mediâ secreta religio! But Cumæ was not yet built; and the lines (l. vi. 96, 97) would become ridiculous if Æneas were actually in a Greek city.

3 There is some difficulty in connecting the 35th chapter of the fourth book of the Gothic War of Procopius with the first book of the history of Agathias. We must now relinquish a statesman and soldier to attend the footsteps of a poet and rhetorician (l. i. p. 11, l. ii. p. 51, edit. Louvre).

4 Among the fabulous exploits of Buccelin, he discomfited and slew Belisarius, subdued Italy and *Sicily*, etc. See in the Historians of France, Gregory of Tours (tom. ii. l. iii. c. 32, p. 201), and Aimoin (tom. iii. l. ii. de Gestis Francorum, c. 23, p. 59).

stood forth as the leaders of the Italian war, and seventy-five thousand Germans descended in the autumn from the Rhætian Alps into the plain of Milan. The vanguard of the Roman army was stationed near the Po under the conduct of Fulcaris, a bold Herulian, who rashly conceived that personal bravery was the sole duty and merit of a commander. As he marched without order or precaution along the Æmilian way, an ambuscade of Franks suddenly rose from the amphitheatre of Parma; his troops were surprised and routed, but their leader refused to fly, declaring to the last moment that death was less terrible than the angry countenance of Narses. The death of Fulcaris, and the retreat of the surviving chiefs, decided the fluctuating and rebellious temper of the Goths; they flew to the standard of their deliverers, and admitted them into the cities which still resisted the arms of the Roman general. The conqueror of Italy opened a free passage to the irresistible torrent of barbarians. They passed under the walls of Cesena, and answered by threats and reproaches the advice of Aligern, that the Gothic treasures could no longer repay the labour of an invasion. Two thousand Franks were destroyed by the skill and valour of Narses himself, who sallied from Rimini at the head of three hundred horse to chastise the licentious rapine of their march. On the confines of Samnium the two brothers divided their forces. With the right wing Buccelin assumed the spoil of Campania, Lucania, and Bruttium; with the left, Lothaire accepted the plunder of Apulia and Calabria. They followed the coast of the Mediterranean and the Hadriatic as far as Rhegium and Otranto, and the extreme lands of Italy were the term of their destructive progress. The Franks, who were Christians and catholics, contented themselves with simple pillage and occasional murder. But the churches which their piety had spared were stripped by the sacrilegious hands of the Alemanni, who sacrificed horses' heads to their native deities of the woods and rivers;[1] they melted or profaned the consecrated vessels, and the ruins of shrines and altars were

1 Agathias notices their superstition in a philosophic tone (l. i. p. 18 [c. 28, *sq.*, ed. Bonn]). At Zug, in Switzerland, idolatry still prevailed in the year 613: St. Columban and St. Gall were the apostles of that rude country; and the latter founded an hermitage, which has swelled into an ecclesiastical principality and a populous city, the seat of freedom and commerce.

stained with the blood of the faithful. Buccelin was actuated by ambition, and Lothaire by avarice. The former aspired to restore the Gothic kingdom; the latter, after a promise to his brother of speedy succours, returned by the same road to deposit his treasure beyond the Alps. The strength of their armies was already wasted by the change of climate and contagion of disease; the Germans revelled in the vintage of Italy, and their own intemperance avenged in some degree the miseries of defenceless people.

At the entrance of the spring the Imperial troops who had guarded the cities assembled, to the number of eighteen thousand men, in the neighbourhood of Rome. Their winter hours had not been consumed in idleness. By the command and after the example of Narses, they repeated each day their military exercise on foot and on horseback, accustomed their ear to obey the sound of the trumpet, and practised the steps and evolutions of the Pyrrhic dance. From the straits of Sicily, Buccelin with thirty thousand Franks and Alemanni slowly moved towards Capua, occupied with a wooden tower the bridge of Casilinum, covered his right by the stream of the Vulturnus, and secured the rest of his encampment by a rampart of sharp stakes, and a circle of waggons whose wheels were buried in the earth. He impatiently expected the return of Lothaire; ignorant, alas! that his brother could never return, and that the chief and his army had been swept away by a strange disease[1] on the banks of the lake Benacus, between Trent and Verona. The banners of Narses soon approached the Vulturnus, and the eyes of Italy were anxiously fixed on the event of this final contest. Perhaps the talents of the Roman general were most conspicuous in the calm operations which precede the tumult of a battle. His skilful movements intercepted the subsistence of the barbarian, deprived him of the advantage of the bridge and river, and in the choice of

1 See the death of Lothaire in Agathias (l. ii. p. 38 [p. 70, ed. Bonn]) and Paul Warnefrid, surnamed Diaconus (l. ii. c. 2, p. 775). The Greek makes him rave and tear his flesh. He had plundered churches.

[A body of Lothaire's troops was defeated near Fano: some were driven down precipices into the sea, others fled to the camp: many prisoners seized the opportunity of making their escape; and the barbarians lost much of their booty in their precipitate retreat. – O. S.]

the ground and moment of action reduced him to comply with
the inclination of his enemy. On the morning of the important
day, when the ranks were already formed, a servant for some
trivial fault was killed by his master, one of the leaders of the
Heruli. The justice or passion of Narses was awakened: he summoned the offender to his presence, and without listening to his
excuses gave the signal to the minister of death. If the cruel
master had not infringed the laws of his nation, this arbitrary
execution was not less unjust than it appears to have been imprudent. The Heruli felt the indignity; they halted: but the
Roman general, without soothing their rage or expecting their
resolution, called aloud, as the trumpets sounded, that, unless
they hastened to occupy their place, they would lose the honour
of the victory. His troops were disposed[1] in a long front; the
cavalry on the wings; in the centre the heavy-armed foot; the
archers and slingers in the rear. The Germans advanced in a
sharp-pointed column of the form of a triangle or solid wedge.
They pierced the feeble centre of Narses, who received them
with a smile into the fatal snare, and directed his wings of cavalry
insensibly to wheel on their flanks and encompass their rear. The
host of the Franks and Alemanni consisted of infantry: a sword
and buckler hung by their side, and they used as their weapons
of offence a weighty hatchet and a hooked javelin, which were
only formidable in close combat or at a short distance. The
flower of the Roman archers, on horseback and in complete
armour, skirmished without peril round this immovable phalanx,
supplied by active speed the deficiency of number, and aimed
their arrows against a crowd of barbarians who, instead of a
cuirass and helmet, were covered by a loose garment of fur or
linen. They paused, they trembled, their ranks were confounded,
and in the decisive moment the Heruli, preferring glory to
revenge, charged with rapid violence the head of the column.
Their leader Sindbal, and Aligern the Gothic prince, deserved
the prize of superior valour; and their example incited the victorious troops to achieve with swords and spears the destruction

    1 Père Daniel (Hist. de la Milice Françoise, tom. i. p. 17–21) has exhibited
a fanciful representation of this battle, somewhat in the manner of the Chevalier
Folard, the once famous editor of Polybius, who fashioned to his own habits
and opinions all the military operations of antiquity.

of the enemy. Buccelin and the greatest part of his army perished
on the field of battle, in the waters of the Vulturnus, or by the
hands of the enraged peasants; but it may seem incredible that
a victory[1] which no more than five of the Alemanni survived
could be purchased with the loss of fourscore Romans. Seven
thousand Goths, the relics of the war, defended the fortress of
Campsa till the ensuing spring; and every messenger of Narses
announced the reduction of the Italian cities, whose names were
corrupted by the ignorance or vanity of the Greeks.[2] After the
battle of Casilinum Narses entered the capital; the arms and
treasures of the Goths, the Franks, and the Alemanni were displayed; his soldiers, with garlands in their hands, chanted the
praises of the conqueror; and Rome for the last time beheld the
semblance of a triumph.

After a reign of sixty years the throne of the Gothic kings
was filled by the exarchs of Ravenna, the representatives in peace
and war of the emperor of the Romans. Their jurisdiction was
soon reduced to the limits of a narrow province; but Narses
himself, the first and most powerful of the exarchs, administered
above fifteen years the entire kingdom of Italy. Like Belisarius,
he had deserved the honours of envy, calumny, and disgrace: but
the favourite eunuch still enjoyed the confidence of Justinian; or
the leader of a victorious army awed and repressed the ingratitude of a timid court. Yet it was not by weak and mischievous
indulgence that Narses secured the attachment of his troops.
Forgetful of the past, and regardless of the future, they abused
the present hour of prosperity and peace. The cities of Italy
resounded with the noise of drinking and dancing: the spoils of
victory were wasted in sensual pleasures; and nothing (says Agathias) remained unless to exchange their shields and helmets for
the soft lute and the capacious hogshead.[3] In a manly oration,

1 Agathias (l. ii. p. 47 [p. 87, ed. Bonn]) has produced a Greek epigram of
six lines on this victory of Narses, which is favourably compared to the battles of Marathon and Platæa. The chief difference is indeed in their consequences – so trivial in the former instance – so permanent and glorious in
the latter.

2 The Beroia and Brincas of Theophanes or his transcriber (p. 201 [tom. i.
p. 367, ed. Bonn]) must be read or understood Verona and Brixia.

3 Ἐλείπετο γὰρ, οἶμαι, αὐτοῖς ὑπὸ ἀβελτερίας τὰς ἀσπίδας τυχὸν καὶ
τὰ κράνη ἀμφορέως οἴνου ἢ καὶ βαρβίτου ἀποδόσθαι (Agathias, l. ii. [c. 11]

not unworthy of a Roman censor, the eunuch reproved these disorderly vices, which sullied their fame and endangered their safety. The soldiers blushed, and obeyed; discipline was confirmed; the fortifications were restored; a *duke* was stationed for the defence and military command of each of the principal cities;[1] and the eye of Narses pervaded the ample prospect from Calabria to the Alps. The remains of the Gothic nation evacuated the country, or mingled with the people: the Franks, instead of revenging the death of Buccelin, abandoned, without a struggle, their Italian conquests; and the rebellious Sindbal, chief of the Heruli, was subdued, taken, and hung on a lofty gallows, by the inflexible justice of the exarch.[2] The civil state of Italy, after the agitation of a long tempest, was fixed by a pragmatic sanction, which the emperor promulgated at the request of the pope. Justinian introduced his own jurisprudence into the schools and tribunals of the West: he ratified the acts of Theodoric and his immediate successors, but every deed was rescinded and abolished which force had extorted or fear had subscribed under the usurpation of Totila. A moderate theory was framed to reconcile the rights of property with the safety of prescription, the claims of the state with the poverty of the people, and the pardon of offences with the interest of virtue and order of society. Under the exarchs of Ravenna, Rome was degraded to the second rank. Yet the senators were gratified by the permission of visiting their estates in Italy, and of approaching without obstacle the throne of Constantinople: the regulation of weights and measures was delegated to the pope and senate; and the salaries of lawyers and physicians, of orators and grammarians, were destined to preserve or rekindle the light of science in the ancient capital. Justinian

---

p. 48 [p. 88, ed. Bonn]). In the first scene of Richard III our English poet has beautifully enlarged on this idea, for which, however, he was not indebted to the Byzantine historian.

1 Maffei has proved (Verona Illustrata, P. i. l. x. p. 257, 289), against the common opinion, that the dukes of Italy were instituted before the conquest of the Lombards, by Narses himself. In the Pragmatic Sanction (No. 23) Justinian restrains the *judices militares*.

2 See Paulus Diaconus, l. iii. c. 3, p. 776. Menander (in Excerpt. Legat. p. 133 [p. 345, ed. Bonn]) mentions some risings in Italy by the Franks, and Theophanes (p. 201 [tom. i. p. 367, ed. Bonn]) hints at some Gothic rebellions.

might dictate benevolent edicts,[1] and Narses might second his wishes by the restoration of cities, and more especially of churches. But the power of kings is most effectual to destroy: and the twenty years of the Gothic war had consummated the distress and depopulation of Italy. As early as the fourth campaign, under the discipline of Belisarius himself, fifty thousand labourers died of hunger[2] in the narrow region of Picenum;[3] and a strict interpretation of the evidence of Procopius would swell the loss of Italy above the total sum of her present inhabitants.[4]

I desire to believe, but I dare not affirm, that Belisarius sincerely rejoiced in the triumph of Narses. Yet the consciousness of his own exploits might teach him to esteem, without jealousy, the merit of a rival; and the repose of the aged warrior was crowned by a last victory, which saved the emperor and the capital. The barbarians, who annually visited the provinces of Europe, were less discouraged by some accidental defeats than they were excited by the double hope of spoil and of subsidy. In the thirty-second winter of Justinian's reign the Danube was deeply frozen; Zabergan led the cavalry of the Bulgarians, and his standard was followed by a promiscuous multitude of Sclavonians. The savage chief passed, without opposition, the river and the mountains, spread his troops over Macedonia and Thrace, and advanced with no more than seven thousand horse to the long walls which should have defended the territory of

1 The Pragmatic Sanction of Justinian, which restores and regulates the civil state of Italy, consists of xxvii articles: it is dated August 15, A.D. 554; is addressed to Narses, V. J. Præpositus Sacri Cubiculi, and to Antiochus Præfectus Prætorio Italiæ; and has been preserved by Julian Antecessor, and in the Corpus Juris Civilis, after the novels and edicts of Justinian, Justin, and Tiberius.

2 A still greater number was consumed by famine in the southern provinces, without ('έκτος) the Ionian Gulf. Acorns were used in the place of bread. Procopius had seen a deserted orphan suckled by a she-goat [Goth. ii. c. 17]. Seventeen passengers were lodged, murdered, and eaten, by two women, who were detected and slain by the eighteenth, etc.

3 Quinta regio Piceni est; quondam uberrimæ multitudinis, ccclx millia Picentium in fidem P. R. venere (Plin. Hist. Natur. iii. 18). In the time of Vespasian this ancient population was already diminished.

4 Perhaps fifteen or sixteen millions. Procopius (Anecdot. c. 18) computes that Africa lost five millions, that Italy was thrice as extensive, and that the depopulation was in a larger proportion. But his reckoning is inflamed by passion, and clouded with uncertainty.

Constantinople. But the works of man are impotent against the assaults of nature: a recent earthquake had shaken the foundations of the walls; and the forces of the empire were employed on the distant frontiers of Italy, Africa, and Persia. The seven *schools,*[1] or companies, of the guards or domestic troops had been augmented to the number of five thousand five hundred men, whose ordinary station was in the peaceful cities of Asia. But the places of the brave Armenians were insensibly supplied by lazy citizens, who purchased an exemption from the duties of civil life without being exposed to the dangers of military service. Of such soldiers few could be tempted to sally from the gates; and none could be persuaded to remain in the field, unless they wanted strength and speed to escape from the Bulgarians. The report of the fugitives exaggerated the numbers and fierceness of an enemy who had polluted holy virgins and abandoned new-born infants to the dogs and vultures; a crowd of rustics, imploring food and protection, increased the consternation of the city; and the tents of Zabergan were pitched at the distance of twenty miles,[2] on the banks of a small river which encircles Melanthias and afterwards falls into the Propontis.[3] Justinian trembled: and those who had only seen the emperor in his old age were pleased to suppose that he had *lost* the alacrity and vigour of his youth. By his command the vessels of gold and silver were removed from the churches in the neighbourhood, and even the suburbs, of Constantinople: the ramparts were lined with trembling spectators; the golden gate was crowded with useless generals and tribunes; and the senate shared the fatigues and the apprehensions of the populace.

1 In the decay of these military schools, the satire of Procopius (Anecdot. c. 24 [tom. iii. p. 135, ed. Bonn]; Aleman. p. 102, 103) is confirmed and illustrated by Agathias (l. v. p. 159 [p. 310, ed. Bonn]), who cannot be rejected as an hostile witness.

2 The distance from Constantinople to Melanthias, Villa Cæsariana (Ammian. Marcellin. xxxi. 11), is variously fixed at 120 or 140 stadia (Suidas, tom. ii. p. 522, 523; Agathias, l. v. [c. 14] p. 158 [p. 308, ed. Bonn]), or xviii or xix miles (Itineraria, p. 138, 230, 323, 332, and Wesseling's Obervations). The first xii miles, as far as Rhegium, were paved by Justinian, who built a bridge over a morass or gullet between a lake and the sea (Procop. de Ædif. l. iv. c. 8).

3 The Atyras (Pompon. Mela, l. ii. c. 2, p. 169, edit. Voss.). At the river's mouth a town or castle of the same name was fortified by Justinian (Procop. de Ædif. l. iv. c. 2; Itinerar. p. 570; and Wesseling).

But the eyes of the prince and people were directed to a feeble veteran, who was compelled by the public danger to resume the armour in which he had entered Carthage and defended Rome. The horses of the royal stables, of private citizens, and even of the circus, were hastily collected; the emulation of the old and young was roused by the name of Belisarius, and his first encampment was in the presence of a victorious enemy. His prudence, and the labour of the friendly peasants, secured, with a ditch and rampart, the repose of the night; innumerable fires and clouds of dust were artfully contrived to magnify the opinion of his strength; his soldiers suddenly passed from despondency to presumption; and, while ten thousand voices demanded the battle, Belisarius dissembled his knowledge that in the hour of trial he must depend on the firmness of three hundred veterans. The next morning the Bulgarian cavalry advanced to the charge. But they heard the shouts of multitudes, they beheld the arms and discipline of the front; they were assaulted on the flanks by two ambuscades which rose from the woods; their foremost warriors fell by the hand of the aged hero and his guards; and the swiftness of their evolutions was rendered useless by the close attack and rapid pursuit of the Romans. In this action (so speedy was their flight) the Bulgarians lost only four hundred horse: but Constantinople was saved; and Zabergan, who felt the hand of a master, withdrew to a respectful distance. But his friends were numerous in the councils of the emperor, and Belisarius obeyed with reluctance the commands of envy and Justinian, which forbade him to achieve the deliverance of his country. On his return to the city, the people, still conscious of their danger, accompanied his triumph with acclamations of joy and gratitude, which were imputed as a crime to the victorious general. But when he entered the palace the courtiers were silent, and the emperor, after a cold and thankless embrace, dismissed him to mingle with the train of slaves. Yet so deep was the impression of his glory on the minds of men, that Justinian, in the seventy-seventh year of his age, was encouraged to advance near forty miles from the capital, and to inspect in person the restoration of the long wall. The Bulgarians wasted the summer in the plains of Thrace; but they were inclined to peace by the failure of their rash attempts on Greece and the Chersonesus. A menace of killing their prisoners quickened the payment of heavy ransoms; and the departure of Zabergan was hastened by the report that double-prowed vessels were built on the Danube to intercept his passage. The danger was soon forgotten; and a vain question, whether their sovereign had shown more wisdom or weakness, amused the idleness of the city.[1]

About two years after the last victory of Belisarius, the emperor returned from a Thracian journey of health, or business, or devotion. Justinian was afflicted by a pain in his head; and his private entry countenanced the rumour of his death. Before the third hour of the day, the bakers' shops were plundered of their bread, the houses were shut, and every citizen, with hope or terror, prepared for the impending tumult. The senators themselves, fearful and suspicious, were convened at the ninth hour; and the præfect received their commands to visit every quarter of the city and proclaim a general illumination for the recovery of the emperor's health. The ferment subsided; but every accident betrayed the impotence of the government and the factious temper of the people: the guards were disposed to mutiny as often as their quarters were changed, or their pay was withheld: the frequent calamities of fires and earthquakes afforded the opportunities of disorder; the disputes of the blues and greens, of the orthodox and heretics, degenerated into bloody battles; and, in the presence of the Persian ambassador, Justinian blushed for himself and for his subjects. Capricious pardon and arbitrary punishment embittered the irksomeness and discontent of a long reign: a conspiracy was formed in the palace; and, unless we are deceived by the names of Marcellus and Sergius, the most virtuous and the most profligate of the courtiers were associated in the same designs. They had fixed the time of the execution; their rank gave them access to the royal banquet; and their black slaves[2] were

1 The Bulgarian war, and the last victory of Belisarius, are imperfectly represented in the prolix declamation of Agathias (l. v. p. 154–174 [p. 299 *sqq.*, ed. Bonn]) and the dry Chronicle of Theophanes (p. 197, 198 [tom. i. p. 360 *sq.*, ed. Bonn]).

2 "Ινδους. They could scarcely be real Indians; and the Æthiopians, sometimes known by that name, were never used by the ancients as guards or followers: they were the trifling, though costly, objects of female and royal luxury (Terent. Eunuch. act i. scene ii. [v. 88]; Sueton. in August. c. 83, with a good note of Casaubon, in Caligulâ, c. 57).

stationed in the vestibule and porticoes to announce the death of the tyrant, and to excite a sedition in the capital. But the indiscretion of an accomplice saved the poor remnant of the days of Justinian. The conspirators were detected and seized with daggers hidden under their garments; Marcellus died by his own hand, and Sergius was dragged from the sanctuary.[1] Pressed by remorse, or tempted by the hopes of safety, he accused two officers of the household of Belisarius, and torture forced them to declare that they had acted according to the secret instructions of their patron.[2] Posterity will not hastily believe that a hero who in the vigour of life had disdained the fairest offers of ambition and revenge should stoop to the murder of his prince, whom he could not long expect to survive. His followers were impatient to fly; but flight must have been supported by rebellion, and he had lived enough for nature and for glory. Belisarius appeared before the council with less fear than indignation: after forty years' service the emperor had prejudged his guilt; and injustice was sanctified by the presence and authority of the patriarch. The life of Belisarius was graciously spared, but his fortunes were sequestered; and, from December to July, he was guarded as a prisoner in his own palace. At length his innocence was acknowledged; his freedom and honours were restored; and death, which might be hastened by resentment and grief, removed him from the world about eight months after his deliverance. The name of Belisarius can never die: but, instead of the funeral, the monuments, the statues, so justly due to his memory, I only read that his treasures, the spoils of the Goths and Vandals, were immediately confiscated by the emperor. Some decent portion was reserved, however, for the use of his widow: and as Antonina had much to repent, she devoted the last remains of her life and fortune to the foundation of a convent. Such is the simple and genuine narrative of the fall of Belisarius and the ingratitude of Justinian.[3]

---

1 The Sergius (Vandal. l. ii. c. 21, 22, Anecdot. c. 5) and Marcellus (Goth. l. iii. c. 32) are mentioned by Procopius. See Theophanes, p. 197, 201 [tom. i. p. 360, 367, ed. Bonn].

2 Alemannus (p. 3) quotes an old Byzantine MS., which has been printed in the Imperium Orientale of Banduri [tom. iii. p. 349, ed. Bonn].

3 Of the disgrace and restoration of Belisarius, the genuine original record is preserved in the Fragment of John Malala (tom. ii. p. 234–243 [p. 494 *sq.*,

That he was deprived of his eyes, and reduced by envy to beg
his bread, 'Give a penny to Belisarius the general!' is a fiction of
later times,¹ which has obtained credit, or rather favour, as a
strange example of the vicissitudes of fortune.²

If the emperor could rejoice in the death of Belisarius, he
enjoyed the base satisfaction only eight months, the last period
of a reign of thirty-eight and a life of eighty-three years. It would
be difficult to trace the character of a prince who is not the most
conspicuous object of his own times: but the confessions of an

ed. Bonn]) and the exact Chronicle of Theophanes (p. 194–204 [tom. i. p. 368
sqq., ed. Bonn]). Cedrenus (Compend. p. 387, 388 [tom. i. p. 680, ed. Bonn])
and Zonaras (tom. ii. l. xiv. [c. 9] p. 69) seem to hesitate between the obsolete
truth and the growing falsehood.

1 The source of this idle fable may be derived from a miscellaneous work
of the twelfth century, the Chiliads of John Tzetzes, a monk (Basil. 1546, ad
calcem Lycophront. Colon. Allobrog. 1614, in Corp. Poet. Græc.). He relates
the blindness and beggary of Belisarius in ten vulgar or *political* verses (Chiliad
iii. No. 88, 339–348, in Corp. Poet. Græc. tom. ii. p. 311).

  Ἔκπωμα ξύλινον κρατῶν, ἐβόα τῷ μιλίῳ,
  Βελισαρίῳ ὀβολὸν δότε τῷ στρατηλάτῃ
  Ὃν τύχη μὲν ἐδόξασεν, ἀποτυφλοῖ δ' ὁ φθόνος.

This moral or romantic tale was imported into Italy with the language and
manuscripts of Greece; repeated before the end of the fifteenth century by
Crinitus, Pontanus, and Volaterranus; attacked by Alciat, for the honour of
the law; and defended by Baronius (A.D. 561, No. 2, etc.), for the honour of
the church. Yet Tzetzes himself had read in *other* chronicles that Belisarius did not
lose his sight, and that he recovered his fame and fortunes.

[John Tzetzes was not a monk, and he relates the story of the blindness
and the beggary of Belisarius in his Cheliads, iii. No. 88. 339–348. But the story
is to be found earlier than he, viz., in the Πάτρια τῆς πόλεως of Codinus
compiled in the time of Basil II. The earliest writer who mentions the disgrace
of Belisarius is Theophanes, who lived in the ninth century, and he expressly
adds that Belisarius was restored to his freedom and honours. Two theories
have been started to account for the origin of the story of Belisarius. The first
is that of Le Beau, who supposes that Belisarius was confounded with his
contemporary John of Cappadocia, who was reduced to such poverty that he
begged his bread from province to province. The second is that of Mr. Finlay,
who suggests that the story took its rise from the fate of Symbatius and Peganes,
who, having formed a conspiracy against Michael III. in the ninth century, were
deprived of their sight and exposed as common beggars in Constantinople. (See
Finlay, *Hist. of Byzantine Empire*.) – O. S.]

2 The statue in the villa Borghese at Rome, in a sitting posture, with an
open hand, which is vulgarly given to Belisarius, may be ascribed with more
dignity to Augustus in the act of propitiating Nemesis (Winckelman, Hist. de
l'Art, tom. iii. p. 266). Ex nocturno visû etiam stipem, quotannis, die certo,

enemy may be received as the safest evidence of his virtues. The
resemblance of Justinian to the bust of Domitian is maliciously
urged,[1] with the acknowledgment, however, of a well-propor-
tioned figure, a ruddy complexion, and a pleasing countenance.
The emperor was easy of access, patient of hearing, courteous
and affable in discourse, and a master of the angry passions
which rage with such destructive violence in the breast of a
despot. Procopius praises his temper, to reproach him with calm
and deliberate cruelty: but in the conspiracies which attacked his
authority and person, a more candid judge will approve the justice, or admire the clemency, of Justinian. He excelled in the
private virtues of chastity and temperance; but the impartial love
of beauty would have been less mischievous than his conjugal
tenderness for Theodora; and his abstemious diet was regulated,
not by the prudence of a philosopher, but the superstition of a
monk. His repasts were short and frugal: on solemn fasts he
contented himself with water and vegetables; and such was his
strength as well as fervour, that he frequently passed two days,
and as many nights, without tasting any food. The measure of
his sleep was not less rigorous: after the repose of a single hour,
the body was awakened by the soul, and, to the astonishment of
his chamberlains, Justinian walked or studied till the morning
light. Such restless application prolonged his time for the acquisition of knowledge[2] and the despatch of business; and he might
seriously deserve the reproach of confounding, by minute and
preposterous diligence, the general order of his administration.
The emperor professed himself a musician and architect, a poet

emendicabat a populo, cavam manum asses porrigentibus præbens (Sueton. in
August. c. 91, with an excellent note of Casaubon).

[It should be noted that the statue formerly in the villa Borghese at Rome
is now in the Louvre. – O. S.]

1 The *rubor* of Domitian is stigmatised, quaintly enough, by the pen of
Tacitus (in Vit. Agricol. c. 45), and has been likewise noticed by the younger
Pliny (Panegyr. c. 48) and Suetonius (in Domitian, c. 18, and Casaubon ad
locum). Procopius (Anecdot. c. 8 [tom. iii. p. 55, ed. Bonn]) foolishly believes
that only *one* bust of Domitian had reached the sixth century.

2 The studies and science of Justinian are attested by the confession (Anecdot. c. 8, 13), still more than by the praises (Gothic. l. iii. c. 31, de Ædific.
l. i. Proem. c. 7) of Procopius. Consult the copious index of Alemannus, and
read the Life of Justinian by Ludewig (p. 135–142).

and philosopher, a lawyer and theologian; and if he failed in the enterprise of reconciling the Christian sects, the review of the Roman jurisprudence is a noble monument of his spirit and industry. In the government of the empire he was less wise, or less successful: the age was unfortunate; the people was oppressed and discontented; Theodora abused her power; a succession of bad ministers disgraced his judgment; and Justinian was neither beloved in his life nor regretted at his death. The love of fame was deeply implanted in his breast, but he condescended to the poor ambition of titles, honours, and contemporary praise; and while he laboured to fix the admiration, he forfeited the esteem and affection, of the Romans. The design of the African and Italian wars was boldly conceived and executed; and his penetration discovered the talents of Belisarius in the camp, of Narses in the palace. But the name of the emperor is eclipsed by the names of his victorious generals; and Belisarius still lives to upbraid the envy and ingratitude of his sovereign. The partial favour of mankind applauds the genius of a conqueror who leads and directs his subjects in the exercise of arms. The characters of Philip the Second and of Justinian are distinguished by the cold ambition which delights in war, and declines the dangers of the field. Yet a colossal statue of bronze represented the emperor on horseback, preparing to march against the Persians in the habit and armour of Achilles. In the great square before the church of St. Sophia, this monument was raised on a brass column and a stone pedestal of seven steps; and the pillar of Theodosius, which weighed seven thousand four hundred pounds of silver, was removed from the same place by the avarice and vanity of Justinian. Future princes were more just or indulgent to *his* memory; the elder Andronicus, in the beginning of the fourteenth century, repaired and beautified his equestrian statue: since the fall of the empire it has been melted into cannon by the victorious Turks.[1]

I shall conclude this chapter with the comets, the earthquakes, and the plague, which astonished or afflicted the age of Justinian.

---

1 See in the C. P. Christiana of Ducange (l. i. c. 24, No. 1) a chain of original testimonies, from Procopius in the sixth, to Gyllius in the sixteenth, century.

1. In the fifth year of his reign, and in the month of September, a comet[1] was seen during twenty days in the western quarter of the heavens, and which shot its rays into the north. Eight years afterwards, while the sun was in Capricorn, another comet appeared to follow in the Sagittary: the size was gradually increasing; the head was in the east, the tail in the west, and it remained visible above forty days. The nations, who gazed with astonishment, expected wars and calamities from their baleful influence; and these expectations were abundantly fulfilled. The astronomers dissembled their ignorance of the nature of these blazing stars, which they affected to represent as the floating meteors of the air; and few among them embraced the simple notion of Seneca and the Chaldæans, that they are only planets of a longer period and more eccentric motion.[2] Time and science have justified the conjectures and predictions of the Roman sage: the telescope has opened new worlds to the eyes of astronomers;[3] and, in the narrow space of history and fable, one and the same comet is already found to have revisited the earth in *seven* equal revolutions of five hundred and seventy-five years. The *first*,[4] which ascends beyond the Christian era one thousand seven hundred and sixty-seven years, is coëval with Ogyges, the father of Grecian antiquity. And this appearance explains the tradition

1 The first comet is mentioned by John Malala (tom. ii. p. 190, 219 [p. 454, 477, ed. Bonn]) and Theophanes (p. 154 [tom. i. p. 278, ed. Bonn]); the second by Procopius (Persic. l. ii. c. 4). Yet I strongly suspect their identity. The paleness of the sun (Vandal. l. ii. c. 14) is applied by Theophanes (p. 158) to a different year.

2 Seneca's seventh book of Natural Questions displays in the theory of comets a philosophic mind. Yet should we not too candidly confound a vague prediction, a veniet tempus, etc., with the merit of real discoveries.

3 Astronomers may study Newton and Halley. I draw my humble science from the article COMÈTE, in the French Encyclopédie, by M. d'Alembert.

[The identity of the comet of A.D. 1680, with the comets of A.D. 1106, A.D. 531, B.C. 44, etc., was an ingenious speculation of Halley. The observations made upon the eccentricity of a comet's orbit, whether it was a parabola or an ellipse with great eccentricity, have recently been made with such accuracy as to warrant almost exact conclusions being obtained. Cf. John Williams, *Observations of Comets from Chinese Annals.* − O. S.]

4 Whiston, the honest, pious, visionary Whiston, had fancied, for the era of Noah's flood (2242 years before Christ), a prior apparition of the same comet which drowned the earth with its tail.

which Varro has preserved, that under his reign the planet Venus changed her colour, size, figure, and course; a prodigy without example either in past or succeeding ages.[1] The *second* visit, in the year eleven hundred and ninety-three, is darkly implied in the fable of Electra, the seventh of the Pleiads, who have been reduced to six since the time of the Trojan war. That nymph, the wife of Dardanus, was unable to support the ruin of her country: she abandoned the dances of her sister orbs, fled from the zodiac to the north pole, and obtained, from her dishevelled locks, the name of the *comet*. The *third* period expires in the year six hundred and eighteen, a date that exactly agrees with the tremendous comet of the Sibyl, and perhaps of Pliny, which arose in the West two generations before the reign of Cyrus. The *fourth* apparition, forty-four years before the birth of Christ, is of all others the most splendid and important. After the death of Cæsar, a long-haired star was conspicuous to Rome and to the nations during the games which were exhibited by young Octavian in honour of Venus and his uncle. The vulgar opinion, that it conveyed to heaven the divine soul of the dictator, was cherished and consecrated by the piety of a statesman; while his secret superstition referred the comet to the glory of his own times.[2] The *fifth* visit has been already ascribed to the fifth year of Justinian, which coincides with the five hundred and thirty-first of the Christian era. And it may deserve notice, that in this, as in the preceding instance, the comet was followed, though at a longer interval, by a remarkable paleness of the sun. The *sixth* return, in the year eleven hundred and six, is recorded by the chronicles of Europe and China: and in the first fervour of the Crusades, the Christians and the Mahometans might surmise,

1 A Dissertation of Fréret (Mémoires de l'Académie des Inscriptions, tom. x. p. 357–377) affords a happy union of philosophy and erudition. The phenomenon in the time of Ogyges was preserved by Varro (apud Augustin. de Civitate Dei, xxi. 8), who quotes Castor, Dion of Naples, and Adrastus of Cyzicus – nobiles mathematici. The two subsequent periods are preserved by the Greek mythologists and the spurious books of Sibylline verses.

2 Pliny (Hist. Nat. ii. 23) has transcribed the original memorial of Augustus. Mairan, in his most ingenious letters to the P. Parennin, missionary in China, removes the games and the comet of September from the year 44 to the year 43 before the Christian era; but I am not totally subdued by the criticism of the astronomer (Opuscules, p. 275–351).

with equal reason, that it portended the destruction of the Infidels. The *seventh* phenomenon, of one thousand six hundred and eighty, was presented to the eyes of an enlightened age.[1] The philosophy of Bayle dispelled a prejudice which Milton's muse had so recently adorned, that the comet, 'from its horrid hair shakes pestilence and war.'[2] Its road in the heavens was observed with exquisite skill by Flamsteed and Cassini: and the mathematical science of Bernoulli, Newton, and Halley investigated the laws of its revolutions. At the *eighth* period, in the year two thousand three hundred and fifty-five, their calculations may perhaps be verified by the astronomers of some future capital in the Siberian or American wilderness.

II. The near approach of a comet may injure or destroy the globe which we inhabit; but the changes on its surface have been hitherto produced by the action of volcanoes and earthquakes.[3] The nature of the soil may indicate the countries most exposed to these formidable concussions, since they are caused by subterraneous fires, and such fires are kindled by the union and fermentation of iron and sulphur. But their times and effects appear to lie beyond the reach of human curiosity; and the philosopher will discreetly abstain from the prediction of earthquakes, till he has counted the drops of water that silently filtrate on the inflammable mineral, and measured the caverns which increase by resistance the explosion of the imprisoned air. Without assigning the cause, history will distinguish the periods in which these calamitous events have been rare or frequent, and will observe that this fever of the earth raged with uncommon

1 This last comet was visible in the month of December, 1680. Bayle, who began his Pensées sur la Comète in January, 1681 (Œuvres, tom. iii.), was forced to argue that a *supernatural* comet would have confirmed the ancients in their idolatry. Bernoulli (see his *Eloge*, in Fontenelle, tom. v. p. 99) was forced to allow that the tail, though not the head, was a *sign* of the wrath of God.

2 Paradise Lost was published in the year 1667; and the famous lines (l. ii. 708, etc.), which startled the licenser, may allude to the recent comet of 1664, observed by Cassini at Rome in the presence of queen Christina (Fontenelle, in his *Eloge*, tom. v. p. 338). Had Charles II. betrayed any symptoms of curiosity or fear?

3 For the cause of earthquakes, see Buffon (tom. i. p. 502–536; Supplément à l'Hist. Naturelle, tom. v. p. 382–390, edition in 4to.), Valmont de Bomare (Dictionnaire d'Histoire Naturelle, *Tremblemens de Terre, Pyrites*), Watson (Chemical Essays, tom. i. p. 181–209).

violence during the reign of Justinian.[1] Each year is marked by
the repetition of earthquakes, of such duration that Constantinople has been shaken above forty days; of such extent that
the shock has been communicated to the whole surface of the
globe, or at least of the Roman empire. An impulsive or vibratory
motion was felt, enormous chasms were opened, huge and heavy
bodies were discharged into the air, the sea alternately advanced
and retreated beyond its ordinary bounds, and a mountain was
torn from Libanus[2] and cast into the waves, where it protected,
as a mole, the new harbour of Botrys[3] in Phœnicia. The stroke
that agitates an ant-hill may crush the insect-myriads in the dust;
yet truth must extort a confession that man has industriously
laboured for his own destruction. The institution of great cities,
which include a nation within the limits of a wall, almost realises
the wish of Caligula that the Roman people had but one neck.
Two hundred and fifty thousand persons are said to have perished
in the earthquake of Antioch, whose domestic multitudes were
swelled by the conflux of strangers to the festival of the Ascen-
sion. The loss of Berytus[4] was of smaller account, but of much
greater value. That city, on the coast of Phœnicia, was illustrated
by the study of the civil law, which opened the surest road to
wealth and dignity: the schools of Berytus were filled with the

1 The earthquakes that shook the Roman world in the reign of Justinian
are described or mentioned by Procopius (Goth. l. iv. c. 25 [tom. ii. p. 594, ed.
Bonn]; Anecdot. c. 18), Agathias (l. ii. p. 52, 53, 54; l. v. p. 145–152 [p. 96–101,
281–294, ed. Bonn]), John Malala (Chron. tom. ii. p. 140–146, 176, 177, 183,
193, 220, 229, 231, 233, 234 [p. 419 sq., 442 sq., 448, 456, 478, 485 sq., 488 sq.,
ed. Bonn]), and Theophanes (p. 151, 183, 189, 191–196 [tom. i. p. 272, 336,
347, 350, 357, ed. Bonn]).

2 An abrupt height, a perpendicular cape, between Aradus and Botrys,
named by the Greeks θεῶν πρόσωπον, and εὐπρόσωπον or λιθοπρόσωπον by
the scrupulous Christians (Polyb. l. v. [c. 68] p. 411; Pompon. Mela, l. i. c. 12,
p. 87, cum Isaac Voss. Observat. Maundrell, Journey, p. 32, 33; Pocock's Description, vol. ii. p. 99).

3 Botrys was founded (ann. ante Christ. 935–903) by Ithobal, king of Tyre
(Marsham, Canon Chron. p. 387, 388). Its poor representative, the village of
Patrone, is now destitute of an harbour.

4 The university, splendour, and ruin of Berytus, are celebrated by Heineccius (p. 351–356) as an essential part of the history of the Roman law. It was
overthrown in the twenty-fifth year of Justinian, A.D. 551, July 9 (Theophanes,
p. 192); but Agathias (l. ii. p. 51, 52 [p. 95 sq., ed. Bonn]) suspends the earthquake till he has achieved the Italian war.

rising spirits of the age, and many a youth was lost in the earthquake who might have lived to be the scourge or the guardian
of his country. In these disasters the architect becomes the enemy
of mankind. The hut of a savage, or the tent of an Arab, may
be thrown down without injury to the inhabitant; and the Peru-
vians had reason to deride the folly of their Spanish conquerors,
who with so much cost and labour erected their own sepulchres.
The rich marbles of a patrician are dashed on his own head; a
whole people is buried under the ruins of public and private
edifices; and the conflagration is kindled and propagated by the
innumerable fires which are necessary for the subsistence and
manufactures of a great city. Instead of the mutual sympathy
which might comfort and assist the distressed, they dreadfully
experience the vices and passions which are released from the
fear of punishment; the tottering houses are pillaged by intrepid
avarice; revenge embraces the moment and selects the victim;
and the earth often swallows the assassin, or the ravisher, in the
consummation of their crimes. Superstition involves the present
danger with invisible terrors; and if the image of death may
sometimes be subservient to the virtue or repentance of individuals, an affrighted people is more forcibly moved to expect the
end of the world, or to deprecate with servile homage the wrath
of an avenging Deity.

III. Æthiopia and Egypt have been stigmatised in every age
as the original source and seminary of the plague.[1] In a damp,
hot, stagnating air, this African fever is generated from the putrefaction of animal substances, and especially from the swarms
of locusts, not less destructive to mankind in their death than in
their lives. The fatal disease which depopulated the earth in the
time of Justinian and his successors[2] first appeared in the neighbourhood of Pelusium, between the Serbonian bog and the eastern

1 I have read with pleasure Mead's short, but elegant, treatise concerning
Pestilential Disorders, the seventh edition, London, 1722.

2 The great plague which raged in 542 and the following years (Pagi,
Critica, tom. ii. p. 518) must be traced in Procopius (Persic. l. ii. c. 22, 23),
Agathias (l. v. p. 153, 154 [p. 297 sq., ed. Bonn]), Evagrius (l. iv. c. 29), Paul
Diaconus (l. ii. c. 4, p. 776, 777), Gregory of Tours (tom. ii. l. iv. c. 5, p. 205),
who styles it *Lues Inguinaria*, and the Chronicles of Victor Tunnunensis (p. 9 in
Thesaur. Temporum), of Marcellinus (p. 54), and of Theophanes (p. 153).

channel of the Nile. From thence, tracing as it were a double
path, it spread to the East, over Syria, Persia, and the Indies, and
penetrated to the West, along the coast of Africa and over the
continent of Europe. In the spring of the second year Constantinople, during three or four months, was visited by the pestilence; and Procopius, who observed its progress and symptoms
with the eyes of a physician,[1] has emulated the skill and diligence
of Thucydides in the description of the plague of Athens.[2] The
infection was sometimes announced by the visions of a distempered fancy, and the victim despaired as soon as he had heard
the menace and felt the stroke of an invisible spectre. But the
greater number, in their beds, in the streets, in their usual occupation, were surprised by a slight fever; so slight, indeed, that
neither the pulse nor the colour of the patient gave any signs of
the approaching danger. The same, the next, or the succeeding
day, it was declared by the swelling of the glands, particularly
those of the groin, of the armpits, and under the ear; and when
these buboes or tumours were opened, they were found to contain a *coal*, or black substance, of the size of a lentil. If they came
to a just swelling and suppuration, the patient was saved by this
kind and natural discharge of the morbid humour; but if they
continued hard and dry, a mortification quickly ensued, and the
fifth day was commonly the term of his life. The fever was often
accompanied with lethargy or delirium; the bodies of the sick
were covered with black pustules or carbuncles, the symptoms
of immediate death; and in the constitutions too feeble to produce an eruption, the vomiting of blood was followed by a
mortification of the bowels. To pregnant women the plague was
generally mortal; yet one infant was drawn alive from his dead
mother, and three mothers survived the loss of their infected
fœtus. Youth was the most perilous season, and the female sex

1 Dr. Friend (Hist. Medicin. in Opp. p. 416–420, Lond. 1733) is satisfied
that Procopius must have studied physic, from his knowledge and use of the
technical words. Yet many words that are now scientific were common and
popular in the Greek idiom.

2 See Thucydides, l. ii. c. 47–54, p. 127–133, edit. Duker, and the poetical
description of the same plague by Lucretius (l. vi. 1136–1284). I was indebted
to Dr. Hunter for an elaborate commentary on this part of Thucydides, a quarto
of 600 pages (Venet. 1603, apud Juntas), which was pronounced in St. Mark's
library by Fabius Paullinus Utinensis, a physician and philosopher.

was less susceptible than the male; but every rank and profession was attacked with indiscriminate rage, and many of those who escaped were deprived of the use of their speech, without being secure from a return of the disorder.[1] The physicians of Constantinople were zealous and skilful; but their art was baffled by the various symptoms and pertinacious vehemence of the disease: the same remedies were productive of contrary effects, and the event capriciously disappointed their prognostics of death or recovery. The order of funerals and the right of sepulchres were confounded; those who were left without friends or servants lay unburied in the streets, or in their desolate houses; and a magistrate was authorised to collect the promiscuous heaps of dead bodies, to transport them by land or water, and to inter them in deep pits beyond the precincts of the city. Their own danger and the prospect of public distress awakened some remorse in the minds of the most vicious of mankind: the confidence of health again revived their passions and habits; but philosophy must disdain the observation of Procopius, that the lives of such men were guarded by the peculiar favour of fortune or Providence. He forgot, or perhaps he secretly recollected, that the plague had touched the person of Justinian himself; but the abstemious diet of the emperor may suggest, as in the case of Socrates, a more rational and honourable cause for his recovery.[2] During his sickness the public consternation was expressed in the habits of the citizens; and their idleness and despondence occasioned a general scarcity in the capital of the East.

Contagion is the inseparable symptom of the plague; which, by mutual respiration, is transfused from the infected persons to the lungs and stomach of those who approach them. While philosophers believe and tremble, it is singular that the existence of

1 Thucydides (c. 51) affirms that the infection could only be once taken; but Evagrius, who had family experience of the plague, observes that some persons, who had escaped the first, sunk under the second attack; and this repetition is confirmed by Fabius Paullinus (p. 588). I observe that on this head physicians are divided; and the nature and operation of the disease may not always be similar.

2 It was thus that Socrates had been saved by his temperance, in the plague of Athens (Aul. Gellius, Noct. Attic. ii. 1). Dr. Mead accounts for the peculiar salubrity of religious houses by the two advantages of seclusion and abstinence (p. 18, 19).

a real danger should have been denied by a people most prone to vain and imaginary terrors.[1] Yet the fellow-citizens of Procopius were satisfied, by some short and partial experience, that the infection could not be gained by the closest conversation;[2] and this persuasion might support the assiduity of friends or physicians in the care of the sick, whom inhuman prudence would have condemned to solitude and despair. But the fatal security, like the predestination of the Turks, must have aided the progress of the contagion; and those salutary precautions to which Europe is indebted for her safety were unknown to the government of Justinian. No restraints were imposed on the free and frequent intercourse of the Roman provinces: from Persia to France the nations were mingled and infected by wars and emigrations; and the pestilential odour which lurks for years in a bale of cotton was imported, by the abuse of trade, into the most distant regions. The mode of its propagation is explained by the remark of Procopius himself, that it always spread from the sea-coast to the inland country: the most sequestered islands and mountains were successively visited; the places which had escaped the fury of its first passage were alone exposed to the contagion of the ensuing year. The winds might diffuse that subtle venom; but unless the atmosphere be previously disposed for its reception, the plague would soon expire in the cold or temperate climates of the earth. Such was the universal corruption of the air, that the pestilence which burst forth in the fifteenth year of Justinian was not checked or alleviated by any difference of the seasons. In time its first malignity was abated and dispersed; the disease alternately languished and revived; but it was not till the end of a calamitous period of fifty-two years that mankind recovered their health, or the air resumed its pure and salubrious quality. No facts have been preserved to sustain

1 Mead proves that the plague is contagious, from Thucydides, Lucretius, Aristotle, Galen, and common experience (p. 10–20); and he refutes (Preface, p. ii.–xiii.) the contrary opinion of the French physicians who visited Marseilles in the year 1720. Yet these were the recent and enlightened spectators of a plague which, in a few months, swept away 50,000 inhabitants (sur la Peste de Marseille, Paris, 1786), of a city that, in the present hour of prosperity and trade, contains no more than 90,000 souls (Necker, sur les Finances, tom. i. p. 231).

2 The strong assertions of Procopius – οὔτε γὰρ ἰατρῷ οὔτε ἰδιώτῃ – are overthrown by the subsequent experience of Evagrius.

an account, or even a conjecture, of the numbers that perished in this extraordinary mortality. I only find that, during three months, five and at length ten thousand persons died each day at Constantinople; that many cities of the East were left vacant; and that in several districts of Italy the harvest and the vintage withered on the ground. The triple scourge of war, pestilence, and famine afflicted the subjects of Justinian; and his reign is disgraced by a visible decrease of the human species, which has never been repaired in some of the fairest countries of the globe.[1]

CHAPTER XLIV

Idea of the Roman Jurisprudence – The Laws of the Kings – The Twelve Tables of the Decemvirs – The Laws of the People – The Decrees of the Senate – The Edicts of the Magistrates and Emperors – Authority of the Civilians – Code, Pandects, Novels, and Institutes of Justinian: – I. Rights of Persons – II. Rights of Things – III. Private Injuries and Actions – IV. Crimes and Punishments

THE vain titles of the victories of Justinian are crumbled into dust, but the name of the legislator is inscribed on a fair and everlasting monument. Under his reign, and by his care, the civil jurisprudence was digested in the immortal works of the CODE, the PANDECTS, and the INSTITUTES:[2] the public reason of the Romans has been silently or studiously transfused into the

1 After some figures of rhetoric, the sands of the sea, etc., Procopius (Anecdot. c. 18) attempts a more definite account; that μυριάδας μυριάδων μυρίας had been exterminated under the reign of the Imperial demon. The expression is obscure in grammar and arithmetic; and a literal interpretation would produce several millions of millions. Alemannus (p. 80) and Cousin (tom. iii. p. 178) translate this passage 'two hundred millions;' but I am ignorant of their motives. If we drop the μυριάδας, the remaining μυριάδων μυριάς, a myriad of myriads, would furnish one hundred millions, a number not wholly inadmissible.

2 The civilians of the darker ages have established an absurd and incomprehensible mode of quotation, which is supported by authority and custom. In their references to the Code, the Pandects, and the Institutes, they mention the number, not of the *book*, but only of the *law*; and content themselves with reciting the first words of the *title* to which it belongs; and of these titles there

domestic institutions of Europe,[1] and the laws of Justinian still command the respect or obedience of independent nations. Wise or fortunate is the prince who connects his own reputation with the honour and interest of a perpetual order of men. The defence of their founder is the first cause which in every age has exercised the zeal and industry of the civilians. They piously commemorate his virtues, dissemble or deny his failings, and fiercely chastise the guilt or folly of the rebels who presume to sully the majesty of the purple. The idolatry of love has provoked, as it usually happens, the rancour of opposition; the character of Justinian has been exposed to the blind vehemence of flattery and invective; and the injustice of a sect (the *Anti-Tribonians*) has refused all praise and merit to the prince, his ministers, and his laws.[2] Attached to no party, interested only for the truth and candour of history, and directed by the most temperate and skilful guides,[3] I enter with just diffidence on the subject of civil law, which has exhausted so many learned lives and clothed the walls of such spacious libraries. In a single, if possible in a short, chapter, I shall trace the Roman jurisprudence from Romulus to

are more than a thousand. Ludewig (Vit. Justiniani, p. 268) wishes to shake off this pedantic yoke; and I have dared to adopt the simple and rational method of numbering the book, the title, and the law.

1 Germany, Bohemia, Hungary, Poland, and Scotland, have received them as common law or reason; in France, Italy, etc., they possess a direct or indirect influence; and they were respected in England from Stephen to Edward I., our national Justinian (Duck. de Usû et Auctoritate Juris Civilis, l. ii. c. 1, 8–15; Heineccius, Hist. Juris Germanici, c. 3, 4, No. 55–124, and the legal historians of each country).

2 Francis Hottoman, a learned and acute lawyer of the sixteenth century, wished to mortify Cujacius and to please the Chancellor de l'Hôpital. His Anti-Tribonianus (which I have never been able to procure) was published in French in 1609; and his sect was propagated in Germany (Heineccius, Op. tom. iii. sylloge iii. p. 171–183).

3 At the head of these guides I shall respectfully place the learned and perspicuous Heineccius, a German professor, who died at Halle in the year 1741 (see his Eloge in the Nouvelle Bibliothèque Germanique, tom. ii. p. 51–64). His ample works have been collected in eight volumes in 4to, Geneva, 1743–1748. The treatises which I have separately used are, 1. Historia Juris Romani et Germanici, Lugd. Batav. 1740, in 8vo. 2. Syntagma Antiquitatum Romanam Jurisprudentiam illustrantium, 2 vols. in 8vo. Traject. ad Rhenum. 3. Elementa Juris Civilis secundum Ordinem Institutionum, Lugd. Bat. 1751, in 8vo. 4. Elementa J. C. secundum Ordinem Pandectarum, Traject. 1772, in 8vo, 2 vols.

Justinian,[1] appreciate the labours of that emperor, and pause to contemplate the principles of a science so important to the peace and happiness of society. The laws of a nation form the most instructive portion of its history; and, although I have devoted myself to write the annals of a declining monarchy, I shall embrace the occasion to breathe the pure and invigorating air of the republic.

The primitive government of Rome[2] was composed with some political skill of an elective king, a council of nobles, and a general assembly of the people. War and religion were administered by the supreme magistrate, and he alone proposed the laws which were debated in the senate, and finally ratified or rejected by a majority of votes in the thirty *curiæ* or parishes of the city. Romulus, Numa, and Servius Tullius are celebrated as the most ancient legislators; and each of them claims his peculiar part in the threefold division of jurisprudence.[3] The laws of marriage, the education of children, and the authority of parents, which may seem to draw their origin from *nature* itself, are ascribed to the untutored wisdom of Romulus. The law of *nations* and of religious worship, which Numa introduced, was derived from his nocturnal converse with the nymph Egeria. The *civil* law is attributed to the experience of Servius; he balanced the rights and fortunes of the seven classes of citizens, and guarded by fifty new regulations the observance of contracts and the punishment of crimes. The state, which he had inclined towards a democracy, was changed by the last Tarquin into lawless despotism; and when the kingly office was abolished, the patricians engrossed the benefits of freedom. The royal laws became odious or obsolete,

1 Our original text is a fragment de Origine Juris (Pandect. l. i. tit. ii.) of Pomponius, a Roman lawyer, who lived under the Antonines (Heinecc. tom. iii. syl. iii. p. 66–126). It has been abridged, and probably corrupted, by Tribonian, and since restored by Bynkershoek (Opp. tom. i. p. 279–304).

2 The constitutional history of the kings of Rome may be studied in the first book of Livy, and more copiously in Dionysius Halicarnassensis (l. ii. [c. 4–25] p. 80–96, 119–130 [c. 57–70]; l. iv. [c. 15, etc.] p. 198–220), who sometimes betrays the character of a rhetorician and a Greek.

3 This threefold division of the law was applied to the three Roman kings by Justus Lipsius (Opp. tom. iv. p. 279); is adopted by Gravina (Origines Juris Civilis, p. 28, edit. Lips. 1737); and is reluctantly admitted by Mascou, his German editor.

the mysterious deposit was silently preserved by the priests and nobles, and at the end of sixty years the citizens of Rome still complained that they were ruled by the arbitrary sentence of the magistrates. Yet the positive institutions of the kings had blended themselves with the public and private manners of the city; some fragments of that venerable jurisprudence[1] were compiled by the diligence of antiquarians;[2] and above twenty texts still speak the rudeness of the Pelasgic idiom of the Latins.[3]

1 The most ancient Code or Digest was styled *Jus Papirianum*, from the first compiler, Papirius, who flourished somewhat before or after the *Regifugium* (Pandect. l. i. tit. ii.). The best judicial critics, even Bynkershoek (tom. i. p. 284, 285) and Heineccius (Hist. J. C. R. l. i. c. 16, 17, and Opp. tom. iii. sylloge iv. p. 1–8), give credit to this tale of Pomponius, without sufficiently adverting to the value and rarity of such a monument of the third century of the *illiterate* city. I much suspect that the Caius Papirius, the Pontifex Maximus, who revived the laws of Numa (Dionys. Hal. l. iii. [c. 36] p. 171), left only an oral tradition; and that the Jus Papirianum of Granius Flaccus (Pandect. l. l. tit. xvi. leg. 144) was not a commentary, but an original work, compiled in the time of Cæsar (Censorin. de Die Natali, c. iii. p. 13; Duker de Latinitate J. C. p. 157).

[Much has been written since the time of Gibbon respecting this compilation of Papirius, but nothing certain is known, and all conjecture is fruitless. The name of the compiler given is not quite certain, as he is variously called Caius, Sextus, and Publius. Dionysius says (iii. 36) that Caius Papirius, the Pontifex Maximus, made a collection of the religious ordinances of Numa, after the expulsion of the last Tarquin, viz., Tarquinius Superbus; and Pomponius (*Pandects*, lib. i. tit. ii. leg. 2, §2, 36) states that Sextus or Publius Papirius made a compilation of all the Leges Regiæ. Cf. Dircksen, *Versuchen zur Kritik und Auslegung der Quellen des Römischen Rechts*; Zimmern, *Geschichte des Römischen Privatrechts*. – O. S.]

2 A pompous, though feeble, attempt to restore the original, is made in the Histoire de la Jurisprudence Romaine of Terrasson, p. 22–72; Paris, 1750, in folio; a work of more promise than performance.

3 In the year 1444 seven or eight tables of brass were dug up between Cortona and Gubbio. A part of these, for the rest is Etruscan, represents the primitive state of the Pelasgic letters and language, which are ascribed by Herodotus to that district of Italy (l. i. c. 56, 57, 58); though this difficult passage may be explained of a Crestona in Thrace (Notes de Larcher, tom. i. p. 256–261). The savage dialect of the Eugubine Tables has exercised, and may still elude, the divination of criticism; but the root is undoubtedly Latin, of the same age and character as the Saliare Carmen, which, in the time of Horace, none could understand. The Roman idiom, by an infusion of Doric and Æolic Greek, was gradually ripened into the style of the twelve tables, of the Duilian column, of Ennius, of Terence, and of Cicero (Gruter. Inscript. tom. i. p. cxlii.; Scipion Maffei, Istoria Diplomatica, p. 241–258; Bibliothèque Italique, tom. iii. p. 30–41, 174–205, tom. xiv. p. 1–52).

I shall not repeat the well-known story of the Decemvirs,[1] who sullied by their actions the honour of inscribing on brass, or wood, or ivory, the TWELVE TABLES of the Roman laws.[2] They were dictated by the rigid and jealous spirit of an aristocracy which had yielded with reluctance to the just demands of the people. But the substance of the Twelve Tables was adapted to the state of the city, and the Romans had emerged from barbarism, since they were capable of studying and embracing the institutions of their more enlightened neighbours. A wise Ephesian was driven by envy from his native country: before he could reach the shores of Latium, he had observed the various forms of human nature and civil society; he imparted his knowledge to the legislators of Rome, and a statue was erected in the forum to the perpetual memory of Hermodorus.[3] The names and divisions of the copper money, the sole coin of the infant state, were of Dorian origin;[4] the harvests of Campania and Sicily relieved the wants of a people whose agriculture was often interrupted by war and faction; and since the trade was established,[5] the deputies who sailed from the Tiber might return

[The language of the Eugubine Tables, which contain four inscriptions in Etruscan characters, two in Latin, and one partially in Etruscan and partially in Latin, has recently been the subject of study. The best modern scholars are agreed that the language which is here found is Umbrian, who are represented by all ancient writers as nationally distinct from both the Etruscan and Sabellian races. – O. S.]

1 Compare Livy (l. iii. c. 31–59) with Dionysius Halicarnassensis (l. x. [c. 55] p. 644 – xi. [c. 1, *sqq.*] p. 691). How concise and animated is the Roman – how prolix and lifeless the Greek! Yet he has admirably judged the masters, and defined the rules, of historical composition.

2 From the historians, Heineccius (Hist. J. R. l. i. No. 26) maintains that the twelve tables were of brass – *æreas*: in the text of Pomponius we read *eboreas*; for which Scaliger has substituted *roboreas* (Bynkershoek, p. 286). Wood, brass, and ivory, might be successively employed.

3 His exile is mentioned by Cicero (Tusculan. Quæstion. v. 36); his statue by Pliny (Hist. Nat. xxxiv. 11). The letter, dream, and prophecy of Heraclitus are alike spurious (Epistolæ Græc. Divers. p. 337).

4 This intricate subject of the Sicilian and Roman money is ably discussed by Dr. Bentley (Dissertation on the Epistles of Phalaris, p. 427–479), whose powers in this controversy were called forth by honour and resentment.

5 The Romans, or their allies, sailed as far as the fair promontory of Africa (Polyb. l. iii. [c. 22] p. 177, ed. Casaubon, in folio). Their voyages to Cumæ, etc., are noticed by Livy and Dionysius.

from the same harbours with a more precious cargo of political wisdom. The colonies of Great Greece had transported and improved the arts of their mother-country. Cumæ and Rhegium, Crotona and Tarentum, Agrigentum and Syracuse, were in the rank of the most flourishing cities. The disciples of Pythagoras applied philosophy to the use of government, the unwritten laws of Charondas accepted the aid of poetry and music,¹ and Zaleucus framed the republic of the Locrians, which stood without alteration above two hundred years.² From a similar motive of national pride, both Livy and Dionysius are willing to believe that the deputies of Rome visited Athens under the wise and splendid administration of Pericles, and the laws of Solon were transfused into the Twelve Tables. If such an embassy had indeed been received from the barbarians of Hesperia, the Roman name would have been familiar to the Greeks before the reign of Alexander,³ and the faintest evidence would have been explored and celebrated by the curiosity of succeeding times. But the Athenian monuments are silent, nor will it seem credible that the patricians should undertake a long and perilous navigation

1 This circumstance would alone prove the antiquity of Charondas, the legislator of Rhegium and Catana, who, by a strange error of Diodorus Siculus (tom. i. l. xii. [c. 11 *sq.*] p. 485–492), is celebrated long afterwards as the author of the policy of Thurium.

2 Zaleucus, whose existence has been rashly attacked, had the merit and glory of converting a band of outlaws (the Locrians) into the most virtuous and orderly of the Greek republics. (See two Mémoires of the Baron de St. Croix, sur la Législation de la Grande Grèce; Mém. de l'Académie, tom. xlii. p. 276–333.) But the laws of Zaleucus and Charondas, which imposed on Diodorus and Stobæus, are the spurious composition of a Pythagorean sophist, whose fraud has been detected by the critical sagacity of Bentley, p. 335–377.

3 I seize the opportunity of tracing the progress of this national intercourse: 1. Herodotus and Thucydides (A.U.C. 300–350) appear ignorant of the name and existence of Rome (Joseph. contra Apion. tom. ii. l. i. c. 12, p. 444, edit. Havercamp.). 2. Theopompus (A.U.C. 400, Plin. iii. 9) mentions the invasion of the Gauls, which is noticed in looser terms by Heraclides Ponticus (Plutarch in Camillo [c. 15], p. 292, edit. H. Stephan.). 3 The real or fabulous embassy of the Romans to Alexander (A.U.C. 430) is attested by Clitarchus (Plin. iii. 9), by Aristus and Asclepiades (Arrian, l. vii. [c. 15] p. 294, 295), and by Memnon of Heraclea (apud Photium, cod. ccxxiv. p. 725 [p. 229, ed. Bekker]), though tacitly denied by Livy. 4. Theophrastus (A.U.C. 440) primus externorum aliqua de Romanis diligentius scripsit (Plin. iii. 9). 5. Lycophron (A.U.C. 480–500) scattered

to copy the purest model of a democracy. In the comparison of the tables of Solon with those of the Decemvirs, some casual resemblance may be found; some rules which nature and reason have revealed to every society; some proofs of a common descent from Egypt or Phœnicia.[1] But in all the great lines of public and private jurisprudence the legislators of Rome and Athens appear to be strangers or adverse to each other.

Whatever might be the origin or the merit of the Twelve Tables,[2] they obtained among the Romans that blind and partial reverence which the lawyers of every country delight to bestow on their municipal institutions. The study is recommended by Cicero[3] as equally pleasant and instructive. 'They amuse the mind by the remembrance of old words, and the portrait of ancient manners; they inculcate the soundest principles of government and morals; and I am not afraid to affirm that the brief composition of the Decemvirs surpasses in genuine value the libraries of Grecian philosophy. How admirable,' says Tully, with honest or affected prejudice, 'is the wisdom of our ancestors! We alone are the masters of civil prudence, and our superiority is the more conspicuous if we deign to cast our eyes on the rude and almost ridiculous jurisprudence of Draco, of Solon, and of Lycurgus.' The Twelve Tables were committed to the memory of the young and the meditation of the old; they were transcribed and illustrated with learned diligence: they had escaped the flames of the

the first seed of a Trojan colony and the fable of the Æneid (Cassandra, 1226–1280):

$$\Gamma \tilde{\eta} \varsigma \; \kappa \alpha i \; \theta \alpha \lambda \acute{\alpha} \sigma \sigma \eta \varsigma \; \sigma \kappa \tilde{\eta} \pi \tau \rho \alpha \; \kappa \alpha i \; \mu o \nu \alpha \rho \chi i \alpha \nu$$
$$\Lambda \alpha \beta \acute{o} \nu \tau \epsilon \varsigma.$$

A bold prediction before the end of the first Punic war.

1 The tenth table, de modo sepulturæ, was borrowed from Solon (Cicero de Legibus, ii. 23–26): the furtum per lancem et licium conceptum is derived by Heineccius from the manners of Athens (Antiquitat. Rom. tom. ii. p. 167–175). The right of killing a nocturnal thief was declared by Moses, Solon, and the Decemvirs (Exodus xxii. 2; Demosthenes contra Timocratem, tom. i. p. 736, edit. Reiske; Macrob. Saturnalia, l. i. c. 4; Collatio Legum Mosaicarum et Romanarum, tit. vii. No. i. p. 218, edit. Cannegieter [Lugd. Bat. 1774]).

2 Βραχέως καὶ ἀπερίττως is the praise of Diodorus (tom. i. l. xii. [c. 26] p. 494), which may be fairly translated by the eleganti atque absolutâ brevitate verborum of Aulus Gellius (Noct. Attic. xx. 1).

3 Listen to Cicero (de Legibus, ii. 23) and his representative Crassus (de Oratore, i. 43, 44).

Gauls, they subsisted in the age of Justinian, and their subsequent loss has been imperfectly restored by the labours of
modern critics.[1] But although these venerable monuments were
considered as the rule of right and the fountain of justice,[2] they
were overwhelmed by the weight and variety of new laws which,
at the end of five centuries, became a grievance more intolerable
than the vices of the city.[3] Three thousand brass plates, the acts
of the senate and people, were deposited in the Capitol;[4] and
some of the acts, as the Julian law against extortion, surpassed
the number of a hundred chapters.[5] The Decemvirs had
neglected to import the sanction of Zaleucus, which so long
maintained the integrity of his republic. A Locrian who proposed
any new law stood forth in the assembly of the people with a
cord round his neck, and if the law was rejected the innovator
was instantly strangled.

The Decemvirs had been named, and their tables were approved, by an assembly of the *centuries*, in which riches preponderated against numbers. To the first class of Romans, the
proprietors of one hundred thousand pounds of copper,[6]

1 See Heineccius (Hist. J. R. No. 29–33). I have followed the restoration
of the twelve tables by Gravina (Origines J. C. p. 280–307) and Terrasson (Hist.
de la Jurisprudence Romaine, p. 94–205).

2 Finis æqui juris (Tacit. Annal. iii. 27). Fons omnis publici et privati juris
(T. Liv. iii. 34).

3 De principiis juris, et quibus modis ad hanc multitudinem infinitam ac
varietatem legum perventum sit *altius* disseram (Tacit. Annal. iii. 25). This deep
disquisition fills only two pages, but they are the pages of Tacitus. With equal
sense, but with less energy, Livy (iii. 34) had complained, in hoc immenso
aliarum super alias acervatarum legum cumulo, etc.

4 Suetonius in Vespasiano, c. 8.

5 Cicero ad Familiares, viii. 8.

6 Dionysius, with Arbuthnot, and most of the moderns (except Eisenschmidt de Ponderibus, etc., p. 137–140), represent the 100,000 *asses* by 10,000
Attic drachmæ, or somewhat more than 300 pounds sterling. But their calculation can apply only to the later times, when the *as* was diminished to 1-24th
of its ancient weight: nor can I believe that in the first ages, however destitute
of the precious metals, a single ounce of silver could have been exchanged for
seventy pounds of copper or brass. A more simple and rational method is to
value the copper itself according to the present rate, and, after comparing the
mint and the market-price, the Roman and avoirdupois weight, the primitive *as*
or Roman pound of copper may be appreciated at one English shilling, and the
100,000 *asses* of the first class amounted to 5000 pounds sterling. It will appear
from the same reckoning that an ox was sold at Rome for five pounds, a sheep

ninety-eight votes were assigned, and only ninety-five were left
for the six inferior classes, distributed according to their substance
by the artful policy of Servius. But the tribunes soon established
a more specious and popular maxim, that every citizen has an
equal right to enact the laws which he is bound to obey. Instead
of the *centuries*, they convened the *tribes;* and the patricians, after
an impotent struggle, submitted to the decrees of an assembly
in which their votes were confounded with those of the meanest
plebeians. Yet as long as the tribes successively passed over
narrow *bridges*,[1] and gave their voices aloud, the conduct of each
citizen was exposed to the eyes and ears of his friends and
countrymen. The insolvent debtor consulted the wishes of his
creditor, the client would have blushed to oppose the views of
his patron, the general was followed by his veterans, and the
aspect of a grave magistrate was a living lesson to the multitude.
A new method of secret ballot abolished the influence of fear
and shame, of honour and interest; and the abuse of freedom
accelerated the progress of anarchy and despotism.[2] The Romans
had aspired to be equal, they were levelled by the equality of
servitude, and the dictates of Augustus were patiently ratified by
the formal consent of the tribes or centuries. Once, and once
only, he experienced a sincere and strenuous opposition. His
subjects had resigned all political liberty; they defended the freedom of domestic life. A law which enforced the obligation and
strengthened the bonds of marriage was clamorously rejected;
Propertius, in the arms of Delia, applauded the victory of licentious love; and the project of reform was suspended till a new
and more tractable generation had arisen in the world.[3] Such an

for ten shillings, and a quarter of wheat for one pound ten shillings (Festus,
p. 330, edit. Dacier; Plin. Hist. Natur. xviii. 4): nor do I see any reason to reject
these consequences, which moderate our ideas of the poverty of the first Romans.

1 Consult the common writers on the Roman Comitia, especially Sigonius
and Beaufort. Spanheim (de Præstantiâ et Usû Numismatum, tom. ii. dissert. x.
p. 192, 193) shows, on a curious medal, the Cista, Pontes, Septa, Diribitor, etc.

2 Cicero (de Legibus, iii. 16, 17, 18) debates this constitutional question,
and assigns to his brother Quintus the most unpopular side.

3 Præ tumultu recusantium perferre non potuit (Sueton. in August. c. 34).
See Propertius, l. ii. eleg. 6 [or 7]. Heineccius, in a separate history, has exhausted the whole subject of the Julian and Papian-Poppæan laws (Opp.
tom. vii. P. i. p. 1–479).

example was not necessary to instruct a prudent usurper of the mischief of popular assemblies; and their abolition, which Augustus had silently prepared, was accomplished without resistance, and almost without notice, on the accession of his successor.[1] Sixty thousand plebeian legislators, whom numbers made formidable and poverty secure, were supplanted by six hundred senators, who held their honours, their fortunes, and their lives by the clemency of the emperor. The loss of executive power was alleviated by the gift of legislative authority; and Ulpian might assert, after the practice of two hundred years, that the decrees of the senate obtained the force and validity of laws. In the times of freedom the resolves of the people had often been dictated by the passion or error of the moment: the Cornelian, Pompeian, and Julian laws were adapted by a single hand to the prevailing disorders; but the senate, under the reign of the Cæsars, was composed of magistrates and lawyers, and in questions of private jurisprudence the integrity of their judgment was seldom perverted by fear or interest.[2]

The silence or ambiguity of the laws was supplied by the occasional EDICTS of those magistrates who were invested with the *honours* of the state.[3] This ancient prerogative of the Roman kings was transferred in their respective offices to the consuls

1 Tacit. Annal. i. 15; Lipsius, Excursus E, in Tacitum.

2 Non ambigitur senatum jus facere posse, is the decision of Ulpian (l. xvi. ad Edict. in Pandect. l. i. tit. iii. leg. 9). Pomponius taxes the *comitia* of the people as a turba hominum (Pandect. l. i. tit. ii. leg. 9).

[Gibbon adopts the opinion that under the emperors alone the senate had a share in the legislative power. They had nevertheless participated in it under the republic, since *senatus-consulta* relating to civil rights have been preserved which are much earlier than the reigns of Augustus or Tiberius. It is true that under the emperors the senate exercised this right more frequently, and that the assemblies of the people had become much more rare, though in law they were still permitted in the time of Ulpian. (See the Fragments of Ulpian.) Bach has clearly shown that the senate had the same power in the time of the republic. It is natural that the senatus-consulta should be more frequent under the emperors, because they employed those means of flattering the pride of the senators by granting them the right of deliberating on all affairs which did not trench on the imperial power. – O. S.]

3 The jus honorarium of the prætors and other magistrates is strictly defined in the Latin text of the Institutes (l. i. tit. ii. No. 7), and more loosely explained in the Greek paraphrase of Theophilus (p. 33–38, edit. Reitz), who drops the important word *honorarium*.

and dictators, the censors and prætors; and a similar right was assumed by the tribunes of the people, the ædiles, and the proconsuls. At Rome, and in the provinces, the duties of the subject and the intentions of the governor were proclaimed; and the civil jurisprudence was reformed by the annual edicts of the supreme judge, the prætor of the city. As soon as he ascended his tribunal, he announced by the voice of the crier, and afterwards inscribed on a white wall, the rules which he proposed to follow in the decision of doubtful cases, and the relief which his equity would afford from the precise rigour of ancient statutes. A principle of discretion more congenial to monarchy was introduced into the republic: the art of respecting the name and eluding the efficacy of the laws was improved by successive prætors; subtleties and fictions were invented to defeat the plainest meaning of the Decemvirs; and where the end was salutary, the means were frequently absurd. The secret or probable wish of the dead was suffered to prevail over the order of succession and the forms of testaments; and the claimant, who was excluded from the character of heir, accepted with equal pleasure from an indulgent prætor the possession of the goods of his late kinsman or benefactor. In the redress of private wrongs, compensations and fines were substituted to the obsolete rigour of the Twelve Tables; time and space were annihilated by fanciful suppositions; and the

[In his note upon the *jus honorarium*, Gibbon here follows the opinion of Heineccius, who, following his master Thomasius, was unwilling to suppose that magistrates exercising a judicial function could share in the legislative power. Heineccius was opposed by the learned Ritter, Professor at Wittenberg, and was followed by the celebrated Bach. But the most light on this question has been thrown by M. Hugo (*History of Roman Law*), who contended that the edicts of the prætors were the true organs of public opinion, and that their edicts furnished the salutary means of perpetually harmonising the legislation with the spirit of the times. It was not according to their caprice that they framed their regulations, but according to the manners and to the opinions of the great civil lawyers of the day who were invited by the prætor to assist in framing this annual law, which, according to its principle, was only a declaration which the prætor made to the public to announce the way in which he was to judge, and to guard against every charge of partiality. The prætor was responsible for all the faults he committed. He was strictly bound to follow the regulation published by him at the commencement of his year of office. Cf. the brief but admirable sketch of the growth of Roman jurisprudence, etc., in the first chapter of Savigny's *Geschichte des Römischen Rechts im Mittelalter.* – O. S.]

plea of youth, or fraud, or violence, annulled the obligation or excused the performance of an inconvenient contract. A juris-diction thus vague and arbitrary was exposed to the most dangerous abuse; the substance, as well as the form of justice, were often sacrificed to the prejudices of virtue, the bias of laudable affection, and the grosser seductions of interest or resentment. But the errors or vices of each prætor expired with his annual office; such maxims alone as had been approved by reason and practice were copied by succeeding judges; the rule of proceeding was defined by the solution of new cases; and the temptations of injustice were removed by the Cornelian law, which compelled the prætor of the year to adhere to the letter and spirit of his first proclamation.[1] It was reserved for the curiosity and learning of Hadrian to accomplish the design which had been conceived by the genius of Cæsar; and the prætorship of Salvius Julian, an eminent lawyer, was immortalised by the composition of the PERPETUAL EDICT. This well-digested code was ratified by the emperor and the senate; the long divorce of law and equity was at length reconciled; and, instead of the Twelve Tables, the Perpetual Edict was fixed as the invariable standard of civil juris-prudence.[2]

From Augustus to Trajan, the modest Cæsars were content to promulgate their edicts in the various characters of a Roman magistrate; and in the decrees of the senate the *epistles* and *orations* of the prince were respectfully inserted. Hadrian[3] appears to have been the first who assumed without disguise the plenitude of legislative power. And this innovation, so agreeable to his active

1 Dion Cassius (tom. i. l. xxxvi. [c. 23] p. 100) fixes the perpetual edicts in the year of Rome 686. Their institution, however, is ascribed to the year 585 in the Acta Diurna, which have been published from the papers of Ludovicus Vives. Their authenticity is supported or allowed by Pighius (Annal. Roman. tom. ii. p. 377, 378), Grævius (ad Sueton. p. 778), Dodwell (Prælection. Camb-den, p. 665), and Heineccius: but a single word, Scutum *Cimbricum*, detects the forgery (Moyle's Works, vol. i. p. 303).

2 The history of edicts is composed, and the text of the perpetual edict is restored, by the master-hand of Heineccius (Opp. tom. vii. P. ii. p. 1–564); in whose researches I might safely acquiesce. In the Academy of Inscriptions, M. Bouchaud has given a series of memoirs to this interesting subject of law and literature.

3 His laws are the first in the Code. See Dodwell (Prælect. Cambden, p. 319–340), who wanders from the subject in confused reading and feeble paradox.

mind, was countenanced by the patience of the times and his long absence from the seat of government. The same policy was embraced by succeeding monarchs, and, according to the harsh metaphor of Tertullian, 'the gloomy and intricate forest of ancient laws was cleared away by the axe of royal mandates and *constitutions*.'[1] During four centuries, from Hadrian to Justinian, the public and private jurisprudence was moulded by the will of the sovereign, and few institutions, either human or divine, were permitted to stand on their former basis. The origin of Imperial legislation was concealed by the darkness of ages and the terrors of armed despotism; and a double fiction was propagated by the servility, or perhaps the ignorance, of the civilians who basked in the sunshine of the Roman and Byzantine courts. 1. To the prayer of the ancient Cæsars the people or the senate had sometimes granted a personal exemption from the obligation and penalty of particular statutes, and each indulgence was an act of jurisdiction exercised by the republic over the first of her citizens. His humble privilege was at length transformed into the prerogative of a tyrant; and the Latin expression of 'released from the laws'[2] was supposed to exalt the emperor above *all* human restraints, and to leave his conscience and reason as the sacred measure of his conduct. 2. A similar dependence was implied in the decrees of the senate, which in every reign defined the titles and powers of an elective magistrate. But it was not before the ideas and even the language of the Romans had been corrupted that a *royal* law,[3] and an irrevocable gift of the people, were created by the fancy of Ulpian, or more probably of Tribonian himself;[4] and

1 Totam illam veterem et squalentem silvam legum novis principalium rescriptorum et edictorum securibus truncatis et cæditis (Apologet. c. 4, p. 50, edit. Havercamp.). He proceeds to praise the recent firmness of Severus, who repealed the useless or pernicious laws, without any regard to their age or authority.

2 The constitutional style of *Legibus solutus* is misinterpreted by the art or ignorance of Dion Cassius (tom. i. l. liii. [c. 18] p. 713). On this occasion his editor, Reimar, joins the universal censure which freedom and criticism have pronounced against that slavish historian.

3 The *word* (*Lex Regia*) was still more recent than the *thing*. The slaves of Commodus or Caracalla would have started at the name of royalty.

4 See Gravina (Opp. p. 501–512) and Beaufort (République Romaine, tom. i. p. 255–274). He has made a proper use of two dissertations by John

the origin of Imperial power, though false in fact and slavish in its consequence, was supported on a principle of freedom and justice. 'The pleasure of the emperor has the vigour and effect of law, since the Roman people, by the royal law, have transferred to their prince the full extent of their own power and sovereignty.'[1] The will of a single man, of a child, perhaps, was allowed to prevail over the wisdom of ages and the inclinations of millions, and the degenerate Greeks were proud to declare that in his hands alone the arbitrary exercise of legislation could be safely deposited. 'What interest or passion,' exclaims Theophilus in the court of Justinian, 'can reach the calm and sublime elevation of the monarch? he is already master of the lives and fortunes of his subjects, and those who have incurred his displeasure are already numbered with the dead.'[2] Disdaining the language of flattery, the historian may confess that in questions of private jurisprudence the absolute sovereign of a great empire can seldom be influenced by any personal considerations. Virtue, or even reason, will suggest to his impartial mind that he is the guardian of peace and equity, and that the interest of society is inseparably connected with his own. Under the weakest and most vicious reign, the seat of justice was filled by the wisdom and integrity of Papinian and Ulpian,[3] and the purest materials of the Code and Pandects are inscribed with the names of Caracalla and his ministers.[4] The tyrant of Rome was sometimes

Frederick Gronovius and Noodt, both translated, with valuable notes, by Barbeyrac, 2 vols. in 12mo, 1731.

1 Institut. l. i. tit. ii. No. 6; Pandect. l. 1. tit. iv. leg. 1; Cod. Justinian. l. i. tit. xvii. leg. 1, No. 7. In his Antiquities and Elements, Heineccius has amply treated de constitutionibus principum, which are illustrated by Godefroy (Comment. ad. Cod. Theodos. l. i. tit. i. ii. iii.) and Gravina (p. 87–90).

[Imperial authority and legislative power were conferred even upon the early emperors by a law called 'Lex Imperii' or 'Lex de Imperio.' Hence Gaius says, 'Cum Imperator ipse per legem imperium accipiat.' – O. S.]

2 Theophilus, in Paraphras. Græc. Institut. p. 33, 34, edit. Reitz. For his person, time, writings, see the Theophilus of J. H. Mylius, Excurs. iii. p. 1034–1073.

3 There is more envy than reason in the complaint of Macrinus (Jul. Capitolin. c. 13). Nefas esse leges videri Commodi et Caracallæ et hominum imperitorum voluntates. Commodus was made a Divus by Severus (Dodwell, Prælect. viii. p. 324, 325). Yet he occurs only twice in the Pandects.

4 Of Antoninus Caracalla alone 200 constitutions are extant in the Code, and with his father 160. These two princes are quoted fifty times in the Pandects and eight in the Institutes (Terrasson, p. 265).

the benefactor of the provinces. A dagger terminated the crimes
of Domitian; but the prudence of Nerva confirmed his acts,
which, in the joy of their deliverance, had been rescinded by an
indignant senate.[1] Yet in the *rescripts*,[2] replies to the consultations
of the magistrates, the wisest of princes might be deceived by a
partial exposition of the case. And this abuse, which placed their
hasty decisions on the same level with mature and deliberate acts
of legislation, was ineffectually condemned by the sense and
example of Trajan. The *rescripts* of the emperor, his *grants* and
decrees, his *edicts* and *pragmatic sanctions*, were subscribed in purple
ink,[3] and transmitted to the provinces as general or special laws,
which the magistrates were bound to execute and the people to
obey. But as their number continually multiplied, the rule of
obedience became each day more doubtful and obscure, till the
will of the sovereign was fixed and ascertained in the Gregorian,
the Hermogenian, and the Theodosian codes. The two first, of
which some fragments have escaped, were framed by two private
lawyers to preserve the constitutions of the Pagan emperors
from Hadrian to Constantine. The third, which is still extant,
was digested in sixteen books by the order of the younger Theodosius to consecrate the laws of the Christian princes from

1 Plin. Secund. Epistol. x. 66; Sueton. in Domitian, c. 23.

2 It was a maxim of Constantine, contra jus rescripta non valeant (Cod.
Theodos. l. i. tit. ii. leg. 1). The emperors reluctantly allow some scrutiny into
the law and the fact, some delay, petition, etc.; but these insufficient remedies
are too much in the discretion and at the peril of the judge.

3 A compound of vermilion and cinnabar, which marks the Imperial diplo-
mas from Leo I. (A.D. 470) to the fall of the Greek empire (Bibliothèque
Raisonnée de la Diplomatique, tom. i. p. 509–514; Lami, de Eruditione Apos-
tolorum, tom. ii. p. 720–726).

[Savigny states the following as the authorities for the Roman law at the
beginning of the fifth century:–

1. The writings of the jurists according to the regulations of the constitution
of Valentinian III., first promulgated in the West, but by its introduction into
the Theodosian code established likewise in the East. This constitution established the authority of the five great jurists, Papinian, Paulus, Caius, Ulpian, and
Modestinus, as interpreters of the ancient law. In case of difference of opinion
among these five, a majority decided the case; when they were equal, the
opinion of Papinian; when he was silent, the judge.

2. The Gregorian and Hermogenian Collection of Imperial Rescripts.

3. The Code of Theodosius II.

4. The particular Novellæ, as additions and supplements to this Code. – O. S.]

Constantine to his own reign. But the three codes obtained an equal authority in the tribunals, and any act which was not included in the sacred deposit might be disregarded by the judge as spurious or obsolete.[1]

Among savage nations the want of letters is imperfectly supplied by the use of visible signs, which awaken attention and perpetuate the remembrance of any public or private transaction. The jurisprudence of the first Romans exhibited the scenes of a pantomime; the words were adapted to the gestures, and the slightest error or neglect in the *forms* of proceeding was sufficient to annul the *substance* of the fairest claim. The communion of the marriage-life was denoted by the necessary elements of fire and water;[2] and the divorced wife resigned the bunch of keys, by the delivery of which she had been invested with the government of the family. The manumission of a son or a slave was performed by turning him round with a gentle blow on the cheek; a work was prohibited by the casting of a stone; prescription was interrupted by the breaking of a branch; the clenched fist was the symbol of a pledge or deposit; the right hand was the gift of faith and confidence. The indenture of covenants was a broken straw; weights and scales were introduced into every payment; and the heir who accepted a testament was sometimes obliged to snap his fingers, to cast away his garments, and to leap and dance with real or affected transport.[3] If a citizen pursued any stolen goods into a neighbour's house, he concealed his nakedness with a linen towel, and hid his face with a mask or basin, lest he should encounter the eyes of a virgin or a matron.[4] In a civil action, the plantiff touched the ear of his

1 Schulting, Jurisprudentia Ante-Justinianea, p. 681–718. Cujacius assigned to Gregory the reigns from Hadrian to Gallienus, and the continuation to his fellow-labourer Hermogenes. This general division may be just, but they often trespassed on each other's ground.

2 Scævola, most probably Q. Cervidius Scævola, the master of Papinian, considers this acceptance of fire and water as the essence of marriage (Pandect. l. xxiv. tit. 1. leg. 66. See Heineccius, Hist. J. R. No. 317).

3 Cicero (de Officiis, iii. 19) may state an ideal case, but St. Ambrose (de Officiis, iii. 2) appeals to the practice of his own times, which he understood as a lawyer and a magistrate (Schulting ad Ulpian. Fragment. tit. xxii. No. 28, p. 643, 644 [Jurispr. Ante-Justin.]).

4 The furtum lance licioque conceptum was no longer understood in the time of the Antonines (Aulus Gellius, xvi. 10). The Attic derivation of

witness, seized his reluctant adversary by the neck, and implored, in solemn lamentation, the aid of his fellow-citizens. The two competitors grasped each other's hand as if they stood prepared for combat before the tribunal of the prætor; he commanded them to produce the object of the dispute; they went, they returned with measured steps, and a clod of earth was cast at his feet to represent the field for which they contended. This occult science of the words and actions of law was the inheritance of the pontiffs and patricians. Like the Chaldæan astrologers, they announced to their clients the days of business and repose; these important trifles were interwoven with the religion of Numa, and after the publication of the Twelve Tables the Roman people was still enslaved by the ignorance of judicial proceedings. The treachery of some plebeian officers at length revealed the profitable mystery; in a more enlightened age the legal actions were derided and observed, and the same antiquity which sanctified the practice, obliterated the use and meaning, of this primitive language.[1]

A more liberal art was cultivated, however, by the sages of Rome, who, in a stricter sense, may be considered as the authors of the civil law. The alteration of the idiom and manners of the Romans rendered the style of the Twelve Tables less familiar to each rising generation, and the doubtful passages were imperfectly explained by the study of legal antiquarians. To define the ambiguities, to circumscribe the latitude, to apply the principles, to extend the consequences, to reconcile the real or apparent contradictions, was a much nobler and more important task; and the province of legislation was silently invaded by the expounders of ancient statutes. Their subtle interpretations concurred with the equity of the prætor to reform the tyranny of the darker ages; however strange or intricate the means, it was the aim of artificial jurisprudence to restore the simple dictates of nature and reason, and the skill of private citizens was usefully employed to undermine the public institutions of their country. The revolution of

Heineccius (Antiquitat. Rom. l. iv. tit. i. No. 13–21) is supported by the evidence of Aristophanes, his scholiast, and Pollux.

1 In his Oration for Murena (c. 9–13) Cicero turns into ridicule the forms and mysteries of the civilians, which are represented with more candour by Aulus Gellius (Noct. Attic. xx. 10), Gravina (Opp. p. 265, 266, 267), and Heineccius (Antiquitat. l. iv. tit. vi.).

almost one thousand years, from the Twelve Tables to the reign of Justinian, may be divided into three periods almost equal in duration, and distinguished from each other by the mode of instruction and the character of the civilians.¹ Pride and ignorance contributed, during the first period, to confine within narrow limits the science of the Roman law. On the public days of market or assembly the masters of the art were seen walking in the forum, ready to impart the needful advice to the meanest of their fellow-citizens, from whose votes, on a future occasion, they might solicit a grateful return. As their years and honours increased, they seated themselves at home on a chair or throne, to expect, with patient gravity, the visits of their clients, who at the dawn of day, from the town and country, began to thunder at their door. The duties of social life and the incidents of judicial proceeding were the ordinary subject of these consultations, and the verbal or written opinion of the *juris-consults* was framed according to the rules of prudence and law. The youths of their own order and family were permitted to listen; their children enjoyed the benefit of more private lessons, and the Mucian race was long renowned for the hereditary knowledge of the civil law. The second period, the learned and splendid age of jurisprudence, may be extended from the birth of Cicero to the reign of Severus Alexander. A system was formed, schools were instituted, books were composed, and both the living and the dead became subservient to the instruction of the student. The *tripartite* of Ælius Pætus, surnamed Catus, or the Cunning, was preserved as the oldest work of jurisprudence. Cato the censor derived some additional fame from his legal studies and those of his son; the

1 The series of the civil lawyers is deduced by Pomponius (de Origine Juris Pandect. l. i. tit. ii. [§ 35 *sqq.*]). The moderns have discussed, with learning and criticism, this branch of literary history; and among these I have chiefly been guided by Gravina (p. 41–79) and Heineccius (Hist. J. R. No. 113–351). Cicero, more especially in his books de Oratore, de Claris Oratoribus, de Legibus, and the Clavis Ciceroniana of Ernesti (under the names of *Mucius*, etc.), afford much genuine and pleasing information. Horace often alludes to the morning labours of the civilians (Serm. I. i. 10, Epist. II. i. 103, etc.).

> Agricolam laudat juris legumque peritus,
> Sub galli cantum consultor ubi ostia pulsat.
> .   .   .   .   .   .
> Romæ dulce diu fuit et solemne, reclusâ
> Mane domo vigilare, clienti promere jura.

kindred appellation of Mucius Scævola was illustrated by three
sages of the law, but the perfection of the science was ascribed
to Servius Sulpicius, their disciple, and the friend of Tully; and
the long succession, which shone with equal lustre under the
republic and under the Cæsars, is finally closed by the respectable
characters of Papinian, of Paul, and of Ulpian. Their names, and
the various titles of their productions, have been minutely
preserved, and the example of Labeo may suggest some idea of
their diligence and fecundity. That eminent lawyer of the Augustan age divided the year between the city and country, between
business and composition, and four hundred books are enumerated as the fruit of his retirement. Of the collections of his
rival Capito, the two hundred and fifty-ninth book is expressly
quoted, and few teachers could deliver their opinions in less than
a century of volumes. In the third period, between the reigns of
Alexander and Justinian, the oracles of jurisprudence were almost mute. The measure of curiosity had been filled; the throne
was occupied by tyrants and barbarians; the active spirits were
diverted by religious disputes; and the professors of Rome, Constantinople, and Berytus, were humbly content to repeat the
lessons of their more enlightened predecessors. From the slow
advances and rapid decay of these legal studies, it may be inferred that they require a state of peace and refinement. From
the multitude of voluminous civilians who fill the intermediate
space, it is evident that such studies may be pursued, and such
works may be performed, with a common share of judgment,
experience, and industry. The genius of Cicero and Virgil was
more sensibly felt, as each revolving age had been found incapable of producing a similar or a second; but the most eminent
teachers of the law were assured of leaving disciples equal or
superior to themselves in merit and reputation.

The jurisprudence which had been grossly adapted to the
wants of the first Romans was polished and improved in the
seventh century of the city by the alliance of Grecian philosophy.
The Scævolas had been taught by use and experience; but Servius
Sulpicius was the first civilian who established his art on a certain
and general theory.[1] For the discernment of truth and falsehood

1 Crassus, or rather Cicero himself, proposes (de Oratore, i. 41, 42) an idea
of the art or science of jurisprudence, which the eloquent, but illiterate, Antonius

he applied, as an infallible rule, the logic of Aristotle and the
stoics, reduced particular cases to general principles, and diffused
over the shapeless mass the light of order and eloquence. Cicero,
his contemporary and friend, declined the reputation of a professed lawyer; but the jurisprudence of his country was adorned
by his incomparable genius, which converts into gold every object that it touches. After the example of Plato, he composed a
republic; and, for the use of his republic, a treatise of laws, in
which he labours to deduce from a celestial origin the wisdom
and justice of the Roman constitution. The whole universe, according to his sublime hypothesis, forms one immense common-
wealth: gods and men, who participate of the same essence, are
members of the same community; reason prescribes the law of
nature and nations; and all positive institutions, however modified by accident or custom, are drawn from the rule of right,
which the Deity has inscribed on every virtuous mind. From
these philosophical mysteries he mildly excludes the sceptics who
refuse to believe, and the epicureans who are unwilling to act.
The latter disdain the care of the republic: he advises them to
slumber in their shady gardens. But he humbly entreats that the
new Academy would be silent, since her bold objections would
too soon destroy the fair and well-ordered structure of his lofty
system.[1] Plato, Aristotle, and Zeno he represents as the only
teachers who arm and instruct a citizen for the duties of social
life. Of these, the armour of the stoics[2] was found to be of the

---

(i. 58) affects to deride. It was partly executed by Servius Sulpicius (in Bruto,
c. 41), whose praises are elegantly varied in the classic Latinity of the Roman
Gravina (p. 60).

[With regard to the Institutes of Justinian, M. Hugo, in his *Histoire du Droit
Romain,* vol. ii. p. 119, thinks that the ingenious system of the Institutes adopted
by a great many of the ancient lawyers and by Justinian himself dates from
Servius Sulpicius. – O. S.]

1 Perturbatricem autem omnium harum rerum Academiam, hanc ab Ar-
cesila et Carneade recentem, exoremus ut sileat, nam si invaserit in hæc, quæ
satis scite instructa et composita videntur, nimias edet ruinas, quam quidem ego
placare cupio, submovere non audeo (de Legibus, i. 13). From this passage
alone, Bentley (Remarks on Freethinking, p. 250) might have learned how
firmly Cicero believed in the specious doctrines which he has adorned.

2 The stoic philosophy was first taught at Rome by Panætius, the friend of
the younger Scipio (see his Life in the Mém. de l'Académie des Inscriptions,
tom. x. p. 75–89).

firmest temper; and it was chiefly worn, both for use and ornament, in the schools of jurisprudence. From the Portico the Roman civilians learned to live, to reason, and to die: but they imbibed in some degree the prejudices of the sect; the love of paradox, the pertinacious habits of dispute, and a minute attachment to words and verbal distinctions. The superiority of *form* to *matter* was introduced to ascertain the right of property: and the equality of crimes is countenanced by an opinion of Trebatius,[1] that he who touches the ear touches the whole body; and that he who steals from a heap of corn or a hogshead of wine is guilty of the entire theft.[2]

Arms, eloquence, and the study of the civil law promoted a citizen to the honours of the Roman state; and the three professions were sometimes more conspicuous by their union in the same character. In the composition of the edict a learned prætor gave a sanction and preference to his private sentiments; the opinion of a censor or a consul was entertained with respect; and a doubtful interpretation of the laws might be supported by the virtues or triumphs of the civilian. The patrician arts were long protected by the veil of mystery; and in more enlightened times the freedom of inquiry established the general principles of jurisprudence. Subtle and intricate cases were elucidated by the disputes of the forum; rules, axioms, and definitions[3] were admitted as the genuine dictates of reason; and the consent of the legal professors was interwoven into the practice of the tribunals. But these interpreters could neither enact nor execute the laws of the republic; and the judges might disregard the authority of the Scævolas themselves, which was often overthrown by the eloquence or sophistry of an ingenious pleader.[4] Augustus and

1 As he is quoted by Ulpian (leg. 40 ad Sabinum in Pandect. l. xlvii. tit. ii. leg. 21). Yet Trebatius, after he was a leading civilian, qui [quod] familiam duxit, became an epicurean (Cicero ad Fam. vii. 5). Perhaps he was not constant or sincere in his new sect.

2 See Gravina (p. 45–51) and the ineffectual cavils of Mascou. Heineccius (Hist. J. R. No. 125) quotes and approves a dissertation of Everard Otto, de Stoicâ Jurisconsultorum Philosophiâ.

3 We have heard of the Catonian rule, the Aquilian stipulation, and the Manilian forms, of 211 maxims, and of 247 definitions (Pandect. l. L. tit. xvi. xvii.).

4 Read Cicero, l. i. de Oratore, Topica, pro Murena.

Tiberius were the first to adopt, as a useful engine, the science of the civilians; and their servile labours accommodated the old system to the spirit and views of despotism. Under the fair pretence of securing the dignity of the art, the privilege of sub-scribing legal and valid opinions was confined to the sages of senatorian or equestrian rank, who had been previously approved by the judgment of the prince; and this monopoly prevailed till Hadrian restored the freedom of the profession to every citizen conscious of his abilities and knowledge. The discretion of the prætor was now governed by the lessons of his teachers; the judges were enjoined to obey the comment as well as the text of the law; and the use of codicils was a memorable innovation, which Augustus ratified by the advice of the civilians.[1]

The most absolute mandate could only require that the judges should agree with the civilians, if the civilians agreed among themselves. But positive institutions are often the result of cus-tom and prejudice; laws and language are ambiguous and arbi-trary; where reason is incapable of pronouncing, the love of argument is inflamed by the envy of rivals, the vanity of masters, the blind attachment of their disciples; and the Roman juris-prudence was divided by the once famous sects of the *Proculians* and *Sabinians*.[2] Two sages of the law, Ateius Capito and Antistius Labeo,[3] adorned the peace of the Augustan age: the former dis-tinguished by the favour of his sovereign; the latter more illus-trious by his contempt of that favour, and his stern though harmless opposition to the tyrant of Rome. Their legal studies were in-fluenced by the various colours of their temper and principles.

1 See Pomponius (de Origine Juris Pandect. l. i. tit. ii. leg. 2, No. 47), Heineccius (ad Institut. l. i. tit. ii. No. 8, l. ii. tit. xxv. in Element. et Antiquitat.), and Gravina (p. 41–45). Yet the monopoly of Augustus, a harsh measure, would appear with some softening in contemporary evidence; and it was probably veiled by a decree of the senate.

2 I have perused the Diatribe of Gotfridus Mascovius, the learned Mascou, de Sectis Jurisconsultorum (Lipsiæ, 1728, in 12mo. p. 276), a learned treatise on a narrow and barren ground.

3 See the character of Antistius Labeo in Tacitus (Annal. iii. 75) and in an epistle of Ateius Capito (Aul. Gellius, xiii. 12), who accuses his rival of libertas nimia et *vecors*. Yet Horace would not have lashed a virtuous and respectable senator; and I must adopt the emendation of Bentley, who reads *Labieno* insan-ior (Serm I. iii. 82). See Mascou, de Sectis (c. i. p. 1–24).

Labeo was attached to the form of the old republic; his rival embraced the more profitable substance of the rising monarchy. But the disposition of a courtier is tame and submissive; and Capito seldom presumed to deviate from the sentiments, or at least from the words, of his predecessors; while the bold republican pursued his independent ideas without fear of paradox or innovations. The freedom of Labeo was enslaved, however, by the rigour of his own conclusions, and he decided, according to the letter of the law, the same questions which his indulgent competitor resolved with a latitude of equity more suitable to the common sense and feelings of mankind. If a fair exchange had been substituted to the payment of money, Capito still considered the transaction as a legal sale;[1] and he consulted nature for the age of puberty, without confining his definition to the precise period of twelve or fourteen years.[2] This opposition of sentiments was propagated in the writings and lessons of the two founders; the schools of Capito and Labeo maintained their inveterate conflict from the age of Augustus to that of Hadrian;[3] and the two sects derived their appellations from Sabinus and Proculus, their most celebrated teachers. The names of *Cassians* and *Pegasians* were likewise applied to the same parties; but by a strange reverse, the popular cause was in the hands of

1 Justinian (Institut. l. iii. tit. 23, and Theophil. Vers. Græc. p. 677, 680) has commemorated this weighty dispute, and the verses of Homer that were alleged on either side as legal authorities. It was decided by Paul (leg. 33, ad Edict. in Pandect. l. xviii. tit. i. leg. 1), since, in a simple exchange, the buyer could not be discriminated from the seller.

2 This controversy was likewise given for the Proculians, to supersede the indecency of a search, and to comply with the aphorism of Hippocrates, who was attached to the septenary number of two weeks of years, or 700 of days (Institut. l. i. tit. xxii.). Plutarch and the Stoics (de Placit. Philosoph. l. v. c. 24) assign a more natural reason. Fourteen years is the age – περὶ ἥν ὁ σπερματικὸς κρίνεται ἀῤῥός. See the *vestigia* of the sects in Mascou, c. ix. p. 145–276.

3 The series and conclusion of the sects are described by Mascou (c. ii.–vii. p. 24–120); and it would be almost ridiculous to praise his equal justice to these obsolete sects.

[The work of Gaius subsequent to Hadrian's time furnishes us with some information about the rival legal schools of Capito and Labeo. The disputes which arose between them have been very numerous. Gaius avows himself a disciple of Sabinus and of Caius, though on controverted points he not infrequently follows the opinion of the opposite school. – O. S.]

Pegasus,[1] a timid slave of Domitian, while the favourite of the Cæsars was represented by Cassius,[2] who gloried in his descent from the patriot assassin. By the perpetual edict the controversies of the sects were in a great measure determined. For that important work the emperor Hadrian preferred the chief of the Sabinians: the friends of monarchy prevailed; but the moderation of Salvius Julian insensibly reconciled the victors and the vanquished. Like the contemporary philosophers, the lawyers of the age of the Antonines disclaimed the authority of a master, and adopted from every system the most probable doctrines.[3] But their writings would have been less voluminous, had their choice been more unanimous. The conscience of the judge was perplexed by the number and weight of discordant testimonies, and every sentence that his passion or interest might pronounce was justified by the sanction of some venerable name. An indulgent edict of the younger Theodosius excused him from the labour of comparing and weighing their arguments. Five civilians, Caius, Papinian, Paul, Ulpian, and Modestinus, were established as the oracles of jurisprudence: a majority was decisive; but if their opinions were equally divided, a casting vote was ascribed to the superior wisdom of Papinian.[4]

When Justinian ascended the throne, the reformation of the Roman jurisprudence was an arduous but indispensable task. In

1 At the first summons he flies to the turbot-council; yet Juvenal (Satir. iv. 75–81) styles the præfect or *bailiff* of Rome sanctissimus legum interpres. From his science, says the old scholiast, he was called, not a man, but a book. He derived the singular name of Pegasus from the galley which his father commanded.

2 Tacit. Annal. xvi. 7. Sueton. in Nerone, c. xxxvii.

3 Mascou, de Sectis, c. viii. p. 120–144, de Herciscundis, a legal term which was applied to these eclectic lawyers: *herciscere* is synonymous to dividere.

4 See the Theodosian Code, l. i. tit. iv. with Godefroy's Commentary, tom. i. p. 31–35. This decree might give occasion to Jesuitical disputes like those in the Lettres Provinciales, whether a judge was obliged to follow the opinion of Papinian, or of a majority, against his judgment, against his conscience, etc. Yet a legislator might give that opinion, however false, the validity, not of truth, but of law.

[We possess since 1824 (says Milman) some interesting information as to the framing of the Theodosian Code and its ratification at Rome in the year 438. M. Closius, late professor at Dorpat in Russia, and M. Peyron, member of the Academy at Turin, discovered the one at Milan, the other at Turin, a great part of the first five books of the Code, which were wanting, and besides this the space of ten centuries the infinite variety of laws and legal opinions had filled many thousand volumes, which no fortune could purchase and no capacity could digest. Books could not easily be found; and the judges, poor in the midst of riches, were reduced to the exercise of their illiterate discretion. The subjects of the Greek provinces were ignorant of the language that disposed of their lives and properties; and the *barbarous* dialect of the Latins was imperfectly studied in the academies of Berytus and Constantinople. As an Illyrian soldier, that idiom was familiar to the infancy of Justinian; his youth had been instructed by the lessons of jurisprudence, and his Imperial choice selected the most learned civilians of the East, to labour with their sovereign in the work of reformation.[1] The theory of professors was assisted by the practice of advocates and the experience of magistrates; and the whole undertaking was animated by the spirit of Tribonian.[2] This extraordinary man, the object of so much praise and censure, was a native of Side in Pamphylia; and his genius, like that of Bacon, embraced, as his own, all the business and knowledge of the age. Tribonian composed, both in prose and verse, on a strange diversity of curious and abstruse subjects:[3] a

the reports (gesta) of the sitting of the senate at Rome in which the Code was published, in the year after the marriage of Valentinian III. From this we gather that Theodosius designed a great reform in the legislation; to add to the Gregorian and Hermogenian codes all the new constitutions from Constantine to his own day; and to frame a second code for common use, with extracts from the three codes, and from the works of the civil lawyers. All laws either abrogated or fallen into disuse were to be noted under their proper heads. – O. S.]

1 For the legal labours of Justinian, I have studied the Preface to the Institutes; the 1st, 2nd and 3rd Prefaces to the Pandects; the 1st and 2nd Preface to the Code; and the Code itself (l. i. tit. xvii. de Veteri Jure enucleando). After these original testimonies, I have consulted, among the moderns, Heineccius (Hist. J. R. No. 383–404), Terrasson (Hist. de la Jurisprudence Romaine, p. 295–356), Gravina (Opp. p. 93–100), and Ludewig, in his Life of Justinian (p. 19–123, 318–321; for the Code and Novels, p. 209–261; for the Digest or Pandects, p. 262–317).

2 For the character of Tribonian, see the testimonies of Procopius (Persic. l. i. c. 23, 24 [24, 25]; Anecdot. c. 13, 20) and Suidas (tom. iii. p. 501, edit. Kuster). Ludewig (in Vit. Justinian. p. 175–209) works hard, very hard, to whitewash – the blackamoor.

3 I apply the two passages of Suidas to the same man; every circumstance so exactly tallies. Yet the lawyers appear ignorant; and Fabricius is inclined to separate the two characters (Biblioth. Græc. tom. i. p. 341, ii. p. 518, iii. p. 418, xii. p. 346, 353, 474).

double panegyric of Justinian and the Life of the philosopher Theodotus; the nature of happiness and the duties of government; Homer's catalogue and the four-and-twenty sorts of metre; the astronomical canon of Ptolemy; the changes of the months; the houses of the planets; and the harmonic system of the world. To the literature of Greece he added the use of the Latin tongue; the Roman civilians were deposited in his library and in his mind; and he most assiduously cultivated those arts which opened the road of wealth and preferment. From the bar of the prætorian præfects he raised himself to the honours of quæstor, of consul, and of master of the offices: the council of Justinian listened to his eloquence and wisdom; and envy was mitigated by the gentleness and affability of his manners. The reproaches of impiety and avarice have stained the virtues or the reputation of Tribonian. In a bigoted and persecuting court, the principal minister was accused of a secret aversion to the Christian faith, and was supposed to entertain the sentiments of an Atheist and a Pagan, which have been imputed, inconsistently enough, to the last philosophers of Greece. His avarice was more clearly proved and more sensibly felt. If he were swayed by gifts in the administration of justice, the example of Bacon will again occur; nor can the merit of Tribonian atone for his baseness, if he degraded the sanctity of his profession, and if laws were every day enacted, modified, or repealed, for the base consideration of his private emolument. In the sedition of Constantinople, his removal was granted to the clamours, perhaps to the just indignation, of the people: but the quæstor was speedily restored, and, till the hour of his death, he possessed, above twenty years, the favour and confidence of the emperor. His passive and dutiful submission has been honoured with the praise of Justinian himself, whose vanity was incapable of discerning how often that submission degenerated into the grossest adulation. Tribonian adored the virtues of his gracious master: the earth was unworthy of such a prince; and he affected a pious fear, that Justinian, like Elijah or Romulus, would be snatched into the air, and translated alive to the mansions of celestial glory.[1]

1 This story is related by Hesychius (de Viris Illustribus), Procopius (Anecdot. c. 13 [tom. iii. p. 84, ed. Bonn]), and Suidas (tom. iii. p. 501). Such flattery is incredible!

If Cæsar had achieved the reformation of the Roman law, his creative genius, enlightened by reflection and study, would have given to the world a pure and original system of jurisprudence. Whatever flattery might suggest, the emperor of the East was afraid to establish his private judgment as the standard of equity: in the possession of legislative power, he borrowed the aid of time and opinion; and his laborious compilations are guarded by the sages and legislators of past times. Instead of a statue cast in a simple mould by the hand of an artist, the works of Justinian represent a tesselated pavement of antique and costly, but too often of incoherent, fragments. In the first year of his reign, he directed the faithful Tribonian, and nine learned associates, to revise the ordinances of his predecessors, as they were contained, since the time of Hadrian, in the Gregorian, Hermogenian, and Theodosian codes; to purge the errors and contradictions, to retrench whatever was obsolete or superfluous, and to select the wise and salutary laws best adapted to the practice of the tribunals and the use of his subjects. The work was accomplished in fourteen months; and the twelve books or *tables*, which the new decemvirs produced, might be designed to imitate the labours of their Roman predecessors. The new CODE of Justinian was honoured with his name, and confirmed by his royal signature: authentic transcripts were multiplied by the pens of notaries and scribes; they were transmitted to the magistrates of the European, the Asiatic, and afterwards the African provinces; and the law of the empire was proclaimed on solemn festivals at the doors of churches. A more arduous operation was still behind – to extract the spirit of jurisprudence from the decisions and conjectures, the questions and disputes, of the Roman civilians. Seventeen lawyers, with Tribonian at their head, were appointed by the emperor to exercise an absolute jurisdiction over the works of their predecessors. If they had obeyed his commands in ten years, Justinian would have been satisfied with their diligence;

—— Nihil est quod credere de se
Non possit, cum laudatur Diis æqua potestas.

Fontenelle (tom. i. p. 32–39) has ridiculed the impudence of the modest Virgil. But the same Fontenelle places his king above the divine Augustus; and the sage Boileau has not blushed to say, 'Le destin à ses yeux n'oseroit balancer.' Yet neither Augustus nor Louis XIV. were fools.

and the rapid composition of the DIGEST or PANDECTS[1] in three years will deserve praise or censure according to the merit of the execution. From the library of Tribonian they chose forty, the most eminent civilians of former times:[2] two thousand treatises were comprised in an abridgment of fifty books; and it has been carefully recorded that three millions of lines or sentences[3] were reduced, in this abstract, to the moderate number of one hundred and fifty thousand. The edition of this great work was delayed a month after that of the INSTITUTES; and it seemed reasonable that the elements should precede the digest of the Roman law. As soon as the emperor had approved their labours, he ratified, by his legislative power, the speculations of these private citizens: their commentaries on the Twelve Tables, the Perpetual Edict, the laws of the people, and the decrees of the senate, succeeded to the authority of the text; and the text was abandoned, as a useless, though venerable, relic of antiquity. The *Code*, the *Pandects*, and the *Institutes* were declared to be the legitimate system of civil jurisprudence; they alone were admitted in the tribunals, and they alone were taught in the academies, of Rome, Constantinople, and Berytus. Justinian addressed to the senate and provinces his *eternal oracles:* and his pride, under the mask of piety, ascribed the consummation of this great design to the support and inspiration of the Deity.

1 Πάνδεκται (general receivers) was a common title of the Greek miscellanies (Plin. Præfat. ad Hist. Natur.). The *Digesta* of Scævola, Marcellinus, Celsus, were already familiar to the civilians: but Justinian was in the wrong when he used the two appellations as synonymous. Is the word *Pandects* Greek or Latin − masculine or feminine? The diligent Brenckman will not presume to decide these momentous controversies (Hist. Pandect. Florentin. p. 300–304).

2 Angelus Politianus (l. v. Epist. ult.) reckons thirty-seven (p. 192–200) civilians quoted in the Pandects − a learned, and for his times, an extraordinary list. The Greek index to the Pandects enumerates thirty-nine, and forty are produced by the indefatigable Fabricius (Biblioth. Græc. tom. iii. p. 488–502). Antoninus Augustus [Antonius Augustinus] (de Nominibus Propriis Pandect. apud Ludewig, p. 283) is said to have added fifty-four names; but they must be vague or secondhand references.

3 The Στιχοὶ of the ancient MSS. may be strictly defined as sentences or periods of a complete sense, which, on the breadth of the parchment rolls or volumes, composed as many lines of unequal length. The number of Στιχοὶ in each book served as a check on the errors of the scribes (Ludewig, p. 211–215; and his original author Suicer. Thesaur. Ecclesiast. tom. i. p. 1021–1036).

Since the emperor declined the fame and envy of original composition, we can only require at his hands method, choice, and fidelity – the humble, though indispensable, virtues of a compiler. Among the various combinations of ideas it is difficult to assign any reasonable preference; but, as the order of Justinian is different in his three works, it is possible that all may be wrong, and it is certain that two cannot be right. In the selection of ancient laws he seems to have viewed his predecessors without jealousy and with equal regard: the series could not ascend above the reign of Hadrian, and the narrow distinction of Paganism and Christianity, introduced by the superstition of Theodosius, had been abolished by the consent of mankind. But the jurisprudence of the Pandects is circumscribed within a period of a hundred years, from the Perpetual Edict to the death of Severus Alexander: the civilians who lived under the first Cæsars are seldom permitted to speak, and only three names can be attributed to the age of the republic. The favourite of Justinian (it has been fiercely urged) was fearful of encountering the light of freedom and the gravity of Roman sages. Tribonian condemned to oblivion the genuine and native wisdom of Cato, the Scævolas, and Sulpicius; while he invoked spirits more congenial to his own, the Syrians, Greeks, and Africans, who flocked to the Imperial court to study Latin as a foreign tongue, and jurisprudence as a lucrative profession. But the ministers of Justinian[1] were instructed to labour not for the curiosity of antiquarians, but for the immediate benefit of his subjects. It was their duty to select the useful and practical parts of the Roman law; and the writings of the old republicans, however curious or excellent, were no longer suited to the new system of manners, religion, and government. Perhaps, if the preceptors and friends of Cicero were still alive, our candour would acknowledge that, except in purity of language,[2] their intrinsic merit was excelled by the

1 An ingenious and learned oration of Schultingius (Jurisprudentia Ante-Justinianea, p. 883–907) justifies the choice of Tribonian against the passionate charges of Francis Hottoman and his sectaries.

2 Strip away the crust of Tribonian, and allow for the use of technical words, and the Latin of the Pandects will be found not unworthy of the *silver* age. It has been vehemently attacked by Laurentius Valla, a fastidious grammarian of the fifteenth century, and by his apologist Floridus Sabinus. It has been

school of Papinian and Ulpian. The science of the laws is the
slow growth of time and experience, and the advantage both of
method and materials is naturally assumed by the most recent
authors. The civilians of the reign of the Antonines had studied
the works of their predecessors: their philosophic spirit had mitigated the rigour of antiquity, simplified the forms of proceeding,
and emerged from the jealousy and prejudice of the rival sects.
The choice of the authorities that compose the Pandects
depended on the judgment of Tribonian; but the power of his
sovereign could not absolve him from the sacred obligations of
truth and fidelity. As the legislator of the empire, Justinian might
repeal the acts of the Antonines, or condemn as seditious the
free principles which were maintained by the last of the *Roman*
lawyers.[1] But the existence of past facts is placed beyond the
reach of despotism; and the emperor was guilty of fraud and
forgery when he corrupted the integrity of their text, inscribed
with their venerable names the words and ideas of his servile
reign,[2] and suppressed by the hand of power the pure and authentic copies of their sentiments. The changes and interpolations
of Tribonian and his colleagues are excused by the pretence of
uniformity: but their cares have been insufficient, and the *antinomies*, or contradictions, of the Code and Pandects, still exercise
the patience and subtlety of modern civilians.[3]

defended by Alciat, and a nameless advocate (most probably James Capellus).
Their various treatises are collected by Duker (Opuscula de Latinitate veterum
Jurisconsultorum, Lugd. Bat. 1721, in 12mo).

[Gibbon is wrong here with respect to Valla, who, though he inveighs
against the barbarous style of the civilians of his day, lavishes high praise
on the admirable purity of the language of the ancient writers on civil law.
M. Warnkönig quotes a long passage of Valla in justification of this observation.
Since his time this truth has been recognised by men of high eminence, such
as Erasmus, David Hume, and Ruhnkenius. – O. S.]

1   Nomina quidem veteribus servavimus, legum autem veritatem nostram
fecimus. Itaque siquid erat in illis *seditiosum*, multa autem talia erant ibi reposita,
hoc decisum est et definitum, et in perspicuum finem deducta est quæque lex
(Cod. Justinian. l. i. tit. xvii. leg. 3, No. 10). A frank confession!

2   The number of these *emblemata* (a polite name for forgeries) is much
reduced by Bynkershoek (in the four last books of his Observations), who
poorly maintains the right of Justinian and the duty of Tribonian.

3   The *antinomies*, or opposite laws of the Code and Pandects, are sometimes
the cause, and often the excuse, of the glorious uncertainty of the civil law,

A rumour, devoid of evidence, has been propagated by the enemies of Justinian, that the jurisprudence of ancient Rome was reduced to ashes by the author of the Pandects, from the vain persuasion that it was now either false or superfluous. Without usurping an office so invidious, the emperor might safely commit to ignorance and time the accomplishment of this destructive wish. Before the invention of printing and paper, the labour and the materials of writing could be purchased only by the rich; and it may reasonably be computed that the price of books was a hundred-fold their present value.[1] Copies were slowly multiplied and cautiously renewed: the hopes of profit tempted the sacrilegious scribes to erase the characters of antiquity, and Sophocles or Tacitus were obliged to resign the parchment to missals, homilies, and the golden legend.[2] If such was the fate of the most beautiful compositions of genius, what stability could be expected for the dull and barren works of an obsolete science? The books of jurisprudence were interesting to few and entertaining to none; their value was connected with present use, and they sunk for ever as soon as that use was superseded by the innovations of fashion, superior merit, or public authority. In the age of peace and learning, between Cicero and the last of the Antonines, many losses had been already sustained, and some luminaries of the school or forum were known only to the curious by tradition and report. Three hundred and sixty years of disorder and decay accelerated the progress of oblivion; and it may fairly be presumed that, of the writings which Justinian is accused of neglecting, many were no longer to be found in the libraries of the East.[3]

which so often affords what Montaigne calls 'Questions pour l'Ami.' See a fine passage of Franciscus Balduinus in Justinian (l. ii. p. 259, etc., apud Ludewig, p. 305, 306).

1 When Fust, or Faustus, sold at Paris his first printed Bibles as manuscripts, the price of a parchment copy was reduced from four or five hundred to sixty, fifty, and forty crowns. The public was at first pleased with the cheapness, and at length provoked by the discovery of the fraud (Mattaire, Annal. Typograph. tom. i. p. 12; first edition).

2 This execrable practice prevailed from the eighth, and more especially from the twelfth century, when it became almost universal (Montfaucon, in the Mémories de l'Académie, tom. vi. p. 606, etc.; Bibliothèque Raisonnée de la Diplomatique, tom. i. p. 176).

3 Pomponius (Pandect. l. i. tit. ii. leg. 2 [§ 39]) observes, that of the three founders of the civil law, Mucius, Brutus, and Manilus, extant volumina,

The copies of Papinian or Ulpian, which the reformer had proscribed, were deemed unworthy of future notice; the Twelve Tables and prætorian edict insensibly vanished; and the monuments
of ancient Rome were neglected or destroyed by the envy and
ignorance of the Greeks. Even the Pandects themselves have
escaped with difficulty and danger from the common ship-
wreck, and criticism has pronounced that *all* the editions
and manuscripts of the West are derived from *one* original.[1] It
was transcribed at Constantinople in the beginning of the
seventh century,[2] was successively transported by the accidents
of war and commerce to Amalphi,[3] Pisa,[4] and Florence,[5] and is

[in-]scripta Manilii monumenta; that of some old republican lawyers, hæc ver-
santur eorum scripta inter manus hominum. Eight of the Augustan sages were
reduced to a compendium: of Cascellius, scripta non extant sed unus liber, etc.
[§ 45]; of Trebatius, minus frequentatur [ib.]; of Tubero, libri parum grati
sunt [§ 46]. Many quotations in the Pandects are derived from books which
Tribonian never saw; and, in the long period from the seventh to the thirteenth
century of Rome, the *apparent* reading of the moderns successively depends on
the knowledge and veracity of their predecessors.

1 *All*, in several instances, repeat the errors of the scribe and the transposi-
tions of some leaves in the Florentine Pandects. This fact, if it be true, is
decisive. Yet the Pandects are quoted by Ivo of Chartres (who died in 1117),
by Theobald, archbishop of Canterbury, and by Vacarius, our first professor,
in the year 1140 (Selden ad Fletam, c. 7, tom. ii. p. 1080–1085). Have our British
MSS. of the Pandects been collated?

2 See the description of this original in Brenckman (Hist. Pandect. Florent.
l. i. c. 2, 3, p. 4–17, and l. ii.). Politian, an enthusiast, revered it as the authentic
standard of Justinian himself (p. 407, 408); but this paradox is refuted by the
abbreviations of the Florentine MS. (l. ii. c. 3, p. 117–130). It is composed of
two quarto volumes, with large margins, on a thin parchment, and the Latin
characters betray the hand of a Greek scribe.

3 Brenckman, at the end of his history, has inserted two dissertations on
the republic of Amalphi, and the Pisan war in the year 1135, etc.

4 The discovery of the Pandects at Amalphi (A.D. 1137) is first noticed (in
1501) by Ludovicus Bologninus (Brenckman, l. i. c. 11. p. 73, 74; l. iv. c. 2,
p. 417–425), on the faith of a Pisan chronicle (p. 409, 410) without a name or
a date. The whole story, though unknown to the twelfth century, embellished
by ignorant ages, and suspected by rigid criticism, is not, however, destitute of
much internal probability (l. i. c. 4–8, p. 17–50). The Liber Pandectarum of
Pisa was undoubtedly consulted in the fourteenth century by the great Bartolus
(p. 406, 407. See l. i. c. 9, p. 50–62).

5 Pisa was taken by the Florentines in the year 1406; and in 1411 the
Pandects were transported to the capital. These events are authentic and
famous.

now deposited as a sacred relic[1] in the ancient palace of the republic.[2]

It is the first care of a reformer to prevent any future reformation. To maintain the text of the Pandects, the Institutes, and the Code, the use of ciphers and abbreviations was rigorously proscribed; and as Justinian recollected that the Perpetual Edict had been buried under the weight of commentators, he denounced the punishment of forgery against the rash civilians who should presume to interpret or pervert the will of their sovereign. The scholars of Accursius, of Bartolus, of Cujacius, should blush for their accumulated guilt, unless they dare to dispute his right of binding the authority of his successors and the native freedom of the mind. But the emperor was unable to fix his own inconstancy; and, while he boasted of renewing the exchange of Diomede, of transmuting brass into gold,[3] he discovered the necessity of purifying his gold from the mixture of baser alloy. Six years had not elapsed from the publication of the Code before he condemned the imperfect attempt by a new and more accurate edition of the same work, which he enriched with two hundred of his own laws and fifty decisions of the darkest and most intricate points of jurisprudence. Every year, or, according to Procopius, each day, of his long reign was marked by some legal innovation. Many of his acts were rescinded by himself; many were rejected by his successors; many have been obliterated by time; but the number of sixteen EDICTS, and one

1 They were new bound in purple, deposited in a rich casket, and shown to curious travellers by the monks and magistrates bare-headed, and with lighted tapers (Brenckman, l. i. c. 10, 11, 12, p. 62–93).

2 After the collations of Politian, Bologninus, and Antoninus Augustinus, and the splendid edition of the Pandects by Taurellus (in 1551), Henry Brenckman, a Dutchman, undertook a pilgrimage to Florence, where he employed several years in the study of a single manuscript. His Historia Pandectarum Florentinorum (Utrecht, 1722, in 4to.), though a monument of industry, is a small portion of his original design.

[Two mistakes must be corrected in this note. The edition of the Pandects was edited by Taurellius, not Taurellus, and in 1553, not 1551. Also the name of the third collator should be Antonius Augustinus, not Antoninus. – O. S.]

3 Χρύσεα χαλκείων, ἑκατόμβοὶ ἐννεαβοίων, apud Homerum patrem omnis virtutis (1st Præfat. ad Pandect.). A line of Milton or Tasso would surprise us in an act of parliament. Quæ omnia obtinere sancimus in omne ævum. Of the first Code he says (2nd Præfat.) in æternum valiturum. Man and for ever!

hundred and sixty-eight NOVELS,[1] has been admitted into the authentic body of the civil jurisprudence. In the opinion of a philosopher superior to the prejudices of his profession, these incessant, and for the most part trifling alterations, can be only explained by the venal spirit of a prince who sold without shame his judgments and his laws.[2] The charge of the secret historian is indeed explicit and vehement; but the sole instance which he produces may be ascribed to the devotion as well as to the avarice of Justinian. A wealthy bigot had bequeathed his inheritance to the church of Emesa, and its value was enhanced by the dexterity of an artist, who subscribed confessions of debt and promises of payment with the names of the richest Syrians. They pleaded the established prescription of thirty or forty years; but their defence was overruled by a retrospective edict, which extended the claims of the church to the term of a century – an edict so pregnant with injustice and disorder, that, after serving this occasional purpose, it was prudently abolished in the same reign.[3] If candour will acquit the emperor himself, and transfer the corruption to his wife and favourites, the suspicion of so foul a vice must still degrade the majesty of his laws; and the advocates of Justinian may acknowledge that such levity, whatsoever be the motive, is unworthy of a legislator and a man.

Monarchs seldom condescend to become the preceptors of their subjects; and some praise is due to Justinian, by whose command an ample system was reduced to a short and elementary treatise. Among the various institutes of the Roman law,[4]

1 *Novellæ* is a classic adjective, but a barbarous substantive (Ludewig, p. 245). Justinian never collected them himself; the nine collations, the legal standard of modern tribunals, consist of ninety-eight Novels; but the number was increased by the diligence of Julian, Haloander, and Contius (Ludewig, p. 249, 258; Aleman. Not. in Anecdot. p. 98).

2 Montesquieu, Considérations sur la Grandeur et la Décadence des Romains, c. 20, tom. iii. p. 501, in 4to. On this occasion he throws aside the gown and cap of a President à Mortier.

3 Procopius, Anecdot. c. 28 [tom. iii. p. 155, ed. Bonn]. A similar privilege was granted to the church of Rome (Novel. ix.). For the general repeal of these mischievous indulgences, see Novel. cxi. and Edict. v.

4 Lactantius, in his Institutes of Christianity, an elegant and specious work, proposes to imitate the title and method of the civilians. Quidam prudentes et arbitri æquitatis Institutiones Civilis Juris compositas ediderunt (Institut. Divin. l. i. c. 1). Such as Ulpian, Paul, Florentinus, Marcian.

those of Caius[1] were the most popular in the East and West; and their use may be considered as an evidence of their merit. They were selected by the Imperial delegates, Tribonian, Theophilus, and Dorotheus; and the freedom and purity of the Antonines was incrusted with the coarser materials of a degenerate age. The same volume which introduced the youth of Rome, Constantinople, and Berytus to the gradual study of the Code and Pandects, is still precious to the historian, the philosopher, and the magistrate. The INSTITUTES of Justinian are divided into four books: they proceed, with no contemptible method, from I. *Persons*, to, II. *Things*, and from things to, III. *Actions;* and the article IV., of *Private Wrongs*, is terminated by the principles of *Criminal Law.*

The distinction of ranks and *persons* is the firmest basis of a mixed and limited government. In France the remains of liberty are kept alive by the spirit, the honours, and even the prejudices of fifty thousand nobles.[2] Two hundred families supply, in lineal descent, the second branch of the English legislature, which maintains, between the king and commons, the balance of the constitution. A gradation of patricians and plebeians, of strangers and subjects, has supported the aristocracy of Genoa, Venice, and ancient Rome. The perfect equality of men is the point in which the extremes of democracy and despotism are confounded; since the majesty of the prince or people would be

1 The emperor Justinian calls him *suum*, though he died before the end of the second century. His Institutes are quoted by Servius, Boethius, Priscian, etc.; and the Epitome by Arrian is still extant. (See the Prolegomena and notes to the edition of Schulting, in the Jurisprudentia Ante-Justinianea, Lugd. Bat. 1717; Heineccius, Hist. J. R. No. 313; Ludewig, in Vit. Just. p. 199.)

[The three great works in Roman jurisprudence prior to Justinian are (*a*) Ulpian's Fragments discovered in 1544; (*b*) the Institutes or Commentaries of Gaius or Caius were found by Niebuhr in 1816 in a palimpsest MS., preserved in the Cathedral Library of Verona, and was first published by Goeschen in 1821; (*c*) the Sententiæ of Paulus, preserved as a portion of the Visigothic Breviarium of Alaric II. – O. S.]

2 See the Annales Politiques de l'Abbé de St. Pierre, tom. i. p. 25, who dates in the year 1735. The most ancient families claim the immemorial possession of arms and fiefs. Since the Crusades, some, the most truly respectable, have been created by the king for merit and services. The recent and vulgar crowd is derived from the multitude of venal offices, without trust or dignity, which continually ennoble the wealthy plebeians.

offended if any heads were exalted above the level of their fellow-slaves or fellow-citizens. In the decline of the Roman empire, the proud distinctions of the republic were gradually abolished, and the reason or instinct of Justinian completed the simple form of an absolute monarchy. The emperor could not eradicate the popular reverence which always waits on the possession of hereditary wealth or the memory of famous ancestors. He delighted to honour with titles and emoluments his generals, magistrates, and senators; and his precarious indulgence communicated some rays of their glory to the persons of their wives and children. But in the eye of the law all Roman citizens were equal, and all subjects of the empire were citizens of Rome. That inestimable character was degraded to an obsolete and empty name. The voice of a Roman could no longer enact his laws, or create the annual ministers of his power: his constitutional rights might have checked the arbitrary will of a master; and the bold adventurer from Germany or Arabia was admitted, with equal favour, to the civil and military command, which the citizen alone had been once entitled to assume over the conquests of his fathers. The first Cæsars had scrupulously guarded the distinction of *ingenuous* and *servile* birth, which was decided by the condition of the mother; and the candour of the laws was satisfied if *her* freedom could be ascertained, during a single moment, between the conception and the delivery. The slaves who were liberated by a generous master immediately entered into the middle class of *libertines* or freedmen; but they could never be enfranchised from the duties of obedience and gratitude: whatever were the fruits of their industry, their patron and his family inherited the third part; or even the whole of their fortune if they died without children and without a testament. Justinian respected the rights of patrons; but his indulgence removed the badge of disgrace from the two inferior orders of freedmen: whoever ceased to be a slave obtained, without reserve or delay, the station of a citizen; and at length the dignity of an ingenuous birth, which nature had refused, was created, or supposed, by the omnipotence of the emperor. Whatever restraints of age, or forms, or numbers, had been formerly introduced to check the abuse of manumissions and the too rapid increase of vile and indigent Romans, he finally abolished; and the spirit of his laws promoted the extinction of domestic servitude. Yet the eastern provinces were filled, in the time of Justinian, with multitudes of slaves, either born or purchased for the use of their masters; and the price, from ten to seventy pieces of gold, was determined by their age, their strength, and their education.[1] But the hardships of this dependent state were continually diminished by the influence of government and religion; and the pride of a subject was no longer elated by his absolute dominion over the life and happiness of his bondsman.[2]

The law of nature instructs most animals to cherish and educate their infant progeny. The law of reason inculcates to the human species the returns of filial piety. But the exclusive, absolute, and perpetual dominion of the father over his children is peculiar to the Roman jurisprudence,[3] and seems to be coeval with the foundation of the city.[4] The paternal power was

1 If the option of a slave was bequeathed to several legatees, they drew lots, and the losers were entitled to their share of his value: ten pieces of gold for a common servant or maid under ten years; if above that age, twenty; if they knew a trade, thirty; notaries or writers, fifty; midwives or *physicians*, sixty; eunuchs under ten years, thirty pieces; above, fifty; if tradesmen, seventy (Cod. l. vi. tit. xliii. leg. 3). These legal prices are generally below those of the market.

2 For the state of slaves and freedmen see Institutes, l. i. tit. iii.–viii., l. ii. tit. ix., l. iii. tit. viii. ix. [vii. viii.]; Pandects or Digest, l. i. tit. v. vi., l. xxxviii. tit. i.–iv., and the whole of the fortieth book; Code, l. vi. tit. iv. v., l. vii. tit. i.–xxiii. Be it henceforward understood that, with the original text of the Institutes and Pandects, the correspondent articles in the Antiquities and Elements of Heineccius are implicity quoted; and with the twenty-seven first books of the Pandects, the learned and rational Commentaries of Gerard Noodt (Opera, tom. ii. p. 1–590, the end, Lugd. Bat. 1724).

3 See the patria potestas in the Institutes (l. i. tit. ix.), the Pandects (l. i. tit. vi. vii.), and the Code (l. viii. tit. xlvii. xlviii. xlix. [tit. xlvi. xlvii. xlviii.]). Jus potestatis quod in liberos habemus proprium est civium Romanorum. Nulli enim alii sunt homines, qui talem in liberos habeant potestatem qualem not habemus.

[Gaius in his Institutes asserts that the absolute dominion of the father over his children supposed to be peculiar to the Roman law was also possessed by the Galatians, i. 55, while Cæsar (Bell. Gall. vi. 19) states that it also existed in Gaul. – O. S.]

4 Dionysius Hal. l. ii. [c. 26] p. 94, 95. Gravina (Opp. p. 286) produces the words of the twelve tables. Papinian (in Collatione Legum Roman. et Mosaicarum, tit. iv. p. 204 [ed. Cannegieter, 1774]) styles this patria potestas, lex regia: Ulpian (ad Sabin. l. xxvi. in Pandect. l. i. tit. vi. leg. 8) says, jus potestatis moribus receptum; and furiosus filium in potestate habetit. How sacred – or rather, how absurd!

instituted or confirmed by Romulus himself; and, after the practice of three centuries, it was inscribed on the fourth table of the
Decemvirs. In the forum, the senate, or the camp, the adult son
of a Roman citizen enjoyed the public and private rights of a
person: in his father's house he was a mere *thing;* confounded by
the laws with the movables, the cattle, and the slaves, whom the
capricious master might alienate or destroy without being responsible to any earthly tribunal. The hand which bestowed the
daily sustenance might resume the voluntary gift, and whatever
was acquired by the labour or fortune of the son was immediately lost in the property of the father. His stolen goods (his
oxen or his children) might be recovered by the same action of
theft;[1] and if either had been guilty of a trespass, it was in his
own option to compensate the damage, or resign to the injured
party the obnoxious animal. At the call of indigence or avarice,
the master of a family could dispose of his children or his slaves.
But the condition of the slave was far more advantageous, since
he regained, by the first manumission, his alienated freedom: the
son was again restored to his unnatural father; he might be
condemned to servitude a second and a third time, and it was
not till after the third sale and deliverance[2] that he was enfranchised from the domestic power which had been so repeatedly
abused. According to his discretion, a father might chastise the
real or imaginary faults of his children by stripes, by imprisonment, by exile, by sending them to the country to work in chains
among the meanest of his servants. The majesty of a parent was
armed with the power of life and death;[3] and the examples of
such bloody executions, which were sometimes praised and
never punished, may be traced in the annals of Rome, beyond
the times of Pompey and Augustus. Neither age, nor rank, nor
the consular office, nor the honours of a triumph, could exempt

1 Pandect. l. xlvii. tit. ii. leg. 14, No. 13, leg. 38, No. 1. Such was the
decision of Ulpian and Paul.

2 The trina mancipatio is most clearly defined by Ulpian (Fragment. x.
p. 591, 592, edit. Schulting); and best illustrated in the Antiquities of Heineccius.

3 By Justinian, the old law, the jus necis of the Roman father (Institut. l. iv.
tit. ix. [viii.] No. 7), is reported and reprobated. Some legal vestiges are left in
the Pandects (l. xliii. tit. xxix. leg. 3, No. 4) and the Collatio Legum Romanarum
et Mosaicarum (tit. ii. No. 3, p. 189).

the most illustrious citizen from the bonds of filial subjection:[1] his own descendants were included in the family of their common ancestor; and the claims of adoption were not less sacred or less rigorous than those of nature. Without fear, though not without danger of abuse, the Roman legislators had reposed an unbounded confidence in the sentiments of paternal love; and the oppression was tempered by the assurance that each generation must succeed in its turn to the awful dignity of parent and master.

The first limitation of paternal power is ascribed to the justice and humanity of Numa; and the maid who, with *his* father's consent, had espoused a freeman, was protected from the disgrace of becoming the wife of a slave. In the first ages, when the city was pressed and often famished by her Latin and Tuscan neighbours, the sale of children might be a frequent practice; but as a Roman could not legally purchase the liberty of his fellow-citizen, the market must gradually fail, and the trade would be destroyed by the conquests of the republic. An imperfect right of property was at length communicated to sons; and the threefold distinction of *profectitious*, *adventitious*, and *professional* was ascertained by the jurisprudence of the Code and Pandects.[2] Of all that proceeded from the father he imparted only the use, and reserved the absolute dominion; yet, if his goods were sold, the filial portion was excepted, by a favourable interpretation, from the demands of the creditors. In whatever accrued by marriage, gift, or collateral succession, the property was secured to the son; but the father, unless he had been specially excluded, enjoyed the usufruct during his life. As a just and prudent reward of military virtue, the spoils of the enemy were acquired, possessed, and bequeathed by the soldier alone; and the fair analogy was

1 Except on public occasions and in the actual exercise of his office. In publicis locis atque muneribus, atque actionibus patrum, jura cum filiorum qui in magistratû sunt, potestatibus collata interquiescere paullulum et connivere, etc. (Aul. Gellius, Noctes Atticæ, ii. 2). The Lessons of the philosopher Taurus were justified by the old and memorable example of Fabius; and we may contemplate the same story in the style of Livy (xxiv. 44) and the homely idiom of Claudius Quadrigarius the annalist.

2 See the gradual enlargement and security of the filial *peculium* in the Institutes (l. ii. tit. ix.), the Pandects (l. xv. tit. i, l. xli. tit. i.), and the Code (l. iv. tit. xxvi. xxvii.).

extended to the emoluments of any liberal profession, the salary
of public service, and the sacred liberality of the emperor or the
empress. The life of a citizen was less exposed than his fortune
to the abuse of paternal power. Yet his life might be adverse to
the interest or passions of an unworthy father: the same crimes
that flowed from the corruption, were more sensibly felt by the
humanity of the Augustan age; and the cruel Erixo, who
whipped his son till he expired, was saved by the emperor from
the just fury of the multitude.[1] The Roman father, from the
licence of servile dominion, was reduced to the gravity and
moderation of a judge. The presence and opinion of Augustus
confirmed the sentence of exile pronounced against an inten-
tional parricide by the domestic tribunal of Arius. Hadrian transported to an island the jealous parent, who, like a robber, had
seized the opportunity of hunting to assassinate a youth, the
incestuous lover of his stepmother.[2] A private jurisdiction is
repugnant to the spirit of monarchy; the parent was again reduced from a judge to an accuser; and the magistrates were
enjoined by Severus Alexander to hear his complaints and execute his sentence. He could no longer take the life of a son
without incurring the guilt and punishment of murder; and the
pains of parricide, from which he had been excepted by the
Pompeian law, were finally inflicted by the justice of Constantine.[3] The same protection was due to every period of existence;
and reason must applaud the humanity of Paulus for imputing
the crime of murder to the father who strangles, or starves, or
abandons his new-born infant, or exposes him in a public place
to find the mercy which he himself had denied. But the exposition of children was the prevailing and stubborn vice of

1 The examples of Erixo and Arius are related by Seneca (de Clementia, i.
14, 15), the former with horror, the latter with applause.

2 Quod latronis magis quam patris jure eum interfecisset, nam patria potestas in pietate debet non in atrocitate consistere (Marcian, Institut. l. xiv. in
Pandect. l. xlviii. tit. ix. leg. 5).

3 The Pompeian and Cornelian laws de *sicariis* and *parricidis*, are repeated,
or rather abridged, with the last supplements of Alexander Severus, Constantine, and Valentinian, in the Pandects (l. xlviii. tit. viii. ix.), and Code (l. ix.
tit. xvi. xvii.). See likewise the Theodosian Code (l. ix. tit. xiv. xv.), with Godefroy's Commentary (tom. iii. p. 84–113), who pours a flood of ancient and
modern learning over these penal laws.

antiquity: it was sometimes prescribed, often permitted, almost always practised with impunity by the nations who never entertained the Roman ideas of paternal power; and the dramatic poets, who appeal to the human heart, represent with indifference a popular custom which was palliated by the motives of economy and compassion.[1] If the father could subdue his own feelings, he might escape, though not the censure, at least the chastisement, of the laws; and the Roman empire was stained with the blood of infants, till such murders were included by Valentinian and his colleagues in the letter and spirit of the Cornelian law. The lessons of jurisprudence[2] and Christianity had been insufficient to eradicate this inhuman practice, till their gentle influence was fortified by the terrors of capital punishment.[3]

Experience has proved that savages are the tyrants of the female sex, and that the condition of women is usually softened by the refinements of social life. In the hope of a robust progeny, Lycurgus had delayed the season of marriage: it was fixed by Numa at the tender age of twelve years, that the Roman husband might educate to his will a pure and obedient virgin.[4] According to the custom of antiquity, he bought his bride of her parents, and she fulfilled the *coemption* by purchasing, with three pieces of

1 When the Chremes of Terence reproaches his wife for not obeying his orders and exposing their infant, he speaks like a father and a master and silences the scruples of a foolish woman. See Apuleius (Metamorph. l. x. p. 337, edit. Delphin.).

2 The opinion of the lawyers, and the discretion of the magistrates, had introduced in the time of Tacitus some legal restraints, which might support his contrast of the boni mores of the Germans to the bonæ leges alibi – that is to say, at Rome (de Moribus Germanorum, c. 19). Tertullian (ad Nationes, l. i. c. 15) refutes his own charges, and those of his brethren, against the heathen jurisprudence.

3 The wise and humane sentence of the civilian Paul (l. ii. Sententiarum in Pandect. l. xxv. tit. iii. leg. 4) is represented as a mere moral precept by Gerard Noodt (Opp. tom. i. in Julius Paulus, p. 567–588, and Amica Responsio, p. 591–606), who maintains the opinion of Justus Lipsius (Opp. tom. ii. p. 409, ad Belgas, cent. i. epist. 85), and as a positive binding law by Bynkershoek (de Jure occidendi Liberos, Opp. tom. i. p. 318–340; Curæ Secundæ, p. 391–427). In a learned but angry controversy the two friends deviated into the opposite extremes.

4 Dionys. Hal. l. ii. p. 92, 93; Plutarch, in Numa, p. 140, 141. Τὸ σῶμα καὶ τὸ ἦθος κάθαρον καὶ ἄθικτον ἐπὶ τῷ γαμοῦντι γένεσθαι. [Comp. Lycurg. cum Numâ, tom. i. p. 310, ed. Reiske.]

copper, a just introduction to his house and household deities.
A sacrifice of fruits was offered by the pontiffs in the presence
of ten witnesses; the contracting parties were seated on the same
sheepskin; they tasted a salt cake of *far*, or rice; and this *confarreation*,[1] which denoted the ancient food of Italy, served as an
emblem of their mystic union of mind and body. But this union
on the side of the woman was rigorous and unequal; and she
renounced the name and worship of her father's house, to embrace a new servitude, decorated only by the title of adoption: a
fiction of the law, neither rational nor elegant, bestowed on the
mother of a family[2] (her proper appellation) the strange characters of sister to her own children and of daughter to her husband
or master, who was invested with the plenitude of paternal
power. By his judgment or caprice her behaviour was approved,
or censured, or chastised; he exercised the jurisdiction of life and
death; and it was allowed that in the cases of adultery or drunkenness[3] the sentence might be properly inflicted. She acquired
and inherited for the sole profit of her lord; and so clearly was
woman defined, not as a *person*, but as a *thing*, that, if the original
title were deficient, she might be claimed, like other movables,
by the *use* and possession of an entire year. The inclination of
the Roman husband discharged or withheld the conjugal debt,
so scrupulously exacted by the Athenian and Jewish laws:[4] but
as polygamy was unknown, he could never admit to his bed a
fairer or more favoured partner.

1 Among the winter *frumenta*, the *triticum*, or bearded wheat; the *siligo*, or
the unbearded; the *far*, *adorea*, *oryza*, whose description perfectly tallies with the
rice of Spain and Italy. I adopt this identity on the credit of M. Paucton in his
useful and laborious Métrologie (p. 517–529).

2 Aulus Gellius (Noctes Atticæ, xviii. 6) gives a ridiculous definition of
Ælius Melissus, Matrona, quæ semel, *materfamilias* quæ sæpius peperit, as porce-
tra, and scropha in the sow kind. He then adds the genuine meaning, quæ in
matrimonium vel in manum convenisset.

[By marriage a female passed wholly into the power of her husband, and
this state was called *manas*. By this authority he had complete jurisdiction over
her actions, yet he could only divorce her on the grounds of drunkenness,
adultery, and carrying false keys. – O. S.]

3 It was enough to have tasted wine, or to have stolen the key of the cellar
(Plin. Hist. Nat. xiv. 14).

4 Solon requires three payments per month. By the Misna, a daily debt was
imposed on an idle, vigorous, young husband; twice a week on a citizen; once

After the Punic triumphs the matrons of Rome aspired to the
common benefits of a free and opulent republic; their wishes
were gratified by the indulgence of fathers and lovers, and their
ambition was unsuccessfully resisted by the gravity of Cato the
Censor.[1] They declined the solemnities of the old nuptials, defeated the annual prescription by an absence of three days, and,
without losing their name or independence, subscribed the liberal and definite terms of a marriage contract. Of their private
fortunes, they communicated the use and secured the property:
the estates of a wife could neither be alienated nor mortgaged
by a prodigal husband; their mutual gifts were prohibited by the
jealousy of the laws; and the misconduct of either party might
afford, under another name, a future subject for an action of
theft. To this loose and voluntary compact religious and civil
rites were no longer essential, and between persons of a similar
rank the apparent community of life was allowed as sufficient
evidence of their nuptials. The dignity of marriage was restored
by the Christians, who derived all spiritual grace from the prayers
of the faithful and the benediction of the priest or bishop. The
origin, validity, and duties of the holy institution were regulated
by the tradition of the synagogue, the precepts of the Gospel,
and the canons of general or provincial synods;[2] and the conscience of the Christians was awed by the decrees and censures
of their ecclesiastical rulers. Yet the magistrates of Justinian were
not subject to the authority of the church; the emperor consulted
the unbelieving civilians of antiquity; and the choice of matrimonial laws in the Code and Pandects is directed by the earthly

on a peasant; once in thirty days on a camel-driver; once in six months on a
seaman. But the student or doctor was free from tribute; and *no* wife, if she
received a *weekly* sustenance, could sue for a divorce; for one week a vow of
abstinence was allowed. Polygamy divided, without multiplying, the duties of
the husband (Selden, Uxor Ebraica, l. iii. c. 6, in his works, vol. ii. p. 717–720).

1 On the Oppian law we may hear the mitigating speech of Valerius Flaccus
and the severe censorial oration of the elder Cato (Liv. xxxiv. 1–8). But we
shall rather hear the polished historian of the eighth, than the rough orators of
the sixth, century of Rome. The principles, and even the style, of Cato are more
accurately preserved by Aulus Gellius (x. 23).

2 For the system of Jewish and Catholic matrimony, see Selden (Uxor
Ebraica, Opp. vol. ii. p. 529–860), Bingham (Christian Antiquities, l. xxii.), and
Chardon (Hist. des Sacremens, tom. vi.).

motives of justice, policy, and the natural freedom of both sexes.[1]

Besides the agreement of the parties, the essence of every rational contract, the Roman marriage required the previous approbation of the parents. A father might be forced by some recent laws to supply the wants of a mature daughter, but even his insanity was not generally allowed to supersede the necessity of his consent. The causes of the dissolution of matrimony have varied among the Romans;[2] but the most solemn sacrament, the confarreation itself, might always be done away by rites of a contrary tendency. In the first ages the father of a family might sell his children, and his wife was reckoned in the number of his children: the domestic judge might pronounce the death of the offender, or his mercy might expel her from his bed and house; but the slavery of the wretched female was hopeless and perpetual, unless he asserted for his own convenience the manly prerogative of divorce. The warmest applause has been lavished on the virtue of the Romans, who abstained from the exercise of this tempting privilege above five hundred years;[3] but the same fact evinces the unequal terms of a connection in which the slave was unable to renounce her tyrant, and the tyrant was unwilling to relinquish his slave. When the Roman matrons became the equal and voluntary companions of their lords, a new jurisprudence was introduced, that marriage, like other partnerships,

1 The civil laws of marriage are exposed in the Institutes (l. i. tit. x.), the Pandects (l. xxiii. xxiv. xxv.), and the Code (l. v.); but as the title de ritû nuptiarum is yet imperfect, we are obliged to explore the fragments of Ulpian (tit. ix. p. 590, 591), and the Collatio Legum Mosaicarum (tit. xvi. p. 790, 791) with the notes of Pithæus and Schulting [Jurispr. Ante-Justin.]. They find, in the Commentary of Servius (on the 1st Georgic and the 4th Æneid), two curious passages.

2 According to Plutarch (p. 57 [Rom. c. 22]) Romulus allowed only three grounds of a divorce – drunkenness, adultery, and false keys. Otherwise, the husband who abused his supremacy forfeited half his goods to the wife, and half to the goddess Ceres, and offered a sacrifice (with the remainder?) to the terrestrial deities. This strange law was either imaginary or transient.

3 In the year of Rome 523, Spurius Carvilius Ruga repudiated a fair, a good, but a barren wife (Dionysius Hal. l. ii. [c. 25] p. 93; Plutarch, in Numa [comp. Lycurg. cum Numâ, c. 3], p. 141; Valerius Maximus, l. ii. c. 1 [§ 4]; Aulus Gellius, iv. 3). He was questioned by the censors, and hated by the people; but his divorce stood unimpeached in law.

might be dissolved by the abdication of one of the associates. In three centuries of prosperity and corruption, this principle was enlarged to frequent practice and pernicious abuse. Passion, interest, or caprice suggested daily motives for the dissolution of marriage; a word, a sign, a message, a letter, the mandate of a freedman, declared the separation; the most tender of human connections was degraded to a transient society of profit or pleasure. According to the various conditions of life, both sexes alternately felt the disgrace and injury: an inconstant spouse transferred her wealth to a new family, abandoning a numerous, perhaps a spurious, progeny to the paternal authority and care of her late husband; a beautiful virgin might be dismissed to the world, old, indigent, and friendless; but the reluctance of the Romans, when they were pressed to marriage by Augustus, sufficiently marks that the prevailing institutions were least favourable to the males. A specious theory is confuted by this free and perfect experiment, which demonstrates that the liberty of divorce does not contribute to happiness and virtue. The facility of separation would destroy all mutual confidence, and inflame every trifling dispute: the minute difference between a husband and a stranger, which might so easily be removed, might still more easily be forgotten; and the matron who in five years can submit to the embraces of eight husbands must cease to reverence the chastity of her own person.[1]

Insufficient remedies followed with distant and tardy steps the rapid progress of the evil. The ancient worship of the Romans afforded a peculiar goddess to hear and reconcile the complaints of a married life; but her epithet of *Viriplaca*,[2] the appeaser of husbands, too clearly indicates on which side

1   —— Sic fiunt octo mariti
        Quinque per autumnos.   (Juvenal, Satir. vi. 229.)
A rapid succession, which may yet be credible, as well as the non consulum numero, sed maritorum annos suos computant, of Seneca (de Beneficiis, iii. 16). Jerom saw at Rome a triumphant husband bury his twenty-first wife, who had interred twenty-two of his less sturdy predecessors (Opp. tom. i. p. 90, ad Gerontiam). But the ten husbands in a month of the poet Martial is an extravagant hyperbole (l. vi. epigram 7).

2 Sacellum Viriplacæ (Valerius Maximus, l. ii. c. 1 [§ 6], in the Palatine region, appears in the time of Theodosius, in the description of Rome by Publius Victor.

submission and repentance were always expected. Every act of
a citizen was subject to the judgment of the *censors;* the first who
used the privilege of divorce assigned at their command the
motives of his conduct;[1] and a senator was expelled for dismissing his virgin spouse without the knowledge or advice of his
friends. Whenever an action was instituted for the recovery of a
marriage-portion, the *prætor*, as the guardian of equity, examined
the cause and the characters, and gently inclined the scale in
favour of the guiltless and injured party. Augustus, who united
the powers of both magistrates, adopted their different modes
of repressing or chastising the licence of divorce.[2] The presence
of seven Roman witnesses was required for the validity of this
solemn and deliberate act: if any adequate provocation had been
given by the husband, instead of the delay of two years, he was
compelled to refund immediately or in the space of six months;
but if he could arraign the manners of his wife, her guilt or levity
was expiated by the loss of the sixth or eighth part of her marriage-portion. The Christian princes were the first who specified
the just causes of a private divorce; their institutions, from Constantine to Justinian, appear to fluctuate between the custom of
the empire and the wishes of the church;[3] and the author of the
Novels too frequently reforms the jurisprudence of the Code and
Pandects. In the most rigorous laws a wife was condemned to
support a gamester, a drunkard, or a libertine, unless he were
guilty of homicide, poison, or sacrilege; in which cases the marriage, as it should seem, might have been dissolved by the hand
of the executioner. But the sacred right of the husband was
invariably maintained to deliver his name and family from the
disgrace of adultery; the list of *mortal* sins, either male or female,
was curtailed and enlarged by successive regulations, and the
obstacles of incurable impotence, long absence, and monastic
profession, were allowed to rescind the matrimonial obligation.

1 Valerius Maximus, l. ii. c. 9 [§ 2]. With some propriety he judges divorce
more criminal than celibacy: illo namque conjugalia sacra spreta tantum, hoc
etiam injuriose tractata.

2 See the laws of Augustus and his successors, in Heineccius, ad Legem
Papiam-Poppæam, c. 19, in Opp. tom. vi. P. i. p. 323–333.

3 Aliæ sunt leges Cæsarum, aliæ Christi; aliud Papinianus, aliud Paulus *noster*
præcipit (Jerom, tom. i. p. 198; Selden, Uxor Ebraica, l. iii. c. 31, p. 847–853).

Whoever transgressed the permission of the law was subject to various and heavy penalties. The woman was stripped of her wealth and ornaments, without excepting the bodkin of her hair; if the man introduced a new bride into his bed, *her* fortune might be lawfully seized by the vengeance of his exiled wife. Forfeiture was sometimes commuted to a fine; the fine was sometimes aggravated by transportation to an island, or imprisonment in a monastery; the injured party was released from the bonds of marriage, but the offender, during life or a term of years, was disabled from the repetition of nuptials. The successor of Justinian yielded to the prayers of his unhappy subjects, and restored the liberty of divorce by mutual consent; the civilians were unanimous,[1] the theologians were divided,[2] and the ambiguous word which contains the precept of Christ is flexible to any interpretation that the wisdom of a legislator can demand.

The freedom of love and marriage was restrained among the Romans by natural and civil impediments. An instinct, almost innate and universal, appears to prohibit the incestuous commerce[3] of parents and children in the infinite series of ascending and descending generations. Concerning the oblique and collateral

1 The Institutes are silent; but we may consult the Codes of Theodosius (l. iii. tit. xvi. with Godefroy's Commentary, tom. i. p. 311–313) and Justinian (l. v. tit. xvii.), the Pandects (l. xxiv. tit. ii.) and the Novels (xxii. cxvii. cxxvii. cxxxiv. cxl.). Justinian fluctuated to the last between civil and ecclesiastical law.

2 In pure Greek, πορνεία is not a common word; nor can the proper meaning, fornication, be strictly applied to matrimonial sin. In a figurative sense, how far, and to what offences, may it be extended? Did Christ speak the Rabbinical or Syriac tongue? Of what original word is πορνεία the translation? How variously is that Greek word translated in the versions ancient and modern! There are two (Mark x. 11, Luke xvi. 18) to one (Matthew xix. 9) that such ground of divorce was not excepted by Jesus. Some critics have presumed to think, by an evasive answer, he avoided the giving offence either to the school of Sammai or to that of Hillel (Selden, Uxor Ebraica, l. iii. c. 18–22, 28, 31).

3 The principles of the Roman jurisprudence are exposed by Justinian (Institut. l. i. tit. x.); and the laws and manners of the different nations of antiquity concerning forbidden degrees, etc., are copiously explained by Dr. Taylor in his Elements of Civil Law (p. 108, 314–339), a work of amusing though various reading, but which cannot be praised for philosophical precision.

[In consequence of the marriage of the emperor Claudius with his niece Agrippina, the daughter of his brother Germanicus, it became lawful for a man to marry the daughter of his brother, but it was unlawful for him to marry the daughter of his sister. – O. S.]

branches nature is indifferent, reason mute, and custom various and arbitrary. In Egypt the marriage of brothers and sisters was admitted without scruple or exception: a Spartan might espouse the daughter of his father; an Athenian, that of his mother; and the nuptials of an uncle with his niece were applauded at Athens as a happy union of the dearest relations. The profane lawgivers of Rome were never tempted by interest or superstition to multiply the forbidden degrees; but they inflexibly condemned the marriage of sisters and brothers, hesitated whether first-cousins should be touched by the same interdict, revered the parental character of aunts and uncles, and treated affinity and adoption as a just imitation of the ties of blood. According to the proud maxims of the republic, a legal marriage could only be contracted by free citizens; an honourable, at least an ingenuous, birth was required for the spouse of a senator: but the blood of kings could never mingle in legitimate nuptials with the blood of a Roman; and the name of Stranger degraded Cleopatra and Berenice[1] to live the *concubines* of Mark Antony and Titus.[2] This appellation, indeed, so injurious to the majesty, cannot without indulgence be applied to the manners, of these Oriental queens. A concubine, in the strict sense of the civilians, was a woman of servile or plebeian extraction, the sole and faithful companion of a Roman citizen, who continued in a state of celibacy. Her modest station, below the honours of a wife, above the infamy of a prostitute, was acknowledged and approved by the laws: from the age of Augustus to the tenth century the use of this secondary marriage prevailed both in the West and East; and the humble virtues of a concubine were often preferred to the pomp and insolence of a noble matron. In this connection the two Antonines, the best of princes and of men, enjoyed the comforts of domestic love; the example was imitated by many citizens impatient of celibacy, but regardful of

1 When her father Agrippa died (A.D. 44), Berenice was sixteen years of age (Joseph. tom. i. Antiquit. Judaic. l. xix. c. 9, p. 952, edit. Havercamp.). She was therefore above fifty years old when Titus (A.D. 79) invitus invitam invisit. This date would not have adorned the tragedy or pastoral of the tender Racine.

2 The *Ægyptia conjux* of Virgil (Æneid, viii. 688) seems to be numbered among the monsters who warred with Mark Antony against Augustus, the senate, and the gods of Italy.

their families. If at any time they desired to legitimate their natural children, the conversion was instantly performed by the celebration of their nuptials with a partner whose fruitfulness and
fidelity they had already tried.[1] By this epithet of *natural* the
offspring of the concubine were distinguished from the spurious
brood of adultery, prostitution, and incest, to whom Justinian
reluctantly grants the necessary aliments of life; and these natural
children alone were capable of succeeding to a sixth part of the
inheritance of their reputed father. According to the rigour of
law, bastards were entitled only to the name and condition of
their mother, from whom they might derive the character of a
slave, a stranger, or a citizen. The outcasts of every family were
adopted, without reproach, as the children of the state.[2]

The relation of guardian and ward, or, in Roman words, of
tutor and *pupil*, which covers so many titles of the Institutes and
Pandects,[3] is of a very simple and uniform nature. The person
and property of an orphan must always be trusted to the custody
of some discreet friend. If the deceased father had not signified
his choice, the *agnats*, or paternal kindred of the nearest degree,
were compelled to act as the natural guardians: the Athenians
were apprehensive of exposing the infant to the power of those
most interested in his death; but an axiom of Roman jurisprudence

1 [The edict of Constantine first conferred this right of marriage after trial
and experience of fecundity; for Augustus had prohibited the taking as a concubine the woman who might afterwards be taken as a wife: if marriage took
place afterwards, this made no difference in the rights of the children born
before it: recourse was then had to adoption, properly called arrogation. – O. S.]

2 The humble but legal rights of concubines and natural children are stated
in the Institutes (l. i. tit. x.), the Pandects (l. i. tit. vii.), the Code (l. v. tit. xxv.),
and the Novels (lxxiv. lxxxix.). The researches of Heineccius and Giannone
(ad Legem Juliam et Papiam-Poppæam, c. iv. p. 164–175, Opere Posthume,
p. 108–158) illustrate this interesting and domestic subject.

[By the first law of Constantine the legitimate offspring could alone inherit:
where there were no near legitimate relatives, the inheritance went to the fiscus.
By the second law, all persons, even of the highest rank, senators, perfectissimi,
decemvirs, were to be declared infamous, and out of the protection of the
Roman law if born ex ancillâ, vel ancillcæ filiâ, vel libertâ, vel libertæ filiâ, sive
Romanâ factâ, seu Latinâ, vel scænicœ filiâ, etc. Whatever a fond father had
conferred on such children was revoked, and either restored to the legitimate
children or confiscated to the state. – O. S.]

3 See the article of guardians and wards in the Institutes (l. i. tit. xiii.–xxvi.),
the Pandects (l. xxvi. xxvii.), and the Code (l. v. tit. xxviii.–lxx.).

has pronounced that the charge of tutelage should constantly attend the emolument of succession. If the choice of the father and the line of consanguinity afforded no efficient guardian, the failure was supplied by the nomination of the prætor of the city or the president of the province; but the person whom they named to this *public* office might be legally excused by insanity or blindness, by ignorance or inability, by previous enmity or adverse interest, by the number of children or guardianships with which he was already burthened, and by the immunities which were granted to the useful labours of magistrates, lawyers, physicians, and professors. Till the infant could speak and think, he was represented by the tutor,[1] whose authority was finally determined by the age of puberty. Without his consent, no act of the pupil could bind himself to his own prejudice, though it might oblige others for his personal benefit. It is needless to observe that the tutor often gave security, and always rendered an account; and that the want of diligence or integrity exposed him to a civil and almost criminal action for the violation of his sacred trust. The age of puberty had been rashly fixed by the civilians at fourteen;[2] but, as the faculties of the

1 [Gibbon's theory of pupillage does not seem correct according to Dr. W. Smith. The tutor did not represent the 'pupillus.' His office is always described as 'augere auctoritatem, interponere, auctor fieri,' *i.e.*, to fill out or complete the defective legal personality of the ward. All formal words essential to a legal transaction had to be pronounced by the ward himself, and then the tutor, by his assent, added the *animus*, or intention, of which the child was not capable. – O. S.]

2 ['The civilians had rashly fixed the age of puberty at fourteen,' but it is probable that the doctrine attributed generally to the civilians was quite unknown to the older law. As the 'pupillus' was in theory a defectus paterfamilias, it is more than likely that the tutelage ceased at the epoch of actual physical manhood. We learn from Gaius (l. i. §. 196) and Ulpian (Reg. ii. 28) that the Sabinians still maintained this view, while the Proculeians were in favour of the age of puberty being fixed at fourteen. It was not until the legislation of Justinian that the question was finally settled in favour of the latter opinion. In the case of females, the age of puberty was fixed at twelve from the earliest times.

As regards the function of the curator, there has been considerable dispute, but the following seems to be the most consistent accout of the matter: The law of the 'Twelve Tables' provided for the appointment of curators in the case of madmen and prodigals, but did not make any provision for the protection of young persons who had attained the age of puberty. The first enactment on the subject of which we have any knowledge is the *Lex Plætoria* (not *Lætoria* as often

mind ripen more slowly than those of the body, a *curator* was interposed to guard the fortunes of a Roman youth from his own inexperience and headstrong passions. Such a trustee had been first instituted by the prætor to save a family from the blind havoc of a prodigal or madman; and the minor was compelled by the laws to solicit the same protection to give validity to his acts till he accomplished the full period of twenty-five years. Women were condemned to the perpetual tutelage of parents, husbands, or guardians; a sex created to please and obey was never supposed to have attained the age of reason and experience. Such at least was the stern and haughty spirit of the ancient law, which had been insensibly mollified before the time of Justinian.

II. The original right of property can only be justified by the accident or merit of prior occupancy; and on this foundation it is wisely established by the philosophy of the civilians.[1] The savage who hollows a tree, inserts a sharp stone into a wooden handle, or applies a string to an elastic branch, becomes in a state of nature the just proprietor of the canoe, the bow, or the hatchet. The materials were common to all; the new form, the produce of his time and simple industry, belongs solely to himself. His hungry brethren cannot, without a sense of their own injustice, extort from the hunter the game of the forest overtaken or slain by his personal strength and dexterity. If his provident care preserves and multiplies the tame animals, whose nature is

written), passed before the time of Plautus, which, fixing the age of the perfecta ætas at twenty-five years, provided that any one defrauding a person under that age should be liable to a criminal prosecution and to infamy (Cicero de Natura Deorum, iii. 30; de Officiis, iii. 15); and probably permitted the appointment of curators in cases where a good reason for the appointment was given. The prætor subsequently provided a remedy which was a great protection to persons under twenty-five years of age who came before him, by directing in all cases a *restitutio in integrum*: viz., that the applicant should be placed exactly in the position in which he would have been had not the fraud been practised against him. Finally, Marcus Antoninus ordered that curators should be given in all cases without inquiry on the application of the pubes. Cf. Julius Capitolinus, in Vita Marc. Aurel. Anton. c. 10. – O. S.]

1 Institut. l. ii. tit. i. ii. Compare the pure and precise reasoning of Caius and Heineccius (l. ii. tit. i. p. 69–91) with the loose prolixity of Theophilus (p. 207–265). The opinions of Ulpian are preserved in the Pandects (l. i. tit. viii. leg. 41, No. 1).

tractable to the arts of education, he acquires a perpetual title to the use and service of their numerous progeny, which derives its existence from him alone. If he encloses and cultivates a field for their sustenance and his own, a barren waste is converted into a fertile soil; the seed, the manure, the labour, create a new value, and the rewards of harvest are painfully earned by the fatigues of the revolving year. In the successive states of society, the hunter, the shepherd, the husbandman, may defend their possessions by two reasons which forcibly appeal to the feelings of the human mind: that whatever they enjoy is the fruit of their own industry; and that every man who envies their felicity may purchase similar acquisitions by the exercise of similar diligence. Such, in truth, may be the freedom and plenty of a small colony cast on a fruitful island. But the colony multiplies, while the space still continues the same; the common rights, the equal inheritance of mankind, are engrossed by the bold and crafty; each field and forest is circumscribed by the landmarks of a jealous master; and it is the peculiar praise of the Roman juris-prudence that it asserts the claim of the first occupant to the wild animals of the earth, the air, and the waters. In the progress from primitive equity to final injustice, the steps are silent, the shades are almost imperceptible, and the absolute monopoly is guarded by positive laws and artificial reason. The active, insat-iate principle of self-love can alone supply the arts of life and the wages of industry; and as soon as civil government and exclusive property have been introduced, they become necessary to the existence of the human race. Except in the singular in-stitutions of Sparta, the wisest legislators have disapproved an agrarian law as a false and dangerous innovation. Among the Romans, the enormous disproportion of wealth surmounted the ideal restraints of a doubtful tradition and an obsolete statute – a tradition that the poorest follower of Romulus had been en-dowed with the perpetual inheritance of two *jugera;*[1] a statute which confined the richest citizen to the measure of five hundred jugera, or three hundred and twelve acres of land. The original

1 The *heredium* of the first Romans is defined by Varro (de Re Rusticâ, l. i. c. ii. p. 141, c. x. p. 160, 161, edit. Gesner), and clouded by Pliny's declamation (Hist. Natur. xviii. 2). A just and learned comment is given in the Administra-tion des Terres chez les Romains (p. 12–66).

territory of Rome consisted only of some miles of wood and meadow along the banks of the Tiber; and domestic exchange could add nothing to the national stock. But the goods of an alien or enemy were lawfully exposed to the first hostile occupier; the city was enriched by the profitable trade of war; and the blood of her sons was the only price that was paid for the Volscian sheep, the slaves of Britain, or the gems and gold of Asiatic kingdoms. In the language of ancient jurisprudence, which was corrupted and forgotten before the age of Justinian, these spoils were distinguished by the name of *manceps* or *mancipium*, taken with the hand; and whenever they were sold or *emancipated*, the purchaser required some assurance that they had been the property of an enemy, and not of a fellow-citizen.[1] A citizen could only forfeit his rights by apparent dereliction, and such dereliction of a valuable interest could not easily be presumed. Yet, according to the Twelve Tables, a prescription of one year for movables, and of two years for immovables, abolished the claim of the ancient master, if the actual possessor had acquired them by a fair transaction from the person whom he believed to be the lawful proprietor.[2] Such conscientious injustice, without any mixture of fraud or force, could seldom injure the members of a small republic; but the various periods of three, of ten, or of twenty years, determined by Justinian, are more suitable to the latitude of a great empire. It is only in the term of prescription that the distinction of real and personal fortune has been remarked by the civilians; and their general idea of property is that of simple, uniform, and absolute dominion.

1 The *res mancipi* is explained from faint and remote lights by Ulpian (Fragment. tit. xviii. [xix.] p. 618, 619] and Bynkershoek (opp. tom. i. p. 306–315). The definition is somewhat arbitrary; and as none except myself have assigned a reason, I am diffident of my own.

[Since the time of Gibbon it has been proved incontestably that the agrarian laws of Rome related only to the Ager Publicus, or domains of the state, and that the laws of Lucinius and of Gracchus limited a Roman citizen to the possession of 500 jugera of such land, but that he might become the proprietor of any amount of private land. – O. S.]

2 From this short prescription, Hume (Essays, vol. i. p. 423) infers that there could not *then* be more order and settlement in Italy than *now* amongst the Tartars. By the civilian of his adversary Wallace he is reproached, and not without reason, for overlooking the conditions (Institut. l. ii. tit. vi.).

The subordinate exceptions of *use*, of *usufruct*,[1] of *servitudes*,[2] imposed for the benefit of a neighbour on lands and houses, are abundantly explained by the professors of jurisprudence. The claims of property, as far as they are altered by the mixture, the division, or the transformation of substances, are investigated with metaphysical subtlety by the same civilians.

The personal title of the first proprietor must be determined by his death; but the possession, without any appearance of change, is peaceably continued in his children, the associates of his toil, and the partners of his wealth. This natural inheritance has been protected by the legislators of every climate and age, and the father is encouraged to persevere in slow and distant improvements, by the tender hope that a long posterity will enjoy the fruits of his labour. The *principle* of hereditary succession is universal; but the *order* has been variously established by convenience or caprice, by the spirit of national institutions, or by some partial example which was originally decided by fraud or violence. The jurisprudence of the Romans appears to have deviated from the equality of nature much less than the Jewish,[3] the Athenian,[4] or the English institutions.[5] On the death of a citizen, all his descendants, unless they were already freed from his paternal power, were called to the inheritance of his possessions. The insolent prerogative of primogeniture was unknown; the two

1 See the Institutes (l. i. [ii.] tit. iv. v.) and the Pandects (l. vii.). Noodt has composed a learned and distinct treatise *de Usufructû* (Opp. tom. i p. 387–478).

2 The questions *de Servitutibus* are discussed in the Institutes (l. ii. tit. iii.) and Pandects (l. viii). Cicero (pro Murenâ, c. 9) and Lactantius (Institut. Divin. l. i. c. i.) affect to laugh at the insignificant doctrine, de aquâ pluviâ arcendâ, etc. Yet it might be of frequent use among litigious neighbours, both in town and country.

3 Among the patriarchs, the first-born enjoyed a mystic and spiritual primogeniture (Genesis xxv. 31). In the land of Canaan he was entitled to a double portion of inheritance (Deuteronomy xxi. 17, with Le Clerc's judicious Commentary).

4 At Athens the sons were equal; but the poor daughters were endowed at the discretion of their brothers. See the κληρικοί pleadings of Isæus (in the seventh volume of the Greek Orators), illustrated by the version and comment of Sir William Jones, a scholar, a lawyer, and a man of genius.

5 In England, the eldest son alone inherits *all* the land; a law, says the orthodox Judge Blackstone (Commentaries on the Laws of England, vol. ii. p. 215), unjust only in the opinion of younger brothers. It may be of some political use in sharpening their industry.

sexes were placed on a just level; all the sons and daughters were entitled to an equal portion of the patrimonial estate; and if any of the sons had been intercepted by a premature death, his person was represented, and his share was divided, by his surviving children. On the failure of the direct line, the right of succession must diverge to the collateral branches. The degrees of kindred[1] are numbered by the civilians, ascending from the last possessor to a common parent, and descending from the common parent to the next heir: my father stands in the first degree, my brother in the second, his children in the third, and the remainder of the series may be conceived by fancy, or pictured in a genealogical table. In this computation a distinction was made, essential to the laws and even the constitution of Rome: the *agnats*, or persons connected by a line of males, were called, as they stood in the nearest degree, to an equal partition; but a female was incapable of transmitting any legal claims; and the *cognats* of every rank, without excepting the dear relation of a mother and a son, were disinherited by the Twelve Tables, as strangers and aliens. Among the Romans a *gens* or lineage was united by a common *name* and domestic rites; the various *cognomens* or *surnames* of Scipio or Marcellus distinguished from each other the subordinate branches or families of the Cornelian or Claudian race: the default of the *agnats* of the same surname was supplied by the larger denomination of *gentiles*; and the vigilance of the laws maintained, in the same name, the perpetual descent of religion and property. A similar principle dictated the Voconian law,[2] which abolished the right of female inheritance. As long as virgins were given or sold in marriage, the adoption of the wife extinguished the hopes of the daughter. But the equal succession of independent matrons supported their pride and

1 Blackstone's Tables (vol. ii. p. 202) represent and compare the decrees of the civil with those of the canon and common law. A separate tract of Julius Paulus, de gradibus et affinibus, is inserted or abridged in the Pandects (l. xxxviii. tit. x. [leg. 10]). In the seventh degrees he computes (No. 18) 1024 persons.

2 The Voconian law was enacted in the year of Rome 584. The younger Scipio, who was then 17 years of age (Freinsheimius, Supplement. Livian. xlvi. 44), found an occasion of exercising his generosity to his mother, sisters, etc. (Polybius, tom. ii. l. xxxi. p. 1453–1464, edit. Gronov. [xxxii. 12], a domestic witness.)

luxury, and might transport into a foreign house the riches of their fathers. While the maxims of Cato[1] were revered, they tended to perpetuate in each family a just and virtuous mediocrity: till female blandishments insensibly triumphed, and every salutary restraint was lost in the dissolute greatness of the republic. The rigour of the decemvirs was tempered by the equity of the prætors. Their edicts restored emancipated and posthumous children to the rights of nature; and upon the failure of the *agnats*, they preferred the blood of the *cognats* to the name of the gentiles, whose title and character were insensibly covered with oblivion. The reciprocal inheritance of mothers and sons was established in the Tertullian and Orphitian decrees by the humanity of the senate. A new and more impartial order was introduced by the novels of Justinian, who affected to revive the jurisprudence of the Twelve Tables. The lines of masculine and female kindred were confounded: the descending, ascending, and collateral series was accurately defined; and each degree, according to the proximity of blood and affection, succeeded to the vacant possessions of a Roman citizen.[2]

The order of succession is regulated by nature, or at least by the general and permanent reason of the lawgiver; but this order is frequently violated by the arbitrary and partial *wills*, which prolong the dominion of the testator beyond the grave.[3] In the simple state of society this last use or abuse of the right of property is seldom indulged; it was introduced at Athens by the laws of Solon, and the private testaments of the father of a family are authorised by the Twelve Tables. Before the time of

1 Legem Voconiam (Ernesti, Clavis Ciceroniana) voce magnâ bonis lateribus (at sixty-five years of age) suasissem, says old Cato (de Senectute, c. 5). Aulus Gellius (vii. 13, xvii. 6) has saved some passages.

2 See the law of succession in the Institutes of Caius (l. ii. tit. viii. p. 130–144, [Schulting, Jurispr. Ante-Justin. Lips. 1737]) and Justinian (l. iii. tit. i.–vi. with the Greek version of Theophilus, p. 515–575, 588–600), the Pandects (l. xxxviii. tit. vi.–xvii.), the Code (l. vi. tit. lv.–lx.), and the Novels (cxviii.).

3 That succession was the *rule*, testament the *exception*, is proved by Taylor (Elements of Civil Law, p. 519–527), a learned, rambling, spirited writer. In the second and third books the method of the Institutes is doubtless preposterous; and the chancellor Daguesseau (Œuvres, tom. i. p. 275) wishes his countryman Domat in the place of Tribonian. Yet *covenants* before *successions* is not surely *the natural order of the civil laws*.

the decemvirs,[1] a Roman citizen exposed his wishes and motives to the assembly of the thirty curiæ or parishes, and the general law of inheritance was suspended by an occasional act of the legislature. After the permission of the decemvirs, each private lawgiver promulgated his verbal or written testament in the presence of five citizens, who represented the five classes of the Roman people; a sixth witness attested their concurrence; a seventh weighed the copper money, which was paid by an imaginary purchaser, and the estate was emancipated by a fictitious sale and immediate release. This singular ceremony,[2] which excited the wonder of the Greeks, was still practised in the age of Severus; but the prætors had already approved a more simple testament, for which they required the seals and signatures of seven witnesses, free from all legal exception, and purposely summoned for the execution of that important act. A domestic monarch, who reigned over the lives and fortunes of his children, might distribute their respective shares according to the degrees of their merit or his affection; his arbitrary displeasure chastised an unworthy son by the loss of his inheritance, and the mortifying preference of a stranger. But the experience of unnatural parents recommended some limitations of their testamentary powers. A son, or, by the laws of Justinian, even a daughter, could no longer be disinherited by their silence: they were compelled to name the criminal, and to specify the offence; and the justice of the emperor enumerated the sole causes that could justify such a violation of the first principles of nature and society.[3] Unless a legitimate portion, a fourth part, had been reserved for the children, they were entitled to institute an action or complaint of *inofficious* testament – to suppose that their

1 Prior examples of testaments are perhaps fabulous. At Athens a *childless* father only could make a will (Plutarch. in Solone, tom. i. [c. 21] p. 164. See Isæus and Jones).

2 The testament of Augustus is specified by Suetonius (in August. c. 101, in Neron. c. 4), who may be studied as a code of Roman antiquities. Plutarch (Opuscul. tom. ii. p. 976) is surprised ὅταν δὲ διαθήκας γράφουσιν, ἑτέροι μὲν ἀπολείπουσι κληρονόμους, ἕτεροι δὲ πωλοῦσι τὰς οὐσίας. The language of Ulpian (Fragment. tit. xx. [§ 2] p. 627, edit. Schulting) is almost too exclusive – solum in usû est.

3 Justinian (Novell. cxv. c. 3, 4) enumerates only the public and private crimes, for which a son might likewise disinherit his father.

father's understanding was impaired by sickness or age, and respectfully to appeal from his rigorous sentence to the deliberate wisdom of the magistrate. In the Roman jurisprudence an essential distinction was admitted between the inheritance and the legacies. The heirs who succeeded to the entire unity, or to any of the twelve fractions of the substance of the testator, represented his civil and religious character, asserted his rights, fulfilled his obligations, and discharged the gifts of friendship or liberality which his last will had bequeathed under the name of legacies. But as the imprudence or prodigality of a dying man might exhaust the inheritance, and leave only risk and labour to his successor, he was empowered to retain the *Falcidian* portion; to deduct, before the payment of the legacies, a clear fourth for his own emolument. A reasonable time was allowed to examine the proportion between the debts and the estate, to decide whether he should accept or refuse the testament; and if he used the benefit of an inventory, the demands of the creditors could not exceed the valuation of the effects. The last will of a citizen might be altered during his life, or rescinded after his death: the persons whom he named might die before him, or reject the inheritance, or be exposed to some legal disqualification. In the contemplation of these events, he was permitted to substitute second and third heirs, to replace each other according to the order of the testament; and the incapacity of a madman or an infant to bequeath his property might be supplied by a similar substitution.[1] But the power of the testator expired with the acceptance of the testament: each Roman of mature age and discretion acquired the absolute dominion of his inheritance, and the simplicity of the civil law was never clouded by the long and intricate entails which confine the happiness and freedom of unborn generations.

Conquest and the formalities of law established the use of *codicils.* If a Roman was surprised by death in a remote province

---

1 The *substitutions fidei-commissaires* of the modern civil law is a feudal idea grafted on the Roman jurisprudence, and bears scarcely any resemblance to the ancient fidei-commissa (Institutions du Droit François, tom. i. p. 347–383; Denissart, Décisions de Jurisprudence, tom. iv. p. 577–604). They were stretched to the fourth degree by an abuse of the clixth Novel; a partial, perplexed, declamatory law.

of the empire, he addressed a short epistle to his legitimate or testamentary heir, who fulfilled with honour, or neglected with impunity, this last request, which the judges before the age of Augustus were not authorised to enforce. A codicil might be expressed in any mode or in any language, but the subscription of five witnesses must declare that it was the genuine composition of the author. His intention, however laudable, was sometimes illegal, and the invention of *fidei-commissa*, or trusts, arose from the struggle between natural justice and positive jurisprudence. A stranger of Greece or Africa might be the friend or benefactor of a childless Roman, but none, except a fellow-citizen, could act as his heir. The Voconian law, which abolished female succession, restrained the legacy or inheritance of a woman to the sum of one hundred thousand sesterces;[1] and an only daughter was condemned almost as an alien in her father's house. The zeal of friendship and parental affection suggested a liberal artifice: a qualified citizen was named in the testament, with a prayer or injunction that he would restore the inheritance to the person for whom it was truly intended. Various was the conduct of the trustees in this painful situation; they had sworn to observe the laws of their country, but honour prompted them to violate their oath; and, if they preferred their interest under the mask of patriotism, they forfeited the esteem of every virtuous mind. The declaration of Augustus relieved their doubts, gave a legal sanction to confidential testaments and codicils, and gently unravelled the forms and restraints of the republican jurisprudence.[2] But as the new practice of trusts degenerated into some abuse, the trustee was enabled, by the Trebellian and Pegasian decrees, to reserve one fourth of the estate, or to transfer on the head of the real heir all the debts and actions of the succession. The interpretation of testaments was strict and literal; but the language of *trusts* and codicils was delivered from the minute and technical accuracy of the civilians.[3]

1 Dion Cassius (tom. ii. l. lvi. [c. 10] p. 814, with Reimar's Notes) specifies in Greek money the sum of 25,000 drachms.

2 The revolutions of the Roman laws of inheritance are finely, though sometimes fancifully, deduced by Montesquieu (Esprit des Loix, l. xxvii.).

3 Of the civil jurisprudence of successions, testaments, codicils, legacies, and trusts, the principles are ascertained in the Institutes of Caius (l. ii.

III. The general duties of mankind are imposed by their public and private relations, but their specific *obligations* to each other can only be the effect of, 1, a promise; 2, a benefit; or 3, an injury; and when these obligations are ratified by law, the interested party may compel the performance by a judicial *action*. On this principle the civilians of every country have erected a similar jurisprudence, the fair conclusion of universal reason and justice.[1]

1. The goddess of *faith* (of human and social faith) was worshipped, not only in her temples, but in the lives of the Romans; and if that nation was deficient in the more amiable qualities of benevolence and generosity, they astonished the Greeks by their sincere and simple performance of the most burdensome engagements.[2] Yet among the same people, according to the rigid maxims of the patricians and decemvirs, a *naked pact*, a promise, or even an oath, did not create any civil obligation, unless it was confirmed by the legal form of a *stipulation*. Whatever might be the etymology of the Latin word, it conveyed the idea of a firm and irrevocable contract, which was always expressed in the mode of a question and answer. Do you promise to pay me one hundred pieces of gold? was the solemn interrogation of Seius. I do promise – was the reply of Sempronius. The friends of Sempronius, who answered for his ability and inclination, might be separately sued at the option of Seius; and the benefit of partition, or order of reciprocal actions, insensibly deviated from the strict theory of stipulation. The most cautious and deliberate consent was justly required to sustain the validity of a gratuitous promise, and the citizen who might have obtained a legal security incurred the suspicion of fraud, and paid the forfeit of his neglect. But the ingenuity of the civilians successfully laboured to convert simple engagements into the form of solemn stipulations. The prætors, as the guardians of social faith, admitted every

tit. ii.–viii. p. 91–144), Justinian (l. ii. tit. x.–xxv.), and Theophilus (p. 328, 514); and the immense detail occupies twelve books (xxviii.–xxxix.) of the Pandects.

1 The Institutes of Caius (l. ii. tit. ix. x. p. 144–214), of Justinian (l. iii. tit. xiv.–xxx. [xiii.–xxix.] l. iv. tit. i.–vi.), and of Theophilus (p. 616–837), distinguish four sorts of obligations – aut *re*, aut *verbis*, aut *literis*, aut *consensû*: but I confess myself partial to my own division.

2 How much is the cool, rational evidence of Polybius (l. vi. [c. 56] p. 693, l. xxxi. p. 1459, 1460) superior to vague, indiscriminate applause – omnium maxime et præcipue fidem coluit (A. Gellius, xx. 1 [tom. ii. p. 289, ed. Bipont.]).

rational evidence of a voluntary and deliberate act, which in their tribunal produced an equitable obligation, and for which they gave an action and a remedy.[1]

2. The obligations of the second class, as they were contracted by the delivery of a thing, are marked by the civilians with the epithet of real.[2] A grateful return is due to the author of a benefit; and whoever is intrusted with the property of another has bound himself to the sacred duty of restitution. In the case of a friendly loan, the merit of generosity is on the side of the lender only; in a deposit, on the side of the receiver; but in a *pledge*, and the rest of the selfish commerce of ordinary life, the benefit is compensated by an equivalent, and the obligation to restore is variously modified by the nature of the transaction. The Latin language very happily expresses the fundamental difference between the *commodatum* and the *mutuum*, which our poverty is reduced to confound under the vague and common appellation of a loan. In the former, the borrower was obliged to restore the same individual thing with which he had been *accommodated* for the temporary supply of his wants; in the latter, it was destined for his use and consumption, and he discharged this *mutual* engagement by substituting the same specific value according to a just estimation of number, of weight, and of measure. In the contract of *sale*, the absolute dominion is transferred to the purchaser, and he repays the benefit with an adequate sum of gold or silver, the price and universal standard of all earthly possessions. The obligation of another contract, that of *location*, is of a more complicated kind. Lands or houses, labour or talents, may be hired for a definite term; at the expiration of the time, the thing itself must be restored to the owner with an additional reward for the beneficial occupation and employment. In these lucrative contracts, to which may be added those

1 The Jus Prætorium de Pactis et Transactionibus is a separate and satisfactory treatise of Gerard Noodt (Opp. tom. i. p. 483–564). And I will here observe that the universities of Holland and Brandenburg, in the beginning of the present century, appear to have studied the civil law on the most just and liberal principles.

2 The nice and various subject of contracts by consent is spread over four books (xvii.–xx.) of the Pandects, and is one of the parts best deserving of the attention of an English student.

of partnership and commissions, the civilians sometimes imagine the delivery of the object, and sometimes presume the consent of the parties. The substantial pledge has been refined into the invisible rights of a mortgage or *hypotheca;* and the agreement of sale for a certain price imputes, from that moment, the chances of gain or loss to the account of the purchaser. It may be fairly supposed that every man will obey the dictates of his interest; and if he accepts the benefit, he is obliged to sustain the expense, of the transaction. In this boundless subject, the historian will observe the *location* of land and money, the rent of the one and the interest of the other, as they materially affect the prosperity of agriculture and commerce. The landlord was often obliged to advance the stock and instruments of husbandry, and to content himself with a partition of the fruits. If the feeble tenant was oppressed by accident, contagion, or hostile violence, he claimed a proportionable relief from the equity of the laws: five years were the customary term, and no solid or costly improvements could be expected from a farmer who, at each moment, might be ejected by the sale of the estate.[1] Usury,[2] the inveterate griev-ance of the city, had been discouraged by the Twelve Tables,[3] and abolished by the clamours of the people. It was revived by

1 The covenants of rent are defined in the Pandects (l. xix.) and the Code (l. iv. tit. lxv.). The quinquennium, or term of five years, appears to have been a custom rather than a law; but in France all leases of land were determined in nine years. This limitation was removed only in the year 1775 (Encyclopédie Méthodique, tom. i. de la Jurisprudence, p. 668, 669); and I am sorry to observe that it yet prevails in the beauteous and happy country where I am permitted to reside.

2 I might implicitly acquiesce in the sense and learning of the three books of G. Noodt, de fœnore et usuris (Opp. tom. i. p. 175–268). The interpretation of the *asses* or *centesimæ usuræ* at twelve, the *unciariæ* at one per cent., is maintained by the best critics and civilians: Noodt (l. ii. c. 2, p. 207), Gravina (Opp. p. 205, etc., 210), Heineccius (Antiquitat. ad Institut. l. iii. tit. xv.), Montesquieu (Esprit des Loix, l. xxii. c. 22, tom. ii. p. 36; Défense de l'Esprit des Loix, tom. iii. p. 478, etc.), and above all John Frederic Gronovius (de Pecunia Veteri, l. iii. c. 13, p. 213–227, and his three Antexegeses, p. 455–655), the founder, or at least the champion, of this probable opinion, which is, however, perplexed with some difficulties.

3 Primo xii Tabulis sancitum est ne quis unciario fœnore amplius exerceret (Tacit. Annal. vi. 16). Pour peu (says Montesquieu, Esprit des Loix, l. xxii. c. 22) qu'on soit versé dans l'histoire de Rome, on verra qu'une pareille loi ne devoit pas être l'ouvrage des décemvirs. Was Tacitus ignorant – or stupid? But the

their wants and idleness, tolerated by the discretion of the prætors, and finally determined by the Code of Justinian. Persons of illustrious rank were confined to the moderate profit of *four per cent.;* six was pronounced to be the ordinary and legal standard of interest; eight was allowed for the convenience of manufacturers and merchants; twelve was granted to nautical insurance, which the wiser ancients had not attempted to define; but, except in this perilous adventure, the practice of exorbitant usury was severely restrained.[1] The most simple interest was condemned by the clergy of the East and West;[2] but the sense of mutual benefit, which had triumphed over the laws of the republic, has resisted with equal firmness the decrees of the church, and even the prejudices of mankind.[3]

3. Nature and society impose the strict obligation of repairing an injury; and the sufferer by private injustice acquires a personal right and a legitimate action. If the property of another be intrusted to our care, the requisite degree of care may rise and fall according to the benefit which we derive from such temporary possession; we are seldom made responsible for inevitable accident, but the consequences of a voluntary fault must always be imputed to the author.[4] A Roman pursued and recovered his stolen goods by a civil action of theft; they might pass through

---

wiser and more virtuous patricians might sacrifice their avarice to their ambition, and might attempt to check the odious practice by such interest as no lender would accept, and such penalties as no debtor would incur.

1 Justinian has not condescended to give usury a place in his Institutes; but the necessary rules and restrictions are inserted in the Pandects (l. xxii. tit. i. ii.) and the Code (l. iv. tit. xxxii. xxxiii.).

2 The fathers are unanimous (Barbeyrac, Morale des Pères, p. 144, etc.): Cyprian, Lactantius, Basil, Chrysostom (see his frivolous arguments in Noodt, l. i. c. 7, p. 188), Gregory of Nyssa, Ambrose, Jerom, Augustin, and a host of councils and casuists.

3 Cato, Seneca, Plutarch, have loudly condemned the practice or abuse of usury. According to the etymology of *fœnus* and τοκός, the principal is supposed to *generate* the interest: a breed of barren metal, exclaims Shakspeare – and the stage is the echo of the public voice.

4 Sir William Jones has given an ingenious and rational Essay on the Law of Bailment (London, 1781, p. 127, in 8vo.). He is perhaps the only lawyer equally conversant with the year-books of Westminster, the Commentaries of Ulpian, the Attic pleadings of Isæus, and the sentences of Arabian and Persian cadhis.

a succession of pure and innocent hands, but nothing less than
a prescription of thirty years could extinguish his original claim.
They were restored by the sentence of the prætor, and the injury
was compensated by double, or three-fold, or even quadruple
damages, as the deed had been perpetrated by secret fraud or
open rapine, as the robber had been surprised in the fact or
detected by a subsequent research. The Aquilian law[1] defended
the living property of a citizen, his slaves and cattle, from the
stroke of malice or negligence: the highest price was allowed that
could be ascribed to the domestic animal at any moment of the
year preceding his death; a similar latitude of thirty days was
granted on the destruction of any other valuable effects. A personal injury is blunted or sharpened by the manners of the times
and the sensibility of the individual: the pain or the disgrace of
a word or blow cannot easily be appreciated by a pecuniary
equivalent. The rude jurisprudence of the decemvirs had confounded all hasty insults, which did not amount to the fracture
of a limb, by condemning the aggressor to the common penalty
of twenty-five *asses*. But the same denomination of money was
reduced, in three centuries, from a pound to the weight of half
an ounce; and the insolence of a wealthy Roman indulged himself in the cheap amusement of breaking and satisfying the law
of the Twelve Tables. Veratius ran through the streets striking
on the face the inoffensive passengers, and his attendant purse-
bearer immediately silenced their clamours by the legal tender of
twenty-five pieces of copper, about the value of one shilling.[2]
The equity of the prætors examined and estimated the distinct
merits of each particular complaint. In the adjudication of civil
damages, the magistrate assumed a right to consider the various
circumstances of time and place, of age and dignity, which may
aggravate the shame and sufferings of the injured person; but if
he admitted the idea of a fine, a punishment, an example, he
invaded the province, though perhaps he supplied the defects,
of the criminal law.

1 Noodt (Opp. tom. i. p. 137–172) has composed a separate treatise, ad
Legem Aquiliam (Pandect. l. ix. tit. ii.).
2 Aulus Gellius (Noct. Attic. xx. 1 [tom. ii. p. 284]) borrowed this story
from the Commentaries of Q. Labeo on the twelve tables.

The execution of the Alban dictator, who was dismembered by eight horses, is represented by Livy as the first and the last instance of Roman cruelty in the punishment of the most atrocious crimes.[1] But this act of justice or revenge was inflicted on a foreign enemy in the heat of victory, and at the command of a single man. The Twelve Tables afford a more decisive proof of the national spirit, since they were framed by the wisest of the senate and accepted by the free voices of the people; yet these laws, like the statutes of Draco,[2] are written in characters of blood.[3] They approve the inhuman and unequal principle of retaliation; and the forfeit of an eye for an eye, a tooth for a tooth, a limb for a limb, is rigorously exacted, unless the offender can redeem his pardon by a fine of three hundred pounds of copper. The decemvirs distributed with much liberality the slighter chastisements of flagellation and servitude; and nine crimes of a very different complexion are adjudged worthy of death. 1. Any act of *treason* against the state, or of correspondence with the public enemy. The mode of execution was painful and ignominious: the head of the degenerate Roman was shrouded in a veil, his hands were tied behind his back, and, after he had been scourged by the lictor, he was suspended in the midst of the forum on a cross, or inauspicious tree. 2. Nocturnal meetings in the city, whatever might be the pretence – of pleasure, or religion, or the public good. 3. The murder of a citizen; for which the common feelings of mankind demand the blood of the murderer. Poison is still more odious than the sword or dagger; and we are surprised to discover, in two flagitious events, how early such subtle wickedness had infected the simplicity of the republic

1 The narrative of Livy (i. 28) is weighty and solemn. At tu dictis, Albane, maneres, is a harsh reflection, unworthy of Virgil's humanity (Æneid. viii. 643). Heyne, with his usual good taste, observes that the subject was too horrid for the shield of Æneas (tom. iii. p. 229).

2 The age of Draco (Olympiad xxxix. 1) is fixed by Sir John Marsham (Canon Chronicus, p. 593–596) and Corsini (Fasti Attici, tom. iii. p. 62). For his laws, see the writers on the government of Athens, Sigonius, Meursius, Potter, etc.

3 The seventh, de delictis, of the twelve tables is delineated by Gravina (Opp. p. 292, 293, with a commentary, p. 214–230). Aulus Gellius (xx. 1) and the Collatio Legum Mosaicarum et Romanarum afford much original information.

and the chaste virtues of the Roman matrons.[1] The parricide, who violated the duties of nature and gratitude, was cast into the river or the sea, enclosed in a sack; and a cock, a viper, a dog, and a monkey, were successively added as the most suitable companions.[2] Italy produces no monkeys; but the want could never be felt till the middle of the sixth century first revealed the guilt of a parricide.[3] 4. The malice of an *incendiary*. After the previous ceremony of whipping, he himself was delivered to the flames; and in this example alone our reason is tempted to applaud the justice of retaliation. 5. *Judicial perjury*. The corrupt or malicious witness was thrown headlong from the Tarpeian rock to expiate his falsehood, which was rendered still more fatal by the severity of the penal laws and the deficiency of written evidence. 6. The corruption of a judge, who accepted bribes to pronounce an iniquitous sentence. 7. Libels and satires, whose rude strains sometimes disturbed the peace of an illiterate city. The author was beaten with clubs, a worthy chastisement; but it is not certain that he was left to expire under the blows of the executioner.[4] 8. The nocturnal mischief of damaging or destroying a neighbour's corn. The criminal was suspended as a

1 Livy mentions two remarkable and flagitious eras, of 3000 persons accused, and of 190 noble matrons convicted, of the crime of poisoning (xl. 43, viii. 18). Mr. Hume discriminates the ages of private and public virtue (Essays, vol. i. p. 22, 23). I would rather say that such ebullitions of mischief (as in France in the year 1680) are accidents and prodigies which leave no marks on the manners of a nation.

2 The twelve tables and Cicero (pro Roscio Amerino, c. 25, 26) are content with the sack; Seneca (Excerpt. Controvers. v. 4) adorns it with serpents; Juvenal pities the guiltless monkey (innoxia simia – Satir. xiii. 156). Adrian (apud Dositheum Magistrum, l. iii. c. 16, p. 874–876, with Schulting's Note), Modestinus (Pandect. xlviii. tit. ix. leg. 9), Constantine (Cod. l. ix. tit. xvii.), and Justinian (Institut. l. iv. tit. xviii.), enumerate all the companions of the parricide. But this fanciful execution was simplified in practice. Hodie tamen vivi exuruntur vel ad bestias dantur (Paul. Sentent. Recept. l. v. tit. xxiv. p. 512, edit. Schulting [Jurispr. Ante-Justin.]).

3 The first parricide at Rome was L. Ostius, after the second Punic war (Plutarch in Romulo [c. 22], tom. i. p. 57). During the Cimbric, P. Malleolus was guilty of the first matricide (Liv. Epitom. l. lxviii.).

4 Horace talks of the formidine fustis (l. ii. Epist. i. 154), but Cicero (de Republicâ, l. iv. apud Augustin. de Civitat. Dei, ix. 6, in Fragment. Philosoph. tom. iii. p. 393, edit. Olivet) affirms that the decemvirs made libels a capital offence: cum perpaucas res capite sanxissent – *perpaucas!*

grateful victim to Ceres. But the sylvan deities were less implacable, and the extirpation of a more valuable tree was compensated by the moderate fine of twenty-five pounds of copper.
9. Magical incantations; which had power, in the opinion of the
Latian shepherds, to exhaust the strength of an enemy, to extinguish his life, and to remove from their seats his deep-rooted
plantations. The cruelty of the Twelve Tables against insolvent
debtors still remains to be told; and I shall dare to prefer the
literal sense of antiquity to the specious refinements of modern
criticism.[1] After the judicial proof or confession of the debt,
thirty days of grace were allowed before a Roman was delivered
into the power of his fellow-citizen. In this private prison twelve
ounces of rice were his daily food; he might be bound with a
chain of fifteen pounds weight; and his misery was thrice exposed in the market-place, to solicit the compassion of his
friends and countrymen. At the expiration of sixty days the debt
was discharged by the loss of liberty or life; the insolvent debtor
was either put to death or sold in foreign slavery beyond the
Tiber: but, if several creditors were alike obstinate and unrelenting, they might legally dismember his body, and satiate their
revenge by this horrid partition. The advocates for this savage
law have insisted that it must strongly operate in deterring idleness and fraud from contracting debts which they were unable
to discharge; but experience would dissipate this salutary terror,
by proving that no creditor could be found to exact this unprofitable penalty of life or limb. As the manners of Rome were
insensibly polished, the criminal code of the decemvirs was abolished by the humanity of accusers, witnesses, and judges; and
impunity became the consequence of immoderate rigour. The
Porcian and Valerian laws prohibited the magistrates from inflicting on a free citizen any capital, or even corporal, punishment; and the obsolete statutes of blood were artfully, and
perhaps truly, ascribed to the spirit, not of patrician, but of regal,
tyranny.

1 Bynkershoek (Observat. Juris Rom. l. i. c. 1, in Opp. tom. i. p. 10, 11)
labours to prove that the creditors divided not the *body*, but the *price*, of the
insolvent debtor. Yet his interpretation is one perpetual harsh metaphor; nor
can he surmount the Roman authorities of Quintilian, Cæcilius, Favonius, and
Tertullian. See Aulus Gellius, Noct. Attic. xx. 1 [tom. ii. p. 285].

In the absence of penal laws and the insufficiency of civil
actions, the peace and justice of the city were imperfectly maintained by the private jurisdiction of the citizens. The malefactors
who replenish our gaols are the outcasts of society, and the
crimes for which they suffer may be commonly ascribed to ignorance, poverty, and brutal appetite. For the perpetration of
similar enormities, a vile plebeian might claim and abuse the
sacred character of a member of the republic; but on the proof
or suspicion of guilt the slave or the stranger was nailed to a
cross, and this strict and summary justice might be exercised
without restraint over the greatest part of the populace of Rome.
Each family contained a domestic tribunal, which was not confined, like that of the prætor, to the cognisance of external actions: virtuous principles and habits were inculcated by the
discipline of education, and the Roman father was accountable
to the state for the manners of his children, since he disposed
without appeal of their life, their liberty, and their inheritance.
In some pressing emergencies, the citizen was authorised to
avenge his private or public wrongs. The consent of the Jewish,
the Athenian, and the Roman laws, approved the slaughter of
the nocturnal thief; though in open daylight a robber could not
be slain without some previous evidence of danger and complaint. Whoever surprised an adulterer in his nuptial bed might
freely exercise his revenge;[1] the most bloody or wanton outrage
was excused by the provocation;[2] nor was it before the reign of
Augustus that the husband was reduced to weigh the rank of the
offender, or that the parent was condemned to sacrifice his
daughter with her guilty seducer. After the expulsion of the
kings, the ambitious Roman who should dare to assume their
title or imitate their tyranny was devoted to the infernal gods:
each of his fellow-citizens was armed with the sword of justice;

1 The first speech of Lysias (Reiske, Orator. Græc. tom. v. p. 2–48) is in
defence of a husband who had killed the adulterer. The rights of husbands and
fathers at Rome and Athens are discussed with much learning by Dr. Taylor
(Lectiones Lysiacæ, c. xi. in Reiske, tom. vi. p. 301–308).

2 See Casaubon ad Athenæum, l. i. c. 5, p. 19. Percurrent raphanique
mugilesque (Catull. [xv. 18] p. 41, 42, edit. Vossian.). Hunc mugilis intrat (Juvenal. Satir. x. 317). Hunc perminxere calones (Horat. l. i. Satir. ii. 44). Familiæ
stuprandum dedit [objecit] . . . fraudi non fuit (Val. Maxim. l. vi. c. 1, No. 13).

and the act of Brutus, however repugnant to gratitude or
prudence, had been already sanctified by the judgment of his
country.[1] The barbarous practice of wearing arms in the midst
of peace,[2] and the bloody maxims of honour, were unknown to
the Romans; and during the two purest ages, from the establishment of equal freedom to the end of the Punic wars, the city
was never disturbed by sedition, and rarely polluted with atrocious crimes. The failure of penal laws was more sensibly felt
when every vice was inflamed by faction at home and dominion abroad. In the time of Cicero each private citizen enjoyed
the privilege of anarchy — each minister of the republic was
exalted to the temptations of regal power, and their virtues are
entitled to the warmest praise as the spontaneous fruits of nature or philosophy. After a triennial indulgence of lust, rapine,
and cruelty, Verres, the tyrant of Sicily, could only be sued for
the pecuniary restitution of three hundred thousand pounds sterling; and such was the temper of the laws, the judges, and perhaps the accuser himself,[3] that, on refunding a thirteenth part
of his plunder, Verres could retire to an easy and luxurious
exile.[4]

The first imperfect attempt to restore the proportion of
crimes and punishments was made by the dictator Sylla, who, in
the midst of his sanguinary triumph, aspired to restrain the
licence rather than to oppress the liberty of the Romans. He
gloried in the arbitrary proscription of four thousand seven

1 This law is noticed by Livy (ii. 8) and Plutarch (in Publicola [c. 12], tom.
i. p. 187), and it fully justifies the public opinion on the death of Cæsar, which
Suetonius could publish under the Imperial government. Jure cæsus existimatur
(in Julio, c. 76). Read the letters that passed between Cicero and Matius a few
months after the ides of March (ad Fam. xi. 27, 28).

2 Πρῶτοι δὲ Ἀθηναῖοι τόν τε σίδηρον κατέθεντο. Thucydid. l. i. c. 6. The
historian who considers this circumstance as the test of civilisation would disdain the barbarism of a European court.

3 He first rated at *millies* (£800, 000) the damages of Sicily (Divinatio in
Cæcilium, c. 5), which he afterwards reduced to *quadringenties* (£320,000 — 1 Actio
in Verrem, c. 18), and was finally content with *tricies* (£24,000). Plutarch (in
Ciceron. [c. 8] tom. iii. p. 1584) has not dissembled the popular suspicion and
report.

4 Verres lived near thirty years after his trial, till the second triumvirate,
when he was proscribed by the taste of Mark Antony for the sake of his
Corinthian plate (Plin. Hist. Natur. xxxiv. 3).

hundred citizens.[1] But, in the character of a legislator, he respected the prejudices of the times; and instead of pronouncing
a sentence of death against the robber or assassin, the general
who betrayed an army or the magistrate who ruined a province,
Sylla was content to aggravate the pecuniary damages by the
penalty of exile, or, in more constitutional language, by the in-
terdiction of fire and water. The Cornelian, and afterwards the
Pompeian and Julian laws, introduced a new system of criminal
jurisprudence;[2] and the emperors, from Augustus to Justinian,
disguised their increasing rigour under the names of the original
authors. But the invention and frequent use of *extraordinary pains*
proceeded from the desire to extend and conceal the progress
of despotism. In the condemnation of illustrious Romans, the
senate was always prepared to confound, at the will of their
masters, the judicial and legislative powers. It was the duty of
the governors to maintain the peace of their province by the
arbitrary and rigid administration of justice; the freedom of the
city evaporated in the extent of empire, and the Spanish malefactor who claimed the privilege of a Roman was elevated by
the command of Galba on a fairer and more lofty cross.[3] Occasional rescripts issued from the throne to decide the questions
which, by their novelty or importance, appeared to surpass the
authority and discernment of a proconsul. Transportation and
beheading were reserved for honourable persons; meaner criminals were either hanged, or burnt, or buried in the mines, or
exposed to the wild beasts of the amphitheatre. Armed robbers

1 Such is the number assigned by Valerius Maximus (l. ix. c. 2, No. 1).
Florus (iii. 21) distinguishes 2000 senators and knights. Appian (de Bell. Civil
l. i. c. 95, tom. ii. p. 133, edit. Schweighaüser) more accurately computes 40
victims of the senatorian rank and 1600 of the equestrian census or order.

2 For the penal laws (Leges Corneliæ, Pompeiæ, Juliæ, of Sylla, Pompey,
and the Cæsars), see the sentences of Paulus (l. iv. tit. xviii.–xxx. p. 497–528,
edit. Schulting), the Gregorian Code (Fragment. l. xix. p. 705, 706, in Schulting),
the Collatio Legum Mosaicarum et Romanarum (tit. i.–xv.), the Theodosian
Code (l. ix.), the Code of Justinian (l. ix.), the Pandects (xlviii.), the Institutes
(l. iv. tit. xviii.), and the Greek version of Theophilus (p. 917–926).

3 It was a guardian who had poisoned his ward. The crime was atrocious: yet the punishment is reckoned by Suetonius (c. 9) among the acts
in which Galba showed himself acer, vehemens, et in delictis coercendis im-
modicus.

were pursued and extirpated as the enemies of society; the driving away horses or cattle was made a capital offence;[1] but simple theft was uniformly considered as a mere civil and private injury. The degrees of guilt and the modes of punishment were too often determined by the discretion of the rulers, and the subject was left in ignorance of the legal danger which he might incur by every action of his life.

A sin, a vice, a crime, are the objects of theology, ethics, and jurisprudence. Whenever their judgments agree, they corroborate each other; but as often as they differ, a prudent legislator appreciates the guilt and punishment according to the measure of social injury. On this principle the most daring attack on the life and property of a private citizen is judged less atrocious than the crime of treason or rebellion, which invades the *majesty* of the republic: the obsequious civilians unanimously pronounced that the republic is contained in the person of its chief, and the edge of the Julian law was sharpened by the incessant diligence of the emperors. The licentious commerce of the sexes may be tolerated as an impulse of nature, or forbidden as a source of disorder and corruption; but the fame, the fortunes, the family of the husband, are seriously injured by the adultery of the wife. The wisdom of Augustus, after curbing the freedom of revenge, applied to this domestic offence the animadversion of the laws; and the guilty parties, after the payment of heavy forfeitures and fines, were condemned to long or perpetual exile in two separate islands.[2] Religion pronounces an equal censure against the infidelity of the husband, but, as it is not accompanied by the same civil effects, the wife was never permitted to vindicate her

1 The abactores or abigeatores, who drove one horse, or two mares or oxen, or five hogs, or ten goats, were subject to capital punishment (Paul. Sentent. Recept. l. iv. tit. xviii. p. 497, 498). Hadrian (ad Concil. Bæticæ), most severe where the offence was most frequent, condemns the criminals, ad gladium, ludi damnationem (Ulpian, de Officio Proconsulis, l. viii. in Collatione Legum Mosaic. et Rom. tit. xi. p. 236 [ed. Cannegieter, 1774]).

2 Till the publication of the Julius Paulus of Schulting (l. ii. tit. xxvi. p. 317–323), it was affirmed and believed that the Julian laws punished adultery with death; and the mistake arose from the fraud or error of Tribonian. Yet Lipsius had suspected the truth from the narratives of Tacitus (Annal. iii. 50, iii. 24, iv. 42), and even from the practice of Augustus, who distinguished the *treasonable* frailties of his female kindred.

wrongs;[1] and the distinction of simple or double adultery, so familiar and so important in the canon law, is unknown to the jurisprudence of the Code and Pandects. I touch with reluctance, and despatch with impatience, a more odious vice, of which modesty rejects the name, and nature abominates the idea. The primitive Romans were infected by the example of the Etruscans[2] and Greeks;[3] in the mad abuse of prosperity and power every pleasure that is innocent was deemed insipid; and the Scatinian law,[4] which had been extorted by an act of violence, was insensibly abolished by the lapse of time and the multitude of criminals. By this law the rape, perhaps the seduction, of an ingenuous youth was compensated as a personal injury by the poor damages of ten thousand sesterces, or fourscore pounds; the ravisher might be slain by the resistance or revenge of chastity; and I wish to believe that at Rome, as in Athens, the voluntary and effeminate deserter of his sex was degraded from the honours and the rights of a citizen.[5] But the practice of vice was not discouraged by the severity of opinion: the indelible stain of manhood was confounded with the more venial transgressions of fornication and adultery; nor was the licentious lover exposed to the same dishonour which he impressed on the male or female

1 In cases of adultery Severus confined to the husband the right of public accusation (Cod. Justinian. l. ix. tit. ix. leg. 1). Nor is this privilege unjust – so different are the effects of male or female infidelity.

2 Timon [Timæus] (l. i.) and Theopompus (l. xliii. apud Athenæum, l. xii. p. 517 [c. 14, tom. iv. p. 422, ed. Schweigh.]) describe the luxury and lust of the Etruscans: πολὺ μέν τοι γε χαίρουσι συνόντες τοῖς παισὶ καὶ τοῖς μειρακίοις. About the same period (A.U.C. 445) the Roman youth studied in Etruria (liv. ix. 36).

3 The Persians had been corrupted in the same school: ἀπ᾽ Ἑλλήνων μαθόντες παισὶ μίσγονται (Herodot. l. i. c. 135). A curious dissertation might be formed on the introduction of pæderasty after the time of Homer, its progress among the Greeks of Asia and Europe, the vehemence of their passions, and the thin device of virtue and friendship which amused the philosophers of Athens. But, scelera ostendi oportet dum puniuntur, abscondi flagitia.

4 The name, the date, and the provisions of this law are equally doubtful (Gravina, Opp. p. 432, 433; Heineccius, Hist. Jur. Rom. No. 108; Ernesti, Clav. Ciceron. in Indice Legum). But I will observe that the *nefanda* Venus of the honest German is styled *aversa* by the more polite Italian.

5 See the oration of Æschines against the catamite Timarchus (in Reiske, Orator. Græc. tom. iii. p. 21–184).

partner of his guilt. From Catullus to Juvenal,[1] the poets accuse and celebrate the degeneracy of the times; and the reformation of manners was feebly attempted by the reason and authority of the civilians, till the most virtuous of the Cæsars proscribed the sin against nature as a crime against society.[2]

A new spirit of legislation, respectable even in its error, arose in the empire with the religion of Constantine.[3] The laws of Moses were received as the divine original of justice, and the Christian princes adapted their penal statutes to the degrees of moral and religious turpitude. Adultery was first declared to be a capital offence: the frailty of the sexes was assimilated to poison or assassination, to sorcery or parricide; the same penalties were inflicted on the passive and active guilt of pæderasty; and all criminals, of free or servile condition, were either drowned, or beheaded, or cast alive into the avenging flames. The adulterers were spared by the common sympathy of mankind; but the lovers of their own sex were pursued by general and pious indignation: the impure manners of Greece still prevailed in the cities of Asia, and every vice was fomented by the celibacy of the monks and clergy. Justinian relaxed the punishment at least of female infidelity: the guilty spouse was only condemned to solitude and penance, and at the end of two years she might be recalled to the arms of a forgiving husband. But the same emperor declared himself the implacable enemy of unmanly lust, and the cruelty of his persecution can scarcely be excused by the purity of his motives.[4] In defiance of every principle of justice,

1 A crowd of disgraceful passages will force themselves on the memory of the classic reader: I will only remind him of the cool declaration of Ovid: —
Odi concubitus qui non utrumque resolvunt.
Hoc est quod puerûm tangar amore *minus*.

2 Ælius Lampridius, in Vit. Heliogabal. in Hist. August. p. 112. Aurelius Victor, in Philippo [de Cæsar. c. 28], Codex Theodos. l. ix. tit. vii. leg. 6, and Godefroy's Commentary, tom. iii. p. 63. Theodosius abolished the subterraneous brothels of Rome, in which the prostitution of both sexes was acted with impunity.

3 See the laws of Constantine and his successors against adultery, sodomy, etc., in the Theodosian (l. ix. tit. vii. leg. 7, l. xi. tit. xxxvi. leg. 1, 4) and Justinian Codes (l. ix. tit. ix. leg. 30, 31). These princes speak the language of passion as well as of justice, and fraudulently ascribe their own severity to the first Cæsars.

4 Justinian, Novel. lxxvii. cxxxiv. cxli.; Procopius in Anecdot. c. 11, 16 [tom. iii. p. 76, 99, ed. Bonn], with the notes of Alemannus; Theophanes, p. 151 [ed.

he stretched to past as well as future offences the operations of his edicts, with the previous allowance of a short respite for confession and pardon. A painful death was inflicted by the amputation of the sinful instrument, or the insertion of sharp reeds into the pores and tubes of most exquisite sensibility; and Justinian defended the propriety of the execution, since the criminals would have lost their hands had they been convicted of sacrilege. In this state of disgrace and agony two bishops, Isaiah of Rhodes and Alexander of Diospolis, were dragged through the streets of Constantinople, while their brethren were admonished by the voice of a crier to observe this awful lesson, and not to pollute the sanctity of their character. Perhaps these prelates were innocent. A sentence of death and infamy was often founded on the slight and suspicious evidence of a child or a servant: the guilt of the green faction, of the rich, and of the enemies of Theodora, was presumed by the judges, and pæderasty became the crime of those to whom no crime could be imputed. A French philosopher[1] has dared to remark that whatever is secret must be doubtful, and that our natural horror of vice may be abused as an engine of tyranny. But the favourable persuasion of the same writer, that a legislator may confide in the taste and reason of mankind, is impeached by the unwelcome discovery of the antiquity and extent of the disease.[2]

The free citizens of Athens and Rome enjoyed in all criminal cases the invaluable privilege of being tried by their country.[3]

Par.; tom. i. p. 271, ed. Bonn]; Cedrenus, p. 368 [ed. Par.; tom. i. p. 645, ed. Bonn]; Zonaras, l. xiv. [c. 7] p. 64.

1 Montesquieu, Esprit des Loix, l. xii. c. 6. That eloquent philosopher conciliates the rights of liberty and of nature, which should never be placed in opposition to each other.

2 For the corruption of Palestine, 2000 years before the Christian era, see the history and laws of Moses. Ancient Gaul is stigmatised by Diodorus Siculus (tom. i. l. v. [c. 32] p. 356), China by the Mahometan and Christian travellers (Ancient Relations of India and China, p. 34, translated by Renaudot, and his bitter critic the Père Premare, Lettres Edifiantes, tom. xix. p. 435), and native America by the Spanish historians (Garcilasso de la Vega, l. iii. c. 13, Rycaut's translation; and Dictionnaire de Bayle, tom. iii. p. 88). I believe, and hope, that the negroes, in their own country, were exempt from this moral pestilence.

3 The important subject of the public questions and judgments at Rome is explained with much learning, and in a classic style, by Charles Sigonius (l. iii. de Judiciis, in Opp. tom. iii. p. 679–864); and a good abridgment may be found

1. The administration of justice is the most ancient office of a prince: it was exercised by the Roman kings, and abused by Tarquin, who alone, without law or council, pronounced his arbitrary judgments. The first consuls succeeded to this regal prerogative; but the sacred right of appeal soon abolished the jurisdiction of the magistrates, and all public causes were decided by the supreme tribunal of the people. But a wild democracy, superior to the forms, too often disdains the essential principles, of justice; the pride of despotism was envenomed by plebeian envy; and the heroes of Athens might sometimes applaud the happiness of the Persian, whose fate depended on the caprice of a *single* tyrant. Some salutary restraints, imposed by the people on their own passions, were at once the cause and effect of the gravity and temperance of the Romans. The right of accusation was confined to the magistrates. A vote of the thirty-five tribes could inflict a fine; but the cognisance of all capital crimes was reserved by a fundamental law to the assembly of the centuries, in which the weight of influence and property was sure to preponderate. Repeated proclamations and adjournments were interposed, to allow time for prejudice and resentment to subside; the whole proceeding might be annulled by a seasonable omen or the opposition of a tribune, and such popular trials were commonly less formidable to innocence than they were favourable to guilt. But this union of the judicial and legislative powers left it doubtful whether the accused party was pardoned or acquitted; and, in the defence of an illustrious client, the orators of Rome and Athens address their arguments to the policy and benevolence, as well as to the justice, of their sovereign. 2. The task of convening the citizens for the trial of each offender became more difficult, as the citizens and the offenders continually multiplied, and the ready expedient was adopted of delegating the jurisdiction of the people to the ordinary magistrates or to extraordinary *inquisitors*. In the first ages these questions were rare and occasional. In the beginning of the seventh century of Rome they were made perpetual: four prætors were annually

in the République Romaine of Beaufort (tom. ii. l. v. p. 1–121). Those who wish for more abstruse law may study Noodt (de Jurisdictione et Imperio Libri duo, tom. i. p. 93–134), Heineccius (ad Pandect. l. i. et ii. ad Institut. l. iv. tit. xvii. Element. ad Antiquitat.), and Gravina (Opp. 230–251).

empowered to sit in judgment on the state offences of treason, extortion, peculation, and bribery; and Sylla added new prætors and new questions for those crimes which more directly injure the safety of individuals. By these *inquisitors* the trial was prepared and directed; but they could only pronounce the sentence of the majority of *judges*, who, with some truth and more prejudice, have been compared to the English juries.[1] To discharge this important though burdensome office, an annual list of ancient and respectable citizens was formed by the prætor. After many constitutional struggles, they were chosen in equal numbers from the senate, the equestrian order, and the people; four hundred and fifty were appointed for single questions, and the various rolls or *decuries* of judges must have contained the names of some thousand Romans, who represented the judicial authority of the state. In each particular cause a sufficient number was drawn from the urn; their integrity was guarded by an oath; the mode of ballot secured their independence; the suspicion of partiality was removed by the mutual challenges of the accuser and defendant; and the judges of Milo, by the retrenchment of fifteen on each side, were reduced to fifty-one voices or tablets, of acquittal, of condemnation, or of favourable doubt.[2] 3. In his civil jurisdiction the prætor of the city was truly a judge, and almost a legislator; but, as soon as he had prescribed the action of law, he often referred to a delegate the determination of the fact. With the increase of legal proceedings, the tribunal of the centumvirs, in which he presided, acquired more weight and reputation. But whether he acted alone or with the advice of his council, the most absolute powers might be trusted to a magistrate who was annually chosen by the votes of the people. The rules and precautions of freedom have required some explanation; the order of despotism is simple and inanimate. Before the

1   The office, both at Rome and in England, must be considered as an occasional duty, and not a magistracy or profession. But the obligation of a unanimous verdict is peculiar to our laws, which condemn the juryman to undergo the torture from whence they have exempted the criminal.

2   We are indebted for this interesting fact to a fragment of Asconius Pedianus, who flourished under the reign of Tiberius. The loss of his Commentaries on the Orations of Cicero has deprived us of a valuable fund of historical and legal knowledge.

age of Justinian, or perhaps of Diocletian, the decuries of Roman judges had sunk to an empty title; the humble advice of the assessors might be accepted or despised; and in each tribunal the civil and criminal jurisdiction was administered by a single magistrate, who was raised and disgraced by the will of the emperor.

A Roman accused of any capital crime might prevent the sentence of the law by voluntary exile or death. Till his guilt had been legally proved, his innocence was presumed and his person was free; till the votes of the last *century* had been counted and declared, he might peaceably secede to any of the allied cities of Italy, or Greece, or Asia.[1] His fame and fortunes were preserved, at least to his children, by this civil death; and he might still be happy in every rational and sensual enjoyment, if a mind accustomed to the ambitious tumult of Rome could support the uniformity and silence of Rhodes or Athens. A bolder effort was required to escape from the tyranny of the Cæsars; but this effort was rendered familiar by the maxims of the Stoics, the example of the bravest Romans, and the legal encouragements of suicide. The bodies of condemned criminals were exposed to public ignominy, and their children, a more serious evil, were reduced to poverty by the confiscation of their fortunes. But, if the victims of Tiberius and Nero anticipated the decree of the prince or senate, their courage and despatch were recompensed by the applause of the public, the decent honours of burial, and the validity of their testaments.[2] The exquisite avarice and cruelty of Domitian appears to have deprived the unfortunate of this last consolation, and it was still denied even by the clemency of the Antonines. A voluntary death, which, in the case of a capital offence, intervened between the accusation and the sentence, was admitted as a confession of guilt, and the spoils of the deceased were seized by the inhuman claims of the treasury.[3] Yet

1 Polyb. l. vi. [c. 14] p. 643. The extension of the empire and *city* of Rome obliged the exile to seek a more distant place of retirement.

2 Qui de se statuebant, humabantur corpora, manebant testamenta; pretium festinandi. Tacit. Annal. vi. 29, with the Notes of Lipsius.

3 Julius Paulus (Sentent. Recept. l. v. tit. xii. p. 476), the Pandects (l. xlviii. tit. xxi.), the Code (l. ix. tit. L.), Bynkershoek (tom. i. p. 59, Observat. J. C. R. iv. 4), and Montesquieu (Esprit des Loix, l. xxix. c. 9), define the civil limitations of the liberty and privileges of suicide. The criminal penalties are the production of a later and darker age.

the civilians have always respected the natural right of a citizen
to dispose of his life; and the posthumous disgrace invented by
Tarquin[1] to check the despair of his subjects was never revived
or imitated by succeeding tyrants. The powers of this world have
indeed lost their dominion over him who is resolved on death,
and his arm can only be restrained by the religious apprehension
of a future state. Suicides are enumerated by Virgil among the
unfortunate, rather than the guilty,[2] and the poetical fables of the
infernal shades could not seriously influence the faith or practice
of mankind. But the precepts of the Gospel or the church have
at length imposed a pious servitude on the minds of Christians,
and condemn them to expect, without a murmur, the last stroke
of disease or the executioner.

The penal statues form a very small proportion of the sixty-
two books of the Code and Pandects, and in all judicial proceeding the life or death of a citizen is determined with less caution
and delay than the most ordinary question of covenant or inheritance. This singular distinction, though something may be
allowed for the urgent necessity of defending the peace of society, is derived from the nature of criminal and civil jurisprudence. Our duties to the state are simple and uniform; the
law by which he is condemned is inscribed not only on brass or
marble, but on the conscience of the offender, and his guilt is
commonly proved by the testimony of a single fact. But our
relations to each other are various and infinite; our obligations
are created, annulled, and modified by injuries, benefits, and
promises; and the interpretation of voluntary contracts and testaments, which are often dictated by fraud or ignorance, affords
a long and laborious exercise to the sagacity of the judge. The
business of life is multiplied by the extent of commerce and
dominion, and the residence of the parties in the distant provinces of an empire is productive of doubt, delay, and inevitable

1 Plin. Hist. Natur. xxxvi. 24. When he fatigued his subjects in building the
Capitol, many of the labourers were provoked to despatch themselves: he nailed
their dead bodies to crosses.

2 The sole resemblance of a violent and premature death has engaged Virgil
(Æneid. vi. 434–439) to confound suicides with infants, lovers, and persons
unjustly condemned. Heyne, the best of his editors, is at a loss to deduce the
idea, or ascertain the jurisprudence, of the Roman poet.

appeals from the local to the supreme magistrate. Justinian, the Greek emperor of Constantinople and the East, was the legal successor of the Latian shepherd who had planted a colony on the banks of the Tiber. In a period of thirteen hundred years the laws had reluctantly followed the changes of government and manners; and the laudable desire of conciliating ancient names with recent institutions destroyed the harmony, and swelled the magnitude, of the obscure and irregular system. The laws which excuse on any occasions the ignorance of their subjects, confess their own imperfections; the civil jurisprudence, as it was abridged by Justinian, still continued a mysterious science and a profitable trade, and the innate perplexity of the study was involved in tenfold darkness by the private industry of the practitioners. The expense of the pursuit sometimes exceeded the value of the prize, and the fairest rights were abandoned by the poverty or prudence of the claimants. Such costly justice might tend to abate the spirit of litigation, but the unequal pressure serves only to increase the influence of the rich, and to aggravate the misery of the poor. By these dilatory and expensive proceedings the wealthy pleader obtains a more certain advantage than he could hope from the accidental corruption of his judge. The experience of an abuse from which our own age and country are not perfectly exempt may sometimes provoke a generous indignation, and extort the hasty wish of exchanging our elaborate jurisprudence for the simple and summary decrees of a Turkish cadhi. Our calmer reflection will suggest that such forms and delays are necessary to guard the person and property of the citizen; that the discretion of the judge is the first engine of tyranny; and that the laws of a free people should foresee and determine every question that may probably arise in the exercise of power and the transactions of industry. But the government of Justinian united the evils of liberty and servitude, and the Romans were oppressed at the same time by the multiplicity of their laws and the arbitrary will of their master.

CHAPTER XLV

Reign of the younger Justin – Embassy of the Avars – Their Settlement on the Danube – Conquest of Italy by the Lombards – Adoption and Reign of Tiberius – Of Maurice – State of Italy under the Lombards and the Exarchs – Of Ravenna – Distress of Rome – Character and Pontificate of Gregory the First

DURING the last years of Justinian, his infirm mind was devoted to heavenly contemplation, and he neglected the business of the lower world. His subjects were impatient of the long continuance of his life and reign: yet all who were capable of reflection apprehended the moment of his death, which might involve the capital in tumult and the empire in civil war. Seven nephews[1] of the childless monarch, the sons or grandsons of his brother and sister, had been educated in the splendour of a princely fortune; they had been shown in high commands to the provinces and armies; their characters were known, their followers were zealous, and, as the jealousy of age postponed the declaration of a successor, they might expect with equal hopes the inheritance of their uncle. He expired in his palace, after a reign of thirty-eight years; and the decisive opportunity was embraced by the friends of Justin, the son of Vigilantia.[2] At the hour of midnight his domestics were awakened by an importunate crowd, who thundered at his door, and obtained admittance by revealing themselves to be the principal members of the senate. These welcome deputies announced the recent and momentous secret of the emperor's decease; reported, or perhaps invented, his dying choice of the best beloved and most deserving of his nephews; and conjured Justin to prevent the disorders of the multitude, if they should perceive, with the return of light, that they were left without a master. After composing his

---

1 See the family of Justin and Justinian in the Familiæ Byzantinæ of Du-cange, p. 89–101. The devout civilians, Ludewig (in Vit. Justinian. p. 131) and Heineccius (Hist. Juris Roman. p. 374) have since illustrated the genealogy of their favourite prince.

2 In the story of Justin's elevation I have translated into simple and concise prose the eight hundred verses of the two first books of Corippus, De Laudibus Justini, Appendix Hist. Byzant. p. 401–416, Rome, 1777 [p. 166–187, ed. Bonn].

countenance to surprise, sorrow, and decent modesty, Justin, by the advice of his wife Sophia, submitted to the authority of the senate. He was conducted with speed and silence to the palace; the guards saluted their new sovereign; and the martial and religious rites of his coronation were diligently accomplished. By the hands of the proper officers he was invested with the Imperial garments, the red buskins, white tunic, and purple robe. A fortunate soldier, whom he instantly promoted to the rank of tribune, encircled his neck with a military collar; four robust youths exalted him on a shield; he stood firm and erect to receive the adoration of his subjects; and their choice was sanctified by the benediction of the patriarch, who imposed the diadem on the head of an orthodox prince. The hippodrome was already filled with innumerable multitudes; and no sooner did the emperor appear on his throne than the voices of the blue and the green factions were confounded in the same loyal acclamations. In the speeches which Justin addressed to the senate and people he promised to correct the abuses which had disgraced the age of his predecessor, displayed the maxims of a just and beneficent government, and declared that, on the approaching calends of January,[1] he would revive in his own person the name and liberality of a Roman consul. The immediate discharge of his uncle's debts exhibited a solid pledge of his faith and generosity: a train of porters, laden with bags of gold, advanced into the midst of the hippodrome, and the hopeless creditors of Justinian accepted this equitable payment as a voluntary gift. Before the end of three years his example was imitated and surpassed by the empress Sophia, who delivered many indigent citizens from the weight of debt and usury: an act of benevolence the best entitled to gratitude, since it relieves the most intolerable distress; but in which the bountry of a prince is the most liable to be abused by the claims of prodigality and fraud.[2]

1 It is surprising how Pagi (Critica, in Annal. Baron. tom. ii. p. 639) could be tempted by any chronicles to contradict the plain and decisive text of Corippus (vicina dona, l. ii. 354, vicina dies, l. iv. 1), and to postpone, till A.D. 567, the consulship of Justin.

2 Theophan. Chronograph. p. 205 [tom. i. p. 374, ed. Bonn]. Whenever Cedrenus or Zonaras are mere transcribers, it is superfluous to allege their testimony.

On the seventh day of his reign Justin gave audience to the ambassadors of the Avars, and the scene was decorated to impress the barbarians with astonishment, veneration, and terror. From the palace gate, the spacious courts and long porticoes were lined with the lofty crests and gilt bucklers of the guards, who presented their spears and axes with more confidence than they would have shown in a field of battle. The officers who exercised the power, or attended the person, of the prince, were attired in their richest habits, and arranged according to the military and civil order of the hierarchy. When the veil of the sanctuary was withdrawn, the ambassadors beheld the emperor of the East on his throne, beneath a canopy, or dome, which was supported by four columns, and crowned with a winged figure of Victory. In the first emotions of surprise, they submitted to the servile adoration of the Byzantine court; but, as soon as they rose from the ground, Targetius, the chief of the embassy, expressed the freedom and pride of a barbarian. He extolled, by the tongue of his interpreter, the greatness of the chagan, by whose clemency the kingdoms of the South were permitted to exist, whose victorious subjects had traversed the frozen rivers of Scythia, and who now covered the banks of the Danube with innumerable tents. The late emperor had cultivated, with annual and costly gifts, the friendship of a grateful monarch, and the enemies of Rome had respected the allies of the Avars. The same prudence would instruct the nephew of Justinian to imitate the liberality of his uncle, and to purchase the blessings of peace from an invincible people, who delighted and excelled in the exercise of war. The reply of the emperor was delivered in the same strain of haughty defiance, and he derived his confidence from the God of the Christians, the ancient glory of Rome, and the recent triumphs of Justinian. 'The empire,' said he, 'abounds with men and horses, and arms sufficient to defend our frontiers and to chastise the barbarians. You offer aid, you threaten hostilities: we despise your enmity and your aid. The conquerors of the Avars solicit our alliance; shall we dread their fugitives and exiles?' The bounty of our

1 Corippus, l. iii. 390. The unquestionable sense relates to the Turks, the conquerors of the Avars; but the word *scultor* has no apparent meaning, and the sole MS. of Corippus, from whence the first edition (1581, apud Plantin) was

uncle was granted to your misery, to your humble prayers. From us you shall receive a more important obligation, the knowledge of your own weakness. Retire from our presence; the lives of ambassadors are safe; and, if you return to implore our pardon, perhaps you will taste of our benevolence.'[1] On the report of his ambassadors, the chagan was awed by the apparent firmness of a Roman emperor of whose character and resources he was ignorant. Instead of executing his threats against the Eastern empire, he marched into the poor and savage countries of Germany, which were subject to the dominion of the Franks. After two doubtful battles he consented to retire, and the Austrasian king relieved the distress of his camp with an immediate supply of corn and cattle.[2] Such repeated disappointments had chilled the spirit of the Avars, and their power would have dissolved away in the Sarmatian desert, if the alliance of Alboin, king of the Lombards, had not given a new object to their arms, and a lasting settlement to their wearied fortunes.

While Alboin served under his father's standard, he encountered in battle, and transpierced with his lance, the rival prince of the Gepidæ. The Lombards, who applauded such early prowess, requested his father, with unanimous acclamations, that the heroic youth, who had shared the dangers of the field, might be admitted to the feast of victory. 'You are not unmindful,' replied the inflexible Audoin, 'of the wise customs of our ancestors. Whatever may be his merit, a prince is incapable of sitting at table with his father till he has received his arms from a

printed, is no longer visible. The last editor, Foggini of Rome, has inserted the conjectural emendation of *soldan*: but the proofs of Ducange (Joinville, Dissert. xvi. p. 238–240), for the early use of this title among the Turks and Persians, are weak or ambiguous. And I must incline to the authority of D'Herbelot (Bibliothèque Orient. p. 825), who ascribes the word to the Arabic and Chaldæan tongues, and the date to the beginning of the eleventh century, when it was bestowed by the khalif of Bagdad on Mahmud, prince of Gazna, and conqueror of India.

1 For these characteristic speeches, compare the verse of Corippus (l. iii. 266–401) with the prose of Menander (Excerpt. Legation. p. 102, 103 [ed. Par.; p. 287 *sq.*, ed. Bonn]). Their diversity proves that they did not copy each other; their resemblance, that they drew from a common original.

2 For the Austrasian war, see Menander (Excerpt. Legat. p. 110 [c. 11, p. 303, de. Bonn]), Gregory of Tours (Hist. Franc. l. iv. c. 29), and Paul the Deacon (de Gest. Langobard. l. ii. c. 10).

foreign and royal hand.' Alboin bowed with reverence to the institutions of his country, selected forty companions, and boldly visited the court of Turisund, king of the Gepidæ, who embraced and entertained, according to the laws of hospitality, the murderer of his son. At the banquet, whilst Alboin occupied the seat of the youth whom he had slain, a tender remembrance arose in the mind of Turisund. 'How dear is that place – how hateful is that person!' were the words that escaped, with a sigh, from the indignant father. His grief exasperated the national resentment of the Gepidæ; and Cunimund, his surviving son, was provoked by wine, or fraternal affection, to the desire of vengeance. 'The Lombards,' said the rude barbarian, 'resemble, in figure and in smell, the mares of our Sarmatian plains.' And this insult was a coarse allusion to the white bands which enveloped their legs. 'Add another resemblance,' replied an audacious Lombard; 'you have felt how strongly they kick. Visit the plain of Asfeld, and seek for the bones of thy brother: they are mingled with those of the vilest animals.' The Gepidæ, a nation of warriors, started from their seats, and the fearless Alboin, with his forty companions, laid their hands on their swords. The tumult was appeased by the venerable interposition of Turisund. He saved his own honour, and the life of his guest; and, after the solemn rites of investiture, dismissed the stranger in the bloody arms of his son, the gift of a weeping parent. Alboin returned in triumph; and the Lombards, who celebrated his matchless intrepidity, were compelled to praise the virtues of an enemy.' In this extraordinary visit he had probably seen the daughter of Cunimund, who soon after ascended the throne of the Gepidæ. Her name was Rosamond, an appellation expressive of female beauty, and which our own history or romance has consecrated to amorous tales. The king of the Lombards (the father of Alboin no longer lived) was contracted to the grand-daughter of Clovis; but the restraints of faith and policy soon yielded to the hope of possessing the fair Rosamond, and of insulting her family and nation. The arts of persuasion were tried without success; and the impatient lover, by force and stratagem, obtained the object of

1 Paul Warnefrid. the deacon of Friuli, de Gest. Langobard. l. i. c. 23, 24. His pictures of national manners, though rudely sketched, are more lively and faithful than those of Bede or Gregory of Tours.

his desires. War was the consequence which he foresaw and solicited; but the Lombards could not long withstand the furious assault of the Gepidæ, who were sustained by a Roman army. And, as the offer of marriage was rejected with contempt, Alboin was compelled to relinquish his prey, and to partake of the disgrace which he had inflicted on the house of Cunimund.[1]

When a public quarrel is envenomed by private injuries, a blow that is not mortal or decisive can be productive only of a short truce, which allows the unsuccessful combatant to sharpen his arms for a new encounter. The strength of Alboin had been found unequal to the gratification of his love, ambition, and revenge: he condescended to implore the formidable aid of the chagan; and the arguments that he employed are expressive of the art and policy of the barbarians. In the attack of the Gepidæ he had been prompted by the just desire of extirpating a people whom their alliance with the Roman empire had rendered the common enemies of the nations, and the personal adversaries of the chagan. If the forces of the Avars and the Lombards should unite in this glorious quarrel, the victory was secure and the reward inestimable: the Danube, the Hebrus, Italy, and Constantinople would be exposed, without a barrier, to their invincible arms. But, if they hesitated or delayed to prevent the malice of the Romans, the same spirit which had insulted would pursue the Avars to the extremity of the earth. These specious reasons were heard by the chagan with coldness and disdain: he detained the Lombard ambassadors in his camp, protracted the negotiation, and by turns alleged his want of inclination, or his want of ability, to undertake this important enterprise. At length he signified the ultimate price of his alliance, that the Lombards should immediately present him with the tithe of their cattle; that the spoils and captives should be equally divided; but that the lands of the Gepidæ should become the sole patrimony of the Avars. Such hard conditions were eagerly accepted by the passions of Alboin; and, as the Romans were dissatisfied with the ingratitude and perfidy of the Gepidæ, Justin abandoned that incorrigible

---

1 The story is told by an impostor (Theophylact. Simocat. l. vi. c. 10 [p. 261, ed. Bonn]); but he had art enough to build his fictions on public and notorious facts.

people to their fate, and remained the tranquil spectator of this unequal conflict. The despair of Cunimund was active and dangerous. He was informed that the Avars had entered his confines; but, on the strong assurance that after the defeat of the Lombards these foreign invaders would easily be repelled, he rushed forwards to encounter the implacable enemy of his name and family. But the courage of the Gepidæ could secure them no more than an honourable death. The bravest of the nation fell in the field of battle: the king of the Lombards contemplated with delight the head of Cunimund, and his skull was fashioned into a cup to satiate the hatred of the conqueror, or perhaps to comply with the savage custom of his country.[1] After this victory no farther obstacle could impede the progress of the confederates, and they faithfully executed the terms of their agreement.[2] The fair countries of Wallachia, Moldavia, Transylvania, and the parts of Hungary beyond the Danube, were occupied without resistance by a new colony of Scythians; and the Dacian empire of the chagans subsisted with splendour above two hundred and thirty years. The nation of the Gepidæ was dissolved; but, in the distribution of the captives, the slaves of the Avars were less fortunate than the companions of the Lombards, whose generosity adopted a valiant foe, and whose freedom was incompatible with cool and deliberate tyranny. One moiety of the spoil introduced into the camp of Alboin more wealth than a barbarian could readily compute. The fair Rosamond was persuaded or compelled to acknowledge the rights of her victorious lover; and the daughter of Cunimund appeared to forgive those crimes which might be imputed to her own irresistible charms.

The destruction of a mighty kingdom established the fame of Alboin. In the days of Charlemagne the Bavarians, the Saxons, and the other tribes of the Teutonic language, still repeated the

---

1 It appears from Strabo [l. vii.], Pliny [l. vii. c. 11], and Ammianus Marcellinus [l. xxvii.], that the same practice was common among the Scythian tribes (Muratori, Scriptores Rer. Italic. tom. i. p. 424). The *scalps* of North America are likewise trophies of valour. The skull of Cunimund was preserved above two hundred years among the Lombards; and Paul himself was one of the guests to whom Duke Ratchis exhibited this cup on a high festival (l. ii. c. 28).

2 Paul, l. i. c. 27. Menander, in Excerpt. Legat. p. 110, 111 [p. 303, 304, ed. Bonn].

songs which described the heroic virtues, the valour, liberality, and fortune of the king of the Lombards.[1] But his ambition was yet unsatisfied; and the conqueror of the Gepidæ turned his eyes from the Danube to the richer banks of the Po and the Tiber. Fifteen years had not elapsed since his subjects, the confederates of Narses, had visited the pleasant climate of Italy; the mountains, the rivers, the highways, were familiar to their memory; the report of their success, perhaps the view of their spoils, had kindled in the rising generation the flame of emulation and enterprise. Their hopes were encouraged by the spirit and eloquence of Alboin; and it is affirmed that he spoke to their senses by producing at the royal feast the fairest and most exquisite fruits that grew spontaneously in the garden of the world. No sooner had he erected his standard than the native strength of the Lombards was multiplied by the adventurous youth of Germany and Scythia. The robust peasantry of Noricum and Pannonia had resumed the manners of barbarians; and the names of the Gepidæ, Bulgarians, Sarmatians, and Bavarians may be distinctly traced in the provinces of Italy.[2] Of the Saxons, the old allies of the Lombards, twenty thousand warriors, with their wives and children, accepted the invitation of Alboin. Their bravery contributed to his success; but the accession or the absence of their numbers was not sensibly felt in the magnitude of his host. Every mode of religion was freely practised by its respective votaries. The king of the Lombards had been educated in the Arian heresy, but the catholics in their public worship were allowed to pray for his conversion; while the more stubborn barbarians sacrificed a she-goat, or perhaps a captive, to the gods

1 Ut hactenus etiam tam apud Bajoariorum gentem, quam et Saxonum, sed et alios ejusdem linguæ homines . . . in eorum carminibus celebretur. Paul. l. i. c. 27. He died A.D. 799 (Muratori, in Præfat. tom. i. p. 397). These German songs, some of which might be as old as Tacitus (de Moribus Germ. c. 2), were compiled and transcribed by Charlemagne. Barbara et antiquissima carmina, quibus veterum regum actus et bella canebantur scripsit memoriæque mandavit (Eginard, in Vit. Carol. Magn. c. 29, p. 130, 131). The poems, which Goldast commends (Animadvers. ad Eginard. p. 207), appear to be recent and contemptible romances.

2 The other nations are rehearsed by Paul (l. ii. c. 6, 26). Muratori (Antichità Italiane, tom. i. dissert. i. p. 4) has discovered the village of the Bavarians, three miles from Modena.

of their fathers.[1] The Lombards and their confederates were united by their common attachment to a chief who excelled in all the virtues and vices of a savage hero; and the vigilance of Alboin provided an ample magazine of offensive and defensive arms for the use of the expedition. The portable wealth of the Lombards attended the march; their lands they cheerfully relinquished to the Avars, on the solemn promise, which was made and accepted without a smile, that if they failed in the conquest of Italy these voluntary exiles should be reinstated in their former possessions.

They might have failed if Narses had been the antagonist of the Lombards; and the veteran warriors, the associates of his Gothic victory, would have encountered with reluctance an enemy whom they dreaded and esteemed. But the weakness of the Byzantine court was subservient to the barbarian cause; and it was for the ruin of Italy that the emperor once listened to the complaints of his subjects. The virtues of Narses were stained with avarice; and in his provincial reign of fifteen years he accumulated a treasure of gold and silver which surpassed the modesty of a private fortune. His government was oppressive or unpopular, and the general discontent was expressed with freedom by the deputies of Rome. Before the throne of Justin they boldly declared that their Gothic servitude had been more tolerable than the despotism of a Greek eunuch; and that, unless their tyrant were instantly removed, they would consult their own happiness in the choice of a master. The apprehension of a revolt was urged by the voice of envy and detraction, which had so recently triumphed over the merit of Belisarius. A new exarch, Longinus, was appointed to supersede the conqueror of Italy; and the base motives of his recall were revealed in the insulting mandate of the empress Sophia, 'that he should leave to *men* the exercise of arms, and return to his proper station among the maidens of the palace, where a distaff should be again placed in the hand of the eunuch.' 'I will spin her such a thread as she shall not easily unravel!' is said to have been the reply which

1 Gregory the Roman (Dialog. l. iii. c. 27, 28, apud Baron. Annal. Eccles. A.D. 579, No. 10) supposes that they likewise adored this she-goat. I know but of one religion in which the god and the victim are the same.

indignation and conscious virtue extorted from the hero. Instead
of attending, a slave and a victim, at the gate of the Byzantine
palace, he retired to Naples, from whence (if any credit is due
to the belief of the times) Narses invited the Lombards to chastise the ingratitude of the prince and people.[1] But the passions
of the people are furious and changeable, and the Romans soon
recollected the merits, or dreaded the resentment, of their victorious general. By the mediation of the pope, who undertook a
special pilgrimage to Naples, their repentance was accepted; and
Narses, assuming a milder aspect and a more dutiful language,
consented to fix his residence in the Capitol. His death,[2] though
in the extreme period of old age, was unseasonable and premature, since *his* genius alone could have repaired the last and fatal
error of his life. The reality, or the suspicion, of a conspiracy
disarmed and disunited the Italians. The soldiers resented the
disgrace, and bewailed the loss, of their general. They were ignorant of their new exarch; and Longinus was himself ignorant
of the state of the army and the province. In the preceding years
Italy had been desolated by pestilence and famine, and a disaffected people ascribed the calamities of nature to the guilt or
folly of their rulers.[3]

Whatever might be the grounds of his security, Alboin neither
expected nor encountered a Roman army in the field. He ascended the Julian Alps, and looked down with contempt and
desire on the fruitful plains to which his victory communicated
the perpetual appellation of LOMBARDY. A faithful chieftain and

1 The charge of the deacon against Narses (l. ii. c. 5) may be groundless;
but the weak apology of the cardinal (Baron. Annal. Eccles. A.D. 567, No. 8–12)
is rejected by the best critics – Pagi (tom. ii. p. 639, 640), Muratori (Annali
d'Italia, tom. v. p. 160–163), and the last editors, Horatius Blancus (Script.
Rerum Italic. tom. i. p. 427, 428) and Philip Argelatus (Sigon. Opera, tom. ii.
p. 11, 12). The Narses who assisted at the coronation of Justin (Corippus, l. iii.
221) is clearly understood to be a different person.

2 The death of Narses is mentioned by Paul, l. ii. c. 11. Anastas. in Vit.
Johan. iii. p. 43. Agnellus, Liber Pontifical. Raven. [c. 3 *fin.*] in Script. Rer.
Italicarum, tom. ii. part i. p. 114, 124. Yet I cannot believe with Agnellus that
Narses was ninety-five years of age. Is it probable that all his exploits were
performed at fourscore?

3 The designs of Narses and of the Lombards for the invasion of Italy are
exposed in the last chapter of the first book, and the seven first chapters of
the second book, of Paul the Deacon.

a select band were stationed at Forum Julii, the modern Friuli, to guard the passes of the mountains. The Lombards respected the strength of Pavia, and listened to the prayers of the Trevisans: their slow and heavy multitudes proceeded to occupy the palace and city of Verona; and Milan, now rising from her ashes, was invested by the powers of Alboin five months after his departure from Pannonia. Terror preceded his march: he found everywhere, or he left, a dreary solitude; and the pusillanimous Italians presumed, without a trial, that the stranger was invincible. Escaping to lakes, or rocks, or morasses, the affrighted crowds concealed some fragments of their wealth, and delayed the moment of their servitude. Paulinus, the patriarch of Aquileia, removed his treasures, sacred and profane, to the isle of Grado,[1] and his successors were adopted by the infant republic of Venice, which was continually enriched by the public calamities. Honoratus, who filled the chair of St. Ambrose, had credulously accepted the faithless offers of a capitulation; and the archbishop, with the clergy and nobles of Milan, were driven by the perfidy of Alboin to seek a refuge in the less accessible ramparts of Genoa. Along the maritime coast the courage of the inhabitants was supported by the facility of supply, the hopes of relief, and the power of escape; but, from the Trentine hills to the gates of Ravenna and Rome, the inland regions of Italy became, without a battle or a siege, the lasting patrimony of the Lombards. The submission of the people invited the barbarian to assume the character of a lawful sovereign, and the helpless exarch was confined to the office of announcing to the emperor Justin the rapid and irretrievable loss of his provinces and cities.[2] One city, which had been diligently fortified by the Goths,

1 Which from this translation was called New Aquileia (Chron. Venet. p. 3). The patriarch of Grado soon became the first citizen of the republic (p. 9, etc.), but his seat was not removed to Venice till the year 1450. He is now decorated with titles and honours; but the genius of the church has bowed to that of the state, and the government of a catholic city is strictly presbyterian. Thomassin, Discipline de l'Eglise, tom. i. p. 156, 157, 161–165. Amelot de la Houssaye, Gouvernement de Venise, tom. i. p. 256–261.

2 Paul has given a description of Italy, as it was then divided, into eighteen regions (l. ii. c. 14–24). The Dissertatio Chorographica de Italiâ Medii Ævi, by Father Beretti, a Benedictine monk, and regius professor at Pavia, has been usefully consulted.

resisted the arms of a new invader; and, while Italy was subdued by the flying detachments of the Lombards, the royal camp was fixed above three years before the western gate of Ticinum, or Pavia. The same courage which obtains the esteem of a civilised enemy provokes the fury of a savage; and the impatient besieger had bound himself by a tremendous oath that age, and sex, and dignity should be confounded in a general massacre. The aid of famine at length enabled him to execute his bloody vow; but as Alboin entered the gate his horse stumbled, fell, and could not be raised from the ground. One of his attendants was prompted by compassion, or piety, to interpret this miraculous sign of the wrath of Heaven: the conqueror paused and relented; he sheathed his sword, and, peacefully reposing himself in the palace of Theodoric, proclaimed to the trembling multitude that they should live and obey. Delighted with the situation of a city which was endeared to his pride by the difficulty of the purchase, the prince of the Lombards disdained the ancient glories of Milan; and Pavia during some ages was respected as the capital of the kingdom of Italy.[1]

The reign of the founder was splendid and transient; and, before he could regulate his new conquests, Alboin fell a sacrifice to domestic treason and female revenge. In a palace near Verona, which had not been erected for the barbarians, he feasted the companions of his arms; intoxication was the reward of valour, and the king himself was tempted by appetite or vanity to exceed the ordinary measure of his intemperance. After draining many capacious bowls of Rhætian or Falernian wine he called for the skull of Cunimund, the noblest and most precious ornament of his sideboard. The cup of victory was accepted with horrid applause by the circle of the Lombard chiefs. 'Fill it again with wine!' exclaimed the inhuman conqueror, 'fill it to the brim! carry this goblet to the queen, and request in my name that she would rejoice with her father.' In an agony of grief and rage, Rosamond had strength to utter, 'Let the will of my lord be obeyed!' and, touching it with her lips, pronounced a silent imprecation that

1 For the conquest of Italy, see the original materials of Paul (l. ii. c. 7–10, 12, 14, 25, 26, 27), the eloquent narrative of Sigonius (tom. ii. de Regno Italiæ, l. i. p. 13–19), and the correct and critical review of Muratori (Annali d'Italia, tom. v. p. 164–180).

the insult should be washed away in the blood of Alboin. Some indulgence might be due to the resentment of a daughter, if she had not already violated the duties of a wife. Implacable in her enmity, or inconstant in her love, the queen of Italy had stooped from the throne to the arms of a subject, and Helmichis, the king's armour-bearer, was the secret minister of her pleasure and revenge. Against the proposal of the murder he could no longer urge the scruples of fidelity or gratitude; but Helmichis trembled when he revolved the danger as well as the guilt, when he rec-ollected the matchless strength and intrepidity of a warrior whom he had so often attended in the field of battle. He pressed, and obtained, that one of the bravest champions of the Lom-bards should be associated to the enterprise; but no more than a promise of secrecy could be drawn from the gallant Peredeus, and the mode of seduction employed by Rosamond betrays her shameless insensibility both to honour and love. She supplied the place of one of her female attendants who was beloved by Peredeus, and contrived some excuse for darkness and silence till she could inform her companion that he had enjoyed the queen of the Lombards, and that his own death or the death of Alboin must be the consequence of such treasonable adultery. In this alternative he chose rather to be the accomplice than the victim of Rosamond,[1] whose undaunted spirit was incapable of fear or remorse. She expected and soon found a favourable moment, when the king, oppressed with wine, had retired from the table to his afternoon slumbers. His faithless spouse was anxious for his health and repose; the gates of the palace were shut, the arms removed, the attendants dismissed, and Rosa-mond, after lulling him to rest by her tender caresses, unbolted the chamber-door and urged the reluctant conspirators to the instant execution of the deed. On the first alarm the warrior started from his couch: his sword, which he attempted to draw, had been fastened to the scabbard by the hand of Rosamond; and a small stool, his only weapon, could not long protect him

1 The classical reader will recollect the wife and murder of Candaules, so agreeably told in the first book of Herodotus [c. 8, *sqq.*]. The choice of Gyges, αἱρέεται αὐτὸς περιεῖναι, may serve as the excuse of Peredeus; and this soft insinuation of an odious idea has been imitated by the best writers of antiquity (Grævius, ad Ciceron. Orat. pro Milone, c. 10).

from the spears of the assassins. The daughter of Cunimund smiled in his fall: his body was buried under the staircase of the palace; and the grateful posterity of the Lombards revered the tomb and the memory of their victorious leader.

The ambitious Rosamond aspired to reign in the name of her lover; the city and palace of Verona were awed by her power; and a faithful band of her native Gepidæ was prepared to applaud the revenge and to second the wishes of their sovereign. But the Lombard chiefs, who fled in the first moments of consternation and disorder, had resumed their courage and collected their powers; and the nation, instead of submitting to her reign, demanded with unanimous cries that justice should be executed on the guilty spouse and the murderers of their king. She sought a refuge among the enemies of her country, and a criminal who deserved the abhorrence of mankind was protected by the selfish policy of the exarch. With her daughter, the heiress of the Lombard throne, her two lovers, her trusty Gepidæ, and the spoils of the palace of Verona, Rosamond descended the Adige and the Po, and was transported by a Greek vessel to the safe harbour of Ravenna. Longinus beheld with delight the charms and the treasures of the widow of Alboin: her situation and her past conduct might justify the most licentious proposals, and she readily listened to the passion of a minister who, even in the decline of the empire, was respected as the equal of kings. The death of a jealous lover was an easy and grateful sacrifice, and as Helmichis issued from the bath he received the deadly potion from the hand of his mistress. The taste of the liquor, its speedy operation, and his experience of the character of Rosamond, convinced him that he was poisoned; he pointed his dagger to her breast, compelled her to drain the remainder of the cup, and expired in a few minutes with the consolation that she could not survive to enjoy the fruits of her wickedness. The daughter of Alboin and Rosamond, with the richest spoils of the Lombards, was embarked for Constantinople: the surprising strength of Peredeus amused and terrified the Imperial court; his blindness and revenge exhibited an imperfect copy of the adventures of Samson. By the free suffrage of the nation in the assembly of Pavia, Clepho, one of their noblest chiefs, was elected as the successor of Alboin. Before the end of eighteen months the throne was polluted by a second murder: Clepho was stabbed by the hand of a domestic; the regal office was suspended above ten years during the minority of his son Autharis, and Italy was divided and oppressed by a ducal aristocracy of thirty tyrants.[1]

When the nephew of Justinian ascended the throne, he proclaimed a new era of happiness and glory. The annals of the second Justin[2] are marked with disgrace abroad and misery at home. In the West the Roman empire was afflicted by the loss of Italy, the desolation of Africa, and the conquests of the Persians. Injustice prevailed both in the capital and the provinces: the rich trembled for their property, the poor for their safety; the ordinary magistrates were ignorant or venal, the occasional remedies appear to have been arbitrary and violent, and the complaints of the people could no longer be silenced by the splendid names of a legislator and a conqueror. The opinion which imputes to the prince all the calamities of his times may be countenanced by the historian as a serious truth or a salutary prejudice. Yet a candid suspicion will arise that the sentiments of Justin were pure and benevolent, and that he might have filled his station without reproach if the faculties of his mind had not been impaired by disease, which deprived the emperor of the use of his feet and confined him to the palace, a stranger to the complaints of the people and the vices of the government. The tardy knowledge of his own impotence determined him to lay down the weight of the diadem, and in the choice of a worthy substitute he showed some symptoms of a discerning and even magnanimous spirit. The only son of Justin and Sophia died in his infancy; their daughter Arabia was the wife of Baduarius,[3]

---

1 See the history of Paul, l. ii. c. 28–32. I have borrowed some interesting circumstances from the Liber Pontificalis of Agnellus [c. 4] in Script. Rer. Ital. tom. ii. p. 124. Of all chronological guides Muratori is the safest.

2 The original authors for the reign of Justin the younger are Evagrius, Hist. Eccles. l. v. c. 1–12; Theophanes, in Chronograph. p. 204–210 [tom. i. p. 373, *sqq.*, ed. Bonn]; Zonaras, tom. ii. l. xiv. [c. 10] p. 70–72; Cedrenus, in Compend. p. 388–392 [tom. i. p. 680–688, ed. Bonn].

      3 Dispositorque novus sacræ Baduarius aulæ.
        Successor soceri mox factus Cura-palatî. – Corippus.

Baduarius is enumerated among the descendants and allies of the house of Justinian. A family of noble Venetians (Casa *Badoero*) built churches and gave

superintendent of the palace, and afterwards commander of the Italian armies, who vainly aspired to confirm the rights of marriage by those of adoption. While the empire appeared an object of desire, Justin was accustomed to behold with jealousy and hatred his brothers and cousins, the rivals of his hopes; nor could he depend on the gratitude of those who would accept the purple as a restitution rather than a gift. Of these competitors one had been removed by exile, and afterwards by death; and the emperor himself had inflicted such cruel insults on another, that he must either dread his resentment or despise his patience. This domestic animosity was refined into a generous resolution of seeking a successor, not in his family, but in the republic; and the artful Sophia recommended Tiberius,[1] his faithful captain of the guards, whose virtues and fortune the emperor might cherish as the fruit of his judicious choice. The ceremony of his elevation to the rank of Cæsar or Augustus was performed in the portico of the palace in the presence of the patriarch and the senate. Justin collected the remaining strength of his mind and body; but the popular belief that his speech was inspired by the Deity betrays a very humble opinion both of the man and of the times.[2] 'You behold,' said the emperor, 'the ensigns of supreme power. You are about to receive them, not from my hand, but from the hand of God. Honour them, and from them you will derive honour. Respect the empress your mother; you are now her son; before, you were her servant. Delight not in blood; abstain from revenge; avoid those actions by which I have incurred the public hatred; and consult the experience, rather than the example, of your predecessor. As a man, I have sinned; as a sinner, even in

dukes to the republic as early as the ninth century; and, if their descent be admitted, no kings in Europe can produce a pedigree so ancient and illustrious. Ducange, Fam. Byzantin. p. 99. Amelot de la Houssaye, Gouvernement de Venise, tom. ii. p. 555.

1 The praise bestowed on princes before their elevation is the purest and most weighty. Corippus has celebrated Tiberius at the time of the accession of Justin (l. i. 212–222). Yet even a captain of the guards might attract the flattery of an African exile.

2 Evagrius (l. v. c. 13) has added the reproach to his ministers. He applies this speech to the ceremony when Tiberius was invested with the rank of Cæsar. The loose expression, rather than the positive error, of Theophanes, etc., has delayed it to his *Augustan* investiture, immediately before the death of Justin.

this life, I have been severely punished: but these servants (and he pointed to his ministers), who have abused my confidence and inflamed my passions, will appear with me before the tribunal of Christ. I have been dazzled by the splendour of the diadem: be thou wise and modest; remember what you have been, remember what you are. You see around us your slaves and your children; with the authority, assume the tenderness of a parent. Love your people like yourself; cultivate the affections, maintain the discipline, of the army; protect the fortunes of the rich, relieve the necessities of the poor." The assembly, in silence and in tears, applauded the counsels and sympathised with the repentance of their prince; the patriarch rehearsed the prayers of the church; Tiberius received the diadem on his knees; and Justin, who in his abdication appeared most worthy to reign, addressed the new monarch in the following words: – 'If you consent, I live; if you command, I die: may the God of heaven and earth infuse into your heart whatever I have neglected or forgotten.' The four last years of the emperor Justin were passed in tranquil obscurity: his conscience was no longer tormented by the remembrance of those duties which he was incapable of discharging, and his choice was justified by the filial reverence and gratitude of Tiberius.

Among the virtues of Tiberius,[2] his beauty (he was one of the tallest and most comely of the Romans) might introduce him to the favour of Sophia; and the widow of Justin was persuaded that she should preserve her station and influence under the reign of a second and more youthful husband. But if the ambitious candidate had been tempted to flatter and dissemble, it was no longer in his power to fulfil her expectations or his own promise. The factions of the hippodrome demanded with some impatience the name of their new empress; both the people and

1 Theophylact Simocatta (l. iii. c. 11 [p. 136, ed. Bonn]) declares that he shall give to posterity the speech of Justin as it was pronounced, without attempting to correct the imperfections of language or rhetoric. Perhaps the vain sophist would have been incapable of producing such sentiments.

2 For the character and reign of Tiberius see Evagrius, l. v. c. 13; Theophylact. l. iii. c. 12, etc.; Theophanes, in Chron. p. 210–213 [ed. Par.; tom. i. p. 382–388, ed. Bonn]; Zonaras, tom. ii. l. xiv. [c. 11] p. 72; Cedrenus, p. 392 [tom. i. p. 688, ed. Bonn]; Paul Warnefrid, de Gestis Langobard. l. iii. c. 11, 12. The deacon of Forum Julii appears to have possessed some curious and authentic facts.

Sophia were astonished by the proclamation of Anastasia, the secret though lawful wife of the emperor Tiberius. Whatever could alleviate the disappointment of Sophia, imperial honours, a stately palace, a numerous household, was liberally bestowed by the piety of her adopted son; on solemn occasions he attended and consulted the widow of his benefactor, but her ambition disdained the vain semblance of royalty, and the respectful appellation of mother served to exasperate rather than appease the rage of an injured woman. While she accepted and repaid with a courtly smile the fair expressions of regard and confidence, a secret alliance was concluded between the dowager empress and her ancient enemies; and Justinian, the son of Germanus, was employed as the instrument of her revenge. The pride of the reigning house supported with reluctance the dominion of a stranger: the youth was deservedly popular, his name after the death of Justin had been mentioned by a tumultuous faction, and his own submissive offer of his head, with a treasure of sixty thousand pounds, might be interpreted as an evidence of guilt, or at least of fear. Justinian received a free pardon and the command of the eastern army. The Persian monarch fled before his arms, and the acclamations which accompanied his triumph declared him worthy of the purple. His artful patroness had chosen the month of the vintage, while the emperor in a rural solitude was permitted to enjoy the pleasures of a subject. On the first intelligence of her designs he returned to Constantinople, and the conspiracy was suppressed by his presence and firmness. From the pomp and honours which she had abused, Sophia was reduced to a modest allowance; Tiberius dismissed her train, intercepted her correspondence, and committed to a faithful guard the custody of her person. But the services of Justinian were not considered by that excellent prince as an aggravation of his offences: after a mild reproof his treason and ingratitude were forgiven, and it was commonly believed that the emperor entertained some thoughts of contracting a double alliance with the rival of his throne. The voice of an angel (such a fable was propagated) might reveal to the emperor that he should always triumph over his domestic foes, but Tiberius derived a firmer assurance from the innocence and generosity of his own mind.

With the odious name of Tiberius he assumed the more popular appellation of Constantine, and imitated the purer virtues of the Antonines. After recording the vice or folly of so many Roman princes, it is pleasing to repose for a moment on a character conspicuous by the qualities of humanity, justice, temperance, and fortitude; to contemplate a sovereign affable in his palace, pious in the church, impartial on the seat of judgment, and victorious, at least by his generals, in the Persian war. The most glorious trophy of his victory consisted in a multitude of captives, whom Tiberius entertained, redeemed, and dismissed to their native homes with the charitable spirit of a Christian hero. The merit or misfortunes of his own subjects had a dearer claim to his beneficence, and he measured his bounty not so much by their expectations as by his own dignity. This maxim, however dangerous in a trustee of the public wealth, was balanced by a principle of humanity and justice, which taught him to abhor, as of the basest alloy, the gold that was extracted from the tears of the people. For their relief, as often as they had suffered by natural or hostile calamities, he was impatient to remit the arrears of the past or the demands of future taxes: he sternly rejected the servile offerings of his ministers, which were compensated by tenfold oppression; and the wise and equitable laws of Tiberius excited the praise and regret of succeeding times. Constantinople believed that the emperor had discovered a treasure; but his genuine treasure consisted in the practice of liberal economy, and the contempt of all vain and superfluous expense. The Romans of the East would have been happy if the best gift of heaven, a patriot king, had been confirmed as a proper and permanent blessing. But in less than four years after the death of Justin, his worthy successor sunk into a mortal disease, which left him only sufficient time to restore the diadem, according to the tenure by which he held it, to the most deserving of his fellow-citizens. He selected Maurice from the crowd – a judgment more precious than the purple itself: the patriarch and senate were summoned to the bed of the dying prince; he bestowed his daughter and the empire, and his last advice was solemnly delivered by the voice of the quæstor. Tiberius expressed his hope that the virtues of his son and successor would erect the noblest mausoleum to his memory. His memory was embalmed by the public affliction; but the most sincere grief evaporates in the tumult of a new reign, and the eyes and acclamations of mankind were speedily directed to the rising sun.

The emperor Maurice derived his origin from ancient Rome;[1] but his immediate parents were settled at Arabissus in Cappadocia, and their singular felicity preserved them alive to behold and partake the fortune of their *august* son. The youth of Maurice was spent in the profession of arms: Tiberius promoted him to the command of a new and favourite legion of twelve thousand confederates; his valour and conduct were signalised in the Persian war; and he returned to Constantinople to accept, as his just reward, the inheritance of the empire. Maurice ascended the throne at the mature age of forty-three years; and he reigned above twenty years over the East and over himself;[2] expelling from his mind the wild democracy of passions, and establishing (according to the quaint expression of Evagrius) a perfect aristocracy of reason and virtue. Some suspicion will degrade the testimony of a subject, though he protests that his secret praise should never reach the ear of his sovereign,[3] and some failings seem to place the character of Maurice below the purer merit of his predecessor. His cold and reserved demeanour might be imputed to arrogance; his justice was not always exempt from cruelty, nor his clemency from weakness; and his rigid economy too often exposed him to the reproach of avarice. But the rational wishes of an absolute monarch must tend to the happiness of his people: Maurice was endowed with sense and courage to

1 It is therefore singular enough that Paul (l. iii. c. 15) should distinguish him as the first Greek emperor – primus ex Græcorum genere in Imperio constitutus [confirmatus]. His immediate predecessors had indeed been born in the Latin provinces of Europe: and a various reading, in Græcorum Imperio, would apply the expression to the empire rather than the prince.

2 Consult, for the character and reign of Maurice, the fifth and sixth books of Evagrius, particularly l. vi. c. 1; the eight books of his prolix and florid history by Theophylact Simocatta; Theophanes, p. 213, etc. [tom. i. p. 288, *sqq.*, ed. Bonn]; Zonaras, tom. ii. l. xiv. [c. 12] p. 73; Cedrenus, p. 394 [tom. i. p. 691, ed. Bonn].

3 Αὐτοκράτωρ οὕτως γενόμενος τὴν μὲν ὀχλοκρατείαν τῶν παθῶν ἐκ τῆς οἰκείας ἐξενηλάτησε ψυχῆς· ἀριστοκρατείαν δὲ ἐν τοῖς ἑαυτοῦ λογισμοῖς καταστησάμενος [l. vi. c. 1]. Evagrius composed his history in the twelfth year of Maurice; and he had been so wisely indiscreet that the emperor knew and rewarded his favourable opinion (l. vi. c. 24).

promote that happiness, and his administration was directed by
the principles and example of Tiberius. The pusillanimity of the
Greeks had introduced so complete a separation between the
offices of king and of general, that a private soldier, who had
deserved and obtained the purple, seldom or never appeared at
the head of his armies. Yet the emperor Maurice enjoyed the
glory of restoring the Persian monarch to his throne; his lieutenants waged a doubtful war against the Avars of the Danube; and
he cast an eye of pity, of ineffectual pity, on the abject and
distressful state of his Italian provinces.

From Italy the emperors were incessantly tormented by tales
of misery and demands of succour, which extorted the humiliating confession of their own weakness. The expiring dignity of
Rome was only marked by the freedom and energy of her complaints: 'If you are incapable,' she said, 'of delivering us from the
sword of the Lombards, save us at least from the calamity of
famine.' Tiberius forgave the reproach, and relieved the distress:
a supply of corn was transported from Egypt to the Tiber; and
the Roman people, invoking the name, not of Camillus, but of
St. Peter, repulsed the barbarians from their walls. But the relief
was accidental, the danger was perpetual and pressing; and the
clergy and senate, collecting the remains of their ancient
opulence, a sum of three thousand pounds of gold, despatched
the patrician Pamphronius to lay their gifts and their complaints
at the foot of the Byzantine throne. The attention of the court,
and the forces of the East, were diverted by the Persian war; but
the justice of Tiberius applied the subsidy to the defence of the
city; and he dismissed the patrician with his best advice, either
to bribe the Lombard chiefs, or to purchase the aid of the kings
of France. Notwithstanding this weak invention, Italy was still
afflicted, Rome was again besieged, and the suburb of Classe,
only three miles from Ravenna, was pillaged and occupied by the
troops of a simple duke of Spoleto. Maurice gave audience to a
second deputation of priests and senators: the duties and the
menaces of religion were forcibly urged in the letters of the
Roman pontiff; and his nuncio, the deacon Gregory, was alike
qualified to solicit the powers either of heaven or of the earth.
The emperor adopted, with stronger effect, the measures of his
predecessor: some formidable chiefs were persuaded to embrace

the friendship of the Romans; and one of them, a mild and faithful barbarian, lived and died in the service of the exarch: the passes of the Alps were delivered to the Franks; and the pope encouraged them to violate, without scruple, their oaths and engagements to the misbelievers. Childebert, the great-grandson of Clovis, was persuaded to invade Italy by the payment of fifty thousand pieces; but, as he had viewed with delight some Byzantine coin of the weight of one pound of gold, the king of Austrasia might stipulate that the gift should be rendered more worthy of his acceptance by a proper mixture of these respectable medals. The dukes of the Lombards had provoked by frequent inroads their powerful neighbours of Gaul. As soon as they were apprehensive of a just retaliation, they renounced their feeble and disorderly independence: the advantages of regal government, union, secrecy, and vigour, were unanimously confessed; and Autharis, the son of Clepho, had already attained the strength and reputation of a warrior. Under the standard of their new king, the conquerors of Italy withstood three successive invasions, one of which was led by Childebert himself, the last of the Merovingian race who descended from the Alps. The first expedition was defeated by the jealous animosity of the Franks and Alemanni. In the second they were vanquished in a bloody battle, with more loss and dishonour than they had sustained since the foundation of their monarchy. Impatient for revenge, they returned a third time with accumulated force, and Autharis yielded to the fury of the torrent. The troops and treasures of the Lombards were distributed in the walled towns between the Alps and the Apennine. A nation, less sensible of danger than of fatigue and delay, soon murmured against the folly of their twenty commanders; and the hot vapours of an Italian sun infected with disease those tramontane bodies which had already suffered the vicissitudes of intemperance and famine. The powers that were inadequate to the conquest, were more than sufficient for the desolation, of the country; nor could the trembling natives distinguish between their enemies and their deliverers. If the junction of the Merovingian and Imperial forces had been effected in the neighbourhood of Milan, perhaps they might have subverted the throne of the Lombards; but the Franks expected six days the signal of a flaming village, and the

arms of the Greeks were idly employed in the reduction of
Modena and Parma, which were torn from them after the retreat
of their transalpine allies. The victorious Autharis asserted his
claim to the dominion of Italy. At the foot of the Rhætian Alps,
he subdued the resistance, and rifled the hidden treasures, of a
sequestered island in the lake of Comum. At the extreme point
of Calabria, he touched with his spear a column on the sea-shore
of Rhegium,[1] proclaiming that ancient landmark to stand the
immovable boundary of his kingdom.[2]

During a period of two hundred years Italy was unequally
divided between the kingdom of the Lombards and the exarchate of Ravenna. The offices and professions which the jealousy
of Constantine had separated were united by the indulgence of
Justinian; and eighteen successive exarchs were invested, in the
decline of the empire, with the full remains of civil, of military,
and even of ecclesiastical power. Their immediate jurisdiction,
which was afterwards consecrated as the patrimony of St. Peter,
extended over the modern Romagna, the marshes or valleys of
Ferrara and Commachio,[3] five maritime cities from Rimini to
Ancona, and a second inland Pentapolis, between the Hadriatic
coast and the hills of the Apennine. Three subordinate provinces, of Rome, of Venice, and of Naples, which were divided by
hostile lands from the palace of Ravenna, acknowledged, both
in peace and war, the supremacy of the exarch. The duchy of
Rome appears to have included the Tuscan, Sabine, and Latin
conquests of the first four hundred years of the city, and the

1 The Columna Rhegina, in the narrowest part of the Faro of Messina, one
hundred stadia from Rhegium itself, is frequently mentioned in ancient geography. Cluver. Ital. Antiq. tom. ii. p. 1295; Lucas Holsten. Annotat. ad Cluver.
p. 301; Wesseling, Itinerar. p. 106.

2 The Greek historians afford some faint hints of the wars of Italy (Menander, in Excerpt. Legat. p. 124, 126 [p. 327, 331, ed. Bonn]; Theophylact,
l. iii. c. 4 [p. 120, ed. Bonn]). The Latins are more satisfactory; and especially
Paul Warnefrid (l. iii. c. 13–34), who had read the more ancient histories of
Secundus and Gregory of Tours. Baronius produces some letters of the popes,
etc.; and the times are measured by the accurate scale of Pagi and Muratori.

3 The papal advocates, Zacagni and Fontanini, might justly claim the valley
or morass of Commachio as a part of the exarchate. But the ambition of
including Modena, Reggio, Parma, and Placentia, has darkened a geographical
question somewhat doubtful and obscure. Even Muratori, as the servant of the
house of Este, is not free from partiality and prejudice.

limits may be distinctly traced along the coast, from Civita Vec-
chia to Terracina, and with the course of the Tiber from Ameria
and Narni to the port of Ostia. The numerous islands from
Grado to Chiozza composed the infant dominion of Venice; but
the more accessible towns on the continent were overthrown by
the Lombards, who beheld with impotent fury a new capital
rising from the waves. The power of the dukes of Naples was
circumscribed by the bay and the adjacent isles, by the hostile
territory of Capua, and by the Roman colony of Amalphi,[1] whose
industrious citizens, by the invention of the mariner's compass,
have unveiled the face of the globe. The three islands of Sardinia,
Corsica, and Sicily still adhered to the empire; and the acquisition
of the farther Calabria removed the landmark of Autharis from
the shore of Rhegium to the isthmus of Consentia. In Sardinia
the savage mountaineers preserved the liberty and religion of their
ancestors; but the husbandmen of Sicily were chained to their rich
and cultivated soil. Rome was oppressed by the iron sceptre of
the exarchs, and a Greek, perhaps a eunuch, insulted with impunity the ruins of the Capitol. But Naples soon acquired
the privilege of electing her own dukes:[2] the independence of
Amalphi was the fruit of commerce; and the voluntary attachment of Venice was finally ennobled by an equal alliance with
the Eastern empire. On the map of Italy the measure of the
exarchate occupies a very inadequate space, but it included an
ample proportion of wealth, industry, and population. The most
faithful and valuable subjects escaped from the barbarian yoke;
and the banners of Pavia and Verona, of Milan and Padua, were
displayed in their respective quarters by the new inhabitants of
Ravenna. The remainder of Italy was possessed by the Lombards; and from Pavia, the royal seat, their kingdom was extended to the east, the north, and the west, as far as the confines
of the Avars, the Bavarians, and the Franks of Austrasia and
Burgundy. In the language of modern geography, it is now represented by the Terra Firma of the Venetian republic, Tyrol, the
Milanese, Piedmont, the coast of Genoa, Mantua, Parma, and

1 See Brenckman, Dissert. Ima. de Republicâ Amalphitanâ, p. 1–42, ad
calcem Hist. Pandect. Florent.

2 Gregor. Magn. l. iii. Epist. 23, 25, 26, 27.

Modena, the grand duchy of Tuscany, and a large portion of the ecclesiastical state from Perugia to the Hadriatic. The dukes, and at length the princes, of Beneventum, survived the monarchy, and propagated the name of the Lombards. From Capua to Tarentum, they reigned near five hundred years over the greatest part of the present kingdom of Naples.[1]

In comparing the proportion of the victorious and the vanquished people, the change of language will afford the most probable inference. According to this standard it will appear that the Lombards of Italy, and the Visigoths of Spain, were less numerous than the Franks or Burgundians; and the conquerors of Gaul must yield, in their turn, to the multitude of Saxons and Angles who almost eradicated the idioms of Britain. The modern Italian has been insensibly formed by the mixture of nations: the awkwardness of the barbarians in the nice management of declensions and conjugations reduced them to the use of articles and auxiliary verbs; and many new ideas have been expressed by Teutonic appellations. Yet the principal stock of technical and familiar words is found to be of Latin derivation;[2] and, if we were sufficiently conversant with the obsolete, the rustic, and the muncipal dialects of ancient Italy, we should trace the origin of many terms which might, perhaps, be rejected by the classic purity of Rome. A numerous army constitutes but a small nation, and the powers of the Lombards were soon diminished by the retreat of twenty thousand Saxons, who scorned a dependent situation, and returned, after many bold and perilous adventures, to their native country.[3] The camp of Alboin was of formidable extent, but the extent of a camp would be easily circumscribed within the limits of a city; and its martial inhabitants must be

1 I have described the state of Italy from the excellent Dissertation of Beretti. Giannone (Istoria Civile, tom. i. p. 374–387) has followed the learned Camillo Pellegrini in the geography of the kingdom of Naples. After the loss of the true Calabria the vanity of the Greeks substituted that name instead of the more ignoble appellation of Bruttium; and the change appears to have taken place before the time of Charlemagne (Eginard, p. 75 [c. 15]).

2 Maffei (Verona Illustrata, part i. p. 310–321) and Muratori (Antichità Italiane, tom. ii. Dissertazione xxxii. xxxiii. p. 71–365) have asserted the native claims of the Italian idiom: the former with enthusiasm, the latter with discretion: both with learning, ingenuity, and truth.

3 Paul, de Gest. Langobard. l. iii. c. 5, 6, 7.

thinly scattered over the face of a large country. When Alboin descended from the Alps, he invested his nephew, the first duke of Friuli, with the command of the province and the people: but the prudent Gisulf would have declined the dangerous office, unless he had been permitted to choose, among the nobles of the Lombards, a sufficient number of families[1] to form a perpetual colony of soldiers and subjects. In the progress of conquest, the same option could not be granted to the dukes of Brescia or Bergamo, of Pavia or Turin, of Spoleto or Beneventum; but each of these, and each of their colleagues, settled in his appointed district with a band of followers who resorted to his standard in war and his tribunal in peace. Their attachment was free and honourable: resigning the gifts and benefits which they had accepted, they might emigrate with their families into the jurisdiction of another duke; but their absence from the kingdom was punished with death, as a crime of military desertion.[2] The posterity of the first conquerors struck a deeper root into the soil, which, by every motive of interest and honour, they were bound to defend. A Lombard was born the soldier of his king and his duke; and the civil assemblies of the nation displayed the banners, and assumed the appellation, of a regular army. Of this army the pay and the rewards were drawn from the conquered provinces; and the distribution, which was not effected till after the death of Alboin, is disgraced by the foul marks of injustice and rapine. Many of the most wealthy Italians were slain or banished; the remainder were divided among the strangers, and a tributary obligation was imposed (under the name of hospitality) of paying to the Lombards a third part of the fruits of the earth. Within less than seventy years this artificial system was abolished by a more simple and solid tenure.[3] Either the Roman landlord was expelled by his strong and insolent guest, or the

---

1 Paul, l. ii. c. 9. He call these families or generations by the Teutonic name of *Faras*, which is likewise used in the Lombard laws. The humble deacon was not insensible of the nobility of his own race. See l. iv. c. 39.

2 Compare No. 3 and 177 of the Laws of Rotharis.

3 Paul, l. ii. c. 31, 32, l. iii. c. 16. The Laws of Rotharis, promulgated A.D. 643, do not contain the smallest vestige of this payment of thirds; but they preserve many curious circumstances of the state of Italy and the manners of the Lombards.

annual payment, a third of the produce, was exchanged by a more equitable transaction for an adequate proportion of landed property. Under these foreign masters, the business of agriculture, in the cultivation of corn, vines, and olives, was exercised with degenerate skill and industry by the labour of the slaves and natives. But the occupations of a pastoral life were more pleasing to the idleness of the barbarians. In the rich meadows of Venetia they restored and improved the breed of horses, for which that province had once been illustrious;[1] and the Italians beheld with astonishment a foreign race of oxen or buffaloes.[2] The depopulation of Lombardy, and the increase of forests, afforded an ample range for the pleasures of the chase.[3] That marvellous art which teaches the birds of the air to acknowledge the voice, and execute the commands, of their master had been unknown to the ingenuity of the Greeks and Romans.[4] Scandinavia and Scythia produce the boldest and most tractable falcons:[5] they were tamed and educated by the roving inhabitants, always on

1 The studs of Dionysius of Syracuse, and his frequent victories in the Olympic games, had diffused among the Greeks the fame of the Venetian horses; but the breed was extinct in the time of Strabo (l. v. p. 325 [p. 212, ed. Casaub.]). Gisulf obtained from his uncle generosarum equarum greges. Paul, l. ii. c. 9. The Lombards afterwards introduced caballi silvatici – wild horses. Paul. l. iv. c. 11.

2 Tunc (A.D. 596) primum, *bubali* in Italiam delati Italiæ populis miracula fuere (Paul Warnefrid, l. iv. c. 11). The buffaloes, whose native climate appears to be Africa and India, are unknown to Europe, except in Italy, where they are numerous and useful. The ancients were ignorant of these animals, unless Aristotle (Hist. Anim. l. ii. c. 1, p. 58, Paris, 1783) has described them as the wild oxen of Arachosia. See Buffon, Hist. Naturelle, tom. xi. and Supplement, tom. vi. Hist. Générale des Voyages, tom. i. p. 7, 481, ii. 105, iii. 291, iv. 234, 461, v. 193, vi. 491, viii. 400, x. 666; Pennant's Quadrupedes, p. 24; Dictionnaire d'Hist. Naturelle, par Valmont de Bomare, tom. ii. p. 74. Yet I must not conceal the suspicion that Paul, by a vulgar error, may have applied the name of *bubalus* to the aurochs, or wild bull, of ancient Germany.

3 Consult the twenty-first Dissertation of Muratori.

4 Their ignorance is proved by the silence even of those who professedly treat of the arts of hunting and the history of animals. Aristotle (Hist. Animal. l. ix. c. 36, tom. i. p. 586, and the Notes of his last editor, M. Camus, tom. ii. p. 314), Pliny (Hist. Natur. l. x. c. 10), Ælian (de Natur. Animal. l. ii. c. 42), and perhaps Homer (Odyss. xxii. 302–306), describe with astonishment a tacit league and common chase between the hawks and the Thracian fowlers.

5 Particularly the gerfaut, or gyrfalcon, of the size of a small eagle. See the animated description of M. de Buffon, Hist. Naturelle, tom. xvi. p. 239, etc.

horseback and in the field. This favourite amusement of our ancestors was introduced by the barbarians into the Roman provinces: and the laws of Italy esteem the sword and the hawk as of equal dignity and importance in the hands of a noble Lombard.[1]

So rapid was the influence of climate and example, that the Lombards of the fourth generation surveyed with curiosity and affright the portraits of their savage forefathers.[2] Their heads were shaven behind, but the shaggy locks hung over their eyes and mouth, and a long beard represented the name and character of the nation. Their dress consisted of loose linen garments, after the fashion of the Anglo-Saxons, which were decorated, in their opinion, with broad stripes of variegated colours. The legs and feet were clothed in long hose and open sandals, and even in the security of peace a trusty sword was constantly girt to their side. Yet this strange apparel and horrid aspect often concealed a gentle and generous disposition; and as soon as the rage of battle had subsided, the captives and subjects were sometimes surprised by the humanity of the victor. The vices of the Lombards were the effect of passion, of ignorance, of intoxication; their virtues are the more laudable, as they were not affected by the hypocrisy of social manners, nor imposed by the rigid constraint of laws and education. I should not be apprehensive of deviating from my subject, if it were in my power to delineate the private life of the conquerors of Italy; and I shall relate with pleasure the adventurous gallantry of Autharis, which breathes the true spirit of chivalry and romance.[3] After the loss of his

1 Script. Rerum Italicarum, tom. i. part ii. p. 129. This is the sixteenth law of the emperor Lewis the Pious. His father Charlemagne had falconers in his household as well as huntsmen (Mémories sur l'Ancienne Chevalerie, par M. de St. Palaye, tom. iii. p. 175). I observe in the Laws of Rotharis a more early mention of the art of hawking (No. 322); and in Gaul, in the fifth century, it is celebrated by Sidonius Apollinaris among the talents of Avitus (202–207).

2 The epitaph of Droctulf (Paul, l. iii. c. 19) may be applied to many of his countrymen: –

> Terribilis visu facies, sed mente benignus
> Longaque robusto pectore barba fuit.

The portraits of the old Lombards might still be seen in the palace of Monza, twelve miles from Milan, which had been founded or restored by queen Theudelinda (l. iv. 22, 23). See Muratori, tom. i. dissertaz. xxiii. p. 300.

3 The story of Autharis and Theudelinda is related by Paul, l. iii. c. 29, 34; and any fragment of Bavarian antiquity excites the indefatigable diligence of the

promised bride, a Merovingian princess, he sought in marriage
the daughter of the king of Bavaria, and Garibald accepted the
alliance of the Italian monarch. Impatient of the slow progress
of negotiation, the ardent lover escaped from his palace and
visited the court of Bavaria in the train of his own embassy. At
the public audience the unknown stranger advanced to the
throne, and informed Garibald that the ambassador was indeed
the minister of state, but that he alone was the friend of Autharis, who had trusted him with the delicate commission of making a faithful report of the charms of his spouse. Theudelinda
was summoned to undergo this important examination, and,
after a pause of silent rapture, he hailed her as the queen of Italy,
and humbly requested that, according to the custom of the nation, she would present a cup of wine to the first of her new
subjects. By the command of her father she obeyed: Autharis
received the cup in his turn, and, in restoring it to the princess,
he secretly touched her hand, and drew his own finger over his
face and lips. In the evening Theudelinda imparted to her nurse
the indiscreet familiarity of the stranger, and was comforted by
the assurance that such boldness could proceed only from the
king her husband, who, by his beauty and courage, appeared
worthy of her love. The ambassadors were dismissed: no sooner
did they reach the confines of Italy than Autharis, raising himself
on his horse, darted his battle-axe against a tree with incomparable strength and dexterity: 'Such,' said he to the astonished
Bavarians, 'such are the strokes of the king of the Lombards.'
On the approach of a French army, Garibald and his daughter
took refuge in the dominions of their ally, and the marriage
was consummated in the palace of Verona. At the end of one
year it was dissolved by the death of Autharis; but the virtues
of Theudelinda[1] had endeared her to the nation, and she was
permitted to bestow, with her hand, the sceptre of the Italian
kingdom.

Count de Buat, Hist. des Peuples de l'Europe, tom. xi. p. 595–635, tom. xii.
p. 1–53.

    1 Giannone (Istoria Civile di Napoli, tom. i. p. 263) has justly censured
the impertinence of Boccaccio (Gio. iii. Novel. 2), who, without right, or
truth, or pretence, has given the pious queen Theudelinda to the arms of a
muleteer.

From this fact, as well as from similar events,[1] it is certain that the Lombards possessed freedom to elect their sovereign, and sense to decline the frequent use of that dangerous privilege. The public revenue arose from the produce of land and the profits of justice. When the independent dukes agreed that Autharis should ascend the throne of his father, they endowed the regal office with a fair moiety of their respective domains. The proudest nobles aspired to the honours of servitude near the person of their prince; he rewarded the fidelity of his vassals by the precarious gift of pensions and *benefices*, and atoned for the injuries of war by the rich foundation of monasteries and churches. In peace a judge, a leader in war, he never usurped the powers of a sole and absolute legislator. The king of Italy convened the national assemblies in the palace, or more probably in the fields, of Pavia; his great council was composed of the persons most eminent by their birth and dignities; but the validity, as well as the execution, of their decrees depended on the approbation of the *faithful* people, the *fortunate* army of the Lombards. About fourscore years after the conquest of Italy their traditional customs were transcribed in Teutonic Latin,[2] and ratified by the consent of the prince and people; some new regulations were introduced, more suitable to their present condition; the example of Rotharis was imitated by the wisest of his successors: and the laws of the Lombards have been esteemed the least imperfect of the barbaric codes.[3] Secure by their courage in the possession of liberty, these rude and hasty legislators were incapable of balancing the powers of the constitution, or of discussing the nice theory of political government. Such crimes as threatened the life of the sovereign or the safety of the state were adjudged worthy of death; but their attention was principally

1 Paul, l. iii. c. 16. The first dissertations of Muratori, and the first volume of Giannone's history, may be consulted for the state of the kingdom of Italy.

2 The most accurate edition of the Laws of the Lombards is to be found in the Scriptores Rerum Italicarum, tom. i. part ii. p. 1–181, collated from the most ancient MSS., and illustrated by the critical notes of Muratori.

3 Montesquieu, Esprit des Loix, l. xxviii. c. 1. Les loix des Bourguignons sont assez judicieuses; celles de Rotharis et des autres princes Lombards le sont encore plus.

confined to the defence of the person and property of the subject. According to the strange jurisprudence of the times, the guilt of blood might be redeemed by a fine; yet the high price of nine hundred pieces of gold declares a just sense of the value of a simple citizen. Less atrocious injuries, a wound, a fracture, a blow, an opprobrious word, were measured with scrupulous and almost ridiculous diligence; and the prudence of the legislator encouraged the ignoble practice of bartering honour and revenge for a pecuniary compensation. The ignorance of the Lombards in the state of Paganism or Christianity gave implicit credit to the malice and mischief of witchcraft: but the judges of the seventeenth century might have been instructed and confounded by the wisdom of Rotharis, who derides the absurd superstition, and protects the wretched victims of popular or judicial cruelty.[1] The same spirit of a legislator superior to his age and country may be ascribed to Liutprand, who condemns while he tolerates the impious and inveterate abuse of duels,[2] observing, from his own experience, that the juster cause had often been oppressed by successful violence. Whatever merit may be discovered in the laws of the Lombards, they are the genuine fruit of the reason of the barbarians, who never admitted the bishops of Italy to a seat in their legislative councils. But the succession of their kings is marked with virtue and ability; the troubled series of their annals is adorned with fair intervals of peace, order, and domestic happiness; and the Italians enjoyed a milder and more equitable government than any of the other kingdoms which had been founded on the ruins of the Western empire.[3]

1 See Leges Rotharis, No. 379, p. 47. Striga is used as the name of a witch. It is of the purest classic origin (Horat. epod. v. 20; Petron. c. 134); and from the words of Petronius (quæ striges comederunt nervos tuos?) it may be inferred that the prejudice was of Italian rather than barbaric extraction.

2 Quia incerti sumus de judicio Dei, et multos audivimus per pugnam sine justâ causâ suam causam perdere. Sed propter consuetudinem gentem nostram Langobardorum legem impiam vetare non possumus. See p. 74, No. 65, of the Laws of Liutprand, promulgated A.D. 724.

3 Read the history of Paul Warnefrid; particularly l. iii. c. 16. Baronius rejects the praise, which appears to contradict the invectives, of pope Gregory the Great; but Muratori (Annali d'Italia, tom. v. p. 217) presumes to insinuate that the saint may have magnified the faults of Arians and enemies.

Amidst the arms of the Lombards, and under the despotism of the Greeks, we again inquire into the fate of Rome,[1] which had reached, about the close of the sixth century, the lowest period of her depression. By the removal of the seat of empire and the successive loss of the provinces, the sources of public and private opulence were exhausted: the lofty tree, under whose shade the nations of the earth had reposed, was deprived of its leaves and branches, and the sapless trunk was left to wither on the ground. The ministers of command and the messengers of victory no longer met on the Appian or Flaminian way, and the hostile approach of the Lombards was often felt and continually feared. The inhabitants of a potent and peaceful capital, who visit without an anxious thought the garden of the adjacent country, will faintly picture in their fancy the distress of the Romans: they shut or opened their gates with a trembling hand, beheld from the walls the flames of their houses, and heard the lamentations of their brethren, who were coupled together like dogs, and dragged away into distant slavery beyond the sea and the mountains. Such incessant alarms must annihilate the pleasures and interrupt the labours of a rural life; and the Campagna of Rome was speedily reduced to the state of a dreary wilderness, in which the land is barren, the waters are impure, and the air is infectious. Curiosity and ambition no longer attracted the nations to the capital of the world; but, if chance or necessity directed the steps of a wandering stranger, he contemplated with horror the vacancy and solitude of the city, and might be tempted to ask, where is the senate, and where are the people? In a season of excessive rains the Tiber swelled above its banks, and rushed with irresistible violence into the valleys of the seven hills. A pestilential disease arose from the stagnation of the deluge, and so rapid was the contagion that fourscore persons expired in an hour in the midst of a solemn procession which implored the mercy of Heaven.[2] A society in which marriage is encouraged and industry prevails soon repairs the accidental

1 The passages of the homilies of Gregory which represent the miserable state of the city and country are transcribed in the Annals of Baronius, A.D. 590, No. 16, A.D. 595, No. 2, etc. etc.

2 The inundation and plague were reported by a deacon, whom his bishop, Gregory of Tours, had despatched to Rome for some relics. The ingenious

losses of pestilence and war; but, as the far greater part of the Romans was condemned to hopeless indigence and celibacy, the depopulation was constant and visible, and the gloomy enthusiasts might expect the approaching failure of the human race.[1] Yet the number of citizens still exceeded the measure of subsistence: their precarious food was supplied from the harvests of Sicily or Egypt, and the frequent repetition of famine betrays the inattention of the emperor to a distant province. The edifices of Rome were exposed to the same ruin and decay; the mouldering fabrics were easily overthrown by inundations, tempests, and earthquakes; and the monks, who had occupied the most advantageous stations, exulted in their base triumph over the ruins of antiquity.[2] It is commonly believed that pope Gregory the First attacked the temples and mutilated the statues of the city; that, by the command of the barbarian, the Palatine library was reduced to ashes, and that the history of Livy was the peculiar mark of his absurd and mischievous fanaticism. The writings of Gregory himself reveal his implacable aversion to the monuments of classic genius, and he points his severest censure against the profane learning of a bishop who taught the art of grammar, studied the Latin poets, and pronounced with the same voice the praises of Jupiter and those of Christ. But the evidence of his destructive rage is doubtful and recent: the Temple of Peace or the Theatre of Marcellus have been demolished by the slow operation of ages, and a formal proscription would have multiplied the copies of Virgil and Livy in the countries which were not subject to the ecclesiastical dictator.[3]

messenger embellished his tale and the river with a great dragon and a train of little serpents (Greg. Turon. l. x. c. 1).

1 Gregory of Rome (Dialog. l. ii. c. 15) relates a memorable prediction of St. Benedict. Roma à Gentilibus [gentibus] non exterminabitur sed tempestatibus, corusis turbinibus ac terræ motû [fatigata] in semetipsa marcescet. Such a prophecy melts into true history, and becomes the evidence of the fact after which it was invented.

2 Quia in uno se ore cum Jovis laudibus, Christi laudes non capiunt, et quam grave nefandumque sit episcopis canere quod nec laico religioso conveniat, ipse considera (l. ix. Ep. 4). The writings of Gregory himself attest his innocence of any classic taste or literature.

3 Bayle (Dictionnaire Critique, tom. ii. p. 598, 599), in a very good article of *Grégoire* I., has quoted, for the buildings and statues, Platina in Gregorio I.;

Like Thebes, or Babylon, or Carthage, the name of Rome
might have been erased from the earth, if the city had not been
animated by a vital principle, which again restored her to honour
and dominion. A vague tradition was embraced, that two Jewish
teachers, a tent-maker and a fisherman, had formerly been executed in the circus of Nero, and at the end of five hundred
years their genuine or fictitious relics were adored as the Palla-
dium of Christian Rome. The pilgrims of the East and West
resorted to the holy threshold; but the shrines of the apostles
were guarded by miracles and invisible terrors, and it was not
without fear that the pious catholic approached the object of his
worship. It was fatal to touch, it was dangerous to behold, the
bodies of the saints; and those who, from the purest motives,
presumed to disturb the repose of the sanctuary were affrighted
by visions or punished with sudden death. The unreasonable
request of an empress, who wished to deprive the Romans of
their sacred treasure, the head of St. Paul, was rejected with the
deepest abhorrence; and the pope asserted, most probably with
truth, that a linen which had been sanctified in the neighbourhood of his body, or the filings of his chain, which it was sometimes easy and sometimes impossible to obtain, possessed an
equal degree of miraculous virtue.[1] But the power as well as
virtue of the apostles resided with living energy in the breast of
their successors: and the chair of St. Peter was filled under the
reign of Maurice by the first and greatest of the name of
Gregory.[2] His grandfather Felix had himself been pope, and, as

for the Palatine library, John of Salisbury (de Nugis Curialium, l. ii. c. 26); and
for Livy, Antoninus of Florence: the oldest of the three lived in the twelfth
century.

1 Gregor. l. iii. Epist. 24, Indict. 12, etc. [l. iv. Ep. 30, ed. Bened.]. From the
Epistles of Gregory, and the eighth volume of the Annals of Baronius, the pious
reader may collect the particles of holy iron which were inserted in keys or
crosses of gold, and distributed in Britain, Gaul, Spain, Africa, Constantinople,
and Egypt. The pontifical smith who handled the file must have understood
the miracles which it was in his own power to operate or withhold; a circumstance which abates the superstition of Gregory at the expense of his veracity.

2 Besides the Epistles of Gregory himself, which are methodised by Dupin
(Bibliothèque Ecclés. tom. v. p. 103–126), we have three Lives of the pope; the
two first written in the eighth and ninth centuries (de Triplici Vita St. Greg.
Preface to the fourth volume of the Benedictine edition) by the deacons Paul
(p. 1–18) and John (p. 19–188), and containing much original, though doubtful,

the bishops were already bound by the law of celibacy, his consecration must have been preceded by the death of his wife. The
parents of Gregory, Sylvia and Gordian, were the noblest of the
senate and the most pious of the church of Rome; his female
relations were numbered among the saints and virgins, and his
own figure, with those of his father and mother, were represented near three hundred years in a family portrait[1] which he
offered to the monastery of St. Andrew. The design and colour-
ing of this picture afford an honourable testimony that the art
of painting was cultivated by the Italians of the sixth century;
but the most abject ideas must be entertained of their taste and
learning, since the epistles of Gregory, his sermons, and his
dialogues, are the work of a man who was second in erudition
to none of his contemporaries:[2] his birth and abilities had raised
him to the office of præfect of the city, and he enjoyed the merit
of renouncing the pomp and vanities of this world. His ample
patrimony was dedicated to the foundation of seven monasteries,[3] one in Rome[4] and six in Sicily; and it was the wish of

evidence; the third, a long and laboured compilation by the Benedictine editors
(p. 199–305). The Annals of Baronius are a copious but partial history. His
papal prejudices are tempered by the good sense of Fleury. (Hist. Ecclés.
tom. viii.), and his chronology has been rectified by the criticism of Pagi and
Muratori.

1 John the deacon has described them like an eye-witness (l. iv. c. 83, 84);
and his description is illustrated by Angelo Rocca, a Roman antiquary (St. Greg.
Opera, tom. iv. p. 312–326), who observes that some mosaics of the popes of
the seventh century are still preserved in the old churches of Rome (p. 321–323).
The same walls which represented Gregory's family are now decorated with the
martyrdom of St. Andrew, the noble contest of Domenichino and Guido.

2 Disciplinis vero liberalibus, hoc est grammaticâ, rhetoricâ, dialecticâ ita a
puero est institutus, ut quamvis eo tempore florerent adhuc Romæ studia literarum,
tamen nulli in urbe ipsâ secundus putaretur. Paul. Diacon. in Vit. S. Gregor. c. 2.

3 The Benedictines (Vit. Greg. l. i. p. 205–208) labour to reduce the monasteries of Gregory within the rule of their own order; but as the question is
confessed to be doubtful, it is clear that these powerful monks are in the wrong.
See Butler's Lives of the Saints, vol. iii. p. 145; a work of merit: the sense and
learning belong to the author – his prejudices are those of his profession.

4 Monasterium Gregorianum in ejusdem Beati Gregorii ædibus ad clivum
Scauri prope ecclesiam SS. Johannis et Pauli in honorem St. Andræ (John, in Vit.
Greg. l. i. c. 6; Greg. l. vii. Epist. 13). This house and monastery were situate on
the side of the Cælian hill which fronts the Palatine; they are now occupied by the
Camaldoli: San Gregorio triumphs, and St. Andrew has retired to a small chapel.
Nardini, Roma Antica, l. iii. c. 6, p. 100; Descrizione di Roma, tom. i. p. 442–446.

Gregory that he might be unknown in this life and glorious only in the next. Yet his devotion, and it might be sincere, pursued the path which would have been chosen by a crafty and ambitious statesman. The talents of Gregory, and the splendour which accompanied his retreat, rendered him dear and useful to the church, and implicit obedience has been always inculcated as the first duty of a monk. As soon as he had received the character of deacon, Gregory was sent to reside at the Byzantine court, the nuncio or minister of the apostolic see; and he boldly assumed, in the name of St. Peter, a tone of independent dignity which would have been criminal and dangerous in the most illustrious layman of the empire. He returned to Rome with a just increase of reputation, and, after a short exercise of the monastic virtues, he was dragged from the cloister to the papal throne by the unanimous voice of the clergy, the senate, and the people. He alone resisted, or seemed to resist, his own elevation; and his humble petition that Maurice would be pleased to reject the choice of the Romans could only serve to exalt his character in the eyes of the emperor and the public. When the fatal mandate was proclaimed, Gregory solicited the aid of some friendly merchants to convey him in a basket beyond the gates of Rome, and modestly concealed himself some days among the woods and mountains, till his retreat was discovered, as it is said, by a celestial light.

The pontificate of Gregory the *Great*, which lasted thirteen years, six months, and ten days, is one of the most edifying periods of the history of the church. His virtues, and even his faults, a singular mixture of simplicity and cunning, of pride and humility, of sense and superstition, were happily suited to his station and to the temper of the times. In his rival, the patriarch of Constantinople, he condemned the antichristian title of universal bishop, which the successor of St. Peter was too haughty to concede and too feeble to assume; and the ecclesiastical jurisdiction of Gregory was confined to the triple character of Bishop of Rome, Primate of Italy, and Apostle of the West. He frequently ascended the pulpit, and kindled, by his rude though pathetic eloquence, the congenial passions of his audience: the language of the Jewish prophets was interpreted and applied; and the minds of a people depressed by their present calamities were directed to the hopes and fears of the invisible world. His precepts and example defined the model of the Roman liturgy;[1] the distribution of the parishes, the calendar of festivals, the order of processions, the service of the priests and deacons, the variety and change of sacerdotal garments. Till the last days of his life he officiated in the canon of the mass, which continued above three hours: the Gregorian chant[2] has preserved the vocal and instrumental music of the theatre, and the rough voices of the barbarians attempted to imitate the melody of the Roman school.[3] Experience had shown him the efficacy of these solemn and pompous rites to soothe the distress, to confirm the faith, to mitigate the fierceness, and to dispel the dark enthusiasm of the vulgar, and he readily forgave their tendency to promote the reign of priesthood and superstition. The bishops of Italy and the adjacent islands acknowledged the Roman pontiff as their special metropolitan. Even the existence, the union, or the translation of episcopal seats was decided by his absolute discretion: and his successful inroads into the provinces of Greece, of Spain, and of Gaul, might countenance the more lofty pretensions of succeeding popes. He interposed to prevent the abuses of popular elections; his jealous care maintained the purity of faith and discipline; and the apostolic shepherd assiduously watched over the faith and discipline of the subordinate pastors. Under his reign the Arians of Italy and Spain were

---

1 The Lord's prayer consists of half a dozen lines; the Sacramentarius and Antiphonarius of Gregory fill 880 folio pages (tom. iii. P. i. p. 1–880); yet these only constitute a part of the *Ordo Romanus*, which Mabillon has illustrated and Fleury has abridged (Hist. Ecclés. tom. viii. p. 139–152).

2 I learn from the Abbé Dubos (Réflexions sur la Poésie et la Peinture, tom. iii. p. 174, 175) that the simplicity of the Ambrosian chant was confined to four *modes*, while the more perfect harmony of the Gregorian comprised the eight modes or fifteen chords of the ancient music. He observes (p. 332) that the connoisseurs admire the preface and many passages of the Gregorian office.

3 John the deacon (in Vit. Greg. l. ii. c. 7) expresses the early contempt of the Italians for tramontane singing. Alpina scilicet corpora vocum suarum tonitruis altisone perstrepentia, susceptæ modulationis dulcedinem proprie non resultant: quia bibuli gutturis barbara feritas dum inflexionibus et repercussionibus mitem nititur edere cantilenam, naturali quodam fragore, quasi plaustra per gradus confuse sonantia, rigidas voces jactat, etc. In the time of Charlemagne, the Franks, though with some reluctance, admitted the justice of the reproach. Muratori, Dissert. xxv.

reconciled to the catholic church, and the conquest of Britain reflects less glory on the name of Cæsar than on that of Gregory the First. Instead of six legions, forty monks were embarked for that distant island, and the pontiff lamented the austere duties which forbade him to partake the perils of their spiritual warfare. In less than two years he could announce to the archbishop of Alexandria that they had baptised the king of Kent with ten thousand of his Anglo-Saxons; and that the Roman missionaries, like those of the primitive church, were armed only with spiritual and supernatural powers. The credulity or the prudence of Gregory was always disposed to confirm the truths of religion by the evidence of ghosts, miracles, and resurrections;[1] and posterity has paid to *his* memory the same tribute which he freely granted to the virtue of his own or the preceding generation. The celestial honours have been liberally bestowed by the authority of the popes, but Gregory is the last of their own order whom they have presumed to inscribe in the calendar of saints.

Their temporal power insensibly arose from the calamities of the times; and the Roman bishops, who have deluged Europe and Asia with blood, were compelled to reign as the ministers of charity and peace. I. The church of Rome, as it has been formerly observed, was endowed with ample possessions in Italy, Sicily, and the more distant provinces; and her agents, who were commonly subdeacons, had acquired a civil and even criminal jurisdiction over their tenants and husbandmen. The successor of St. Peter administered his patrimony with the temper of a vigilant and moderate landlord;[2] and the epistles of Gregory are filled with salutary instructions to abstain from doubtful or vexatious lawsuits, to preserve the integrity of weights and measures, to grant every reasonable delay, and to reduce the capitation of the slaves of the glebe, who purchased the right of marriage by

1 A French critic (Petrus Gussanvillus, Opera, tom. ii. p. 105–112) has vindicated the right of Gregory to the entire nonsense of the Dialogues. Dupin (tom. v. p. 138) does not think that any one will vouch for the truth of all these miracles: I should like to know *how many* of them he believed himself.

2 Baronius is unwilling to expatiate on the care of the patrimonies, lest he should betray that they consisted not of *kingdoms* but *farms*. The French writers, the Benedictine editors (tom. iv. l. iii. p. 272, etc.), and Fleury (tom. viii. p. 29, etc.), are not afraid of entering into these humble, though useful, details; and the humanity of Fleury dwells on the social virtues of Gregory.

the payment of an arbitrary fine.¹ The rent or the produce of
these estates was transported to the mouth of the Tiber, at the
risk and expense of the pope: in the use of wealth he acted like
a faithful steward of the church and the poor, and liberally applied to their wants the inexhaustible resources of abstinence and
order. The voluminous account of his receipts and disburse-
ments was kept above three hundred years in the Lateran, as the
model of Christian economy. On the four great festivals he
divided their quarterly allowance to the clergy, to his domestics,
to the monasteries, the churches, the places of burial, the alms-
houses, and the hospitals of Rome, and the rest of the diocese.
On the first day of every month he distributed to the poor,
according to the season, their stated portion of corn, wine,
cheese, vegetables, oil, fish, fresh provisions, clothes, and money;
and his treasurers were continually summoned to satisfy, in his
name, the extraordinary demands of indigence and merit. The
instant distress of the sick and helpless, of strangers and pilgrims,
was relieved by the bounty of each day and of every hour; nor
would the pontiff indulge himself in a frugal repast till he had
sent the dishes from his own table to some objects deserving of
his compassion. The misery of the times had reduced the nobles
and matrons of Rome to accept, without a blush, the benevolence of the church: three thousand virgins received their food
and raiment from the hand of their benefactor; and many
bishops of Italy escaped from the barbarians to the hospitable
threshold of the Vatican. Gregory might justly be styled the
Father of his country; and such was the extreme sensibility of
his conscience, that, for the death of a beggar who had perished
in the streets, he interdicted himself during several days from the
exercise of sacerdotal functions. II. The misfortunes of Rome
involved the apostolical pastor in the business of peace and war;
and it might be doubtful to himself whether piety or ambition
prompted him to supply the place of his absent sovereign.
Gregory awakened the emperor from a long slumber; exposed

1 I much suspect that this pecuniary fine on the marriages of villains
produced the famous, and often fabulous, right, *de cuissage, de marquette*, etc. With
the consent of her husband, a handsome bride might commute the payment in
the arms of a young landlord, and the mutual favour might afford a precedent
of local rather than legal tyranny.

the guilt or incapacity of the exarch and his inferior ministers; complained that the veterans were withdrawn from Rome for the defence of Spoleto; encouraged the Italians to guard their cities and altars; and condescended, in the crisis of danger, to name the tribunes and to direct the operations of the provincial troops. But the martial spirit of the pope was checked by the scruples of humanity and religion: the imposition of tribute, though it was employed in the Italian war, he freely condemned as odious and oppressive; whilst he protected, against the Imperial edicts, the pious cowardice of the soldiers who deserted a military for a monastic life. If we may credit his own declarations, it would have been easy for Gregory to exterminate the Lombards by their domestic factions, without leaving a king, a duke, or a count, to save that unfortunate nation from the vengeance of their foes. As a Christian bishop, he preferred the salutary offices of peace; his mediation appeased the tumult of arms; but he was too conscious of the arts of the Greeks and the passions of the Lombards to engage his sacred promise for the observance of the truce. Disappointed in the hope of a general and lasting treaty, he presumed to save his country without the consent of the emperor or the exarch. The sword of the enemy was suspended over Rome; it was averted by the mild eloquence and seasonable gifts of the pontiff, who commanded the respect of heretics and barbarians. The merits of Gregory were treated by the Byzantine court with reproach and insult; but in the attachment of a grateful people he found the purest reward of a citizen, and the best right of a sovereign.[1]

---

1 The temporal reign of Gregory I. is ably exposed by Sigonius in the first book, de Regno Italiæ. See his works, tom. ii. p. 44–75.

CHAPTER XLVI

Revolutions of Persia after the Death of Chosroes or Nushirvan – His Son Hormouz, a Tyrant, is deposed – Usurpation of Bahram – Flight and Restoration of Chosroes II. – His Gratitude to the Romans – The Chagan of the Avars – Revolt of the Army against Maurice – His Death – Tyranny of Phocas – Elevation of Heraclius – The Persian War – Chosroes subdues Syria, Egypt, and Asia Minor – Siege of Constantinople by the Persians and Avars – Persian Expeditions – Victories and Triumph of Heraclius

THE conflict of Rome and Persia was prolonged from the death of Crassus to the reign of Heraclius. An experience of seven hundred years might convince the rival nations of the impossibility of maintaining their conquests beyond the fatal limits of the Tigris and Euphrates. Yet the emulation of Trajan and Julian was awakened by the trophies of Alexander, and the sovereigns of Persia indulged the ambitious hope of restoring the empire of Cyrus.[1] Such extraordinary efforts of power and courage will always command the attention of posterity; but the events by which the fate of nations is not materially changed leave a faint impression on the page of history, and the patience of the reader would be exhausted by the repetition of the same hostilities, undertaken without cause, prosecuted without glory, and terminated without effect. The arts of negotiation, unknown to the simple greatness of the senate and the Cæsars, were assiduously cultivated by the Byzantine princes; and the memorials of their perpetual embassies[2] repeat, with the same uniform prolixity, the language of falsehood and declamation, the insolence of the barbarians, and the servile temper of the tributary Greeks. Lamenting the barren superfluity of materials, I have studied to compress the narrative of these uninteresting transactions: but the just Nushirvan is still applauded as the model of Oriental

1 Missisqui ... reposcerent ... veteres Persarum ac Macedonum terminos, seque invasurum possessa Cyro et post Alexandro, per vaniloquentiam ac minas jaciebat. Tacit. Annal. vi. 31. Such was the language of the *Arsacides*. I have repeatedly marked the lofty claims of the *Sassanians*.

2 See the embassies of Menander, extracted and preserved in the tenth century by the order of Constantine Porphyrogenitus.

kings, and the ambition of his grandson Chosroes prepared the revolution of the East, which was speedily accomplished by the arms and the religion of the successors of Mohammed.

In the useless altercations that precede and justify the quarrels of princes, the Greeks and the barbarians accused each other of violating the peace which had been concluded between the two empires about four years before the death of Justinian. The sovereign of Persia and India aspired to reduce under his obedience the province of Yemen, or Arabia[1] Felix; the distant land of myrrh and frankincense, which had escaped, rather than opposed, the conquerors of the East. After the defeat of Abrahah under the walls of Mecca, the discord of his sons and brothers gave an easy entrance to the Persians: they chased the strangers of Abyssinia beyond the Red Sea; and a native prince of the ancient Homerites was restored to the throne as the vassal or viceroy of the great Nushirvan.[2] But the nephew of Justinian

1 The general independence of the Arabs, which cannot be admitted without many limitations, is blindly asserted in a separate dissertation of the authors of the Universal History, vol. xx. p. 196–250. A perpetual miracle is supposed to have guarded the prophecy in favour of the posterity of Ishmael; and these learned bigots are not afraid to risk the truth of Christianity on this frail and slippery foundation.

[It certainly seems difficult, as Milman says, to extract a prediction of the perpetual independence of the Arabs from the text in Genesis, which would have received an ample fulfilment during centuries of uninvaded freedom. But the disputants appear to forget the inseparable connection, in the prediction of the wild, the Bedoween habits of the Ismaelites, with their national independence. The stationary and civilised descendant of Ishmael, forfeited, as it were, his birthright, and ceased to be a genuine son of the 'wild man.' The phrase, 'dwelling in the presence of his brethren,' is interpreted by Rosenmüller (in loc.) and others, according to the Hebrew geography, 'to the east' of his brethren, the legitimate descendants of Abraham. – O. S.]

2 D'Herbelot, Biblioth. Orient. p. 477; Pocock, Specimen Hist. Arabum, p. 64, 65. Father Pagi (Critica, tom. ii. p. 646) has proved that, after ten years' peace, the Persian war, which continued twenty years, was renewed A.D. 571. Mahomet was born A.D. 569, in the year of the elephant, or the defeat of Abrahah (Gagnier, Vie de Mahomet, tom. i. p. 89, 90, 98); and this account allows two years for the conquest of Yemen.

[Clinton has conclusively proved, with regard to the renewal of the Persian war, that it was resumed in the seventh year of Justin's reign = 572 A.D. Abrahah is said to have been succeeded by his son Taksoum, who reigned seventeen years; his brother Mascouh, who was slain in battle against the Persians, twelve; but this chronology is irreconcilable with the Arabian conquests of Nushirvan

declared his resolution to avenge the injuries of his Christian ally the prince of Abyssinia, as they suggested a decent pretence to discontinue the annual *tribute*, which was poorly disguised by the name of pension. The churches of Persarmenia were oppressed by the intolerant spirit of the Magi;[1] they secretly invoked the protector of the Christians, and, after the pious murder of their satraps, the rebels were avowed and supported as the brethren and subjects of the Roman emperor. The complaints of Nushirvan were disregarded by the Byzantine court; Justin yielded to the importunities of the Turks, who offered an alliance against the common enemy; and the Persian monarchy was threatened at the same instant by the united forces of Europe, of Æthiopia, and of Scythia. At the age of fourscore the sovereign of the East would perhaps have chosen the peaceful enjoyment of his glory and greatness; but as soon as war became inevitable he took the field with the alacrity of youth, whilst the aggressor trembled in the palace of Constantinople. Nushirvan or Chosroes conducted in person the siege of Dara; and although that important fortress had been left destitute of troops and magazines, the valour of the inhabitants resisted above five months the archers, the elephants, and the military engines of the Great King. In the meanwhile his general Adarman advanced from Babylon, traversed the desert, passed the Euphrates, insulted the suburbs of Antioch, reduced to ashes the city of Apamea, and laid the spoils of Syria at the feet of his master, whose perseverance in the midst of winter at length subverted the bulwark of the East. But these

the Great. Either Seif, or his son Maadi Karb, was the native prince placed on the throne by the Persians. – O. S.]

1 [Persarmenia was long maintained in peace by the tolerant administration of Mejej, prince of the Gnounians. On his death he was succeeded by a persecutor, a Persian, named Ten-Schahpour, who attempted to propagate Zoroastrianism by violence. Nushirvan, on an appeal to the throne by the Armenian clergy, replaced Ten-Schahpour, in 552, by Veschnas-Vahram. The new governor was instructed to repress the bigoted Magi in their persecutions of the Armenians, but the Persian converts to Christianity underwent great sufferings. The most distinguished of them, Izdbouzid, was crucified at Dovin in the presence of a vast multitude. The fame of the martyr spread to the West. Armenia remained long at peace under Veschnas-Vahram and his successor Varazdat. The tyranny of his successor Surena led to the rising under Vartan, who revenged the death of his brother on Surena, and put the whole Magian party in Dovin to the sword. – O. S.]

losses, which astonished the provinces and the court, produced a salutary effect in the repentance and abdication of the emperor Justin: a new spirit arose in the Byzantine councils; and a truce of three years was obtained by the prudence of Tiberius. That seasonable interval was employed in the preparations of war; and the voice of rumour proclaimed to the world that from the distant countries of the Alps and the Rhine, from Scythia, Mæsia, Pannonia, Illyricum, and Isauria, the strength of the Imperial cavalry was reinforced with one hundred and fifty thousand soldiers. Yet the king of Persia, without fear or without faith, resolved to prevent the attack of the enemy; again passed the Euphrates, and, dismissing the ambassadors of Tiberius, arrogantly commanded them to await his arrival at Cæsarea, the metropolis of the Cappadocian provinces. The two armies encountered each other in the battle of Melitene: the barbarians, who darkened the air with a cloud of arrows, prolonged their line and extended their wings across the plain; while the Romans, in deep and solid bodies, expected to prevail in closer action by the weight of their swords and lances. A Scythian chief, who commanded their right wing, suddenly turned the flank of the enemy, attacked their rear-guard in the presence of Chosroes, penetrated to the midst of the camp, pillaged the royal tent, profaned the eternal fire, loaded a train of camels with the spoils of Asia, cut his way through the Persian host, and returned with songs of victory to his friends, who had consumed the day in single combats or ineffectual skirmishes. The darkness of the night and the separation of the Romans afforded the Persian monarch an opportunity of revenge; and one of their camps was swept away by a rapid and impetuous assault. But the review of his loss and the consciousness of his danger determined Chosroes to a speedy retreat: he burnt in his passage the vacant town of Melitene; and, without consulting the safety of his troops, boldly swam the Euphrates on the back of an elephant. After this unsuccessful campaign, the want of magazines, and perhaps some inroad of the Turks, obliged him to disband or divide his forces; the Romans were left masters of the field, and their general Justinian, advancing to the relief of the Persarmenian rebels, erected his standard on the banks of the Araxes. The great Pompey had formerly halted within three days' march of the Caspian:[1] that inland sea was explored for the first time by a hostile fleet,[2] and seventy thousand captives were transplanted from Hyrcania to the isle of Cyprus. On the return of spring Justinian descended into the fertile plains of Assyria; the flames of war approached the residence of Nushirvan; the indignant monarch sunk into the grave; and his last edict restrained his successors from exposing their person in a battle against the Romans. Yet the memory of this transient affront was lost in the glories of a long reign; and his formidable enemies, after indulging their dream of conquest, again solicited a short respite from the calamities of war.[3]

The throne of Chosroes Nushirvan was filled by Hormouz, or Hormisdas, the eldest or the most favoured of his sons. With the kingdoms of Persia and India, he inherited the reputation and example of his father, the service, in every rank, of his wise and valiant officers, and a general system of administration harmonised by time and political wisdom to promote the happiness of the prince and people. But the royal youth enjoyed a still more valuable blessing, the friendship of a sage who had presided over his education, and who always preferred the honour to the interest of his pupil, his interest to his inclination. In a dispute with the Greek and Indian philosophers, Buzurg[4] had once

1 He had vanquished the Albanians, who brought into the field 12,000 horse and 60,000 foot; but he dreaded the multitude of venomous reptiles, whose existence may admit of some doubt, as well as that of the neighbouring Amazons. Plutarch, in Pompeio [c. 36], tom. ii. p. 1165, 1166.

2 In the history of the world I can only perceive two navies on the Caspian: 1. Of the Macedonians, when Patrocles, the admiral of the kings of Syria, Seleucus and Antiochus, descended most probably the river Oxus, from the confines of India (Plin. Hist. Natur. vi. 21). 2. Of the Russians, when Peter the First conducted a fleet and army from the neighbourhood of Moscow to the coast of Persia (Bell's Travels, vol. ii. p. 325–352). He justly observes that such martial pomp had never been displayed on the Volga.

3 For these Persian wars and treaties, see Menander, in Excerpt. Legat. p. 113–125 [p. 311–331, ed. Bonn]; Theophanes Byzant. apud Photium, cod. lxiv. p. 77, 80, 81 [p. 26, 27, ed. Bekk.]; Evagrius, l. v. c. 7–15; Theophylact, l. iii. c. 9–16; Agathias, l. iv. [c. 29] p. 140 [p. 271, ed. Bonn].

4 Buzurg Mihir may be considered, in his character and station, as the Seneca of the East; but his virtues, and perhaps his faults, are less known than those of the Roman, who appears to have been much more loquacious. The Persian sage was the person who imported from India the game of chess and

maintained that the most grievous misfortune of life is old age without the remembrance of virtue; and our candour will presume that the same principle compelled him during three years to direct the councils of the Persian empire. His zeal was rewarded by the gratitude and docility of Hormouz, who acknowledged himself more indebted to his preceptor than to his parent: but when age and labour had impaired the strength, and perhaps the faculties, of this prudent counsellor, he retired from court and abandoned the youthful monarch to his own passions and those of his favourites. By the fatal vicissitude of human affairs the same scenes were renewed at Ctesiphon which had been exhibited in Rome after the death of Marcus Antoninus. The ministers of flattery and corruption, who had been banished by the father, were recalled and cherished by the son; the disgrace and exile of the friends of Nushirvan established their tyranny; and virtue was driven by degrees from the mind of Hormouz, from his palace, and from the government of the state. The faithful agents, the eyes and ears of the king, informed him of the progress of disorder, that the provincial governors flew to their prey with the fierceness of lions and eagles, and that their rapine and injustice would teach the most loyal of his subjects to abhor the name and authority of their sovereign. The sincerity of this advice was punished with death; the murmurs of the cities were despised, their tumults were quelled by military execution; the intermediate powers between the throne and the people were abolished; and the childish vanity of Hormouz, who affected the daily use of the tiara, was fond of declaring that he alone would be the judge as well as the master of his kingdom. In every word and in every action the son of Nushirvan degenerated from the virtues of his father. His avarice defrauded the troops; his jealous caprice degraded the satraps; the palace, the tribunals, the waters of the Tigris, were stained with the blood of the innocent, and the tyrant exulted in the sufferings and execution of thirteen thousand victims. As the excuse of his cruelty, he sometimes condescended to observe that the fears of the Persians would be

the fables of Pilpay. Such has been the fame of his wisdom and virtues, that the Christians claim him as a believer in the Gospel; and the Mohammedans revere Buzurg as a premature Musulman. D'Herbelot, Bibliothèque Orientale, p. 218.

productive of hatred, and that their hatred must terminate in rebellion; but he forgot that his own guilt and folly had inspired the sentiments which he deplored, and prepared the event which he so justly apprehended. Exasperated by long and hopeless oppression, the provinces of Babylon, Susa, and Carmania erected the standard of revolt; and the princes of Arabia, India, and Scythia refused the customary tribute to the unworthy successor of Nushirvan. The arms of the Romans, in slow sieges and frequent inroads, afflicted the frontiers of Mesopotamia and Assyria: one of their generals professed himself the disciple of Scipio; and the soldiers were animated by a miraculous image of Christ, whose mild aspect should never have been displayed in the front of battle.[1] At the same time the eastern provinces of Persia were invaded by the great khan, who passed the Oxus at the head of three or four hundred thousand Turks. The imprudent Hormouz accepted their perfidious and formidable aid; the cities of Khorassan or Bactriana were commanded to open their gates; the march of the barbarians towards the mountains of Hyrcania revealed the correspondence of the Turkish and Roman arms; and their union must have subverted the throne of the house of Sassan.

Persia had been lost by a king; it was saved by a hero. After his revolt, Varanes or Bahram is stigmatised by the son of Hormouz as an ungrateful slave: the proud and ambiguous reproach of despotism, since he was truly descended from the ancient princes of Rei,[2] one of the seven families whose splendid, as well as substantial, prerogative exalted them above the heads of the

---

1 See the imitation of Scipio in Theophylact, l. i. c. 14; the image of Christ, l. ii. c. 3. Hereafter I shall speak more amply of the Christian *images* – I had almost said *idols*. This, if I am not mistaken, is the oldest ἀχειροποίητος of divine manufacture; but in the next thousand years, many others issued from the same workshop.

2 Ragæ, or Rei, is mentioned in the apocryphal book of Tobit as already flourishing 700 years before Christ, under the Assyrian empire. Under the foreign names of Europus and Arsacia, this city, 500 stadia to the south of the Caspian gates, was successively embellished by the Macedonians and Parthians (Strabo, l. xi. p. 796 [p. 524, ed. Casaub.]). Its grandeur and populousness in the ninth century is exaggerated beyond the bounds of credibility; but Rei has been since ruined by wars and the unwholesomeness of the air. Chardin, Voyage en Perse, tom. i. p. 279, 280; D'Herbelot, Biblioth. Oriental. p. 714.

Persian nobility.[1] At the siege of Dara the valour of Bahram was signalised under the eyes of Nushirvan, and both the father and son successively promoted him to the command of armies, the government of Media, and the superintendence of the palace. The popular prediction which marked him as the deliverer of Persia might be inspired by his past victories and extraordinary figure: the epithet *Giubin* is expressive of the quality of *dry wood*; he had the strength and stature of a giant; and his savage countenance was fancifully compared to that of a wild cat. While the nation trembled, while Hormouz disguised his terror by the name of suspicion, and his servants concealed their disloyalty under the mask of fear, Bahram alone displayed his undaunted courage and apparent fidelity: and as soon as he found that no more than twelve thousand soldiers would follow him against the enemy, he prudently declared that to this fatal number Heaven had reserved the honours of the triumph. The steep and narrow descent of the Pule Rudbar,[2] or Hyrcanian rock, is the only pass through which an army can penetrate into the territory of Rei and the plains of Media. From the commanding heights a band of resolute men might overwhelm with stones and darts the myriads of the Turkish host: their emperor and his son were transpierced with arrows; and the fugitives were left, without counsel or provisions, to the revenge of an injured people. The patriotism of the Persian general was stimulated by his affection for the city of his forefathers; in the hour of victory every peasant became a soldier, and every soldier a hero; and their ardour was kindled by the gorgeous spectacle of beds, and thrones, and

1 Theophylact, l. iii. c. 18 [p. 153, ed. Bonn]. The story of the seven Persians is told in the third book of Herodotus; and their noble descendants are often mentioned, especially in the fragments of Ctesias. Yet the independence of Otanes (Herodot. l. iii. c. 83, 84) is hostile to the spirit of despotism, and it may not seem probable that the seven families could survive the revolutions of eleven hundred years. They might however be represented by the seven ministers (Brisson, de Regno Persico, l. i. p. 190); and some Persian nobles, like the kings of Pontus (Polyb. l. v. [c. 43] p. 540) and Cappadocia (Diodor. Sicul. l. xxxi. [c. 19] tom. ii. p. 517), might claim their descent from the bold companions of Darius.

2 See an accurate description of this mountain by Olearius (Voyage en Perse, p. 997, 998), who ascended it with much difficulty and danger in his return from Ispahan to the Caspian Sea.

tables of massy gold, the spoils of Asia and the luxury of the hostile camp. A prince of a less malignant temper could not easily have forgiven his benefactor; and the secret hatred of Hormouz was envenomed by a malicious report that Bahram had privately retained the most precious fruits of his Turkish victory. But the approach of a Roman army on the side of the Araxes compelled the implacable tyrant to smile and to applaud; and the toils of Bahram were rewarded with the permission of encountering a new enemy, by their skill and discipline more formidable than a Scythian multitude. Elated by his recent success, he despatched a herald with a bold defiance to the camp of the Romans, requesting them to fix a day of battle, and to choose whether they would pass the river themselves, or allow a free passage to the arms of the Great King. The lieutenant of the emperor Maurice preferred the safer alternative; and this local circumstance, which would have enhanced the victory of the Persians, rendered their defeat more bloody and their escape more difficult. But the loss of his subjects, and the danger of his kingdom, were over-balanced in the mind of Hormouz by the disgrace of his personal enemy; and no sooner had Bahram collected and reviewed his forces than he received from a royal messenger the insulting gift of a distaff, a spinning-wheel, and a complete suit of female apparel. Obedient to the will of his sovereign, he showed himself to the soldiers in this unworthy disguise: they resented his ignominy and their own; a shout of rebellion ran through the ranks; and the general accepted their oath of fidelity and vows of revenge. A second messenger, who had been commanded to bring the rebel in chains, was trampled under the feet of an elephant, and manifestos were diligently circulated, exhorting the Persians to assert their freedom against an odious and contemptible tyrant. The defection was rapid and universal; his loyal slaves were sacrificed to the public fury; the troops deserted to the standard of Bahram; and the provinces again saluted the deliverer of his country.

As the passes were faithfully guarded, Hormouz could only compute the number of his enemies by the testimony of a guilty conscience, and the daily defection of those who, in the hour of his distress, avenged their wrongs or forgot their obligations. He proudly displayed the ensigns of royalty; but the city and palace of Modain had already escaped from the hand of the tyrant. Among the victims of his cruelty, Bindoes, a Sassanian prince, had been cast into a dungeon: his fetters were broken by the zeal and courage of a brother; and he stood before the king at the head of those trusty guards who had been chosen as the ministers of his confinement, and perhaps of his death. Alarmed by the hasty intrusion and bold reproaches of the captive, Hormouz looked round, but in vain, for advice or assistance; discovered that his strength consisted in the obedience of others; and patiently yielded to the single arm of Bindoes, who dragged him from the throne to the same dungeon in which he himself had been so lately confined. At the first tumult, Chosroes, the eldest of the sons of Hormouz, escaped from the city; he was persuaded to return by the pressing and friendly invitation of Bindoes, who promised to seat him on his father's throne, and who expected to reign under the name of an inexperienced youth. In the just assurance that his accomplices could neither forgive nor hope to be forgiven, and that every Persian might be trusted as the judge and enemy of the tyrant, he instituted a public trial without a precedent and without a copy in the annals of the East. The son of Nushirvan, who had requested to plead in his own defence, was introduced as a criminal into the full assembly of the nobles and satraps.[1] He was heard with decent attention as long as he expatiated on the advantages of order and obedience, the danger of innovation, and the inevitable discord of those who had encouraged each other to trample on their lawful and hereditary sovereign. By a pathetic appeal to their humanity he extorted that pity which is seldom refused to the fallen fortunes of a king; and while they beheld the abject posture and squalid appearance of the prisoner, his tears, his chains, and the marks of ignominious stripes, it was impossible to forget how recently they had adored the divine splendour of his diadem and purple. But an angry murmur arose in the assembly as soon as he presumed to vindicate his conduct, and to applaud the victories of his reign. He defined the duties of a king, and the Persian nobles listened with a smile of contempt; they were fired with indignation

1 The Orientals suppose that Bahram convened this assembly and proclaimed Chosroes; but Theophylact is, in this instance, more distinct and credible.

when he dared to vilify the character of Chosroes; and by the indiscreet offer of resigning the sceptre to the second of his sons, he subscribed his own condemnation and sacrificed the life of his innocent favourite. The mangled bodies of the boy and his mother were exposed to the people; the eyes of Hormouz were pierced with a hot needle; and the punishment of the father was succeeded by the coronation of his eldest son. Chosroes had ascended the throne without guilt, and his piety strove to alleviate the misery of the abdicated monarch; from the dungeon he removed Hormouz to an apartment of the palace, supplied with liberality the consolations of sensual enjoyment, and patiently endured the furious sallies of his resentment and despair. He might despise the resentment of a blind and unpopular tyrant, but the tiara was trembling on his head, till he could subvert the power, or acquire the friendship, of the great Bahram, who sternly denied the justice of a revolution in which himself and his soldiers, the true representatives of Persia, had never been consulted. The offer of a general amnesty, and of the second rank in his kingdom, was answered by an epistle from Bahram, friend of the gods, conqueror of men, and enemy of tyrants, the satrap of satraps, general of the Persian armies, and a prince adorned with the title of eleven virtues.[1] He commands Chosroes, the son of Hormouz, to shun the example and fate of his father, to confine the traitors who had been released from their chains, to deposit in some holy place the diadem which he had usurped, and to accept from his gracious benefactor the pardon of his faults and the government of a province. The rebel might not be proud, and the king most assuredly was not humble; but the one was conscious of his strength, the other was sensible of his weakness; and even the modest language of his reply still left room for treaty and reconciliation. Chosroes led into the field the slaves of the palace and the populace of the capital: they beheld with terror the banners of a veteran army; they were encompassed and surprised by the evolutions of the general; and

---

1 See the words of Theophylact, l. iv. c. 7 [p. 173, ed. Bonn]. Βαρὰμ φίλος τοῖς θεοῖς, νικητής, ἐπιφανής, τυράννων ἐχθρὸς, σατράπης μεγιστάνων, τῆς Περσικῆς ἄρχων δυνάμεως, etc. In his answer Chosroes styles himself τῇ νυκτὶ χαριζόμενος ὄμματα ... ὁ τοὺς Ἀσωνας (the genii) μισθούμενος [p. 175]. This is genuine Oriental bombast.

the satraps who had deposed Hormouz received the punishment of their revolt, or expiated their first treason by a second and more criminal act of disloyalty. The life and liberty of Chosroes were saved, but he was reduced to the necessity of imploring aid or refuge in some foreign land; and the implacable Bindoes, anxious to secure an unquestionable title, hastily returned to the palace, and ended, with a bow-string, the wretched existence of the son of Nushirvan.[1]

While Chosroes despatched the preparations of his retreat, he deliberated with his remaining friends[2] whether he should lurk in the valleys of Mount Caucasus, or fly to the tents of the Turks, or solicit the protection of the emperor. The long emulation of the successors of Artaxerxes and Constantine increased his reluctance to appear as a suppliant in a rival court; but he weighed the forces of the Romans, and prudently considered that the neighbourhood of Syria would render his escape more easy and their succours more effectual. Attended only by his concubines and a troop of thirty guards, he secretly departed from the capital, followed the banks of the Euphrates, traversed the desert, and halted at the distance of ten miles from Circesium. About the third watch of the night the Roman præfect was informed of his approach, and he introduced the royal stranger to the fortress at the dawn of day. From thence the king of Persia was conducted to the more honourable residence of Hierapolis; and Maurice dissembled his pride, and displayed his benevolence, at the reception of the letters and ambassadors of the grandson of Nushirvan. They humbly represented the vicissitudes of fortune and the common interest of princes, exaggerated the ingratitude of Bahram, the agent of the evil principle, and urged, with specious argument, that it was for the advantage of the Romans

1 Theophylact (l. iv. c. 7 [p. 173, ed. Bonn]) imputes the death of Hormouz to his son, by whose command he was beaten to death with clubs. I have followed the milder account of Khondemir and Eutychius, and shall always be content with the slightest evidence to extenuate the crime of parricide.

2 After the battle of Pharsalia, the Pompey of Lucan (l. viii. 256–455) holds a similar debate. He was himself desirous of seeking the Parthians: but his companions abhorred the unnatural alliance; and the adverse prejudices might operate as forcibly on Chosroes and his companions, who could describe, with the same vehemence, the contrast of laws, religion, and manners, between the East and West.

themselves to support the two monarchies which balance the world, the two great luminaries by whose salutary influence it is vivified and adorned. The anxiety of Chosroes was soon relieved by the assurance that the emperor had espoused the cause of justice and royalty; but Maurice prudently declined the expense and delay of his useless visit to Constantinople. In the name of his generous benefactor, a rich diadem was presented to the fugitive prince, with an inestimable gift of jewels and gold; a powerful army was assembled on the frontiers of Syria and Armenia, under the command of the valiant and faithful Narses;[1] and this general, of his own nation, and his own choice, was directed to pass the Tigris, and never to sheathe his sword till he had restored Chosroes to the throne of his ancestors. The enterprise, however splendid, was less arduous than it might appear. Persia had already repented of her fatal rashness, which betrayed the heir of the house of Sassan to the ambition of a rebellious subject: and the bold refusal of the Magi to consecrate his usurpation compelled Bahram to assume the sceptre, regardless of the laws and prejudices of the nation. The palace was soon distracted with conspiracy, the city with tumult, the provinces with insurrection; and the cruel execution of the guilty and the suspected served to irritate rather than subdue the public discontent. No sooner did the grandson of Nushirvan display his own and the Roman banners beyond the Tigris, than he was joined, each day, by the increasing multitudes of the nobility and people; and as he advanced, he received from every side the grateful offerings of the keys of his cities and the heads of his enemies. As soon as Modain was freed from the presence of the usurper, the loyal inhabitants obeyed the first summons of Mebodes at the head of only two thousand horse, and Chosroes accepted the sacred and precious ornaments of the palace as the

---

1 In this age there were three warriors of the name of *Narses*, who have been often confounded (Pagi, Critica, tom. ii. p. 640); 1. A Persarmenian, the brother of Isaac and Armatius, who, after a successful action against Belisarius, deserted from his Persian sovereign, and afterwards served in the Italian war. 2. The eunuch who conquered Italy. 3. The restorer of Chosroes, who is celebrated in the poem of Corippus (l. iii. 220–227) as excelsus super omnia vertice agmina . . . habitu modestus . . . morum probitate placens, virtute verendus; fulmineus, cautus, vigilans, etc.

pledge of their truth and a presage of his approaching success. After the junction of the Imperial troops, which Bahram vainly struggled to prevent, the contest was decided by two battles on the banks of the Zab and the confines of Media. The Romans, with the faithful subjects of Persia, amounted to sixty thousand, while the whole force of the usurper did not exceed forty thousand men: the two generals signalised their valour and ability; but the victory was finally determined by the prevalence of numbers and discipline. With the remnant of a broken army, Bahram fled towards the eastern provinces of the Oxus: the enmity of Persia reconciled him to the Turks; but his days were shortened by poison, perhaps the most incurable of poisons, the stings of remorse and despair, and the bitter remembrance of lost glory. Yet the modern Persians still commemorate the exploits of Bahram; and some excellent laws have prolonged the duration of his troubled and transitory reign.[1]

The restoration of Chosroes was celebrated with feasts and executions; and the music of the royal banquet was often disturbed by the groans of dying or mutilated criminals. A general pardon might have diffused comfort and tranquillity through a country which had been shaken by the late revolutions; yet, before the sanguinary temper of Chosroes is blamed, we should learn whether the Persians had not been accustomed either to dread the rigour or to despise the weakness of their sovereign. The revolt of Bahram and the conspiracy of the satraps were impartially punished by the revenge or justice of the conqueror; the merits of Bindoes himself could not purify his hand from the guilt of royal blood; and the son of Hormouz was desirous to assert his own innocence and to vindicate the sanctity of kings. During the vigour of the Roman power several princes were seated on the throne of Persia by the arms and the authority of the first Cæsars. But their new subjects were soon disgusted with the vices or virtues which they had imbibed in a

1 [According to Mirkhond and the Oriental writers, Bahram received the daughter of the Khakan in marriage, and commanded a body of Turks in an invasion of Persia. Some say that he was assassinated; Malcolm adopts the opinion that he was poisoned. His sister Gourdieh, the companion of his flight, is celebrated in the Shah Nameh. She was afterwards one of the wives of Chosroes. – O. S.]

foreign land; the instability of their dominion gave birth to a vulgar observation, that the choice of Rome was solicited and rejected with equal ardour by the capricious levity of Oriental slaves.[1] But the glory of Maurice was conspicuous in the long and fortunate reign of his *son* and his ally. A band of a thousand Romans, who continued to guard the person of Chosroes, proclaimed his confidence in the fidelity of the strangers; his growing strength enabled him to dismiss this unpopular aid, but he steadily professed the same gratitude and reverence to his adopted father; and, till the death of Maurice, the peace and alliance of the two empires were faithfully maintained. Yet the mercenary friendship of the Roman prince had been purchased with costly and important gifts; the strong cities of Martyropolis and Dara were restored, and the Persarmenians became the willing subjects of an empire whose eastern limit was extended, beyond the example of former times, as far as the banks of the Araxes and the neighbourhood of the Caspian. A pious hope was indulged that the church as well as the state might triumph in this revolution: but if Chosroes had sincerely listened to the Christian bishops, the impression was erased by the zeal and eloquence of the Magi; if he was armed with philosophic indifference, he accommodated his belief, or rather his professions, to the various circumstances of an exile and a sovereign. The imaginary conversion of the king of Persia was reduced to a local and superstitious veneration for Sergius,[2] one of the saints of Antioch, who heard his prayers and appeared to him in dreams; he enriched the shrine with offerings of gold and silver, and ascribed to this invisible patron the success of his arms, and the pregnancy of Sira, a devout Christian and the best beloved of

1 Experimentis cognitum est barbaros malle Româ petere reges quam habere. These experiments are admirably represented in the invitation and expulsion of Vonones (Annal. ii. 1–3), Tiridates (Annal. vi. 32–44), and Meherdates (Annal. xi. 10, xii. 10–14). The eye of Tacitus seems to have transpierced the camp of the Parthians and the walls of the harem.

2 Sergius and his companion Bacchus, who are said to have suffered in the persecution of Maximian, obtained divine honour in France, Italy, Constantinople, and the East. Their tomb at Rasaphe was famous for miracles, and that Syrian town acquired the more honourable name of Sergiopolis. Tillemont, Mém. Ecclés. tom. v. p. 491–496; Butler's Saints, vol. x. p. 155.

his wives.[1] The beauty of Sira, or Schirin,[2] her wit, her musical
talents, are still famous in the history, or rather in the romances,
of the East: her own name is expressive, in the Persian tongue,
of sweetness and grace; and the epithet of *Parviz* alludes to the
charms of her royal lover. Yet Sira never shared the passion
which she inspired, and the bliss of Chosroes was tortured by a
jealous doubt, that while he possessed her person she had bestowed her affections on a meaner favourite.[3]

   While the majesty of the Roman name was revived in the
East, the prospect of Europe is less pleasing and less glorious.
By the departure of the Lombards and the ruin of the Gepidæ
the balance of power was destroyed on the Danube; and the
Avars spread their permanent dominion from the foot of the Alps
to the sea-coast of the Euxine. The reign of Baian is the brightest
era of their monarchy; their chagan, who occupied the rustic
palace of Attila, appears to have imitated his character and
policy;[4] but as the same scenes were repeated in a smaller circle,

   1 Evagrius (l. v. c. 21) and Theophylact (l. v. c. 13, 14 [p. 230, *sqq.*, ed.
Bonn]) have preserved the original letters of Chosroes, written in Greek, signed
with his own hand, and afterwards inscribed on crosses and tables of gold,
which were deposited in the church of Sergiopolis. They had been sent to the
bishop of Antioch, as primate of Syria.

   2 The Greeks only describe her as a Roman by birth, a Christian by religion;
but she is represented as the daughter of the emperor Maurice in the Persian
and Turkish romances which celebrate the love of Khosrou for Schirin, of
Schirin for Ferhad, the most beautiful youth of the East. D'Herbelot, Biblioth.
Orient. p. 789, 997, 998.

   3 The whole series of the tyranny of Hormouz, the revolt of Bahram, and
the flight and restoration of Chosroes, is related by two contemporary Greeks –
more concisely by Evagrius (l. vi. c. 16, 17, 18, 19), most diffusely by Theophylact Simocatta (l. iii. c. 6–18, l. iv. c. 1–16, l. v. c. 1–15): succeeding
compilers, Zonaras and Cedrenus, can only transcribe and abridge. The Christian Arabs, Eutychius (Annal. tom. ii. p. 200–208) and Abulpharagius (Dynast.
p. 96–98), appear to have consulted some particular memoirs. The great Persian
historians of the fifteenth century, Mirkhond and Khondemir, are only known
to me by the imperfect extracts of Schikard (Tarikh, p. 150–155), Texeira, or
rather Stevens (Hist. of Persia, p. 182–186), a Turkish MS. translated by the
Abbé Fourmont (Hist. de l'Académie des Inscriptions, tom. vii. p. 325–334),
and D'Herbelot (aux mots, *Hormouz*, p. 457–459; Bahram, p. 174; Khosrou
Parviz, p. 996). Were I perfectly satisfied of their authority, I could wish these
Oriental materials had been more copious.

   4 A general idea of the pride and power of the chagan may be taken from
Menander (Excerpt. Legat. p. 113, etc. [p. 308, *sq.*, ed. Bonn]), and Theophylact

a minute representation of the copy would be devoid of the greatness and novelty of the original. The pride of the second Justin, of Tiberius, and Maurice was humbled by a proud barbarian, more prompt to inflict than exposed to suffer the injuries of war; and as often as Asia was threatened by the Persian arms, Europe was oppressed by the dangerous inroads or costly friendship of the Avars. When the Roman envoys approached the presence of the chagan, they were commanded to wait at the door of his tent till, at the end perhaps of ten or twelve days, he condescended to admit them. If the substance or the style of their message was offensive to his ear, he insulted, with real or affected fury, their own dignity and that of their prince; their baggage was plundered, and their lives were only saved by the promise of a richer present and more respectful address. But *his* sacred ambassadors enjoyed and abused an unbounded licence in the midst of Constantinople: they urged, with importunate clamours, the increase of tribute, or the restitution of captives and deserters: and the majesty of the empire was almost equally degraded by a base compliance, or by the false and fearful excuses with which they eluded such insolent demands. The chagan had never seen an elephant; and his curiosity was excited by the strange, and perhaps fabulous, portrait of that wonderful animal. At his command, one of the largest elephants of the Imperial stables was equipped with stately caparisons, and conducted by a numerous train to the royal village in the plains of Hungary. He surveyed the enormous beast with surprise, with disgust, and possibly with terror; and smiled at the vain industry of the Romans, who in search of such useless rarities could explore the limits of the land and sea. He wished, at the expense of the emperor, to repose in a golden bed. The wealth of Constantinople, and the skilful diligence of her artists, were instantly devoted to the gratification of his caprice; but when the work was finished, he rejected with scorn a present so unworthy the

(l. i. c. 3, l. vii. c. 15), whose eight books are much more honourable to the Avar than to the Roman prince. The predecessors of Baian had tasted the liberality of Rome, and *he* survived the reign of Maurice (Buat, Hist. des Peuples Barbares, tom. xi. v. p. 545). The chagan who invaded Italy A.D. 611 (Muratori, Annali, tom. v. p. 305) was then juvenili ætate florentem (Paul Warnefrid, de Gest. Langobard. l. iv. c. 38), the son, perhaps, or the grandson, of Baian.

majesty of a great king.[1] These were the casual sallies of his pride; but the avarice of the chagan was a more steady and tractable passion: a rich and regular supply of silk apparel, furniture, and plate introduced the rudiments of art and luxury among the tents of the Scythians; their appetite was stimulated by the pepper and cinnamon of India;[2] the annual subsidy or tribute was raised from fourscore to one hundred and twenty thousand pieces of gold; and, after each hostile interruption, the payment of the arrears, with exorbitant interest, was always made the first condition of the new treaty. In the language of a barbarian, without guile, the prince of the Avars affected to complain of the insincerity of the Greeks;[3] yet he was not inferior to the most civilised nations in the refinements of dissimulation and perfidy. As the successor of the Lombards, the chagan asserted his claim to the important city of Sirmium, the ancient bulwark of the Illyrian provinces.[4] The plains of the Lower Hungary were covered with the Avar horse; and a fleet of large boats was built in the Hercynian wood, to descend the Danube, and to transport into the Save the materials of a bridge. But as the strong garrison of Singidunum, which commanded the conflux of the two rivers, might have stopped their passage and baffled his designs, he dispelled their apprehensions by a solemn oath that his views were not hostile to the empire. He swore by his sword, the symbol of the god of war, that he did not, as the enemy of Rome, construct a bridge upon the Save. 'If I violate my oath,' pursued the intrepid Baian, 'may I myself, and the last of my

1 Theophylact, l. i. c. 5, 6.

2 Even in the field the chagan delighted in the use of these aromatics. He solicited, as a gift, Ἰνδικὰς καρυκείας, and received πέπερι καὶ φύλλον Ἰνδῶν, κασίαν τε καὶ τόν λεγόμενον κόστον. Theophylact, l. vii. c. 13 [p. 294, ed. Bonn]. The Europeans of the ruder ages consumed more spices in their meat and drink than is compatible with the delicacy of a modern palate. Vie Privée des François, tom. ii. p. 162, 163.

3 Theophylact, l. vi. c. 6, l vii. c. 15 [p. 251, 299, ed. Bonn]. The Greek historian confesses the truth and justice of his reproach.

4 Menander (in Excerpt. Legat. p. 126–132, 174, 175 [p. 332–342, 424, 425, ed. Bonn]) describes the perjury of Baian and the surrender of Sirmium. We have lost his account of the siege, which is commended by Theophylact, l. i. c. 3. Τὸ δ' ὅπως Μενάνδρῳ τῷ περιφανεῖ σαφῶς διηγόρευται [p. 38, ed. Bonn].

nation, perish by the sword! May the heavens, and fire, the deity of the heavens, fall upon our heads! May the forests and mountains bury us in their ruins; and the Save, returning, against the laws of nature, to his source, overwhelm us in his angry waters!' After this barbarous imprecation he calmly inquired what oath was most sacred and venerable among the Christians; what guilt of perjury it was most dangerous to incur. The bishop of Singidunum presented the Gospel, which the chagan received with devout reverence. 'I swear,' said he, 'by the God who has spoken in this holy book, that I have neither falsehood on my tongue nor treachery in my heart.' As soon as he rose from his knees he accelerated the labour of the bridge, and despatched an envoy to proclaim what he no longer wished to conceal. 'Inform the emperor,' said the perfidious Baian, 'that Sirmium is invested on every side. Advise his prudence to withdraw the citizens and their effects, and to resign a city which it is now impossible to relieve or defend.' Without the hope of relief, the defence of Sirmium was prolonged above three years: the walls were still untouched; but famine was enclosed within the walls, till a merciful capitulation allowed the escape of the naked and hungry inhabitants. Singidunum, at the distance of fifty miles, experienced a more cruel fate: the buildings were razed, and the vanquished people was condemned to servitude and exile. Yet the ruins of Sirmium are no longer visible; the advantageous situation of Singidunum soon attracted a new colony of Sclavonians; and the conflux of the Save and Danube is still guarded by the fortifications of Belgrade, or the *White City*, so often and so obstinately disputed by the Christian and Turkish arms.¹ From Belgrade to the walls of Constantinople a line may be measured of six hundred miles: that line was marked with flames and with blood; the horses of the Avars were alternately bathed in the Euxine and the Hadriatic; and the Roman pontiff, alarmed by the approach of a more savage enemy,² was reduced to cherish

---

1 See D'Anville, in the Mémoires de l'Acad. des Inscriptions, tom. xxviii. p. 412–443. The Sclavonic name of *Belgrade* is mentioned in the tenth century by Constantine Porphyrogenitus: the Latin appellation of *Alba Græca* is used by the Franks in the beginning of the ninth (p. 414).

2 Baron. Annal. Eccles. A.D. 600, No. 1. Paul Warnefrid (l. iv. c. 38) relates their irruption into Friuli, and (c. 39) the captivity of his ancestors, about

the Lombards as the protectors of Italy. The despair of a captive whom his country refused to ransom disclosed to the Avars the invention and practice of military engines.[1] But in the first attempts they were rudely framed and awkwardly managed; and the resistance of Diocletianopolis and Berœa, of Philippopolis and Adrianople, soon exhausted the skill and patience of the besiegers. The warfare of Baian was that of a Tartar; yet his mind was susceptible of a humane and generous sentiment: he spared Anchialus, whose salutary waters had restored the health of the best beloved of his wives; and the Romans confess that their starving army was fed and dismissed by the liberality of a foe. His empire extended over Hungary, Poland, and Prussia, from the mouth of the Danube to that of the Oder;[2] and his new subjects were divided and transplanted by the jealous policy of the conqueror.[3] The eastern regions of Germany, which had been left vacant by the emigration of the Vandals, were replenished with Sclavonian colonists; the same tribes are discovered in the neighbourhood of the Hadriatic and of the Baltic; and with the name of Baian himself, the Illyrian cities of Neyss and Lissa are again found in the heart of Silesia. In the disposition both of his troops and provinces the chagan exposed the vassals, whose lives he disregarded,[4] to the first assault; and the swords of the enemy were blunted before they encountered the native valour of the Avars.

A.D. 632. The Sclavi traversed the Hadriatic cum multitudine navium, and made a descent in the territory of Sipontum (c. 47).

1 Even the helepolis, or movable turret. Theophylact, l. ii. 16, 17.

2 The arms and alliances of the chagan reached to the neighbourhood of a western sea, fifteen months' journey from Constantinople. The emperor Maurice conversed with some itinerant harpers from that remote country, and only seems to have mistaken a trade for a nation. Theophylact, l. vi. c. 2 [p. 243, sq., ed. Bonn].

3 This is one of the most probable and luminous conjectures of the learned Count de Buat (Hist. des Peuples Barbares, tom. xi. p. 546–568). The Tzechi and Serbi are found together near Mount Caucasus, in Illyricum, and on the lower Elbe. Even the wildest traditions of the Bohemians, etc., afford some colour to his hypothesis.

4 See Fredegarius, in the Historians of France, tom. ii. p. 432. Baian did not conceal his proud insensibility. Ὅτι τοιουτοῦς (not τοσουτοῦς, according to a foolish emendation) ἐπαφήσω τῇ Ῥωμαϊκῇ, ὡς εἰ καὶ συμβαίη γε σφισί θανατῷ ἁλῶναι, ἀλλ᾿ ἐμοί γε μὴ γένεσθαι συναίσθησιν.

The Persian alliance restored the troops of the East to the defence of Europe; and Maurice, who had supported ten years the insolence of the chagan, declared his resolution to march in person against the barbarians. In the space of two centuries none of the successors of Theodosius had appeared in the field; their lives were supinely spent in the palace of Constantinople; and the Greeks could no longer understand that the name of *emperor*, in its primitive sense, denoted the chief of the armies of the republic. The martial ardour of Maurice was opposed by the grave flattery of the senate, the timid superstition of the patriarch, and the tears of the empress Constantina; and they all conjured him to devolve on some meaner general the fatigues and perils of a Scythian campaign. Deaf to their advice and entreaty, the emperor boldly advanced[1] seven miles from the capital; the sacred ensign of the cross was displayed in the front, and Maurice reviewed with conscious pride the arms and numbers of the veterans who had fought and conquered beyond the Tigris. Anchialus was the last term of his progress by sea and land; he solicited without success a miraculous answer to his nocturnal prayers; his mind was confounded by the death of a favourite horse, the encounter of a wild boar, a storm of wind and rain, and the birth of a monstrous child; and he forgot that the best of omens is to unsheathe our sword in the defence of our country.[2] Under the pretence of receiving the ambassadors of Persia, the emperor returned to Constantinople, exchanged the thoughts of war for those of devotion, and disappointed the public hope by his absence and the choice of his lieutenants. The blind partiality of fraternal love might excuse the promotion of his brother Peter, who fled with equal disgrace from the barbarians, from his own soldiers, and from the inhabitants of a Roman city. That city, if we may credit the resemblance of name and character, was the famous Azimuntium,[3] which had alone

1 See the march and return of Maurice, in Theophylact, l. v. c. 16, l. vi. c. 1, 2, 3. If he were a writer of taste or genius, we might suspect him of an elegant irony; but Theophylact is surely harmless.

2 Εἷς οἰωνὸς ἄριστος ἀμύνεσθαι περὶ πάτρης. Iliad, xii. 243.
This noble verse, which unites the spirit of a hero with the reason of a sage, may prove that Homer was in every light superior to his age and country.

3 Theophylact, l. vii. c. 3 [p. 274, ed. Bonn]. On the evidence of this fact, which had not occurred to my memory, the candid reader will correct and

repelled the tempest of Attila. The example of her warlike youth was propagated to succeeding generations; and they obtained, from the first or the second Justin, an honourable privilege that their valour should be always reserved for the defence of their native country. The brother of Maurice attempted to violate this privilege, and to mingle a patriot band with the mercenaries of his camp; they retired to the church; he was not awed by the sanctity of the place; the people rose in their cause, the gates were shut, the ramparts were manned; and the cowardice of Peter was found equal to his arrogance and injustice. The military fame of Commentiolus[1] is the object of satire or comedy rather than of serious history, since he was even deficient in the vile and vulgar qualification of personal courage. His solemn counsels, strange evolutions, and secret orders, always supplied an apology for flight or delay. If he marched against the enemy, the pleasant valleys of Mount Hæmus opposed an insuperable barrier; but in his retreat he explored with fearless curiosity the most difficult and obsolete paths, which had almost escaped the memory of the oldest native. The only blood which he lost was drawn, in a real or affected malady, by the lancet of a surgeon; and his health, which felt with exquisite sensibility the approach of the barbarians, was uniformly restored by the repose and safety of the winter season. A prince who could promote and support this unworthy favourite must derive no glory from the accidental merit of his colleague Priscus.[2] In five successive battles, which seem to have been conducted with skill and resolution, seventeen thousand two hundred barbarians were made prisoners; near sixty thousand, with four sons of the chagan, were slain: the Roman general surprised a peaceful district of the Gepidæ, who slept under the protection of the Avars; and his last trophies were erected on the banks of the Danube and the Theiss. Since the death of Trajan the arms of the empire had not penetrated so deeply into the old Dacia; yet the success of

excuse a note in Chapter XXXIV., vol. iii. p. 411, of this History, which hastens the decay of Asimus, or Azimuntium: another century of patriotism and valour is cheaply purchased by such a confession.

1 See the shameful conduct of Commentiolus, in Theophylact, l. ii. c. 10–15, l. vii. c. 13, 14, l. viii. c. 2, 4.

2 See the exploits of Priscus, l. viii. c. 2, 3.

Priscus was transient and barren, and he was soon recalled by the apprehension that Baian, with dauntless spirit and recruited forces, was preparing to avenge his defeat under the walls of Constantinople.[1]

The theory of war was not more familiar to the camps of Cæsar and Trajan than to those of Justinian and Maurice.[2] The iron of Tuscany or Pontus still received the keenest temper from the skill of the Byzantine workmen. The magazines were plentifully stored with every species of offensive and defensive arms. In the construction and use of ships, engines, and fortifications, the barbarians admired the superior ingenuity of a people whom they so often vanquished in the field. The science of tactics, the order, evolutions, and stratagems of antiquity, was transcribed and studied in the books of the Greeks and Romans. But the solitude or degeneracy of the provinces could no longer supply a race of men to handle those weapons, to guard those walls, to navigate those ships, and to reduce the theory of war into bold and successful practice. The genius of Belisarius and Narses had been formed without a master, and expired without a disciple. Neither honour, nor patriotism, nor generous superstition, could animate the lifeless bodies of slaves and strangers who had succeeded to the honours of the legions: it was in the camp alone that the emperor should have exercised a depotic command; it was only in the camps that his authority was disobeyed and insulted: he appeased and inflamed with gold the licentiousness of the troops; but their vices were inherent, their victories were accidental, and their costly maintenance exhausted the substance of a state which they were unable to defend. After a long and pernicious indulgence, the cure of this inveterate evil was undertaken by Maurice; but the rash attempt, which drew destruction on his own head, tended only to aggravate the disease. A

1 The general detail of the war against the Avars may be traced in the first, second, sixth, seventh, and eighth books of the History of the Emperor Maurice, by Theophylact Simocatta. As he wrote in the reign of Heraclius, he had no temptation to flatter; but his want of judgment renders him diffuse in trifles, and concise in the most interesting facts.

2 Maurice himself composed twelve books on the military art, which are still extant, and have been published (Upsal, 1664) by John Scheffer, at the end of the Tactics of Arrian (Fabricius, Biblioth. Græca, l. iv. c. 8, tom. iii. p. 278), who promises to speak more fully of his work in its proper place.

reformer should be exempt from the suspicion of interest, and he must possess the confidence and esteem of those whom he proposes to reclaim. The troops of Maurice might listen to the voice of a victorious leader; they disdained the admonitions of statesmen and sophists; and when they received an edict which deducted from their pay the price of their arms and clothing, they execrated the avarice of a prince insensible of the dangers and fatigues from which he had escaped. The camps both of Asia and Europe were agitated with frequent and furious seditions;[1] the enraged soldiers of Edessa pursued with reproaches, with threats, with wounds, their trembling generals; they overturned the statues of the emperor, cast stones against the miraculous image of Christ, and either rejected the yoke of all civil and military laws, or instituted a dangerous model of voluntary subordination. The monarch, always distant and often deceived, was incapable of yielding or persisting, according to the exigence of the moment. But the fear of a general revolt induced him too readily to accept any act of valour, or any expression of loyalty, as an atonement for the popular offence; the new reform was abolished as hastily as it had been announced; and the troops, instead of punishment and restraint, were agreeably surprised by a gracious proclamation of immunities and rewards. But the soldiers accepted without gratitude the tardy and reluctant gifts of the emperor: their insolence was elated by the discovery of his weakness and their own strength, and their mutual hatred was inflamed beyond the desire of forgiveness or the hope of reconciliation. The historians of the times adopt the vulgar suspicion that Maurice conspired to destroy the troops whom he had laboured to reform; the misconduct and favour of Commentiolus are imputed to this malevolent design; and every age must condemn the inhumanity or avarice[2] of a prince who, by the trifling

---

1 See the mutinies under the reign of Maurice, in Theophylact, l. iii. c. 1–4, l. vi. c. 7, 8, 10, l. vii. c. 1. l. viii. c. 6, etc.

2 Theophylact and Theophanes seem ignorant of the conspiracy and avarice of Maurice. These charges, so unfavourable to the memory of that emperor, are first mentioned by the author of the Paschal Chronicle (p. 379, 380 [ed. Par.; tom. i. p. 695, ed. Bonn]); from whence Zonaras (tom. ii. l. xiv. [c. 13] p. 77, 78) has transcribed them. Cedrenus (p. 399 [tom. i. p. 700, ed. Bonn]) has followed another computation of the ransom.

ransom of six thousand pieces of gold, might have prevented the
massacre of twelve thousand prisoners in the hands of the chagan. In the just fervour of indignation, an order was signified to
the army of the Danube that they should spare the magazines
of the province, and establish their winter quarters in the hostile
country of the Avars. The measure of their grievances was full:
they pronounced Maurice unworthy to reign, expelled or slaughtered his faithful adherents, and under the command of Phocas,
a simple centurion, returned by hasty marches to the neighbourhood of Constantinople. After a long series of legal succession,
the military disorders of the third century were again revived; yet
such was the novelty of the enterprise that the insurgents were
awed by their own rashness. They hesitated to invest their favourite with the vacant purple; and while they rejected all treaty
with Maurice himself, they held a friendly correspondence with
his son Theodosius and with Germanus, the father-in-law of the
royal youth. So obscure had been the former condition of Phocas,
that the emperor was ignorant of the name and character of his
rival; but as soon as he learned that the centurion, though bold
in sedition, was timid in the face of danger, 'Alas!' cried the desponding prince, 'if he is a coward, he will surely be a murderer.'

Yet if Constantinople had been firm and faithful, the murderer might have spent his fury against the walls; and the rebel
army would have been gradually consumed or reconciled by the
prudence of the emperor. In the games of the circus, which he
repeated with unusual pomp, Maurice disguised with smiles of
confidence the anxiety of his heart, condescended to solicit the
applause of the *factions*, and flattered their pride by accepting
from their respective tribunes a list of nine hundred *blues* and
fifteen hundred *greens*, whom he affected to esteem as the solid
pillars of his throne. Their treacherous or languid support betrayed his weakness and hastened his fall: the green faction were
the secret accomplices of the rebels, and the blues recommended
lenity and moderation in a contest with their Roman brethren.
The rigid and parsimonious virtues of Maurice had long since
alienated the hearts of his subjects: as he walked barefoot in a
religious procession he was rudely assaulted with stones, and his
guards were compelled to present their iron maces in the defence
of his person. A fanatic monk ran through the streets with a

drawn sword, denouncing against him the wrath and the sentence of God; and a vile plebeian, who represented his countenance and apparel, was seated on an ass and pursued by the imprecations of the multitude.[1] The emperor suspected the popularity of Germanus with the soldiers and citizens: he feared, he threatened, but he delayed to strike; the patrician fled to the sanctuary of the church; the people rose in his defence, the walls were deserted by the guards, and the lawless city was abandoned to the flames and rapine of a nocturnal tumult. In a small bark the unfortunate Maurice, with his wife and nine children, escaped to the Asiatic shore, but the violence of the wind compelled him to land at the church of St. Autonomus,[2] near Chalcedon, from whence he despatched Theodosius, his eldest son, to implore the gratitude and friendship of the Persian monarch. For himself, he refused to fly: his body was tortured with sciatic pains,[3] his mind was enfeebled by superstition; he patiently awaited the event of the revolution, and addressed a fervent and public prayer to the Almighty, that the punishment of his sins might be inflicted in this world rather than in a future life. After the abdication of Maurice, the two factions disputed the choice of an emperor; but the favourite of the blues was rejected by the jealousy of their antagonists, and Germanus himself was hurried along by the crowds who rushed to the palace of Hebdomon, seven miles from the city, to adore the majesty of Phocas the centurion. A modest wish of resigning the purple to the rank and merit of Germanus was opposed by *his* resolution, more

1 In their clamours against Maurice the people of Constantinople branded him with the name of Marcionite or Marcionist: a heresy (says Theophylact, l. viii. c. 9 [p. 331, ed. Bonn]) μετά τινος μωρᾶς εὐλαβείας, εὐήθης τε καὶ καταγέλαστος. Did they only cast out a vague reproach – or had the emperor really listened to some obscure teacher of those ancient Gnostics?

2 The church of St. Autonomus (whom I have not the honour to know) was 150 stadia from Constantinople (Theophylact, l. viii. c. 9). The port of Eutropius, where Maurice and his children were murdered, is described by Gyllius (de Bosphoro Thracio, l. iii. c. xi.) as one of the two harbours of Chalcedon.

3 The inhabitants of Constantinople were generally subject to the νόσοι ἀρθρίτιδες; and Theophylact insinuates (l. viii. c. 9 [p. 332, ed. Bonn], that, if it were consistent with the rules of history, he could assign the medical cause. Yet such a digression would not have been more impertinent than his inquiry (l. vii. c. 16, 17) into the annual inundations of the Nile, and all the opinions of the Greek philosophers on that subject.

obstinate and equally sincere; the senate and clergy obeyed his summons; and as soon as the patriarch was assured of his orthodox belief, he consecrated the successful usurper in the church of St. John the Baptist. On the third day, amidst the acclamations of a thoughtless people, Phocas made his public entry in a chariot drawn by four white horses: the revolt of the troops was rewarded by a lavish donative, and the new sovereign, after visiting the palace, beheld from his throne the games of the hippodrome. In a dispute of precedency between the two factions, his partial judgment inclined in favour of the greens. 'Remember that Maurice is still alive' resounded from the opposite side; and the indiscreet clamour of the blues admonished and stimulated the cruelty of the tyrant. The ministers of death were despatched to Chalcedon: they dragged the emperor from his sanctuary, and the five sons of Maurice were successively murdered before the eyes of their agonising parent. At each stroke, which he felt in his heart, he found strength to rehearse a pious ejaculation: 'Thou art just, O Lord! and thy judgments are righteous.' And such in the last moments was his rigid attachment to truth and justice, that he revealed to the soldiers the pious falsehood of a nurse who presented her own child in the place of a royal infant.[1] The tragic scene was finally closed by the execution of the emperor himself, in the twentieth year of his reign, and the sixty-third of his age. The bodies of the father and his five sons were cast into the sea; their heads were exposed at Constantinople to the insults or pity of the multitude; and it was not till some signs of putrefaction had appeared that Phocas connived at the private burial of these venerable remains. In that grave the faults and errors of Maurice were kindly interred. His fate alone was remembered; and at the end of twenty years, in the recital of the history of Theophylact, the mournful tale was interrupted by the tears of the audience.[2]

1 From this generous attempt Corneille has deduced the intricate web of his tragedy of *Heraclius*, which requires more than one representation to be clearly understood (Corneille de Voltaire, tom. v. p. 300); and which, after an interval of some years, is said to have puzzled the author himself (Anecdotes Dramatiques, tom. i. p. 422).

2 The revolt of Phocas and death of Maurice are told by Theophylact Simocatta (l. viii. c. 7–12), the Paschal Chronicle (p. 379, 380 [tom. i. p. 694,

Such tears must have flowed in secret, and such compassion would have been criminal, under the reign of Phocas, who was peaceably acknowledged in the provinces of the East and West. The images of the emperor and his wife Leontia were exposed in the Lateran to the veneration of the clergy and senate of Rome, and afterwards deposited in the palace of the Cæsars, between those of Constantine and Theodosius. As a subject and a Christian, it was the duty of Gregory to acquiesce in the established government; but the joyful applause with which he salutes the fortune of the assassin has sullied, with indelible disgrace, the character of the saint. The successor of the apostles might have inculcated with decent firmness the guilt of blood and the necessity of repentance; he is content to celebrate the deliverance of the people and the fall of the oppressor; to rejoice that the piety and benignity of Phocas have been raised by Providence to the Imperial throne; to pray that his hands may be strengthened against all his enemies; and to express a wish, perhaps a prophecy, that, after a long and triumphant reign, he may be transferred from a temporal to an everlasting kingdom.[1] I have already traced the steps of a revolution so pleasing, in Gregory's opinion, both to heaven and earth; and Phocas does not appear less hateful in the exercise than in the acquisition of power. The pencil of an impartial historian has delineated the portrait of a monster:[2] his diminutive and deformed person, the closeness of his shaggy eyebrows, his red hair, his beardless chin, and his cheek disfigured and discoloured by a formidable scar. Ignorant of letters, of laws, and even of arms, he indulged in the

---

sq., ed. Bonn]), Theophanes (Chronograph. p. 238–244 [tom. i. p. 432–448, ed. Bonn]), Zonaras (tom. ii. l. xiv. [c. 13, 14] p. 77–80), and Cedrenus (p. 399–404 [tom. i. p. 700–708, ed. Bonn]).

1 Gregor. l. xi. Epist. 38 [l. xiii. Ep. 31, ed. Bened.] indict. vi. Benignitatem vestræ pietatis ad Imperiale fastigium pervenisse gaudemus. Lætentur cœli et exultet terra, et de vestris benignis actibus universæ reipublicæ populus nunc usque vehementer afflictus hilarescat, etc. This base flattery, the topic of Protestant invective, is justly censured by the philosopher Bayle (Dictionnaire Critique, Grégoire I. Not. H. tom. ii. p. 597, 598). Cardinal Baronius justifies the pope at the expense of the fallen emperor.

2 The images of Phocas were destroyed; but even the malice of his enemies would suffer one copy of such a portrait or caricature (Cedrenus, p. 404 [tom. i. p. 708, ed. Bonn]) to escape the flames.

supreme rank a more ample privilege of lust and drunkenness, and his brutal pleasures were either injurious to his subjects or disgraceful to himself. Without assuming the office of a prince, he renounced the profession of a soldier, and the reign of Phocas afflicted Europe with ignominious peace and Asia with desolating war. His savage temper was inflamed by passion, hardened by fear, exasperated by resistance or reproach. The flight of Theodosius to the Persian court had been intercepted by a rapid pursuit or a deceitful message: he was beheaded at Nice, and the last hours of the young prince were soothed by the comforts of religion and the consciousness of innocence. Yet his phantom disturbed the repose of the usurper; a whisper was circulated through the East that the son of Maurice was still alive; the people expected their avenger, and the widow and daughters of the late emperor would have adopted as their son and brother the vilest of mankind. In the massacre of the Imperial family,[1] the mercy, or rather the discretion, of Phocas had spared these unhappy females, and they were decently confined to a private house. But the spirit of the empress Constantina, still mindful of her father, her husband, and her sons, aspired to freedom and revenge. At the dead of night she escaped to the sanctuary of St. Sophia, but her tears and the gold of her associate Germanus were insufficient to provoke an insurrection. Her life was forfeited to revenge, and even to justice; but the patriarch obtained and pledged an oath for her safety, a monastery was allotted for her prison, and the widow of Maurice accepted and abused the lenity of his assassin. The discovery or the suspicion of a second conspiracy dissolved the engagements, and rekindled the fury, of Phocas. A matron who commanded the respect and pity of mankind, the daughter, wife, and mother of emperors, was tortured like the vilest malefactor, to force a confession of her designs and associates; and the empress Constantina, with her three innocent daughters, was beheaded at Chalcedon, on the same ground which had been stained with the blood of her husband

1 The family of Maurice is represented by Ducange (Familiæ Byzantinæ, p. 106, 107, 108): his eldest son Theodosius had been crowned emperor when he was no more than four years and a half old, and he is always joined with his father in the salutations of Gregory. With the Christian daughters, Anastasia and Theocteste, I am surprised to find the Pagan name of Cleopatra.

and five sons. After such an example, it would be superfluous to enumerate the names and sufferings of meaner victims. Their condemnation was seldom preceded by the forms of trial, and their punishment was embittered by the refinements of cruelty: their eyes were pierced, their tongues were torn from the root, the hands and feet were amputated; some expired under the lash, others in the flames, others again were transfixed with arrows, and a simple speedy death was mercy which they could rarely obtain. The hippodrome, the sacred asylum of the pleasures and the liberty of the Romans, was polluted with heads and limbs and mangled bodies; and the companions of Phocas were the most sensible that neither his favour nor their services could protect them from a tyrant, the worthy rival of the Caligulas and Domitians of the first age of the empire.[1]

A daughter of Phocas, his only child, was given in marriage to the patrician Crispus,[2] and the *royal* images of the bride and bridegroom were indiscreetly placed in the circus by the side of the emperor. The father must desire that his posterity should inherit the fruit of his crimes, but the monarch was offended by this premature and popular association; the tribunes of the green faction, who accused the officious error of their sculptors, were condemned to instant death; their lives were granted to the prayers of the people, but Crispus might reasonably doubt whether a jealous usurper could forget and pardon his involuntary competition. The green faction was alienated by the ingratitude of Phocas and the loss of their privileges: every province of the empire was ripe for rebellion; and Heraclius, exarch of Africa, persisted above two years in refusing all tribute and obedience to the centurion who disgraced the throne of Constantinople. By the secret emissaries of Crispus and the senate, the independent exarch was solicited to save and to govern his country: but his ambition was chilled by age, and he resigned the

1 Some of the cruelties of Phocas are marked by Theophylact, l. viii. c. 13, 14, 15. George of Pisidia, the poet of Heraclius, styles him (Bell. Abaricum, p. 46, Rome, 1777) τῆς τυραννίδος ὁ δυσκάθεκτος καὶ βιοφθόρος δράκων [v. 49]. The latter epithet is just – but the corrupter of life was easily vanquished.

2 In the writers, and in the copies of those writers, there is such hesitation between the names of *Priscus* and *Crispus* (Ducange, Fam. Byzant. p. 111), that I have been tempted to identify the son-in-law of Phocas with the hero five times victorious over the Avars.

dangerous enterprise to his son Heraclius, and to Nicetas, the son of Gregory, his friend and lieutenant. The powers of Africa were armed by the two adventurous youths: they agreed that the one should navigate the fleet from Carthage to Constantinople, that the other should lead an army through Egypt and Asia, and that the Imperial purple should be the reward of diligence and success. A faint rumour of their undertaking was conveyed to the ears of Phocas, and the wife and mother of the younger Heraclius were secured as the hostages of his faith; but the treacherous heart of Crispus extenuated the distant peril, the means of defence were neglected or delayed, and the tyrant supinely slept till the African navy cast anchor in the Hellespont. Their standard was joined at Abydus by the fugitives and exiles who thirsted for revenge: the ships of Heraclius, whose lofty masts were adorned with the holy symbols of religion,[1] steered their triumphant course through the Propontis; and Phocas beheld from the windows of the palace his approaching and inevitable fate. The green faction was tempted, by gifts and promises, to oppose a feeble and fruitless resistance to the landing of the Africans; but the people, and even the guards, were determined by the well-timed defection of Crispus, and the tyrant was seized by a private enemy, who boldly invaded the solitude of the palace. Stripped of the diadem and purple, clothed in a vile habit, and loaded with chains, he was transported in a small boat to the Imperial galley of Heraclius, who reproached him with the crimes of his abominable reign. 'Wilt thou govern better?' were the last words of the despair of Phocas. After suffering each variety of insult and torture, his head was severed from his body, the mangled trunk was cast into the flames, and the same treatment was inflicted on the statues of the vain usurper and the seditious banner of the green faction. The voice of the clergy, the senate, and the people invited Heraclius to ascend the throne which he had purified from guilt and ignominy; after some

---

1 According to Theophanes [tom. i. p. 459, ed. Bonn], κιβώτια and εἰκόνας [τῆς] θεομήτορος. Cedrenus adds an ἀχειροποίητον εἴκονα τοῦ κυρίου, which Heraclius bore as a banner in the first Persian expedition [tom. i. p. 719]. See George Pisid. Acroas. i. 140. The manufacture seems to have flourished, but Foggini, the Roman editor (p. 26), is at a loss to determine whether this picture was an original or a copy.

graceful hesitation he yielded to their entreaties. His coronation was accompanied by that of his wife Eudoxia, and their posterity, till the fourth generation, continued to reign over the empire of the East.¹ The voyage of Heraclius had been easy and prosperous; the tedious march of Nicetas was not accomplished before the decision of the contest, but he submitted without a murmur to the fortune of his friend, and his laudable intentions were rewarded with an equestrian statue and a daughter of the emperor. It was more difficult to trust the fidelity of Crispus, whose recent services were recompensed by the command of the Cappadocian army. His arrogance soon provoked, and seemed to excuse, the ingratitude of his new sovereign. In the presence of the senate, the son-in-law of Phocas was condemned to embrace the monastic life; and the sentence was justified by the weighty observation

1 The following is the genealogical table of the family of Heraclius:—

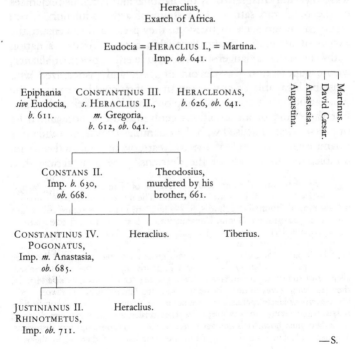

—S.

of Heraclius, that the man who had betrayed his father could never be faithful to his friend.[1]

Even after his death the republic was afflicted by the crimes of Phocas, which armed with a pious cause the most formidable of her enemies. According to the friendly and equal forms of the Byzantine and Persian courts, he announced his exaltation to the throne; and his ambassador Lilius, who had presented him with the heads of Maurice and his sons, was the best qualified to describe the circumstances of the tragic scene.[2] However it might be varnished by fiction or sophistry, Chosroes turned with horror from the assassin, imprisoned the pretended envoy, disclaimed the usurper, and declared himself the avenger of his father and benefactor. The sentiments of grief and resentment, which humanity would feel and honour would dictate, promoted on this occasion the interest of the Persian king, and his interest was powerfully magnified by the national and religious prejudices of the Magi and satraps. In a strain of artful adulation, which assumed the language of freedom, they presumed to censure the excess of his gratitude and friendship for the Greeks, a nation with whom it was dangerous to conclude either peace or alliance, whose superstition was devoid of truth and justice, and who must be incapable of any virtue since they could perpetrate the most atrocious of crimes, the impious murder of their sovereign.[3] For the crime of an ambitious centurion the nation which he oppressed was chastised with the calamities of war, and the same calamities, at the end of twenty years, were retaliated and redoubled on the heads of the Persians.[4] The general who had

1 See the tyranny of Phocas and the elevation of Heraclius, in Chron. Paschal. p. 380–383 [tom. i. p. 694–701, ed. Bonn]; Theophanes, p. 242–250 [tom. i. p. 446–459, ed. Bonn]; Nicephorus, p. 3–7 [ed. Par. 1648]; Cedrenus, p. 404–407 [tom. i. p. 708–714, ed. Bonn]; Zonaras, tom ii. l. xiv. [c. 14, 15] p. 80–82.

2 Theophylact, l. viii. c. 15 [p. 346, ed. Bonn]. The Life of Maurice was composed about the year 628 (l. viii. c. 13) by Theophylact Simocatta, expræfect, a native of Egypt. Photius, who gives an ample extract of the work (cod. lxv. p. 81–100 [p. 27–33, ed. Bekk.]), gently reproves the affectation and allegory of the style. His preface is a dialogue between Philosophy and History; they seat themselves under a plane-tree, and the latter touches her lyre.

3 Christianis nec pactum esse, nec fidem nec fœdus . . . quod si ulla ipsis fides fuisset, regem suum non occidissent. Eutych. Annales, tom. ii. p. 211, vers. Pocock.

4 We must now, for some ages, take our leave of contemporary historians, and descend, if it be a descent, from the affectation of rhetoric to the rude

restored Chosroes to the throne still commanded in the East, and the name of Narses was the formidable sound with which the Assyrian mothers were accustomed to terrify their infants. It is not improbable that a native subject of Persia should encourage his master and his friend to deliver and possess the provinces of Asia. It is still more probable that Chosroes should animate his troops by the assurance that the sword which they dreaded the most would remain in its scabbard or be drawn in their favour. The hero could not depend on the faith of a tyrant, and the tyrant was conscious how little he deserved the obedience of a hero. Narses was removed from his military command; he reared an independent standard at Hierapolis, in Syria; he was betrayed by fallacious promises, and burnt alive in the market-place of Constantinople. Deprived of the only chief whom they could fear or esteem, the bands which he had led to victory were twice broken by the cavalry, trampled by the elephants, and pierced by the arrows of the barbarians; and a great number of the captives were beheaded on the field of battle by the sentence of the victor, who might justly condemn these seditious mercenaries as the authors or accomplices of the death of Maurice. Under the reign of Phocas, the fortifications of Merdin, Dara, Amida, and Edessa were successively besieged, reduced, and destroyed by the Persian monarch; he passed the Euphrates, occupied the Syrian cities, Hierapolis, Chalcis, and Berrhœa or Aleppo, and soon encompassed the walls of Antioch with his irresistible arms. The rapid tide of success discloses the decay of the empire, the incapacity of Phocas, and the disaffection of his subjects; and Chosroes provided a decent apology for their submission or revolt by an impostor who attended his camp as the son of Maurice[1] and the lawful heir of the monarchy.

simplicity of chronicles and abridgments. Those of Theophanes (Chronograph. p. 244–279 [tom. i. p. 449–516, ed. Bonn] and Nicephorus (p. 3–16) supply a regular, but imperfect, series of the Persian war; and for any additional facts I quote my special authorities. Theophanes, a courtier who became a monk, was born A.D. 748; Nicephorus, patriarch of Constantinople, who died A.D. 829, was somewhat younger: they both suffered in the cause of images. Hankius, de Scriptoribus Byzantinis, p. 200–246.

1 The Persian historians have been themselves deceived; but Theophanes (p. 244 [tom. i. p. 449, ed. Bonn]) accuses Chosroes of the fraud and falsehood;

The first intelligence from the East which Heraclius received[1] was that of the loss of Antioch; but the aged metropolis, so often overturned by earthquakes and pillaged by the enemy, could supply but a small and languid stream of treasure and blood. The Persians were equally successful and more fortunate in the sack of Cæsarea, the capital of Cappadocia; and as they advanced beyond the ramparts of the frontier, the boundary of ancient war, they found a less obstinate resistance and a more plentiful harvest. The pleasant vale of Damascus has been adorned in every age with a royal city: her obscure felicity has hitherto escaped the historian of the Roman empire: but Chosroes reposed his troops in the paradise of Damascus before he ascended the hills of Libanus or invaded the cities of the Phœnician coast. The conquest of Jerusalem,[2] which had been meditated by Nushirvan, was achieved by the zeal and avarice of his grandson; the ruin of the proudest monument of Christianity was vehemently urged by the intolerant spirit of the Magi; and he could enlist for this holy warfare an army of six-and-twenty thousand Jews, whose furious bigotry might compensate in some degree for the want of valour and discipline. After the reduction of Galilee and the region beyond the Jordan, whose resistance appears to have delayed the fate of the capital, Jerusalem itself was taken by assault. The sepulchre of Christ and the stately churches of Helena and Constantine were consumed, or at least damaged, by the flames; the devout offerings of three hundred years were rifled in one sacrilegious day; the patriach Zachariah and the *true cross* were transported into Persia; and the massacre

and Eutychius believes (Annal. tom. ii. p. 211) that the son of Maurice, who was saved from the assassins, lived and died a monk on Mount Sinai.

1 Eutychius dates all the losses of the empire under the reign of Phocas; an error which saves the honour of Heraclius, whom he brings not from Carthage, but Salonica, with a fleet laden with vegetables for the relief of Constantinople (Annal. tom. ii. p. 223, 224). The other Christians of the East, Barhebræus (apud Asseman, Bibliothec. Oriental. tom. iii. p. 412, 413), Elmacin (Hist. Saracen. p. 13–16), Abulpharagius (Dynast. p. 98, 99), are more sincere and accurate. The years of the Persian war are disposed in the chronology of Pagi.

2 On the conquest of Jerusalem, an event so interesting to the church, see the Annals of Eutychius (tom. ii. p. 212–223), and the lamentations of the monk Antiochus (apud Baronium, Annal. Eccles. A.D. 614, No. 16–26), whose one hundred and twenty-nine homilies are still extant, if what no one reads may be said to be extant.

of ninety thousand Christians is imputed to the Jews and Arabs, who swelled the disorder of the Persian march. The fugitives of Palestine were entertained at Alexandria by the charity of John the archbishop, who is distinguished among a crowd of saints by the epithet of *almsgiver*:[1] and the revenues of the church, with a treasure of three hundred thousand pounds, were restored to the true proprietors, the poor of every country and every denomination. But Egypt itself, the only province which had been exempt since the time of Diocletian from foreign and domestic war, was again subdued by the successors of Cyrus. Pelusium, the key of that impervious country, was surprised by the cavalry of the Persians: they passed with impunity the innumerable channels of the Delta, and explored the long valley of the Nile from the pyramids of Memphis to the confines of Æthiopia. Alexandria might have been relieved by a naval force, but the archbishop and the præfect embarked for Cyprus; and Chosroes entered the second city of the empire, which still preserved a wealthy remnant of industry and commerce.[2] His western trophy was erected, not on the walls of Carthage,[3] but in the neighbourhood of Tripoli: the Greek colonies of Cyrene were finally extirpated; and the conqueror, treading in the footsteps of Alexander, returned in triumph through the sands of the Libyan desert. In the same campaign another army advanced from the Euphrates to the Thracian Bosphorus; Chalcedon surrendered after a long siege, and a Persian camp was maintained above ten years in the presence of Constantinople. The sea-coast of Pontus, the city of Ancyra, and the isle of Rhodes are enumerated among the last conquests of the Great King; and if Chosroes had possessed any maritime power, his boundless ambition would have spread slavery and desolation over the provinces of Europe.

1 The Life of this worthy saint is composed by Leontius, a contemporary bishop; and I find in Baronius (Annal. Eccles. A.D. 610, No. 10, etc.) and Fleury (tom. viii. p. 235–242) sufficient extracts of this edifying work.

2 [Theophanes gives the date of the conquest of Egypt as A.M. 6107 = A.D. 615. – O. S.]

3 The error of Baronius, and many others who have carried the arms of Chosroes to Carthage instead of Chalcedon, is founded on the near resemblance of the Greek words Καλχήδονα and Καρχήδονα, in the text of Theophanes, etc., which have been sometimes confounded by transcribers, and sometimes by critics.

From the long-disputed banks of the Tigris and Euphrates, the reign of the grandson of Nushirvan was suddenly extended to the Hellespont and the Nile, the ancient limits of the Persian monarchy. But the provinces, which had been fashioned by the habits of six hundred years to the virtues and vices of the Roman government, supported with reluctance the yoke of the barbarians. The idea of a republic was kept alive by the institutions, or at least by the writings, of the Greeks and Romans, and the subjects of Heraclius had been educated to pronounce the words of liberty and law. But it has always been the pride and policy of Oriental princes to display the titles and attributes of their omnipotence; to upbraid a nation of slaves with their true name and abject condition; and to enforce, by cruel and insolent threats, the rigour of their absolute commands. The Christians of the East were scandalised by the worship of fire and the impious doctrine of the two principles: the Magi were not less intolerant than the bishops; and the martyrdom of some native Persians who had deserted the religion of Zoroaster[1] was conceived to be the prelude of a fierce and general persecution. By the oppressive laws of Justinian the adversaries of the church were made the enemies of the state; the alliance of the Jews, Nestorians, and Jacobites had contributed to the success of Chosroes, and his partial favour to the sectaries provoked the hatred and fears of the catholic clergy. Conscious of their fear and hatred, the Persian conqueror governed his new subjects with an iron sceptre; and, as if he suspected the stability of his dominion, he exhausted their wealth by exorbitant tributes and licentious rapine; despoiled or demolished the temples of the East; and transported to his hereditary realms the gold, the silver, the precious marbles, the arts, and the artists of the Asiatic cities. In the obscure picture of the calamities of the empire[2] it is not easy to discern the figure of Chosroes himself, to separate his

1 The *genuine* acts of St. Anastasius are published in those of the seventh general council, from whence Baronius (Annal. Eccles. A.D. 614, 626, 627) and Butler (Lives of the Saints, vol. i. p. 242–248) have taken their accounts. The holy martyr deserted from the Persian to the Roman army, became a monk at Jerusalem, and insulted the worship of the Magi, which was then established at Cæsarea in Palestine.

2 Abulpharagius, Dynast. p. 99; Elmacin, Hist. Saracen. p. 14.

actions from those of his lieutenants, or to ascertain his personal merit in the general blaze of glory and magnificence. He enjoyed with ostentation the fruits of victory, and frequently retired from the hardships of war to the luxury of the palace. But, in the space of twenty-four years, he was deterred by superstition or resentment from approaching the gates of Ctesiphon: and his favourite residence of Artemita, or Dastagerd, was situate beyond the Tigris, about sixty miles to the north of the capital.[1] The adjacent pastures were covered with flocks and herds: the paradise or park was replenished with pheasants, peacocks, ostriches, roebucks, and wild boars; and the noble game of lions and tigers was sometimes turned loose for the bolder pleasures of the chase. Nine hundred and sixty elephants were maintained for the use or splendour of the Great King; his tents and baggage were carried into the field by twelve thousand great camels and eight thousand of a smaller size;[2] and the royal stables were filled with six thousand mules and horses, among whom the names of Shebdiz and Barid are renowned for their speed or beauty. Six thousand guards successively mounted before the palace gate; the service of the interior apartments was performed by twelve thousand slaves; and in the number of three thousand virgins, the fairest of Asia, some happy concubine might console her master for the age or the indifference of Sira. The various treasures of gold, silver, gems, silk, and aromatics were deposited in a hundred subterraneous vaults; and the chamber *Badaverd* denoted the accidental gift of the winds which had wafted the spoils of Heraclius into one of the Syrian harbours of his rival. The voice of flattery, and perhaps of fiction, is not ashamed to compute the thirty thousand rich hangings that adorned the walls; the forty thousand columns of silver, or more probably of marble, and plated wood, that supported the roof; and the thousand globes of gold suspended

1 D'Anville, Mém. de l'Académie des Inscriptions, tom. xxxii. p. 568–571.

2 The difference between the two races consists in one or two humps; the dromedary has only one; the size of the proper camel is larger; the country he comes from, Turkistan or Bactriana; the dromedary is confined to Arabia and Africa. Buffon, Hist. Naturelle, tom. xi. p. 211, etc.; Aristot. Hist. Animal. tom. i. l. ii. c. 1, tom. ii. p. 185.

in the dome, to imitate the motions of the planets and the constellations of the zodiac.[1] While the Persian monarch contemplated the wonders of his art and power, he received an epistle from an obscure citizen of Mecca, inviting him to acknowledge Mohammed as the apostle of God. He rejected the invitation, and tore the epistle. 'It is thus,' exclaimed the Arabian prophet, 'that God will tear the kingdom and reject the supplications of Chosroes.'[2] Placed on the verge of the two great empires of the East, Mohammed observed with secret joy the progress of their mutual destruction; and in the midst of the Persian triumphs he ventured to foretell that, before many years should elapse, victory would again return to the banners of the Romans.[3]

At the time when this prediction is said to have been delivered, no prophecy could be more distant from its accomplishment, since the first twelve years of Heraclius announced the approaching dissolution of the empire. If the motives of Chosroes had been pure and honourable, he must have ended the quarrel with the death of Phocas, and he would have embraced, as his best ally, the fortunate African who had so generously avenged the injuries of his benefactor Maurice. The prosecution

1 Theophanes, Chronograph. p. 268 [tom. i. p. 494, ed. Bonn]. D'Herbelot, Bibliothèque Orientale, p. 997. The Greeks describe the decay, the Persians the splendour, of Dastagerd; but the former speak from the modest witness of the eye, the latter from the vague report of the ear.

2 The historians of Mohammed, Abulfeda (in Vit. Mohammed, p. 92, 93) and Gagnier (Vie de Mohammed, tom. ii. p. 247), date this embassy in the seventh year of the Hegira, which commenced A.D. 628, May 11. Their chronology is erroneous, since Chosroes died in the month of February of the same year (Pagi, Critica, tom. ii. p. 779). The Count de Boulainvilliers (Vie de Mahomed, p. 327, 328) places this embassy about A.D. 615, soon after the conquest of Palestine. Yet Mohammed would scarcely have ventured so soon on so bold a step.

[Chosroes (Khoosroo Purveez) was encamped on the banks of the Karasoo river when he received the letter, which he tore up and threw into the Karasoo. For this action to this day, as Sir John Malcolm records, he is regarded as an outcast by all pious Mohammedans. – O. S.]

3 See the thirtieth chapter of the Koran, entitled *the Greeks*. Our honest and learned translator, Sale (p. 330, 331), fairly states this conjecture, guess, wager, of Mohammed; but Boulainvilliers (p. 329–344), with wicked intentions, labours to establish this evident prophecy of a future event, which must, in his opinion, embarrass the Christian polemics.

of the war revealed the true character of the barbarian; and the suppliant embassies of Heraclius to beseech his clemency, that he would spare the innocent, accept a tribute, and give peace to the world, were rejected with contemptuous silence or insolent menace. Syria, Egypt, and the provinces of Asia were subdued by the Persian arms; while Europe, from the confines of Istria to the long wall of Thrace, was oppressed by the Avars, unsatiated with the blood and rapine of the Italian war. They had coolly massacred their male captives in the sacred field of Pannonia; the women and children were reduced to servitude, and the noblest virgins were abandoned to the promiscuous lust of the barbarians. The amorous matron who opened the gates of Friuli passed a short night in the arms of her royal lover; the next evening Romilda was condemned to the embraces of twelve Avars; and, the third day, the Lombard princess was impaled in the sight of the camp, while the chagan observed, with a cruel smile, that such a husband was the fit recompense of her lewdness and perfidy.[1] By these implacable enemies Heraclius, on either side, was insulted and besieged: and the Roman empire was reduced to the walls of Constantinople, with the remnant of Greece, Italy, and Africa, and some maritime cities, from Tyre to Trebizond, of the Asiatic coast. After the loss of Egypt the capital was afflicted by famine and pestilence; and the emperor, incapable of resistance and hopeless of relief, had resolved to transfer his person and government to the more secure residence of Carthage. His ships were already laden with the treasures of the palace; but his flight was arrested by the patriarch, who armed the powers of religion in the defence of his country, led Heraclius to the altar of St. Sophia, and extorted a solemn oath that he would live and die with the people whom God had intrusted to his care. The chagan was encamped in the plains of Thrace; but he dissembled his perfidious designs, and solicited an interview with the emperor near the town of Heraclea. Their reconciliation was celebrated with equestrian games; the senate and people, in their gayest apparel, resorted to the festival of peace; and the Avars beheld, with envy and desire, the spectacle

1 Paul Warnefrid, de Gestis Langobardorum, l. iv. c. 38, 42; Muratori, Annali d'Italia, tom. v. p. 305, etc.

of Roman luxury. On a sudden the hippodrome was encompassed by the Scythian cavalry, who had pressed their secret and
nocturnal march: the tremendous sound of the chagan's whip
gave the signal of the assault; and Heraclius, wrapping his diadem round his arm, was saved, with extreme hazard, by the
fleetness of his horse. So rapid was the pursuit, that the Avars
almost entered the golden gate of Constantinople with the flying
crowds:[1] but the plunder of the suburbs rewarded their treason,
and they transported beyond the Danube two hundred and
seventy thousand captives. On the shore of Chalcedon the emperor held a safer conference with a more honourable foe, who,
before Heraclius descended from his galley, saluted with reverence and pity the majesty of the purple. The friendly offer of
Sain, the Persian general, to conduct an embassy to the presence
of the Great King was accepted with the warmest gratitude; and
the prayer for pardon and peace was humbly presented by the
prætorian præfect, the præfect of the city, and one of the first
ecclesiastics of the patriarchal church.[2] But the lieutenant of
Chosroes had fatally mistaken the intentions of his master. 'It
was not an embassy,' said the tyrant of Asia, 'it was the person
of Heraclius, bound in chains, that he should have brought to
the foot of my throne. I will never give peace to the emperor of
Rome till he has abjured his crucified God and embraced the
worship of the sun.' Sain was flayed alive, according to the inhuman practice of his country; and the separate and rigorous
confinement of the ambassadors violated the law of nations and
the faith of an express stipulation. Yet the experience of six years
at length persuaded the Persian monarch to renounce the conquest of Constantinople, and to specify the annual tribute or

1 The Paschal Chronicle, which sometimes introduces fragments of history
into a barren list of names and dates, gives the best account of the treason of
the Avars, p. 389, 390 [tom. i. p. 712 *sq.*, ed. Bonn]. The number of captives is
added by Nicephorus.

[Theophanes dates the attack of the Avars on Constantinople as 619 A.D.,
while others place it at 623. It was during this campaign that the clothing of
the Holy Virgin was discovered at Blachern. – O. S.]

2 Some original pieces, such as the speech or letter of the Roman ambassadors (p. 386–388 [ed. Par.; tom. i. p. 707–709, ed. Bonn]), likewise constitute
the merit of the Paschal Chronicle, which was composed, perhaps at Alexandria,
under the reign of Heraclius.

ransom of the Roman empire: a thousand talents of gold, a thousand talents of silver, a thousand silk robes, a thousand horses, and a thousand virgins. Heraclius subscribed these ignominious terms; but the time and space which he obtained to collect such treasures from the poverty of the East was industriously employed in the preparations of a bold and desperate attack.

Of the characters conspicuous in history, that of Heraclius is one of the most extraordinary and inconsistent. In the first and the last years of a long reign the emperor appears to be the slave of sloth, of pleasure, or of superstition; the careless and impotent spectator of the public calamities. But the languid mists of the morning and evening are separated by the brightness of the meridian sun: the Arcadius of the palace arose the Cæsar of the camp; and the honour of Rome and Heraclius was gloriously retrieved by the exploits and trophies of six adventurous campaigns. It was the duty of the Byzantine historians to have revealed the causes of his slumber and vigilance. At this distance we can only conjecture that he was endowed with more personal courage than political resolution; that he was detained by the charms, and perhaps the arts, of his niece Martina, with whom, after the death of Eudocia, he contracted an incestuous marriage;[1] and that he yielded to the base advice of the counsellors who urged, as a fundamental law, that the life of the emperor should never be exposed in the field.[2] Perhaps he was awakened by the last insolent demand of the Persian conqueror; but at the moment when Heraclius assumed the spirit of a hero, the only hopes of the Romans were drawn from the vicissitudes of fortune, which might threaten the proud prosperity of Chosroes, and must be favourable to those who had attained the lowest

1 Nicephorus (p. 10, 11), who brands this marriage with the names of ἄθεσμον and ἀθέμιτον, is happy to observe, that of two sons, its incestuous fruit, the elder was marked by Providence with a stiff neck, the younger with the loss of hearing.

2 George of Pisidia (Acroas. i. 112–125, p. 5), who states the opinions, acquits the pusillanimous counsellors of any sinister views. Would he have excused the proud and contemptuous admonition of Crispus? Ἐπιθωπτάζων οὐκ ἔξον βασιλεῖ ἔφασκε καταλιμπάνειν βασίλεια, καὶ τοῖς πόρρω ἐπιχωριάζειν δυνάμεσιν.

period of depression.[1] To provide for the expenses of war was the first care of the emperor; and for the purpose of collecting the tribute he was allowed to solicit the benevolence of the Eastern provinces. But the revenue no longer flowed in the usual channels; the credit of an arbitrary prince is annihilated by his power; and the courage of Heraclius was first displayed in daring to borrow the consecrated wealth of churches, under the solemn vow of restoring, with usury, whatever he had been compelled to employ in the service of religion and of the empire. The clergy themselves appear to have sympathised with the public distress; and the discreet patriarch of Alexandria, without admitting the precedent of sacrilege, assisted his sovereign by the miraculous or seasonable revelation of a secret treasure.[2] Of the soldiers who had conspired with Phocas, only two were found to have survived the stroke of time and of the barbarians;[3] the loss even of these seditious veterans was imperfectly supplied by the new levies of Heraclius; and the gold of the sanctuary united, in the same camp, the names, and arms, and languages of the East and West. He would have been content with the neutrality of the Avars; and his friendly entreaty that the chagan would act not as the enemy, but as the guardian of the empire, was accompanied with a more persuasive donative of two hundred thousand pieces of gold. Two days after the festival of Easter, the emperor, exchanging his purple for the simple garb of a penitent and

> 1 Εἰ τὰς ἐπ᾽ ἄκρον ἡρμένας εὐεξίας
> Ἐσφαλμένας λέγουσιν οὐκ ἀπεικότως,
> Κείσθω τὸ   λοιπὸν ἐν κακοῖς τὰ Πέρσιδος,
> Ἀντιστρόψως δὲ, etc.
>> George Pisid. Acroas. i. 51, etc., p. 4.

The Orientals are not less fond of remarking this strange vicissitude; and I remember some story of Khosrou Parviz, not very unlike the ring of Polycrates of Samos.

2 Baronius gravely relates this discovery, or rather transmutation, of barrels, not of honey, but of gold (Annal. Eccles. A.D. 620, No. 3, etc.). Yet the loan was arbitrary, since it was collected by soldiers, who were ordered to leave the patriarch of Alexandria no more than one hundred pounds of gold. Nicephorus (p. 11), two hundred years afterwards, speaks with ill-humour of this contribution, which the church of Constantinople might still feel.

3 Theophylact Simocatta, l. viii. c. 12 [p. 340, ed. Bonn]. This circumstance need not excite our surprise. The muster-roll of a regiment, even in time of peace, is renewed in less than twenty or twenty-five years.

warrior,[1] gave the signal of his departure. To the faith of the people Heraclius recommended his children; the civil and military powers were vested in the most deserving hands; and the discretion of the patriarch and senate was authorised to save or surrender the city, if they should be oppressed in his absence by the superior forces of the enemy.

The neighbouring heights of Chalcedon were covered with tents and arms; but if the new levies of Heraclius had been rashly led to the attack, the victory of the Persians in the sight of Constantinople might have been the last day of the Roman empire. As imprudent would it have been to advance into the provinces of Asia, leaving their innumerable cavalry to intercept his convoys, and continually to hang on the lassitude and disorder of his rear. But the Greeks were still masters of the sea; a fleet of galleys, transports, and store-ships was assembled in the harbour; the barbarians consented to embark; a steady wind carried them through the Hellespont; the western and southern coast of Asia Minor lay on their left hand; the spirit of their chief was first displayed in a storm; and even the eunuchs of his train were excited to suffer and to work by the example of their master. He landed his troops on the confines of Syria and Cilicia, in the gulf of Scanderoon, where the coast suddenly turns to the south;[2] and his discernment was expressed in the choice of this important

1 He changed his *purple*, for *black*, buskins, and dyed them *red* in the blood of the Persians (George. Pisid. Acroas. iii. 118, 121, 122. See the Notes of Foggini, p. 35).

2 George of Pisidia (Acroas. ii. 10, p. 8) has fixed this important point of the Syrian and Cilician gates. They are elegantly described by Xenophon, who marched through them a thousand years before. A narrow pass of three stadia, between steep high rocks (πέτραι ἠλίβατοι) and the Mediterranean, was closed at each end by strong gates, impregnable to the land (παρελθεῖν οὐκ ἦν βίᾳ), accessible by sea (Anabasis, l. i. [c. 4] p. 35, 36, with Hutchinson's Geographical Dissertation, p. vi.). The gates were thirty-five parasangs, or leagues, from Tarsus (Anabasis, l. i. [c. 4] p. 33, 34), and eight or ten from Antioch. Compare Itinerar. Wesseling. p. 580, 581; Schultens, Index Geograph. ad calcem Vit. Saladin. p. 9; Voyage en Turquie et en Perse, par M. Otter, tom. i. p. 78, 79.

[This place where Heraclius pitched his camp has been called the Πύλαι by George of Pisidia, and translated as well as identified as 'the Cilician Gates.' But Tafel has shown that this identification is not correct, and that the locality indicated is Pylæ on the southern side of the Nicomedian Bay, which Heraclius had reached by sailing round the cape of Heræum. – O. S.]

post.[1] From all sides the scattered garrisons of the maritime cities and the mountains might repair with speed and safety to his Imperial standard. The natural fortifications of Cilicia protected and even concealed the camp of Heraclius, which was pitched near Issus, on the same ground where Alexander had vanquished the host of Darius. The angle which the emperor occupied was deeply indented into a vast semicircle of the Asiatic, Armenian, and Syrian provinces; and to whatsoever point of the circumference he should direct his attack, it was easy for him to dissemble his own motions, and to prevent those of the enemy. In the camp of Issus the Roman general reformed the sloth and disorder of the veterans, and educated the new recruits in the knowledge and practice of military virtue. Unfolding the miraculous image of Christ, he urged them to *revenge* the holy altars which had been profaned by the worshippers of fire; addressing them by the endearing appellations of sons and brethren, he deplored the public and private wrongs of the republic. The subjects of a monarch were persuaded that they fought in the cause of freedom, and a similar enthusiasm was communicated to the foreign mercenaries, who must have viewed with equal indifference the interest of Rome and of Persia. Heraclius himself, with the skill and patience of a centurion, inculcated the lessons of the school of tactics, and the soldiers were assiduously trained in the use of their weapons and the exercises and evolutions of the field. The cavalry and infantry, in light or heavy armour, were divided into two parties; the trumpets were fixed in the centre, and their signals directed the march, the charge, the retreat or pursuit, the direct or oblique order, the deep or extended phalanx, to represent in fictitious combat the operations of genuine war. Whatever hardship the emperor imposed on the troops, he inflicted with equal severity on himself; their labour, their diet, their sleep, were measured by the inflexible rules of discipline; and, without despising the enemy, they were taught to repose an implicit confidence in their own valour and

---

1 Heraclius might write to a friend in the modest words of Cicero: 'Castra habuimus ea ipsa quæ contra Darium habuerat apud Issum Alexander, imperator haud paulo melior quam aut tu aut ego.' Ad Atticum, V. 20. Issus, a rich and flourishing city in the time of Xenophon, was ruined by the prosperity of Alexandria or Scanderoon, on the other side of the bay.

the wisdom of their leader. Cilicia was soon encompassed with the Persian arms, but their cavalry hesitated to enter the defiles of Mount Taurus till they were circumvented by the evolutions of Heraclius, who insensibly gained their rear, whilst he appeared to present his front in order of battle. By a false motion, which seemed to threaten Armenia, he drew them against their wishes to a general action. They were tempted by the artful disorder of his camp; but when they advanced to combat, the ground, the sun, and the expectation of both armies, were unpropitious to the barbarians: the Romans successfully repeated their tactics in a field of battle,[1] and the event of the day declared to the world that the Persians were not invincible, and that a hero was invested with the purple. Strong in victory and fame, Heraclius boldly ascended the heights of Mount Taurus, directed his march through the plains of Cappadocia, and established his troops for the winter season in safe and plentiful quarters on the banks of the river Halys.[2] His soul was superior to the vanity of entertaining Constantinople with an imperfect triumph; but the presence of the emperor was indispensably required to soothe the restless and rapacious spirit of the Avars.

Since the days of Scipio and Hannibal, no bolder enterprise has been attempted than that which Heraclius achieved for the deliverance of the empire.[3] He permitted the Persians to oppress for awhile the provinces, and to insult with impunity the capital of the East, while the Roman emperor explored his perilous way through the Black Sea[4] and the mountains of Armenia, penetrated

1 Foggini (Annotat. p. 31) suspects that the Persians were deceived by the φάλαγξ πεπληγμένη of Ælian (Tactic. c. 48), an intricate spiral motion of the army. He observes (p. 28) that the military descriptions of George of Pisidia are transcribed in the Tactics of the emperor Leo.

2 George of Pisidia, an eye-witness (Acroas. ii. 122, etc.), described, in three acroaseis or cantos, the first expedition of Heraclius. The poem has been lately (1777) published at Rome; but such vague and declamatory praise is far from corresponding with the sanguine hopes of Pagi, D'Anville, etc.

3 Theophanes (p. 256) carries Heraclius swiftly (κατά ταχὸς) into Armenia. Nicephorus (p. 11), though he confounds the two expeditions, defines the province of Lazica. Eutychius (Annal. tom. ii. p. 231) has given the 5000 men, with the more probable station of Trebizond.

4 From Constantinople to Trebizond, with a fair wind, four or five days; from thence to Erzerom, five; to Erivan, twelve; to Tauris, ten: in all, thirty-two. Such is the Itinerary of Tavernier (Voyages, tom. i. p. 12–56), who was perfectly

into the heart of Persia,[1] and recalled the armies of the Great King to the defence of their bleeding country.

With a select band of five thousand soldiers, Heraclius sailed from Constantinople to Trebizond; assembled his forces which had wintered in the Pontic regions; and from the mouth of the Phasis to the Caspian Sea, encouraged his subjects and allies to march with the successor of Constantine under the faithful and victorious banner of the cross. When the legions of Lucullus and Pompey first passed the Euphrates, they blushed at their easy victory over the natives of Armenia. But the long experience of war had hardened the minds and bodies of that effeminate people; their zeal and bravery were approved in the service of a declining empire; they abhorred and feared the usurpation of the house of Sassan, and the memory of persecution envenomed their pious hatred of the enemies of Christ. The limits of Armenia, as it had been ceded to the emperor Maurice, extended as far as the Araxes: the river submitted to the indignity of a bridge,[2] and Heraclius, in the footsteps of Mark Antony, advanced towards the city of Tauris or Gandzaca,[3] the ancient and modern capital of one of the provinces of Media. At the head of forty thousand men, Chosroes himself had returned from some distant expedition to oppose the progress of the Roman arms; but

conversant with the roads of Asia. Tournefort, who travelled with a pasha, spent ten or twelve days between Trebizond and Erzerom (Voyage du Levant, tom. iii. lettre xviii.); and Chardin (Voyages, tom. i. p. 249–254) gives the more correct distance of fifty-three parasangs, each of 5000 paces (what paces?), between Erivan and Tauris.

1 The expedition of Heraclius into Persia is finely illustrated by M. D'Anville (Mémoires de l'Académie des Inscriptions, tom. xxxviii. p. 559–573). He discovers the situation of Gandzaca, Thebarma, Dastagerd, etc., with admirable skill and learning; but the obscure campaign of 624 he passes over in silence.

2 Et pontem indignatus Araxes. – Virgil, Æneid, viii. 728.
The river Araxes is noisy, rapid, vehement, and, with the melting of the snows, irresistible: the strongest and most massy bridges are swept away by the current' and its *indignation* is attested by the ruins of many arches near the old town of Zulfa. Voyages de Chardin, tom. i. p. 252.

3 Chardin, tom. i. p. 255–259. With the Orientals (D'Herbelot, Biblioth. Orient. p. 834), he ascribes the foundation of Tauris, or Tebris, to Zobeide, the wife of the famous Khalif Haroun Alrashid; but it appears to have been more ancient; and the names of Gandzaca, Gazaca, Gaza, are expressive of the royal treasure. The number of 550,000 inhabitaants is reduced by Chardin from 1,100,000, the popular estimate.

he retreated on the approach of Heraclius, declining the generous alternative of peace or of battle. Instead of half a million of
inhabitants, which have been ascribed to Tauris under the reign
of the Sophys, the city contained no more than three thousand
houses; but the value of the royal treasures was enhanced by a
tradition that they were the spoils of Crœsus, which had been
transported by Cyrus from the citadel of Sardes. The rapid conquests of Heraclius were suspended only by the winter season;
a motive of prudence or superstition[1] determined his retreat into
the province of Albania, along the shores of the Caspian; and
his tents were most probably pitched in the plains of Mogan,[2]
the favourite encampment of Oriental princes. In the course of
this successful inroad he signalised the zeal and revenge of a
Christian emperor: at his command the soldiers extinguished the
fire, and destroyed the temples, of the Magi; the statues of Chosroes, who aspired to divine honours, were abandoned to the
flames; and the ruin of Thebarma or Ormia,[3] which had given
birth to Zoroaster himself, made some atonement for the injuries
of the holy sepulchre. A purer spirit of religion was shown in
the relief and deliverance of fifty thousand captives. Heraclius
was rewarded by their tears and grateful acclamations; but this
wise measure, which spread the fame of his benevolence, diffused the murmurs of the Persians against the pride and obstinacy of their own sovereign.

Amidst the glories of the succeeding campaign, Heraclius is
almost lost to our eyes, and to those of the Byzantine historians.[4]

1 He opened the Gospel and applied or interpreted the first casual passage
to the name and situation of Albania. Theophanes, p. 258 [tom. i. p. 474, ed. Bonn].

2 The heath of Mogan, between the Cyrus and the Araxes, is sixty parasangs in length and twenty in breadth (Olearius, p. 1023, 1024), abounding in
waters and fruitful pastures (Hist. de Nadir Shah, translated by Mr. Jones from
a Persian MS. Part ii. p. 2, 3). See the encampments of Timur (Hist. par
Sherefeddin Ali, l. v. c. 37, l. vi. c. 13) and the coronation of Nadir Shah (Hist.
Persanne, p. 3–13, and the English Life by Mr. Jones, p. 64, 65).

3 Thebarma and Ormia, near the lake Spauta, are proved to be the same city
by D'Anville (Mémoires de l'Académie, tom. xxviii. p. 564, 565). It is honoured
as the birthplace of Zoroaster, according to the Persians (Schultens, index Geograph. p. 48); and their tradition is fortified by M. Perron d'Anquetil (Mém. de
l'Acad. des Inscript. tom. xxxi. p. 375), with some texts from *his*, or *their*, Zendavesta.

4 I cannot find, and (what is much more) M. D'Anville does not attempt
to seek, the Salban, Tarantum, territory of the Huns, etc., mentioned by

From the spacious and fruitful plains of Albania, the emperor appears to follow the chain of Hyrcanian mountains, to descend into the province of Media or Irak, and to carry his victorious arms as far as the royal cities of Casbin and Ispahan, which had never been approached by a Roman conqueror. Alarmed by the danger of his kingdom, the powers of Chosroes were already recalled from the Nile and the Bosphorus, and three formidable armies surrounded, in a distant and hostile land, the camp of the emperor. The Colchian allies prepared to desert his standard; and the fears of the bravest veterans were expressed, rather than concealed, by their desponding silence. 'Be not terrified,' said the intrepid Heraclius, 'by the multitude of your foes. With the aid of Heaven, one Roman may triumph over a thousand barbarians. But if we devote our lives for the salvation of our brethren, we shall obtain the crown of martyrdom, and our immortal reward will be liberally paid by God and posterity.' These magnanimous sentiments were supported by the vigour of his actions. He repelled the threefold attack of the Persians, improved the divisions of their chiefs, and, by a well-concerted train of marches, retreats, and successful actions, finally chased them from the field into the fortified cities of Media and Assyria. In the severity of the winter season, Sarbaraza deemed himself secure in the walls of Salban: he was surprised by the activity of Heraclius, who divided his troops, and performed a laborious march in the silence of the night. The flat roofs of the houses were defended with useless valour against the darts and torches of the Romans: the satraps and nobles of Persia, with their wives and children, and the flower of their martial youth, were either slain or made prisoners. The general escaped by a precipitate flight, but his golden armour was the prize of the conqueror; and the soldiers of Heraclius enjoyed the wealth and repose which they had so nobly deserved. On the return of spring, the emperor traversed in seven days the mountains of Curdistan, and passed without resistance the rapid stream of the Tigris. Oppressed by the weight of their spoils and captives, the Roman army halted under

Theophanes (p. 260–262). Eutychius (Annal. tom. ii. p. 231, 232), an insufficient author, names Asphahan; and Casbin is most probably the city of Sapor. Ispahan is twenty-four days' journey from Tauris, and Casbin half way between them (Voyages de Tavernier, tom. i. p. 63–82).

the walls of Amida; and Heraclius informed the senate of Constantinople of his safety and success, which they had already felt by the retreat of the besiegers. The bridges of the Euphrates were destroyed by the Persians; but as soon as the emperor had discovered a ford, they hastily retired to defend the banks of the Sarus,[1] in Cilicia. That river, an impetuous torrent, was about three hundred feet broad; the bridge was fortified with strong turrets; and the banks were lined with barbarian archers. After a bloody conflict, which continued till the evening, the Romans prevailed in the assault; and a Persian of gigantic size was slain and thrown into the Sarus by the hand of the emperor himself. The enemies were dispersed and dismayed; Heraclius pursued his march to Sebaste in Cappadocia; and at the expiration of three years, the same coast of the Euxine applauded his return from a long and victorious expedition.[2]

Instead of skirmishing on the frontier, the two monarchs who disputed the empire of the East aimed their desperate strokes at the heart of their rival. The military force of Persia was wasted by the marches and combats of twenty years, and many of the veterans, who had survived the perils of the sword and the climate, were still detained in the fortresses of Egypt and Syria. But the revenge and ambition of Chosroes exhausted his kingdom; and the new levies of subjects, strangers, and slaves, were divided into three formidable bodies.[3] The first army of fifty thousand men, illustrious by the ornament and title of the *golden spears*, was destined to march against Heraclius; the second was stationed to prevent his junction with the troops of his brother Theodorus; and the third was commanded to besiege Constantinople, and to second the operations of the chagan, with whom the Persian king had ratified a treaty of alliance and partition. Sarbar, the general of the third army, penetrated through the

---

1 At ten parasangs from Tarsus the army of the younger Cyrus passed the Sarus, three plethra in breadth: the Pyramus, a stadium in breadth, ran five parasangs farther to the east (Xenophon, Anabas. l. i. p. 33, 34 [c. 4 *init.*]).

2 George of Pisidia (Bell. Abaricum, 246–265, p. 49) celebrates with truth the persevering courage of the three campaigns (τρεῖς περιδρόμους) against the Persians.

3 Petavius (Annotationes ad Nicephorum, p. 62, 63, 64) discriminates the names and actions of five Persian generals who were successively sent against Heraclius.

provinces of Asia to the well-known camp of Chalcedon, and amused himself with the destruction of the sacred and profane buildings of the Asiatic suburbs, while he impatiently waited the arrival of his Scythian friends on the opposite side of the Bosphorus. On the twenty-ninth of June, thirty thousand barbarians, the vanguard of the Avars, forced the long wall, and drove into the capital a promiscuous crowd of peasants, citizens, and soldiers. Fourscore thousand[1] of his native subjects, and of the vassal tribes of Gepidæ, Russians, Bulgarians, and Sclavonians, advanced under the standard of the chagan; a month was spent in marches and negotiations, but the whole city was invested on the thirty-first of July, from the suburbs of Pera and Galata to the Blachernæ and seven towers; and the inhabitants descried with terror the flaming signals of the European and Asiatic shores. In the meanwhile the magistrates of Constantinople repeatedly strove to purchase the retreat of the chagan; but their deputies were rejected and insulted; and he suffered the patricians to stand before his throne, while the Persian envoys, in silk robes, were seated by his side. 'You see,' said the haughty barbarian, 'the proofs of my perfect union with the Great King; and his lieutenant is ready to send into my camp a select band of three thousand warriors. Presume no longer to tempt your master with a partial and inadequate ransom: your wealth and your city are the only presents worthy of my acceptance. For yourselves, I shall permit you to depart, each with an undergarment and a shirt; and, at my entreaty, my friend Sarbar will not refuse a passage through his lines. Your absent prince, even now a captive or a fugitive, has left Constantinople to its fate; nor can you escape the arms of the Avars and Persians, unless you could soar into air like birds, unless like fishes you could like dive into the waves.'[2] During ten successive days the capital was assaulted by the Avars, who had made some progress in the science of attack;

1 This number of eight myriads is specified by George of Pisidia (Bell. Abar. 219). The poet (50–88) clearly indicates that the old chagan lived till the reign of Heraclius, and that his son and successor was born of a foreign mother. Yet Foggini (Annotat. p. 57) has given another interpretation to this passage.

2 A bird, a frog, a mouse, and five arrows, had been the present of the Scythian king to Darius (Herodot. l. iv. c. 131, 132). Substituez une lettre à ces signes (says Rousseau, with much good taste), plus elle sera menaçante moins

they advanced to sap or batter the wall, under the cover of the impenetrable tortoise; their engines discharged a perpetual volley of stones and darts; and twelve lofty towers of wood exalted the combatants to the height of the neighbouring ramparts. But the senate and people were animated by the spirit of Heraclius, who had detached to their relief a body of twelve thousand cuirassiers; the powers of fire and mechanics were used with superior art and success in the defence of Constantinople; and the galleys, with two and three ranks of oars, commanded the Bosphorus, and rendered the Persians the idle spectators of the defeat of their allies. The Avars were repulsed; a fleet of Sclavonian canoes was destroyed in the harbour; the vassals of the chagan threatened to desert, his provisions were exhausted, and, after burning his engines, he gave the signal of a slow and formidable retreat. The devotion of the Romans ascribed this signal deliverance to the Virgin Mary; but the mother of Christ would surely have condemned their inhuman murder of the Persian envoys, who were entitled to the rights of humanity, if they were not protected by the laws of nations.[1]

After the division of his army, Heraclius prudently retired to the banks of the Phasis, from whence he maintained a defensive war against the fifty thousand gold spears of Persia. His anxiety was relieved by the deliverance of Constantinople; his hopes were confirmed by a victory of his brother Theodorus; and to the hostile league of Chosroes with the Avars, the Roman emperor opposed the useful and honourable alliance of the Turks. At his liberal invitation, the horde of Chozars[2] transported their tents from the plains of the Volga to the mountains of Georgia;

elle effrayera: ce ne sera qu'une fanfaronnade dont Darius n'eut fait que rire (Emile, tom. iii. p. 146). Yet I much question whether the senate and people of Constantinople *laughed* at this message of the chagan.

1 The Paschal Chronicle (p. 392–397 [tom. i. p. 716–726, ed. Bonn]) gives a minute and authentic narrative of the siege and deliverance of Constantinople. Theophanes (p. 264) adds some circumstances; and a faint light may be obtained from the smoke of George of Pisidia, who has composed a poem (de Bello Abarico, p. 45–54) to commemorate this auspicious event.

2 The power of the Chozars prevailed in the seventh, eighth, and ninth centuries. They were known to the Greeks, the Arabs, and, under the name of *Kosa*, to the Chinese themselves. De Guignes, Hist. des Huns, tom. ii. part. ii. p. 507–509.

Heraclius received them in the neighbourhood of Teflis, and the khan with his nobles dismounted from their horses, if we may credit the Greeks, and fell prostrate on the ground to adore the purple of the Cæsar. Such voluntary homage and important aid were entitled to the warmest acknowledgments, and the emperor, taking off his own diadem, placed it on the head of the Turkish prince, whom he saluted with a tender embrace and the appellation of son. After a sumptuous banquet he presented Ziebel with the plate and ornaments, the gold, the gems, and the silk which had been used at the Imperial table, and, with his own hand, distributed rich jewels and earrings to his new allies. In a secret interview he produced the portrait of his daughter Eudocia,[1] condescended to flatter the barbarian with the promise of a fair and *august* bride, obtained an immediate succour of forty thousand horse, and negotiated a strong diversion of the Turkish arms on the side of the Oxus.[2] The Persians, in their turn, retreated with precipitation; in the camp of Edessa Heraclius reviewed an army of seventy thousand Romans and strangers; and some months were successfully employed in the recovery of the cities of Syria, Mesopotamia, and Armenia, whose fortifications had been imperfectly restored. Sarbar still maintained the important station of Chalcedon, but the jealousy of Chosroes, or the artifice of Heraclius, soon alienated the mind of that powerful satrap from the service of his king and country. A messenger was intercepted with a real or fictitious mandate to the cadarigan, or second in command, directing him to send, without delay, to the throne the head of a guilty or unfortunate general. The despatches were transmitted to Sarbar himself, and, as soon as he read the sentence of his own death, he dexterously inserted

1 Epiphania, or Eudocia, the only daughter of Heraclius and his first wife Eudocia, was born at Constantinople on the 7th of July A.D. 611, baptised the 15th of August, and crowned (in the oratory of St. Stephen in the palace) the 4th of October of the same year. At this time she was about fifteen. Eudocia was afterwards sent to her Turkish husband, but the news of his death stopped her journey, and prevented the consummation (Ducange, Familiæ Byzantin. p. 118).

2 Elmacin (Hist. Saracen. p. 13–16) gives some curious and probable facts: but his numbers are rather too high – 300,000 Romans assembled at Edessa – 500,000 Persians killed at Nineveh. The abatement of a cipher is scarcely enough to restore his sanity.

the names of four hundred officers, assembled a military council, and asked the *cadarigan* whether he was prepared to execute the commands of their tyrant? The Persians unanimously declared that Chosroes had forfeited the sceptre; a separate treaty was concluded with the government of Constantinople; and if some considerations of honour or policy restrained Sarbar from joining the standard of Heraclius, the emperor was assured that he might prosecute without interruption his designs of victory and peace.

Deprived of his firmest support, and doubtful of the fidelity of his subjects, the greatness of Chosroes was still conspicuous in its ruins. The number of five hundred thousand may be interpreted as an Oriental metaphor to describe the men and arms, the horses and elephants, that covered Media and Assyria against the invasion of Heraclius. Yet the Romans boldly advanced from the Araxes to the Tigris, and the timid prudence of Rhazates was content to follow them by forced marches through a desolate country, till he received a peremptory mandate to risk the fate of Persia in a decisive battle. Eastward of the Tigris, at the end of the bridge of Mosul, the great Nineveh had formerly been erected:[1] the city, and even the ruins of the city, had long since disappeared;[2] the vacant space afforded a spacious field for the operations of the two armies. But these operations are neglected by the Byzantine historians, and, like the authors of epic poetry and romance, they ascribe the victory, not to the military conduct, but to the personal valour, of their favourite hero. On this memorable day Heraclius, on his horse Phallas, surpassed the bravest of his warriors; his lip was pierced with a spear, the steed was wounded in the thigh, but he carried his master safe and

1 Ctesias (apud Diodor. Sicul. tom. i. l. ii. [c. 3] p. 115, edit. Wesseling) assigns 480 stadia (perhaps only 32 miles) for the circumference of Nineveh. Jonas talks of three days' journey: the 120,000 persons described by the prophet as incapable of discerning their right hand from their left may afford about 700,000 persons of all ages for the inhabitants of that ancient capital (Goguet, Origines des Loix, etc., tom. iii. part i. p. 92, 93), which ceased to exist 600 years before Christ. The western suburb still subsisted, and is mentioned under the name of Mosul, in the first age of the Arabian khalifs.

2 Niebuhr (Voyage en Arabie, etc., tom. ii. p. 286) passed over Nineveh without perceiving it. He mistook for a ridge of hills the old rampart of brick or earth. It is said to have been 100 feet high, flanked with 1500 towers, each of the height of 200 feet.

victorious through the triple phalanx of the barbarians. In the heat of the action three valiant chiefs were successively slain by the sword and lance of the emperor: among these was Rhazates himself; he fell like a soldier, but the sight of his head scattered grief and despair through the fainting ranks of the Persians. His armour of pure and massy gold, the shield of one hundred and twenty plates, the sword and belt, the saddle and cuirass, adorned the triumph of Heraclius; and if he had not been faithful to Christ and his mother, the champion of Rome might have offered the fourth *opime* spoils to the Jupiter of the Capitol.[1] In the battle of Nineveh, which was fiercely fought from daybreak to the eleventh hour, twenty-eight standards, besides those which might be broken or torn, were taken from the Persians; the greatest part of their army was cut in pieces; and the victors, concealing their own loss, passed the night on the field. They acknowledged that, on this occasion, it was less difficult to kill than to discomfit the soldiers of Chosroes; amidst the bodies of their friends, no more than two bow-shots from the enemy, the remnant of the Persian cavalry stood firm till the seventh hour of the night; about the eighth hour they retired to their unrifled camp, collected their baggage, and dispersed on all sides from the want of orders rather than of resolution. The diligence of Heraclius was not less admirable in the use of victory; by a march of forty-eight miles in four-and-twenty hours his vanguard occupied the bridges of the great and the lesser Zab, and the cities and palaces of Assyria were open for the first time to the Romans. By a just gradation of magnificent scenes they penetrated to the royal seat of Dastagerd, and, though much of the treasure had been removed and much had been expended, the remaining wealth appears to have exceeded their hopes, and even to have satiated their avarice. Whatever could not be easily transported they consumed with fire, that Chosroes might feel the anguish of those wounds which he had so often inflicted on the

1 Rex regia arma fero (says Romulus, in the first consecration) ... bina postea (continues Livy, i. 10) inter tot bella, opima parta sunt spolia, adeo rara ejus fortuna decoris. If Varro (apud Pomp. Festum, p. 306, edit. Dacier) could justify his liberality in granting the *opime* spoils even to a common soldier who had slain the king or general of the enemy, the honour would have been much more cheap and common.

provinces of the empire; and justice might allow the excuse, if the desolations had been confined to the works of regal luxury – if national hatred, military licence, and religious zeal had not wasted with equal rage the habitations and the temples of the guiltless subject. The recovery of three hundred Roman standards and the deliverance of the numerous captives of Edessa and Alexandria reflect a purer glory on the arms of Heraclius. From the palace of Dastagerd he pursued his march within a few miles of Modain or Ctesiphon, till he was stopped, on the banks of the Arba, by the difficulty of the passage, the rigour of the season, and perhaps the fame of an impregnable capital. The return of the emperor is marked by the modern name of the city of Sherhzour: he fortunately passed Mount Zara before the snow, which fell incessantly thirty-four days; and the citizens of Gandzaca, or Tauris, were compelled to entertain his soldiers and their horses with an hospitable reception.[1]

When the ambition of Chosroes was reduced to the defence of his hereditary kingdom, the love of glory, or even the sense of shame, should have urged him to meet his rival in the field. In the battle of Nineveh his courage might have taught the Persians to vanquish, or he might have fallen with honour by the lance of a Roman emperor. The successor of Cyrus chose rather, at a secure distance, to expect the event, to assemble the relics of the defeat, and to retire by measured steps before the march of Heraclius, till he beheld with a sigh the once loved mansions of Dastagerd. Both his friends and enemies were persuaded that it was the intention of Chosroes to bury himself under the ruins of the city and palace: and as both might have been equally adverse to his flight, the monarch of Asia, with Sira and three concubines, escaped through a hole in the wall nine days before the arrival of the Romans. The slow and stately procession in which he showed himself to the prostrate crowd was changed to a rapid and secret journey; the first evening he lodged in the cottage of a peasant, whose humble door would

1 In describing this last expedition of Heraclius, the facts, the places and the dates of Theophanes (p. 265–271 [tom. i. p. 487–502, ed. Bonn]) are so accurate and authentic, that he must have followed the original letters of the emperor, of which the Paschal Chronicle has preserved (p. 398–402 [tom. i. p. 727–734, ed. Bonn]) a very curious specimen.

scarcely give admittance to the Great King.[1] His superstition was subdued by fear: on the third day he entered with joy the fortifications of Ctesiphon; yet he still doubted of his safety till he had opposed the river Tigris to the pursuit of the Romans. The discovery of his flight agitated with terror and tumult the palace, the city, and the camp of Dastagerd: the satraps hesitated whether they had most to fear from their sovereign or the enemy; and the females of the harem were astonished and pleased by the sight of mankind, till the jealous husband of three thousand wives again confined them to a more distant castle. At his command the army of Dastagerd retreated to a new camp: the front was covered by the Arba and a line of two hundred elephants; the troops of the more distant provinces successively arrived; and the vilest domestics of the king and satraps were enrolled for the last defence of the throne. It was still in the power of Chosroes to obtain a reasonable peace; and he was repeatedly pressed by the messengers of Heraclius to spare the blood of his subjects, and to relieve a humane conqueror from the painful duty of carrying fire and sword through the fairest countries of Asia. But the pride of the Persian had not yet sunk to the level of his fortune; he derived a momentary confidence from the retreat of the emperor; he wept with impotent rage over the ruins of his Assyrian palaces; and disregarded too long the rising murmurs of the nation, who complained that their lives and fortunes were sacrificed to the obstinacy of an old man. That unhappy old man was himself tortured with the sharpest pains both of mind and body; and, in the consciousness of his approaching end, he resolved to fix the tiara on the head of Merdaza, the most favoured of his sons. But the will of Chosroes was no longer revered, and Siroes, who gloried in the rank and merit of his mother Sira, had conspired with the malcontents to assert and anticipate the rights of primogeniture.[2] Twenty-two

1 The words of Theophanes are remarkable: εἰσῆλθεν Χοσρόης εἰς οἶκον γεωργοῦ μεδαμινοῦ μεῖναι, μόλις χωρηθεὶς ἐν τῇ τούτου θύρᾳ, ἣν ἰδὼν ἔσχατον Ἡράκλειος ἐθαύμασεν (p. 269 [p. 496, ed. Bonn]). Young princes who discover a propensity to war should repeatedly transcribe and translate such salutary texts.

2 The authentic narrative of the fall of Chosroes is contained in the letter of Heraclius (Chron. Paschal. p. 398 [tom. i. p. 727, ed. Bonn]) and the history of Theophanes (p. 271 [tom. i. p. 500, sq., ed. Bonn]).

satraps, they styled themselves patriots, were tempted by the
wealth and honours of a new reign: to the soldiers the heir of
Chosroes promised an increase of pay; to the Christians, the free
exercise of their religion; to the captives, liberty and rewards; and
to the nation, instant peace and the reduction of taxes. It was
determined by the conspirators that Siroes, with the ensigns of
royalty, should appear in the camp; and if the enterprise should
fail, his escape was contrived to the Imperial court. But the new
monarch was saluted with unanimous acclamations; the flight of
Chosroes (yet where could he have fled?) was rudely arrested,
eighteen sons were massacred before his face, and he was thrown
into a dungeon, where he expired on the fifth day. The Greeks
and modern Persians minutely describe how Chosroes was insulted, and famished, and tortured, by the command of an inhuman son, who so far surpassed the example of his father; but at
the time of his death what tongue would relate the story of the
parricide? what eye could penetrate into the *tower of darkness?*
According to the faith and mercy of his Christian enemies, he
sunk without hope into a still deeper abyss,[1] and it will not be
denied that tyrants of every age and sect are the best entitled to
such infernal abodes. The glory of the house of Sassan ended
with the life of Chosroes; his unnatural son enjoyed only eight
months the fruit of his crimes; and in the space of four years
the regal title was assumed by nine candidates, who disputed,
with the sword or dagger, the fragments of an exhausted monarchy. Every province and each city of Persia was the scene of
independence, of discord, and of blood; and the state of anarchy
prevailed about eight years longer, till the factions were silenced
and united under the common yoke of the Arabian caliphs.[2]

1 On the first rumour of the death of Chosroes, an Heracliad in two cantos
was instantly published at Constantinople by George of Pisidia (p. 97–105). A
priest and a poet might very properly exult in the damnation of the public
enemy (ἐμπεσὼν τῷ Ταρτάρῳ, v. 56): but such mean revenge is unworthy of a
king and a conqueror; and I am sorry to find so much black superstition
(θεομάχος Χοσρόης ἔπεσεν καὶ ἐππωματίσθη εἰς τὰ καταχθόνια . . . εἰς
τὸ πῦρ τὸ ἀκατάσβεστον, etc.) in the letter of Heraclius [Chron. Pasch. p. 728
sq., ed. Bonn]: he almost applauds the parricide of Siroes as an act of piety and
justice.

2 The best Oriental accounts of this last period of the Sassanian kings are
found in Eutychius (Annal. tom. ii. p. 251–256), who dissembles the parricide

As soon as the mountains became passable the emperor received the welcome news of the success of the conspiracy, the death of Chosroes, and the elevation of his eldest son to the throne of Persia. The authors of the revolution, eager to display their merits in the court or camp of Tauris, preceded the ambassadors of Siroes, who delivered the letters of their master to his *brother* the emperor of the Romans.[1] In the language of the usurpers of every age, he imputes his own crimes to the Deity, and, without degrading his equal majesty, he offers to reconcile the long discord of the two nations by a treaty of peace and alliance more durable than brass or iron. The conditions of the treaty were easily defined and faithfully executed. In the recovery of the standards and prisoners which had fallen into the hands of the Persians, the emperor imitated the example of Augustus; their care of the national dignity was celebrated by the poets of the times, but the decay of genius may be measured by the distance between Horace and George of Pisidia; the subjects and brethren of Heraclius were redeemed from persecution, slavery, and exile; but, instead of the Roman eagles, the true wood of the holy cross was restored to the importunate demands of the successor of Constantine. The victor was not ambitious of enlarging the weakness of the empire; the son of Chosroes abandoned without regret the conquests of his father; the Persians who evacuated the cities of Syria and Egypt were honourably conducted to the frontier; and a war which had wounded the vitals of the two monarchies produced no change in their external and relative situation. The return of Heraclius from Tauris to Constantinople was a perpetual triumph, and after the exploits of six glorious campaigns he peaceably enjoyed the sabbath of his toils. After a long impatience, the senate, the clergy, and the people went forth to meet their hero with tears and acclamations, with olive-branches and innumerable lamps; he entered the capital in a chariot drawn by four elephants, and, as soon as the emperor could disengage himself from the tumult of public joy, he tasted

of Siroes. D'Herbelot (Bibliothèque Orientale, p. 789), and Assemanni (Bibliothec. Oriental. tom. iii. p. 415–420).

1 The letter of Siroes in the Paschal Chronicle (p. 402 [tom. i. p. 735, ed. Bonn]) unfortunately ends before he proceeds to business. The treaty appears in its execution in the histories of Theophanes and Nicephorus.

more genuine satisfaction in the embraces of his mother and his son.[1]

The succeeding year was illustrated by a triumph of a very different kind, the restitution of the true cross to the holy sepulchre. Heraclius performed in person the pilgrimage of Jerusalem: the identity of the relic was verified by the discreet patriarch,[2] and this august ceremony has been commemorated by the annual festival of the exaltation of the cross. Before the emperor presumed to tread the consecrated ground he was instructed to strip himself of the diadem and purple, the pomp and vanity of the world; but in the judgment of his clergy, the persecution of the Jews was more easily reconciled with the precepts of the Gospel. He again ascended his throne to receive the congratulations of the ambassador of France and India; and the fame of Moses, Alexander, and Hercules[3] was eclipsed, in the popular estimation, by the superior merit and glory of the great Heraclius. Yet the deliverer of the East was indigent and feeble. Of the Persian spoils the most valuable portion had been expended in the war, distributed to the soldiers, or buried, by an unlucky tempest, in the waves of the Euxine. The conscience of the emperor was oppressed by the obligation of restoring the wealth of the clergy, which he had borrowed for their own defence: a perpetual fund was required to satisfy these inexorable creditors; the provinces, already wasted by the arms and avarice of the Persians, were compelled to a second payment of the same taxes; and the arrears of a simple citizen, the treasurer of

1 The burthen of Corneille's song,

'Montrez Heraclius au peuple qui l'attend,'

is much better suited to the present occasion. See his triumph in Theophanes (p. 272, 273 [tom. i. p. 503 *sq.*, ed. Bonn]) and Nicephorus (p. 15, 16). The life of the mother and tenderness of the son are attested by George of Pisidia (Bell. Abar. 255, etc. p. 49). The metaphor of the Sabbath is used, somewhat profanely, by these Byzantine Christians.

2 See Baronius (Annal. Eccles. A.D. 628, No.1–4), Eutychius (Annal. tom. ii. p. 240–248), Nicephorus (Brev. p. 15). The seals of the case had never been broken; and this preservation of the cross is ascribed (under God) to the devotion of queen Sira.

3 George of Pisidia, Acroas. iii. de Expedit. contra Persas, 415, etc. [p. 21], and Heracliad. Acroas. i. 65–138. I neglect the meaner parallels of Daniel, Timotheus, etc.; Chosroes and the chagan were of course compared to Belshazzar, Pharaoh, the old serpent, etc.

Damascus, were commuted to a fine of one hundred thousand pieces of gold. The loss of two hundred thousand soldiers,[1] who had fallen by the sword, was of less fatal importance than the decay of arts, agriculture, and population in this long and destructive war; and although a victorious army had been formed under the standard of Heraclius, the unnatural effort appears to have exhausted rather than exercised their strength. While the emperor triumphed at Constantinople or Jerusalem, an obscure town on the confines of Syria was pillaged by the Saracens, and they cut in pieces some troops who advanced to its relief; an ordinary and trifling occurrence, had it not been the prelude of a mighty revolution. These robbers were the apostles of Mohammed; their fanatic valour had emerged from the desert; and in the last eight years of his reign Heraclius lost to the Arabs the same provinces which he had rescued from the Persians.

1 Suidas (in Excerpt. Hist. Byzant. p. 46) gives this number; but either the *Persian* must be read for the *Isaurian* war, or this passage does not belong to the *emperor* Heraclius.

ABOUT THE INTRODUCER

HUGH TREVOR-ROPER, Lord Dacre of Glanton, was formerly Regius Professor of History in the University of Oxford and Master of Peterhouse, Cambridge. He has written many distinguished works on seventeenth-century and twentieth-century history, including *Archbishop Laud*, *The Gentry, 1540–1640*, and *The Last Days of Hitler*.

CHINUA ACHEBE
Things Fall Apart

THE ARABIAN NIGHTS
(tr. Husain Haddawy)

MARCUS AURELIUS
Meditations

JANE AUSTEN
Emma
Mansfield Park
Northanger Abbey
Persuasion
Pride and Prejudice
Sense and Sensibility

HONORÉ DE BALZAC
Cousin Bette
Eugénie Grandet
Old Goriot

SIMONE DE BEAUVOIR
The Second Sex

WILLIAM BLAKE
Poems and Prophecies

JORGE LUIS BORGES
Ficciones

JAMES BOSWELL
The Life of Samuel Johnson

CHARLOTTE BRONTË
Jane Eyre
Villette

EMILY BRONTË
Wuthering Heights

MIKHAIL BULGAKOV
The Master and Margarita

SAMUEL BUTLER
The Way of all Flesh

ITALO CALVINO
If on a winter's night a traveler

ALBERT CAMUS
The Stranger

WILLA CATHER
Death Comes for the Archbishop

MIGUEL DE CERVANTES
Don Quixote

GEOFFREY CHAUCER
Canterbury Tales

ANTON CHEKHOV
The Steppe and Other Stories
My Life and Other Stories

KATE CHOPIN
The Awakening

CARL VON CLAUSEWITZ
On War

SAMUEL TAYLOR COLERIDGE
Poems

WILKIE COLLINS
The Moonstone
The Woman in White

JOSEPH CONRAD
Heart of Darkness
Lord Jim
Nostromo
The Secret Agent
Typhoon and Other Stories
Under Western Eyes

DANTE ALIGHIERI
The Divine Comedy

DANIEL DEFOE
Moll Flanders
Robinson Crusoe

CHARLES DICKENS
Bleak House
David Copperfield
Dombey and Son
Great Expectations
Hard Times
Little Dorrit
Martin Chuzzlewit
Nicholas Nickleby
Oliver Twist
Our Mutual Friend
A Tale of Two Cities

DENIS DIDEROT
Memoirs of a Nun